DEFEASIBLE DEONTIC LOGIC

SYNTHESE LIBRARY

STUDIES IN EPISTEMOLOGY,

LOGIC, METHODOLOGY, AND PHILOSOPHY OF SCIENCE

Managing Editor:

JAAKKO HINTIKKA, *Boston University*

Editors:

DIRK VAN DALEN, *University of Utrecht, The Netherlands*
DONALD DAVIDSON, *University of California, Berkeley*
THEO A.F. KUIPERS, *University of Groningen, The Netherlands*
PATRICK SUPPES, *Stanford University, California*
JAN WOLEŃSKI, *Jagiellonian University, Kraków, Poland*

VOLUME 263

DEFEASIBLE DEONTIC LOGIC

Edited by

DONALD NUTE

*The University of Georgia,
Athens, U.S.A.*

KLUWER ACADEMIC PUBLISHERS

DORDRECHT / BOSTON / LONDON

A C.I.P. Catalogue record for this book is available from the Library of Congress

ISBN 0-7923-4630-0

Published by Kluwer Academic Publishers,
P.O. Box 17, 3300 AA Dordrecht, The Netherlands.

Sold and distributed in the U.S.A. and Canada
by Kluwer Academic Publishers,
101 Philip Drive, Norwell, MA 02061, U.S.A.

In all other countries, sold and distributed
by Kluwer Academic Publishers Group,
P.O. Box 322, 3300 AH Dordrecht, The Netherlands.

Printed on acid-free paper

CONTENTS

Preface   vii

Acknowledgements   ix

INTRODUCTION   1
Donald Nute and Xiaochang Yu

NONMONOTONIC FOUNDATIONS FOR DEONTIC LOGIC   17
John F. Horty

DEONTIC LOGICS OF DEFEASIBILITY   45
Marvin Belzer and Barry Loewer

SYSTEMATIC FRAME CONSTANTS IN DEFEASIBLE DEONTIC LOGIC   59
Lennart Åqvist

THE MANY FACES OF DEFEASIBILITY IN DEFEASIBLE DEONTIC LOGIC   79
Leendert W.N. van der Torre and Yao-Hua Tan

DEONTIC LOGIC VIEWED AS DEFEASIBLE REASONING   123
Y. U. Ryu and R. M. Lee

REASONS TO THINK AND ACT   139
Michael Morreau

COMMON SENSE OBLIGATION   159
Nicholas Asher and Daniel Bonevac

DEFEASIBLE REASONING AND MORAL DILEMMAS   205
Robert C. Koons and T. K. Seung

DYADIC DEONTIC LOGIC AND CONTRARY-TO-DUTY OBLIGATIONS   223
Henry Prakken and Marek Sergot

DEFEASBILE REASONING WITH LEGAL RULES   263
Lamber Royakkers and Frank Dignum

APPARENT OBLIGATION   287
Donald Nute

A NEW APPROACH TO CONTRARY-TO-DUTY OBLIGATIONS 317
José Carmo and Andrew J. I. Jones

**ALCHOURRÓN AND VON WRIGHT ON CONFLICT AMONG
NORMS**   345
R. P. Loui

Index   353

PREFACE

The notion of defeasibility in normative reasoning is quite old. Surely the discussion of the nature of justice between Socrates and Cephalas in *The Republic* demonstrates that reasons for believing an act to be just can be overriden by other morally relevant reasons. Of course it is also clear that Plato sought a characterization of justice and the other virtues that admitted of no exceptions. Nevertheless, his dialogs are replete with examples of defeasible normative reasoning.

Ron Loui tells me he has tried to find the source of the term "defeasible" in the philosophical literature. He has traced it back to the writings of H. L. A. Hart. Whether it occurs earlier is uncertain. But despite the long-time interest in defeasible reasoning within the philosophical community, it can hardly be denied that the investigation of defeasible or "nonmonotonic" reasoning received a huge impetus when the artificial intelligence community discovered it. Since a special issue of the journal *Artificial Intelligence* containing seminal papers by McCarthy, Reiter, McDermott and Doyle, and others, nonmonotonicity has been a favorite topic for those interested in knowledge representation and automated reasoning.

With a better understanding of the requirements for an adequate treatment of defeasibility, attention is turned again to normative reasoning. Yet all the work on nonmonotonic reasoning in the past twenty years or so has not produced a convergence of systems or even of intuitions. The variety of approaches is evident in this collection of papers by researchers from business, computer science, law, and philosophy. While most of the papers propose some version of defeasible deontic logic, a few consider alternatives to defeasibility for solving some of the puzzles of normative reasoning. I hope this book will provide readers from many disciplines with quite different concerns a variety of useful tools and a sense of both the accomplishments and the stubborn problems that remain in this field.

ACKNOWLEDGEMENTS

The Society for Exact Philosophy served as midwife for this volume. The theme of the SEP meeting held at York University in May of 1993 was deontic logic. Papers presented at that meeting by Dan Bonevac, Rob Koons, and Marvin Belzer integrated defeasible reasoning and deontic logic. This was something I had been thinking about for some time. The subject of defeasible deontic logic came up again during a chance meeting with Ms. Annie Kuipers of Kluwer Academic Press at the American Philosophical Association conference in Atlanta in December of 1993. She encouraged me to pursue the idea of a volume of essays beginning with papers presented at the 1993 SEP meeting. In May, 1994, the SEP met at the University of Texas. There I recruited Asher and Bonevac, Koons and Seung, Michael Morreau, and a few others who ultimately were not able to provide papers. By the SEP meeting at the University of Calgary in May of 1995, essentially the entire slate of contributors had been established. I had an opportunity to present a first draft of my own paper at this meeting and to discuss the volume with Jeff Horty and Michael Morreau. The goal was to finish the volume by the end of 1995. This turned out to be overly ambitious. The last few papers weren't received until shortly before the SEP meeting at East Tennessee University in October of 1996. At that meeting, Dan Bonevac and I presented second drafts of our papers.

A group of colleagues and students at the Artificial Intelligence Center at the University of Georgia formed a year-long seminar that read and discussed drafts of the papers in this volume as they were received. This group provided the comments which were collected and sent to the authors to guide their revisions. At different times, the group included Victor Bancroft, David Billington, Charles Cross, Frank Price, David Goodman, Christopher Henderson, Zachary Hunter, Hong-gee Kim, Henry Prakken, and Guo-qiang Zhang. My former student and the co-author of the introduction to this volume, Xiaochang Yu, also served as a reader for several of the papers.

My graduate assistant, Zac Hunter, is responsible for getting these papers into their final form in LATEXand for compiling the index of names. His work ranged from a light tune-up for some papers to producing LATEXsource files from a typed manuscript in others. He did an outstanding job. Angie Paul, secretary of the Artificial Intelligence Center at the University of Georgia, provided valuable assistance communicating with the authors at different stages of this project. The Artificial Intelligence Center provided support for myself and Zac Hunter while we prepared this volume.

My wife, Jane, sometimes asks me, "What are you working on?" Often, my reply is, "The book." Near the beginning of this project, she said, "I thought you had finished the book." "I did," I said. "This is another book." For more than twenty years, "the book" in one incarnation or another has been a member of our family. I thank all the authors represented in this volume and all the other individuals and organizations mentioned here. I also thank those colleagues who put their time and effort into work on papers for the volume but for one reason or another were finally not able to contribute. And as always, I appreciate the support and the encouragement from Jane while I worked on "the book."

DONALD NUTE AND XIAOCHANG YU

INTRODUCTION

In one way or another, the papers in this volume investigate the intersection and interaction of defeasible reasoning and normative reasoning. Various notions from normative reasoning, including the notions of *prima facie* obligation, contrary-to-duty obligations, and moral dilemmas have raised serious problems for deontic logicians, problems which have defied solution within standard deontic logic and its extensions. As a result, deontic logic has fallen into ill-repute with those who must actually engage in normative reasoning. An underlying thesis of this volume is that nonmonotonic or defeasible methods may provide the way to solve some of these thorny problems. A *defeasible* deontic logic may not only solve some of the familiar paradoxes of deontic logic, but may actually be attractive to moral philosophers, jurists, and others who would seem to be the natural clients of the deontic logician.

The very expression "*prima facie* obligation" cries out for a defeasible or nonmonotonic analysis. Such an obligation binds unless it is overriden by appropriate considerations – usually a higher obligation. *Prima facie* obligations may be overriden and defeasible arguments may be defeated. Perhaps we can capitalize on this parallel. If we represent *prima facie* obligations correctly within a defeasible theory, then perhaps we can take the defeasible consequences of the theory to represent our actual obligations, or at least those duties we should perform so far as we can determine. Part of the attraction of such an approach is that some of the obligations represented initially in the theory may not be derivable from the theory. The argument to support it is defeated by another element of the theory representing overriding considerations.

The papers in this volume take a variety of approaches to the task of integrating normative and defeasible reasoning. Many of the papers refer to something called *standard deontic logic*. We will summarize what we take that system to be. Many of the papers also propose solutions to well-known paradoxes in deontic logic. We will review the most important of these and examine some of the attempts that have been made at resolving them without resorting to defeasible reasoning. Finally, we will point out some of the themes arising out of the treatment of defeasible reasoning that relate some of the papers in this volume to each other.

D. Nute (ed.), Defeasible Deontic Logic, 1–16.
© 1997 *Kluwer Academic Publishers. Printed in the Netherlands.*

1. CLASSICAL AND STANDARD DEONTIC LOGIC

Von Wright (1951) laid a foundation for the development of modern deontic logic. This is one of the earliest treatments of deontic logic as a branch of modal logic. The primitive deontic concept for this work is "permission". "ϕ is permitted" is symbolized as $\mathcal{P}\phi$. Other operators are defined in terms of the operator $\mathcal{P}$.

$\mathcal{F}\phi =_{df} \neg\mathcal{P}\phi$ Something forbidden is not permitted.

$\bigcirc\phi =_{df} \neg\mathcal{P}\neg\phi$ Something obligatory is not permitted not to do.

There are two axioms in von Wright's system which he calls the Principle of Deontic Distribution and the Principle of Permission.

VW1: $\mathcal{P}(\phi \vee \psi) \leftrightarrow \mathcal{P}\phi \vee \mathcal{P}\psi$

VW2: $\mathcal{P}\phi \vee \mathcal{P}\neg\phi$

It's not clear whether von Wright endorsed a deontic inheritance rule:

VW3:   if $\vdash \phi \supset \psi$ then $\vdash \bigcirc\phi \supset \bigcirc\psi$

Von Wright calls theorems *deontic tautologies* or *laws of deontic logic*. He lists four laws for the "dissolution" of deontic operators, e.g., $\bigcirc(\phi \wedge \psi) \leftrightarrow \bigcirc\phi \wedge \bigcirc\psi$, and six laws on "commitment". Some examples are

VW4: $(\bigcirc\phi \wedge \bigcirc(\phi \supset \psi)) \supset \bigcirc\psi$

VW5: $(\neg\mathcal{P}\psi \wedge \bigcirc(\phi \supset \psi)) \supset \neg\mathcal{P}\phi$

VW6: $(\bigcirc(\phi \supset \psi \vee \chi) \wedge \neg\mathcal{P}\psi \wedge \neg\mathcal{P}\chi) \supset \neg\mathcal{P}\phi$

VW7: $\neg(\bigcirc(\phi \vee \psi) \wedge \neg\mathcal{P}\phi \wedge \neg\mathcal{P}\psi)$

Neither $\bigcirc(\phi \vee \neg\phi)$ nor $\mathcal{F}(\phi \wedge \neg\phi)$ can be derived from von Wright's two axioms (principles). This means that in von Wright's system, unlike most later systems, a tautology is not necessarily obligatory and a contradiction is not necessarily forbidden. von Wright's monadic system, sometimes referred to as the "classical deontic logic", is decidable.

The standard system of deontic logic, a modification of von Wright's system, uses $\bigcirc$ (ought) as the primary operator. A permission operator $\mathcal{P}$ is defined by

$\mathcal{P}\phi =_{df} \neg \bigcirc \neg\phi$

One version of the standard system called **OK+** by Åqvist (Åqvist, 1984, pp. 615-6) has the following axiom schemata and rules of proof.

SD0:   Axiom schemata for propositional logic

SD1: $\bigcirc\phi \supset \neg \bigcirc \neg\phi$

SD2: $\bigcirc(\phi \supset \psi) \supset (\bigcirc\phi \supset \bigcirc\psi)$

SD3:   if $\vdash \phi$ and $\vdash \phi \supset \psi$ then $\vdash \psi$

SD4:   if $\vdash \phi$ then $\vdash \bigcirc \phi$

SD1 is equivalent to von Wright's VW2. Either of SD1 or VW2 will lead to what we will call the principle deontic consistency.

SD5: $\neg(\bigcirc\phi \wedge \bigcirc\neg\phi)$

SD2 is derivable from von Wright's system and is equivalent to his theorem VW4. We will refer to this system as **SDL** for "standard deontic logic".

One of the main differences between von Wright's classical deontic logic and the standard deontic logic lies in SD4 ($\bigcirc$-necessitation). The addition of SD4 makes deontic logic a normal system. Every logically true proposition, therefore, is obligatory. In particular, the theorem $\bigcirc(\phi \vee \neg\phi)$, explicitly rejected by von Wright, is derivable.

According to von Wright, deontic operators are predicates which attach to act-qualifying properties. An act-qualifying property is also called a generic act in contrast to individual actions. For example, theft is an act-qualifying property or generic act, but individual thefts are not: they are act-individuals. This treatment of the objects of deontic operators is different from that of most later deontic logicians; for them, deontic operators are deontic modalities which take sentences describing state of affairs as their arguments. Thus, $\mathcal{P}\phi$ for von Wright means it is permitted to do ϕ, while for most later logicians, $\mathcal{P}\phi$ means it is permitted that ϕ.

Von Wright's conception of modal notions as act-qualifying properties raises questions about how truth-functional connectives can be used to form compounds of variables ranging over generic acts. Quite a few systems that we will discuss take the opposite position. Since it is more natural to use expressions like "ought to do ϕ" than "it is obligatory that ϕ", we will follow most writers and use both forms interchangeably in our discussion. Whenever it is convenient, for example, we will use "John ought to help his neighbors" instead of the somewhat cumbersome expression "It ought to be the case that John help his neighbors".

The standard system of deontic logic receives more attention than von Wright's classical system. But there is disagreement about which system offers a more reasonable approach to moral reasoning. One of the essential disputes concerns which rule of deontic logic is more reasonable, SD4 of standard deontic logic or the more restrictive VW3 (which we tentatively attribute to von Wright, also called the principle of inheritance of obligations) which is derivable from SD4.

Writers on deontic logic use the word "paradox" in a loose sense. Some paradoxes discussed in the literature of deontic logic are actually dilemmas or counter-intuitive results. Prior's Paradox of Derived Obligation, discussed below, is such an example. These are not paradoxes in the sense of logical contradictions. But a great number of deontic paradoxes are themselves logic paradoxes or lead directly to logical contradictions. Chisholm's Paradox is an example of this kind. We will follow the customary usage of the word "paradox" in the literature of deontic logic and refer to cases of both types as deontic paradoxes. We will review several classes of deontic paradoxes that arise within standard deontic logic.

2. DEONTIC PARADOXES RELATED TO MATERIAL IMPLICATION

Ross' Paradox (1930) involves the theorem

RP1: $\bigcirc\phi \supset \bigcirc(\phi \vee \psi)$

The paradox is named after Alf Ross whose example was "If I ought to mail a letter, I ought to mail or burn it."

Prior's Paradox (1954) of Derived Obligation concerns the theorem

PP1: $\neg P\phi \supset \bigcirc(\phi \supset \psi)$, or

PP2: $\bigcirc\neg\phi \supset \bigcirc(\phi \supset \psi)$

This theorem is interpreted as making the counterintuitive claim that performing a forbidden act commits us to any other act. An example is "If it is forbidden to kill a man, then it is obligatory that if I kill a man, I rob him."

Both Ross' Paradox and Prior's Paradox are closely related to the paradoxes of material implication in sentential logic. Some authors suggest that the oddness of the conclusions in Ross' Paradox and Prior's Paradox lies in the ambiguity of normative phrases in natural language. As for Ross' Paradox, in ordinary language when we say something like "it ought to be that ϕ or ψ", this seems to indicate that we have a free choice to decide which proposition to bring about. However, in **SDL**, although we can derive $\bigcirc(\phi \vee \psi)$ from $\bigcirc\phi$ and $\bigcirc\phi \supset \bigcirc(\phi \vee \psi)$, we cannot derive $\bigcirc\psi$. So the theorem in question does not allow us to infer that ψ ought to be the case or is even permitted. Castañeda (1981, p. 38) claimed that "(s)ome 'paradoxes' – like Alf Ross's – are nothing but elementary confusion."

The same is true for Prior's Paradox. $\bigcirc(\phi \supset \psi)$ is not synonymous with the ordinary language conditional "If ϕ, then it is obligatory that ψ". Deontic logic uses material implication. So $\bigcirc\neg\phi \supset \bigcirc(\phi \supset \psi)$ is equivalent to

PP3: $\bigcirc\neg\phi \supset \bigcirc(\neg\phi \vee \psi)$

This is then simply another version of Ross' Paradox. So we need to stick to the meaning expressed by material implications and "not 'read into' them anything 'beyond' it" (Åqvist, 1984, p. 643).

Some other writers think these paradoxes do reveal a logical difficulty. But it is not necessary for deontic logicians to do much about it. **SDL** is an extension of the traditional propositional logic and employs material implication to express conditional obligations. It is not surprising that it inherits all paradoxes of material implication from propositional logic. Such logical problems are therefore "devoid of any special interest for a student of deontic logic" (hintikka, 1971, p. 88).

3. GOOD SAMARITAN PARADOXES

There is a group of paradoxes called the Good Samaritan Paradoxes. James Forrester (1984) presents a particular version of this group called the Paradox of Gentle Murder. Forrester's version is usually considered a more serious version of the group of Good Samaritan Paradoxes. The paradox runs as follows.

1. It is obligatory that Smith not murder Jones.
2. If Smith murders Jones, it is obligatory that Smith murders Jones gently.
3. Smith murders Jones.
4. Smith murders Jones gently entails that Smith murders Jones.

Notice that (4) represents a strict conditional rather than just a material conditional. Let g stand for "Smith murders Jones gently" and m for "Smith murders Jones". From (2) and (3) we have

GM5: $\bigcirc g$

From (4) and the principle of inheritance of obligations, we have

GM6: $\bigcirc g \supset \bigcirc m$

Now from (1) and GM5 and GM6 we have

GM7: $\bigcirc \neg m \wedge \bigcirc m$

GM7 contradicts the principle of deontic consistency. If we apply the axiom

SD1: $\bigcirc \phi \supset \neg \bigcirc \neg \phi,$

we derive the contradiction

GM8: $\bigcirc m \wedge \neg \bigcirc m$

Approaches to resolving the Paradox of Gentle Murder are basically of two kinds. The first approach tries to explain away the paradox by pointing out the ambiguities of grammatical structures involved in the set of sentences, especially the scope confusion of the deontic operator involved in the sentences (sinnott-Armstrong, 1985; castañeda, 1986). According to this approach, the deontic operator applies only to "gently" and does not apply to "murders" in the sentence "John murders Smith gently." Walter Sinnott-Armstrong, for example, formalizes (2) as:

GM2: $(\exists x) M x s j \supset (\exists x)(M x s j \wedge \bigcirc G x)$

instead of:

GM2': $(\exists x) M x s j \supset \bigcirc (\exists x)(M x s j \wedge G x)$

According to GM2, what is obligatory is merely the character of "gentleness" related to the act rather than the murderous act itself. In that case we cannot reach the conclusion that it is obligatory that Smith murders Jones.

However, this treatment is challenged by Lou Goble (1991). According to Goble, the best solution to the Paradox is simply to give up the principle of inheritance of obligations. A similar position (giving up the principle) is also taken by Frank Jackson (1985) and Sven Hansson (1988), among others.

But the principle of inheritance of obligations is one of the most fundamental principles in **SDL** and has strong intuitive appeal. It requires the agent to take moral responsibility for the logical consequences of what he/she has committed to do. The rejection of the principle, therefore, seems to be contrary to one of our basic moral reasoning patterns.

4. CHISHOLM'S PARADOX OF CONTRARY-TO-DUTY OBLIGATIONS

The problem in standard deontic logic that perhaps has received the most attention in the literature involves obligations which arise only when some other obligation has been violated. These are the Contrary-to-Duty Obligations which play a crucial role in Chisholm's Paradox (chisholm, 1963).

A standard version of Chisholm's Paradox involves the following four claims.

5. Jones ought to go to the aid of his neighbors.
6. If Jones goes to the aid of his neighbors, then he ought to tell them he is coming.
7. If Jones does not go to the aid of his neighbors, then he ought not to tell them he is coming.
8. Jones does not go to the aid of his neighbors.

According to standard deontic logic, these four sentences can be symbolized as follows

$$\text{CD1:} \quad \bigcirc g$$
$$\text{CD2:} \quad \bigcirc(g \supset n)$$
$$\text{CD3:} \quad \neg g \supset \bigcirc \neg n$$
$$\text{CD4:} \quad \neg g$$

Since from CD1 and CD2 we get $\bigcirc n$ and from CD3 and CD4 we get $\bigcirc \neg n$, we derive $\bigcirc n \wedge \bigcirc \neg n$ which contradicts the principle of deontic consistency. An alternative way to symbolize the sentences is either to replace CD2 with

$$\text{CD5:} \quad g \supset \bigcirc n$$

or to replace CD3 with

$$\text{CD6:} \quad \bigcirc(\neg g \supset \neg n)$$

Either way, $\bigcirc n \wedge \bigcirc \neg n$ is no longer derivable. However, CD5 is derivable from CD4 and CD6 is derivable from CD1, and either result is inconsistent with the intuitive non-redundancy of (1)–(4). In standard deontic logic, it seems that we cannot represent the above set of sentences in a way that satisfies both the consistency and the non-redundancy of the original set of English sentences.

Following Patricia Greenspan (1975), let's call the derivation of $\bigcirc \neg n$ from CD3 and CD4 a *factual detachment* and the derivation of $\bigcirc n$ from CD1 and CD2 a *deontic detachment*. The cause of the paradox, it seems, is that standard deontic logic allows both factual and deontic detachments indiscriminately. This has led to attempts to block or modify one or both of these two detachment principles. Since detachments are closely related to conditional statements, it has also led to a reconsideration of the formalization of conditional obligations.

It has become increasingly clear that an adequate system of deontic logic should be able to allow both deontic detachment and factual detachment yet to handle them coherently. It is then not surprising that temporal specification and other parameters have been employed to restrict normative operators and conditional obligations. Within a tensified deontic logic, the paradoxical results of various deontic paradoxes can be avoided by assigning different time parameters to the obligations involved. The result of Chisholm's story, for example, would be something like $\bigcirc_{t1} n \wedge \bigcirc_{t2} \neg n$. Since these two obligations apply at different times, the result will not violate the principle of deontic consistency. However, some obligations, such as general moral principles, seem not so easily affected by temporal factors, while temporal factors seems to be only one of various factors that might influence conditional obligations and detachments.

The systems of deontic logic can be categorized by different criteria. According to the normative operator they use, they can be divided into monadic (one argument) or dyadic (two argument) deontic logics. According to the types of conditionality used for "if-then" sentences in these systems, they can be characterized as deontic logics with material implication (e.g., **SDL**), deontic logics with necessary implication, deontic logics with counterfactual conditionals, etc. Systems of deontic logic can also be divided into different groups according to their positions regarding their principles of detachments. According to this criterion, different systems can be divided into three groups: the deontic detachment systems, the factual detachment systems, and the systems that allow both detachments. We will use this last criterion to organize the different "pre-defeasibility" attempts to resolve Chisholm's Paradox.

4.1. Deontic Detachment Systems

The most common way for a deontic detachment system to dismiss the principle of factual detachment is to use a dyadic normative operator instead of a monadic normative operator to formalize a conditional obligation. Hence, the deontic detachment systems are closely related to dyadic systems: almost all (if not all) deontic detachment systems are dyadic deontic systems and most dyadic deontic systems are deontic detachment systems.

A conditional obligation is formalized as $\bigcirc(\psi/\phi)$ in a dyadic system. It is read "It ought to be that ψ given that ϕ". The original dyadic system of deontic logic was proposed by von Wright (1956). His system is characterized by the following axioms.

VD1: $\quad \mathcal{P}(\phi/\psi) \vee \mathcal{P}(\neg\phi/\psi)$

VD2: $\quad \mathcal{P}(\phi \wedge \psi/\chi) \equiv \mathcal{P}(\phi/\chi) \wedge \mathcal{P}(\psi/\chi \wedge \phi)$

A deontic system of relative or conditional permission, prohibition, and obligation, according to von Wright, could be developed upon these two axioms. And the new system would include the old, unconditional (monadic) system, with the theorems of the latter under tautologous conditions $\psi \vee \neg\psi$. An unconditional obligation, therefore, would be represented by $O(\phi/\psi \vee \neg\psi)$.

Later von Wright (1971) presented another dyadic system and indicated that it could handle Chisholm's paradox. However, it is not clear whether the system can handle the Paradox since von Wright does not specify which detachment he endorses. For a more general criticism of von Wright's dyadic systems refer to Dagfinn Føllesdal and Risto Hilpinen (1971).

Other logicians offer different dyadic systems that do endorse a deontic detachment. Since Feldman and Mark Vorobej have dealt with Chisholm's Paradox directly, in what follows we will mainly discuss their systems in turn.

Feldman (1986; 1990) offers a deontic detachment approach within the framework of a dyadic system. Feldman thinks that the problem of **SDL** arise from its failure to take into account the fact that obligations devolve upon individuals at times. A person a might have an obligation to do something at a certain time. But doing the same thing might not be an obligation for a person b or even for a himself at a different time.

Feldman characterizes a possible world is a "huge proposition" that describes "some total way the world might have been" (1990, p.311). On Feldman's approach, possible worlds are ranked according to a value-relation with the best worlds ranked highest. In this context, $\bigcirc\phi$ in earlier systems of deontic logic would mean "ϕ is true at all the best worlds". In order to capture the idea that obligations devolve upon individuals at times, Feldman introduces a new relation of accessibility to the semantics. This accessibility relation enables him to relate possible worlds to a person at a time. "Instead of using an unadorned '$\bigcirc$' to express truth at all the best worlds, we can use an '$\bigcirc$' with both a personal and a temporal subscript to indicate truth at all the best worlds accessible to the indicated person as of the indicated time" (1990, p.322). $\bigcirc_{s,t}\phi$ therefore abbreviates "ϕ occurs in all the best worlds accessible to a person s as of a time t". Feldman also introduces the symbol $\rightarrow$ to represent a kind of necessary conditional. Thus, $\phi\rightarrow\psi$, for example, will express "the idea that the material conditional $\phi \supset \psi$ is true at every world" (1990, p.311). The system based on this semantics is called **DBWC** (Doing the Best We Can) which includes the following axioms:

FF1: $\bigcirc_{s,t}\phi \supset \neg \bigcirc_{s,t} \neg\phi$

FF2: $[(\bigcirc_{s,t}\phi) \wedge (\phi\rightarrow\psi)] \supset \bigcirc_{s,t}\psi$

FF3: $\bigcirc_{s,t}(\phi \wedge \psi) \supset \bigcirc_{s,t}\phi \wedge \bigcirc_{s,t}\psi$

A conditional obligation in **DBWC** is symbolized as $\bigcirc_{s,t}\phi/\psi$ which says that ϕ occurs in all the best ψ-worlds accessible to s at t. The straightforward factual detachment

FF4: $\quad [(\bigcirc_{s,t}\phi/\psi) \wedge \psi] \supset \bigcirc_{s,t}\phi$

is not valid in **DBWC** because although ϕ might be true in all the best accessible ψ-worlds, the real world (where ψ is true) might not be one of the best. Only an "unalterability detachment" is valid. If $\mathcal{U}$ stands for unalterability, then an unalterability detachment is represented by the following principle.

FF5: $\quad [(\bigcirc_{s,t}\phi/\psi) \wedge \mathcal{U}_{s,t}\psi] \supset \bigcirc_{s,t}\psi$

The temporal subscripts play an essential role in Feldman's solution to Chisholm's Paradox. He sets t as a time at which Jones is still able to go to help his neighbors and notify them, and is also still able not to go and not to notify them. The four sentences are formalized as follows.

FF6: $\quad \bigcirc_{j,t}g$
FF7: $\quad \bigcirc_{j,t}n/g$
FF8: $\quad \bigcirc_{j,t}\neg n/\neg g$
FF9: $\quad \neg g$

We can derive

FF10: $\quad \bigcirc_{j,t}n$

by applying deontic detachment to FF6 and FF7. But we cannot derive

FF11: $\quad \bigcirc_{j,t}\neg n$

from FF8 and FF9 because factual detachment is not valid in **DBWC**.

Feldman's treatment of Chisholm's Paradox is criticized by Castañeda (1989a; 1989b) and Tomberlin (1990). Castañeda points out that Feldman's treatment has the following result.

FF12: $\quad \neg g \wedge \bigcirc_{j,t}n$

FF12 says that Jones is not going to aid his neighbors but he nevertheless ought to tell them he will go to help them. Feldman admits that FF12 is "a bit strange"; but he insists that it is a reasonable representation of the situation. According to Feldman, $\neg g$ stands for "Jones is not going to the aid of his neighbors" rather than "Jones does not go to the aid of his neighbors". The possible worlds open to Jones at a time of "not going to" are different from the possible worlds open to him at a time of "does not go to". To somebody who is not going to aid his neighbors, he still can go to aid his neighbors. The best worlds accessible to him are still those where he goes to their aid and consequently notifies his neighbors.

Feldman seems to admit that if Jones in fact does not go to their aid, then we can conclude he ought not to notify his neighbors. But suppose this is the case (and it seems to be the case in Chisholm's original example); then, instead of FF9, we have:

FF13: $\quad \mathcal{U}_{j,t}\neg g$

together with FF8 and FF5, we have FF11 which contradicts FF10.

If Feldman does not tell us directly how to resolve the Paradox when $\neg g$ is interpreted as an unalterable fact, Vorobej (1986) does offer a way out. Vorobej presents "a future tensed variant of" Chisholm's story.

9. John ought to help his neighbor tomorrow.
10. If John will help, he ought to tell his neighbor today that he will help.
11. If John will not help, he ought not to tell his neighbor today that he will help.
12. John will not help tomorrow.

Vorobej holds that the revision is important, because a tenseless reading of Chisholm's sentences is inconsistent. It is inconsistent because, according to his understanding of the Kantian "ought implies can" principle, "John does not help", if it is settled, will make "John ought to help" impossible. For "John does not help" entails he is no longer able to (meaningfully) do so. This contradicts that "John ought to help" which entails John is able (it is possible) to do so. The inconsistency will no longer exist in a future tensed version of Chisholm's set. Now "John will not help tomorrow" will not make "John ought to help tomorrow" impossible because he still can help.

Vorobej prefers deontic detachment for it "has a strong intuitive appeal and is provable in the majority of existing deontic systems" (1986, p.16). His main argument against a (straight) factual detachment in the context of Chisholm's Paradox could be summarized as follows. The detachment of "John ought not to tell his neighbor" is permissible only in case "John ought to help" is no longer held. Let h and t abbreviate, respectively, "John helps his neighbor" and "John tells his neighbor that he will help", then the above idea is formalized as follows.

$$\text{MV1:} \qquad (\neg h \wedge \bigcirc(\neg t / \neg h) \wedge \neg \bigcirc h) \supset \bigcirc \neg t$$

But since it is still possible for John to help, it is not the case that $\neg \bigcirc h$. Therefore, we cannot get the conclusion $\bigcirc \neg t$. According to Vorobej,

$$\text{MV2:} \qquad (\neg h \wedge \bigcirc(\neg t / \neg h)) \supset \bigcirc \neg t$$

is invalid because we don't know whether $\bigcirc h$ is still held or not.

However, there are difficulties in Vorobej's account. The first difficulty is whether John's failure to help negates his original obligation to help or his obligation to notify his neighbors that he will help. It seems to us that John's failure to help negates the latter but not the former. Another difficulty is that, if it is not the case that John ought to help his neighbor, MV1 would no longer express a contrary-to-duty obligation. This distorts Chisholm's story, since how to formalize a contrary-to-duty obligation is one of the essential points of Chisholm's Paradox.

Although Feldman and Vorobej have modified the strict deontic detachment system by allowing a restricted factual detachment, they still cannot provide a satisfactory solution to Chisholm's Paradox. Generally speaking, a deontic detachment system has difficulty handling situations where actual obligations and factual statements are involved.

4.2. *Factual Detachment Systems*

Mott (1973), al-Hibri (1978), and Robert McArthur (1982) propose factual detachment systems. We will concentrate on Mott's account.

Mott's system of conditional obligation is based on David Lewis' counterfactual conditional. According to Lewis (1974), a counterfactual conditional $\phi \,\square\!\!\rightarrow \psi$ means that if ϕ were true then ψ also would be true. Semantically, $\phi \,\square\!\!\rightarrow \psi$ is true at a world w if and only if either there is no possible ϕ-world, or some ϕ-worlds where ψ holds are more similar to w than any ϕ-worlds where ψ does not hold. Some well known inference patterns for material conditionals, such as strengthening the antecedent, transitivity and contraposition, are not valid for counterfactual conditionals. The invalidity of these inferences prevents some well-known "paradoxes" associated with material conditional.

Mott's system includes the following axioms and rules of inference subjoined to the propositional calculus:

PM1:	$\bigcirc(\phi \supset \psi) \supset (\bigcirc\phi \supset \bigcirc\psi)$
PM2:	$\bigcirc\phi \supset \neg \bigcirc \neg\phi$
PM3:	$\phi \,\square\!\!\rightarrow \phi$
PM4:	$(\phi \wedge \psi) \supset (\phi \,\square\!\!\rightarrow \psi)$
PM5:	$(\phi \,\square\!\!\rightarrow \psi \wedge \psi \,\square\!\!\rightarrow \phi) \supset (\phi \,\square\!\!\rightarrow \chi \leftrightarrow \psi \,\square\!\!\rightarrow \chi)$
PM6:	$(\phi \,\square\!\!\rightarrow \psi) \supset (\phi \supset \psi)$
PM7:	$(\phi \vee \psi \,\square\!\!\rightarrow \psi) \vee (\phi \vee \psi \,\square\!\!\rightarrow \phi) \vee [(\phi \vee \psi \,\square\!\!\rightarrow \chi) \leftrightarrow$ $((\phi \,\square\!\!\rightarrow \chi) \wedge (\psi \,\square\!\!\rightarrow \chi))]$
PM8:	$(\neg\phi \,\square\!\!\rightarrow \phi) \supset \bigcirc\phi$
PM9:	if $\vdash \phi$ then $\vdash \bigcirc \phi$
PM10:	if $\vdash (\phi \supset \psi) \supset (\phi \supset \chi)$ then $\vdash (\phi \,\square\!\!\rightarrow \psi) \supset (\phi \,\square\!\!\rightarrow \chi)$

Semantically, Mott proposes the concept of the best of practically attainable worlds to replace the more common concept of deontically ideal worlds. Thus, $\bigcirc\phi$ is true in w if and only if ϕ is true in all the best practically attainable worlds from w. A conditional obligation could be formalized either as $\bigcirc(\phi \,\square\!\!\rightarrow \psi)$ or $\phi \,\square\!\!\rightarrow \bigcirc \psi$. $\bigcirc(\phi \,\square\!\!\rightarrow \psi)$ is true at world w if and only if, in all the best of practically attainable worlds from w, there are $(\phi \wedge \psi)$-worlds closer than any $(\phi \wedge \neg\psi)$-worlds. $\phi \,\square\!\!\rightarrow \bigcirc \psi$ is true if and only if some ϕ-worlds where $\bigcirc\psi$ is true, namely, where all the best practically attainable worlds are ψ-worlds, are closer to w than any ϕ-worlds where $\bigcirc\psi$ is not true.

Mott uses Lennart Åqvist's (1967) version of Chisholm's Paradox:

13. Jones robs Smith.
14. Jones ought not to rob Smith.
15. It ought to be that if Jones doesn't rob Smith, he isn't punished.

16. If Jones does rob Smith then he ought to be punished.

Mott proposes three adequacy conditions for formalizing (13) to (16): the representation must be consistent; the entailment between (13) and (16) and "Jones ought to be punished" must be preserved; and the representation of "It ought to be that if Jones doesn't rob Smith then he is punished" must be false. Mott formalizes (13)–(16) as follows.

> PM11: r
> PM12: $\bigcirc \neg r$
> PM13: $\neg r \,\square\!\!\rightarrow \bigcirc \neg p$
> PM14: $r \supset \bigcirc p$

It is apparent that the representation is both consistent and non-redundant. Although we can get $\bigcirc p$ from PM11 and PM14 through *modus ponens,* we cannot derive $\bigcirc \neg p$ from PM12 and PM13. Also, since

> PM15: $\phi \supset (\neg \phi \,\square\!\!\rightarrow \psi)$

is not valid in conditional logic, the counterfactual conditional in PM13 is not derivable from PM11. Consequently, the representation is non-redundant.

The representation also satisfies Mott's requirement that the representation of "It ought to be that if Jones doesn't rob Smith then he is punished" is false. Now if $\neg r \,\square\!\!\rightarrow \bigcirc \neg p$ is true, then the most similar $\neg r$-worlds to ours are $\bigcirc \neg p$-worlds, in which all the "ethically desirable" worlds are $\neg p$-worlds. So $\bigcirc p$ is false at those worlds and $\neg r \,\square\!\!\rightarrow \bigcirc p$ is false at the actual world.

Mott's way of blocking the deontic detachment from PM12 and PM13, as some critics have suggested, seems to be arbitrary. Tomberlin (1981) thinks that it is reasonable to allow a factual detachment, but argues that Mott offers no justification for representing sentence (3) as PM13 instead of

> PM16: $\bigcirc(\neg r \,\square\!\!\rightarrow \neg p)$

PM16 seems more appropriate to represent the original sentence (15) based on Mott's semantics. But if this is the case, from PM12 and PM16 we again get $\bigcirc \neg p$ and the paradox is reinstated. Judith Decew (1967) argues that, $\bigcirc \neg p$ rather than $\bigcirc p$ should be derivable. For it is odd to say that a man has an absolute obligation to be punished rather than not to be punished. In other words, she is arguing for a deontic detachment over a factual detachment. In addition, both Decew and Tomberlin think that it would make better sense if both conditional sentences in the story were represented as counterfactuals.

Generally speaking, those who are against deontic detachments think that deontic detachments are only suited to ideal worlds. Since our world is not an ideal world, they are not valid here. Otherwise, unsolvable paradoxes will be created in deontic logic. McArthur (1982), for example, defends this view. But deontic logic should support reasoning about *prima facie* obligations. To exclude deontic detachments from deontic logic unnecessarily limits the scope of deontic logic. Hence, although we do not agree with Decew's preference of deontic detachment over factual detachment, we think a deontic logic should support deontic detachment in addition to a factual detachment. A mechanism is needed to resolve the conflicts between the two kinds of detachments rather than an arbitrary representation to block either deontic detachment or factual detachment.

5. RECURRING THEMES IN DEFEASIBLE REASONING

Defeasible rules or principles are defeated by other rules or principles which often as not are also defeasible. When two defeasible rules compete, how do we resolve the conflict? Which rule do we apply? Sometimes there is at least a plausible answer to this question. For example, if one of the competing principles is more specific than the other – e.g., "Penguins don't ordinarily fly" is more specific than "Birds normally fly" – we apply the more specific rule and reject the less specific. But often there is no meta-principle to resolve the issue. We have no easy way to decide between "Quakers are normally pacifists" and "Republicans usually are not pacifists" in the familiar Nixon Diamond. If we apply either of these rules for a particular individual, then the consequent of the other rule is falsified for that individual and on pain of contradiction we cannot apply it. So applying one blocks the other. The order in which we apply the rules affects the outcome.

Suppose we have a set of formulas S which includes all the formulas in some defeasible theory T. Suppose S contains all the formulas that can be derived from S using first-order logic. Suppose further that for every defeasible rule r in T, either r isn't satisfied in S, r is blocked in S, or the consequent of r is a member of S. We might want to impose some additional requirements on S as well. Any set like S which meets all these requirements is called an *extension* of the theory T. We can also call S a *fixed-point* for T since we can add nothing new to S using either first-order logic or any of the defeasible rules in T. Depending on how we construct our defeasible theories and the constraints we put on extensions or fixed-points, there may or may not be an algorithm for generating all of the extensions of a given theory. This description of the fixed-point approach to defeasible reasoning is admittedly imprecise. It is difficult to be more precise without talking about the details of a particular fixed-point theory. This kind of approach is essentially syntactic. One of the best known fixed-point approaches to nonmonotonic reasoning is Reiter's (1980) default logic. Horty's paper in this volume is based on Reiter's system. Ryu and Lee present their own fixed-point approach. Asher and Bonevac, Prakken and Sergot, Royakkers and Dignum, and Morreau also present systems which arguably depend upon a fixed-point method.

A semantic approach to defeasible reasoning utilizes the notion of a preference relation on possible worlds. Outside the context of normative reasoning, the preference relation is understood to represent something like *normality* where preferred worlds are more normal than less preferred worlds. In normative contexts, the preference ordering is perhaps more intuitive: preferred worlds are morally better than their less preferred counterparts. Bengt Hansson (1969) and David Lewis (1974) proposed preference semantics for normative contexts well before the recent wave of interest in defeasible reasoning. This kind of semantics seems best suited for conditional obligations. A conditional obligation $\bigcirc(\phi/\psi)$ would be true just in case ϕ is true in all the best worlds in which ψ is true. The papers by Åqvist, Prakken and Sergot, and van der Torre and Tan in this volume all rely on preference semantics.

Principles like *lex superior* and *lex posterior* in law point to the fact that normative reasoning often appeals to an explicit claim that one normative principle takes precedence over another. Some of the authors in this volume make a partial ordering on the rules of the system an integral part of their defeasible deontic formalisms. These include Morreau, Royakkers and Dignum, and Ryu and Lee. Nute proposes using a second defeasible theory to reason about the priority of rules in an original defeasible deontic theory.

Not all the papers in this volume represent defeasible approaches to deontic logic. Belzer and Loewer recognize the importance of defeasible normative principles, but they propose a system for deriving our "all-things-considered" obligations. Clearly, either a moral judgment represents all morally relevant considerations or it does not. If it does, then no further information and no further deliberation can change it. So while defeasible normative principles will be considered in arriving at an "all-things-considered" obligation, this kind of reasoning must by definition be monotonic. Carmo and Jones recognize the importance of defeasible reasoning for certain kinds of normative reasoning, but they offer an alternative modal approach to the solution of Chisholm's Paradox. Finally, Loui provides a defeasibilist's response to modal accounts of conflicting norms due to von Wright and Alchourrón. Carlos Alchourrón had planned to write a paper for this volume, but his death prevented this. We are pleased that his work is represented here Loui's discussion.

Donald Nute
Department of Philosophy and Artificial Intelligence Center
The University of Georgia

Xiaochang Yu
University Library Services
Virginia Commonwealth University

REFERENCES

al-Hibri, Azizah (1978). *Deontic Logic: A Comprehensive Appraisal and a New Proposal.* University Press of America, Washington, D.C.

Åqvist, Lennart (1967). Good samaritans, contrary-to-duty imperatives, and epistemic obligations. *Noûs* 1:361–379.

Åqvist, Lennart (1984). Deontic logic. In D. Gabbay and F. Guenthner (eds.), *Handbook of Philosophical Logic, Vol II*, D. Reidel, Dordrecht.

Castañeda, Hector-Neri (1981). The paradoxes of deontic logic: the simplest solution to all of them in one fell swoop. In Risto Hilpinen (ed.), *New Studies in Deontic Logic: Norms, Actions, and the Foundations of Ethics*, D. Reidel, Dordrecht.

Castañeda, Hector-Neri (1986). Obligations, aspectual actions and circumstances, *Philosophical Papers* 15:155–170.

Castañeda, Hector-Neri (1989a). Paradoxes of moral reparation: deontic foci and circumstances. *Philosophical Studies* 57:1–21.

Castañeda, Hector-Neri (1989b). Moral obligation, circumstances, and deontic foci (a rejoinder to Fred Feldman). *Philosophical Studies* 57:157–174.

Chisholm, Roderick M. (1963). Contrary-to-duty imperatives and deontic logic. *Analysis* 24:33–36.

Decew, Judith W. (1981). Conditional obligation and counterfactuals. *Journal of Philosophical Logic* 10:55–72.

Feldman, Fred (1986). *Doing the Best We Can*. D. Reidel, Dordrecht.

Feldman, Fred (1990). A simpler solution to the paradoxes of deontic logic. In James Tomberlin (ed.), *Philosophical Perspectives, 4: Action Theory and Philosophy of Mind*, Ridgeview, Atascadero.

Forrester, James(1984). Gentle murder, or the adverbial samaritan. *The Journal of Philosophy* 81:193–197.

Føllesdal, Dagfinn and Risto Hilpinen (1971). Deontic logic: an introduction. In Risto Hilpinen (ed.), *Deontic Logic: Introduction and Systematic Readings*, D. Reidel, Dordrecht.

Goble, Lou (1991). Murder most gentle: the paradox deepens. *Philosophical Studies* 64:217–227.

Greenspan, Patricia (1975). Conditional oughts and hypothetical imperatives. *The Journal of Philosophy* 72:259–276.

Hansson, Bengt (1969). An analysis of some deontic logics. *Noûs* 3:373–398. Reprinted in Risto Hilpinen (ed.), *Deontic Logic: Introduction and Systematic Readings*, D. Reidel, Dordrecht, 1971.

Hansson, Sven (1988). Deontic logic without misleading alethic analogies. *Logique et Analyse* 31:337–370.

Hintikka, Jaakko (1971). Some main problems of deontic logic. In Risto Hilpinen (ed.), *Deontic Logic: Introduction and Systematic Readings*, D. Reidel, Dordrecht.

Jackson, Frank (1985). On the semantics and logic of obligation. *Mind* 94:177–195.

Lewis, David (1974). Semantic analysis for dyadic deontic logic. *Logical Theory and Semantic Analysis: Essays Dedicated to Stig Kanger on his Fiftieth Birthday*, Søren Stenlund (ed.), D. Reidel, Dordrecht.

McArthur, Robert (1982). Defeasible obligation. *Pacific Philosophical Quarterly* 63:157–167.

Mott, Peter L. (1973). On Chisholm's paradox. *Journal of Philosophical Logic* 2:197–211.

Prior, Arthur N. (1954). The paradoxes of derived obligation. *Mind* 63:64–65.

Reiter, Raymond (1980). A logic for default reasoning. *Artificial Intelligence* 13:81–132.

Ross, W. D. (1930). *The Right and the Good*, Clarendon Press, Oxford.

Sinnott-Armstrong, Walter (1985). A solution to Forrester's paradox of gentle murder. *The Journal of Philosophy* 82:162–168.

Tomberlin, James E. (1981). Contrary-to-duty imperatives and conditional obligations. *Noûs* 15:357–375.

Tomberlin, James E. (1990). Deontic paradox and conditional obligation. *Philosophy and Phenomenological Research* 50:107–114.

von Wright, Georg Henrik (1951). Deontic logic. *Mind* 60:1–15.
von Wright, Georg Henrik (1956). A note on deontic logic and derived obligation. *Mind* 65:507–509.
von Wright, Georg Henrik (1971). A new system of deontic logic. In Risto Hilpinen (ed.), *Deontic Logic: Introduction and Systematic Readings,* D. Reidel, Dordrecht.
Vorobej, Mark I. (1986). Conditional obligation and detachment. *Canadian Journal of Philosophy* 16:11–26.

JOHN F. HORTY

NONMONOTONIC FOUNDATIONS FOR DEONTIC LOGIC

1. INTRODUCTION

Ever since its inception in the work of G. H. von Wright (von Wright, 1951), deontic logic has been developed primarily as a species of modal logic. I argue in this paper, however, that, at least for certain purposes, the techniques recently developed within the field of nonmonotonic logic may provide a better theoretical framework for the formal study of normative reasoning than the usual modal treatment.

The two subjects of deontic and nonmonotonic logic have evolved within different disciplines. Deontic logic was developed, for the most part, by philosophers concerned with valid patterns of ethical and legal reasoning. The study of nonmonotonic logic, on the other hand, was initiated, much more recently, by researchers in artificial intelligence who felt that the logical theories then available could not be used to represent the kind of defeasible generalizations that constitute so much of our commonsense knowledge. Still, even though they have evolved within such different disciplines, it is not really surprising that there might be illuminating connections between these two subjects, for it is natural to view the rules underlying much of our ethical and legal reasoning as themselves carrying the kind of defeasible quality that motivated the development of nonmonotonic logic.

In the past few years, much of the research in nonmonotonic logic has concentrated on conflicts among defeasible generalizations, and also on situations in which one of two conflicting generalization might be taken to override another. Accordingly, I focus here on two particular areas of normative reasoning in which the techniques of nonmonotonic logic promise improved understanding: the first is the logic of conflicting oughts statements; the second is the logic governing those conditionals taken as expressing prima facie oughts.

The paper is organized as follows. Section 2 reviews three logical approaches to conflicting oughts: the accounts provided by standard modal logic and by a weaker modal logic, and then an account set out by Bas van Fraassen in (van Fraassen, 1973). I argue that, of these options, only van Fraassen's account is intuitively adequate; but as it turns out, this approach cannot be interpreted in any natural way within the framework of modal logic. Section 3 introduces one of the most familiar formalisms for nonmonotonic reasoning, Raymond Reiter's default logic (Reiter, 1980), and then reviews a result, first presented in (Horty, 1994), that justifies an interpretation of

17

D. Nute (ed.), Defeasible Deontic Logic, 17–44.

van Fraassen's deontic logic into Reiter's default logic. Section 4 explores some technical points concerning van Fraassen's account, and then develops three variant approaches. I believe that these variants approaches, like van Fraassen's original account, likewise reflect stable and coherent strategies for reasoning with conflicting oughts; but again, they cannot be interpreted naturally within modal logic.

Section 5 reviews two ways in which conditional ought statements have been formalized within the framework of modal logic, and then points out a shared difficulty that renders each of these treatments inadequate as a formalization of prima facie oughts. Section 6 begins by sketching a way in which this problem might be addressed within the framework of nonmonotonic logic. A number of issues concerning conditional reasoning in the nonmonotonic framework are still unsettled, however, and so the section concludes by surveying some of the ways in which these open questions bear upon the preliminary sketch.

2. NORMATIVE CONFLICTS

2.1. *Standard deontic logic*

On the usual approach to deontic logic, obligation is interpreted as a kind of necessity, which can be modeled using possible worlds techniques. The most familiar theory of this kind, known as *standard deontic logic*, is based on models of the form $\mathcal{M} = \langle W, f, v \rangle$, with W a set of possible worlds, v a valuation mapping sentence letters into sets of worlds at which they are true, and f a function mapping each world into a nonempty set of worlds. Where α is an individual world, $f(\alpha)$ can be thought of as the set of worlds ideal from the standpoint of α, those in which all the oughts in force at α are satisfied; or if we follow the common practice of identifying propositions with sets of worlds, $f(\alpha)$ can then be viewed as a proposition expressing the standard of obligation at work in α.

Against the background of these standard deontic models, the evaluation rule for the connective $\bigcirc$, representing 'It ought to be the case that ...', is given as

$$\mathcal{M}, \alpha \models \bigcirc A \text{ if and only if } f(\alpha) \subseteq |A|,$$

with $|A|$ representing the set of worlds in which A is true. The idea is that $\bigcirc A$ should hold just in case A is a necessary condition for things turning out as they should—just in case A is entailed by the relevant standard of obligation.

Let us say that a situation gives rise to a *normative conflict* if it presents each of two conflicting propositions as obligatory—if, for example, it supports the truth of both $\bigcirc A$ and $\bigcirc B$ where A and B cannot hold jointly; or, as an extreme case, if it supports the truth of both $\bigcirc A$ and $\bigcirc \neg A$. We often seem to face conflicts like this in everyday life, and there are a number of vivid examples in philosophy and literature. Perhaps the best known of these is Sartre's description (Sartre, 1946) of a student during the Second World War who felt for reasons of patriotism and vengeance (his brother had been killed by the Germans) that he ought to leave home in order to join the Free French, but who felt also, for reasons of sympathy and personal devotion, that he ought to stay at home in order to care for his mother.

Sartre presents this student's situation in a compelling way that really does make it seem as if he had been confronted with conflicting, and perhaps irreconcilable, moral principles. However, if standard deontic logic is correct, Sartre is mistaken: the student did not face a moral conflict—no one ever does, because according to standard deontic logic, such a conflict is impossible. This is easy to see. In order for the two statements $\bigcirc A$ and $\bigcirc B$ to be supported at a world α, we need both $f(\alpha) \subseteq |A|$ and $f(\alpha) \subseteq |B|$, from which it follows, of course, that $f(\alpha) \subseteq |A| \cap |B|$. If the statements A and B were inconsistent, however, we would have $|A| \cap |B| = \emptyset$, from which it would then follow that $f(\alpha) = \emptyset$ as well; but in standard deontic models, the sole requirement on f is that it should map each world into a nonempty set. Apart from what is presupposed by the background framework of normal modal logic, then, the entire content of standard deontic logic seems to be simply that there are no normative conflicts; and in fact, validity in these standard models can be axiomatized by supplementing the basic modal logic K with the statement

$$\neg(\bigcirc A \wedge \bigcirc \neg A)$$

as an additional axiom schema. The resulting system is known as *KD*.

Now this feature of standard deontic logic—that it rules out normative conflicts—has received extensive discussion in the philosophical literature. There is currently no consensus among moral theorists on the question whether an ideal ethical theory could actually be structured in such a way that moral dilemmas might arise.[1] Still, it can seem like an objectionable feature of standard deontic logic that it rules out this possibility. Because the question is open, and the possibility of moral dilemmas is a matter for substantive ethical discussion, it seems to be inappropriate for a position on this issue to be built into the logic of the subject. And even if it does turn out, ultimately, that research in ethics is able to exclude the possibility of conflicts in a correct moral theory, it may be useful all the same to have a logic that allows for conflicting oughts.

One reason for this is that the task of actually applying a correct moral theory to each of the ethical decisions we face every day would be difficult and time-consuming; and it seems unlikely, for most of us, that such a theory could have any more bearing upon our day to day ethical reasoning than

---

[1] The issue has been addressed, for example, in (Donagan, 1984), (Foot, 1983), (Lemmon, 1962), (Marcus, 1980), and (Williams, 1965).

physics has upon our everyday reasoning about objects in the world. Most of our commonsense ethical thinking seems to be guided instead, not by the dictates of moral theory, but by simple rules of thumb—'Return what you borrow', 'Don't cause harm'—and it is not hard to generate conflicts among these.[2] Moreover, normative reasoning more generally is conditioned by a number of oughts, many of which are founded in a concern with matters other than morality—etiquette, aesthetics, fun—and of course, these lead to other conflicts both among themselves and with the oughts of morality. Even if we do eventually conclude, then, that there can be no clashes among the oughts generated by a correct ethical theory, it would still seem necessary to allow for conflicting oughts in any logic that aims to represent either our everyday moral thinking or our normative reasoning more broadly.

Finally, the need for a deontic logic that tolerates conflicting norms can be motivated from a different perspective if we imagine an intelligent system that is designed to reason about and achieve certain goals supplied to it by its users, and that represents those goals as ought statements. It is always possible for different users (or even for the same user) to supply the system with conflicting goals; and in such a case, we would not want the mechanisms for reasoning about goals to break down entirely, as it would if it were guided by standard deontic logic. This kind of situation is analogous to that envisioned by Nuel Belnap in (Belnap, 1977a) and (Belnap, 1977b) as a way of motivating the applicability of a contradiction tolerating logic (a relevance logic, as it happens) in the area of automated reasoning. Belnap imagines a computer designed to reason from data supplied by its users; and he argues that there are situations in which, even if the users inadvertently supply the machine with inconsistent information—say, A and $\neg A$—we would not want it to conclude that everything is true. In the same way, we can easily imagine a situation in which, even if a machine happens to be supplied by its users with inconsistent goals—say, $\bigcirc A$ and $\bigcirc \neg A$—we would not want it to conclude, as in standard deontic logic, that it should regard every proposition as a goal.

2.2. *A weak modal logic*

One strategy for adapting deontic logic to reason sensibly in the face of conflicting norms is to continue the attempt to develop the subject within a modal framework, but simply to move to a weaker, non-normal modal logic. The clearest example of this is Brian Chellas's suggestion, in (Chellas, 1974) and (Chellas, 1980, Sections 6.5 and 10.2), that we base our deontic logic on a class of minimal models for modal logic, in which the accessibility relation maps individual worlds, not into sets of worlds, but into sets of propositions—

---

[2]The relation between moral theory and the rules of thumb that guide everyday ethical decisions has recently been discussed in (Dennett, 1986).

sets of sets of worlds. More exactly, Chellas recommends a deontic logic based on models of the form $\mathcal{M} = \langle W, N, v \rangle$, with W and v as before, but with N a function from W into $\wp(\wp(W))$, subject to the condition that, for each of the propositions X and Y in $\wp(W)$, if $X \in N(\alpha)$ and $X \subseteq Y$, then $Y \in N(\alpha)$.[3] Intuitively, the various propositions belonging to $N(\alpha)$ can be thought of as expressing the variety of different ways in which things ought to turn out at α, the variety of different normative standards in force at α.

In these models, the truth conditions for ought statements can be presented through the rule

$$\mathcal{M}, \alpha \models \bigcirc A \text{ if and only if } |A| \in N(\alpha) \; ;$$

the idea is that $\bigcirc A$ should hold just in case A is entailed by some normative standard at work in α. And validity is axiomatized by the system EM, which results from supplementing ordinary propositional logic with the rule schema

$$A \supset B$$
$$\overline{\bigcirc A \supset \bigcirc B.}$$

In fact, this logic is weak enough to tolerate normative conflicts: the statements $\bigcirc A$ and $\bigcirc \neg A$ are jointly satisfiable, without entailing $\bigcirc B$. However, in weakening standard deontic logic to allow conflicts, it seems that we have now arrived at a system that is too weak: it fails to validate intuitively desirable inferences. Suppose, for example, that an agent is subject to the following two norms, the first issuing perhaps from some legal authority, the second from religion or conscience:

You ought either to fight in the army or perform alternative service,
You ought not to fight in the army.

We can represent these norms through the formulas $\bigcirc(F \vee S)$ and $\bigcirc \neg F$. Now it seems intuitively that the agent should conclude from these premises that he ought to perform alternative service. However, the inference from $\bigcirc(F \vee S)$ and $\bigcirc \neg F$ to $\bigcirc S$ is not valid in the logic EM.

Let us look at this problem a bit more closely. Any logical consequence of an ought derivable in EM is itself derivable as an ought in this system; and of course, S is a logical consequence of $(F \vee S) \wedge \neg F$. Therefore, we would be able to derive $\bigcirc S$ from our premise set if we could somehow merge the

---

[3]Chellas recommends also the further condition that $\emptyset \notin N(\alpha)$. I ignore this condition because it seems like an overly strong constraint for many application areas, particularly the case in which the oughts of a deontic logic represent goals supplied to an intelligent system by its users. We would not want to rule out the possibility that a fallible user might present an intelligent system with an impossible goal ("Find a rational root for this equation"), or to abandon sensible reasoning in such a case.

individual oughts $\bigcirc(F \lor S)$ and $\bigcirc \neg F$ together into a joint ought of the form

$$\bigcirc((F \lor S) \land \neg F).$$

But how could we get this latter statement? It seems possible to derive it from our premises only through a rule of the form

$$\frac{\bigcirc A \qquad \bigcirc B}{\bigcirc(A \land B),}$$

dubbed by Bernard Williams as the rule of *agglomeration* (Williams, 1965). However, such a rule is not admissible in *EM*, and in fact, it is exactly the kind of thing that this logic is designed to avoid: from $\bigcirc A$ and $\bigcirc \neg A$, agglomeration would allow us to conclude $\bigcirc(A \land \neg A)$, and so $\bigcirc B$ for arbitrary B, due to closure of ought under logical consequence.

Evidently, the issue of agglomeration is crucial for a proper logical understanding of normative conflicts. We do not want to allow unrestricted agglomeration, as in the standard deontic logic *KD*; this would force us to treat conflicting oughts as incoherent. On the other hand, we do not want to block agglomeration entirely, as in the weak deontic logic *EM*; we would then miss some desirable consequences in cases in which conflict is not a problem.

2.3. Van Fraassen's proposal

As far as I know, the first intuitively adequate account of reasoning in the presence of normative conflicts was presented in (van Fraassen, 1973), a paper that is largely devoted to more broadly philosophical issues. Suppose that Γ is a set of oughts, possibly conflicting, and let us say that a statement of the form $\bigcirc B$ is fulfilled in some situation just in case B is true in that situation. The basic idea behind van Fraassen's suggestion, then, is that the statement $\bigcirc A$ should follow from Γ just in case the truth of A is a necessary condition for fulfilling some maximal set of the ought statements contained in Γ.

As van Fraassen presents it, the account relies formally on a notion of *score*. Where $\mathcal{M}$ is an (ordinary, classical) model of an underlying, ought-free language, the score of $\mathcal{M}$, relative to a set of ought statements Γ, is defined as the set of statements from Γ that $\mathcal{M}$ fulfills:

$$score_\Gamma(\mathcal{M}) = \{\bigcirc B \in \Gamma : \mathcal{M} \models B\}.$$

In this non-modal framework, we now let $|A|$ represent the ordinary model class of A: $|A| = \{\mathcal{M} : \mathcal{M} \models A\}$. Van Fraassen's notion of deontic consequence, which we represent as the relation $\vdash_F$, is then defined as follows.

Definition 1 $\Gamma \vdash_F \bigcirc A$ if and only if there is a model $\mathcal{M}_1 \in |A|$ for which there is no model $\mathcal{M}_2 \in |\neg A|$ such that $score_\Gamma(\mathcal{M}_1) \subseteq score_\Gamma(\mathcal{M}_2)$.

As in the logic *EM*, this notion of consequence is weak enough that conflicting oughts do not imply arbitrary oughts: we cannot derive $\bigcirc B$ from $\bigcirc A$ and $\bigcirc \neg A$. However, unlike *EM*, this way of characterizing deontic consequence does allow what seems to be the right degree of agglomeration: we can agglomerate individual oughts as long as this does not lead to the introduction of an inconsistent formula within the scope of an ought. For example, although we do not get

$$\bigcirc A, \bigcirc \neg A \vdash_F \bigcirc (A \wedge \neg A),$$

we do have

$$\bigcirc (F \vee S), \bigcirc \neg F \vdash_F \bigcirc ((F \vee S) \wedge \neg F);$$

and then, since any logical consequence of an ought is itself an ought, this tells us that

$$\bigcirc (F \vee S), \bigcirc \neg F \vdash_F \bigcirc S.$$

Although this proposal of van Fraassen's does appear to capture an intuitively attractive and stable account of reasoning in the presence of conflicting norms, and although the general topic of normative conflict has been an issue of intense concern in philosophy for well over a decade, it is hard to find any discussion of the proposal in either the philosophical or the logical literature on the topic. I feel that part of the reason for this neglect is that both philosophers and logicians are accustomed to approaching deontic logic from the perspective of modal logic; and as we will see, van Fraassen's proposal does not fit naturally within this framework. It turns out, however, that the proposal can be interpreted in a straightforward way within the theoretical framework provided by nonmonotonic logic.

3. AN INTERPRETATION WITHIN DEFAULT LOGIC

3.1. *Default logic*

Although nonmonotonic logics have found applications in areas as diverse as database theory and automated diagnosis, an important initial motive in their development was the need felt within artificial intelligence for a formalism more naturally suited than ordinary logical systems to model the tentative nature of commonsense reasoning. Often, it seems, we want to draw conclusions from a given body of data that we would be willing to abandon if that data were supplemented with further information. To take a standard example, if we were told that Tweety is a bird, most of us would conclude that Tweety can fly—since we believe that, as a general rule, birds can fly. However, we would abandon this conclusion, and we would not feel that we had been presented with any kind of inconsistency, if we were then told in addition that Tweety cannot fly.

By now, a number of different formalisms have evolved with the field of nonmonotonic reasoning, but we focus here on one of the most familiar: the default logic defined in (Reiter, 1980), which supplements standard classical logic with new rules of inference, known as *default rules*. In order to characterize the conclusion sets of theories involving these new default rules, Reiter then modifies the standard, monotonic notion of logical consequence.

An ordinary rule of inference (with a single premise) can be depicted simply as a premise-conclusion pair, such as (A/B). This rule commits a reasoner to B once A has been established. By contrast, a default rule is a triple, such as $(A : C \ / \ B)$. Very roughly, this rule can be thought of as committing the reasoner to B once A has been established and, in addition, C is consistent with the reasoner's conclusion set. The formula A is referred to as the *prerequisite* of this default rule, B as its *consequent*, and C as its *justification*. A *default theory* is a pair $\Delta = \langle W, \mathcal{D} \rangle$, in which is W is a set of ordinary formulas and $\mathcal{D}$ is a set of default rules.

Before going on to set out the new concept of a conclusion set defined by Reiter for default theories, let us see how the information given above about Tweety might be represented in default logic. The first case, in which we are told only that Tweety is a bird, can be represented by the default theory $\Delta_1 = \langle W_1, \mathcal{D}_1 \rangle$, where $W_1 = \{Bt\}$ and $\mathcal{D}_1 = \{(Bt : Ft \ / \ Ft)\}$. Here the default rule says that if we know Tweety is a bird, and it is consistent with what we know that Tweety can fly, then we should conclude that Tweety can fly. (The generic statement 'Birds fly' can be taken to mean that, once we learn of some object that it is a bird, we should conclude that it flies, unless we happen to know that it does not. The default rule can then be thought of as an instantiation for Tweety of this generic truth.) In this case, because we do know that Bt, and there is no reason to think that Ft is inconsistent with what we know, the default rule yields Ft as a conclusion. Where Cn is a function mapping any set of formulas to its logical closure, then, the appropriate conclusion set based on Δ_1 seems to be $Cn[\{Bt, Ft\}]$, the logical closure of what we are told to begin with together with the conclusions of the applicable defaults. In the second case, however, when we are told in addition that Tweety does not fly, we move to the default theory $\Delta_2 = \langle W_2, \mathcal{D}_2 \rangle$, with $\mathcal{D}_2 = \mathcal{D}_1$ and $W_2 = W_1 \cup \{\neg Ft\}$. Here the default rule cannot be applied, because its justification is inconsistent with what we know. So the appropriate conclusion set based on Δ_2 seems to be $Cn[W_2]$.

These two examples illustrate, in some simple and natural cases, the kind of conclusion sets desired from given default theories. The task of arriving at a general definition of this notion, however, is not trivial; the trick is to find a way of capturing the intended meaning of the new component—the justification—present in default rules. A default rule is supposed to be applicable only if its justification is consistent with the conclusion set; but what can consistency mean in this setting? Consistency is usually defined in terms of logical consequence (a set is consistent if there is no explicit contradiction among its consequences), and so there is a danger of circularity here. In fact, the very application of a default rule might undermine its own justification, or the justification of some other rule that has already been applied. As an example, consider the theory $\Delta_3 = \langle W_3, \mathcal{D}_3 \rangle$, with $W_3 = \{A, B \supset \neg C\}$ and $\mathcal{D}_3 = \{(A : C \ / \ B)\}$. Before any new conclusions are drawn from this information, the rule $(A : C \ / \ B)$ seems to be applicable, since its prerequisite already belongs to the initial data set W_3, and its justification is consistent with this set. The effect of applying this rule, though, is to introduce B into the conclusion set; just a bit of additional reasoning then shows that the conclusion set must contain $\neg C$ as well, and so the applicability of the default rule is undermined.

Of course, a chain of reasoning like this showing that some default rule is undermined can be arbitrarily long; and so we cannot really be sure that a default rule is applicable in some context until we have applied it, along with all the other rules that seem applicable, and then surveyed the logical closure of the result. Because of this, the conclusion set associated with a default theory cannot be defined in the usual iterative way, by successively adding to the original data the conclusions of the applicable rules of inference, and then taking the limit of this process.

Instead, Reiter is forced to adopt a fixed point approach in specifying the conclusion sets of default theories. He first defines an operator Φ that uses the information from a particular default theory Δ to map each formula set S into the formula set $\Phi_\Delta(S)$, as follows.

Definition 2 Where $\Delta = \langle W, \mathcal{D} \rangle$ is a default theory and S is some set of formulas, $\Phi_\Delta(S)$ is the minimal set satisfying the following three conditions:

1. $W \subseteq \Phi_\Delta(S)$,
2. $Cn[\Phi_\Delta(S)] = \Phi_\Delta(S)$,
3. For each $(A : B \ / \ C) \in \mathcal{D}$, if $A \in \Phi_\Delta(S)$ and $\neg B \notin S$, then $C \in \Phi_\Delta(S)$.

The first two conditions in this definition tell us simply that $\Phi_\Delta(S)$ contains the information provided by the original theory, and that it is closed under logical consequence; the third condition tells us that it contains the conclusions of the default rules applicable in S; and the minimality constraint prevents unwarranted conclusions from creeping in.

Where $\Delta = \langle W, \mathcal{D} \rangle$ is a default theory, the operator Φ_Δ maps any formula set S into the minimal superset of W that is closed under both ordinary logical consequence and the default rules from $\mathcal{D}$ that are applicable in S. The appropriate conclusion sets of default theories—known as *extensions*—are then defined as the fixed points of this operator.

Definition 3 The set $\mathcal{E}$ is an extension of the default theory Δ if and only if $\Phi_\Delta(\mathcal{E}) = \mathcal{E}$.

As the reader can verify, the default theories Δ_1 and Δ_2 above have the advertised conclusion sets as their extensions. In addition, it should be clear that the notion of an extension defined here is a conservative generalization of the corresponding notion of a conclusion set from ordinary logic: the extension of a default theory $\langle \mathcal{W}, \mathcal{D} \rangle$ in which $\mathcal{D}$ is empty is simply $Cn[\mathcal{W}]$.

3.2. *Multiple extensions*

In contrast to the situation in ordinary logic, however, not every default theory leads to a single set of appropriate conclusions. Some default theories, such as Δ_3 above, can be shown to have no extensions; these theories are often viewed as incoherent. More interesting, for our purposes, some default theories lead to multiple extensions. A standard example arises when we try to encode within default logic the following set of facts:

> Nixon is a Quaker,
> Nixon is a republican,
> Quakers tend to be pacifists,
> Republicans tend not to be pacifists.

If we instantiate for Nixon the general statements expressed here about Quakers and republicans, the resulting theory is $\Delta_4 = \langle \mathcal{W}_4, \mathcal{D}_4 \rangle$, with $\mathcal{W}_4 = \{Qn, Rn\}$ and $\mathcal{D}_4 = \{(Qn : Pn \ / \ Pn), (Rn : \neg Pn \ / \ \neg Pn)\}$. This theory allows both $Cn[\mathcal{W}_4 \cup \{Pn\}]$ and $Cn[\mathcal{W}_4 \cup \{\neg Pn\}]$ as extensions. Initially, before we draw any new conclusions, both of the default rules from $\mathcal{D}_4$ are applicable, but once we adopt the conclusion of either, the applicability of the other is blocked.

In cases like this, when a default theory leads to more than one extension, it is hard to decide what conclusions a reasoner should actually draw from the information contained in the theory. Two broad reasoning strategies have been suggested in the literature. According to the first, sometimes described as the *credulous* strategy, the reasoner should arbitrarily select one of the theory's several extensions and endorse the conclusions contained in that extension; according to the second, now generally described as the *skeptical* strategy, the reasoner should endorse a conclusion only if it is contained in the intersection of the theory's extensions.[4] For the purpose of modeling commonsense reasoning, the multiple extensions associated with default theories can sometimes seem like an embarrassment: what we really want is a unique conclusion set, and so we are forced either to select nondeterministically from among these various extensions, or else to combine them somehow into a unique set.

---

[4] The use of the *credulous/skeptical* terminology to characterize these two broad reasoning strategies was first introduced in (Touretzky *et al.* , 1987), but the distinction is older than this; it was noted already in Section 2.2 of (Reiter, 1980), and was described in (McDermott, 1982) as the distinction between *brave* and *cautious* reasoning.

As we shall see, however, the multiple extensions provided by default logic are no longer embarrassing when it comes to interpreting deontic ideas; they give us exactly what we need.

3.3. *Oughts as defaults*

Often, and in all of our examples so far, default rules seem to represent something like commonsense probabilistic generalizations. The defaults concerning birds or Quakers, for instance, seem to mean simply that a large majority of birds can fly, or that a large majority of Quakers are pacifists. The connection between defaults and generalizations of this kind has suggested to many that default reasoning can best be understood as a kind of qualitative probabilistic reasoning, a view that is most thoroughly developed by Judea Pearl (Pearl, 1988).

There are, however, some important examples of default reasoning that do not seem to fit so naturally into the probabilistic framework. In driving along a narrow country road, for instance, it is best, whenever one approaches the crest of a hill, to adopt the default that there will be traffic in the oncoming lane, even if the road is deserted and the actual likelihood of traffic is low. Again, the presumption of innocence in a legal system is a kind of default that overrides probabilistic considerations: even if the most salient reference class to which an individual belongs is one among which the proportion of criminals is very high, we are to presume that he has committed no crime unless there is conclusive evidence to the contrary.[5]

Those who favor a probabilistic understanding of defaults can attempt to account for discrepancies like these between defaults and commonsense generalizations by supposing that default rules might reflect, in addition, information concerning utilities of the outcomes. (For example, it could be argued that the default concerning oncoming traffic is reasonable, even though the likelihood is low, because the cost of a false negative in this case is potentially so high.) But there is also another explanation of the differences here between defaults and commonsense probabilistic generalizations. What these examples suggest is that default rules can be used to represent *norms* quite generally. When the norms involved have a probabilistic basis, it is natural to expect default reasoning to resemble probabilistic reasoning. But default rules can be used also, it seems, to represent other kinds of norms—such as legal or ethical norms—and in that case, any relation with probabilistic reasoning will be more distant.

---

[5]The notion of presumption is discussed in (Ullman-Margalit, 1973), who argues that specific presumptions are justified by a mixture of probabilistic and "value-related" considerations, and cites the presumption of innocence as one in whose justification the value-related considerations seem to outweigh those of probability.

It is this reading of defaults as representing norms in general that moti-
vates the connection, first established in (Horty, 1994), between default and
deontic logics: if the norms generated by ought statements are represented
through default rules, it turns out that van Fraassen's theory of oughts can be
interpreted in a straightforward way within Reiter's default logic.

Formally, the interpretation is developed as follows. Where Γ is some
set of ought statements, we first define the corresponding default theory as
$\Delta_\Gamma = \langle \mathcal{W}, \mathcal{D} \rangle$, with $\mathcal{W} = \emptyset$ and $\mathcal{D} = \{(\top : B \mathbin{/} B) : \bigcirc B \in \Gamma\}$, and with
$\top$ representing the universal truth. The interpretation of ought statements as
defaults is then justified by the following result.

Theorem 1 $\Gamma \vdash_F \bigcirc A$ if and only if $A \in \mathcal{E}$ for some extension $\mathcal{E}$ of Δ_Γ.

This result suggests a way of understanding the extensions of a default theory
as descriptions of situations in which the norms expressed by the defaults are
fulfilled; a default theory that contains conflicting norms, which cannot all be
fulfilled at once, will then give rise to multiple extensions.

It is interesting to note that this particular way of defining a deontic logic
within default logic, aimed at interpreting van Fraassen's theory, relies upon a
credulous treatment of multiple extensions: a statement of the form $\bigcirc A$ is said
to follow from a set of oughts Γ just in case A belongs to any extension of the
corresponding default theory. A deontic consequence relation that relies upon
a skeptical treatment of multiple extensions will be motivated and defined in
Section 4.3.

4. EXPLORING THE THEORY

4.1. *The consequence relation*

Although, as we have seen, van Fraassen's notion of deontic consequence
fits naturally within the framework of nonmonotonic logic, the consequence
relation $\vdash_F$ is itself monotonic: from the fact that $\Gamma \vdash_F \bigcirc A$ we can conclude
that $\Gamma \cup \Gamma' \vdash_F \bigcirc A$. This result follows at once from our Theorem 1 together
with Theorem 3.2 of (Reiter, 1980), and also, more directly, from Theorem 2
below; what it suggests is that, in relating van Fraassen's account of oughts
to default logic, we are not yet relying on the actual nonmonotonicity of this
theory, but only on its ability to yield multiple, mutually inconsistent sets of
sentences as consequence sets for a given set of premises. This will change
in Section 4.3, where we consider some alternatives to the present treatment,
and also in in Section 6, where we extend the present treatment to deal with
conditional oughts.

It is easy to see both that the logical truths follow as oughts from any
premise set, and also, as mentioned earlier, that any logical consequence of a
generated ought is itself generated as an ought: $\vdash A$ implies $\Gamma \vdash_F \bigcirc A$; and
$\Gamma \vdash_F \bigcirc A$ and $A \vdash B$ together imply $\Gamma \vdash_F \bigcirc B$. Moreover, van Fraassen's

consequence relation allows us to derive only consistent formulas as oughts (a form of ought implies can), no matter what ought statements it is supplied with as premises: if $\Gamma \vdash_F \bigcirc A$, then A is consistent.

Because only consistent formulas are derivable as oughts, we can see at once that the consequence relation $\vdash_F$ is not reflexive. Although an inconsistent ought might appear among some set of premises, it cannot appear as a conclusion of those premises; and so we do not have

$$\bigcirc(A \wedge \neg A) \vdash_F \bigcirc(A \wedge \neg A),$$

for example. From this, it follows that van Fraassen's theory cannot be captured in a natural way within a conventional modal logic, since any such logic carries a reflexive consequence relation.

In addition, the $\vdash_F$ relation fails to satisfy the cut rule; for example, although we have

$$\bigcirc(A \wedge B) \vdash_F \bigcirc A$$

and

$$\bigcirc A, \bigcirc\neg B \vdash_F \bigcirc(A \wedge \neg B),$$

we do not have

$$\bigcirc(A \wedge B), \bigcirc\neg B \vdash_F \bigcirc(A \wedge \neg B).^6$$

4.2. *Some comparisons*

As might be expected, van Fraassen's consequence relation $\vdash_F$ generally lies between $\vdash_{EM}$ and $\vdash_{KD}$, the consequence relations associated with *EM* and *KD*; it generally allows us to derive more oughts from a given set of premises than *EM* and fewer than *KD*. But there are exceptions to this general rule, and we need to introduce some technical vocabulary in order to describe the situation exactly.

First, let us officially characterize an *ought statement* as a statement of the form $\bigcirc A$ in which A is $\bigcirc$-free. Since the modal theories allow for iterated deontic operators and van Fraassen's theory does not, we must restrict ourselves in comparisons to the shared sub-language of ought statements. Where Γ is a set of ought statements, we will let $\overline{\Gamma} = \{B : \bigcirc B \in \Gamma\}$ represent the content of the oughts contained in that set. We can then define a set of ought statements Γ as *unit consistent* if each individual ought belonging to the set is itself satisfiable—that is, if B is consistent for each $B \in \overline{\Gamma}$. And we will say that Γ is not just unit consistent but *consistent* if the oughts belonging to Γ are jointly satisfiable—that is, if $\overline{\Gamma}$ itself is consistent.

---

[6]I owe this observation, along with the example, is due to Johan van Benthem (personal correspondence).

Before working out the exact relations among these different deontic logics, we offer yet another characterization, perhaps the most straightforward, of the consequence relation $\vdash_F$.

Theorem 2 Let Γ be a set of ought statements. Then $\Gamma \vdash_F \bigcirc A$ if and only if there a consistent subset $\mathcal{G}$ of $\overline{\Gamma}$ such that $\mathcal{G} \vdash A$.

Proof First, suppose $\Gamma \vdash_F \bigcirc A$. Let $\mathcal{M}_1$ be as in Definition 1, and let $\mathcal{G} = Th(\mathcal{M}_1) \cap \overline{\Gamma}$. Clearly, $\mathcal{G}$ is consistent and a subset of $\overline{\Gamma}$; and it is clear also that $score_\Gamma(\mathcal{M}) = score_\Gamma(\mathcal{M}')$ for any $\mathcal{M}, \mathcal{M}' \in |\mathcal{G}|$. To see that $\mathcal{G} \vdash A$, suppose otherwise: then there exists a model $\mathcal{M}_2 \in |\mathcal{G}| \cap |\neg A|$; but in that case we have $score_\Gamma(\mathcal{M}_2) = score_\Gamma(\mathcal{M}_1)$, contrary to the definition of $\vdash_F$. Next, suppose $\mathcal{G} \vdash A$ for some consistent subset $\mathcal{G}$ of $\overline{\Gamma}$. Standard techniques allow us to define a maximal consistent subset $\mathcal{G}^*$ of $\overline{\Gamma}$ containing $\mathcal{G}$. Since $\mathcal{G}^*$ is consistent, and since it must also entail A, we have some model $\mathcal{M}_1 \in |\mathcal{G}^*| \subseteq |A|$; and then since $\mathcal{G}^*$ is maximal, it is easy to see that there can be no $\mathcal{M}_2 \in |\neg A|$ such that $score_\Gamma(\mathcal{M}_1) \subseteq score_\Gamma(\mathcal{M}_2)$. So $\Gamma \vdash_F \bigcirc A$. ∎

We consider first the relations between van Fraassen's theory and *EM*. If a set of ought statements Γ is not even unit consistent, we must have $\Gamma \vdash_{EM} \bigcirc A$ for every A; and so *EM* is stronger than van Fraassen's theory, since this theory allows us to derive only consistent oughts. As we have seen from the army example discussed above in Sections 2.2 and 2.3, however, van Fraassen's theory does allow us to draw conclusions from certain unit consistent sets that cannot be derived in *EM*; and together with the following theorem, this shows that the theory is properly stronger than *EM* for unit consistent sets of oughts.

Theorem 3 Let Γ be a unit consistent set of ought statements. Then if $\Gamma \vdash_{EM} \bigcirc A$, it follows that $\Gamma \vdash_F \bigcirc A$.

Proof We begin by constructing a model for the modal language in which the possible worlds are ordinary models of the underlying classical language. Let $\mathcal{M} = \langle W, N, v \rangle$, where W is the set of models of the underlying classical language, and in which $N(\alpha) = \{X : |B| \subseteq X \text{ and } \bigcirc B \in \Gamma\}$ for each $\alpha \in W$, and $v(p) = |p|$ for each proposition letter p. It is clear that $\mathcal{M}$ is a minimal model satisfying the condition that, if $X \in N(\alpha)$ and $X \subseteq Y$, then $Y \in N(\alpha)$; and clear also that $\mathcal{M}, \alpha \models \Gamma$ for each $\alpha \in W$. Therefore, since $\Gamma \vdash_{EM} \bigcirc A$, we know that $\mathcal{M} \models \bigcirc A$; that is, $|A| \in N(\alpha)$ for each $\alpha \in W$. From this and the definition of N, we can conclude that $|B| \subseteq |A|$ for some $\bigcirc B \in \Gamma$. However, since Γ is unit consistent, $\{B\}$ is then a consistent subset of $\overline{\Gamma}$ that entails A; and so we can conclude that $\Gamma \vdash_F \bigcirc A$ from Theorem 2. ∎

We turn now to *KD*. Of course, anything can be derived in *KD* from an inconsistent set of oughts; and so, together with the following theorem, this shows that, as expected, *KD* is properly stronger than van Fraassen's theory.

Theorem 4 Let Γ be a set of ought statements. Then if $\Gamma \vdash_F \bigcirc A$, it follows that $\Gamma \vdash_{KD} \bigcirc A$.

Proof Suppose $\Gamma \vdash_F \bigcirc A$. By Theorem 2, it follows that $\mathcal{G} \vdash A$ for some subset $\mathcal{G}$ of Γ; and so $\vdash (B_1 \wedge \ldots \wedge B_n) \supset A$, for some $B_1, \ldots, B_n \in \overline{\Gamma}$. Since *KD* is a normal modal logic, we can conclude from this that $\vdash_{KD} (\bigcirc B_1 \wedge \ldots \wedge \bigcirc B_n) \supset \bigcirc A$; and so $\Gamma \vdash_{KD} \bigcirc A$, since $\bigcirc B_1, \ldots, \bigcirc B_n \in \Gamma$. ∎

It is reassuring to see, however, that, unlike *EM*, van Fraassen's theory differs from *KD* only when applied to an inconsistent set of ought statements; otherwise, the two theories yield exactly the same results.

Theorem 5 Let Γ be a consistent set of ought statements. Then if $\Gamma \vdash_{KD} \bigcirc A$, it follows that $\Gamma \vdash_F \bigcirc A$.

Proof As in the proof of Theorem 3, we construct a model for the modal language with the ordinary models of the underlying classical language as its possible worlds. Let $\mathcal{M} = \langle W, f, v \rangle$, with W and v as before, but in which $f(\alpha) = |\overline{\Gamma}|$ for each $\alpha \in W$. Since Γ is consistent, $f(\alpha)$ is always a nonempty set; and so $\mathcal{M}$ is a standard deontic model. Moreover, $\mathcal{M} \models \Gamma$, and so since $\Gamma \vdash_{KD} \bigcirc A$, we have $\mathcal{M} \models \bigcirc A$; that is, $f(\alpha) \subseteq |A|$ for each $\alpha \in W$. From this and the definition of f, we can conclude that $|\overline{\Gamma}| \subseteq |A|$; and since $\overline{\Gamma}$ is itself consistent, Theorem 2 allows us to conclude that $\Gamma \vdash_F \bigcirc A$. ∎

4.3. *Some variations*

Although van Fraassen's account embodies an intuitively coherent and stable approach to reasoning in the presence of normative conflicts, it is not the only such approach. In this section, I simply mention some variations on van Fraassen's original account—one based on a skeptical reasoning strategy, one based a strategy of articulating the premise set, and one that combines these two ideas.

Suppose, first, that an agent is given $\bigcirc A$ and $\bigcirc \neg A$ as premises. We have assumed so far that these premises should yield as conclusions both $\bigcirc A$ and $\bigcirc \neg A$, though not the agglomerate $\bigcirc (A \wedge \neg A)$. But there is another option. It seems possible to imagine that, in this case, a sensible agent might want to resist the conclusion $\bigcirc A$ precisely because he has reason to believe that $\bigcirc \neg A$, and that he might likewise want to resist the conclusion that $\bigcirc \neg A$ because he has reason to believe that $\bigcirc A$. More generally, it seems possible to imagine that a sensible agent might want to conclude that a proposition ought to hold just in case he has reason for thinking that it ought to hold, and no reason for thinking otherwise.

There are, in fact, several different ways of making precise logical sense of this suggestion, but the one that seems most attractive can be set out quite simply, by modifying the idea underlying Theorem 1 to reflect a skeptical reasoning strategy. Rather than supposing that $\bigcirc A$ should follow from the premise set Γ just in case A belongs to some extension of corresponding default theory Δ_Γ, we might choose to conclude $\bigcirc A$ only if A belongs to each of these extensions. The resulting skeptical notion of deontic consequence, represented through the relation $\vdash_S$, is defined as follows.

Definition 4 $\Gamma \vdash_S \bigcirc A$ if and only if $A \in \mathcal{E}$ for each extension $\mathcal{E}$ of Δ_Γ.

It can then be shown, in parallel with Theorem 2, that $\Gamma \vdash_S \bigcirc A$ just in case $\mathcal{G} \vdash A$ for each consistent subset $\mathcal{G}$ of $\overline{\Gamma}$.

To illustrate this skeptical theory, let us consider an example suggested by Ruth Barcan Marcus (Marcus, 1980) involving symmetrical but conflicting oughts: we suppose that an agent is faced with a situation in which he has equally weighty reasons for saving the lives of two identical twins, but is able to save only one. The premises conditioning the agent's deliberations in this situation can be represented through the set $\Gamma_1 = \{\bigcirc A, \bigcirc B\}$, where A represents the statement that the agent saves the first twin and B represents the statement that he saves the second, and where we take A and B, therefore, to be individually but not jointly consistent.

According to van Fraassen's theory, the premise set Γ_1 yields as consequences both $\bigcirc A$ and $\bigcirc B$—and then also, since in the situation A entails $\neg B$ and B entails $\neg A$—both $\bigcirc \neg A$ and $\bigcirc \neg B$. On this theory, then, no matter which of the twins the agent chooses to save, he is both neglecting to fulfill certain oughts that are generated by his premises and actually violating other generated oughts. According to the skeptical theory, on the other hand, none of the above ought statements follows from Γ_1, since none of the formulas A, B, $\neg A$, or $\neg B$ are found in all extensions of Δ_{Γ_1}. Instead, the strongest conclusion that can be drawn from Γ_1 is the statement $\bigcirc(A \vee B)$. The skeptical theory, then, will still constrain the agent's actions: he cannot simply walk away, saving neither twin. But as long as the agent saves one twin or the other, he will satisfy all the oughts generated by his premises.[7]

Like van Fraassen's consequence relation $\vdash_F$, the skeptical consequence relation $\vdash_S$ fails to satisfy the structural rules of reflexivity and cut; the examples supplied in Section 4.1 to establish these failures for $\vdash_F$ suffice here as well. However, unlike $\vdash_F$, the skeptical consequence relation $\vdash_S$ is itself nonmonotonic: although we might have

$$\bigcirc A \vdash_S \bigcirc A,$$

---

[7]An approach to Marcus's twins problem along the lines suggested here was sketched in (Donagan, 1984).

for example, we cannot have

$$\bigcirc A, \bigcirc \neg A \vdash_S \bigcirc A.$$

It is interesting to note, also, that this consequence relation validates a rule of agglomeration: given that $\Gamma \vdash_S \bigcirc A$ and $\Gamma \vdash_S \bigcirc B$, we can conclude that $\Gamma \vdash_S \bigcirc(A \wedge B)$. With the skeptical reasoning strategy, then, implications of the form

$$\bigcirc A, \bigcirc \neg A \vdash_S \bigcirc(A \wedge \neg A)$$

are avoided not, as before, through the failure of agglomeration, but instead, through the failure of monotonicity.

To motivate our second variation on van Fraassen's account, consider a situation in which an agent is issued the following command by some author-itative but confused source:

Square the circle, and go to the store for some milk.

Such a command might enter into the agent's reasoning through the premise set

$$\Gamma_2 = \{\bigcirc((A \wedge \neg A) \wedge B)\},$$

in which the formula $A \wedge \neg A$ represents the inconsistent first conjunct of the command, and the formula B represents its consistent second conjunct.

Now, what should the agent conclude? As we have noted, van Fraassen's suggestion is simply to ignore inconsistent oughts that occur among premises; according to this policy, no oughts at all could be concluded from Γ_2 other than the logical truths. But there seems to be another coherent option. We can imagine that an agent provided with an inconsistent ought statement as a premise, which cannot be satisfied entirely, might still wish to satisfy "as much" of this statement as possible. Returning to our example, the agent here might want to draw from the premise set Γ_2 at least the conclusion $\bigcirc B$, that he ought to go to the store for some milk.

In order to develop a reasoning strategy that embodies this idea—satisfying as much as possible even of inconsistent premises—we adapt to the present setting a procedure developed for another purpose by Belnap, and defended in detail in (Anderson *et al.* , 1992, Section 82.4). Given a set of premises, rather than drawing conclusions immediately, we first articulate the premise set in a way that is supposed to represent its intended meaning more explicitly, and then apply van Fraassen's approach to this articulated set of premises in order to reach the appropriate conclusions.

Adapting the procedure described in (Anderson *et al.* , 1992), we define the *articulation* of a premise set of ought statements as follows. Implica-tion is first eliminated, so that the resulting formulas are written in $\wedge$, $\vee$, and $\neg$; and an occurrence of a subformula in an ought statement is de-fined as *positive* or *negative* depending on whether it lies within the scope of an even or odd number of negations. Given a premise set Γ, the articulated set Γ^* is then defined as the smallest superset of Γ that contains both $\bigcirc(\ldots B \ldots)$ and $\bigcirc(\ldots C \ldots)$ whenever it contains either a formula of the form $\bigcirc(\ldots (B \wedge C) \ldots)$ with the occurrence of the conjunction positive, or a formula of the form $\bigcirc(\ldots (B \vee C) \ldots)$ with the occurrence of the disjunction negative. As an example, the articulated set corresponding to Γ_2 would be

$$\Gamma_2^* = \Gamma \cup \{\bigcirc(A \wedge B), \bigcirc(\neg A \wedge B), \bigcirc A, \bigcirc \neg A, \bigcirc B\}.$$

It is now a straightforward matter to define the consequence relation $\vdash_{FA}$, representing an articulated variant of van Fraassen's original notion.

Definition 5 $\Gamma \vdash_{FA} \bigcirc A$ if and only if $\Gamma^* \vdash_F \bigcirc A$.

This new consequence notion would allow us to draw the following conclusions from Γ_2, none of which is generated by Fraassen's original definition: $\bigcirc(A \wedge B)$, $\bigcirc(\neg A \wedge B)$, $\bigcirc A$, $\bigcirc \neg A$, and $\bigcirc B$.

Of course, the two variations suggested here—the skeptical variation and the articulation variation—run in orthogonal directions, and they can be combined without interference: in reasoning from a premise set Γ, an agent might first extend this to the articulated set Γ^*, and then, reasoning skeptically, draw only those conclusions contained in each extension of the corresponding default theory Δ_{Γ^*}. The notion $\vdash_{SA}$ of articulated skeptical consequence that reflects this reasoning strategy can be defined in the obvious way.

Definition 6 $\Gamma \vdash_{SA} \bigcirc A$ if and only if $\Gamma^* \vdash_S \bigcirc A$.

Focusing again on Γ_2, an agent reasoning with this new notion of consequence would have to abandon all the conclusions listed above except $\bigcirc B$.

5. CONDITIONAL OUGHTS

Much of our normative reasoning involves ought statements that are conditional rather than absolute, as in 'Given A, it ought to be that B', which we represent through the standard notation $\bigcirc(B/A)$.

Within the framework of modal logic, two general styles of analysis have been proposed for conditional oughts. Some writers have advanced an analysis involving a combination of an ordinary ought and an ordinary material conditional. Von Wright (von Wright, 1951) originally suggested, for example, that a conditional ought statement should be analyzed through a formula of the form $\bigcirc(A \supset B)$, and A. N. Prior (Prior, 1962) suggested $A \supset \bigcirc B$; these two proposals are compared by in (Hintikka, 1969). Other writers—such as Bengt Hansson (Hansson, 1971), David Lewis (Lewis, 1973, Section 5.1), and van Fraassen (van Fraassen, 1972)—have suggested that a conditional ought operator should be analyzed instead as a primitive dyadic construction within the general framework of conditional logic; a number of proposals along these lines are surveyed by in (Lewis, 1974). As usual in conditional logics, this kind of analysis relies on a background ordering of the possible worlds, here intended to represent some relation of comparative goodness, or value; the basic idea is that $\bigcirc(B/A)$ should be true at a world just in case, with respect to the value ordering that is operative there, B is true at the best worlds in which A is true.

As it turns out, neither of these two general lines of approach seems promising as an analysis of prima facie ought statements.[8] At least when statements of the form $\bigcirc(B/A)$ are taken to express a prima facie oughts, problems then arise for both approaches concerning the degree of strengthening, or monotonicity, to be allowed in the antecedent of the conditional.

Consider the first approach. If $\bigcirc(B/A)$ is analyzed either as $A \supset \bigcirc B$ or as $\bigcirc(A \supset B)$, then conditional ought statements allow unrestricted strengthening in their antecedents; on either of these analyses, a rule of the form

$$\frac{\bigcirc(B/A)}{\bigcirc(B/A \wedge C)}$$

is admissible. (This is easy to see. The statement $(A \wedge C) \supset \bigcirc B$ is an immediate consequence of $A \supset \bigcirc B$; and since $(A \wedge C) \supset B$ is a consequence of $A \supset B$ and oughts are closed under consequence, $\bigcirc((A \wedge C) \supset B)$ follows from $\bigcirc(A \supset B)$.) If we follow the second general approach, on the other hand, analyzing conditional oughts within the general framework of conditional logic, the rule of antecedent strengthening must then be abandoned entirely. There is no way to conclude $\bigcirc(B/A \wedge C)$ from $\bigcirc(B/A)$; there is no reason to think, just because B holds at all the best worlds in which A is true, that it should hold also at the best worlds in which $A \wedge C$ is true.

It seems, however, that, at least for an analysis of prima facie reasoning, neither of these extreme approaches to strengthening in the antecedent of a conditional ought is correct: we do not want the rule of antecedent strengthening to hold without restriction, but neither do we want to abandon this rule entirely. This can be seen through an example drawn from (Horty, 1994). Suppose that an agent, having studied the proprieties, believes that his behavior at mealtime should be governed by the following three prima facie oughts:

> You ought not to eat with your fingers,
> You ought to put your napkin on your lap,
> If you are served asparagus, you ought to eat it with your fingers.

---

[8]It is often unclear to what extent the various writers concerned with conditional oughts intend for their analyses to apply to prima facie ought statements, rather than some other style of deontic conditional. However, at least (Hintikka, 1969) explicitly suggests that statements of the form $\bigcirc(A \supset B)$ should be taken to represent prima facie oughts; and it is conjectured in (Stalnaker and Richmond, 1970) that the general techniques of conditional logic can be used to analyze prima facie obligation.

Taking an unconditional ought, in the usual way, as an ought conditional on the universal truth $\top$, we can then represent the premises governing the agent's deliberations as the set

$$\Gamma_3 = \{\bigcirc(\neg F/\top), \bigcirc(N/\top), \bigcirc(F/A)\}.$$

Now it seems, intuitively, that the third of these oughts should override the first when asparagus is served, so that, in this special case, the agent should not conclude that he ought not to eat with his fingers; but even if asparagus is served, nothing interferes with the second of these oughts, and so, even in this special case, the agent should still conclude that he ought to put his napkin on his lap. That is: from the premise set Γ_3, we would want to derive $\bigcirc(N/A)$, but not $\bigcirc(\neg F/A)$.

The only plausible way to derive $\bigcirc(N/A)$ in this situation, it seems, is by strengthening the antecedent of the second premise; a treatment of conditional oughts that simply rules out this kind of strengthening, such as those based on conditional logic, will not allow us to derive this conclusion. On the other hand, a treatment that allows unrestricted strengthening, such as those suggested by von Wright and Prior, will incorrectly yield $\bigcirc(\neg F/A)$ from the first premise. What is needed, apparently, is a certain amount of strengthening, but not too much: in order to model prima facie reasoning, we want to allow oughts formulated explicitly only for very general circumstances to apply also by default in more specific situations, unless they are overridden in those situations.

As far as I know, no treatment of conditional oughts based on any of the standard philosophical logics is able to model this kind of reasoning. It appears, for example, that the consequence relation associated with any appropriate theory would have to be nonmonotonic. To see this, suppose the statement

> If you are served asparagus, you ought to eat it with your fingers

were deleted from the list of rules displayed above, resulting in the new premise set

$$\Gamma_4 = \Gamma_3 - \{\bigcirc(F/A)\}.$$

In that case, since the general injunction against eating with one's fingers is not explicitly overridden in the particular situation in which asparagus is served, it should apply here by default also; and so we would now want to derive $\bigcirc(\neg F/A)$ from Γ_4. But as we have seen, with $\bigcirc(F/A)$ present as a premise, the general injunction is overridden, and so $\bigcirc(\neg F/A)$ is no longer acceptable. Even though Γ_4 yields $\bigcirc(F/A)$, then, and Γ_4 is a subset of Γ_3, we do not want Γ_3 to yield $\bigcirc(F/A)$; adding a premise leads us to withdraw a conclusion.

The idea of analyzing conditional oughts within the general semantic framework of conditional logic led to certain departures from the earlier treatment that involved mixing ordinary oughts with material conditionals; but at least as an analysis of prima facie oughts, these departures now seem to be both too radical and too conservative. The way in which the departures seem to be too radical is by forcing us entirely to abandon a rule of strengthening in the antecedent of a conditional ought; for it appears that we do want to admit a certain amount of strengthening as a default. But the departures also seem to be too conservative because, although these conditional logics do abandon the rule of strengthening, or antecedent monotonicity, within conditional ought statements, they nevertheless treat conditional oughts within an ordinary logical framework, with a monotonic consequence relation; and it appears that the consequence relation that governs our reasoning with prima facie oughts is itself nonmonotonic.

6.   A NONMONOTONIC APPROACH TO CONDITIONAL OUGHTS

Because it seems to demand a nonmonotonic consequence relation, it is natural to hope that a useful theory of conditional oughts could be developed within the framework of nonmonotonic logic. In order to illustrate how such a development might proceed, this section first sketches a preliminary analysis of conditional oughts, which generalizes the theory of simple oughts set out earlier, and then explores some problems with the preliminary proposal.

6.1. *Conditioned extensions*

We focus on *ought contexts*: structures of the form $\langle W, \Gamma \rangle$, like default theories, except that the set of defaults is replaced by a set Γ of conditional ought statements. The two components of an ought context are supposed to represent the background set of conditional oughts and the particular facts relevant to an agent's normative reasoning in that context.

Let us say that a conditional ought $\bigcirc(B/A)$ is *overridden* in the context $\langle W, \Gamma \rangle$ just in case there is a statement $\bigcirc(D/C) \in \Gamma$ such that (i) $|W| \subseteq |C|$, (ii) $|C| \subset |A|$, and (iii) $W \cup \{D, B\}$ is inconsistent. The idea here is that a conditional ought should be overridden in some context whenever another ought is applicable, more specific than the original, and inconsistent with the original. In the definition, clause (i) tells us that us that $\bigcirc(D/C)$ is applicable in the context, in the sense that its antecedent condition is satisfied; clause (ii) tells us that $\bigcirc(D/C)$ is more specific than $\bigcirc(B/A)$, in the sense that the antecedent condition C is more restrictive than the antecedent condition A; and clause (iii) tells us $\bigcirc(D/C)$ and $\bigcirc(B/A)$ are inconsistent in the context, in the sense that their consequents B and D cannot both be realized along with the background information W.

Using this characterization of the circumstances under which conditional oughts are overridden, we can now define a new kind of extension for ought contexts—known as a *conditioned extensions*—as follows.

Definition 7 The set $\mathcal{E}$ is a conditioned extension of the ought context $\langle \mathcal{W}, \Gamma \rangle$ just in case there is a set $\mathcal{F}$ such that

$$
\mathcal{F} = \{ B : \bigcirc(B/A) \in \Gamma, \\
|\mathcal{W}| \subseteq |A|, \\
\bigcirc(B/A) \text{ is not overridden in } \langle \mathcal{W}, \Gamma \rangle, \\
\neg B \notin \mathcal{E} \},
$$

and $\mathcal{E} = Cn[\{\mathcal{W}\} \cup \mathcal{F}]$.

This is, of course, a fixed point definition; and so there is reason to suspect, just as certain default theories lack conventional extensions, that certain ought contexts might lack conditioned extensions. Fortunately, the suspicion turns out to be unfounded.

Theorem 6 Every ought context $\langle \mathcal{W}, \Gamma \rangle$ has a conditioned extension $\mathcal{E}$.

Proof Given $\langle \mathcal{W}, \Gamma \rangle$, first define

$$
\mathcal{F}_1 = \{ B : \bigcirc(B/A) \in \Gamma, \\
|\mathcal{W}| \subseteq |A|, \\
\bigcirc(B/A) \text{ is not overridden in } \langle \mathcal{W}, \Gamma \rangle \},
$$

and then let $\mathcal{F}_2$ be some maximal subset of $\mathcal{F}_1$ that is consistent with $\mathcal{W}$; these are guaranteed to exist. Let $\mathcal{E} = Cn[\{\mathcal{W}\} \cup \mathcal{F}_2]$. Evidently, $\mathcal{E}$ is a conditioned extension of $\langle \mathcal{W}, \Gamma \rangle$ if and only if $\mathcal{F}_2 = \mathcal{F}$ (where $\mathcal{F}$ is as defined in the text); and it is clear from the definition of $\mathcal{F}_2$ that $\mathcal{F}_2 = \mathcal{F}$ just in case $\mathcal{F}_2 = \mathcal{F}_1 \cap \{ B : \neg B \notin \mathcal{E} \}$. So suppose first that $B \in \mathcal{F}_1$ and $\neg B \notin \mathcal{E}$. Then B is consistent with $\{\mathcal{W}\} \cup \mathcal{F}_2$, and so $B \in \mathcal{F}_2$, since $\mathcal{F}_2$ is maximal. Next, suppose $B \in \mathcal{F}_2$. Of course, $B \in \mathcal{F}_1$; and we must have $\neg B \notin \mathcal{E}$ as well, for otherwise we would have both B and $\neg B$ in $Cn[\{\mathcal{W}\} \cup \mathcal{F}_2]$, and so $\mathcal{F}_2$ would not be consistent with $\mathcal{W}$. ∎

Because conditioned extensions are guaranteed to exist, we can define a consequence relation $\vdash_{CF}$ between ought contexts and conditional ought statements in the following way.

Definition 8 $\langle \mathcal{W}, \Gamma \rangle \vdash_{CF} \bigcirc(B/A)$ if and only if $B \in \mathcal{E}$ for some conditioned extension $\mathcal{E}$ of $\langle \mathcal{W} \cup \{A\}, \Gamma \rangle$.

And it is then natural to define the consequences of a set of conditional oughts by reference to the special case in which the factual component of an ought context is empty.

Definition 9 $\Gamma \vdash_{CF} \bigcirc(B/A)$ if and only if $\langle \emptyset, \Gamma \rangle \vdash_{CF} \bigcirc(B/A)$.

Returning to our earlier asparagus example, we can now see that the present analysis yields the desired results. The unique conditioned extension of the ought context $\langle \{A\}, \Gamma_3 \rangle$ is $Cn[\{A, F, N\}]$; and so we have $\Gamma_3 \vdash_{CF} \bigcirc(N/A)$, as desired, but we do not have $\Gamma_3 \vdash_{CF} \bigcirc(\neg F/A)$. Just as in those theories based on the semantic framework of conditional modal logics, the present account of conditional oughts is nonmonotonic in the antecedent of the conditional. The ought context $\langle \{\top\}, \Gamma_3 \rangle$, for example, has as its unique conditioned extension the set $Cn[\{\neg F, N\}]$, and so we have $\Gamma_3 \vdash_{CF} \bigcirc(\neg F/\top)$; but, as mentioned, we do not have $\Gamma_3 \vdash_{CF} \bigcirc(\neg F/A)$. In addition, however, the consequence relation $\vdash_{CF}$ is itself nonmonotonic. The unique extension of $\langle \{A\}, \Gamma_4 \rangle$ is $Cn[\{A, \neg F, N\}]$, and so we have $\Gamma_4 \vdash_{CF} \bigcirc(\neg F/A)$; but monotonicity fails because, although Γ_4 is a subset of Γ_3, we do not have $\Gamma_3 \vdash_{CF} \bigcirc(\neg F/A)$.

The present account exhibits, also, several properties desirable in a conditional deontic logic. Since conditioned extensions are closed under logical consequence, the consequents of supported ought statements are closed under consequence as well: if $\Gamma \vdash_{CF} \bigcirc(B/A)$ and $B \vdash C$, then $\Gamma \vdash_{CF} \bigcirc(C/A)$. Again, by examining the definition of conditioned extensions we can see that conditional oughts are sensitive only to the propositions expressed by their antecedents, not to the particular sentences expressing those propositions: if $|A| = |B|$, then $\Gamma \vdash_{CF} \bigcirc(C/A)$ just in case $\Gamma \vdash_{CF} \bigcirc(C/B)$. And finally, an ought context $\langle \mathcal{W}, \Gamma \rangle$ will have an inconsistent extension if and only if the set $\mathcal{W}$ is itself inconsistent; and from this we conclude that $\Gamma \vdash_{CF} \bigcirc(\bot/A)$ if and only if $|A| = |\bot|$.[9]

It turns out, moreover, that the consequence relation $\vdash_{CF}$ is a conservative extension of the relation $\vdash_F$ described earlier, in the following sense:

Theorem 7 Where Γ is a set of conditional oughts, let

$$\Gamma' = \{\bigcirc B : \bigcirc(B/A) \in \Gamma \text{ and } |A| = |\top|\}.$$

Then $\Gamma' \vdash_F \bigcirc C$ if and only if $\Gamma \vdash_{CF} \bigcirc(C/\top)$.

Proof (sketch) We know by Theorem 1 that $\Gamma' \vdash_F \bigcirc C$ if and only if $C \in \mathcal{E}$ for some extension $\mathcal{E}$ of the default theory $\Delta_{\Gamma'}$. Reflection on the construction underlying Theorem 2.1 of Reiter (Reiter, 1980) shows that $\mathcal{E}$ is an extension of $\Delta_{\Gamma'}$ just in case there is a set $\mathcal{F}$ such that

$$\mathcal{F} = \{B : \quad \bigcirc B \in \Gamma',$$
$$\neg B \notin \mathcal{E}\},$$

and $\mathcal{E} = Cn[\mathcal{F}]$. It is easy to see that no conditional ought can be overridden in any context of the form $\langle \{\top\}, \Gamma \rangle$; and of course $|\top| \subseteq |A|$ if and only if

---

[9]The three properties described in this paragraph can be compared to the rules RCOEA, RCOM, and COD from (Chellas, 1980, Section 10.2).

$|A| = |\top|$. Therefore, we can conclude that $\mathcal{E}$ is an extension of $\Delta_{\Gamma'}$ just in case there is a set $\mathcal{F}$ such that

$$\mathcal{F} = \{B : \quad \bigcirc(B/A) \in \Gamma,$$
$$|\top| \subseteq |A|,$$
$$\bigcirc(B/A) \text{ is not overridden in } \langle\{\top\}, \Gamma\rangle,$$
$$\neg B \notin \mathcal{E}\},$$

and $\mathcal{E} = Cn[\{\top\} \cup \mathcal{F}]$; that is, just in case $\mathcal{E}$ is a conditioned extension of $\langle\{\top\}, \Gamma\rangle$. The theorem then follows at once from the definition of the relation $\vdash_{CF}$. ■

>From this result and the discussion in Section 4, we can conclude that the consequence relation $\vdash_{CF}$, like $\vdash_F$, satisfies neither reflexivity nor cut.

6.2. *Problems with the theory*

This account of conditional deontic consequence exhibits a number of advantages not found in the usual modal approaches. The consequence relation $\vdash_{CF}$ is itself nonmonotonic, as is the antecedent place in derived conditional oughts; but unlike those accounts based on the the semantic framework of conditional logic, the current account does allow for a certain amount of strengthening, or monotonicity, in the antecedent of these derived oughts. And the theory generalizes the earlier treatment of reasoning in the presence of normative conflict, which already lies beyond the scope of modal approaches to deontic logic.

However, the current account of conditional deontic consequence is beset by several problems, and so can be taken, at best, only as a preliminary. I close simply by mentioning four issues that would have to be confronted in extending this account to a more complete theory.

First and most important, the current account does not allow any kind of transitivity, or chaining, across conditional oughts. We cannot derive $\bigcirc(C/A)$ from a premise set consisting of $\bigcirc(C/B)$ and $\bigcirc(B/A)$; and in particular, taking simple oughts as oughts conditional upon $\top$, we cannot derive $\bigcirc B$ from $\bigcirc(B/A)$ and $\bigcirc A$. Of course, this is similar to the situation in those accounts based on conditional logics, which also forbid transitivity of the conditional, and of the deontic conditional. However, the nonmonotonic framework allows for a new possibility that is not present in these standard logics—the possibility that transitivity should hold as a defeasible rule, subject to override. This is, in fact, exactly how transitivity is supposed to work in a number of application areas of nonmonotonic logics, such as the kind of reasoning supported by defeasible inheritance hierarchies. Here, we would want to conclude, for example, that Tweety flies given only the premises that Tweety is a bird and that birds fly; but we would allow this conclusion to be overridden by the additional information that Tweety is a penguin, where penguins are a particular class of birds that do not fly.

I think that it would be natural to incorporate this kind of defeasible transitivity also into an account of conditional deontic reasoning; but I have not attempted to do so here because the task of combining defeasible transitivity with a proper treatment of overriding (known in the inheritance literature as "preemption") would involve us in technical and conceptual issues intricate enough to obscure the main point of this paper. In spite of the efforts of a number of researchers—including Craig Boutilier (Boutilier, 1992), James Delgrande (Delgrande, 1988), Hector Geffner (Geffner, 1989), and John Pollock (Pollock, 1992)—I know of no solution to these problems for a language as expressive as propositional calculus that is generally accepted; and the matter is not settled even for the very simple language of inheritance hierarchies, as can be seen from (Touretzky et al. , 1987) and (Horty, 1994).

The second issue presented by the current account of conditional deontic consequence concerns the matter of reasoning with disjunctive antecedents. Where $\Gamma_5 = \{\bigcirc(C/A), \bigcirc(C/B)\}$, for example, it seems to some that we should be able to conclude from Γ_5 that $\bigcirc(C/A \vee B)$; but in fact, the only conditioned extension of $\langle\{A \vee B\}, \Gamma_5\rangle$ is $Cn[\{A \vee B\}]$, and so the present account does not yield this result. There seem to be two strategies available for handling this issue. First, we could try to modify the account so as to yield the kind of results that some view as desirable. Problems involving disjunctive reasoning are familiar in the context of default logic; and several proposals, such as that of (Przymusinska et al., 1991), have been put forth for modifying standard default logic so that it allows defaults to be applied on the basis of disjunctive information. Given the similarity between conditional extensions of ought contexts and ordinary extensions of default theories, it should not be too difficult to adapt these proposals to the present context; but it is not simply an exercise, since the adaptation would have to involve extending the notion of overriding to apply properly to disjunctive antecedents. Alternatively, however, we might deny that inferences such as that from $\bigcirc(C/A)$ and $\bigcirc(C/B)$ to $\bigcirc(C/A \vee B)$ should be validated in a deontic setting; a discussion of the conditions under which this kind of inference seems to fail can be found in (Horty, 1996).

The third issue presented by the current theory concerns a detail in the treatment of overridden oughts. According to the this theory, an conditional ought can be overridden only by a single opposing statement, which is both applicable in the context and more specific. However, there are cases in which it is natural to suppose that an ought, although not overridden by a single opposing rule, might be overridden by a set of opposing rules. For example, let

$$\Gamma_6 = \{\bigcirc(Q/\top), \bigcirc(\neg(P \wedge Q)/A), \bigcirc(P/A)\}.$$

Here, it seems that in the context $\langle\{A\}, \Gamma_6\rangle$, the first rule should be overridden by the second two taken together, although it is not overridden by either individually.

The final problem concerns yet another detail in the present treatment of overriding. Suppose an ought statement is overridden by another which is itself overridden. What is the status of the original? According to the present treatment, it remains out of play; but it is also possible to imagine that the original rule should then be reinstated. As an example, let

$$\Gamma_7 = \{\bigcirc(Q/\top), \bigcirc(P/A), \bigcirc(\neg P/A \wedge B)\},$$

and consider the context $\langle\{W\}, \Gamma_7\rangle$, where W is the formula $(A \wedge B) \wedge \neg(P \wedge Q)$. Of course, the first rule in Γ_7 is overridden in this context by the second, but the second is likewise overridden by the third. Since overridden rules remain out of play, according to the the present treatment, this context has $Cn[\{W, \neg P\}]$ as its only conditioned extension; and so we do not have $\bigcirc(Q/W)$. But it does not seem unreasonable to modify the present treatment so that the rule $\bigcirc(Q/\top)$ is reinstated in this context, since the rule that overrides it is itself overridden. In that case, we would have $Cn[\{W, \neg P, Q\}]$ as a conditioned extension; and so we would be able to derive $\bigcirc(Q/W)$ from Γ_7. The issue of reinstatement in inheritance hierarchies is explored in (Touretzky *et al.*, 1991) and (Horty, 1994).

The problems pointed out here with the current account of conditional deontic consequence are serious, but I do not feel that they should lead us to abandon the project of designing a conditional deontic logic using the techniques of nonmonotonic logic. In fact, none of these problems is unique to the deontic interpretation of the background nonmonotonic theory; instead, they reflect more general difficulties in nonmonotonic reasoning, which surface here just as they surface elsewhere. Of course, it is impossible to offer a final evaluation of the nonmonotonic approach to conditional deontic reasoning until these issues with the underlying logical framework are resolved. But the approach does seem to be promising; and it may be that, in bringing the techniques of nonmonotonic logic into contact with the new data provided by normative reasoning, we will not only discover new possibilities for the construction of deontic logics, but gain a deeper understanding of the underlying nonmonotonic logics as well.

ACKNOWLEDGMENTS

This paper is a revision of (Horty, 1993), incorporating also some material from (Horty, 1994). I am very grateful to Nuel Belnap, Craig Boutilier, Jon Doyle, David Etherington, Matt Ginsberg, David Makinson, Judea Pearl, Michael Slote, Rich Thomason, David Touretzky, and Johan van Benthem for discussions or correspondence on these topics. My work in this area has been supported by the National Science Foundation through Grants No. IRI-9003165 and IRI-8907122, by the Army Research Office through Grant No. DAAL-03-88-K0087, and by the National Endowment for Humanities through a Fellowship for University Teachers.

John F. Horty
Department of Philosophy and Institute for Advance Computer Studies
University of Maryland

REFERENCES

Anderson, Alan, Belnap, Nuel, and Dunn, J. Michael (1992). *Entailment: The Logic of Relevance and Necessity, Volume 2.* Princeton University Press.

Belnap, Nuel (1977a). How a computer should think. In Gilbert Ryle (ed.), *Contemporary Aspects of Philosophy,* Oriel Press, Stocksfield, England, pages 30–56.

Belnap, Nuel (1977b). A useful four-valued logic. In J. Michael Dunn and G. Epstein (eds.), *Modern Uses of Multiple-valued Logic,* D. Reidel, Dordrecht, pages 8–37.

Boutilier, Craig (1992). *Conditional Logics for Default Reasoning and Belief Revision.* PhD thesis, Computer Science Department, University of Toronto. Available as Technical Report KRR-TR-92-1.

Chellas, Brian (1974). Conditional obligation. In Søren Stenlund (ed.), *Logical Theory and Semantic Analysis,* D. Reidel, Dordrecht, pages 23–33.

Chellas, Brian (1980). *Modal Logic: An Introduction.* Cambridge University Press, Cambridge, UK.

Delgrande, James (1988). An approach to default reasoning based on a first-order conditional logic: revised report. *Artificial Intelligence* 36:63–90.

Dennett, Daniel (1988). The moral first aid manual. In Daniel Dennett, *The Tanner Lectures on Human Values, Volume VIII,* Cambridge University Press, pages 119–147.

Donagan, Alan (1984). Consistency in rationalist moral systems. *The Journal of Philosophy* 81:291–309.

Foot, Philippa (1983). Moral realism and moral dilemma. *Journal of Philosophy* 80:379–398.

Geffner, Hector (1989). *Default Reasoning: Causal and Conditional Theories.* PhD thesis, Computer Science Department, University of California at Los Angeles.

Hansson, Bengt (1971). An analysis of some deontic logics. In R. Hilpenin (ed.), *Deontic Logic: Introductory and Systematic Readings,* D. Reidel, Dordrecht, pages 121–147.

Hintikka, Jaakko (1969). Deontic logic and its philosophical morals. In *Models for Modalities: Selected Essays,* D. Reidel, Dordrecht, pages 184–214.

Horty, John (1993). Deontic logic as founded on nonmonotonic logic. *Annals of Mathematics and Artificial Intelligence* 9:69–91.

Horty, John (1996). *Agency, Deontic Logic, and Utilitarianism.* Manuscript, Philosophy Department and Institute for Advanced Computer Studies, University of Maryland.

Horty, John (1991). Moral dilemmas and nonmonotonic logic. *Journal of Philosophical Logic,* 23:35–65, 1994. Preliminary version in J.–J. Ch. Meyer and R. M. Wieringa (eds.), *Proceedings of the First International Workshop on Deontic Logic in Computer Science,* Free University of Amsterdam.

Horty, John (1994). Some direct theories of nonmonotonic inheritance. In D. Gabbay, C. J. Hogger, and J. A. Robinson (eds.), *Handbook of Logic in Artificial Intelligence and Logic*

Programming, Volume 3: Nonmonotonic Reasoning and Uncertain Reasoning, Oxford University Press, pages 111–187.

Lemmon, E. J. (1962). Moral dilemmas. *Philosophical Review*, 70:139–158.

Lewis, David (1973). *Counterfactuals*. Blackwells, Oxford.

Lewis, David (1974). Semantic analyses for dyadic deontic logic. In Søren Stenlund (ed.), *Logical Theory and Semantic Analysis*, D. Reidel, Dordrecht, pages 1–14.

Przymusinska, H., Gelfond, M., Lifschitz, V. and Truszczynski, M. (1991). Disjunctive defaults. In *Principles of Knowledge Representation and Reasoning: Proceedings of the Second International Conference (KR-91)*, Morgan Kaufmann, San Mateo, CA.

Marcus, Ruth Barcan (1980). Moral dilemmas and consistency. *Journal of Philosophy* 77:121–136.

McDermott, Drew (1982). Non-monotonic logic II. *Journal of the Association for Computing Machinery* 29:33–57.

Pearl, Judea (1988). *Probabilistic Reasoning in Intelligent Systems*. Morgan Kaufmann, San Mateo, CA.

Pollock, John (1992). How to reason defeasibly. *Artificial Intelligence* 57:1–42.

Prior, Arthur (1962). *Formal Logic*. Oxford University Press.

Reiter, Raymond (1980). A logic for default reasoning. *Artificial Intelligence* 13:81–132.

Sartre, Jean Paul (1946). *L'Existentialisme est un Humanisme*. Nagel. Translated as "Existentialism is a Humanism" in W. Kaufmann (ed.), *Existentialism from Dostoevsky to Sartre*, Meridian Press, 1975.

Stalnaker, Robert and Thomason, Richmond (1970). A semantic analysis of conditional logic. *Theoria* 36:23–42.

Touretzky, David, Horty, John and Thomason, Richmond (1987). A clash of intuitions: the current state of nonmonotonic multiple inheritance systems. In *Proceedings of the Tenth International Joint Conference on Artificial Intelligence(IJCAI-87)*, Morgan Kaufmann, San Mateo, CA, pages 476–482.

Touretzky, David, Thomason, Richmond and Horty, John (1991). A skeptic's menagerie: conflictors, preemptors, reinstaters, and zombies in nonmonotonic inheritance. In *Proceedings of the Twelfth International Joint Conference on Artificial Intelligence (IJCAI-91)*, Morgan Kaufmann, San Mateo, CA, pages 478–483.

Ullman-Margalit, Edna (1973). On presumption. *The Journal of Philosophy* 70:143–163.

van Fraassen, Bas (1972). The logic of conditional obligation. *The Journal of Philosophical Logic* 72:417–438.

van Fraassen, Bas (1973). Values and the heart's command. *The Journal of Philosophy* 70:5–19.

von Wright, Georg Henrik (1951). Deontic logic. *Mind* 60:1–15.

Williams, Bernard (1965). Ethical consistency. *Proceedings of the Aristotelian Society* 39 (supplemental):103–124. A revised version appears in Bernard Williams, *Problems of the Self: Philosophical Papers 1956–1972*, Cambridge University Press, pages 166–186.

MARVIN BELZER AND BARRY LOEWER

DEONTIC LOGICS OF DEFEASIBILITY

1.

A normative rule (for example, "one ought to do A given B") is *defeasible* in a normative system S iff S contains another rule to the effect that one ought not do A given B&C or one is permitted not to do A given B&C. In these cases the latter rules *defeat* the first one. We claim that most normative systems that are complex enough to guide actions in light of the fact that some rules have been violated will contain defeasible rules. For example, the Model Penal Code specifies straightforwardly that one ought not to use force against another person. Yet this rule is defeasible since the code also specifies that one *may* use force in self defense; that is, the rule is defeated when someone violates the rule not to use force. And the rule permitting force in self defense is itself defeasible since one *may not* use force even in self defense if one believes he is being restrained by a policeman (Nozick, 1968).

While a normative system may contain various defeasible rules, we are ultimately interested in what the normative system says we ought, and are permitted, to do all things considered ("all out") in particular situations. If one fails to do what one ought all out to do then one violates the normative rules of the system. But which rules should one follow in determining one's all out obligations? Of course this will depend on the rules in the system and also on what reasons are eligible in the particular situation. This kind of reasoning—from defeasible reasons to what one ought all out to do—is, we believe, the heart of practical and normative reasoning insofar as it takes place within the context of a single normative system.

Additional complications are introduced in reasoning in which distinct normative systems compete. The norms of a legal system may be defeated by those of morality. Phrases like "all out" and "all things considered" often are used relative to the normative status of actions in light of all competing normative systems. Our topic in this paper is *intra*-systematic defeasibility. The modal deontic operators and semantic functions we will introduce are implicitly indexed to a single normative system. We assume that *inter*-systematic defeasibility can be discussed properly only after we understand intra-systematic defeasibility.[1]

---

[1] For a dissenting opinion, see (Castañeda, 1981). Castañeda denied the existence of intra-systematic defeasibility and argued that defeasibility should be understood universally in inter-systematic relations. For our response cf. (Belzer and Loewer, 1994).

D. Nute (ed.), Defeasible Deontic Logic, 45–57.

Promises quite naturally give rise to defeasible norms within a single normative system. In a familiar illustrative story, Sally tells a secret to a friend and asks him not to tell anyone the secret, especially not Ernie, or Hal, or Jerry. But were he to break his promise and tell Ernie, she requests, tell the other two (Hal and Jerry) as well. And, moreover, if he tells Ernie but does not tell Hal, not to tell Jerry. The friend so promises. Now it appears that in this story, which clearly is coherent, the promises create a number of obligations for the friend. First, not to tell anyone at all. But to tell both Hal and Jerry if he tells Ernie. Yet not to tell Jerry if he fails to tell Hal after telling Ernie. Each of these obligations can be expressed by normative rules, and they are defeasible in the sense that they can be overridden, or defeated. The obligation not to tell Hal is overridden by his telling Ernie. (Of course this does not excuse his telling Ernie in the first place). And there may be further relevant rules, for example, that if he tells Ernie but telling Jerry would cause great harm (unforeseen at the time of the promise) then he ought not tell Jerry.

2.

We will use $\bigcirc(A/B)$ to mean that B defeasibly requires (perhaps for a particular person) A. $\bigcirc(A/B)$ does <u>not</u> mean that B is evidence for A's being obligatory all out but rather that B is a deontic consideration in favor of doing A. B is a feature of A or the circumstances that makes A something one ought, defeasibly, to do in just the way that the fact that you promise to do A provides a deontic consideration in favor of your doing A. If $\bigcirc(A/B)$ and B are true then B typically will provide evidence for A's being all out obligatory. But B may provide evidence for A's being all out obligatory without its being a consideration in favor of A; that is to say, there is here a difference between epistemic and deontic reasons. For example, the fact that Jerry looks guilty when asked if he finished writing his report might provide evidence that he ought all out to finish the report, even though it is not a deontic consideration in favor of his finishing it.

Being defeasible means that $\bigcirc(A/B)$ is logically compatible with $\neg\bigcirc(A/B\&C)$ and $\bigcirc(\neg A/B\&C)$ for some C. The conclusions reached in normative reasoning typically are relative to a set of propositions "eligible" for use in such reasoning, such as, for instance, the propositions "settled" as true at a particular time or situation. We will use $\bigcirc_t A$ to mean that at time t (or in situation t) it ought all out to be that A; and $N_t B$ means that B is eligible at t. The connection between $\bigcirc(A/B)$ and $\bigcirc_t A$ is this:

CONN. If $\bigcirc(A/B)$ is true and B is "eligible" at t and $\bigcirc(A/B)$ is not defeated due to some C which is both (a) eligible at t and (b) such that $\neg\bigcirc(A/B\&C)$ or $\bigcirc(\neg A/B\&C)$, then $\bigcirc_t A$ is true.

The basic idea is that what a normative system requires all out in a situation is what its most complete reason eligible in that situation requires. Of course the import of this principle depends on the notion of "eligibility" employed. For now it can be understood as follows. A proposition is eligible at t (in w) if, and only if, it is settled as true at t (in w). Talk of "being settled" presupposes a branching tree structure for world histories, where B is settled as true at t (in w) iff B is true at all histories branching from t (in w). **M3D** is a minimal system for representing the detachment of all out ought statements from defeasible rules. Its "neighborhood" semantics are as follow:

> An **M3D** model structure is a sextuple $\langle W, w, T, f, g, h \rangle$ (to ease presentation we suppress reference to normative systems and worlds when convenient) where W is a set of worlds, w is the actual world, T is a finite set of times ordered by later than, f assigns to each subset B of W a set of subsets of W (these are the propositions that B requires). We will assume that f is defined for each proposition B. g and h are functions from T to subsets of W. $g(t)$ is the set of propositions eligible to be considered at t. We assume that if B belongs to $g(t)$ so do its entailments and that if C and B belong to $g(t)$ so does their intersection and that $g(t)$ is monotonically increasing. $h(t)$ is the set of propositions which are required all out at t.

We will assume that the three functions are connected by the following semantical counterpart to **CONN**:

$B \in h(t)$ iff $B \in f(\cap g(t))$.

Truth conditions for the essential notions are:

$\bigcirc(B/A)$ is true iff $B \in f(A)$.
$N_t A$ is true iff $A \in g(t)$.
$\bigcirc_t B$ is true iff $B \in h(t)$.
$R_t(B,A)$ is true iff for all C, $C \in g(t)$ only if:
   $B \in f(A)$ iff $B \in f(A \cap C)$.

If $\bigcirc(B/A)$ then $R_t(B,A)$ will say that $\bigcirc(B/A)$ is not defeated at t; if $\neg\bigcirc(B/A)$ then $R_t(B,A)$ says that $\neg\bigcirc(B/A)$ is not overridden at t (see below). The following inference schema is valid in **M3D**:

3D $\bigcirc(B/A)$ & $N_t A$ & $R_t(B,A)$ entails $\bigcirc_t B$.

The schema is the formal counterpart of **CONN**. As noted earlier, the basic idea of this schema is that it permits the detachment of $\bigcirc_t B$ from $\bigcirc(B/A)$ when A is eligible at t and $\bigcirc(B/A)$ is not defeated at t. Recall the story involving the promises to Sally. The relevant normative rules in the story are (let the non-indexed $\bigcirc A$ abbreviate $\bigcirc(A/\top)$, for tautology $\top$):

$\bigcirc\neg e$:	He should not tell Ernie.
$\bigcirc\neg h$:	He should not tell Hal.
$\bigcirc\neg j$:	He should not tell Jerry.
$\bigcirc(j/e)$:	He should tell Jerry if he tells Ernie.
$\bigcirc(h/e)$:	He should tell Hal if he tells Ernie.
$\bigcirc(\neg j/e\&\neg h)$:	He should not tell Jerry if he tells Ernie but does not tell Hal.

Suppose that at t=1 the only eligible proposition is the tautology. Then $\bigcirc_1\neg e$ and $\bigcirc_1\neg h$ and $\bigcirc_1\neg j$. But suppose that by t=2 the friend has violated his obligation not to tell Ernie so the proposition e has become eligible. If nothing else relevant is eligible, then $\bigcirc_2 h$ and $\bigcirc_2 j$. Finally if by t=3 h becomes eligible, then $\bigcirc_3\neg j^2$.

M3D can represent B's being a reason for A and the relative strength of B as a reason for A. Because of this it can also represent a number of useful meta-normative notions. While we will not try to argue here that the following definitions fully capture these notions, the definitions should indicate **M3D**'s expressive power.

1. B is an *absolute* reason for A, @(A/B), iff $A \in f(B \& X)$ for all X. Absolute reasons have maximal strength since they cannot be defeated. An absolute unconditional obligation is one for which $\top$ (tautology) is an absolute reason.[3]

2. There is a *prima facie* reason for A at t iff there is some B such that $\bigcirc(A/B)$ and $N_t B$. A is *prima facie* obligatory at t iff there is a *prima facie* reason for A at t.[4]

3. B is a *conclusive* (or, *all out*) reason for A at t iff $\bigcirc(A/B)$ and $N_t B$ and $R_t(B,A)$. If there is a conclusive reason for A at t then $\bigcirc_t A$, it ought all out at t to be the case that A.

---

[2] "Standard deontic logic" (SDL) could not represent this type of story consistently, as Chisholm's well-known "contrary to duty imperative" example made clear. The significant shortcoming of SDL is its inability to represent reasoning with defeasible rules. **M3D**, like **3D**, combines two general approaches developed in response to the problems SDL encountered. The first type is the dyadic deontic logics (of Danielsson, Hansson, Lewis, van Fraasen, Åqvist, and others) that could represent the set of defeasible rules – but not all out obligations – via a dyadic $\bigcirc(-/-)$. The second approach (of Montague, Chellas, Thomason, Humberstone, van Eck, Feldman, and others) ties the semantics of $\bigcirc$ to specific circumstances, enabling them adequately to represent all out obligations, but only clumsily can they represent the background of rules or reasoning with rules. See our "Dyadic deontic detachment," *op. cit.*

[3] Chisholm uses the phrase 'indefeasibly requires' for a similar notion (Chisholm, 1978).

[4] See Chisholm, ibid. Also see (Loewer and Belzer, 1991).

4. $\bigcirc(B/A)$ is *overridden* at t iff there is some C such that N_tC and $\bigcirc(\neg B/A\&C)$, in which case $\bigcirc(B/A)$ is overridden at t by C. $\neg\bigcirc(B/A)$ is overridden at t iff there is some C such that N_tC and $\bigcirc(B/A\&C)$.

5. $\bigcirc(B/A)$ is *undercut* at t iff there is some C such that N_tC and $\neg\bigcirc(B/A\&C)$, in which case $\bigcirc(B/A)$ is undercut at t by C.[5]

6. $\bigcirc(B/A)$ is *defeated* at t iff $\bigcirc(B/A)$ is overridden or undercut at t.

7. B is a *stronger reason* for A than is C iff $\bigcirc(A/B)$ and $\bigcirc(A/C)$ and for all times t, every D that defeats $\bigcirc(A/B)$ at t defeats $\bigcirc(A/C)$ at t but not *vice versa*.

8. $\bigcirc(A/B)$ has *greater relative weight* than $\bigcirc(C/D)$ iff $\bigcirc(A/B\&D\&\neg(A \equiv C))$ and $\neg\bigcirc(C/B\&D\&\neg(A \equiv C))$, cf. (Belzer, 1985a).

9. There is a *prima facie conflict* at t iff there are A,B,C, and D such that N_tB and N_tD and $\bigcirc(A/B)$ and $\bigcirc(C/D)$ and $N_t\neg(A \equiv C)$.

10. There is an *all out conflict* (or, *dilemma*) at t iff there is a *prima facie* conflict at t, as just described, and neither $\bigcirc(A/B)$ nor $\bigcirc(C/D)$ is defeated at t.

A *prima facie* conflict may not be an all out conflict if one of the competing $\bigcirc(-/-)$ statements is defeated at t, as would be the case for instance if $\bigcirc(A/B)$ has greater relative weight than $\bigcirc(C/D)$. (In that case: $\bigcirc(C/D)$ is undercut because $N_t(B\&D\&\neg(A \equiv C))$ and $\neg\bigcirc(C/B\&D\&\neg(A \equiv C))$; see definitions 6 and 8.)

3.

M3D is a very weak logic. There are no logical truths of the form $\bigcirc(X/Y)$ and no logical connections other than truth functional ones involving statements of the form $\bigcirc(X/Y)$ except for substitutions of logical equivalences for A and B in $\bigcirc(B/A)$. Similarly substitution is the only logical principle that holds for $\bigcirc_t$. The weakness of **M3D** is in some ways essential to the formalization of defeasibility. The invalidity of the following schemas is characteristic of defeasibility, so we should not wish to validate any of them in our subsequent strengthenings of **M3D**.

$\bigcirc(B/A) \rightarrow \bigcirc(B/A\&C)$	*strengthening the antecedent*
$\bigcirc(B/A)\&A \rightarrow \bigcirc B$	$\bigcirc$ *modus ponens*
$\bigcirc(B/A)\& N_tA \rightarrow \bigcirc_t B$	*factual detachment*
$\bigcirc(B/A) \rightarrow \bigcirc(\neg A/\neg B)$	*transposition*
$\bigcirc(B/A)\& \bigcirc (C/B) \rightarrow \bigcirc(C/A)$	*chaining*

The invalidity of the *factual detachment* principle is especially interesting for a discussion of defeasibility. Sometimes we may want to draw a conclusion

---

[5]John Pollock uses the term 'undercut' in (Pollock, 1976); Raz uses 'cancelling condition' for a related notion in (Raz, 1978).

about what we ought to do all out from defeasible reasons even when we do not know that our reasons include everything that is relevant, or even when we know that our reasons do *not* include everything that is pertinent at t to the normative status of A. In other words, for some A and B, we accept $\bigcirc$(A/B) and N_tB but not R_t(A,B) – but we infer $\bigcirc_t$A anyway. This reasoning is invalid in **M3D**, since the premise R_t(B,A) also is needed for the entailment of $\bigcirc_t$A. "Factual detachment" is an example of what sometimes has been called "defeasible reasoning" or "non-monotonic reasoning" – the conclusion $\bigcirc_t$A would be withdrawn in light of a further settled fact C which is such that $\neg\bigcirc$(A/B&C). Even though factual detachment is invalid in **M3D** (which is not a non-monotonic system),[6] and even though we would argue that **M3D** is a proper formalization of defeasibility and defeasible reasoning via **CONN** and **3D** , we certainly do not wish to claim that the inference is necessarily irrational. Employment of a system that makes such inferences may be good policy if doing so generally (or probably, or often enough) brings good results.

In what follows we strengthen **M3D** in three steps while maintaining its core representation of defeasibility via **CONN** and its definitions of the ten meta-normative notions.

4.

The following inference is not valid in **M3D**.

$$\bigcirc(A/B), \text{ A entails Q; so } \bigcirc(Q/B)$$

If we conceive of a system of norms as telling us what actions are defeasibly required in various situations then we would want this to be valid. If B is a reason that requires doing A and it is logically impossible to do A without doing Q then it seems that B is also a reason for doing Q, albeit a derivative reason since it is derived from A's entailing Q. Let **M3D+** be the system obtained from **M3D** by adding to its semantics the conditions

ENT   If A entails Q and $A \in f(B)$, then $Q \in f(B)$

and

$A \in f(A)$.

---

[6]There can be no set x of premises that both entails $\bigcirc_{t_1}$A in **M3D** and is such that a superset of x fails to entail $\bigcirc_{t_1}$A. Suppose $\bigcirc$(A/B) and $\bigcirc$($\neg$A/B&C) and no other relevant rules in the normative system, and suppose C is not settled at t_1 but becomes settled by t_2. We have $\bigcirc_{t_1}$A and $\bigcirc_{t_2}\neg$A. $\bigcirc_{t_1}$A is entailed by z={$\bigcirc$(A/B), $\bigcirc$($\neg$A/B&C), N_{t_1}B, R_{t_1}(A,B)} and by any set that includes this one. $\bigcirc_{t_2}\neg$A is entailed by y={$\bigcirc$(A/B), $\bigcirc$($\neg$A/B&C), N_{t_2}B, N_{t_2}C, R_{t_2}(A,B&C)} and any superset of it. Notice that R_{t_2}(A,B) is false. Also, monotonicity is not dependent on the temporal indexing. To see this, drop the indexing and (to avoid ambiguity) do not abbreviate $\bigcirc$(A/$\top$) as $\bigcirc$A. Given parallel truth conditions $\bigcirc$A is entailed by z^* ={$\bigcirc$(A/B), $\bigcirc$($\neg$A/B&C), NB, R(A,B)} and any superset. The trick is that z^*∪NC is inconsistent, entailing both R(A,B) and $\neg$R(A,B). On the other hand, "adding" NC *consistently* it is true we lose the entailment of $\bigcirc$A, but we also "lose" the premise R(A,B).

A number of philosophers have denied the validity of the entailment principle because of the family of so-called Good Samaritan paradoxes. A familiar example is the knower paradox: suppose that at t it is settled that the enemy will attack. It may be that at t the spy Ortcutt should know that the enemy will attack. It follows by entailment that at t it ought to be that the enemy will attack. This seems paradoxical and has led some to deny the validity of entailment principles. But, given their obvious use in planning, this seems an over-reaction. A more satisfactory response is to distinguish in some way primary ought statements from derived ones.[7] We can think of the primary ought statements as being given by the primitive. **M3D** model. If we add the entailment principle then the new ought statements that hold are said to be derived.

5.

Two additional principles not valid in **M3D** or **M3D+** are

$$\bigcirc(B/A) \ \& \ \bigcirc(C/A) \ \rightarrow \ \bigcirc(B\&C/A) \qquad \text{agglomeration}$$

and

$$\bigcirc(C/A) \ \rightarrow \ \Diamond C \qquad \qquad \bigcirc \text{ implies } \Diamond \text{ (for possible A)}$$

Their absence from **M3D** and **M3D+** is related to the consistency of dilemmas in **M3D**, as is the invalidity of both:

$$\bigcirc(B/A) \ \rightarrow \ \neg\bigcirc(\neg B/A)$$
$$\bigcirc_t B \ \rightarrow \ \neg \bigcirc_t \neg B$$

Because dilemmas are consistent in **M3D** and **M3D+** some attention needs to be paid to the representation of permission. For normative systems without dilemmas each of the following may be held valid:

$$P(A/B) \equiv \neg \bigcirc (\neg A/B).$$
$$\bigcirc(A/B) \ \rightarrow P(A/B).$$

If dilemmas are tolerated, however, one of them must be abandoned. In **M3D** and **M3D+** we will use the first as a definition of permission and abandon the second. (Likewise for the corresponding pair concerning $\bigcirc_t$ and P_t).

When we add both agglomeration and "ought implies $\Diamond$" to **M3D+**, dilemmas, as defined above in Definition 10, are not consistent. For instance, $\bigcirc(A/B)$ and $\bigcirc(\neg A/B)$ entail $\bigcirc(A\&\neg A/B)$ by agglomeration, but $A\&\neg A$ is not possible. Whether or not one may coherently think of a particular normative system as giving way to dilemmas is a complicated and much discussed

---

[7]See our (Loewer and Belzer, 1986, p.128).

question. We do not attempt to settle it here for any particular normative system. Indeed, it seems to us that the question of the possibility of dilemmas is a normative, not a logical, question. It does seem clear that a normative system may allow dilemmas without running into logical difficulties, since the "logic" of that system may be minimal. By the same token, there may be good reasons for thinking that certain normative systems do not allow dilemmas, in which case the following logic would be *apropos*.

The system **M3D++** requires that the function f satisfies **ENT** and the conditions

> **AGG**   for any set of propositions $\{A_1, \ldots, A_i\}$ such that each   and
> $A_i \in f(B)$, $\cap \{A_1, \ldots, A_i\} \subseteq f(B)$

if $B \in f(A)$ then there is a w such that w$\in$A.

The resulting semantics can be simplified to a set selection function semantics by defining f^* as a world set-selection function such that

$$f^*(A) = \cap f(A).$$

f^* picks out the set of worlds that are most acceptable given A (that is, the set of A-worlds most acceptable relative to the relevant normative system). Let g^* be a world set-selection function defined in terms of g as $g^*(A) = \cap g(A)$. Truth conditions for our key notions then are given by:

> $\bigcirc(B/A)$ is true iff $f^*(A) \subseteq B$
> $N_t A$ is true iff $g^*(t) \subseteq A$
> $\bigcirc_t A$ is true iff $f^*(g^*(t)) \subseteq A$
> $R_t(B,A)$ is true iff for all C:
>   if $g^*(t) \subseteq C$ then $f^*(A) \subseteq B$ iff $f^*(A \cap C) \subseteq B$.

6.

Consider now the following principles:

> Disjunction(a) $\bigcirc(C/A \vee B) \rightarrow \bigcirc(C/A) \vee \bigcirc(C/B)$.
> Disjunction(b) $\bigcirc(C/A) \, \& \, \bigcirc(C/B) \rightarrow \bigcirc(C/A \vee B)$.

If $\bigcirc(B/A)$ means that A defeasibly requires B (or A is a reason in favor of B) then these two principles seem intuitively valid (if, at any rate, we already have seen fit to accept **M3D++** for a particular normative system). Together they imply that worlds are partially ordered by the value system. An even more interesting principle is

> **vW** $\bigcirc(B/A) \, \& \, P(C/A) \rightarrow \bigcirc(B/A\&C)$.

This principle is interesting both logically and normatively.[8] The corresponding semantical constraint on the function f^* is the following:

$$\text{if } f^*(A) \cap B \neq \emptyset, \text{ then } f^*(A\&B) = f^*(A) \cap B.$$

With this condition, the set selection function can be simplified to a ranking-of-worlds semantics, since this condition on f^* entails that f^* determines a weak ordering of worlds (that is, a total ordering with ties) and gives the logic we called **3D** (Loewer and Belzer, 1983). It uses a weak ordering as in Lewis's *Counterfactuals* (1973) to interpret $\bigcirc(B/A)$, and treats $\bigcirc_t A$ as true at w just in case A is true at all the worlds, of those accessible at t in w, most highly ranked in the Lewis ordering. Even though *strengthening the antecedent*

$$\bigcirc(A/B) \rightarrow \bigcirc(A/B\&C)$$

remains invalid, **vW** offers a restricted form of strengthening the antecedent insofar as $\bigcirc(A/B\&C)$ follows from $\bigcirc(B/A)$ for any C that is permissible given A. The principle **vW** says, in effect, that doing something which is permissible, given A, cannot undercut obligations conditional upon A. Instances of the principle include:

(i) $\bigcirc B \ \& \ PC \ \rightarrow \ \bigcirc(B/C)$
(ii) $PC \ \& \ P(B/C) \rightarrow PB$

(As before, let $\bigcirc B = \text{df } \bigcirc(B/\top)$ and $PB = \text{df } P(B/\top)$, for tautology $\top$). So equally the principle says that one does not violate any obligations (or prohibitions) by doing only what is permissible. Together the two ideas represented in these instances say that doing the permissible neither violates nor undercuts obligations. Suppose that the antecedent of (i) obtains, $\bigcirc B \ \& \ PC$, and there are no other relevant rules. Then (i) guarantees that the order in which one does what is obligatory or permitted makes no difference. If C is done first the obligation to do B remains, and *vice versa*. It is only when something forbidden occurs that obligations and permissions are defeated (and perhaps replaced by new ones). This is the general import of **vW**. Similarly, it says that one cannot get out of an obligation by doing something that is permissible. These strike us as interesting and not unreasonable constraints for normative systems that purport to guide action.

A number of counter-examples to **vW** have been suggested. One has an obligation to give you the money if one promised to do so, $\bigcirc(g/p)$; but one does not have the obligation if after one's promising, you cancel the obligation, $\neg\bigcirc(g/p\&c)$. However, from these and **vW**, which entails

$$\bigcirc(B/A)\&\neg\bigcirc(B/A\&C) \rightarrow \bigcirc(\neg C/A),$$

[8] '**vW**' denotes G. H. von Wright, who in 1982 called it to our attention, asking if it is valid in the *Counterfactuals*-based systems and emphasizing its importance.

it follows that if one promises you some money, you should not cancel their obligation, $\bigcirc(\neg c/p)$. This sounds odd (or worse). Asher and Bonevac point out, "Generalizing, the principle entails that no one should release anyone from a promise or other obligation, which is absurd."[9] Scott Shapiro and Horacio Arlo-Costas suggest the following legal counter-example to **vW**. If you as a judge are confronted with evidence seized without a search warrant, you should not admit it in trial, $\bigcirc(\neg a/\neg s)$; but if the police officer seized the evidence in good faith, even without a search warrant, you may admit it, $P(a/\neg s \& g)$. **vW** gives us $\bigcirc(\neg g/\neg s)$, if the evidence was seized without a search warrant the officer should not have acted in good faith. Another legal example is drawn by Robert Koons and Thomas Seung from *McLoughlin v. O'Brien* (1989): you are legally liable if you injure another person, $\bigcirc(l/i)$; but you are not liable for non-physical injuries, $\bigcirc(\neg l/i \& \neg p)$. As Bonevac and Asher correctly point out, this set with **vW** entails $\bigcirc(p/i)$, if you injure someone, you should injure them physically. It must be acknowledged of course that some normative systems do not respect **vW**, just as some allow dilemmas (or some may reject the entailment principles), and there appear to be no good reasons for thinking these systems are logically incoherent. A minimal logic like **M3D** is appropriate for such systems. But stronger logics may work for others. The logical principles appropriate to a given normative system that is used and presupposed in action will to some extent be determined by the norms of that system and by examining what actions are endorsed in practice.

For this reason, questions about the reality of dilemmas or respect for **vW** are themselves normative, not logical, questions. Should a particular institution or legal system be regarded as respecting **vW**? One way to frame this question is to imagine Dworkin's super-judge and -philosopher choosing a deontic logic, from among those on offer, for his reconstruction of the law or some other practice.

There are two general lines of defense that Hercules might employ, in light of the alleged counterexamples to **vW**, were he to reconstruct the system in **3D** (including **vW**) rather than one of the weaker logics. The first (and perhaps weaker) strategy accepts the specified rules as part of the normative system, and argues that, appearances to the contrary notwithstanding) it *is* reasonable to interpret the system as containing these norms.

About promising: "It is not absurd to say that there is a *prima facie* obligation not to release others from their promises. The existence of the institution of promising requires that promises are not frequently or casually cancelled, for if promises were too easily cancelled, then people would tend not to take seriously enough the promises they make (or receive). Surprisingly, the institution of promising supports a *prima facie* obligation not to cancel the

---

[9]"Two theories of *prima facie* obligation," ms., p. 26.

promises one receives. Of course, this *prima facie* obligation can itself be overridden by other considerations (indeed one's desire to cancel might be sufficient)." About searches: "Evidence seized without a warrant should *not* involve good faith, since officers should know better." About injuries: "The legal system really does have a preference for physical injuries, because they are more easily verified and compensated."

A second strategy denies that the relevant systems contain all of the norms in the examples. The *prima facie* rules of the normative systems have not been correctly identified in the alleged counterexamples. About promising: only uncanceled promises create obligations. So $\bigcirc(g/p)$ is not an instance of any relevant deontic rule regarding promising; but $\bigcirc(g/p\&\neg c)$ may be. About evidence: $\bigcirc(\neg a/\neg s)$ is not a genuine legal rule, although $\bigcirc(\neg a/\neg s\&\neg f)$ is. About injuries: the relevant rule is $\bigcirc(l/i\&p)$, not $\bigcirc(l/i)$. The rejected rules in each of these examples, however, may correspond to acceptable epistemic rules. For instance, "Evidence gathered without a warrant is not admissible" may be an acceptable, though defeasible, epistemic rule, if normally when evidence is gathered without a warrant there is in fact not good faith. Normally promises ought to be kept, because normally they are not cancelled. English conditionals containing 'ought' and 'should' are often ambiguous between epistemic and deontic readings (recall the distinction between Jerry's looking guilty being evidence for what his all out obligations are, and its being a deontic reason).

There are some apparent counterexamples to **vW** that definitely should be handled in the second way. For instance, if you hurt someone, you ought, morally, to compensate them, $\bigcirc(c/h)$; but if you hurt them but not very badly then you need not compensate them, $P(\neg c/h\&\neg b)$. From these, **vW** gives us $\bigcirc(b/h)$, if you hurt someone, you should hurt them very badly. This is not a conclusive counterexample to **vW** (as applied to morality) because obviously the first norm $\bigcirc(c/h)$ should be rejected and replaced by $\bigcirc(c/h\&b)$ – this is what the permission tells us. Not all hurts morally require compensation, although the bad ones do, that is, $\bigcirc(c/h\&b)$. And the new set does not entail $\bigcirc(b/h)$.

Some of our practices may not be definitive enough to establish a fact of the matter about whether they support a principle like **vW**. And even if Hercules rejects the principle for a particular system, a restricted version of the principle may be defensible: nothing one permissibly can do enables one to defeat *one's own* obligations. That is, nothing an agent herself can do permissibly, given A, will defeat any of her A-conditional obligations. Suppose B and C both describe the actions of a given agent, then, and suppose $\bigcirc(B/A)$ and

$P(C/A)$ are true; then so is $\bigcirc(B/A\&C)$.[10]

Marvin Belzer
Department of Philosophy
Bowling Green State University

Barry Loewer
Department of Philosophy
Rutgers University

REFERENCES

Belzer, M. (1985a). Normative kinematics (I): a solution to a problem about permission. *Law and Philosophy* 4:257–287.

Belzer, M. (1985b). Normative kinematics (II): the introduction of imperatives. *Law and Philosophy* 4:377–403.

Belzer, M. (1986a). Reasoning with defeasible principles. *Synthese* 66:1–24.

Belzer, M. (1986b). A logic of deliberation. *Proc. Fifth National Conference on Artificial Intelligence*, vol. 1, pages 38-43.

Belzer, M. and Loewer, B. (1993). Absolute obligations and ordered worlds." *Philosophical Studies* 70:61–74.

Belzer, M. and Loewer, B. (1994). HECTOR meets 3-D: a diaphilosophical epic." In J. Tomberlin (ed.), *Philosophical Perspectives* 8:389–414.

Castañeda, H-N. (1981). The paradoxes of deontic logic: the simplest solution to all of them in one fell swoop. In R. Hilpinen (ed.), *New Studies in Deontic Logic*, D. Reidel, Dordrecht, pages 37–85.

Chellas, B. (1984). *Modal Logic*. Cambridge University Press.

Chisholm, R. (1978). Practical reason and the Logic of Requirement. In J. Raz (ed.), *Practical Reasoning*, Oxford University Press, pages 118–127.

Feldman, F. (1986). *Doing the Best We Can*. D. Reidel, Dordrecht.

Føllesdal, D. and Hilpinen, R. (1971). Deontic logic: an introduction. In R. Hilpinen (ed.), *Deontic Logic: Introductory and Systematic Readings*, D. Reidel, Dordrecht.

Humberstone, I. (1983). The background of circumstances. *Pacific Philosophical Quarterly* 64:19–34.

Lewis, D. (1973). *Counterfactuals*. Blackwell, Oxford.

Lewis, D. (1974). Semantic analyses for dyadic deontic logic. In S. Stenlund (ed.), *Logical Theory and Semantic Analysis*, D. Reidel, Dordrecht, pages 1–14.

Lewis, D. 1979. A problem about permission. In E. Saarinen, R. Hilpinen, I. Niiniluoto, and M. B. Provence (eds), *Essays in Honour of Jaakko Hintikka*, D. Reidel, Dordrecht, pages 163–179.

Loewer, B. and Belzer, M. (1983). Dyadic deontic detachment. *Synthese* 54:295–319.

Loewer, B. and Belzer, M. (1986). Help for the Good Samaritan paradox. *Philosophical Studies* 50:117–127.

---

[10] An earlier version of this paper was presented at the Society for Exact Philosophy meetings held at York University in Toronto, 1993.

Loewer, B. and Belzer, M. (1991). *Prima-facie* obligation: its deconstruction and reconstruction. In E. Lepore and R. van Gulick (eds.), *John Searle and His Critics,* Blackwell, Oxford, pages 359–370.

Nozick, R. (1968). Moral complications and moral structures. *Natural Law Forum* 13:1–50.

Pollock, J. (1976). *Subjunctive Reasoning.* D. Reidel, Dordrecht.

Raz, J. 1978. Introduction. In J. Raz (ed.), *Practical Reasoning,* Oxford University Press, pages 1–17.

Thomason, R. (1970). Indeterminist time and truth value gaps. *Theoria* 36:264–81.

Thomason, R. (1981). Deontic logic as founded on tense logic. In R. Hilpinen (ed.), *New Studies in Deontic Logic,* D. Reidel, Dordrecht.

Sinnott-Armstrong, W. (1989). *Moral Dilemmas.* Blackwell, Oxford.

Tomberlin, J. (1983). Contrary-to-duty imperatives and Castañeda's System of Deontic Logic. In J. Tomberlin(ed.), *Agent, Language, and the Structure of the World: Essays Presented to Hector-Neri Castañeda with His Replies,* Hackett, Indianapolis, pages 231–249.

van Eck, J. (1982). A system of temporally relative modal modal and deontic predicate logic and its applications. *Logique et Analyse* 25:249–290, 339–381.

LENNART ÅQVIST

SYSTEMATIC FRAME CONSTANTS IN DEFEASIBLE DEONTIC LOGIC*

A New Form of Andersonian Reduction

1. INTRODUCTION

The present paper is concerned with the problem of providing adequate semantical foundations for certain systems of *dyadic* ("defeasible", "non-monotonic") deontic logic (logics of *conditional* obligation and permission), and of giving semantically sound and complete axiomatizations of those systems. These dyadic deontic logics are all extensions of the system DSDL3, which was proposed by Bengt Hansson in his well known pioneering paper (Hansson, 1969), where DSDL3 was characterized in purely semantical terms, without any attempt being made by him to characterize it in axiomatic or proof-theoretical terms. In section 2 *infra* we start out by studying an infinite hierarchy of systems of Alethic Modal Logic, to which we intend to add *definitions* of dyadic deontic operators - this is in the spirit of the familiar Andersonian reduction of deontic to alethic modal logic (Anderson, 1956; Anderson, 1958). In section 3, then, we go on to deal with an infinite hierarchy of *dyadic* deontic logics, which we prove to be *representable* in the former hierarchy of alethic systems. This done in section 4, which forms the bulk of the paper. Finally, in the concluding section 5, we announce a result on a certain "core" system of dyadic deontic logic, the detailed proof of which will have to be deferred to another occasion.

The main technical device employed in our two hierarchies of logics is this: in the models of both, we work with a set

$$\{opt_1, opt_2, \ldots, opt_m\}$$

which is to be a *partition* of the set W of "possible worlds" into exactly m non-empty, pairwise disjoint and together exhaustive "optimality" classes, viewed as so many *levels of perfection*. Intuitively, we think of opt_1 as the set of "best" (optimal) members of W as a whole, opt_2 as the set of best members of $W - opt_1$ (the "second best" members of W), opt_3 as the set of best members of $W - (opt_1 \cup opt_2)$ (the "third best" members of W); and so on. Now, we shall represent each level of perfection in the object-language

*The present contribution reports research done under the auspices of the Swedish Council for Research in the Humanities and the Social Sciences (HSFR): Project "On the Legal Concepts of Rights and Duties: an Analysis Based on Deontic and Causal Conditional Logic".

D. Nute (ed.), Defeasible Deontic Logic, 59–77.

of the systems by a so-called *systematic frame constant*. The truth conditions and axioms governing those constants will be seen to play a highly important, characteristic role in our axiomatization.

The approach adopted here to the problem of finding the "right" semantical foundations for dyadic deontic logic deviates from other, related approaches in the literature most conspicuously in the following respect: unlike e.g. (Hansson, 1969; Spohn, 1975), and myself in (Åqvist, 1987, Ch.VI) and (Åqvist, 1993), we do not here take the weak preference relation 'is at least as ideal as' as *primitive* in the models of our systems, but *define* it in terms of the optimality classes $opt_1, \ldots, opt_m$, as done in section 3 below. There are, we take it, definite advantages in doing so.

As to the technique of systematic frame constants as applied to deontic logic (and not only to tense logic), it seems to originate with my (Åqvist, 1984) and (Åqvist, 1987); the applications of that technique in those works were not entirely successful, however.

At this juncture, we may give a brief review of the informal, philosophical motivation for Hansson's work, and notably for his system **DSDL3**. We recall that this dyadic system (and its cognates) were proposed by Hansson as alternatives to the treatments of conditional obligation given in (Rescher, 1958) and in (von Wright, 1964), both of which were criticized by (Hansson, 1969) in so many words:

"In Rescher's system some obligations may disappear and no new are created; in von Wright's system no obligations disappear and some may be created. The robbery of Jones by Smith creates the conditional obligation to restore the money. Therefore Rescher is wrong. And if the circumstance that Smith quits his job comes true, his employer is no longer obligated to pay him a salary. Therefore von Wright is wrong."(Hansson, 1969, section XIII)

Again, (Lewis, 1973) agrees with Hansson that those treatments of conditional obligation are unsatisfactory

".... because they validate inferences from 'Given that ϕ_1, it ought to be that ψ' to 'Given that $\phi_1 \& \phi_2$, it ought to be that ψ', or conversely. Neither direction ought to be valid, since it seems that we can have consistent alternating sequences like this:

> Given that ϕ_1, it ought to be that ψ,
> Given that $\phi_1 \& \phi_2$, it ought to be that $\neg\psi$,
> Given that $\phi_1 \& \phi_2 \& \phi_3$, it ought to be that ψ,
> $\vdots$

along with all their negated opposites. For instance: 'Given that Jesse robbed the bank, he ought to confess; but given in addition that his confession would send his ailing mother to an early grave, he ought not to; but given in addition that an innocent man is on trial for the crime, he ought to after all ...'. .... Bengt Hansson and Bas van Fraassen have given analyses of conditional obligation expressly designed to permit such appearances and disappearances of conditional obligation as are found in my alternating sequence. I have based my analysis on theirs, but with various changes."(Lewis, 1973, section 5.1, p.102 f.)

Against the background of these passages, we may ask: what is the intuitive, pre-theoretical idea embodied in the analyses of conditional obligation proposed by Hansson and Lewis? Well, according to (Hansson, 1969, section XIV):

"The problem of conditional obligation is what happens if somebody nevertheless performs a forbidden act. Ideal worlds are excluded. But, it may be the case that among the still achievable worlds, some are better than others. There should then be an obligation to make the best out of the sad circumstances. The following seems to be a rather straightforward way to generalize the semantics of **SDL** (*sc.* standard deontic logic) to the dyadic case: ... "

And, according to (Lewis, 1974, section I):

"It ought not be be that you are robbed. *A fortiori*, it ought not to be that you are robbed and then helped. But you ought to be helped, given that you have been robbed. The robbing excludes the best possibilities that might otherwise have been actualized, and the helping is needed in order to actualize the best of those that remain. Among the possible worlds marred by the robbing, the best of a bad lot are some of those where the robbing is followed by helping."

Hopefully, the explanations given in these quotations suffice as motivation for our interest in Hansson's work and will facilitate understanding of the enterprise undertaken in the present paper. On the other hand, we cannot here discuss the various complex technical aspects of Lewis's way of developing dyadic deontic logic, as done in (Lewis, 1973) and (Lewis, 1974). However, the following remarks should not be out of place.

Remark 1 : Consider again a partition

$$\{opt_1, opt_2, \ldots, opt_m\}$$

of our set W of possible worlds, designed to represent so many levels of perfection. Let \$ be the set of subsets of W defined by setting

$$\$ = \{opt_1, opt_1 \cup opt_2, \ldots, opt_1 \cup \ldots \cup opt_m\}$$

Then, \$ will be a special kind of finite *system of spheres* over W in the Lewis sense: it will be "universal", "absolute" and "nested", whence, since each member of \$ is properly included in the next one (if any), \$ will be closed under unions and intersections.

Conversely, consider a universal, absolute and finite system of non-empty spheres over W (in the Lewis sense)

$$\$ = \{S_1, S_2, \ldots, S_m\}$$

with $\emptyset \neq S_1 \subset S_2 \subset \ldots \subset S_{m-1} \subset S_m$ (all inclusions proper!). Define $opt_1 = S_1$ and, for each integer i with $1 < i \leq m$, $opt_i = S_i - S_{i-1}$. Then, as thus defined, the set

$$\{opt_1, opt_2, \ldots, opt_m\}$$

will obviously be a partition of W into exactly m non-empty, pairwise disjoint and together exhaustive optimality classes in the sense of this paper.

The present observation then tells us how our levels of perfection can be related to Lewis-style systems-of-spheres of the special kind just considered.

Remark 2 : As a corollary of this result, we observe that Lewis might well have considered infinite hierarchies of dyadic deontic logics, like our systems *Gm* [*m* = 1,2,...], dealt with in section 3 *infra*. A suggestion somehow to this effect (although in the context of counterfactuals) can indeed be found in section 2.1 of (Lewis, 1973), entitled "Multiple Modalities". The technical realization of that suggestion is of course different from the one I develop in the present paper, but that analogy is sufficiently striking to deserve further close study.

Remark 3 : (Nasty Question to the Reader). On p. 121 in section 6.1 of (Lewis, 1973), Lewis asserts that there is no special characteristic axiom corresponding to the so-called Limit Assumption which, in the context of deontic logic, is to the effect that every non-empty subset of W has at least one best, or optimal, element. However, in the axiomatization of our systems *Gm* and *G* given in section 3 *infra*, we naturally select the axiom schema $\alpha 3$ as one that adequately reflects that Limit Assumption. How can this be so?

2. THE ALETHIC MODAL LOGICS $Hm \, (m = 1, 2, \ldots)$: SYNTAX, SEMANTICS AND PROOF THEORY

The *language* of systems *Hm* (with *m* any positive integer) has, in addition to an at most denumerable set $Prop$ of propositional variables and the usual Boolean sentential connectives (including the constants *verum* and *falsum*, i.e. $\top$ and $\bot$), the following characteristic primitive *logical operators*:

N (for universal necessity)
M (for universal possibility)

as well as a family $\{Q_i\} 1 \leq i < \omega$ of *systematic frame constants*, which are indexed by the set of positive integers. The Q_i are to represent different "levels of perfection" in the models of our systems, as explained above. The set $Sent$ of well formed sentences (formulas, wffs) is then defined in the obvious way - we think of the Q_i as zero-place connectives on a par with $\top$ and $\bot$.

Furthermore, we shall be interested in adding to the language of the systems *Hm* the following *definitions* of the dyadic deontic operators $\bigcirc$ (for conditional obligation) and $\mathcal{P}$ (for conditional permission):

Definition 1

$$\bigcirc_B A = df \quad [M(Q_1 \& B) \to N((Q_1 \& B) \to A)] \,\&$$
$$[(\neg M(Q_1 \& B) \& M(Q_2 \& B)) \to N(Q_2 \& B \to A)] \& \ldots \&$$
$$[(\neg M(Q_1 \& B) \& \ldots \& \neg M(Q_{m-1} \& B) \& M(Q_m \& B))$$
$$\to N(Q_m \& B \to A)]$$

Definition 2

$$\mathcal{P}_B A = df \quad M(Q_1\&B\&A) \vee (\neg M(Q_1\&B)\&M(Q_2\&B\&A)) \vee \ldots \vee$$
$$(\neg M(Q_1\&B)\&\ldots\&\neg M(Q_{m-1}\&B)\&M(Q_m\&B\&A)).$$

Remark on Notation for Dyadic Deontic Operators. We write $\bigcirc_B A [\mathcal{P}_B A]$ to render the ordinary language locution "if B, then it ought to be that A" ["if B, then it is permitted that A"]. We prefer this style of notation to the current one $\bigcirc(A/B)[\mathcal{P}(A/B)]$, because (i) it is parenthesis-free, and (ii) the reading goes from left to right, and not the other way around.

Let us next turn to the *semantics* for our alethic modal logics with frame constants. For any positive integer m, let a *Hm-structure* be an ordered quadruple

$$\mathcal{M} = (W, V, \{opt_i\}_{i=1,2,\ldots}, m)$$

where:

(i) $W \neq \emptyset$ (W is a non-empty set of "possible worlds").
(ii) $V : Prop \to pow(W)$ (V is a valuation function which to each propositional variable assigns a subset of W).
(iii) $\{opt_i\}_{i=1,2,\ldots}$ is an infinite sequence of subsets of W.
(iv) m is the positive integer under consideration.

We can now tell what it means for any sentence A to be *true at* a point ("world") $x(\in W)$ *in* a *Hm*-structure $\mathcal{M}$ (in symbols: $\mathcal{M}, x \models A$), starting out with obvious clauses like

$$\mathcal{M}, x \models p \text{ iff } x \in V(p) \text{ (for any } p \text{ in the set } Prop)$$
$$\mathcal{M}, x \models \top$$
$$\text{not: } \mathcal{M}, x \models \bot$$

and so on for molecular sentences having Boolean connectives as their principal sign. We then handle sentences having the characteristic *Hm*-operators as their principal sign as follows:

$$\mathcal{M}, x \models NA \text{ iff for each } y \text{ in } W : \mathcal{M}, y \models A$$
$$\mathcal{M}, x \models Q_i \text{ iff } x \in opt_i \text{ (for all positive integers } i).$$

We now focus our attention on a special kind of *Hm*-structures called "*Hm*-models". By a *Hm-model* we shall mean any *Hm*-structure $\mathcal{M}$, where $\{opt_i\}$ and m satisfy the following additional condition: *Exactly m Non-Empty Levels of Perfection.* This condition requires the set $\{opt_1, opt_2, \ldots, opt_m\}$ to be a *partition* of W in the sense that

(a) $opt_i \cap opt_j = \emptyset$, for all positive integers i, j with $1 \leq i \neq j \leq m$.
(b) $opt_1 \cup \ldots \cup opt_m = W$.
(c) $opt_i \neq \emptyset$, for each i with $1 \leq i \leq m$.
(d) $opt_i = \emptyset$, for each i with $i > m$.

As usual, then, we say that a sentence A is *Hm-valid* iff $\mathcal{M}, x \models A$ for all *Hm*-models $\mathcal{M}$ and all points x in W. And we say that a set Γ of sentences is *Hm-satisfiable* iff there exists a *Hm*-model $\mathcal{M}$ and a member x of W such that for all sentences A in $\Gamma : \mathcal{M}, x \models A$.

It is now time to consider the *proof theory* of the systems *Hm*. Thus, for any positive integer m, the *axiomatic system Hm* is determined by the following rule of inference, rule of proof, and axiom schemata:

Rule of inference

$$mp \text{ (modus ponens)} \quad \frac{A, A \to B}{B}$$

Rule of proof

$$nec \text{ (necessitation for } N) \quad \frac{\vdash A}{\vdash NA}$$

Axiomatic schemata

A0 All tautologies over $Sent$
A1 S5-schemata for $N, M (i.e.\ MA \leftrightarrow \neg N \neg A, N(A \to B) \to$
$\quad (NA \to NB), NA \to A, NA \to NNA, MNA \to A)$
A2 $Q_i \to \neg Q_j$, for all positive integers i, j with $1 \le i \ne j < w$
A3 $Q_1 \vee \ldots \vee Q_m$
A4 $MQ_1 \& \ldots \& MQ_m$

As usual, the above axiom schemata and rules determine syntactic notions of *Hm-provability* and *Hm-deducibility* as follows. We say that a sentence A is *Hm-provable* (in symbols: $\vdash_{Hm} A$) iff A belongs to the smallest subset of $Sent$ which (i) contains every instance of A0 - A4 as its member, and which (ii) is closed under the rule of inference *mp* and the rule of proof *nec*. Again, we say that the sentence A is *Hm-deducible* from the set $\Gamma (\subseteq Sent)$ of *assumptions* (in symbols: $\Gamma \vdash_{Hm} A$) iff there are sentences $B_1, \ldots, B_k$ in Γ, for some natural number $k \ge 0$, such that $\vdash_{Hm} (B_1 \& \ldots \& B_k) \to A$.

Moreover, letting $\Gamma \subseteq Sent$, we say that Γ is *Hm-inconsistent* iff $\Gamma \vdash_{Hm} \perp$, and *Hm-consistent* otherwise. Finally, we say that Γ is *maximal Hm-consistent* iff Γ is *Hm*-consistent and, for each sentence A, either $A \in \Gamma$ or $\neg A \in \Gamma$; where this latter condition is known as requiring Γ to be *negation-complete*.

We leave to the reader the task of verifying the following result, in the absence of which our axiomatic theories would be pointless:

Theorem 1 (Soundness)

Weak version: For any $m = 1, 2, \ldots$: every *Hm*-provable sentence is *Hm*-valid.
Strong version: For any $m = 1, 2, \ldots$: every *Hm*-satisfiable set of sentences is *Hm*-consistent.

A more challenging task is to establish the converse of these results, i.e. to prove, for every positive integer m, the following:

Theorem 2 (Completeness)

Weak version: Every *Hm*-valid sentence is *Hm*-provable.
Strong version: Every *Hm*-consistent set of sentences is *Hm*-satisfiable.

Proof (very sketchy): As the weak version is immediate from the strong one, we concentrate on the latter.

Let Γ be any *Hm*-consistent set of sentences. By Lindenbaum's Lemma Γ has a maximal *Hm*-consistent extension, call it Γ_w. Form the so-called *canonical Hm-structure generated by* Γ_w, in the sense of the structure

$$\mathcal{M}^{\Gamma_w} = (W, V, \{opt_i\}_{i=1,2,\ldots}, m)$$

where

(i) W = the set of maximal *Hm*-consistent sets x of sentences such that for
  all $A \in Sent$, if $NA \in \Gamma_w$, then $A \in x$.
(ii) V = the valuation function such that for all p in $Prop$:
  $V(p) = \{x \in W : p \in x\}$.
(iii) $opt_i = \begin{cases} \{x \in W : Q_i \in x\}, & \text{if } 1 \leq i \leq m \\ \emptyset, & \text{otherwise (i.e., if } m < i < w) \end{cases}$
(iv) m = the positive integer under consideration.

Note that opt_i is well defined by (iii), because the axioms A3 and A2 guarantee the existence in each $x \in W$ of a unique Q_i with $1 \leq i \leq m$.

Omitting details, we can then prove (a) that $\mathcal{M}^{\Gamma_w}$ is a *Hm*-model, and (b) that for each sentence A:

$$\mathcal{M}^{\Gamma_w}, \Gamma_w \models A \text{ iff } A \in \Gamma_w.$$

Hence, since $\Gamma \subseteq \Gamma_w$, we have $\mathcal{M}^{\Gamma_w}, \Gamma_w \models A$ for every $A \in \Gamma$. In other words, assuming Γ to be any *Hm*-consistent set of sentences, we have constructed a *Hm*-model, viz. $\mathcal{M}^{\Gamma_w}$, such that for some x in its universe W, viz. Γ_w, $\mathcal{M}^{\Gamma_w}, x \models A$ for each A in Γ; i.e. we have shown Γ to be *Hm*-satisfiable.
Q.E.D.

3. TWO DYADIC DEONTIC LOGICS: THE SYSTEMS
$Gm[m = 1, 2, \ldots]$ AND G

The *language* of the systems Gm is like that of the Hm, except that its logical vocabulary has the dyadic deontic operators $\bigcirc$ and $\mathcal{P}$ among its *primitive* connectives. And the language of the system G is like that of the Gm except for lacking the systematic frame constants Q_i altogether. The definition of *Sent* is straightforward in both cases.

It is convenient to begin the presentation of those systems by outlining their *proof theory*. The rule of inference *mp* and the rule of proof *nec* (for N) are common to $Gm(m = 1, 2, \ldots)$ and G. Consider next the following list:

Axiom Schemata

A0 - A4
a1 $\mathcal{P}_B A \leftrightarrow \neg \bigcirc_B \neg A$
a2 $\bigcirc_B (A \to C) \to (\bigcirc_B A \to \bigcirc_B C)$
a3 $\bigcirc_B A \to N \bigcirc_B A$
a4 $NA \to \bigcirc_B A$
$\alpha 0$ $N(A \leftrightarrow B) \to (\bigcirc_A C \leftrightarrow \bigcirc_B C)$
$\alpha 1$ $\bigcirc_A A$
$\alpha 2$ $\bigcirc_{A\&B} C \to \bigcirc_A (B \to C)$
$\alpha 3$ $MA \to (\bigcirc_A B \to \mathcal{P}_A B)$
$\alpha 4$ $\mathcal{P}_A B \to (\bigcirc_A (B \to C) \to \bigcirc_{A\&B} C)$
$\alpha 5$ $= A2$
$\alpha 6$ $\mathcal{P}_B Q_i \to ((Q_1 \vee \ldots \vee Q_{i-1}) \to \neg B)$, for all i with $1 < i \le m$
$\alpha 7$ $Q_1 \to (\bigcirc_B A \to (B \to A))$
$\alpha 8$ $(Q_i \& \bigcirc_B A\&B\&\neg A) \to \mathcal{P}_B(Q_1 \vee \ldots \vee Q_{i-1})$, for all $1 < i \le m$

Then the *axiomatic system* $Gm(m = 1, 2, \ldots)$ is determined by *all* these schemata (and the above rules). On the other hand, the axiom schemata of the system G are just A0, A1, a1 - a4, $\alpha 0 - \alpha 4$, i.e. what remains after we have dropped every schema in the Gm containing occurrences of frame constants.

The notions of *Gm-/ G-/* provability, -deducibility, -consistency etc. are introduced in the obvious way.

Turning next to the *semantics* of the logics Gm, we define, for any positive integer m, a *Gm-structure* as an ordered quintuple

$$\mathcal{M} = (W, V, \{opt_i\}_{i=1,2,\ldots}, m, best)$$

where the first four items are as in the definition of a Hm-structure, and where

(v) *best*: $Sent \to pow(W)$ (*best* is a function which to each sentence in the Gm-language assigns a subset of W, heuristically, the set of *best* worlds in the extension (truth-set) of the sentence under consideration).

For $\mathcal{M}$ a *Gm*-structure and $x \in W$, we then define the locution "$\mathcal{M}, x \models A$" recursively just as in the case of *Hm*-structures, except that there are the following fresh clauses in the inductive step governing sentences having $\bigcirc$ and $\mathcal{P}$ as their principal sign:

$$\mathcal{M}, x \models \bigcirc_B A \text{ iff for each } y \text{ in } best(B) : \mathcal{M}, y \models A$$
$$\mathcal{M}, x \models \mathcal{P}_B A \text{ iff for some } y \text{ in } best(B) : \mathcal{M}, y \models A$$

Again, we focus our attention on a special kind of *Gm*-structure: by a *Gm-model* we understand any *Gm*-structure $\mathcal{M}$, where $\{opt_i\}$ and m satisfy the condition *Exactly m Non-Empty Levels of Perfection*, clauses (a) - (d), and where the new function *best* satisfies:

$\gamma 0.$ $x \in best(B)$ iff $\mathcal{M}, x \models B$ and for each y in W :
        if $\mathcal{M}, y \models B$, then $x \succeq y$.

Here, the weak preference relation $\succeq$ is to be understood as follows. First of all, by clauses (a) and (b) in the condition *Exactly m etc.*, we have that for each x in W there is *exactly one* positive integer i with $1 \le i \le m$ such that $x \in opt_i$. We then define a "ranking" function r from W into the closed interval $[1, m]$ of integers by setting

$$r(x) = \text{ the } i, \text{ with } 1 \le i \le m, \text{ such that } x \in opt_i.$$

Finally, we define $\succeq$ as the binary relation on W such that for all x, y in W:

$$x \succeq y \text{ iff } r(x) \le r(y).$$

Note the importance of the new condition $\gamma 0$: it captures well the intuitive meaning of our "choice" function *best*.

Given the notion of a *Gm*-model, those of *Gm*-validity and *Gm*-satisfiability are defined in the usual manner.

Theorem 3 (Soundness & Completeness of the Systems $Gm(m = 1, 2, \ldots)$)

Weak version: For every sentence A: A is *Gm*-provable iff A is *Gm*-valid.
Strong version: For each set Γ of sentences: Γ is *Gm*-consistent iff Γ is *Gm*-satisfiable.

Proof (still rather sketchy). The soundness parts are unproblematic. So we concentrate on the "only if" part of the strong version, from which the "if" part of the weak one is immediate.

Let Γ be any *Gm*-consistent set of sentences, and let Γ_w be a maximal *Gm*-consistent extension of Γ, the existence of which is guaranteed by Lindenbaum's Lemma. Form the *canonical Gm-structure generated by* Γ_w, in the sense of a structure

$$\mathcal{M}^{\Gamma_w} = (W, V, \{opt_i\}_{i=1,2,\ldots}, m, best)$$

satisfying conditions (i)-(iv) in our definition above of the canonical *Hm*-structure except that, of course, W will now be a certain set of maximal

Gm-consistent sets, and where

> (v) $best$ = the function from $Sent$ into $pow(W)$ defined by setting, for all sentences B, $best(B) = \{x \in W : \text{for all } A \in Sent, \text{ if } \bigcirc_B A \in \Gamma_w, \text{ then } A \in x\}$.

Again omitting details, we can prove that $\mathcal{M}^{\Gamma_w}$ is a *Gm*-model and that for each sentence A:

$$\mathcal{M}^{\Gamma_w}, \Gamma_w \models A \text{ iff } A \in \Gamma_w$$

which results suffice to establish the desired strong version of the completeness theorem for the systems *Gm*. We observe that a proof that $\mathcal{M}^{\Gamma_w}$ satisfies our condition $\gamma 0$ on *best* is easily extracted from the proof given in (Åqvist, 1993) and (Åqvist, 1987, Ch. VI, pp.188-191) that the three-place relation $\mathcal{R}$ satisfies essentially the same condition.

We close the present section by a brief consideration of the dyadic deontic logic *G*, which, as we recall, lacks the frame constants in its vocabulary, and which is determined by the axiom schemata A0, A1, a1-a4, and $\alpha 0 - \alpha 4$ (in addition to the rules *mp* and *nec* for N).

As to the *semantics* for *G*: a *G-structure* is an ordered triple

$$\mathcal{M} = (W, V, best)$$

where, as usual, (i) $W \neq \emptyset$, (ii) $V : Prop \rightarrow pow(W)$, and (v) $best : Sent \rightarrow pow(W)$. The relevant clauses in the truth-definition for *G*-sentences have then all been stated. Again, by a *G-model* we mean any *G*-structure $\mathcal{M}$ satisfying the following five conditions paralleling the axioms $\alpha 0 - \alpha 4$ (cf. (Åqvist, 1987, Ch. VI, p.166): for any *G*-sentence A, we let $\|A\|^{\mathcal{M}}$, or $\|A\|$ for short, be the *extension* in $\mathcal{M}$ of A, i.e. $\|A\| = \{x \in W : \mathcal{M}, x \models A\}$):

$\sigma 0$ $\|A\| = \|B\|$ only if $best(A) = best(B)$
$\sigma 1$ $best(A) \subseteq \|A\|$
$\sigma 2$ $best(A) \cap \|B\| \subseteq best(A\&B)$
$\sigma 3$ $\|A\| \neq \emptyset$ only if $best(A) \neq \emptyset$
$\sigma 4$ $best(A) \cap \|B\| \neq \emptyset$ only if $best(A\&B) \subseteq best(A) \cap \|B\|$

for any *G*-sentences A, B. *G*-validity and *G*-satisfiability are as usual.

Theorem 4 (Soundness & Completeness of the System G)

Weak version: For each A in Sent: A is *G*-provable iff A is *G*-valid.
Strong version: For each $\Gamma \subseteq Sent$: Γ is *G*-consistent iff Γ is *G*-satisfiable.

Proof. Omitted and left as an exercise. *Hint*: Pp.160-165 of my (Åqvist, 1987, Ch. VI) are helpful, although the setting is somewhat different from the present one.

4. REPRESENTABILTIY OF DYADIC DEONTIC LOGICS IN ALETHIC MODAL LOGICS WITH SYSTEMATIC FRAME CONSTANTS

In this section we prove two results concerning the relationship between the systems *Gm* and *Hm*, which amount to alternative, but equivalent, ways of *representing* the former in the latter.

Theorem 5 (Deductive Equivalence of *Hm* to *Gm*). For each positive integer m, let *Hm*+Def $\bigcirc$+Def $\mathcal{P}$ be the result of adding the definitions Def $\bigcirc$ and Def $\mathcal{P}$ *supra* to the alethic system *Hm*. Then, *Hm*+Def $\bigcirc$+Def $\mathcal{P}$ is *deductively equivalent* to *Gm* (m=1,2,...) in the sense that the following conditions are satisfied:

(i) *Hm*+Def $\bigcirc$+Def $\mathcal{P}$ contains *Gm*.
(ii) Each of Def $\bigcirc$ and Def $\mathcal{P}$ is provable in the form of an equivalence in *Gm*.

Proof: We show that (i) and (ii) both hold good.

Ad (i). The rules of procedure, *mp* and *nec* (for N), are common to *Gm* and *Hm*. In like manner, the axiom schemata $A0 - A4$ in *Gm* are in *Hm*+Def $\bigcirc$+Def $\mathcal{P}$ as well.

To prove a1 (of *Gm*) in *Hm*+Def $\bigcirc$+Def $\mathcal{P}$, use one of De Morgan's Laws together with elementary principles of alethic modal logic (i.e. A1).

To prove a2 in *Hm*+Def $\bigcirc$+Def $\mathcal{P}$, use A1 once again. As for a3, the proof is an exercise in using S5's reduction theses (see A1). For a4, use one of the so-called "paradoxes of strict implication". The proof of $\alpha 0$ in *Hm*+Def $\bigcirc$+Def $\mathcal{P}$ will involve repeated applications of a principle of substitutability of strict equivalents, familiar in S5.

Again, the proof of $\alpha 1$ uses $\vdash A \to A$ together with a paradox of implication. Let us then do the case of $\alpha 2$ somewhat more in detail.

Assume the *definiens* of Def$\bigcirc$ applied to $\bigcirc_{A\&B}C$ together with the *definiens* of Def$\mathcal{P}$ applied to $\mathcal{P}_A(B\&\neg C)$. This assumption, which we want to reduce *ad absurdum*, is an *m*-termed conjunction of implications conjoined with an *m*-termed disjunction of conjunctions; since & distributes over v, the whole assumption can be written as a certain *m*-termed disjunction; we will be done when each disjunct has been reduced *ad absurdum* (in *Hm*). Well, the first disjunct looks like this:

$$(1) \quad M(Q_1\&A\&B) \to N((Q_1\&A\&B) \to C)$$
$$\& \dots \& \text{ etc.}$$
$$\& M(Q_1\&A\&B\&\neg C)$$

Since the last conjunct in (1) implies (in *Hm*) the antecedent of the initial implication, (1) implies the consequent of that implication. But, that consequent is inconsistent (by A1 etc.) with the last conjunct in (1), whence (1) as a whole must be inconsistent (in *Hm*). The same kind of reasoning works for the remaining m-1 disjuncts, so we are done: $\alpha 2$ is provable in $Hm+\text{Def}\bigcirc$ $+\text{Def}\mathcal{P}$.

To prove $\alpha 3$:

1. MA	hypothesis
2. $N(Q_1 \vee \ldots \vee Q_m)$	A3, *nec*
3. $M(Q_1\&A) \vee \ldots \vee M(Q_m\&A)$	1,2,A1,A0 etc.
4. $M(Q_1\&A) \vee (\neg M(Q_1\&A)\&M(Q_2\&A)) \vee \ldots \vee$	
$(\neg M(Q_1\&A)\& \ldots \&\neg M(Q_{m-1}\&A)\&M(Q_m\&A))$	3,A0,*mp*
5. $\bigcirc_A B$ rewritten in accordance with Def$\bigcirc$	hypothesis
6. $M(Q_1\&A)$	hyp (= 1st
	disjunct in 4)
7. $M(Q_1\&A\&B)$	5,6,A1 etc.
Q.E.D. $\mathcal{P}_A B$ rewritten by means of Def$\mathcal{P}$	7,A0,*mp*
8. $\neg M(Q_1\&A)\&M(Q_2\&A)$	hyp (= 2nd
	disjunct in 4)
9. $\neg M(Q_1\&A)\&M(Q_2\&A\&B)$	5,8,A1 etc.
Q.E.D. $\mathcal{P}_A B$ rewritten by means of Def$\mathcal{P}$	9,A0,*mp*

And so on, down to the mth and last disjunct in 4: in all cases we obtain Q.E.D. using 5 and the relevant disjunct in 4. This completes the proof in $Hm+\text{Def}\bigcirc+\text{Def}\mathcal{P}$ of $\alpha 3$.

The proof of $\alpha 4$ is left as an exercise to the reader, who should also explain why the consequent of $\alpha 4$ by itself, i.e. without the antecedent $\mathcal{P}_A B$, is neither provable in Gm, nor in $Hm+\text{Def} \bigcirc+\text{Def} \mathcal{P}$.

To prove $\alpha 6$ in $Hm+\text{Def} \bigcirc+\text{Def} \mathcal{P}$, for any i between (weakly) 2 and m, set $A = Q_i$ in the *definiens* of Def $\mathcal{P}$ and observe that the only consistent disjunct is the following:

$$\neg M(Q_1\&B)\& \ldots \&\neg M(Q_{i-1}\&B)\&M(Q_i\&B\&Q_i)$$

whence we obtain by A1

$$N(Q_1 \to \neg B), \ldots, N(Q_{i-1} \to \neg B)$$

and, still using A1, the desired conclusion

$$(Q_1 \vee \ldots \vee Q_{i-1}) \to \neg B.$$

By virtue of A2, all the remaining $m - 2$ disjuncts are inconsistent in Hm: hence, they imply the desired conclusion vacuously, so we are done.

To prove $\alpha 7$:

1.	Q_1	hyp
2.	B	hyp
3.	$\bigcirc_B A$ rewritten by means of Def $\bigcirc$	hyp
4.	$M(Q_1 \& B)$	1,2,A1
5.	$N((Q_1 \& B) \to A)$	1st conjunct in 3,4,mp
6.	$Q_1 \to (B \to A)$	5,A1,A0
7.	$B \to A$	1,6,mp
8.	A	2,7,mp

Discharging the three hypotheses, we obtain the desired result $\alpha 7$ as a matter of course.

Finally, we have to prove $\alpha 8$ in Hm+Def $\bigcirc$+Def $\mathcal{P}$. For any integer $i = 2, \ldots, m$, assume

1.	$Q_i \& B \& \neg A$	hyp
2.	$\bigcirc_B A$ rewritten in accordance with Def $\bigcirc$	hyp
3.	MB	1,A0,A1
4.	$M(Q_1 \& B) \vee \ldots \vee (\neg M(Q_1 \& B) \& \ldots \& \neg M(Q_{m-1} \& B) \& M(Q_m \& B))$	3,A3,nec,A1,A0

We must now consider the disjuncts in 4 in turn, and start with

5.	$M(Q_1 \& B)$	hyp (1st disjunct in 4)
6.	$M(Q_1 \& B \& (Q_1 \vee \ldots \vee Q_{i-1}))$	5,A0,A1
7.	$\mathcal{P}_B(Q_1 \vee \ldots \vee Q_{i-1})$ rewritten by Def $\mathcal{P}$	6,A0
8.	$\neg M(Q_1 \& B) \& M(Q_2 \& B)$	hyp (2nd disjunct in 4)
9.	$\neg M(Q_1 \& B) \& M(Q_2 \& B \& (Q_1 \vee \ldots \vee Q_{i-1}))$	8,A0,A1
10.	$\mathcal{P}_B(Q_1 \vee \ldots \vee Q_{i-1})$ rewritten by Def $\mathcal{P}$	9,A0

And so on, down to

11.	$(\neg M(Q_1 \& B) \& \ldots \& \neg M(Q_{i-2} \& B) \& M(Q_{i-1} \& B))$	hyp $(i - 1^{st})$ disjunct in 4
12.	$\mathcal{P}_B(Q_1 \vee \ldots \vee Q_{i-1})$ rewritten by Def $\mathcal{P}$	from 11 similarly

Consider next a crucial case:

13.	$(\neg M(Q_1 \& B) \& \ldots \& \neg M(Q_{i-1} \& B) \& M(Q_i \& B))$	hyp ($= i^{th}$ disjunct in 4)

14. $N(Q_i\&B \to A)$ from 13 by the ith conjunct in 2

15. $Q_i \to (B \to A)$ 14,A1,A0

16. $B \to A$ 1 (1st conjunct),15,mp

17. $\perp$ since 16 contradicts 1 (2nd and 3rd conjuncts)

18. $\mathcal{P}_B(Q_1 \vee \ldots \vee Q_{i-1})$
     rewritten according to Def$\mathcal{P}$ from 17 vacuously

19. $(\neg M(Q_1\&B)\& \ldots \&$
     $\neg M(Q_i\&B)\&M(Q_{i+1}\&B))$ hyp ($= (i+1)^{st}$ disjunct in 4)

20. $N(Q_i \to \neg B)$ i^{th} conjunct in 19, A1, A0

21. $\neg B$ 1 (1st conjunct), 20, A1, A0

22. $\mathcal{P}_B(Q_1 \vee \ldots \vee Q_{i-1})$
     rewritten using Def$\mathcal{P}$ since 21 contradicts 1 (2nd conjunct)

The desired result 22 can also be derived in the remaining cases (if any), where we hypothesize the $(i + 2^{nd}) \ldots$, the mth disjunct in 4. Furthermore, since line 22 = line 18 = line 12 = line 10 = line 7, we have established the desired conclusion in all the cases taken into account by 4. The proof of $\alpha 8$ is complete, and so is the proof that $Hm+$Def$\bigcirc+$Def$\mathcal{P}$ contains Gm, for each positive integer m.

Ad (ii). We are to show that the Hm-definitions Def$\bigcirc$ and Def$\mathcal{P}$ are both provable as equivalences in Gm. Beginning with the *left-to-right* direction in Def$\bigcirc$, we argue as follows.

1. $\bigcirc_B A \to ((Q_1\&B) \to A)$ $\alpha 7$, A0
2. $N \bigcirc_B A \to N((Q_1\&B) \to A)$ 1, *nec*, A1
3. $\bigcirc_B A \to N \bigcirc_B A$ a3
4. $\bigcirc_B A \to (M(Q_1\&B) \to N(Q_1\&B \to A))$ 3, 2, A0 etc.

whence $\bigcirc_B A$ implies in Gm the first conjunct in the *definiens* of Def$\bigcirc$.
As for the remaining conjuncts, assume, for any i, with $1 < i \leq m$:

1. $\bigcirc_B A$ hyp
2. $\neg M(Q_1\&B)\&\neg M(Q_2\&B)\& \ldots \&$
     $\neg M(Q_{i-1}\&B)\&M(Q_i\&B)$ hyp

Then:

3. $N(B \to \neg Q_1)\&N(B \to \neg Q_2)\& \ldots \&$
     $N(B \to \neg Q_{i-1})$ 2,A1,A0
4. $N(B \to \neg(Q_1 \vee \ldots \vee Qi - 1))$ 3,A1,A0
5. $\bigcirc_B(B \to \neg(Q_1 \vee \ldots \vee Qi - 1))$ 4,a4
6. $\bigcirc_B\neg(Q_1 \vee \ldots \vee Qi - 1)$ 5,a2,$\alpha 1$

7. $\bigcirc_B A \to [(\bigcirc_B \neg(Q_1 \vee \ldots \vee Qi - 1) \to$ $\alpha 8$ contraposed,
    $((Q_i \& B) \to A)]$ a1 etc

8. $N\bigcirc_B A \to [N\bigcirc_B \neg(Q_1 \vee \ldots \vee Qi - 1) \to$
    $N(Q_i \& B \to A)]$ 7,nec,A1

9. $N\bigcirc_B \neg(Q_1 \vee \ldots \vee Qi - 1) \to$ 1,a3,8,mp
    $N(Q_i \& B \to A)$

10.$N((Q_i \& B) \to A)$ 6,a3,9,mp

where 10 is our desired conclusion.

In order to handle the *right-to-left* direction in Def $\bigcirc$, we need a *Lemma*.

(1) $\vdash_{Gm} M(Q_1 \& B) \to \bigcirc_B Q_1$.
(2) $\vdash_{Gm} (\neg M(Q_1 \& B) \& M(Q_2 \& B)) \to \bigcirc_B Q_2$.

$\vdots$

(m) $\vdash_{Gm} (\neg M(Q_1 \& B) \& \ldots \& \neg M(Q_{m-1} \& B) \& M(Q_m \& B)) \to \bigcirc_B Q_m$.
$(m+1)$ $\vdash_{Gm} \neg MB \to \bigcirc_B A$.
$(m+2)$ $\vdash_{Gm} P_B A \to M(B \& A)$.

The proof of the *Lemma* is a useful exercise in the proof theory of the systems *Gm*!

We then argue as follows.

1.   *Definiens* of Def $\bigcirc$ hyp
2. $MB \vee \neg MB$ A0
3. MB hyp $(= 1^{st}$ disjunct in 2)
4. $M(Q_1 \& B) \vee \ldots \vee (\neg M(Q_1 \& B)$ 3,A3,nec,A1,A0 -as in
    $\& \ldots \& \neg M(Q_{m-1} \& B) \& M(Q_m \& B))$ the proof of $\alpha 8$ in *Hm*

Considering the disjuncts in 4 in turn we deal explicitly only with

5. $M(Q_1 \& B)$ hyp $(= 1^{st}$ disjunct in 4; note that
                        5 is also the antecedent of the first
                        implication in 1)

6. $N(Q_1 \& B \to A)$ 1 $(1^{st}$ conjunct),5,mp
7. $\bigcirc_{(Q_1 \& B)}(Q_1 \& B \to A)$ 6,a4
8. $\bigcirc_{(Q_1 \& B)} A$ 7,a2,$\alpha 1$
9. $\bigcirc_B(Q_1 \to A)$ 8,$\alpha 0, \alpha 2$
10.$\bigcirc_B Q_1 \to \bigcirc_B A$ 9,a2,mp
11.$\bigcirc_B A$ 5,clause (1) of the Lemma,10,mp

where 11 is the desired conclusion in the present case, i.e. 5. The argument is analogous in the remaining $m - 1$ cases: in the last step we appeal to clause(2)

... clause(m) in our Lemma. Finally,

    12. $\neg MB$ hyp ($= 2^{nd}$ disjunct in 2)

we obtain the desired conclusion $\bigcirc_B A$ directly by means of clause($m + 1$) in the Lemma.

    This completes our proof that the *Hm*-definition Def $\bigcirc$ is provable in the form of an equivalence in *Gm*. The parallel result concerning Def $\mathcal{P}$ is left to the reader.

    We close this section by presenting an alternative, more "semantical", method of representing the dyadic deontic systems *Gm* in the alethic modal logics *Hm*. We start by defining recursively a certain *translation* ϕ from the set of *Gm*-sentences into the set of *Hm*-sentences as follows:

$$\phi(p) = p \qquad \text{for each } p \text{ in the set } Prop$$
$$\text{of propositional variables}$$

$$\phi(\top) = \top$$
$$\phi(\bot) = \bot$$
$$\phi(Q_i) = Q_i \qquad \text{for each } i \text{ with } 1 \leq i < \omega$$
$$\phi(\neg A) = \neg\phi(A)$$
$$\phi(A\&B) = (\phi(A)\&\phi(B))$$

Similarly for *Gm*-sentences having $\vee, \rightarrow, \leftrightarrow$ as their principal sign.

$$\phi(NA) = N\phi(A)$$
$$\phi(MA) = M\phi(A)$$

Finally, we have two characteristic clauses corresponding to Def $\bigcirc$ and Def $\mathcal{P}$:

$$\phi(\bigcirc_B A) = \quad [M(Q_1\&\phi(B)) \rightarrow N((Q_1\&\phi B) \rightarrow \phi(A))]\&$$
$$[(\neg M(Q_1\&\phi(B))\&M(Q_2\&\phi(B))) \rightarrow$$
$$N(Q_2\&\phi(B) \rightarrow \phi(A))]\&\dots\&[\neg M(Q_1\&\phi(B))\&\dots\&$$
$$\neg M(Q_{m-1}\&\phi(B))\&M(Q_m\&\phi(B))) \rightarrow$$
$$N(Q_m\&\phi(B) \rightarrow \phi(A))]$$

Similarly for $\phi(\mathcal{P}_B A)$: write it out as an m-termed disjunction!

    In the sequel we often write ϕA instead of $\phi(A)$. We then have the following result.

Theorem 6 (Translation Theorem for the Systems *Gm*). For each positive integer m, and for each *Gm*-sentence A:

$$\vdash_{Gm} A \text{ iff } \vdash_{Hm} \phi A.$$

Proof.

    Left-to-right ("only if" part). The proof is by induction on the length of the supposed *Gm*-proof of A. If its length = 1 (induction basis), then A is an instance of one or other of the axiom schemata A0-A4, a1-a4, $\alpha 0 - \alpha 8$. In all these cases, the desired *Hm*-proof of ϕA is immediate from the proof of our last theorem, point (i). If the length of the supposed *Gm*-proof of $A > 1$ (cases *mp* and *nec* in the inductive step), our desired results are likewise established without any problems.

   Right-to-left ("if" part). This is less easy: we are to show that if $\vdash_{Hm} \phi A$, then $\vdash_{Gm} A$, or, contrapositively, that if $\nvdash_{Gm} A$ (A is *not Gm*-provable), then $\nvdash_{Hm} \phi A (\phi A$ is *not Hm*-provable). As in my (Åqvist, 1987, Ch. IV), we suggest the following *strategy of argument*:

1. $\nvdash_{Gm} A$	hyp
2. $\nvDash_{Gm} A$ (i.e. A is not *Gm*-valid)	from 1 by completeness of *Gm*
3. $\mathcal{M}, x \nvDash A$, for some *Gm*-model	from 2 by the definition of
$\mathcal{M} = (W, V, \{opt_i\}, m, best)$	*Gm*-validity
and some x in W	

Consider that *Gm*-model $\mathcal{M}$. We claim that the result $\mathcal{M}^-$ of deleting the function *best* in $\mathcal{M}$ is a *Hm*-model (obviously!) satisfying what I called the

> *Crucial Lemma.*   For each *Gm*-sentence A and each x in W:
> $$\mathcal{M}, x \models A \text{ iff } \mathcal{M}^-, x \models \phi A.$$

We then continue our "strategic" argument as follows:

4. $\mathcal{M}^-, x \nvDash \phi A$	from 3 by the Crucial Lemma
5. $\nvDash_{Hm} \phi A$ (ϕA is not *Hm*-valid)	from 4 by def. of *Hm*-validity
6. $\nvdash_{Hm} \phi A$	from 5 by the soundness of *Hm*

where 6 is our desired conclusion.

   Hence, in order to complete the argument, we must show that the *Hm*-model $\mathcal{M}^-$ satisfies the Crucial Lemma. This is done by induction on the length of A. The only interesting cases are those where $A = \bigcirc_B C$ and where $A = \mathcal{P}_B C$ (for some *Gm*-sentences B, C). In the first case we have:

1. $\mathcal{M}, x \models \bigcirc_B C$	iff	for each y in $best(B)$:	by definition of
		$\mathcal{M}, y \models C$	truth at x in $\mathcal{M}$

2. $\mathcal{M}^-, x \models \phi(\bigcirc_B C)$ iff $\begin{cases} \text{if } opt_1 \cap \|\phi B\| \neq \emptyset, \\ \qquad \text{then } opt_1 \cap \|\phi B\| \subseteq \|\phi C\|\,; \quad \textit{and} \\ \text{if } opt_1 \cap \|\phi B\| = \emptyset \\ \qquad \text{but } opt_2 \cap \|\phi B\| \neq \emptyset, \\ \qquad \text{then } opt_2 \cap \|\phi B\| \subseteq \|\phi C\|\,; \quad \textit{and} \\ \qquad\qquad\qquad \vdots \\ \qquad\qquad\qquad\qquad\qquad\qquad \textit{and} \\ \text{if } opt_1 \cap \|\phi B\| = \dots \\ \qquad = opt_{m-1} \cap \|\phi B\| = \emptyset \\ \qquad \text{but } opt_m \cap \|\phi B\| \neq \emptyset, \\ \qquad \text{then } opt_m \cap \|\phi B\| \subseteq \|C\| \end{cases}$

by the definition of truth
at x in $\mathcal{M}^-$; 2 is the result
of "semanticizing" Def $\bigcirc$

3.   For all y in W :

$$\mathcal{M}, y \models B \quad \text{iff} \quad \mathcal{M}^-, y \models \phi B,$$
and
$$\mathcal{M}, y \models C \quad \text{iff} \quad \mathcal{M}^-, y \models \phi C$$

4.   (Right member of 1)   iff   (right member of 2)

by induction
hypothesis
from 3 and $\gamma 0$
(for $\mathcal{M}$) by
elementary
reasoning

5. $\mathcal{M}, x \models \bigcirc_B C$ iff $\mathcal{M}^-, x \models \phi(\bigcirc_B C)$

1,2,4,
transitivity of
"iff"

where 5 is our desired result. The case where $A = \mathcal{P}_B C$ is handled analogously.

This completes the proof of the right-to-left direction in the Translation Theorem for *Gm* as well as that of the theorem as a whole. In our "strategic" argument, note the importance of step 2, where we rely on (the weak version of) our completeness result for the systems *Gm*.

5.   CONCLUSION: A RESULT ON THE "CORE" SYSTEM *G*

In the last section we were concerned about the relation of the deontic logics *Gm* to the alethic modal logics *Hm*. What about the dyadic deontic system *G* without frame constants? How is it related to the *Gm* and *Hm*? We close the present paper by announcing a result on *G*, which answers this question, but cannot be proved here. A few hints about the proof will be given, however.

Theorem 7 For each G-sentence A:

$$\vdash_G A \text{ iff for each positive integer } m, \ \vdash_{Gm} A.$$

The left-to-right direction here is of course trivial, since each Gm is an extension of G. The opposite direction is much harder, as might be seen from its contraposed version. We envisage a proof which utilizes an appropriate notion of the *filtration* of a G-model *through* the set of sub-sentences of $\neg A$, and which profits from the fact that the system G is deductively equivalent to a certain logic *PR* of *preference* (see (Åqvist, 1987, §33) and also (Åqvist, 1986, §5)).

An obvious corollary of the present Theorem and previous ones is the following: For any G-sentence A,

$$\vdash_G A \text{ iff for each positive integer } m, \ \vdash_{Hm} \phi A$$

where ϕ is defined as in the last section except that the clause for the Q_i is deleted.

Lennart Åqvist
Department of Law
Uppsala University
Uppsala, Sweden

REFERENCES

Anderson, A. R. (1956). The formal analysis of normative systems. In N. Rescher (ed.), *The Logic of Decision and Action,* University of Pittsburgh Press, 1967, pages 147–213.

Anderson A. R. (1958). A reduction of deontic logic to alethic modal logics. *Mind* 67:100–103.

Åqvist, L. (1984). Deontic logic. In D. M. Gabbay and F. Guenthner (eds.), *Handbook of Philosophical Logic, Vol.II: Extensions of Classical Logic,* D. Reidel, Dordrecht, pages 605–714.

Åqvist, L. (1986). Some results on dyadic deontic logic and the logic of preference. *Synthese* 66:95–110.

Åqvist, L. (1987). *Introduction to Deontic Logic and the Theory of Normative Systems.* Bibliopolis, Napoli.

Åqvist, L. (1993). A completeness theorem in deontic logic with systematic frame constants. *Logique et Analyse* 36:177–192.

Hansson, B. (1969). An analysis of some deontic logics. *Noûs* 3:373–398. Reprinted in R. Hilpinen (ed.), *Deontic Logic: Introductory and Systematic Readings,* D. Reidel, Dordrecht, pages 121–147.

Lewis, D. K. (1973). *Counterfactuals.* Blackwell, Oxford.

Lewis, D. K. (1974). Semantic analyses for dyadic deontic logic. In S. Stenlund (ed.), *Logical Theory and Semantic Analysis: Essays Dedicated to Stig Kanger,* D. Reidel, Dordrecht, pages 1–14.

Rescher, N. (1958). An axiom system for deontic logic. *Philosophical Studies* 9:24–30.

Spohn, W. (1975). An analysis of Hansson's dyadic deontic logic. *Journal of Philosophical Logic* 4:237–252.

von Wright, G. H. (1964). A new system of deontic logic. *Danish Yearbook of Philosophy* 1:173–182.

LEENDERT W.N. VAN DER TORRE AND YAO-HUA TAN

THE MANY FACES OF DEFEASIBILITY IN DEFEASIBLE
DEONTIC LOGIC

1. INTRODUCTION

Deontic logic is the logic of obligations, i.e. reasoning about what should be the case. Defeasible logic is the logic of default assumptions, i.e. reasoning about what normally is the case. In defeasible deontic logic these two are combined. An example of this combination is the sentence 'normally, you should do p'. Now the problem is what to conclude about somebody who does not do p? Is this an exception to the normality claim, or is it a violation of the obligation to do p? This confusion arises because there is a substantial overlap between deontic and defeasibility aspects. In this article we analyze this overlap, and we also show that this confusion can be avoided if one makes the proper distinctions between different types of defeasibility. Furthermore, we also show that these distinctions are essential for an adequate analysis of notorious contrary-to-duty paradoxes such as the Chisholm and Forrester paradoxes.

The main claim of this article is that the defeasible aspect of defeasible deontic logic is different from the defeasible aspect of, for example, Reiter's default rules (Reiter, 1980). Different types of defeasibility in a logic of defeasible reasoning formalize a single notion, whereas defeasible deontic logics formalize two notions. Consider first the logics of defeasible reasoning and the famous Tweety example. In the case of factual defeasibility, we say that the 'birds fly' default is *cancelled* by the fact $\neg f$, and in the case of overridden defeasibility by the 'penguins do not fly' default. By cancellation we mean, for example, that if $\neg f$ is true, then the default assumption that f is true is null and void. The truth of $\neg f$ implies that the default assumption about f is contradicted.

The fundamental difference between deontic logic and logics for defeasible reasoning is that $\neg p \land \bigcirc p$ is *not* inconsistent. That is the reason why the deontic operator $\bigcirc$ had to be represented as a modal operator with a possible worlds semantics, to make sure that *both* the obligation and its violation could be true at the same time. Although the obligation $\bigcirc p$ is violated by the fact $\neg p$, the obligation still has its force, so to say. This still being in force of an obligation is reflected, for example, by the fact that someone has to pay a fine even if she does $\neg p$. Even if you drive too fast, you should not drive too fast. But if penguins cannot fly, it makes no sense to state that normally they can fly. We will refer to this relation between the obligation and its violation as

79

D. Nute (ed.), Defeasible Deontic Logic, 79–121.
© 1997 *Kluwer Academic Publishers. Printed in the Netherlands.*

overshadowing to distinguish it from *cancellation* in the case of defeasible logics. By the overshadowing of an obligation we mean that it is still in force, but it is no longer to be acted upon.

The conceptual difference between cancelling and overshadowing is analogous to the distinction between 'defeasibility' and 'violability' made by Smith (1993) and by Prakken and Sergot (1994). An essential difference between those articles and this one is that in this article we argue that violability has to be considered as a type of defeasibility too, because it also induces a constraint on strengthening of the antecedent. The main advantage of the violability-as-defeasibility perspective is that it explains the distinctions *as well as the similarities* between cancelling and overshadowing. Moreover, it can be used to analyze complicated phenomena like prima facie obligations, which have cancelling as well as overriding aspects.

In this article we give a general analysis of different types of defeasibility in defeasible deontic logics. We argue that (at least) three types of defeasibility must be distinguished in a defeasible deontic logic. First, we make a distinction between *factual defeasibility*, that formalizes overshadowing of an obligation by a violating fact, and *overridden defeasibility*, that formalizes cancelling of an obligation by other conditional obligations. Second, we show that overridden defeasibility can be further divided into *strong overridden defeasibility*, that formalizes specificity, and *weak overridden defeasibility*, that formalizes the overriding of prima facie obligations. Our general analysis can be applied to any defeasible deontic logic. Moreover, we illustrate the intuitions behind the various distinctions with preference-based semantics. We also show that these distinctions are essential for an adequate analysis of notorious contrary-to-duty paradoxes such as the Chisholm and Forrester paradoxes in a defeasible deontic logic.

1.1. *Defeasible deontic logic*

In this article we only discuss a dyadic version of deontic logic. Dyadic modal logics were introduced to formalize deontic reasoning about contrary-to-duty obligations in, for example, the Chisholm paradox that we will discuss later. See (Lewis, 1974) for an overview of several dyadic deontic logics. An example of a conditional obligation in a dyadic modal logic is $\bigcirc(h \mid r)$, which expresses that "you ought to be helped (h) when you are robbed (r)". Similarly, $\bigcirc(\neg r \mid \top)$ expresses that "you ought not to be robbed", where $\top$ stands for any tautology. If both $\bigcirc(\neg r \mid \top)$ and r are true, then we say that the obligation is *violated* by the fact r. In recent years it was argued by several authors that these dyadic obligations can be formalized in non-monotonic logics (McCarty, 1994; Horty, 1993; Ryu and Lee, 1993).

In this article we argue that contrary-to-duty obligations do have a defeasible aspect, but a different one than is usually thought. The first part of this claim follows directly from Alchourrón's (1994) definition of a defeasible conditional as a conditional that lacks strengthening of the antecedent, represented by the inference pattern

$$\text{SA} : \frac{\bigcirc(\alpha|\beta_1)}{\bigcirc(\alpha|\beta_1 \wedge \beta_2)}$$

Alchourrón's definition is based on the idea that lack of strengthening of the antecedent is a kind of implicit non-monotonicity. The relation between strengthening of the antecedent and non-monotonicity can be made explicit with the following inference pattern *Exact Factual Detachment* EFD.[1] Exact factual detachment can be represented by the inference pattern

$$\text{EFD} : \frac{\bigcirc(\alpha|\beta), \mathcal{A}\beta}{\bigcirc(\alpha)}$$

in which $\bigcirc\alpha$ is a new, monadic modal operator, and $\mathcal{A}$ is an all-that-is-known operator (Levesque, 1990): $\mathcal{A}\phi$ is true if and only if (iff) ϕ is logically equivalent with all factual premises given. The inference pattern EFD is based on the intuition that the antecedent of a dyadic obligation restricts the focus to possible situations in which the antecedent is *assumed* to be factually true, and the consequent represent what is obligatory, given that *only* these facts are assumed. If the facts are equivalent to the antecedent, then the consequent can be considered as an absolute obligation. From the properties of $\mathcal{A}$ follows immediately that EFD is monotonic iff the dyadic obligations have strengthening of the antecedent. Dyadic deontic logics that can represent contrary-to-duty reasoning are defeasible deontic logics, because the dyadic obligations typically lack strengthening of the antecedent.[2] In this sense, contrary-to-duty obligations do have a defeasible aspect.

However, we argue that this defeasible aspect of contrary-to-duty obligations is a different one than is usually proposed. In this article, we analyze defeasibility in defeasible deontic logic by analyzing different conditions on

---

[1] A related idea was proposed by Boutilier (1994): 'to determine preferences based on certain actual facts, we consider only the *most ideal* worlds satisfying those facts, rather than *all* worlds satisfying those facts'. In Boutilier's logic, this means that the antecedent of his conditional is logically equivalent with the premises, i.e. he considers $\vdash \bigcirc(\alpha|KB)$, where KB is the set of premises. Von Wright (1968) proposed two ways to represent monadic obligations $\bigcirc\alpha$ in a dyadic logic: by $\bigcirc(\alpha|\top)$ and by $\bigcirc(\alpha|S)$, where S stands for the actual circumstance. Alchourrón (1994) observes that the former has been followed unanimously by all deontic logicians, although it is wrong (which follows from the semantics). In Alchourrón's words, this misrepresentation is 'the ghost of categorical norms'.

[2] The dyadic obligations can be contrasted to conditional obligations that do validate factual detachment and strengthening of the antecedent, and are typically (see e.g. (Chellas, 1974; Alchourrón, 1994)) represented by a strict implication '$>$' and a monadic operator such that $\bigcirc(\alpha|\beta) =_{\text{def}} \beta > \bigcirc\alpha$.

strengthening of the antecedent. In particular, we analyze the inference relation of defeasible deontic logics with inference patterns, in a similar way as in (Kraus, *et al.*, 1990) logics of defeasible reasoning are analyzed. Moreover, we give preference-based semantic intuitions for the inference patterns. Some of the dyadic modal logics that can represent contrary-to-duty obligations have a preference-based semantics (Hansson, 1971; Makinson, 1993). The advantage of our analysis is that (1) it is applicable to any defeasible deontic logic, because of the generality of the inference patterns, and (2) it gives also a semantic explanation of the intuitions behind the inference patterns by the preference semantics.

1.2. *Different types of defeasibility*

In defeasible reasoning one can distinguish at least three types of defeasibility, based on different semantic intuitions. To illustrate the difference between the different types we discuss the penguin example in Geffner and Pearl's assumption-based default theories (Geffner and Pearl, 1992). In such theories, the 'birds fly' default rule is expressed by a factual sentence $\delta_1 \rightarrow f$ and a default sentence $\top \Rightarrow \delta_1$, and the 'penguins do not fly' default by $p \wedge \delta_2 \rightarrow \neg f$ and $p \Rightarrow \delta_2$. Here, '$\rightarrow$' is the classical material implication and '$\Rightarrow$' a kind of default implication. The δ_i constants are the so-called assumptions; for each default in the set of premises a distinct constant is introduced. Geffner and Pearl's so-called conditional entailment maximizes these assumptions, given certain constraints. In conditional entailment, the 'birds fly' default can be defeated by the fact $\neg f$, or it can be overridden by the more specific 'penguins do not fly' default. The first follows directly from $\neg f \rightarrow \neg \delta_1$, i.e. the contraposition of the factual sentence $\delta_1 \rightarrow f$, and the second follows from the fact that $p \rightarrow \neg \delta_1$ can be derived from the constraints of conditional entailment (we do not give the complicated proof; see (Geffner and Pearl, 1992) for these details). We call the first case *factual defeasibility* and the last case *overridden defeasibility*. The distinction between factual and overridden defeasibility is only the start of a classification of different types of defeasibility. To illustrate the further distinction between different types of overridden defeasibility, we consider the adapted 'penguins do not fly and live on the southern hemisphere' default $p \wedge \delta_2 \rightarrow (\neg f \wedge s)$. In some logics of defeasible reasoning, the 'birds fly' default is overridden whenever p is true. In other logics it is overridden when p is true *but only as long as s is not false*. If s is false, then the penguin default is no longer applicable. In the first logics the 'birds fly' default is not reinstated, whereas in the second logics it is, because it was only suspended. In other words, in the latter case the penguin default overrides the bird default only when it is applicable itself. We call the first case *strong overridden defeasibility* and the second case *weak overridden defeasibility*. The different types of overridden defeasibility are based on different semantic intuitions. Strong overridden defeasibility is usually based on a probabilistic interpretation of defaults (most birds fly, but penguins are exceptional), like in Pearl's ϵ-semantics (Pearl, 1988). Weak overridden defeasibility is usually based on an argument-based conflict resolution interpretation (there is a conflict between the two rules, and the second one has highest priority). Examples are conditional entailment, prioritized default logic (Brewka, 1994) and several argument systems (Vreeswijk, 1993; Dung, 1993; Prakken and Sartor, 1995).

The distinction between different types of defeasibility is crucial in logics that formalize reasoning about obligations which can be overridden by other obligations. Overridden defeasibility becomes relevant when there is a (potential) conflict between two obligations. For example, there is a conflict between $\bigcirc(\alpha_1|\beta_1)$ and $\bigcirc(\alpha_2|\beta_2)$ when α_1 and α_2 are contradictory, and β_1 and β_2 are factually true. There are several different approaches to deal with deontic conflicts. In von Wright's so-called standard deontic logic SDL (Von Wright, 1951) a deontic conflict is inconsistent. In weaker deontic logics, like minimal deontic logic MDL (Chellas, 1974), a conflict is consistent and called a 'deontic dilemma'. In a defeasible deontic logic a conflict can be *resolved*, because one of the obligations overrides the other one. For example, overridden structures can be based on a notion of specificity, like in Horty's well-known example that 'you should not eat with your fingers', but 'if you are served asparagus, then you should eat with your fingers' (Horty, 1993). In such cases, we say that an obligation is *cancelled* when it is overridden, because it is analogous to cancelling in logics of defeasible reasoning. The obligation not to eat with your fingers is cancelled by the exceptional circumstances that you are served asparagus. A different kind of overridden structures have been proposed by Ross (1930) and formalized, for example, by Morreau (1996). In Ross' ethical theory, an obligation which is overridden has not become a 'proper' or actual duty, but it remains in force as a prima facie obligation. For example, the obligation not to break a promise may be overridden to prevent a disaster, but even when it is overridden it remains in force as a prima facie obligation. As actual obligation the overridden obligation is cancelled, but as prima facie obligation it is only overshadowed. Because of this difference between cancellation and overshadowing, it becomes essential not to confuse the different types of defeasibility in analyzing the deontic paradoxes. We show that if they are confused, counterintuitive conclusions follow for the Chisholm and Forrester paradoxes. In the table below the three different types of defeasible deontic logic are represented with their corresponding character (cancelling or overshadowing).

In non-deontic defeasible logic the different types of defeasibility, factual and overridden, all have a cancelling character.

	overshadowing	cancelling
Factual defeasibility	X	
Strong overridden defeasibility		X
Weak overridden defeasibility	X	X

This article is organized as follows. In Section 2 we give a detailed comparison of factual and overridden defeasibility in deontic reasoning, and we show that the Chisholm paradox can be analyzed as a case of factual defeasibility rather than overridden defeasibility. In Section 3 we focus on the overshadowing aspect of factual defeasibility as well as the cancellation aspect of overridden defeasibility by analyzing specificity, and we show that in an adequate analysis of an extension of the Forrester paradox both these aspects have to be combined. In Section 4 we focus on the cancelling aspect and the overshadowing aspect of overridden defeasibility by analyzing prima facie obligations.

2.   OVERRIDDEN VERSUS FACTUAL DEFEASIBILITY

In this section we analyze the fundamental difference between overridden and factual defeasibility in a defeasible deontic logic by formalizing contrary-to-duty reasoning as a kind of overridden defeasibility as well as a kind of factual defeasibility. Moreover, we show that contrary-to-duty reasoning is best formalized by the latter one.

2.1. *Contrary-To-Duty paradoxes*

Deontic logic is hampered by many paradoxes, intuitively consistent sentences which are formally inconsistent, or from which counterintuitive sentences can be derived. The most notorious paradoxes are caused by so-called *Contrary-To-Duty* (CTD) obligations, obligations that refer to sub-ideal situations. For example, Lewis describes the following example of the CTD obligation that you should be helped when you are robbed.

Example 1 (Good Samaritan paradox) "It ought not to be that you are robbed. *A fortiori*, it ought not to be that you are robbed and then helped. But you ought to be helped, given that you have been robbed. This robbing excludes the best possibilities that might otherwise have been actualized, and the helping is needed in order to actualize the best of those that remain. Among the best possible worlds marred by the robbing, the best of the bad lot are some of those where the robbing is followed by helping." *(Lewis, 1974)*

In the early seventies, several dyadic modal systems were introduced to formalize CTD obligations, see (Lewis, 1974) for an overview. Unfortunately, several technical problems related to CTD reasoning persisted in the dyadic logics, see (Tomberlin, 1981). A dyadic obligation $\bigcirc(\alpha \mid \beta)$ can be read as 'if β (the antecedent) is the case then α (the consequent) should be the case'. A CTD obligation is a dyadic obligation of which the antecedent contradicts the consequent of another obligation. For example, if we have $\bigcirc(\alpha_1 \mid \top)$ and $\bigcirc(\alpha_2 \mid \neg\alpha_1)$ then the last one is a CTD (or *secondary*) obligation and the first one is called its *primary* obligation. CTD obligations refer to optimal sub-ideal situations. In the sub-ideal situation that $\bigcirc(\alpha_1 \mid \top)$ is violated by $\neg\alpha_1$, the best thing to do is α_2. Recently, it was observed that this aspect of violations can be formalized in non-monotonic logics (McCarty, 1994; Horty, 1993), theories of diagnosis (Tan and Van der Torre, 1994a; Tan and Van der Torre, 1994b) or qualitative decision theories (Boutilier, 1994) (see also (Powers, 1967; Jennings, 1974; Pearl, 1993; Thomason and Horty, 1996)).

Since the late seventies, several temporal deontic logics and deontic action logics were introduced, which formalize satisfactorily a special type of CTD obligations, see for example (Thomason, 1981; Van Eck, 1982; Loewer and Belzer, 1983; Makinson, 1993; Alchourrón, 1994). Temporal deontic logics formalize conditional obligations in which the consequent occurs later than the antecedent. In this temporal approach, the underlying principle of the formalization of CTD obligations is that facts of the past are not in the 'context of deliberation' (Thomason, 1981). Hence, they can formalize the Good Samaritan paradox in Example 1. However, they cannot formalize the variant of the paradox described by Forrester (see Example 4) and the following Chisholm paradox, because in these paradoxes there are CTD obligations of which the consequent occurs at the same time or even before its antecedent.

The following example describes the notorious Chisholm paradox, also called the CTD paradox, or the paradox of deontic detachment (Chisholm, 1963). The original paradox was given in a monadic modal logic. Here we give the obvious formalization in a non-defeasible dyadic logic. See (Tomberlin, 1981) for a discussion of the Chisholm paradox in several conditional deontic logics. To make our analysis as general as possible, we assume as little as possible about the deontic logic we use. The analyses given in this article in terms of inference patterns are, in principle, applicable to any deontic logic.

Example 2.1 (Chisholm paradox) Assume a dyadic deontic logic that validates at least substitution of logical equivalents and the following inference patterns (unrestricted) *Strengthening of the Antecedent* SA, *Weakening of the Consequent* WC and a version of *Deontic Detachment* DD'.[3]

---

[3] We do not use the 'standard' names of conditional logic (Chellas, 1980), like for example RCM for weakening of the consequent, to emphasize that our inference patterns are analysis tools at the level of inference relations. See for example the inference patterns RSA$_O$ and RSA$_V$ later in this article, which contain conditions C_O and C_V.

$$\text{SA}: \frac{O(\alpha|\beta_1)}{O(\alpha|\beta_1 \wedge \beta_2)} \qquad \text{WC}: \frac{O(\alpha_1|\beta)}{O(\alpha_1 \vee \alpha_2|\beta)} \qquad \text{DD}': \frac{O(\alpha|\beta), O(\beta|\gamma)}{O(\alpha \wedge \beta|\gamma)}$$

Notice that the following inference pattern *Deontic Detachment* (or transitivity) DD can be derived from WC and DD'.

$$\text{DD}: \frac{O(\alpha|\beta), O(\beta|\gamma)}{O(\alpha|\gamma)}$$

Furthermore, assume the premises $O(a \mid \top)$, $O(t \mid a)$ and $O(\neg t \mid \neg a)$, where $\top$ stands for any tautology, a can be read as the fact that a certain man goes to the assistance of his neighbors and t as the fact that he tells them he is coming. The premise $O(\neg t \mid \neg a)$ is a CTD obligation of the (primary) obligation $O(a|\top)$, because its antecedent is inconsistent with the consequent of the latter. Notice that t occurs before a in this interpretation of the propositional atoms. Hence, the example cannot be represented in a temporal deontic logic.

The paradoxical derivation of $O(t \mid \neg a)$ from the Chisholm paradox is represented in Figure 1. The intuitive obligation $O(a \wedge t|\top)$ can be derived by DD' from the first two obligations. It seems intuitive, because in the ideal situation the man goes to the assistance of his neighbors and he tells them he is coming. The obligation $O(t|\top)$ can be derived from $O(a \wedge t|\top)$ by WC (or from the premises by DD). The obligation $O(t|\top)$ expresses that if the man does not tell his neighbors, then the ideal situation is no longer reachable. However, from $O(t|\top)$ the counterintuitive $O(t|\neg a)$ can be derived by SA. This is counterintuitive, because there is no reason to tell the neighbors he is coming when the man does not go. In contrast, in this violation context the man should do the opposite! Moreover, in several deontic logics the set of obligations $\{O(\neg t|\neg a), O(t|\neg a)\}$ is inconsistent.

$$\frac{\dfrac{O(t|a) \quad O(a|\top)}{\dfrac{O(a \wedge t|\top)}{\dfrac{O(t|\top)}{O(t|\neg a)}\text{SA}}\text{WC}}\text{DD}'}{}$$

Fig. 1. Chisholm paradox

In this example the Chisholm paradox is presented in a normal dyadic deontic logic, to show its paradoxical character. In the next section, we analyze the paradox in a defeasible deontic logic that has only overridden defeasibility. This analysis solves the paradox, but for the wrong reasons. Finally, in

Section 2.3 we give an analysis of the Chisholm paradox in terms of factual defeasibility, which is more satisfactory. In Section 2.4 we analyze factual defeasibility with a preference semantics.

2.2. Overridden defeasibility

In recent years several authors have proposed to solve the Chisholm paradox by analyzing its problematic CTD obligation as a type of overridden defeasibility (see e.g. (McCarty, 1994; Ryu and Lee, 1993)).[4] The underlying idea is that a CTD obligation can be considered as a conflicting obligation that overrides a primary obligation. Although this idea seems to be very intuitive at first sight, we claim that the perspective of CTD obligations as a kind of overridden defeasibility is misleading. It is misleading, because although this perspective yields most (but not all!) of the correct conclusions for the Chisholm paradox, it does so for the wrong reasons. We show that it is more appropriate to consider the CTD obligation as a kind of factual defeasibility. This does not mean that there is no place for overridden defeasibility in deontic logic. By a careful analysis of an extended version of another notorious paradox of deontic logic, the Forrester paradox, we show that sometimes combinations of factual and overridden defeasibility are needed to represent defeasible deontic reasoning. But first we give our analysis of the Chisholm paradox. The following example shows that the counterintuitive obligation of Example 2.1 cannot be derived in a defeasible deontic logic with overridden defeasibility. For our argument we use a notion of overridden based on specificity.

Example 2.2 (Chisholm paradox, continued) Assume that SA is replaced by the following Restricted Strengthening of the Antecedent rule RSA_O. RSA_O contains the so-called non-overridden condition C_O, which requires that $\bigcirc(\alpha|\beta_1)$ is not overridden for $\beta_1 \wedge \beta_2$ by some more specific $\bigcirc(\alpha'|\beta')$.[5]

$$RSA_O : \frac{\bigcirc(\alpha|\beta_1), C_O}{\bigcirc(\alpha|\beta_1 \wedge \beta_2)}$$

where condition C_O is defined as follows:

C_O: there is no premise $\bigcirc(\alpha' \mid \beta')$ such that $\beta_1 \wedge \beta_2$ logically implies β', β' logically implies β_1 and not vice versa and α and α' are contradictory.

The 'solution' for the paradox is represented in Figure 2. This figure should be read as follows. The horizontal lines represent *possible* derivation steps.

---

[4]McCarty (1994) does not analyze the Chisholm paradox but the so-called Reykjavic paradox, which he considers to contain 'two instances of the Chisholm paradox, each one interacting with the other'.

[5]The overridden condition C_O is based on a simplified notion of specificity, because background knowledge is not taken into account and an obligation cannot be overridden by

Blocked derivation steps are represented by dashed lines. For example, the last derivation step is blocked, and the cause of the blocking is represented by the obligation $O(\neg t | \neg a)$ above the blocked inference rule. We compare the blocked derivation in Figure 2 with the derivation in Figure 1. The intuitive obligation $O(t | \top)$ can still be derived by DD (hence, by DD$'$ and WC) from the first two obligations. From $O(t | \top)$ the counterintuitive $O(t | \neg a)$ cannot be derived by RSA$_O$, because $O(t | \top)$ is overridden for $\neg a$ by the CTD obligation $O(\neg t | \neg a)$, i.e. C_O is false. Hence, the counterintuitive obligation is cancelled by the exceptional circumstances that the man does not go to the assistance.

$$
\frac{\dfrac{O(t|a) \quad O(a|\top)}{\dfrac{O(a \wedge t | \top)}{O(t|\top)} \text{WC}} \text{DD}'}{- - - - - - - -} \qquad \begin{array}{c} O(\neg t | \neg a) \\ \downarrow \\ (\text{RSA}_O) \end{array}
$$
$$
O(t | \neg a)
$$

Fig. 2. Chisholm paradox solved by overridden defeasibility

Overridden defeasibility yields intuitive results from the Chisholm paradox, but for the wrong reasons. A simple counterargument against the solution of the paradox in Example 2.2 is that overriding based on specificity does not solve the paradox anymore when the premise $O(a | \top)$ is replaced by another premise with a non-tautological antecedent. For example, if it is replaced by $O(a | i)$, where i can be read as the fact that the man is personally invited to assist. Another counterargument against the solution of the paradox for *any* definition of overridden is that the derivation of $O(t | \neg a)$ is also counterintuitive when the set of premises contains only the first two obligations, as is the case in the following example.

Example 2.3 (Chisholm paradox, continued) Assume only the premises $O(a | \top)$ and $O(t | a)$. Again the intuitive obligation $O(t | \top)$ can be derived by DD. From this derived obligation the counterintuitive $O(t | \neg a)$ can be derived by RSA$_O$, because there is no CTD obligation which cancels the counterintuitive obligation.

In (Tan and Van der Torre, 1994b) we dubbed the intuition that the inference of the obligation $O(t | \top)$ is intuitive but not the inference of the obligation

---

more than one obligation. A more sophisticated definition of overridden can be found in the literature of logics of defeasible reasoning. For our purposes this simple definition is enough, because it is a weak definition (most definitions of specificity are extensions of this definition). For a discussion on the distinction between background and factual knowledge, see (Van der Torre, 1994).

$$\frac{\bigcirc(t|a) \quad \bigcirc(a|\top)}{\bigcirc(a \wedge t|\top)} \text{DD}'$$
$$\frac{}{\bigcirc(t|\top)} \text{WC}$$
$$\frac{}{\bigcirc(t|\neg a)} \text{RSA}_O$$

Fig. 3. Chisholm paradox, continued

$\bigcirc(t|\neg a)$ as 'deontic detachment as a defeasible rule'. Unrestricted strengthening of the antecedent cannot be applied to the obligation $\bigcirc(t|\top)$, derived by DD. This restriction is the characteristic property of defeasible conditionals, see the discussion in Section 1.1. The underlying intuition is that the inference of the obligation of the man to tell his neighbors that he is coming is made *on the assumption that he goes to their assistance.* If he does not go, then this assumption is violated and the obligation based on this assumption is factually defeated. We say that the man should tell his neighbors, unless he does not go to their assistance.

The problematic character of DD is well-known from the Chisholm paradox. A popular 'solution' of the paradox is not to accept DD' for a deontic logic. However, this rejection of DD' causes serious semantic problems for these logics. For example, (Tomberlin, 1981) showed that there are semantic problems related to the rejection of DD' for Mott's solution of the Chisholm paradox (Mott, 1973). Moreover, the following so-called apples-and-pears problem (Tan and Van der Torre, 1996) shows that similar problems occur when RSA$_O$, WC and the *Conjunction* inference pattern AND are accepted. This last rule is accepted by many deontic logics. For examples of deontic logics *not* satisfying the AND rule, see Chellas' CKD (Chellas, 1974; Chellas, 1980), which is a nonnormal modal deontic logic, or the minimizing logic $\bigcirc_\exists(\alpha \mid \beta)$ in (Tan and Van der Torre, 1996). For examples not validating the WC rule, see S.O. Hansson's Preference-based Deontic Logic (PDL) (Hansson, 1990), Brown and Mantha's logic (Brown and Mantha, 1991) and the ordering logic $\bigcirc(\alpha|\beta)$ in (Tan and Van der Torre, 1996).[6]

Example 3 (Apples-and-Pears problem) Assume a dyadic deontic logic that validates at least substitution of logical equivalents and the inference

---

[6] An alphabetic variant of Example 3 is the following version of the Chisholm paradox, in which the conditional obligation is represented as an absolute obligation. However, it is usually argued that the premise $\bigcirc(a \rightarrow t|\top)$ does not represent the conditional obligation correctly.

Example 2.4 (Chisholm paradox continued) Consider the premises $\bigcirc(a \mid \top)$ and $\bigcirc(a \rightarrow t|\top)$. The intuitive obligation $\bigcirc(t \mid \top)$ is derived from the two premises by CC (see Example 3). However, from this derived obligation the counterintuitive $\bigcirc(t|\neg a)$ can be derived by SA or RSA$_O$.

patterns RSA$_O$, WC and the following conjunction rule AND.

$$\text{AND} : \frac{\bigcirc(\alpha_1|\beta), \bigcirc(\alpha_2|\beta)}{\bigcirc(\alpha_1 \wedge \alpha_2|\beta)}$$

Notice that the following inference pattern *Consequential Closure* (CC) can be derived from WC and AND.

$$\text{CC} : \frac{\bigcirc(\alpha_1|\beta), \bigcirc(\alpha_1 \to \alpha_2|\beta)}{\bigcirc(\alpha_2|\beta)}$$

Furthermore, assume as premise sets $S = \{\bigcirc(a \vee p|\top), \bigcirc(\neg a|\top)\}$ and $S' = \{\bigcirc(a \vee p|\top), \bigcirc(\neg a|\top), \bigcirc(\neg p|a)\}$, where a can be read as 'buying apples' and p as 'buying pears'. A derivation of the counterintuitive obligation $\bigcirc(p|a)$ from S is represented in Figure 4. This obligation is considered to be counterintuitive, because it is not grounded in the premises. If a is true, then the first premise $\bigcirc(a \vee p|\top)$ is fulfilled and the second premise $\bigcirc(\neg a|\top)$ is violated. Since the first premise is already fulfilled, there is intuitively no reason why p should be obliged given the fact that a. The intuitive obligation $\bigcirc(\neg a \wedge p|\top)$ can be derived by AND. From this obligation, the obligation $\bigcirc(p|\top)$ is derived by WC (hence, from the premise set by CC). From this derived obligation, the counterintuitive obligation $\bigcirc(p|a)$ can be derived by RSA$_O$. The counterintuitive derivation is not derivable from S' by RSA$_O$, because the CTD obligation $\bigcirc(\neg p|a)$ overrides the obligation $\bigcirc(p|\top)$ for a. However, this solution for S' does not suffice for S, just like the solution in Example 2.2 does not suffice for Example 2.3.

$$\frac{\dfrac{\dfrac{\bigcirc(a \vee p|\top) \quad \bigcirc(\neg a|\top)}{\bigcirc(\neg a \wedge p|\top)} \text{ AND}}{\bigcirc(p|\top)} \text{ WC}}{\bigcirc(p|a)} \text{ RSA}_O$$

Fig. 4. Apples-and-pears problem with overridden defeasibility

The examples show that CTD reasoning (i.e., reasoning about sub-ideal behavior) cannot be formalized satisfactorily in a defeasible deontic logic with only overridden defeasibility.

2.3. *Factual defeasibility*

As an illustrative example of a formalization of factual defeasibility, we introduce a deontic version of a labeled deductive system as it was introduced by Gabbay (1991), which is closely related to the proof theoretic approach of the inference patterns. Assume a finite propositional base logic $\mathcal{L}$ and labeled dyadic conditional obligations $\bigcirc(\alpha \mid \beta)_L$, with α and β sentences of $\mathcal{L}$ and L a set of sentences of $\mathcal{L}$. Roughly speaking, the label L is a record of the consequents of all the premises that are used in the derivation of $\bigcirc(\alpha \mid \beta)$. The use of the label can be illustrated by the distinction between explicit and implicit obligations. An explicit obligation is an obligation that has been uttered explicitly (an imperative), and an implicit obligation is an obligation that follows from explicit obligations. The distinction between explicit and implicit obligations is analogous to the distinction between explicit and implicit belief, introduced by Levesque to solve the logical omniscience problem (Levesque, 1984). The consequent of a labeled obligation represents an implicit obligation and its label represents the explicit obligations from which the implicit obligation is derived.

Labeled deontic logic works as follows. Each formula occurring as a premise in the derivation has its own consequent in its label. We assume that the antecedent and the label of an obligation are always consistent. The label of an obligation derived by an inference rule is the union of the labels of the premises used in this inference rule. The labels formalize the assumptions on which an obligation is derived, and the consistency check C_V checks that the assumptions are not violated. Hence, the premises used in the derivation tree are not violated by the antecedent of the derived obligation, or, alternatively, the derived obligation is not a CTD obligation of these premises.[7] Below are some labeled versions of inference schemes.

$$\text{RSA}_V : \frac{\bigcirc(\alpha \mid \beta_1)_L, C_V}{\bigcirc(\alpha \mid \beta_1 \wedge \beta_2)_L}, C_V : L \cup \{\beta_1 \wedge \beta_2\} \text{ is consistent}$$

$$\text{WC}_V : \frac{\bigcirc(\alpha_1 \mid \beta)_L}{\bigcirc(\alpha_1 \vee \alpha_2 \mid \beta)_L}$$

$$\text{DD}'_V : \frac{\bigcirc(\alpha \mid \beta)_{L_1}, \bigcirc(\beta \mid \gamma)_{L_2}, C_V}{\bigcirc(\alpha \wedge \beta \mid \gamma)_{L_1 \cup L_2}}, C_V : L_1 \cup L_2 \cup \{\gamma\} \text{ is consistent}$$

$$\text{AND}_V : \frac{\bigcirc(\alpha_1 \mid \beta)_{L_1}, \bigcirc(\alpha_2 \mid \beta)_{L_2}, C_V}{\bigcirc(\alpha_1 \wedge \alpha_2 \mid \beta)_{L_1 \cup L_2}}, C_V : L_1 \cup L_2 \cup \{\beta\} \text{ is consistent}$$

The following example illustrates that RSA_V is better than RSA_O for modeling the Chisholm paradox, because RSA_V yields all of the intended conclusions of the Examples 2.1-2.4, but none of the counterintuitive conclusions produced by RSA_O.

---

[7] Notice that only the premises are checked from which the obligation is derived. If all premises are checked, then we have some variant of a defeasible reasoning scheme known as System Z (Pearl, 1990; Boutilier, 1994), which has the drawback that it does not validate $\{\bigcirc(p \mid \top), \bigcirc(q \mid \top)\} \vdash \bigcirc(p \mid \neg q)$.

Example 2.5 (Chisholm paradox, continued) Assume a labeled deductive system that validates at least substitution of logical equivalents and the inference patterns RSA_V, WC_V and DD'_V. Furthermore, assume the premises $\bigcirc(a|\top)_{\{a\}}$ and $\bigcirc(t|a)_{\{t\}}$. Figure 5 shows how factual defeasibility blocks the counterintuitive derivation of Figure 1. The obligation $\bigcirc(t \mid \neg a)_{\{a,t\}}$ cannot be derived from $\bigcirc(t \mid \top)_{\{a,t\}}$, because $C_V : \{a,t\} \cup \{\neg a\}$ is not consistent. It does not use a CTD obligation like the blocked derivation in Figure 2, thus it also blocks the counterintuitive derivation in Figure 3.

$$
\cfrac{\cfrac{\bigcirc(t|a)_{\{t\}} \quad \bigcirc(a|\top)_{\{a\}}}{\bigcirc(a \wedge t|\top)_{\{a,t\}}}\ \text{DD}'}{\bigcirc(t|\top)_{\{a,t\}}}\ \text{WC}
$$

$$
- - - - - - \ (\text{RSA}_V)
$$

$$
\bigcirc(t|\neg a)_{\{a,t\}}
$$

Fig. 5. Chisholm paradox solved by factual defeasibility

It can easily be checked that the counterintuitive derivation of $\bigcirc(p|a)$ by RSA_O in Example 3 is blocked by RSA_V too. The examples show that CTD structures sometimes look like overridden defeasible reasoning structures, but a careful analysis shows that they are actually cases of factual defeasibility. There is no difference between the overridden and factual defeasibility analyses of CTD structures in Example 2.2 and 2.5, respectively, because in these examples the two restrictions C_O and C_V coincide for strengthening of the antecedent.

The reader might wonder why we consider condition C_V to be a type of factual defeasibility. In this article, we only discuss conditional obligations, and how these can be derived from each other. Facts do not seem to come into the picture here. However, a closer analysis reveals that factual defeasibility is indeed the underlying mechanism. The antecedent of a dyadic obligation restricts the focus to possibilities in which the antecedent is *assumed* to be factually true, and the consequent represents what is obligatory, given that these facts are assumed. Hence, the consequent refers to 'the best of the bad lot'. As we discussed in the introduction, these facts can be made explicit with a kind of factual detachment, for example with EFD. From the Chisholm paradox $\bigcirc(a|\top), \bigcirc(t|a), \bigcirc(\neg t|\neg a)$ and $\mathcal{A}\top$, we can derive $\bigcirc t$ by EFD, and from $\mathcal{A}\neg a$ we can derive $\bigcirc\neg t$, but not $\bigcirc t$. Hence, by adding a fact $(\neg a)$ we loose a deontic conclusion $(\bigcirc t)$.

Moreover, a comparison with, for example, prioritized default logic (Brewka, 1994) illustrates that C_V is a kind of factual defeasibility. Consider the classical example of non-transitivity of default rules, which consists of the default rules that 'normally, students are adults' ($\frac{s:a}{a}$) and that 'normally, adults are employed' ($\frac{a:e}{e}$). Given that we know that somebody is a student, we can defeat the default conclusion that this person is employed in two ways. Either, it is defeated by the more specific default rule that students are normally unemployed ($\frac{s:\neg e}{\neg e}$), which is a case of overridden defeasibility, or it is defeated by the defeating fact ($\neg a$) that the particular student is known to be no adult. This latter case of defeasibility is the type of factual defeasibility that is analogous to the defeasibility in the Chisholm paradox.

This analogy with default logic also illustrates what we mean by deontic detachment as a defeasible rule. The transitivity of the two default rules above can be blocked either by overridden or factual defeasibility. If neither of the two are the case, then the transitivity holds. In this sense one could say that in default logic transitivity holds as a defeasible rule. Analogously, we say that deontic detachment holds as a defeasible rule. If we only know $\bigcirc(t\,|\,a)_{\{t\}}$ and $\bigcirc(a\,|\,\top)_{\{a\}}$, then we can apply deontic detachment, which results in $\bigcirc(t\,|\,\top)_{\{a,t\}}$. But this detachment is defeated if we assume in the antecedent of this conclusion that $\neg a$ is true.

2.4. *Preference semantics*

In this section we formalize the Chisholm paradox in so-called contextual deontic logic CDL (Van der Torre and Tan, 1996). To illustrate the notion of 'context' of our contextual deontic logic, we consider the following distinction between what we call 'contextual' and 'conditional' obligations for dyadic deontic logics. Technically, the distinction means that a conditional obligation is valid in all cases in which its antecedent is true. It validates strengthening of the antecedent, whereas this is not necessarily the case for contextual obligations. These may be only true in some of these cases.[8] However, in a *dyadic* deontic logic this notion of context is quite restrictive. It only means that in *exactly* the case β the obligation is valid, because any $\beta \wedge \beta'$ can be outside the context. In our contextual deontic logic CDL, dyadic obligations are generalized with an 'unless γ' condition. A contextual obligation is written as $\bigcirc(\alpha|\beta\backslash\gamma)$. The context of a contextual obligation is all cases β except the cases γ. $\bigcirc(\alpha|\beta\backslash\gamma)$ can be compared with the Reiter default rule $\frac{\beta:\neg\gamma}{\alpha}$, where $\neg\gamma$ is the justification of the default rule (Reiter, 1980). For an axiomatization of CDL in Boutilier's modal preference logic CT4O, see (Van der Torre and Tan, 1996).

---

[8]Loewer and Belzer (1983) make another distinction between dyadic deontic logics that validate deontic detachment DD and factual detachment FD. Our reading is related to the reading of so-called 'contextual' obligations by Prakken and Sergot (1996). They call a dyadic obligation $\bigcirc(\alpha|\beta)$ a contextual obligation if its antecedent (called the context) β stands for 'a constellation of acts or situations that agents regard as being settled in determining what they should do'. See also the discussion on circumstances in (Hansson, 1971).

The unless clause formalizes a kind of factual defeasibility, because it blocks strengthening of the antecedent (thus it is defeasibility) and it does not refer to any other obligation for this blocking (thus it is factual). The crucial observation of the Chisholm paradox below is that if the premises are valid in all cases (i.e. have a context 'unless $\perp$', where $\perp$ is a contradiction), then the derived obligations may still be only valid in a restricted context. The context encodes in such a case the assumptions from which an obligation is derived, i.e. when the obligation is factually defeated. The contextual obligations are in a sense similar to labeled obligations, which shows that the labels of the labeled obligations formalize the context in which an obligation is valid.

Moreover, the formalization of the Chisholm paradox in contextual deontic logic gives an intuitive semantic interpretation of factual defeasibility. The preference semantics represent the notion of deontic choice. A preference of α_1 over α_2 means that if an agent can choose between α_1 and α_2, she should choose α_1 (see e.g. (Jennings, 1974)). An obligation for α is formalized by a preference of α over $\neg\alpha$. Thus, if the agent can choose between α and $\neg\alpha$, then she should choose α. Similarly, a conditional obligation for α if β is formalized by a preference of $\alpha \wedge \beta$ over $\neg\alpha \wedge \beta$. This preference is formalized by condition (3) of Definition 1 below. The other conditions (1) and (2) of Definition 1 formalize the condition that in order to choose between α and $\neg\alpha$, these opportunities must be logically possible (called the contingency clause by von Wright). Notice that condition (2) is a difference with labeled obligations, because we did not impose the condition that it is possible to violate a labeled obligation, although we trivially could have done so.

Definition 1 (Contextual obligation) Let $M = \langle W, \leq, V \rangle$ be a Kripke model that consists of W, a set of worlds, $\leq$, a binary reflexive and transitive relation on W, and V, a valuation of the propositions in the worlds. Moreover, let α, β and γ be propositional sentences. The model M satisfies the obligation 'α should be the case if β is the case unless γ is the case', written as $M \models \bigcirc(\alpha|\beta \backslash \gamma)$, iff

1. $W_1 = \{w \in W \mid M, w \models \alpha \wedge \beta \wedge \neg\gamma\}$ is nonempty, and
2. $W_2 = \{w \in W \mid M, w \models \neg\alpha \wedge \beta\}$ is nonempty, and
3. for all $w_1 \in W_1$ and $w_2 \in W_2$, we have $w_2 \not\leq w_1$.

At first sight, it might seem more intuitive to say '$w_1 < w_2$' in condition 3 of Definition 1. However, it is well-known from preference logics (Von Wright, 1963) that such a condition is much too strong. For example, consider this strong definition, two obligations $\bigcirc(p|\top \backslash \perp)$, and $\bigcirc(q|\top \backslash \perp)$ and a model with $p \wedge \neg q$ and $\neg p \wedge q$ worlds. The obligation $\bigcirc(p|\top \backslash \perp)$ says that the first world is strictly preferred over the second one, whereas the obligation $\bigcirc(q|\top\backslash\perp)$ implies the opposite. With other words, a model of the obligations cannot contain $p \wedge \neg q$ and $\neg p \wedge q$ worlds. For a further discussion on this topic, see (Tan and Van der Torre, 1996).

To illustrate the properties of CDL, we compare it with Bengt Hansson's dyadic deontic logic. First we recall some well-known definitions and properties of this logic. In Bengt Hansson's classical preference semantics (Hansson, 1971), as studied by (Lewis, 1974),a dyadic obligation, which we denote by $\bigcirc_{HL}(\alpha|\beta)$, is true in a model iff 'the minimal (or preferred) β worlds satisfy α'. A weaker version of this definition, which allows for moral dilemmas, is that $\bigcirc_{HL}^w(\alpha|\beta)$ is true in a model iff there is an equivalence class of minimal β worlds that satisfy α, or there is an infinite descending chain in which α is true in all β worlds below a certain β world.

Definition 2 (Minimizing) Let $M = \langle W, \leq, V \rangle$ be a Kripke model and $|\alpha|$ be the set of all worlds of W that satisfy α. M satisfies the weak Hansson-Lewis obligation 'α should be the case if β is the case', written as $M \models \bigcirc_{HL}^w(\alpha|\beta)$, iff there is a world $w_1 \in |\alpha \wedge \beta|$ such that for all $w_2 \in |\neg\alpha \wedge \beta|$ we have $w_2 \not\leq w_1$.

The following proposition shows that the expression $\bigcirc_{HL}^w(\alpha|\beta)$ corresponds to a weak Hansson-Lewis minimizing obligation. For simplicity, we assume that there are no infinite descending chains.

Proposition 1 Let $M = \langle W, \leq, V \rangle$ be a Kripke model like in Definition 1, such that there are no infinite descending chains. As usual, we write $w_1 < w_2$ for $w_1 \leq w_2$ and not $w_2 \leq w_1$, and $w_1 \sim w_2$ for $w_1 \leq w_2$ and $w_2 \leq w_1$. A world w is a minimal β-world, written as $M, w \models_< \beta$, iff $M, w \models \beta$ and for all $w' < w$ holds $M, w' \not\models \beta$. A set of worlds is an equivalence class of minimal β-worlds, written as E_β, iff there is a w such that $M, w \models_< \beta$ and $E_\beta = \{w' \mid M, w' \models \beta \text{ and } w \sim w'\}$. We have $M \models \bigcirc_{HL}^w(\alpha|\beta)$ iff there is an E_β such that $E_\beta \subseteq |\alpha|$.

Proof $\Leftarrow$ Follows directly from the definitions. Assume there is a w such that $M, w \models_< \beta$ and $E_\beta = \{w' \mid M, w' \models \beta \text{ and } w \sim w'\}$ and $E_\beta \subseteq |\alpha|$. For all $w_2 \in |\neg\alpha \wedge \beta|$ we have $w_2 \not\leq w$.

$\Rightarrow$ Assume that there is a world $w_1 \in |\alpha \wedge \beta|$ such that for all $w_2 \in |\neg\alpha \wedge \beta|$ we have $w_2 \not\leq w_1$. Let w be a minimal β-world such that $M, w \models_< \beta$ and $w \leq w_1$ (that exists because there are no infinite descending chains), and let $E_\beta = \{w' \mid M, w' \models \beta \text{ and } w \sim w'\}$.

Now we are ready to compare our contextual deontic logic with Bengt Hansson's dyadic deontic logic. The following proposition shows that under a certain condition, the contextual obligation $\bigcirc(\alpha|\beta \setminus \gamma)$ is true in a model if a set of the weak Hansson-Lewis minimizing obligations $\bigcirc_{HL}^w(\alpha|\beta')$ is true in the model.

Proposition 2 Let $M = \langle W, \leq, V \rangle$ be a Kripke model such as in Definition 1, that has no worlds that satisfy the same propositional sentences. Hence, we identify the set of worlds with a set of propositional interpretations, such that there are no duplicate worlds. As usual, for propositional α we say $M \models \alpha$ iff for all $w \in W$ we have $M, w \models \alpha$. $M \models \bigcirc(\alpha|\beta \backslash \gamma)$ iff there are $\alpha \wedge \beta \wedge \neg\gamma$ and $\neg\alpha \wedge \beta$ worlds, and for all propositional β' such that $M \models \beta' \rightarrow \beta$ and $M \not\models \beta' \rightarrow \gamma$, we have $M \models \bigcirc_{HL}^{w}(\alpha|\beta')$.

Proof $\Rightarrow$ Follows directly from the semantic definitions. $\Leftarrow$ Every world is characterized by a unique propositional sentence. Let $\overline{w}$ denote the sentence that uniquely characterizes world w. Proof by contraposition. If we have $M \not\models \bigcirc(\alpha | \beta \backslash \gamma)$, then there are w_1, w_2 such that $M, w_1 \models \alpha \wedge \beta \wedge \neg\gamma$ and $M, w_2 \models \neg\alpha \wedge \beta$ and $w_2 \leq w_1$. Choose $\beta' = \overline{w_1} \vee \overline{w_2}$. The world w_2 is an element of the preferred β' worlds, because there are no duplicate worlds. (If duplicate worlds are allowed, then there could be a β' world w_3 which is a duplicate of w_1, and which is strictly preferred to w_1 and w_2.) We have $M, w_2 \not\models \alpha$ and therefore $M \not\models \bigcirc_{HL}^{w}(\alpha|\beta')$,

In the beginning of this section, we discussed the distinction between conditional and contextual dyadic obligations. In this terminology, the obligations $\bigcirc(\alpha|\beta \backslash \bot)$ are conditional obligations and we write $\bigcirc(\alpha|\beta)$[9] for $\bigcirc(\alpha | \beta \backslash \bot)$. The following corollary for conditional obligations follows directly from Proposition 2.

Corollary 1 Let $M = \langle W, \leq, V \rangle$ be a Kripke model like in Definition 1, that has no worlds that satisfy the same propositional sentences. We have $M \models \bigcirc(\alpha|\beta \backslash \bot)$ iff there are $\alpha \wedge \beta$ and $\neg\alpha \wedge \beta$ worlds, and for all propositional β' such that $M \models \beta' \rightarrow \beta$ and $M \not\models \neg\beta'$, we have $M \models \bigcirc_{HL}^{w}(\alpha|\beta')$.

The following proposition shows several properties of contextual obligations. It shows that strengthening of the antecedent is blocked by γ (besides by the check that the choice alternatives $\alpha \wedge \beta_1 \wedge \beta_2$ and $\neg\alpha \wedge \beta_1 \wedge \beta_2$ are logically possible).

Proposition 3 Contextual deontic logic validates the following inference patterns.[10]

$$\text{RSA}_V : \frac{\bigcirc(\alpha|\beta_1 \backslash \gamma), C_V}{\bigcirc(\alpha|\beta_1 \wedge \beta_2 \backslash \gamma)}, \quad C_V : \quad \begin{array}{l} \alpha \wedge \beta_1 \wedge \beta_2 \wedge \neg\gamma \text{ is consistent, } and \\ \neg\alpha_1 \wedge \beta_1 \wedge \beta_2 \text{ is consistent} \end{array}$$

$$\text{WC}_V : \frac{\bigcirc(\alpha_1 \wedge \alpha_2|\beta \backslash \gamma), C_V}{\bigcirc(\alpha_1|\beta \backslash \gamma \vee \neg\alpha_2)}, C_V : \neg\alpha_1 \wedge \beta \text{ is consistent}$$

---

[9]These so-called *ordering* obligations $\bigcirc(\alpha|\beta)$ lack weakening of the consequent, see (Tan and Van der Torre, 1996) and Proposition 3.

[10]The consistency checks of C_V can also be expressed in the language if we enrich the logic with a modal consistency operator, see (Tan and Van der Torre, 1996; Van der Torre and Tan, 1996).

$$\text{DD}'_V : \frac{\bigcirc(\alpha|\beta\setminus\theta), \bigcirc(\beta|\gamma\setminus\theta), C_V}{\bigcirc(\alpha\wedge\beta|\gamma\setminus\theta)}, C_V : \alpha\wedge\beta\wedge\gamma\wedge\neg\theta \text{ is consistent}$$

Proof The inference patterns can easily be checked in the preference semantics. Consider the inference pattern WC_V. Assume a model M such that $M \models \bigcirc(\alpha_1\wedge\alpha_2|\beta\setminus\gamma)$. Let $W_1 = \{w \mid M, w \models \alpha_1\wedge\alpha_2\wedge\beta\wedge\neg\gamma\}$ and $W_2 = \{w \mid M, w \models \neg(\alpha_1\wedge\alpha_2)\wedge\beta\}$. Definition 1 says that W_1 and W_2 are non-empty, and $w_2 \not\leq w_1$ for every $w_1 \in W_1$ and $w_2 \in W_2$. Moreover, let $W'_1 = \{w \mid M, w \models \alpha_1\wedge\beta\wedge\neg(\gamma\vee\neg\alpha_2)\}$ and $W'_2 = \{w \mid M, w \models \neg\alpha_1\wedge\beta\}$. We have $W'_1 = W_1$ and $W'_2 \subseteq W_2$, and therefore $w_2 \not\leq w_1$ for all $w_1 \in W'_1$ and $w_2 \in W'_2$. Moreover, W'_1 is non-empty, because W_1 is non-empty. Hence, if W'_2 is non-empty (condition C_V), then $M \models \bigcirc(\alpha_1|\beta\setminus\gamma\vee\neg\alpha_2)$. The proofs of the other inference patterns are analogous and left to the reader.

The following example illustrates that now the Chisholm paradox can be analyzed in contextual deontic logic. In the Chisholm paradox, the *premises* do not have exceptions. Hence, the premises are conditional obligations, i.e. contextual obligations with context 'unless $\perp$'. Moreover, the example shows that factual defeasibility of the Chisholm paradox is caused by contextual reasoning, because the *premises* do not have exceptions, only derived obligations have exceptions. Thus, this aspect of factual defeasibility is quite different from defeasibility related to exceptional circumstances or abnormality formalized in logics of defeasible reasoning, because in that case the premises are subject to exceptions.

Example 2.6 (Chisholm paradox, continued) Consider the set of obligations $S = \{\bigcirc(a|\top\setminus\perp), \bigcirc(t|a\setminus\perp)\}$. The solution of the counterintuitive derivation of the Chisholm paradox in Example 2.3 is represented in Figure 6. The obligation $\bigcirc(t \mid \top\setminus\neg a)$ represents that the man should tell his neighbors, unless he does not go to their assistance.

$$\cfrac{\cfrac{\bigcirc(t|a\setminus\perp)\quad\bigcirc(a|\top\setminus\perp)}{\bigcirc(a\wedge t|\top\setminus\perp)}\ \text{DD}'_V}{\cfrac{\bigcirc(t|\top\setminus\neg a)}{\overline{}}\ \text{WC}_V}$$
$$\bigcirc(t|\neg a\setminus\neg a) \qquad (\text{RSA}_V)$$

Fig. 6. Chisholm paradox solved by factual defeasibility

The following example explains the factual defeasibility of the Chisholm paradox by preference semantics.

Example 2.7 (Chisholm paradox, continued) Consider the set of obligations $S = \{\bigcirc(a|\top\setminus\perp), \bigcirc(t|a\setminus\perp), \bigcirc(\neg t|\neg a\setminus\perp)\}$. A typical model M of S is given in Figure 7. This figure should be read as follows. The circles represent non-empty sets of worlds, that satisfy the propositions contained in them. Each circle represents an equivalence class of the partial pre-ordering $\leq$ of the model (the ordering partitions the worlds of the model into a set of equivalence classes). The arrows represent strict preferences for all worlds in the equivalence classes. For example, we have $M \models \bigcirc(\neg t|\neg a \setminus \bot)$, because for all $w_1 \in |\neg t \wedge \neg a|$ and $w_2 \in |t \wedge \neg a|$ we have $w_2 \not\leq w_1$. The condition $\neg a$ corresponds to the semantic concept of zooming in on the ordering. In the figure, this zooming in on the ordering is represented by a dashed box. For the evaluation of $M \models \bigcirc(\neg t|\neg a \setminus \bot)$, only the ordering within the dashed box is considered. As we observed in the analyses of the Chisholm paradox given above, the most important thing is that $\bigcirc(t|\neg a \setminus \gamma)$ does not follow from the premises for any γ. This is true for contextual deontic logic. The crucial observation is that we have $M \not\models \bigcirc(t|\neg a \setminus \gamma)$ for any γ such that $M \not\models t \wedge \neg a \wedge \neg\gamma$, because for all $w_1 \in |t \wedge \neg a \wedge \neg\gamma|$ for any γ, and for all $w_2 \in |\neg t \wedge \neg a|$, we have $w_2 \leq w_1$ (and even $w_2 < w_1$). Furthermore, we have $M \not\models \bigcirc_{HL}^w(t|\neg a \wedge \neg\gamma)$ for any γ such that there exists a $\neg t \wedge \neg a \wedge \neg\gamma$ world. In other words, t is not true in an equivalence class of most preferred $\neg a \wedge \neg\gamma$ worlds.

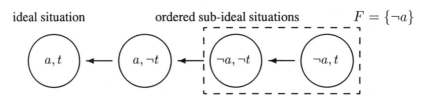

Fig. 7. Preference relation of the Chisholm paradox

Our discussion of the Chisholm paradox showed the fundamental distinction between overridden and factual defeasibility. Contrary-to-duty reasoning can be formalized as a kind of overridden defeasibility as well as a kind of factual defeasibility, and we showed that it is best formalized by the latter. The preference-based semantics illustrates where this type of factual defeasibility comes from. Semantically, the antecedent zooms in on the context of the preference ordering. The inference pattern WC corresponds semantically to introducing exceptions of this context. In the Chisholm paradox, the derivation of $\bigcirc(t|\top \setminus \neg a)$ from $\bigcirc(a \wedge t|\top \setminus \bot)$ says that the preference for t is not valid within the context $\neg a$. As shown in Figure 7, in this violation context the preferences can be the other way around.

Finally, we compare our contextual deontic logic with dyadic deontic logics. First, the Hansson-Lewis minimizing obligations (Hansson, 1971; Lewis, 1974) have too much factual defeasibility, because they do not have any strengthening of the antecedent. This is a result of the fact that every obligation can itself be derived by weakening of the consequent. Thus, it is never safe to apply strengthening of the antecedent, because any strengthening can result in an exceptional context. Second, Chellas-type of dyadic obligations consisting of a strict implication and a monadic operator $\bigcirc(\alpha|\beta) =_{\text{def}} \beta > \bigcirc\alpha$ (Chellas, 1974; Chellas, 1980; Alchourrón, 1994) have too little factual defeasibility, because they have unrestricted strengthening of the antecedent (and factual detachment). Thus they cannot represent contrary-to-duty obligations, because they suffer from the paradoxes.

3. OVERRIDDEN AND FACTUAL DEFEASIBILITY

In this section, we focus on the cancelling aspect of overridden defeasibility and the overshadowing aspect of factual defeasibility. Overridden defeasibility becomes relevant when there is a (potential) conflict between two obligations, i.e. when there are two contradictory obligations. For example, there is a conflict between $\bigcirc(\alpha_1|\beta_1)$ and $\bigcirc(\alpha_2|\beta_2)$ when α_1 and α_2 are contradictory, and β_1 and β_2 are factually true. In a defeasible deontic logic, such a conflict is resolved when one of the obligations overrides the other one. In the language of dyadic deontic logic, the overriding of $\bigcirc(\alpha_1|\beta_1)$ by $\bigcirc(\alpha_2|\beta_2)$ is formalized by the non-derivability of $\bigcirc(\alpha_1 \mid \beta_1 \wedge \beta_2)$. An unresolvable conflict is usually called a 'deontic dilemma', in this case represented by the formula $\bigcirc(\alpha_1|\beta_1 \wedge \beta_2) \wedge \bigcirc(\alpha_2|\beta_1 \wedge \beta_2)$.

In particular, we analyze *violated obligations* in a deontic logic that formalizes reasoning about obligations which can be overridden by other obligations. In the language of dyadic deontic logic, an obligation with a contradictory antecedent and consequent like $\bigcirc(\neg\alpha|\alpha)$ represents 'if α is the case, then it is a violation of the obligation that $\neg\alpha$ should be the case'.[11] This representation of violations is related to the more standard representation $\alpha \wedge \bigcirc\neg\alpha$ in SDL as follows. The standard representation of violations is a combination of monadic obligations and factual detachment, see (Van der Torre and Tan, 1995). With the inference pattern EFD discussed in the introduction the obligation $\bigcirc\neg\alpha$ can be derived from $A\alpha$ and $\bigcirc(\neg\alpha|\alpha)$. Hence, $\bigcirc(\neg\alpha|\alpha)$ can be read as 'if only α is known, then $\bigcirc\neg\alpha$ can be derived' and $\alpha \wedge \bigcirc\neg\alpha$ represents a violation. The contextual obligations we defined in Section 2.4 do not represent violated obligations, but in Section 3.4 we show how the definition of $\bigcirc(\alpha|\beta \setminus \gamma)$ can be adapted to $\bigcirc^r(\alpha|\beta \setminus \gamma)$ to derive violated (i.e. overshadowed) contextual obligations. To keep our analysis as general as possible, in this section we only accept the inference pattern RSA$_O$. Because RSA$_O$ is the only inference pattern we assume, we do not have to formalize contrary-to-duty reasoning and its related problems which we discussed in

---

[11] Alternatively, such an obligation could represent the obligation to update the present state of affairs. For example, the obligation 'if you smoke in a no-smoking area, then you should not smoke in a no-smoking area' (Hansson, 1971) can be read as the obligation to quit smoking.

the previous section. Thus, the analyses in this section are independent from our analysis and our solution of the Chisholm paradox.

3.1. *The Fence example*

The following so-called Fence example was introduced in (Prakken and Sergot, 1994) to illustrate the distinction between contrary-to-duty reasoning and defeasible reasoning (based on exceptional circumstances). It is an extended version of the Forrester (or gentle murderer) paradox: you should not kill, but if you kill, then you should do it gently (Forrester, 1984). In (Van der Torre, 1994) we discussed this Fence example in Horty's defeasible deontic logic. The following example is an alphabetic variant of the original example, because we replaced s, to be read as 'the cottage is by the sea', by d, to be read as 'there is a dog'. The distinction between 'the cottage is by the sea' and 'there is a dog' is that the latter proposition is controllable, whereas the former is not. This important distinction between controllable and uncontrollable propositions has to be formalized in a deontic (or action) logic, if only because for any uncontrollable α the obligation $\bigcirc(\alpha|\top)$ does not make sense, see (Boutilier, 1994) for a discussion. For example, it does not make sense to oblige someone to make the sun rise. In this article, we abstract from this problem and we assume that all propositions are controllable.

Example 4.1 (Fence example) Assume a dyadic deontic logic that validates at least substitution of logical equivalents and the inference pattern RSA$_O$. Furthermore, assume the obligations

$$S = \{\bigcirc(\neg f|\top), \bigcirc(w \wedge f|f), \bigcirc(w \wedge f|d)\},$$

where f can be read as 'there is a fence around your house', $w \wedge f$ as 'there is a white fence around your house' and d as 'you have a dog'. Notice that $\bigcirc(w \wedge f|f)$ is a CTD obligation of $\bigcirc(\neg f|\top)$ and $\bigcirc(w \wedge f|d)$ is not. If there is a fence and a dog ($\mathcal{A}(f \wedge d)$), then the first premise of S is intuitively overridden, and therefore it cannot be violated. Hence, $\bigcirc(\neg f|f \wedge d)$ should *not* be derivable. However, if there is a fence without a dog ($\mathcal{A}f$), then the first premise is intuitively not overridden, and therefore it is violated. Hence, the obligation $\bigcirc(\neg f|f)$ should be derivable. Moreover, this is exactly the difference between cancellation and overshadowing that we discussed in the introduction of this article. Overriding of $\bigcirc(\neg f|\top)$ by $f \wedge d$ and $\bigcirc(w \wedge f|d)$ means that the obligation to have no fence is cancelled and has no force anymore, hence $\bigcirc(\neg f|f \wedge d)$ should not be derivable. Violation of $\bigcirc(\neg f|\top)$ by f means that the obligation to have no fence has still its force, it is only overshadowed and not cancelled, hence $\bigcirc(\neg f|f)$ should be derivable. The possible derivations of $\bigcirc(\neg f \mid f \wedge d)$ and $\bigcirc(\neg f \mid f)$ are represented in Figure 8. In the first derivation, the counterintuitive obligation $\bigcirc(\neg f|f \wedge d)$

is not derived from $\bigcirc(\neg f \mid \top)$ by RSA$_O$, because the latter obligation is overridden by $\bigcirc(w \wedge f \mid d)$ for $f \wedge d$. However, in the second derivation the intuitive obligation $\bigcirc(\neg f \mid f)$ is not derived either from $\bigcirc(\neg f \mid \top)$ by RSA$_O$, because it is overridden by $\bigcirc(w \wedge f \mid f)$ for f, according to C_O.

$$\bigcirc(w \wedge f \mid d) \qquad\qquad \bigcirc(w \wedge f \mid f)$$
$$\bigcirc(\neg f \mid \top) \qquad \downarrow \qquad\qquad \bigcirc(\neg f \mid \top) \qquad \downarrow$$
$$- - - - - - - \ (\text{RSA}_O) \qquad\qquad - - - - - - - \ (\text{RSA}_O)$$
$$\bigcirc(\neg f \mid f \wedge d) \qquad\qquad\qquad\qquad \bigcirc(\neg f \mid f)$$

Fig. 8. Fence example with C_O

The problem in this example is that both $\bigcirc(w \wedge f \mid f)$ and $\bigcirc(w \wedge f \mid d)$ are treated as more specific obligations that override the obligation $\bigcirc(\neg f \mid \top)$, i.e. both are treated as cases of overridden defeasibility. However, this is not correct for $\bigcirc(w \wedge f \mid f)$. This last obligation should be treated as a CTD obligation, i.e. as a case of factual defeasibility. This interference of specificity and CTD is represented in Figure 9. This figure should be read as follows. Each arrow is a condition: a two-headed arrow is a consistency check, and a single-headed arrow is a logical implication. For example, the condition C_O formalizes that an obligation $\bigcirc(\alpha \mid \beta)$ is overridden by $\bigcirc(\alpha' \mid \beta')$ if the conclusions are contradictory (a consistency check, the double-headed arrow) and the condition of the overriding obligation is more specific (β' logically implies β). Case (a) represents criteria for overridden defeasibility, and case (b) represents criteria for CTD. Case (c) shows that the pair of obligations $\bigcirc(\neg f \mid \top)$ and $\bigcirc(w \wedge f \mid f)$ can be viewed as overridden defeasibility as well as CTD.

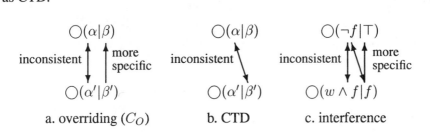

Fig. 9. Specificity and CTD

What is most striking about the Fence example is the observation that when the premise $\bigcirc(\neg f \mid \top)$ is violated by f, then the obligation for $\neg f$ should be derivable, but not when $\bigcirc(\neg f \mid \top)$ is overridden by $f \wedge d$. This means that the CTD or overriding interpretations of $\bigcirc(\neg f \mid \top)$ are quite different in the sense that they have different consequences. This overriding can be viewed as a type of overridden defeasibility and the violation in the CTD as a type of factual defeasibility. Hence, also the Fence example shows that factual and overridden defeasibility lead to different conclusions. This is a kind of factual defeasibility which differs from its counterpart in default logic in the sense that it is overshadowing factual defeasibility rather than cancelling factual defeasibility.

3.2. *Overridden defeasibility*

One obvious analysis of the problem mentioned in Example 4.1 is to observe that condition C_O is too strong. In (Van der Torre, 1994) we gave an ad hoc solution of the problem by weakening the definition of specificity in C_O to C_O^* with an additional condition which represents that a CTD obligation cannot override its primary obligations. The specificity condition C_O^* has three conditions: the two conditions of C_O and the additional condition that the overriding obligation $\bigcirc(\alpha' \mid \beta')$ is not a CTD of $\bigcirc(\alpha \mid \beta)$, i.e. $\beta' \wedge \alpha$ must be consistent. Due to this extra condition the overriding interpretation in case (c) in Figure 9 is no longer valid. The following example shows that the definition of specificity C_O^* gives the intuitive conclusions and avoids the counterintuitive ones.

Example 4.2 (Fence example, continued) Assume that RSA_O is replaced by the following RSA_O^*.

$$\text{RSA}_O^* : \frac{\bigcirc(\alpha \mid \beta_1), C_O^*}{\bigcirc(\alpha \mid \beta_1 \wedge \beta_2)}$$

C_O^*: there is no premise $\bigcirc(\alpha' \mid \beta')$ such that $\beta_1 \wedge \beta_2$ logically implies β', β' logically implies β_1 and not vice versa, α and α' are contradictory and $\alpha \wedge \beta'$ is consistent. (Van der Torre, 1994)

The derivations from S with RSA_O^* are represented in Figure 10. RSA_O^* does not derive the counterintuitive $\bigcirc(\neg f \mid f \wedge d)$, just like RSA_O in Figure 8. However, RSA_O^* does derive the intuitive $\bigcirc(\neg f \mid f)$ from $\bigcirc(\neg f \mid \top)$, in contrast to RSA_O. RSA_O^* solves the problem of Example 4.1, because it does not derive the counterintuitive obligation, but it does derive the intuitive obligation.

This solution of the Fence example is ad hoc, because there is no *a priori* reason to prefer C_O^* and RSA_O^* (the violability interpretation) to C_O and RSA_O (the overridden interpretation). The informal reason given in (Van der Torre, 1994) to prefer the former inference pattern is that with RSA_O, the obligation $\bigcirc(\neg f \mid \top)$ can never be violated, which is a highly counterintuitive property of an obligation. In the following subsection, we give a formal analysis of the Fence example, based on the essential property of obligations that they can be violated.

$$O(w \wedge f | d)$$
$$\downarrow$$

$$\begin{array}{c} O(\neg f | \top) \\ \text{\textemdash}\;\text{\textemdash}\;\text{\textemdash}\;\text{\textemdash}\;\text{\textemdash}\;\text{\textemdash} \quad (\text{RSA}_O^*) \\ O(\neg f | f \wedge d) \end{array}$$

$$\frac{O(\neg f | \top)}{O(\neg f | f)} \ \text{RSA}_O^*$$

Fig. 10. Fence example with C_O^*

3.3. Factual defeasibility

Instead of analyzing the problem of Example 4.1 by examining specificity condition C_O (overridden defeasibility), we can also look at properties of violability (factual defeasibility). The following inference patterns *Contrary-to-Duty* (CD) and *According-to-Duty* (AD) formalize the intuitions that an obligation cannot be defeated by only violating or fulfilling it. The CD rule models the intuition that after violation the obligation to do α is still in force (i.e. overshadowing). Even if you drive too fast, you are still obliged to obey the speed limit.[12]

$$\text{CD}: \ \frac{O(\alpha | \beta)}{O(\alpha | \beta \wedge \neg \alpha)} \qquad \text{AD}: \ \frac{O(\alpha | \beta)}{O(\alpha | \beta \wedge \alpha)}$$

We reconsider the Fence example and we show that CD with RSA_O derives exactly the intuitive conclusions, just like RSA_O^*.

Example 4.3 (Fence example, continued) Assume the inference patterns RSA_O and CD. Figure 11 represents the same two situations as Figure 8. First consider the situation when there is a fence and a dog $(f \wedge d)$. The counterintuitive obligation $O(\neg f \mid f \wedge d)$ cannot be derived, because the derivation via $O(\neg f | d)$ from $O(\neg f | \top)$ is blocked by C_O. Now consider the situation when there is a fence but not a dog (f). The intuitive obligation $O(\neg f | f)$ can be derived from $O(\neg f | \top)$ by CD.

Example 4.2 and 4.3 illustrate that the problem of RSA_O is that it does not imply CD (because its specificity condition C_O is too strong). In other words,

---

[12]The inference patterns CD and AD should not be confused with the following inverses of CD and AD, which seem to say that violations or fulfilled obligations do not come out of the blue.

$$\text{CD}^-: \ \frac{O(\alpha | \beta \wedge \neg \alpha)}{O(\alpha | \beta)} \qquad \text{AD}^-: \ \frac{O(\alpha | \beta \wedge \alpha)}{O(\alpha | \beta)}$$

Although these inference patterns seem intuitive at first sight, they are highly counterintuitive on further inspection. Reconsider the Fence example. There should be a white fence, if there is a fence $O(w \wedge f | f)$. Hence, by AD, there should be a white fence, if there is a white fence $O(w \wedge f | w \wedge f)$ (a fulfilled obligation). However, this does not mean that there is an unconditional obligation that there should be a white fence $O(w \wedge f | \top)$. Hence, the inference pattern AD^- is not valid. A similar argument can be given for CD^-.

$$\frac{O(\neg f | \top)}{\begin{array}{c} O(w \wedge f | d) \\ \downarrow \end{array}} (\text{RSA}_O)$$

$$\frac{O(\neg f | d)}{O(\neg f | f \wedge d)} \text{ CD} \qquad\qquad \frac{O(\neg f | \top)}{O(\neg f | f)} \text{ CD}$$

Fig. 11. Fence example with CD

the problem of RSA$_O$ is that there can be obligations, like $O(\neg f | \top)$, that can never be violated. In Example 4.3, CD and RSA$_O$ yield exactly the same intuitive conclusions as RSA$_O^*$ in Example 4.2. An advantage of CD is that the inference pattern is very intuitive and not an ad hoc like solution of the problem like the adaptation of C_O. Moreover, AD also formalizes an intuitive notion of fulfilled obligations, because it deals with fulfilled obligations in exactly the same way as CD with violated obligations. We illustrate the applicability of our approach by the analysis of the following Reykjavic Scenario, introduced by Belzer (1986).

Example 5.1 (Reykjavic Scenario) Consider the premise set of obligations $S = \{O(\neg r | \top), O(\neg g | \top), O(r | g), O(g | r)\}$, where r can be read as 'the agent tells the secret to Reagan' and g as 'the agent tells the secret to Gorbatsjov'. Figure 12 illustrates that the Reykjavic Scenario is a more complex instance of the Fence example, illustrated in Figure 9. In the Fence example, the obligation $O(w \wedge f | f)$ can be interpreted as a more specific overriding obligation, and it can be interpreted as a CTD obligation. In the Reykjavic Scenario, the latter two obligations of S can be considered as more specific obligations overriding the former two, and they can be considered as CTD obligations.

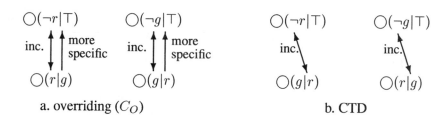

Fig. 12. Specificity and CTD in the Reykjavic Scenario

The Reykjavic Scenario is a highly ambiguous paradox, as a result of the fact that the latter two obligations can be considered as overriding as well as CTD obligations. In (Van der Torre, 1994), we gave the following two interpretations of this paradox.

1. **Overridden interpretation.** In this interpretation, the third sentence of S is an exception to the first sentence, and the fourth sentence is an exception to the second sentence (see Figure 12.a). The agent's primary obligation is not to tell Reagan or Gorbatsjov. When he tells Reagan, he should not tell Reagan but he should tell Gorbatsjov. It is a case of overridden defeasibility, because $\bigcirc(\neg g \,|\, r)$ cannot be derived from $\bigcirc(\neg g \,|\, \top)$ due to the premise $\bigcirc(g \,|\, r)$. When he tells both, he does not violate any obligations because r and g are considered as exceptions.[13]

2. **Violability interpretation.** In this interpretation the two dyadic obligations $\bigcirc(\neg r \,|\, r \wedge g)$ and $\bigcirc(\neg g \,|\, r \wedge g)$ are both derivable from S. Hence, when the agent tells both, he should have told neither of them, $\bigcirc(\neg r \,|\, r \wedge g)$ and $\bigcirc(\neg g \,|\, r \wedge g)$, a case of violability. The third sentence of S is a CTD obligation of the second sentence and the fourth sentence is a CTD obligation of the first sentence (see Figure 12.b).

In our view the violability interpretation is to be preferred to the overridden interpretation, The following example illustrates that the overridden interpretation conflicts with CD.

Example 5.2 (Reykjavic Scenario, continued) Assume a dyadic deontic logic that validates at least substitution of logical equivalents and the inference patterns AND, RSA$_O$, CD and the following disjunction rule OR.

$$\text{OR}: \frac{\bigcirc(\alpha_1 \,|\, \beta), \bigcirc(\alpha_2 \,|\, \beta)}{\bigcirc(\alpha_1 \vee \alpha_2 \,|\, \beta)}$$

Moreover, assume the set of obligations S of Example 5.1. According to the overridden interpretation, there is no violation when the agent tells both Reagan and Gorbatsjov. We cannot use RSA$_O$ to derive a violation from S, because the premises are overridden as represented in Figure 12.a. However, we can use CD to derive the violation $\bigcirc(\neg r \vee \neg g \,|\, r \wedge g)$, as represented in Figure 13. Hence, if we accept CD then we have to reject the overridden interpretation. Since we gave a general motivation for CD that is independent from particular examples, we reject the overridden interpretation.

The examples show that the inference patterns CD and AD are adequate tools to analyze conflicts between overridden and contrary-to-duty interpretations. However, they cannot discriminate between the following two violability

---

[13] According to the overridden interpretation, it might be argued that the paradox is not modeled correctly by the set of obligations S. When the last two conditional obligations should be interpreted as CTD obligations when the agent tells both, the first two obligations should be represented by one conditional obligation $\bigcirc(\neg r \wedge \neg g \,|\, \top)$. In that case, the last two sentences are interpreted as CTD obligations by C_O^*.

$$\dfrac{O(\neg r|\top)\quad O(\neg g|\top)}{\dfrac{O(\neg r \vee \neg g|\top)}{O(\neg r \vee \neg g|r \wedge g)}\ \text{CD}}\ \text{OR} \qquad \dfrac{O(\neg r|\top)\quad O(\neg g|\top)}{\dfrac{O(\neg r \wedge \neg g|\top)}{O(\neg r \wedge \neg g|r \vee g)}\ \text{CD}}\ \text{AND}$$

Fig. 13. Reykjavic scenario with CD

interpretations of the Reykjavic Scenario. McCarty (1994) argues for the first violability interpretation.

2.1 **Violability-1 interpretation** When he tells only Reagan, then one could interpret this as an overridden case, i.e. a case of defeasibility. In this interpretation $O(\neg g|\top)$ is overridden by $O(g|r)$ and the fact r. Hence, in this interpretation $O(\neg g|r)$ is not derivable from the premises. The remarkable thing about this interpretation is that $r \wedge g$ is treated as a violability case, whereas r in isolation is treated as an overridden case.

2.2 **Violability-2 interpretation** If we accept the reasonable principle that if an obligation is overriden for some situation, that it is then also overridden for a more specific situation, then the obligation $O(\neg g|\top)$ cannot be overridden by r only, because it is in the violability interpretation not overridden by the more specific situation $r \wedge g$.[14] According to this interpretation, when the agent tells only Reagan, then he still has the obligation $O(g|r)$ to tell Gorbatsjov, but also he has the derivable obligation not to tell Gorbatsjov $O(\neg g|r)$. The remarkable thing about this interpretation is that if we accept a reasonable principle, then the Reykjavic Scenario becomes a deontic dilemma.

This again illustrates the fact that this scenario is highly ambiguous, and additional principles have to be accepted if we want to decide between these two interpretations 2.1. and 2.2..

3.4. *Preferential semantics:* CD *and* AD

Before we can examine the conflicts between specificity and contrary-to-duty in the semantics, there are two ways in which we have to adapt the definition of contextual obligations. First, in this section we adapt the definition of $O(\alpha|\beta \backslash \gamma)$ to $O^r(\alpha|\beta \backslash \gamma)$. The logic of $O^r(\alpha|\beta \backslash \gamma)$ represents fulfilled and violated obligations, because it validates CD and AD. Second, we have to introduce a semantic notion to model specificity, which is done in Section 3.5 when we introduce obligations $O^{re}(\alpha|\beta \backslash \gamma)$.

---

[14]This principle certainly holds for defeasible logics. For example, if the 'birds fly' default is overridden by the more specific 'penguins do not fly default, then this latter default also holds for the subset super-penguins of penguins, unless it is explicitly stated that by default 'super-penguins do fly'.

The contextual obligations $\bigcirc(\alpha \mid \beta \setminus \gamma)$ do not represent violated and fulfilled obligations, because the first two conditions of Definition 1 say that $\bigcirc(\alpha|\beta\setminus\gamma)$ is false if either $\alpha \wedge \beta \wedge \neg\gamma$ or $\neg\alpha \wedge \beta$ is inconsistent. Obviously, we have to relax these two conditions. We allow the set of worlds W_1' and W_2' of $\bigcirc^r(\alpha|\beta\setminus\gamma)$ to be supersets of W_1 and W_2 from $\bigcirc(\alpha|\beta\setminus\gamma)$. If W_1 and W_2 of Definition 1 are nonempty, then the definition of $\bigcirc$ is equivalent to the definition of $\bigcirc^r$. However, if the set W_1 or W_2 is empty, then we have $M \not\models \bigcirc(\alpha|\beta\setminus\gamma)$, whereas $M \models \bigcirc^r(\alpha|\beta\setminus\gamma)$ if there is any $M \models \bigcirc(\alpha|\beta'\setminus\gamma)$ where β logically implies β' (see Proposition 4 and 5).

Definition 3 (Contextual obligation, with violations) Let $M = \langle W, \leq, V \rangle$ be a Kripke model that consists of W, a set of worlds, $\leq$, a binary reflexive and transitive relation on W, and V, a valuation of the propositions in the worlds. The model M satisfies the obligation 'α should be the case if β is the case unless γ is the case', written as $M \models \bigcirc^r(\alpha|\beta\setminus\gamma)$, iff

1. there is a nonempty $W_1 \subset W$ such that

   - for all $w \in W_1$, we have $M, w \models \alpha \wedge \neg\gamma$, and
   - for all w such that $M, w \models \alpha \wedge \beta \wedge \neg\gamma$, we have $w \in W_1$, and

2. there is a nonempty $W_2 \subset W$ such that

   - for all $w \in W_2$, we have $M, w \models \neg\alpha$, and
   - for all w such that $M, w \models \neg\alpha \wedge \beta$, we have $w \in W_2$, and

3. for all $w_1 \in W_1$ and $w_2 \in W_2$, we have $w_2 \not\leq w_1$.

To give an intuition for the previous formalization of contextual obligations we give the following metaphor, based on a parallel with belief revision. Let $W_1 = \{w \mid M, w \models \alpha \wedge \beta \wedge \neg\gamma\}$ and $W_2 = \{w \mid M, w \models \neg\alpha \wedge \beta\}$ be the choice alternatives of $\bigcirc(\alpha|\beta\setminus\gamma)$. Definition 1 in Section 2.4 says that W_1 and W_2 are non-empty, and $w_2 \not\leq w_1$ for every $w_1 \in W_1$ and $w_2 \in W_2$. Thus, we evaluated $\bigcirc(\alpha|\beta)$ by a choice between $\alpha \wedge \beta$ and $\neg\alpha \wedge \beta$, which can be considered as the AGM expansions of β by α and $\neg\alpha$.[15] Now, we evaluate $\bigcirc^r(\alpha|\beta)$ by a choice between the AGM-style revisions of β by α or $\neg\alpha$, which explains our notation $\bigcirc^r$.[16] Condition (1) and (2) formalize that revision must be possible. The following proposition shows that contextual

---

[15]For details on expansion and etraction, see (Gärdenfors, 1988).

[16]A similar idea is present in a proposal of Tan and Pearl (1994), where a conditional desire $D(l|n \wedge \neg l)$ is interpreted as $D(l|n)$, representing that 'I desire the light to be on if it is night and the light is off' compares night-worlds in which the light is on with those in which the light is off. However, their formalization is problematic, as is shown in (Boutilier, 1994). Moreover, in our case it is violation detection and revision (it refers to deontic alternatives in the past), in their case it is world improvement and update (it refers to alternatives in the future).

Revision can be considered as a combination of retraction and expansion, known as the Levi identity. In (Van der Torre and Tan, 1995), we interpreted the essential mechanism to represent violations in terms of a so-called retraction test. Boutilier and Becher (1995) use a similar

obligations validate strengthening of the antecedent.[17] Hence, the logic also validates CD and AD, because CD and AD follow from SA.

Proposition 4 The logic validates unrestricted strengthening of the antecedent.

$$SA : \frac{\bigcirc^r(\alpha|\beta_1 \setminus \gamma)}{\bigcirc^r(\alpha|\beta_1 \wedge \beta_2 \setminus \gamma)}$$

Proof Assume $M \models \bigcirc^r(\alpha \mid \beta_1 \setminus \gamma)$. There are W_1 and W_2 such that the conditions of Definition 3 are fulfilled. The same W_1 and W_2 also fulfill the conditions for $M \models \bigcirc^r(\alpha|\beta_1 \wedge \beta_2 \setminus \gamma)$.

The following proposition shows the relation between expansion-based contextual obligations in Section 2.4 (Definition 1) and the revision-based contextual obligations (Definition 3).

Proposition 5 The logic validates the following inference pattern.

$$\frac{\bigcirc(\alpha|\beta \setminus \gamma)}{\bigcirc^r(\alpha|\beta \setminus \gamma)}$$

Proof Assume a model M such that $M \models \bigcirc(\alpha|\beta \setminus \gamma)$. Let $W_1 = \{w \mid M, w \models \alpha \wedge \beta \wedge \neg \gamma\}$ and $W_2 = \{w \mid M, w \models \neg \alpha \wedge \beta\}$ be the choice alternatives of Definition 1. Then $M \models \bigcirc^r(\alpha|\beta \setminus \gamma)$, because W_1 and W_2 fulfill the conditions of Definition 3.

3.5. Multi preference semantics

In this section we adapt the definition of contextual obligations to model specificity, i.e. overridden defeasibility. Overridden defeasibility can be formalized by introducing a normality ordering in the semantics. Hence, the logic has a

---

kind of retraction to model predictive explanations: 'In order to evaluate the predictive force of factual explanations, we require that the agent (hypothetically) give up its belief in β and then find some α that would (in this new belief state) restore β. In other words, we contract K by β and evaluate the conditional $\alpha \Rightarrow \beta$ with respect to this contracted belief state: $\beta \in (K_\beta^-)_\alpha^*$. Thus, when we hypothetically suspend belief in β, if α is sufficient to restore this belief then α counts as a valid explanation. The contracted belief set K_β^- might fruitfully be thought of as the belief set held by the agent before it came to accept the observation β'.

[17]For example, we can derive $\bigcirc^r(t|\neg a \setminus \neg a)$ from $\bigcirc^r(t|a \setminus \bot)$ and $\bigcirc^r(a|\top \setminus \bot)$ in the Chisholm paradox (see Figure 6). There are two ways to view this derived obligation. The first is to say it is meaningless, because the antecedent $\neg a$ implies the unless clause $\neg a$. The second way is to say that it is counterintuitive, because it looks like the counterintuitive dyadic obligation $\bigcirc(t|\neg a)$. We can add a fourth condition to Definition 3 if we consider SA too strong, which states that there are worlds $\beta \wedge \neg \gamma$. In that case, there is a condition C_V on SA and $\bigcirc^r(t|\neg a \setminus \neg a)$ is not derivable from the Chisholm paradox.

multi preference semantics: an *ideality ordering* ($\leq_I$) to model contrary-to-duty structures (factual defeasibility) and a *normality ordering* ($\leq_N$) to model exceptional circumstances (overridden defeasibility), see (Tan and Van der Torre, 1995) for details. To facilitate the comparison with the definitions of $\bigcirc(\alpha|\beta\setminus\gamma)$ and $\bigcirc^r(\alpha|\beta\setminus\gamma)$, we assume that the preferential orderings are bounded.[18]

Definition 4 (Contextual obligation, with violations and overriding) Let $M = \langle W, \leq_I, \leq_N, V \rangle$ be a Kripke model that consists of W, a set of worlds, $\leq_I$ and $\leq_N$, two binary reflexive and transitive relations on W, and V, a valuation of the propositions in the worlds, such that there are no infinite descending chains. The model M satisfies the obligation 'α should be the case if β is the case unless γ is the case', written as $M \models \bigcirc^{re}(\alpha|\beta\setminus\gamma)$, iff

1. there is a nonempty $W_1 \subset W$ such that
   - for all $w \in W_1$, we have $M, w \models \alpha \wedge \neg\gamma$, and
   - for all w such that $M, w \models_{\leq_N} \alpha \wedge \beta \wedge \neg\gamma$, we have $w \in W_1$, and
2. there is a nonempty $W_2 \subset W$ such that
   - for all $w \in W_2$, we have $M, w \models \neg\alpha$, and
   - for all w such that $M, w \models_{\leq_N} \neg\alpha \wedge \beta$, we have $w \in W_2$, and
3. for all $w_1 \in W_1$ and $w_2 \in W_2$, we have $w_2 \not\leq_I w_1$.

The following example illustrates the multi preference semantics of the Fence example.

Example 4.4 (Fence example, continued) Consider the set of obligations $S = \{\bigcirc^{re}(\neg f|\top\setminus\bot), \bigcirc^{re}(w \wedge f|d\setminus\bot)\}$. The typical[19] multi preference model of S is given in Figure 14 and can be read as follows. The circles denote equivalence classes of worlds that satisfy the literals inside the circles and the 'horizontal' arrows denote the deontic preference ordering. The boxes denote equivalence classes in the normality ordering and the 'vertical' arrow the normality preference ordering. S constructs two preference orderings on the worlds: one ordering for ideality (like before) and one for normality. The idea of the preference ordering on normality is that the worlds with exceptional circumstances (where you have a dog) are semantically separated from the normal situation (where you do not have a dog). The upper box represents

---

[18]The fact that $\leq_N$ is bounded, ensures that the set of w such that $w \in W_1$ and $M, w \models_{\leq_N} \alpha \wedge \beta \wedge \neg\gamma$ is well-defined. The more general definition for unbounded orderings is: for all w such that $M, w \models \alpha \wedge \beta \wedge \neg\gamma$, there is a world $w' \leq_N w$ such that $M, w' \models \alpha \wedge \beta \wedge \neg\gamma$, and for all w'' such that $M, w'' \models \alpha \wedge \beta \wedge \neg\gamma$ and $w'' \leq_N w'$, we have $w'' \in W_1$. See also Definition 2 and Proposition 1.

[19]Computing these typical models in general is difficult, see (Tan and Van der Torre, 1995). For example, it seems more difficult than defeasible reasoning schemes to complete a single ordering like 'maximally connected' (Tan and Van der Torre, 1996) or System Z (Pearl, 1990).

the 'normal' worlds, which is determined by the fact that d is false, i.e. you do not have a dog. Deontically, the $\neg d$ worlds are ordered according to the obligation that, normally, there should be no fence. The lower box contains the worlds where d is true and which are therefore exceptional. These worlds are deontically ordered by the obligation that in this situation, there should be a white fence. Because of the exceptional circumstances, the worlds are not subject to the obligation that normally, there should not be a fence. In the ideality ordering, the normal $\neg d \wedge \neg f$ worlds and the exceptional $d \wedge w \wedge f$ worlds are equivalent.

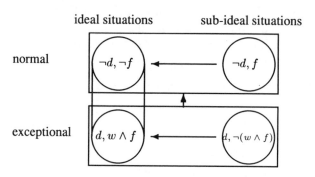

Fig. 14. Multi-preference relation of the Fence example

For example, we have $M \models \bigcirc^{re}(\neg f | \top \setminus \bot)$, because for all $w_1 \in |\neg f \wedge \neg d|$ (the most normal $\neg f$ worlds) and for all $w_2 \in |f \wedge \neg d|$ (the most normal f worlds) we have $w_2 \not\leq_I w_1$. Moreover, we have $M \models \bigcirc^{re}(w \wedge f | d \setminus \bot)$, because we zoom in on the d worlds, and $w \wedge f \wedge d$ worlds are preferred over $\neg(w \wedge f) \wedge d$ worlds.

Notice that we first minimize in the normality ordering when we evaluate the obligation $\bigcirc^{re}(\neg f | \top \setminus \bot)$ in Example 4.4, because we first determine the sets $W_1 = |\neg f \wedge \neg d|$ and $W_2 = |f \wedge \neg d|$, and subsequently we compare the sets W_1 and W_2 in the ideality ordering. We compare the best most normal worlds and we do not compare the most normal best sets $W_1' = |\neg f \wedge \neg d|$ and $W_2' = |w \wedge f \wedge d|$. This is based on the heuristic rule that if an option (like f) can be a violation (like W_2) or an exception (like W_2'), then it is assumed to be a violation. The motivation of this rule is that a criminal should have as little opportunities as possible to excuse herself by claiming that her behavior was exceptional rather than criminal. If an agent has a fence, then it is assumed to be a violation and she cannot excuse herself by claiming that it is an exceptional case (unless, of course, there is a dog).[20] The following proposition shows that the obligations validate CD and AD.

---

[20]However, our approach is quite different from lexicographic minimizing (minimize first $\leq_N$ and then $\leq_I$) like in (Makinson, 1993), because our second step is not minimizing. In fact,

Proposition 6 The logic of the obligations $\bigcirc^{re}$ does not validate SA, but it validates CD and AD.

Proof First, consider the invalidity of SA. The contextual obligation $\bigcirc^{re}(\alpha \mid \beta_1 \wedge \beta_2 \setminus \bot)$ cannot be derived from $\bigcirc^{re}(\alpha \mid \beta_1 \setminus \bot)$, because the most normal worlds $\beta_1 \wedge \beta_2$ can contain worlds not among the most normal β_1 worlds. Thus the logic does not validate SA. Secondly, consider CD and AD. Assume $M \models \bigcirc^{re}(\alpha \mid \beta \setminus \gamma)$. Hence, there are W_1 and W_2 such that the conditions of Definition 4 are fulfilled. The same W_1 and W_2 also satisfy the conditions for $M \models \bigcirc^{re}(\alpha \mid \beta \wedge \neg\alpha \setminus \gamma)$ and $M \models \bigcirc^{re}(\alpha \mid \beta \wedge \alpha \setminus \gamma)$.

The following example illustrates the conflict between overridden and CTD.

Example 4.5 (Fence example, continued) Consider the set of obligations $S' = \{\bigcirc^{re}(\neg f \mid \top \setminus \bot), \bigcirc^{re}(w \wedge f \mid d \setminus \bot), \bigcirc^{re}(w \wedge f \mid f \setminus \bot)\}$. The typical multi preference model M' of S' is given in Figure 15. The normal worlds have deontically been specified more precisely, compared to the model M in Figure 14 of the set of obligations S in Example 4.4. We have $M' \models \bigcirc^{re}(\neg f \mid \top \setminus \bot)$, for similar reasons as $M \models \bigcirc^{re}(\neg f \mid \top \setminus \bot)$ in Example 4.4. We also have $M' \models \bigcirc^{re}(\neg f \mid f \setminus \bot)$, which can be shown as follows. Semantically, the sets W_1 and W_2 must contain the most normal $\neg f \wedge f$ and $f \wedge f$ worlds, respectively. Hence, W_1 can be any subset of $|\neg f|$, and W_2 is a subset of $|f|$ that contains at least $|f \wedge \neg d|$. We can choose W_1 and W_2 as $|\neg f \wedge \neg d|$ and $|f \wedge \neg d|$, and we have $w_2 \not\leq w_1$ for all $w_1 \in W_1$ and $w_2 \in W_2$. However, we do not have $M' \models \bigcirc^{re}(\neg f \mid f \wedge d \setminus \bot)$, as can be verified as follows. The sets W_1 and W_2 must contain the most normal $\neg f \wedge f \wedge d$ and $f \wedge f \wedge d$ worlds, respectively. Hence, W_1 can be any subset of $|\neg f|$, and W_2 is a subset of $|f|$ that contains at least $|f \wedge d|$. Any world $w_2 \in |w \wedge f \wedge d|$ is deontically preferred, hence there cannot be a world $w_1 \in W_1$ such that $w_2 \not\leq w_1$, thus the first condition cannot be fulfilled. This illustrates that the logic does not validate SA, because it does not strengthen $\bigcirc^{re}(\neg f \mid \top \setminus \bot)$ to $\bigcirc^{re}(\neg f \mid f \wedge d \setminus \bot)$ (although it does strengthen to $\bigcirc^{re}(\neg f \mid f \setminus \bot)$). These are precisely the intuitive conclusions that one would draw from S'. If one only knows that there is a fence, then one concludes that the first obligation from S' still holds, hence one derives $\bigcirc^{re}(\neg f \mid f \setminus \bot)$. However, if one knows that there is a dog as well as a fence, then the first obligation is overridden by the second one, and hence one does not derive $\bigcirc(\neg f \mid f \wedge d \setminus \bot)$.

In this section, we focussed on the cancelling aspect of overridden defeasibility and the overshadowing aspect of factual defeasibility. We argued that the distinction should be reflected by two distinct preference orderings

---

under certain assumptions lexicographic minimizing is equivalent to minimizing in a single preference ordering (the lexicographic ordering of $\leq_N$ and $\leq_I$).

ideal situations   ordered sub-ideal situations

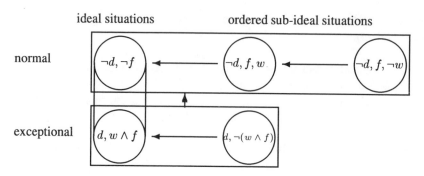

Fig. 15. Extended multi-preference relation of the Fence example

in the semantics: one normality ordering for the cancelling aspect of overridden defeasibility, and one ideality ordering for the overshadowing aspect of factual defeasibility. This is a major distinction between defeasible deontic logics and logics of defeasible reasoning, because in the latter both kinds of defeasibility are cancelling, and they can be modeled by a single preference ordering (see e.g. (Makinson, 1993; Geffner and Pearl, 1992)).

4. STRONG VERSUS WEAK OVERRIDDEN DEFEASIBILITY

In this section we focus on the cancelling aspect and the overriding aspect of overridden defeasibility by formalizing prima facie obligations. First, we show that the overridden defeasibility related to multi preference semantics cannot be used for prima facie obligations. Secondly, we introduce a new kind of preference semantics, based on priorities, to model prima facie obligations. We call the overridden defeasibility related to multi-preference semantics *strong overridden defeasibility*, and the overridden defeasibility based on priorities *weak overridden defeasibility*. The distinction between the different types of overridden defeasibility is shown by three inference patterns which are not valid for the first type, but which are valid for the second type: forbidden conflict and two versions of reinstatement. To distinguish the two types of defeasibility we will use the deontic operator $\bigcirc$ to represent the logic of the first type and $\bigcirc_{pf}$ for the latter one. One of the inferential differences between weak and strong overridden defeasibility is the inference pattern

$$\frac{\bigcirc(\neg f \mid \top), \bigcirc(w \wedge f \mid d)}{\bigcirc(\neg d \mid \top)}$$

which is not valid in strong overridden defeasibility, whereas

$$\frac{\bigcirc_{pf}(k \mid \top), \bigcirc_{pf}(p \wedge \neg k \mid d)}{\bigcirc_{pf}(\neg d \mid \top)}$$

is valid in weak overridden defeasibility. This might look strange, because the premises in both inference schemes have the same syntactic form (obviously the substitution of $\neg k$ for f does not make any difference). However, it simply means that the $\bigcirc$ that represents obligations like 'there should be no fence' is different from the $\bigcirc_{pf}$ that represents prima facie obligations.

4.1. Prima facie obligations

Ross (1930) introduced the notion of so-called prima facie obligations. In his own words: 'I suggest '*prima facie* duty' or 'conditional duty' as a brief way of referring to the characteristic (quite distinct from that of being a duty proper) which an act has, in virtue of being of a certain kind (e.g. the keeping of a promise), of being an act which would be a duty proper if it were not at the same time of another kind which is morally significant' (Ross, 1930, p.19). A prima facie duty is a duty proper when it is not overridden by another prima facie duty. When a prima facie obligation is overridden, it is not a proper duty but it is still in force: 'When we think ourselves justified in breaking, and indeed morally obliged to break, a promise [...] we do not for the moment cease to recognize a prima facie duty to keep our promise' (Ross, 1930, p.28). See (Morreau, 1996) for a formalization of Ross' theory in a deontic logic. The following example describes the typical kind of defeasibility involved in reasoning about prima facie obligations.

Example 6.1 (Promises) Assume the inference pattern RSA$_O$ and the premises $\bigcirc_{pf}(k|\top)$ and $\bigcirc_{pf}(p \wedge \neg k|d)$, where k can be read as 'keeping a promise', p as 'preventing a disaster' and d as 'a disaster will occur if nothing is done to prevent it'. There is a potential conflict between the two obligations, because when the facts imply d then the first obligation says that you should keep your promise and the second one implies that you should not. Assuming that the second obligation is stronger than the first one, the first obligation is overridden by the second one. Hence, the inference

$$\frac{\bigcirc_{pf}(k|\top), \bigcirc_{pf}(p \wedge \neg k|d)}{\bigcirc_{pf}(k|d)}$$

is *not* valid. Important here is that this priority does not depend on specificity. In this example the priority is compatible with specificity, but the converse priority could also have been chosen. You do not have an absolute (alias proper) obligation to keep your promise, but you still have the prima facie obligation. The situation is not ideal anymore. All situations where k is false, i.e. where the prima facie obligation for k is violated, are sub-ideal. This can be verified as follows. Consider a person having the obligation to keep a promise to show up at a birthday party, but she does not want to. So, she does something which might result in a disaster later on (leaving the coffee machine on, for instance) and at the moment of the party, she rushes home to turn off the coffee machine. She has the actual obligation to go home and turn off the machine, but leaving the machine on (on purpose) was a violation already. Hence, the inference

$$\frac{O_{pf}(k|\top), O_{pf}(p \wedge \neg k|d)}{O_{pf}(\neg d|\top)}$$

is valid. It says that it is not permitted to do something that might result in a disaster (remember that all propositions are assumed to be controllable). Finally, assume that there may be a disaster but you do not prevent it. Hence, the second obligation has been violated. In this situation, the proper obligation is not fulfilled, but we can still fulfill the prima facie obligation. Violating one obligation is better than violating both. Hence, the inference

$$\frac{O_{pf}(k|\top), O_{pf}(p \wedge \neg k|d)}{O_{pf}(k|d \wedge \neg p)}$$

is valid.

The following inference pattern is called *Forbidden Conflict* (FC). If the inference pattern is accepted, then it is not allowed to bring about a conflict, because a conflict is sub-ideal, even when it can be resolved.

$$\text{FC}: \frac{O_{pf}(\alpha_1|\beta_1), O_{pf}(\neg\alpha_1 \wedge \alpha_2|\beta_1 \wedge \beta_2)}{O_{pf}(\neg\beta_2|\beta_1)}$$

The situation considered in the following inference pattern *Reinstatement* (RI) is whether an obligation can be overridden by an overriding obligation that itself is factually defeated. The obligation $O_{pf}(\alpha_1|\beta_1)$ is overridden by $O_{pf}(\neg\alpha_1 \wedge \alpha_2|\beta_1 \wedge \beta_2)$ for $\beta_1 \wedge \beta_2$, but is it also overridden for $\beta_1 \wedge \beta_2 \wedge \neg\alpha_2$? If the last conclusion is not accepted, then the first obligation α_1 should be in force again. Hence, the original obligation is reinstated.

$$\text{RI}: \frac{O_{pf}(\alpha_1|\beta_1), O_{pf}(\neg\alpha_1 \wedge \alpha_2|\beta_1 \wedge \beta_2)}{O_{pf}(\alpha_1|\beta_1 \wedge \beta_2 \wedge \neg\alpha_2)}$$

The following inference pattern RIO is a variant of the previous inference pattern RI, in which the overriding obligation is not factually defeated but overridden. $O_{pf}(\alpha_1|\beta_1)$ is overridden by $O_{pf}(\neg\alpha_1 \wedge \alpha_2|\beta_1 \wedge \beta_2)$ for $\beta_1 \wedge \beta_2$, and the latter is overridden by $O_{pf}(\neg\alpha_2|\beta_1 \wedge \beta_2 \wedge \beta_3)$ for $\beta_1 \wedge \beta_2 \wedge \beta_3$. The inference pattern RIO says that an obligation cannot be overridden by an obligation that is itself overridden. Hence, an overridden obligation becomes reinstated when its overriding obligation is itself overridden.

$$\text{RIO}: \frac{O_{pf}(\alpha_1|\beta_1), O_{pf}(\neg\alpha_1 \wedge \alpha_2|\beta_1 \wedge \beta_2), O_{pf}(\neg\alpha_2|\beta_1 \wedge \beta_2 \wedge \beta_3)}{O_{pf}(\alpha_1|\beta_1 \wedge \beta_2 \wedge \beta_3)}$$

Example 6.1 illustrates that the kind of overridden defeasibility related to Ross' notion of 'prima facie' obligations validates the inference patterns FC, RI and RIO.[21] In the next section, we show that the type of overridden defeasibility we used to model specificity in the Fence example does not validate these inference patterns. Hence, there are two different types of overridden defeasibility. We call the type related to prima facie obligations *weak overridden defeasibility* in contrast to *strong overridden defeasibility*. In Section 4.3, we illustrate this new type of defeasibility by a preference ordering with priorities, instead of the multi preference semantics of strong overridden defeasibility in Section 3.5.

4.2. *Strong overridden defeasibility*

In the following example, we reconsider the Fence example and we argue that it should not validate inference patterns similar to FC, RI and RIO. Since this example is based on strong overridden defeasibility, it also shows that these inference patterns are not valid for this type of defeasibility.

Example 4.6 (Fence example, continued) Reconsider the two obligations $O(\neg f \mid \top)$ and $O(w \wedge f \mid d)$ of Example 4.1. There is a potential conflict between the two obligations. When the facts imply d, then there is a conflict, because the first obligation says that there should not be a fence, and the second obligation implies that there should be a fence. However, the first obligation is overridden by the second one, because the second one is more specific. Hence, the conflict is resolved and there should be a white fence. The inference

$$\frac{O(\neg f \mid \top), O(w \wedge f \mid d)}{O(\neg f \mid d)}$$

is *not* valid. The first sentence can be read as: 'normally, there should not be a fence around your house'. Hence, in most situations there should not be a fence, but in exceptional circumstances a fence is allowed. Similarly, the second sentence can be read as 'normally there should be a white fence, when you have a dog'. Hence, the situation when you have a dog is one of the exceptional situations in which the first obligation is not in force. The

---

[21] Alchourrón (1994) criticizes B. Hansson's logic (Hansson, 1971) for being a logic of prima facie obligations instead of a logic of CTD obligations. Hansson's logic validates FC when the antecedent β_1 is $\top$ (establishing a conflict is sub-ideal) but not RI (reinstatement). Actually, there is no strengthening of the antecedent at all in the logic of B. Hansson.

situation is not sub-ideal yet, it is only exceptional. Hence, the inference

$$\frac{\bigcirc(\neg f \mid \top), \bigcirc(w \wedge f \mid d)}{\bigcirc(\neg d \mid \top)}$$

is *not* valid. Finally, assume that there is a dog but there cannot be a white fence (e.g. there might be a black fence or no fence at all). Hence, the second obligation has been violated. In this situation, which is even more specific than the situation where there is a dog (d), nothing is said whether no fence is preferred over a non-white fence. Hence, the inference

$$\frac{\bigcirc(\neg f \mid \top), \bigcirc(w \wedge f \mid d)}{\bigcirc(\neg f \mid d \wedge \neg w)}$$

is *not* valid.

The following example illustrates that the invalidity of the inference patterns FC, RI and RIO can be explained by the multi preference semantics in Section 3.5.

Example 4.7 (Fence example, continued) Reconsider the multi preference model M in Figure 14 of the defeasible contextual obligations $\bigcirc^{re}(\neg f \mid \top\backslash\bot)$ and $\bigcirc^{re}(w \wedge f \mid d\backslash\bot)$ in Example 4.4. Figure 14 shows why the two inference patterns FC and RI are not valid. First of all, the obligation not to establish a conflict is not valid, $M \not\models \bigcirc^{re}(\neg d \mid \top \setminus \bot)$, because the $\neg d$ worlds (the most normal $\neg d$ worlds) are no better than the $d \wedge w \wedge f$ worlds (the optimal most normal d worlds). Secondly, the inference pattern reinstatement is not valid, $M \not\models \bigcirc^{re}(\neg f \mid d \wedge \neg w\backslash\bot)$, because all $d \wedge \neg w$ worlds are equivalent. Hence, if we zoom in on these worlds, there is no preference for f or $\neg f$.

The invalidity of inference patterns similar to FC, RI and RIO shows that strong overridden defeasibility is not sufficient to model reasoning about prima facie obligations. In other words, the obligations that model the Fence example are a different type of obligations than the obligations that model prima facie obligations.

4.3. *Weak overridden defeasibility*

The notion of weak overridden defeasibility can be formalized in a prioritized system. We do not give the formal definitions of a prioritized system, because they can be found in many articles on defeasible reasoning (see e.g. (Brewka, 1994; Geffner and Pearl, 1992; Vreeswijk, 1993)), but we illustrate the idea of a prioritized system by our promises example.

Example 6.2 (Promises, continued) In a prioritized system, a single preference ordering (an ideality ordering) is constructed for the obligations

$O_{pf}(k|\top)$ and $O_{pf}(p \wedge \neg k|d)$. To construct the ordering, a naming mechanism is used, similar to the one in conditional entailment (Geffner and Pearl, 1992). When the ordering is constructed, the prioritization of (the violations of) the obligations is taken into account. A typical prioritized preference ordering of Example 6.1 in Section 4.1 is given in Figure 16. The important relations in this preference model are $w_1 < w_2$ for all $w_1 \in |\neg k \wedge p \wedge d| \cup |\neg k \wedge \neg d|$ and $w_2 \in |k \wedge \neg p \wedge d|$, which state that violating the second obligation is worse than violating the first obligation. Without the prioritization, these worlds would be incomparable. Figure 16 shows why the inference patterns FC and RI are valid. First of all, forbidden conflict FC is valid, because $M \models O_{pf}(\neg d|\top \backslash \bot)$. This follows from the fact that all d worlds are sub-ideal. Secondly, reinstatement is valid because $M \models O_{pf}(k|d \wedge \neg p \backslash \bot)$. The $d \wedge \neg p$ worlds are not equivalent. Hence, if we zoom in on these worlds, as represented by a dashed box, there is an obligation for k.

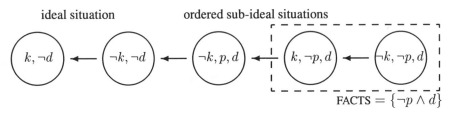

Fig. 16. Prioritized Preference Relation

Weak overridden defeasibility is quite close to overshadowing, but these notions are not identical. The typical case of overshadowing is that an obligation $O(p|\top)$ is violated by the fact $\neg p$. We can introduce the notion of an absolute obligation Op to express that, in spite of the factual violation, the obligation is still in force. In the typical case of weak overridden defeasibility there are two conflicting obligations, say $O_{pf}(p|\top)$ and $O_{pf}(\neg p|q)$ and the fact q, with a preference ordering. To illustrate the difference with overshadowing, let us assume that the second obligation is preferred over the first one. We could generalize the logic of absolute obligations to take preference orderings into account, and then these two obligations would imply the actual obligation $O\neg p$, but not Op. This obligation expresses the duty proper, the obligation that should be acted upon. But these obligations would also imply both prima facie obligations $O_{pf}\neg p$ and $O_{pf}p$, which express that both obligations are still in force. These prima facie obligations resemble the absolute obligations of overshadowing. Hence, overshadowing and weak overridden defeasibility are equivalent from the point of view of 'cue for action': once an obligation is violated, it is still fully in force, but no longer a cue for action. Once an obligation is weakly overridden, it is no longer fully in force, but it is still in force as a prima facie obligation.

5. CONCLUSIONS

In this article we analyzed different types of defeasibility in defeasible deontic logics. We discriminated between two concepts, i.e. overshadowing and cancelling, and three types of defeasibility, i.e. factual defeasibility, strong overridden defeasibility and weak overridden defeasibility. We argued that factual defeasibility should be used to model violability, that strong overridden defeasibility should be used to model specificity and that weak overridden defeasibility should be used to model prima facie obligations. We also showed that the distinction between different types of defeasibility is essential for a better understanding of some of the notorious paradoxes of deontic logic, namely the Chisholm and Forrester paradoxes. Moreover, we introduced several preference-based semantics for deontic logics to analyze the different types of defeasibility.

ACKNOWLEDGEMENTS

This research was partially supported by the ESPRIT III Basic Research Project No.6156 DRUMS II and the ESPRIT III Basic Research Working Group No.8319 MODELAGE. Thanks to Patrick van der Laag, John-Jules Meyer, Henry Prakken and Marek Sergot for useful comments on earlier versions of this article.

Leendert W.N. van der Torre
EURIDIS, Tinbergen Institute and Department of Computer Science
Erasmus University
Rotterdam, The Netherlands

Yao-Hua Tan
EURIDIS
Erasmus University
Rotterdam, The Netherlands

REFERENCES

Alchourrón, C. E. (1994). Philosophical foundations of deontic logic and the logic of defeasible conditionals. In Meyer and Wieringa (eds.), *Deontic Logic in Computer Science: Normative System Specification*, John Wiley & Sons, pages 43–84.

Belzer, M. (1986). A logic of deliberation. In *Proceedings of the Fifth National Conference on Artificial Intelligence*, pages 38–43.

Boutilier, C. (1994). Toward a logic for qualitative decision theory. In *Proceedings of the Fourth International Conference on Principles of Knowledge Representation and Reasoning*, pages 75–86.

Boutilier, C. and Becher, V. (1995). Abduction as belief revision. *Artificial Intelligence* 77:43–94.

Brewka, G. (1994). Adding specificity and priorities to default logic. In *Proceedings of Logics in artificial intelligence : European workshop*, Springer-Verlag.

Brown, A. L. and Mantha, S. (1991). Preferences as normative knowledge: Towards declarative obligations. In *Proceedings of the First Workshop on Deontic Logic in Computer Science*, Amsterdam, pages 142–163.

Chellas, B. F. (1974). Conditional obligation. In Stunland, S. (ed.), *Logical Theory and Semantical Analysis: Essays dedicated to Stig Kauger*, D. Reidel Publishing Company, Dordrecht, Holland, pages 23–33.

Chellas, B. F. (1980). In Stunland S. (ed.), *Modal Logic: An Introduction* Cambridge University Press.

Chisholm, R. M. (1963). Contrary-to-duty imperatives and deontic logic. *Analysis* 24:33–36.

Dung, P. M. (1993). An argumentation semantics for logic programming with explicit negation. In *Proceedings of the Tenth Logic Programming Conference*, MIT Press, pages 616–630.

Forrester, J. W. (1984). Gentle murder, or the adverbial Samaritan. *Journal of Philosophy* 81:193–197.

Gabbay, D. (1991). Labelled deductive systems. *Technical report, Centrum fur Informations und Sprachverarbeitung*, Universität Munchen.

Gärdenfors, P. D. (1988). *Knowledge in Flux*. MIT Press, Cambridge.

Geffner, H. and Pearl, J. (1992). Conditional entailment: bridging two approaches to default reasoning. *Artificial Intelligence* 53:209–244.

Hansson, B. (1971). An analysis of some deontic logics. In Hiplinen (ed.), *Deontic Logic: Introductory and Systematic Readings*, D. Reidel Publishing Company, Dordrecht, Holland, pages 121–147.

Hansson, S. O. (1990). Preference-based deontic logic (PDL). *Journal of Philosophical Logic* 19:75–93.

Horty, J. F. (1993). Deontic logic as founded in nonmonotonic logic. *Annals of Mathematics and Artificial Intelligence* 9:69–91.

Jennings, R. E. (1974). A utilitarian semantics for deontic logic. *Journal of Philosophical Logic* 3:445–465.

Kraus, S., Lehmann, D. and Magidor, M. (1990). Nonmonotonic reasoning, preferential models and cumulative logics. *Artificial Intelligence* 44:167–207.

Levesque, H. J. (1984). A logic of implicit and explicit belief. In *Proceedings of the National Conference on Artificial Intelligence*, pages 198–202.

Levesque, H. J. (1990). All I know: A study in autoepistemic logic. *Artificial Intelligence* 42:263–309.

Lewis, D. (1974). Semantic analysis for dyadic deontic logic. In Stunland (ed.), *Logical Theory and Semantical Analysis* D. Reidel Publishing Company, Dordrecht, Holland, pages 1–14.

Loewer, B. and Belzer, M. (1983). Dyadic deontic detachment. *Synthese* 54:295–318.

Makinson, D. (1993). Five faces of minimality. *Studia Logica* 52:339–379.

McCarty, L. T. (1994). Defeasible deontic reasoning. *Fundamenta Informaticae* 21:125–148.

Morreau, M. (1996). Prima facie and seeming duties. *Studia Logica* 57:47–71.

Mott, P. L. (1973). On Chisholm's paradox. *Journal of Philosophical Logic* 2.

Pearl, J. (1988). *Probabilistic Reasoning in Intelligent Systems*. Morgan Kaufmann, Los Altos, CA.

Pearl, J. (1990). System Z: A natural ordering of defaults with tractable applications to default reasoning. In M. Vardi (ed.), *Proceedings of Theoretical Aspects of Reasoning about Knowledge*, San Mateo, Morgan Kaufmann, pages 121–135.

Pearl, J. (1993). A logic of pragmatic obligation. In *Proceedings of Uncertainty in Artificial Intelligence*,.

Powers, L. (1967). Some deontic logicians. *Noûs* 1:381–400.

Prakken, H. and Sartor, G. (1995). On the relation between legal language and legal argument: assumptions, applicability and dynamic properties. In *Proceedings of the Fifth International Conference on Artificial Intelligence and Law,* ACM Press, pages 1–9.

Prakken, H. and Sergot, M. J. (1996). Contrary-to-duty obligations. *Studia Logica* 57:91–115.

Prakken, H. and Sergot, M. J. (1997). Dyadic deontic logic and contrary-to-duty obligations. In Nute, D. (ed.), *This volume.*

Reiter, R. (1980). A logic for default reasoning. *Artificial Intelligence* 13:81–132.

Ross, D. (1930). *The Right and the Good.* Oxford University Press.

Ryu, Y. U. and Lee, R. M. (1993). Defeasible deontic reasoning: A logic programming model. In Meyer and Wieringa (eds.), *Deontic Logic in Computer Science: Normative System Specification,* John Wiley & Sons, pages 225–241.

Smith, T. (1993). Violation of norms. In *Proceedings of the Fourth International Conference on AI and Law,* ACM, New York, pages 60–65.

Tan, S.-W. and Pearl, J. (1994). Specification and evaluation of preferences under uncertainty. In *Proceedings of the Fourth International Conference on Principles of Knowledge Representation and Reasoning,* pages 530–539.

Tan, Y.-H. and van der Torre, L. W. N. (1994). DIODE: Deontic logic based on diagnosis from first principles. In *Proceedings of the Workshop 'Artificial normative reasoning' of the Eleventh European Conference on Artificial Intelligence,* Amsterdam.

Tan, Y.-H. and van der Torre, L. W. N. (1994). Representing deontic reasoning in a diagnostic framework. In *Proceedings of the Workshop on Legal Applications of Logic Programming of the Eleventh International Conference on Logic Programming,.*

Tan, Y.-H. and van der Torre, L. W. N. (1995). Why defeasible deontic logic needs a multi preference semantics. In *Proceedings of the Symbolic and Quantitative Approaches to Reasoning and Uncertainty,* Springer Verlag, pages 412–419.

Tan, Y.-H. and van der Torre, L. W. N. (1996). How to combine ordering and minimizing in a deontic logic based on preferences. In *Deontic Logic, Agency and Normative Systems. Proceedings of the Third Workshop on Deontic Logic in Computer Science,* Springer Verlag, pages 216–232.

Thomason, R. (1981). Deontic logic as founded on tense logic. In R. Hilpinen (ed.), *New Studies in Deontic Logic,* D. Reidel, pages 165–176.

Thomason, R. and Horty, R. (1996). Nondeterministic action and dominance: foundations for planning and qualitative decision. In *Proceedings of the Sixth Conference on Theoretical Aspects of Rationality and Knowledge,* Morgan Kaufmann, pages 229–250.

Tomberlin, J. E. (1981). Contrary-to-duty imperatives and conditional obligation. *Noûs* 16:357–375.

van der Torre, L. W. N. (1994). Violated obligations in a defeasible deontic logic. In *Proceedings of the Eleventh European Conference on Artificial Intelligence,* John Wiley & Sons, pages 371–375.

van der Torre, L. W. N. and Tan, Y.-H. (1995). Cancelling and overshadowing: two types of defeasibility in defeasible deontic logic. In *Proceedings of the Fourteenth International Joint Conference on Artificial Intelligence,* Morgan Kaufman.

van der Torre, L. W. N. and Tan, Y.-H. (1996). Contextual obligations. *Technical Report 96-04-01,* EURIDIS, Erasmus University Rotterdam.

van Eck, J. (1982). A system of temporally relative modal and deontic predicate logic and its philosophical applications. *Logique et Analyse* 25:249–290 and 339–381.

von Wright, G. H. (1951). Deontic logic. *Mind* 60:1–15.

von Wright, G. H. (1963). *The logic of preference.* Edinburgh University Press.

von Wright, G. H. (1968). *An Essay on Deontic Logic and the General Theory of Action.* North-Holland Publishing Company, Amsterdam.

Vreeswijk, G. (1993). *Studies in Defeasible Argumentation*. PhD thesis, Free University Amsterdam.

Y.U. RYU AND R.M. LEE

DEONTIC LOGIC VIEWED AS DEFEASIBLE REASONING

1. INTRODUCTION

The notion of defeasibility in normative reasoning has been discussed by legal philosophers such as Gardner (1987), Hart (1948, 1958), and MacCormick (1974). For instance, MacCormick, in his 1974 article and also in an unpublished research note "Defeasibility in Law and Logic," stated that an "institutional fact," supporting the validity of a certain legal consequence, is the "ordinarily necessary and presumptively sufficient conditions" of the consequence and thus may be "subject to some kind of invalidating intervention" that brings about its defeasance. Similarly, Gardner (1987) observed "defeasibility of legal consequences." Alchourrón and Makinson (1981) proposed hierarchical reasoning about norms, which showed defeasibility aspects of norms. Ross (1930) distinguished "prima facie norms" and "actual norms," in which a prima facie norm becomes an actual norm after "all things are considered" and there is no reason to rebut it (Bonevac, 1987).

On the other hand, deontic logic, as logic of normative systems, has evolved as a special form of modal logic. Monadic deontic logic is viewed as modal logic without the axiom of necessity (Montague, 1960) or with a weak version of the axiom of necessity (von Wright, 1951; Hansson, 1969; Føllesdal and Hilpinen, 1971). However, monadic deontic logic is known to suffer various logical paradoxes, especially contrary-to-duty imperative paradoxes (Chisholm, 1963; Åqvist, 1967; Føllesdal and Hilpinen, 1971). An effort to resolve paradoxes of deontic logic leads to the formulation of deontic statements as conditionals (von Wright, 1964, 1965; Hansson, 1969; van Fraassen, 1972; Greenspan, 1975) and the study of relationships between deontic conditionals and counterfactuals (Lewis, 1973; Decew, 1981), resulting in dyadic deontic logic. Dyadic deontic logic resolves paradoxes of monadic deontic logic, but does not address rather practical issues of the existence of "unresolvable ethical conflicts" which are "conflicts between what ought to be for one reason and what ought to be for another reason" that cannot be practically resolved (van Fraassen, 1973, p. 8).

Founded on the same conceptual ground as earlier studies of legal philosophy and normative systems, augmentation of deontic logic with defeasible reasoning has been proposed as a way to resolve paradoxes of deontic logic and deal with unresolvable conflicts (Belzer, 1987; Ryu and Lee, 1991; McCarty, 1992; Horty, 1993). A common drawback to these approaches is that the defeasibility of only a single conflicting obligation is considered, but

D. Nute (ed.), Defeasible Deontic Logic, 123–137.
© 1997 Kluwer Academic Publishers. Printed in the Netherlands.

not a group of obligations jointly resulting in a conflicting outcome. Another drawback is that these approaches do not properly deal with "the problem of consistency of contrary-to-duty structures" and often confuse defeasibility with violability (Prakken and Sergot, 1994).

In this paper, we propose another form of defeasible deontic reasoning. Our goal is to build a practical deontic reasoning system that finds enforceable, fulfilled, and violated obligations in a given situation. We adopt Nute's (1985, 1987) specificity-based defeasible logic to address the defeasibility among conflicting deontic modes. We also apply the idea of default extensions (Reiter, 1980) in order to deal with situations in the presence of unresolvable deontic conflicts. Similarly to Horty's (1993) system but differently from others, we take a non-modal approach to deontic reasoning. In addition, we address conflicts between obligations and permissions and defeasance among more than two conflicting deontic conditionals, which are missing in Horty's system.

2. PREFERENCE ON DEONTIC CONDITIONALS

A *deontic conditional* is either $\phi \Rightarrow \psi$ or $\phi \rightsquigarrow \psi$, where ϕ and ψ are first order formulas. We assume that all free variables occurring in a deontic conditional are universally quantified. Especially, $\phi \Rightarrow \psi$ is called a *conditional obligation* and $\phi \rightsquigarrow \psi$ a *conditional permission*. That is, $\phi \Rightarrow \psi$ can be intuitively read that "ψ is obligatory if ϕ"; and $\phi \rightsquigarrow \psi$ can be read that "ψ is permitted if ϕ." We will often use a meta-notation $\phi \gg \psi$ denoting either $\phi \Rightarrow \psi$ or $\phi \rightsquigarrow \psi$.

Let us define a *deontic theory* as a triple:

$$\mathbf{D} = \langle D, W, F \rangle$$

where D is a set of deontic conditionals, W is a set of first order formulas of necessary facts, and F is a set of literals of contingent facts,[1] such that $W \cup F$ is consistent in first order logic.

In deontic logic, the consistency of deontic formulas is defined as follows (Føllesdal and Hilpinen, 1971):

$\{\bigcirc\psi_1, \bigcirc\psi_2, \ldots, \bigcirc\psi_{n-1}, \neg\bigcirc\neg\psi_n\}$ is consistent only if $\{\psi_1, \psi_2, \ldots, \psi_n\}$ is consistent.

Borrowing this definition of consistency of deontic formulas, we define the notion of competition among deontic conditionals.

Definition 2.1

Given a deontic theory $\mathbf{D} = \langle D, W, F \rangle$, a set of deontic conditionals:

$$C = \{\phi_1 \Rightarrow \psi_1, \ \phi_2 \Rightarrow \psi_2, \ \ldots, \ \phi_{n-1} \Rightarrow \psi_{n-1}, \ \phi_n \gg \psi_n\} \subseteq D$$

---

[1]The distinction between necessary facts and contingent facts is borrowed from Poole (1985). They are often called rules and facts (Nute, 1985) and background and evidence (Geffner, 1992).

is called *competing* in $W \cup F$ if and only if $W \cup F \nvdash_{FL} \neg \psi_i$ for $i = 1, 2,$ $\ldots, n$, $W \cup F \cup \{\psi_1, \psi_2, \ldots, \psi_n\}$ is inconsistent, and there does not exist

$$\{\phi'_1 \gg \psi'_1, \phi'_2 \gg \psi'_2, \ldots, \phi'_m \gg \psi'_m\} \subset C$$

such that $W \cup F \cup \{\psi'_1, \psi'_2, \ldots, \psi'_m\}$ is inconsistent. ∎

An important observation of Definition 2.1 is that if a set of deontic conditionals is competing, none of its subset is competing. Note, $\phi \rightsquigarrow \psi$ and $\phi \rightsquigarrow \neg\psi$ are not competing. This is from the intuition that permission of ψ and waiver of ψ (i.e., permission of $\neg\psi$) are not contradictory.

Competing deontic conditionals may potentially lead to deontic conflicts. The first step toward the resolution of logically avoidable deontic conflicts is to define a preference relation over deontic conditionals (cf., Alchourrón and Makinson, 1981). We adopt *specificity* (Nute, 1985, 1987) as the preference ordering criterion. Deontic conditional $\phi \gg \psi$ is preferable to deontic conditional $\phi' \gg \psi'$ if they are competing and ϕ is more specific than ϕ'. More generally, $\phi \gg \psi$ is preferable to a set of deontic conditionals $C = \{\phi_i \gg \psi_i \mid i = 1, 2, \ldots, n\}$ if $\{\phi \gg \psi\} \cup C$ is competing and ϕ is more specific than $\bigwedge_{i=1}^n \phi_i$; similarly C is preferable to $\phi \gg \psi$ if $\{\phi \gg \psi\} \cup C$ is competing and $\bigwedge_{i=1}^n \phi_i$ is more specific than ϕ. We formally define the preference relation as follows.

Definition 2.2
For a deontic theory $\mathbf{D} = \langle D, W, F \rangle$, suppose there exist $\phi \gg \psi \in D$ and $C = \{\phi_i \gg \psi_i \mid i = 1, 2, \ldots, n\} \subset D$ such that $\{\phi \gg \psi\} \cup C$ is competing in $W \cup F$, $W \cup F \vdash_{FL} \phi$, and $W \cup F \vdash_{FL} \phi_i$ $(i = 1, 2, \ldots, n)$, where $\vdash_{FL}$ denotes the deduction of first order logic. If $W \cup \{\phi\} \vdash_{FL} \phi_i$ $(i = 1, 2, \ldots, n)$ and $W \cup \{\phi_i \mid i = 1, 2, \ldots, n\} \nvdash_{FL} \phi$, then $\phi \gg \psi$ is *preferable* to C; if $W \cup \{\phi\} \nvdash_{FL} \phi_i$ $(i = 1, 2, \ldots, n)$ and $W \cup \{\phi_i \mid i = 1, 2, \ldots, n\} \vdash_{FL} \phi$, then C is *preferable* to $\phi \gg \psi$. ∎

We will use the preference relation to formulate the defeasance of deontic conditionals, which is included in the establishment of deontic bases in Definition 3.1 and formally defined in Definition 3.9.

Conditional obligation $\phi \Rightarrow \psi$ is called a *contrary-to-duty imperative* of conditional obligation $\phi' \Rightarrow \psi'$ if $\phi \supset \neg\psi'$. Prakken and Sergot (1994) observed that an obligation should not be defeated by its contrary-to-duty imperative; otherwise, the obligation is never violated. The proposed defeasible deontic reasoning prohibits such defeasance. The following theorem shows that a contrary-to-duty imperative of an obligation is not preferable to the obligation, even though they are competing.

Theorem 2.3
Suppose $\mathbf{D} = \langle D, W, F \rangle$ is a deontic theory and $\{\phi \gg \psi\} \cup C \subseteq D$ is competing in $W \cup F$. For some $\{\phi_1 \gg \psi_1, \ldots, \phi_k \gg \psi_k\} \subseteq C$, if

$W \vdash_{FL} \phi \supset \neg \bigwedge_{i=1}^{k} \psi_i$, then neither $\phi \gg \psi$ is preferable to C nor C is preferable to $\phi \gg \psi$.

Proof. Let $C = \{\phi_1 \gg \psi_1, \ldots, \phi_n \gg \psi_n\}$, where $n \geq k$. Because $\{\phi \gg \psi\} \cup C$ is competing in $W \cup F$, $W \cup F \nvdash_{FL} \neg\psi$ and $W \cup F \nvdash_{FL} \neg\psi_i$ $(i = 1, 2, \ldots, n)$. *Assume* $W \cup F \vdash_{FL} \phi$. Then $W \vdash_{FL} \phi \supset \neg \bigwedge_{i=1}^{k} \psi_i$ implies $W \cup F \vdash_{PL} \neg\psi_i$ for some $i \in \{1, 2, \ldots, n\}$. This contradicts the assumption. Thus, $W \cup F \nvdash_{FL} \phi$, which does not satisfy one of preference conditions of Definition 2.2. That is, neither $\phi \gg \psi$ is preferable to C nor C is preferable to $\phi \gg \psi$.   ∎

For example, suppose deontic theory **D** is given as follows:

$$D = \{\top \Rightarrow \neg p, \ p \Rightarrow q\}$$
$$W = \{q \supset p\}$$
$$F = \{p\}.$$

$p \Rightarrow q$ is a contrary-to-duty imperative of $\top \Rightarrow \neg p$. The former is not preferable to the latter. Similarly, suppose deontic theory **D** is given as follows:

$$D = \{\top \Rightarrow p, \ \top \Rightarrow \neg p \vee q, \ \neg p \Rightarrow \neg q\}$$
$$W = \emptyset$$
$$F = \{\neg p\}.$$

$\neg p \Rightarrow \neg q$ is a contrary-to-duty imperative of $\top \Rightarrow p$. $\neg p \Rightarrow \neg q$ is not preferable to $\{\top \Rightarrow p, \ \top \Rightarrow \neg p \vee q\}$.

A property of the preference relation, formally stated in Lemma 2.4, is that if deontic conditional δ is preferable to set C of deontic conditionals, then for every $\delta' \in C$, $\{\delta\} \cup (C \setminus \{\delta'\})$ is preferable to δ'. This property is an important basis in the claim of consistency in the proposed defeasible deontic reasoning.

Lemma 2.4
Suppose $\mathbf{D} = \langle D, W, F \rangle$ is a deontic theory. If $\phi \gg \psi \in D$ is preferable to $C = \{\phi_i \gg \psi_i \mid i = 1, 2, \ldots, n\} \subset D$, then for every $\phi_i \gg \psi_i \in C$, $\{\phi \gg \psi\} \cup (C \setminus \{\phi_i \gg \psi_i\})$ is preferable to $\phi_i \gg \psi_i$.

Proof. Let $C = \{\phi_1 \gg \psi_1, \ldots, \phi_n \gg \psi_n\}$. If $W \cup \{\phi\} \vdash_{FL} \phi_i$ $(i = 1, 2, \ldots, n)$ and $W \cup \{\phi_1, \ldots, \phi_n\} \nvdash_{FL} \phi$, then for every ϕ_i, $W \cup \{\phi, \phi_1, \ldots, \phi_{i-1}, \phi_{i+1}, \ldots, \phi_n\} \vdash_{FL} \phi_i$ and $W \cup \{\phi_i\} \nvdash_{FL} \phi$. Thus, by Definition 2.2, $\{\phi \gg \psi\} \cup (C \setminus \{\phi_i \gg \psi_i\})$ is preferable to $\phi_i \gg \psi_i$.   ∎

3. DEONTIC BASES AND EXTENSIONS

Given a deontic theory, we define a deontic base as a maximal set of deontic conditionals that are not competing after all things are considered.

Definition 3.1 (Deontic Base)
Suppose $\mathbf{D} = \langle D, W, F \rangle$ is a deontic theory. Define Δ as a maximal subset of D such that for every $\phi \gg \psi \in \Delta$:

1. $W \cup F \vdash_{FL} \phi$,
2. $W \cup F \cup \{\psi\}$ is consistent, and
3. there does not exist $C \subseteq \Delta$ such that $C \cup \{\phi \gg \psi\}$ is competing but $\phi \gg \psi$ is not preferable to C.

We call Δ a *deontic base* of deontic theory $\mathbf{D} = \langle D, W, F \rangle$. ∎

For example, suppose deontic theory $\mathbf{D}$ is:

$$D = \{\top \Rightarrow p,\; r \Rightarrow \neg p \vee q,\; r \wedge s \Rightarrow \neg q\}$$
$$W = \emptyset$$
$$F = \{r, s\}$$

Let $\succ$ denote the preference relation. We can find the following preferences on deontic conditionals:

$$r \wedge s \Rightarrow \neg q \succ \{\top \Rightarrow p,\; r \Rightarrow \neg p \vee q\}$$
$$\{\top \Rightarrow p,\; r \wedge s \Rightarrow \neg q\} \succ r \Rightarrow \neg p \vee q$$
$$\{r \Rightarrow \neg p \vee q,\; r \wedge s \Rightarrow \neg q\} \succ \top \Rightarrow p.$$

(Observe that the above preferences confirm Lemma 2.4.) There exist two deontic bases of $\mathbf{D}$:

$$\Delta_1 = \{\top \Rightarrow p,\; r \wedge s \Rightarrow \neg q\}$$
$$\Delta_2 = \{r \Rightarrow \neg p \vee q,\; r \wedge s \Rightarrow \neg q\}.$$

A deontic base can be intuitively understood as a *maximal* set of conditional obligations (together with compatible permissions) that can be fulfilled *without conflicts*. Lemma 3.2 and Theorem 3.3 verify this intuition.

Lemma 3.2
No subset of a deontic base is competing.

Proof. Suppose Δ is a deontic base of deontic theory $\mathbf{D} = \langle D, W, F \rangle$. *Assume* there exists $C \subseteq \Delta$ such that C is competing. By Definition 3.1, for some $\phi \gg \psi \in C$, $\phi \gg \psi$ is preferable to $C' = C \setminus \{\phi \gg \psi\}$. By Lemma 2.4, for every $\phi_i \gg \psi_i \in C'$, $C \setminus \{\phi_i \gg \psi_i\}$ is preferable to $\phi_i \gg \psi_i$. Therefore, by Definition 3.1 again, $\phi_i \gg \psi_i \notin \Delta$. This contradicts the assumption. ∎

Theorem 3.3
Suppose Δ_1 and Δ_2 are deontic bases of deontic theory $\mathbf{D} = \langle D, W, F \rangle$. If $\Delta_1 \subseteq \Delta_2$, then $\Delta_1 = \Delta_2$.

Proof. *Assume* $\Delta_1 \subset \Delta_2$; that is, there exists $\phi \gg \psi \in \Delta_2$ such that $\phi \gg \psi \notin \Delta_1$. By Definition 3.1, $\phi \gg \psi \notin \Delta_1$ implies that there exists $C \subseteq \Delta_1$ such that $\{\phi \gg \psi\} \cup C$ is competing. By Lemma 3.2, $\{\phi \gg \psi\} \cup C \subseteq \Delta_2$ is not competing. This is contradictory. Therefore, $\Delta_1 = \Delta_2$. ∎

What is implied by Lemma 3.2 and Theorem 3.3 is that if there exist two or more deontic bases of a deontic theory, the union of these deontic bases leads to inconsistency. This is proved in the next theorem.

Theorem 3.4

Suppose Δ_1 and Δ_2 are distinct deontic bases of $\mathbf{D} = \langle D, W, F \rangle$. Then there exists $C \subseteq \Delta_1 \cup \Delta_2$ that is competing.

Proof. Because Δ_1 and Δ_2 are distinct, there exists $\phi \gg \psi \in \Delta_1$ such that $\phi \gg \psi \notin \Delta_2$. By Definition 3.1, $\phi \gg \psi \notin \Delta_2$ implies that there exists $C' \subseteq \Delta_2$ such that $C = \{\phi \gg \psi\} \cup C'$ is competing, where $C \subseteq \Delta_1 \cup \Delta_2$. ∎

Now, we build a deontic extension for a deontic theory as a set of first order formulas closed under the deduction obtained from the deontic base.

Definition 3.5 (Deontic Extension)

Suppose $\mathbf{D} = \langle D, W, F \rangle$ is a deontic theory and Δ is a deontic base of $\mathbf{D}$. A *deontic extension* for $\mathbf{D}$ is

$$\mathcal{E} = \mathrm{Cn}(W \cup F \cup \{\psi_i \mid \text{for all } \phi_i \Rightarrow \psi_i \in \Delta\}),$$

where 'Cn' is the consequence operator of first order logic. We specifically call Δ the deontic base of deontic extension $\mathcal{E}$. ∎

For a deontic extension is built with a deontic base that does not contain competing deontic conditionals, it should be consistent. It is stated in Theorem 3.6, which is easily proved due to Lemma 3.2.

Theorem 3.6

Every deontic extension for a deontic theory is consistent.

Proof. Immediately from Lemma 3.2. ∎

What one can intuitively infer from Theorem 3.6 is that if there are no conflicting deontic conditionals, there should be exactly one deontic extension for the deontic theory. The following theorem formally proves it.

Theorem 3.7

Suppose $\mathbf{D} = \langle D, W, F \rangle$ is a deontic theory. If D's subset $\{\phi \gg \psi \in D \mid W \cup F \vdash_{FL} \psi\}$ is not competing, then $\mathbf{D}$ has a unique deontic extension.

Proof. Let $C = \{\phi \gg \psi \in D \mid W \cup F \vdash_{FL} \phi \text{ and } W \cup F \nvdash_{FL} \neg\psi\}$. Because for every deontic conditional $\phi \gg \psi \in C$ there does not exist $C' \subseteq C$ such that $\{\phi \gg \psi\} \cup C'$ is competing, by Definition 3.1, C is a deontic base of $\mathbf{D}$. By Theorems 3.4 and 3.3, C is the only deontic base of $\mathbf{D}$. Thus $\mathrm{Cn}(W \cup F \cup \{\psi_i \mid \phi_i \Rightarrow \psi_i \in C\})$ is the only deontic extension for $\mathbf{D}$. ∎

A deontic base is a maximal set of conflict-free deontic conditionals and a deontic extension is the result of fulfilling all obligations of the deontic base. With deontic bases and extensions, we can determine three categories of obligations classified by the status of fulfillment: an enforceable obligation that has not been fulfilled yet; a fulfilled obligation; and a violated obligation. Also, we can observe if a deontic conditional is defeated.

Definition 3.8 (Obligation)

Suppose $\mathbf{D} = \langle D, W, F \rangle$ is a deontic theory.

Enforceable obligation: The obligation of ψ is *enforceable* if there exists deontic extension $\mathcal{E}$ for **D** such that $\psi \in \mathcal{E}$ and $W \cup F \nvdash_{FL} \psi$.

Fulfilled obligation: The obligation of ψ is *fulfilled* if there exists deontic base Δ of **D** such that $\{ \psi_i \mid$ for all $\phi_i \Rightarrow \psi_i \in \Delta \} \vdash_{FL} \psi$ and $W \cup F \vdash_{FL} \psi$.

Violated obligation: The obligation of ψ is *violated* if there exists $\phi \Rightarrow \psi \in D$ such that $W \cup F \vdash_{FL} \phi$, $W \cup F \vdash_{FL} \neg\psi$, and for each deontic base Δ of **D**, there does not exist $C \subseteq \Delta$ such that $\{\phi \Rightarrow \psi\} \cup C$ is competing in $W \cup F'$ but $\phi \Rightarrow \psi$ is not preferable to C. (F' is the maximal subset of F such that $W \cup F' \nvdash_{FL} \neg\psi$.)   ∎

Definition 3.9 (Defeasance)

Suppose Δ is the deontic base of deontic extension $\mathcal{E}$ for $\mathbf{D} = \langle D, W, F \rangle$. Deontic conditional $\phi \gg \psi \in D$ is called *defeated* by $C \subseteq \Delta$ in $\mathcal{E}$ if $W \cup F \vdash_{FL} \phi$, $\phi \gg \psi \notin \Delta$, $\{\phi \gg \psi\} \cup C$ is competing in $W \cup F'$, and C is preferable to $\phi \gg \psi$. (F' is the maximal subset of F such that $W \cup F' \nvdash_{FL} \neg\psi$.)
∎

If conditional obligation $\phi \Rightarrow \psi$ is defeated in every deontic extension, there is no obligation of ψ.

Once a deontic conditional is defeated, it is preempted by its defeater and should not defeat other deontic conditionals (cf., Nute, 1985, 1987). The proposed defeasible deontic reasoning supports it.

Theorem 3.10 (Preemption)

Let $\mathbf{D} = \langle D, W, F \rangle$ be a deontic theory. Suppose $C \subseteq D$ is preferable to $\phi \gg \psi \in D$. If $\phi' \gg \psi' \in C$ is defeated in deontic extension $\mathcal{E}$ for **D**, then $\phi \gg \psi$ is not defeated by C in $\mathcal{E}$.

Proof. Let Δ be the deontic base of $\mathcal{E}$. If $\phi' \gg \psi' \in C$ is defeated in $\mathcal{E}$, $\phi' \gg \psi' \notin \Delta$; that is, $C \nsubseteq \Delta$. Thus, $\phi \gg \psi \in \Delta$ is not defeated by C in $\mathcal{E}$. ∎

In our understanding of consistency of deontic modes which is defined in terms of consistency of first order formulas, $\neg\bigcirc\neg\psi$ is viewed as a weak permission, often called *permissibility* (Hintikka, 1970), in that it is compatible with, or does not contradict, all obligations under consideration (Føllesdal and Hilpinen, 1971). The conditional permission $\phi \rightsquigarrow \psi$ adopts this notion of weak permission.

Notice, this weak permission is not as weak as another form of permission that could be defined, with the close world assumption of database (Reiter, 1978) or the 'negation as finite failure' rule of logic programming (Clark, 1978): that is, ψ is permitted if the obligation of $\neg\psi$ does not exist. Whereas this weak permission is not to defeat obligation, we view the permission defined as $\neg\bigcirc\neg\psi$ can defeat obligation. The following definition shows how to determine the permission of a certain thing.

Definition 3.11 (Permission)

Suppose $\mathbf{D} = \langle D, W, F \rangle$ is a deontic theory. ψ is *permissible* if for some deontic extension $\mathcal{E}$ of **D** and its base Δ, either $\psi \in (\text{Cn}(\mathcal{E} \cup \{\psi_i\}) \setminus \text{Cn}(W \cup F))$ for some $\phi_i \rightsquigarrow \psi_i \in \Delta$ or there exists $\phi \gg \psi \in D$ such that $W \cup F \vdash_{FL} \phi$ and $\phi \gg \psi$ is not defeated in $\mathcal{E}$.

Conditional permission $\phi \rightsquigarrow \psi$, in the establishment of deontic bases, is similar to a defeater of Nute's (1985, 1987) defeasible logic and an under-cutting defeater of Pollock's (1987, 1991) defeasible reasoning, in that ϕ of $\phi \rightsquigarrow \psi$ can be a reason to block the inference of the obligation of $\neg\psi$ from $\phi' \Rightarrow \neg\psi$, or to deny the connection between ϕ' and the obligation of $\neg\psi$, but ϕ cannot be a reason to infer the obligation of ψ. Their differences are: First, conditional permissions $\phi \rightsquigarrow \psi$ and $\phi \rightsquigarrow \neg\psi$ are not competing, but defeaters with the same structures are competing. Second, a conditional permission preempts a conditional obligation when the latter is defeated by the former, but a defeater does not preempt a defeasible rule (Nute, 1994). (Note, the earlier defeasible logic (Nute, 1985, 1987) allows preemption by a defeater, but it is corrected in the recent development of defeasible logic (esp., Nute, 1994).)

We now conclude this section with two examples.

Example 1 (Chisholm 1963; Føllesdal and Hilpinen, 1971)

① You should go to the assistance of your neighbors. $\top \Rightarrow p$
② Going to the assistance of them without telling them you are coming is prohibited. $\top \Rightarrow \neg(p \wedge \neg q)$
③ If you don't go, you should not tell them you are coming. $\neg p \Rightarrow \neg q$
④ You don't go. $\neg p$ ■

There exists only one deontic base $\{②, ③\}$, from which we obtain the only deontic extension $\mathcal{E} = \text{Cn}(\{\neg p, \neg(p \wedge \neg q), \neg q\})$.[2] Observe that the obligation of p from ① is violated by ④.

Example 2 (Prakken and Sergot, 1994)

① There should be no fence. $\top \Rightarrow \neg p$
② If the cottage is by the sea, there may be a fence. $q \rightsquigarrow p$
③ The cottage is by the sea. q
④ There is a fence. p ■

① is defeated by ② and there is no obligation of $\neg p$. That is, no obligation is violated.

4. OTHER DEFEASANCE CRITERIA

Though we adopted specificity as the principal criterion of preference on deontic conditionals (Definition 2.2) and thus defeasance, it is possible to

---

[2]Often ② is formulated as $p \Rightarrow q$, instead of $\top \Rightarrow \neg(p \wedge \neg q)$. Then, there exists only one deontic extension $\{\neg p, \neg q\}$ whose deontic base is $\{③\}$. There is no conflict.

adopt other criteria. For instance, in addition to specificity, Loui (1987) uses the amount of supporting evidence as a criterion to determine preferences on defeasible conditionals. Suppose the following defeasible conditionals and first order formulas are given:

$$\phi_1 \Rightarrow \psi, \ \phi_2 \Rightarrow \neg\psi, \ \gamma_1 \Rightarrow \psi_1, \ \gamma_1 \wedge \gamma_2 \Rightarrow \psi_2, \ \gamma_1, \ \gamma_2.$$

The inference of ψ is supported by evidence $E_1 = \gamma_1$ and the inference of $\neg\psi$ by evidence $E_2 = \gamma_1 \wedge \gamma_2$. Suppose $|E_1|$ and E_2 are the sets of all possible worlds in which E_1 and E_2 hold. For $|E_2| \subset |E_1|$, the inference of ψ is blocked. With this, we modify Definition 2.2 as follows.

Definition 2.2'
For a deontic theory $\mathbf{D} = \langle D, W, F \rangle$, suppose there exist $\phi \gg \psi \in D$ and $C = \{ \phi_i \gg \psi_i \mid i = 1, 2, \ldots, n \} \subset D$ such that $\{\phi \gg \psi\} \cup C$ is competing in $W \cup F$, $W \cup F \vdash_{FL} \phi$, and $W \cup F \vdash_{FL} \phi_i$ $(i = 1, 2, \ldots, n)$, where $\vdash_{FL}$ denotes the deduction of first order logic. If for every minimal subset $E' \subseteq F$ such that $W \cup E' \vdash_{FL} \phi'_i$ $(i = 1, 2, \ldots, n)$, there exists a minimal subset $E \subseteq F$ such that $W \cup E \vdash_{FL} \phi$ and $E' \subset E$, then $\phi \gg \psi$ is preferable to C; if for every minimal subset $E \subseteq F$ such that $W \cup E \vdash_{FL} \phi$, there exists a minimal subset $E' \subseteq F$ such that $W \cup E' \vdash_{FL} \phi'_i$ $(i = 1, 2, \ldots, n)$ and $E \subset E'$, then C is preferable to $\phi \gg \psi$. ∎

It can be shown that the replacement of Definition 2.2 by Definition 2.2' satisfies all theorems and lemmas stated and proven previously. It can be also observed and shown that Definition 2.2 and Definition 2.2' are not contradictory. That is, it is never the case that conditional c_1 is preferable to conditional c_2 by Definition 2.2 but c_2 is preferable to c_1 by Definition 2.2'. Thus, we may combine Definition 2.2 and Definition 2.2' and show that it satisfies all previous theorems and lemmas.

Causey's (1994) defeasible reasoning supports different forms of defeasance. Introduced are two types of defeater expressions:

$$\text{defeated}(\psi) \text{ if } \phi$$
$$\text{defeated\_for}(\phi', \psi) \text{ if } \phi' \wedge \phi.$$

We call the first one an absolute defeater and the second one a relative defeater. The absolute defeater says that if ϕ is deducible, block the deduction of ψ; that is, it rebuts the deduction of ψ from any conditional. The relative defeater implements undercutting defeasance; that is, if ϕ is deducible, the deduction of ψ from conditional $\phi' \Rightarrow \psi$ is blocked, or the connection between ϕ' and ψ is denied. This defeasance method can be added to our defeasible deontic reasoning, but it requires some modifications to Definition 3.1.

5. COMPARISON WITH OTHER APPROACHES

Among several defeasible reasoning approaches to deontic reasoning, Ryu and Lee's (1991) and Horty's (1993) systems are non-modal approaches within first order frameworks. In this section, we compare the proposed defeasible deontic reasoning with these two non-modal approaches.

Ryu and Lee's (1991) system implements defeasible deontic reasoning as a variation of logic programming. A program clause is either an indefeasible rule $\phi \rightarrow \psi$ or a defeasible rule $\phi \Rightarrow \psi$,[3] where ϕ is a conjunction of literals and ψ is a literal. A deontic constraint is either $\phi \Rightarrow \text{oblig}(\psi)$, $\phi \Rightarrow \neg\text{oblig}(\psi)$, or commit$(\psi_1, \psi_2)$, where ϕ is a conjunction of literals and ψ, ψ_1, and ψ_2 are literals. $\text{oblig}(\psi)$ corresponds to $\bigcirc\phi$ of deontic logic and commit(ψ_1, ψ_2) to $\bigcirc(\neg\psi_1 \vee \psi_2)$ of deontic logic. Note, commit(ψ_1, ψ_2) is an indefeasible rule with the empty antecedent. A program is a set of rules and facts, where facts are ground literals.

Definition 5.1 (Defeasance)
Suppose P is a program. $\phi \Rightarrow \text{oblig}(\psi_1) \in P$ *defeats* $\phi' \Rightarrow \text{oblig}(\psi_1') \in P$, if $P \vdash_D \phi$, $P \vdash_D \phi'$, ϕ is more specific than ϕ', and either:

- $\psi_1 \wedge \psi_1'$ is inconsistent; or
- there exist commit$(\psi_i, \psi_{i+1}) \in P$ for $i = 1, 2, \ldots, n - 1$ such that $\psi_n \wedge \psi_1'$ is inconsistent; or
- there exist commit$(\psi_j', \psi_{j+1}') \in P$ for $j = 1, 2, \ldots, m - 1$ such that $\psi_1 \wedge \psi_m'$ is inconsistent; or
- there exist commit$(\psi_i, \psi_{i+1}) \in P$ for $i = 1, 2, \ldots, n-1$ and commit$(\psi_j', \psi_{j+1}') \in P$ for $j = 1, 2, \ldots, m - 1$ such that $\psi_n \wedge \psi_m'$ is inconsistent,

where $\vdash_D$ denotes Nute's (1985, 1987) defeasible reasoning. The same defeasibility conditions hold for $\phi \Rightarrow \text{oblig}(\psi_1)$ and $\phi' \Rightarrow \neg\text{oblig}(\neg\psi_1')$, and for $\phi \Rightarrow \neg\text{oblig}(\neg\psi_1)$ and $\phi' \Rightarrow \text{oblig}(\psi_1')$. ∎

Definition 5.2 (Defeasible Deontic Reasoning)
Suppose P is a program. $P \vdash_{DDR} \text{oblig}(\psi)$ if either:

- there exists $\phi \Rightarrow \text{oblig}(\psi) \in P$ such that $P \vdash_D \phi$ and $\phi \Rightarrow \text{oblig}(\psi)$ is not defeated; or
- there exists $\phi \Rightarrow \text{oblig}(\psi_1) \in P$ such that $P \vdash_D \phi$ and $\phi \Rightarrow \text{oblig}(\psi_1)$ is not defeated and there exist commit$(\psi_i, \psi_{i+1}) \in P$ $i = 1, 2, \ldots, n - 1$ such that $\psi_n = \psi$.

The same conditions hold for $P \vdash_{DDR} \neg\text{oblig}(\neg\psi)$. ∎

The fundamental ideas of Ryu and Lee's approach are very similar to those of proposed defeasible deontic reasoning in this paper. Both are non-modal approaches based on Nute's (1985, 1987) defeasible reasoning with specificity. However, the system proposed in this paper overcomes some limitations of Ryu and Lee's approach. The first one is the difference in handling violated obligations. Chisholm's (1963) contrary-to-duty imperative situation of Example 1 is expressed as:

---

[3]Ryu and Lee (1991) viewed that a defeasible rule was a kind of counterfactual; but this was mistaken.

① $\top \Rightarrow \text{oblig}(p)$
② $\text{commit}(p, q)$
③ $\neg p \Rightarrow \text{oblig}(\neg q)$
④ $\neg p$

By Definition 5.1, ③ defeats ①, by which the consistency of the situation is maintained. Here it is assumed that (i) the violated obligation (e.g., ①) can be used in the deduction of $\text{oblig}(q)$ (e.g., with ②), which contradicts ③; and (ii) such inconsistency is resolved by defeating the violated obligation (e.g., ①). A problem of this analysis is that the notions of defeasance and violation are mixed and it is difficult to say if ① is violated or defeated.

Prakken and Sergot's (1994) contrary-to-duty imperative scenario (which is a variation of Example 2) shows this problem more clearly.

Example 3

① There should be no fence. $\top \Rightarrow \text{oblig}(\neg p)$
② If there is a fence, it should be white. $p \Rightarrow \text{oblig}(q)$
③ A white fence is a fence. $q \rightarrow p$.
④ There is a fence. p ∎

Due to ③, $\neg p \wedge q$ is inconsistent and by Definition 5.1, ① is defeated by ②. Thus, ④ does not violate ①; this seems counter-intuitive. In the proposed defeasible deontic reasoning, the examples are analyzed as follows. A contrary-to-duty imperative of an obligation does not defeat the obligation. In Example 1, ③ is a contrary-to-duty imperative of ① and thus it does not defeat ①. Instead ① is violated. Further, the obligation of q is not deduced by ① and ②; that is, there is no inconsistency. In Example 3, it is even clearer. ② does not defeat ① because the former is a contrary-to-duty imperative of the latter. That is, ④ violates ① and there is no inconsistency.

The second limitation of Ryu and Lee's approach is that only a restricted form of compound obligations is supported. That is, ψ in $\text{oblig}(\phi)$ must be a literal; the only expression for compound obligations is $\text{commit}(\psi_1, \psi_2)$, which corresponds to $\bigcirc(\neg\psi_1 \vee \psi_2)$ of deontic logic. The proposed defeasible deontic reasoning does not have this restriction. In conditional obligation $\phi \Rightarrow \psi$, ψ can be any compound first order formula.

Horty (1993) defines deontic logic as a system of Reiter's (1980) default logic. Conditional obligation $\bigcirc(\psi/\phi)$ is viewed as a closed normal default $\phi{:}M\psi/\psi$. A deontic context is default theory $\Delta = \langle \Gamma, W \rangle$, where Γ is a set of conditional obligations and W is a first order formula. Horty's system adopts the concept of overriding (van Fraassen, 1973), which is similar to specificity-based defeasance.

Definition 5.3 (Overriding)
Conditional obligation $\bigcirc(\psi_1/\phi_1) \in \Gamma$ is overridden in deontic context $\Delta = \langle \Gamma, W \rangle$ if there exists $\bigcirc(\psi_2/\phi_2) \in \Gamma$ such that:

- $|W| \subseteq |\phi_2| \subseteq |\phi_1|$,
- $W \wedge \psi_1 \wedge \psi_2$ is inconsistent, and
- $W \wedge \psi_2$ is consistent.   ∎

A conditioned extension for a deontic context is a variation of default extension.

Definition 5.4 (Conditioned Extension)
A conditioned extension for $\Delta = \langle \Gamma, W \rangle$ is $\mathcal{E} = \text{Th}(\{W\} \cup \mathcal{F})$, where:

$$\mathcal{F} = \{\psi \mid \bigcirc(\psi/\phi) \in \Gamma, |W| \subseteq |\phi|, \neg\psi \notin \mathcal{E},$$
$$\bigcirc(\psi/\phi) \text{ is not overridden in } \Delta\},$$

where 'Th' denotes the first order consequence operation.   ∎

Horty's system is the first one in which conflicting, but unresolvable, obligations belong to different extensions (in the sense of Reiter's (1980) default logic), the consistency is maintained in every extension, and no deduction is made across different extensions. We adopt Horty's (i.e., Reiter's) idea of multiple extensions as a way to handle unresolvable conflicts, but further extend reasoning about deontic concepts.

We observe several problems in Horty' system, which are properly addressed in the proposed system. First, there is no default corresponding to $\neg\bigcirc(\psi/\phi)$. Thus it fails to deal with a situation in which we have "you ought to do p if ..." and "you may not do p if ...".

Second, when more than two obligations jointly contradict, their defeasibility is not properly supported. That is, overriding of/by deduced obligations is not addressed. For instance, when a deontic context is given as follows:

$$\Gamma = \{\bigcirc(p_1 \vee p_2/\top), \bigcirc(\neg p_1/q), \bigcirc(\neg p_2/q)\}$$
$$W = q,$$

$\bigcirc(p_1 \vee p_2/\top)$ should be overridden by $\bigcirc(\neg p_1/q)$ and $\bigcirc(\neg p_2/q)$, but Definition 5.3 does not support it. Similarly, in a deontic context of:

$$\Gamma = \{\bigcirc(p_1 \vee p_2/q), \bigcirc(\neg p_1/\top), \bigcirc(\neg p_2/\top)\}$$
$$W = q,$$

Horty's system generates three conditioned extensions:

$$\mathcal{E}_1 = \text{Th}(\{r, p_1 \vee p_2, \neg p_1\})$$
$$\mathcal{E}_2 = \text{Th}(\{r, p_2 \vee p_2, \neg p_2\})$$
$$\mathcal{E}_3 = \text{Th}(\{r, \neg p_1, \neg p_2\}).$$

However, we view $\mathcal{E}_3$ should be excluded, because $\bigcirc(\neg(p_1 \vee p_2)/\top)$, deduced from $\bigcirc(\neg p_1/\top)$ and $\bigcirc(\neg p_2/\top)$, is to be overridden by $\bigcirc(p_1 \vee p_2/q)$.

Third, preemption is not supported in Horty's system. Thus, even if an obligation is overridden, it can still override other obligations.

Finally, Horty's overriding conditions do not properly distinguish violation from defeasance. Assume that violation means not fulfilling an obligation that is not overridden. Then, an obligation can be defeated by its contrary-to-duty imperative and thus the primary obligation is never violated; this seems unacceptable (Prakken and Sergot, 1994).

6. CONCLUSION

We proposed a non-modal deontic reasoning viewed as a form of defeasible reasoning. Specificity defines a preference hierarchy for deontic conditionals, which provides a defeasance mechanism of conflicting deontic conditionals. Unresolvable deontic conflicts lead to the establishment of deontic extensions for a deontic theory. Once a deontic extension is established, we apply first order deductions on it. This two-tiered approach simplifies deontic reasoning and maintains consistency in reasoning in the presence of moral dilemmas.

We aimed at the development of a practical deontic reasoning system, which finds enforceable, fulfilled, and violated obligations in a given situation. We view that an obligation is not enforceable in a given situation if it is violated. The enforceability of an obligation should not be confused with the deducibility in the sense of conditional deontic logic. Example 1 can be expressed as $\bigcirc(p/\top)$, $\bigcirc\neg(p \wedge \neg q/\top)$, $\bigcirc(\neg q/\neg p)$, and $\neg p$ in conditional deontic logic, from which $\bigcirc(p/\top)$ is deducible. However, we view the obligation of p is not enforceable. Further, in conditional deontic logic, even if an obligation is violated, it still can be used to deduce other obligations. That is, $\bigcirc(q/\top)$ is deducible from $\bigcirc(p/\top)$ and $\bigcirc\neg(p \wedge \neg q/\top)$ in conditional deontic logic, where $\bigcirc(p/\top)$ is violated by $\neg p$. In the proposed defeasible deontic reasoning, however, the obligation of q does not hold.

Young U. Ryu
Department of Decision Sciences
The University of Texas at Dallas

Ronald M. Lee
Erasmus University Research Institute for
Decision and Information Systems (EURIDIS)
Erasmus University
Rotterdam, The Netherlands

REFERENCES

Alchourrón, C. E. and Makinson, D. (1981). Hierarchies of regulations and their logic. In Hilpinen, R. (ed.), *New Studies in Deontic Logic,* D. Reidel, Dordrecht, The Netherlands, pages 125–148.

Åqvist, L. (1967). Good Samaritans, contrary-to-duty imperatives, and epistemic obligation. *Noûs* 1(4):361–379.

Belzer, M. (1987). Legal reasoning in 3-D. In *Proceedings of the First International Conference on Artificial Intelligence and Law,* Boston, Massachusetts.

Bonevac, D. (1987). *Deduction: Introductory Symbolic Logic.* Mayfield, Palo Alto, California.

Causey, R. L. (1994). EVID: A system for interactive defeasible reasoning. *Decision Support Systems* 11(2):103–131.

Chisholm, R. M. (1963). Contrary-to-duty imperatives and deontic logic. *Analysis* 24(2):33–36.

Clark, K. L. (1978). Negation as failure. In Gallaire, H. and Minker, J. (eds.), *Logic and Data Bases,* Plenum Press, New York, pages 293–322.

Decew, J. W. (1981). Conditional obligation and counterfactual. *Journal of Philosophical Logic* 10(1):55–72.

Føllesdal, D. and Hilpinen, R. (1971). Deontic logic: An introduction. In Hilpinen, R. (ed.), *Deontic Logic: Introductory and Systematic Readings,* D. Reidel, Dordrecht, The Netherlands.

Gardner, A. v. d. L. (1987). *An Artificial Intelligence Approach to Legal Reasoning.* The MIT Press.

Geffner, H. (1992). *Default Reasoning: Causal and Conditional Theories.* The MIT Press.

Greenspan, P. S. (1975). Conditional oughts and hypothetical imperatives. *The Journal of Philosophy* 22:259–276.

Hansson, B. (1969). An analysis of some deontic logics. *Noûs* 3:373–398.

Hart, H. L. A. (1948). The ascription of responsibility and rights. In *Proceedings of the Aristotelian Society.*

Hart, H. L. A. (1958). Positivism and the separation of law and morals. *Harvard Law Review* 71:593–629.

Hintikka, J. (1970). Deontic logic and its philosophical morals. In Hintikka, J. (ed.), *Models for Modalities: Selected Essays,* D. Reidel, Dordrecht, The Netherlands.

Horty, J. F. (1993). Deontic logic as founded in nonmonotonic logic. *Annals of Mathematics and Artificial Intelligence* 9:69–91.

Lewis, D. (1973). *Counterfactuals.* Harvard University Press.

Loui, R. P. (1987). Defeat among arguments: A system of defeasible inference. *Computational Intelligence* 3:100–106.

MacCormick, D. N. (1974). Law as institutional fact. *Law Quarterly Review* 90:102–129.

McCarty, L. T. (1992). Defeasible deontic reasoning. In *Proceedings of the Fourth International Workshop on Nonmonotonic Reasoning,* Plymouth, Vermont, pages 139–147.

Montague, R. (1960). Logical necessity, physical necessity, ethics, and quantifiers. *Inquiry* 4:259–269.

Nute, D. (1985). A non-monotonic logic based on conditional logic. *Research report 01-0007,* Advanced Computational Methods Center, University of Georgia.

Nute, D. (1987). A logic for defeasible reasoning. In *Proceedings of the Twentieth Annual Hawaii International Conference on System Sciences,* Vol. 3, pages 470–477.

Nute, D. (1994). Defeasible logic. In Gabbay, D., Hogger, C., and Robinson, J. (eds.), *Handbook of Logic in Artificial Intelligence and Logic Programming,* Claredon Press, Oxford, Great Britain, Vol. 3, pages 353–395.

Pollock, J. L. (1987). Defeasible reasoning. *Cognitive Science* 11(4):481–518.

Pollock, J. L. (1991). A theory of defeasible reasoning. *International Journal of Intelligent Systems* 6(1):33–54.

Poole, D. (1985). On the comparison of theories: Preferring the most specific explanation. In *Proceedings of the 1985 International Joint Conference on Artificial Intelligence,* Los Angeles, California, pages 144–147.

Prakken, H. and Sergot, M. (1994). Contrary-to-duty imperatives, defeasibility, and violability. In Jones, A. J. I. and Sergot, M. (eds.), *Proceedings of the Second International Workshop on Deontic Logic in Computer Science,* Norwegian Research Center for Computers and Law, Oslo, Norway, pages 296–318.

Reiter, R. (1978). On closed world data bases. In Gallaire, H. and Minker, J. (eds.), *Logic and Data Bases,* Plenum Press, New York, pages 55–76.

Reiter, R. (1980). A logic for default reasoning. *Artificial Intelligence* 13(1/2):81–132.

Ross, W. D. (1930). *The Right and the Good.* Oxford University, New York.

Ryu, Y. U. and Lee, R. M. (1991). Defeasible deontic reasoning: A logic programming approach. In Meyer, J.-J. Ch. and Wieringa, R. J. (eds.), *Proceedings of the First International Workshop on Deontic Logic in Computer Science,* Free University, Amsterdam, The Netherlands, pages 347–363.

van Fraassen, B. C. (1972). The logic of conditional obligation. *Journal of Philosophical Logic* 1(3/4):417–438.

van Fraassen, B. C. (1973). Values and the heart's command. *Journal of Philosophy* 70(1):5–19.

von Wright, G. H. (1951). Deontic logic. *Mind* 60(237):1–15.

von Wright, G. H. (1964). A new system of deontic logic. *Danish Handbook of Philosophy* 1:173–182.

von Wright, G. H. (1965). A correction to a new system of deontic logic. *Danish Handbook of Philosophy* 2:103–107.

MICHAEL MORREAU

REASONS TO THINK AND ACT

1. INTRODUCTION

That a patient has a characteristic symptom is a reason to think he has the condition itself. It is a *prima facie* reason, not a conclusive reason, since it is possible to have the one without the other. Still, where there is no reason to think the patient doesn't have the condition, it will seem that we can suppose he does. Similarly, that you have promised to meet me is a reason for you to do so. It is a *prima facie* reason since it can happen that, in spite of your promise, you don't have the duty to meet me. Still, where there is no reason to think you don't have this duty, it will seem that you ought to meet me.

Asked why he thinks a patient has a condition, a doctor can give his reason: the patient has the symptom. Pushed further he can point to the evidential relation: that the patient has the symptom is a reason to think he has the condition. We seem in some sense to infer the supposition from the reason. And the inference parallels *modus ponens*, with a *reason sentence* – in this case a sentence expressing the evidential relation between symptom and condition – in the role of *if . . . then. . . .*

Here I will follow this parallel between reason sentences and *if . . . then. . .*, borrowing from studies of conditionals to obtain a formal understanding of reasons. This will lead me in section 2 to paraphrase reason sentences in terms of conditionals. It will lead me in section 3 to present a model-theoretic interpretation for these conditionals. And it will lead me, in section 4, to treat inference from reasons as *allowed argument*, a species of defeasible inference involving conditionals. Allowed argument will be treated there in purely syntactic terms as *allowed consequence*; section 5 provides a model-theoretic characterization, *allowed entailment*. In the illustrations throughout I will continue to slip back and forth between reasons to think something and reasons to do something. Though different in their substance, from a formal perspective these two kinds of reasons are similar.

2. REASONS AND CONDITIONALS

Given that the patient has the symptom, the evidential relation between symptom and condition leads us to suppose he has the condition. That would be accounted for if the reason sentence

> That the patient has the symptom is a reason to suppose he has the condition

D. Nute (ed.), Defeasible Deontic Logic, 139–158.
© 1997 Kluwer Academic Publishers. Printed in the Netherlands.

were to entail

> If the patient has the symptom, then we can suppose he has the condition.

For together with the fact that the patient has the symptom, this conditional entails that we can suppose the patient has the condition. The reason sentence doesn't entail this conditional, however, since it doesn't entail that we can suppose this. That the patient has the symptom is a *prima facie* reason to think he has the condition, not a conclusive one. Where, say, a reliable negative test result is available, we cannot suppose he has the condition.

If the reason sentence entails a conditional then it is a weaker one than this. It is some fainthearted sentence such as

> If a patient has the symptom, then other things being equal we can suppose he has the condition.

We must imagine that "other things" are "equal" if there is no negative test result, the patient is not known to be resistant, and there is nothing else to keep us from thinking the patient has the condition. Similarly, I suggest, the reason sentence concerning promises entails

> If you have promised to meet me, then other things being equal you ought to do so.

Here "other things" are "equal" if we haven't made other arrangements since your promise, you are capable of meeting me, and nothing else keeps you from having the duty to do so.

Arguably talk about "other things being equal" is more obscure than talk about *prima facie* reasons, and no advantage is to be had by exchanging one for the other.[1] I think that there is an advantage to be had, and will go on to analyze reason sentences in terms of conditionals with this qualification. One source of confusion which is best dealt with first is that this phrase is ambiguous between what I will call *comparative* and *ideal* readings.

Consider the sentence

> If one boat looks better than the rest, then other things being equal that is the one you should get.

It seems to amount to this: if among some boats one looks better than the rest, but otherwise the boats are equally good – that is, in all relevant regards besides their looks they are similar – then the better-looking boat is the one to

---

[1] Similarly, many seem reluctant to allow laws with the proviso "other things being equal" a place in science, though Carl Hempel (1988), Jerry Fodor (1991) and others have argued they must have one. Steven Schiffer (1991) does not see a place for them in folk psychology. Presumably this reluctance is in large measure due to difficulties in interpreting this proviso. For a discussion see (Pietroski and Rey, 1995).

get. Used in this comparative sense, "other things being equal" stands in for the proposition that certain contextually determinate individuals are similar in certain contextually determinate ways.[2]

Now consider the following principle of natural selection:

> If an inheritable trait brings an advantage to its bearers, then other things being equal it will become more prevalent.

This sentence expresses, roughly, that if an inheritable trait brings an advantage to its bearers and conditions are favorable – there is no sexual selection against it, the population is not about to be destroyed by a meteorite shower, and so on – then this trait will become more prevalent.

Here the phrase "other things being equal" stands in for a condition which is ideal in much the way that a perfect vacuum, a closed system, a frictionless surface and other such fictions are. On a frictionless surface there is nothing to keep an object from going on indefinitely, once it has been set in motion. Similarly, where there is no adverse sexual selection, no meteorite shower, and so on, there is nothing to keep an advantageous trait from becoming more prevalent. By contrast, the implicit condition of the earlier sentence – that in all relevant regards apart from their looks the boats are similar – does not seem to be ideal in the same way. It is hard to think of an end, analogous to an object's going on indefinitely and a trait's becoming more prevalent, for which conditions are favorable when the only relevant differences between boats are in their looks.

Used in the ideal sense, "other things being equal" stands in for the proposition that conditions are ideal – or close enough to ideal – for some contextually determinate end. It is the proposition that there is nothing that would keep this end from being realized. Under an ideal interpretation,

> If a patient has the symptom, then other things being equal we can suppose he has the condition

says what we can think if a patient has the symptom and no additional circumstance keeps us from thinking he has the condition. Similarly,

> If you have promised to meet me then other things being equal you ought to do so

says what you ought to do if you have promised to meet me and no additional circumstance keeps you from having the duty to do so. I will assume

---

[2]This example came from a boat catalogue. Another example with a comparative interpretation appeared recently in *The Washington Post*. A scientific study on AIDS had indicated that "all other things being equal, oral infection can occur with virus doses 6,000 times smaller than those needed to cause infection via the rectum." Presumably the study reports a finding obtained by comparing on the one hand cases in which viral doses are introduced via the mouth, and on the other hand cases in which they are introduced via the rectum, but which in all other relevant regards – the sizes of the doses, the age and condition of the test animals, and so on – are similar.

that *prima facie* reason sentences entail these corresponding conditionals, qualified "other things being equal" and interpreted in this ideal sense.

Reason sentences cannot simply be paraphrased as the corresponding conditionals, however. They have consequences which these conditionals do not have. For example

That you have promised to meet me is a reason for you to do so

entails

You have promised to meet me.

But the corresponding conditional does not entail this sentence, its own conditional antecedent. A better paraphrase can however be gotten simply by conjoining the antecedent and the conditional. For pragmatic reasons it is then better to replace the *if ... then...* with *since*, obtaining as our paraphrase

You have promised to meet me, and since you have promised to meet me, other things being equal you ought to do so.

Similarly, I suggest, the reason sentence expressing the evidential relation between symptom and condition amounts to

The patient has the symptom, and since he has the symptom, other things being equal we can suppose he has the condition.

So far this discussion raises two main questions. The first is, what are the truth conditions of conditionals qualified "other things being equal"? Section 3 presents a model-theoretic interpretation. The second question concerns the relation between reason sentences, on the one hand, and on the other hand claims about what we can think, and what we ought to do. We have seen that this relation is not entailment – that is what led us in the first place to the qualification "other things being equal". But then what relation is it? In section 4 I will suggest that it is a form of inference studied under the rubric "commonsense reasoning". And I will shore up this suggestion by reconstructing inferences in cases in which we have a firm sense of what we can think, and what we ought to do.

3. FAINTHEARTED CONDITIONALS

It will be helpful to have a formal language in which to represent *if... then...* sentences with the qualification "other things being equal". For this purpose let us introduce the triangle, "... $\triangleright$ ...", as an abbreviation of "if ..., then other things being equal ...". Let L be a countable language of sentential logic. And add $\triangleright$ to L, letting the result be $L_\triangleright$. The sentences of this language are defined in the usual way by recursion over the classical connectives; the additional clause concerning $\triangleright$ is this: if ϕ and ψ are sentences of $L_\triangleright$, so is

$\phi \vartriangleright \psi$. Modal operators expressing justified supposition (B) and obligation ($\bigcirc$) can be added too. Where ϕ is a formula of $L_\vartriangleright$ so are $B(\phi)$ and $\bigcirc(\phi)$.[3]

Let S be "the patient has the symptom" and let C be "the patient has the condition". According with the discussion of the previous section, the reason sentence expressing the evidential relation between symptom and condition can be rendered in $L_\vartriangleright$ as S & (S $\vartriangleright B(C)$). Let P be "you promised to meet me" and let M be "you meet me". The reason sentence concerning your promise can be rendered P & (P $\vartriangleright \bigcirc(M)$).

Certain other reason sentences can also be taken into account which, as far as I know, have not been discussed in the literature. That some fact is a reason to think or do something can itself be a reason to think or do something. For example, that Jones' lateness is a reason to dismiss him is itself a reason for Jones to act; assuming he does not want to be dismissed, it is a reason for him to do what he can to arrive on time. (If on the other hand he does want to be dismissed it is a reason for him to continue being late.) Such embedded reason sentences as

> It is a reason for Jones to get to work earlier that his lateness is a reason to dismiss him

can be taken into account since unlimited embedding of $\vartriangleright$ is allowed in $L_\vartriangleright$. Let L be "Jones is regularly late", let D be "Jones is dismissed" and let A be "Jones attempts to arrive at work on time". The following is a rendering:

$$(L \& (L \vartriangleright \bigcirc(D))) \& ((L \& (L \vartriangleright \bigcirc(D))) \vartriangleright \bigcirc(A)).$$

3.1. An Interpretation of Fainthearted Conditionals

What is the meaning of $\vartriangleright$ and what is its logic? In keeping with the intended interpretation there is a standard axiom scheme of conditional logic which cannot be valid: *modus ponens*, or $(\phi \vartriangleright \psi) \rightarrow (\phi \rightarrow \psi)$. It can happen that other things being equal ψ if ϕ, that ϕ holds, and yet that ψ does not hold. A suitable interpretation of $\vartriangleright$ can be borrowed from the modal-conditional logic of Stalnaker and Thomason (1970) and Lewis (1973), making suitable adjustments so as not to validate *modus ponens*.

The basic notion is that of a *possible-worlds frame*, which is a structure $\langle W, \mathcal{R}_B, \mathcal{R}_\circ, * \rangle$. Here W is a non-empty set of *possible worlds*. The function $\mathcal{R}_B$ maps each world onto a *proposition*, or a subset of W (a proposition p holds in a world w just in case $w \in p$). That is, $\mathcal{R}_B : W \rightarrow \wp(W)$. Informally,

---

[3] I use "B" for "belief" rather than "S" for "supposition" since my interpretation of this operator will just be the classical possible-worlds interpretation of belief. My analysis of obligation will also be the standard one of modal logic. Little depends on these choices however. Other analyses can certainly take the place of the ones I have chosen for this illustration.

$\mathcal{R}_B(w)$ is the strongest supposition that the agent – for simplicity's sake, pretend there is just one agent – is justified in having in w; this function will be used to give an entirely standard interpretation to the operator B. The function $\mathcal{R}_o$ is analogous but has a different significance; informally, $\mathcal{R}_o(w)$ is the set of worlds where everything holds which, in w, ought to hold. This function will be used to give a standard interpretation to the operator $\bigcirc$.

In view of their intended interpretations one familiar constraint can be placed both on $\mathcal{R}_B$ and on $\mathcal{R}_o$. We can require, for each $w \in \mathcal{W}$, that $\mathcal{R}_B(w) \neq \{\}$ and that $\mathcal{R}_o(w) \neq \{\}$. As far as $\mathcal{R}_B$ is concerned this constraint merely reflects the fact that, contradictions always being false, our agent is never justified in supposing them to be true. As far as obligations are concerned this constraint is more significant. It reflects the substantive view in ethics that of necessity duties can be discharged. On some accounts of the grounds of duty this is so, on others it is not, and if we are to remain neutral on this point we cannot place this constraint on the frames. I will place it on them anyway, since the coming examples are more interesting if we're not neutral.

Finally, the *worlds-selection function* $*$ is involved in the interpretation of $\triangleright$. It maps each world and proposition onto a proposition; that is, $* : \mathcal{W} \times \wp(\mathcal{W}) \to \wp(\mathcal{W})$. Informally, $*(w, p)$ is the set of those worlds where things are as they will be, other things being equal, if p. Just which worlds these are depends on w, since how things will be, other things being equal, can vary from time to time and place to place. In keeping with this intended interpretation $*$ is subject to the following basic constraint of modal conditional logic:

Definition 1 Facticity: A frame with selection function $*$ satisfies *facticity* if for each w in the domain $\mathcal{W}$ of $*$, and for each $p \subseteq \mathcal{W}, *(w, p) \subseteq p$.

Clearly p is itself among the propositions which hold, other things being equal, if p. There is another familiar constraint from modal conditional logic which cannot be placed on our frames. Say that w is *centered* if for each p such that $w \in p$ we have $w \in *(w, p)$. The constraint in question is:

Definition 2 Centering: A frame is *centered* if each of its worlds is centered.

We cannot require that frames be centered since w's being a p-world does not guarantee that things are in w as they will be, other things being equal, if p.

The following examples of frames will reappear in later examples. First, consider structures with just a single possible world u, whose selection function is defined $*(u, \{\}) = \{\}; *(u, \{u\}) = \{u\}$. These structures satisfy facticity and are centered. Second, consider structures with two possible worlds u and v, whose selection function is such that for each $x \in \{u, v\}, *(x, \{\}) = \{\}; *(x, \{u\}) = \{u\}$; and $*(x, \{u, v\}) = *(x, \{v\}) = \{v\}$. It is convenient to picture these structures in figure 1. An arrow pointing from one set p of possible worlds to another, q, means that for each $x \in \{u, v\}, *(x, p) = q$. These frames satisfy facticity but

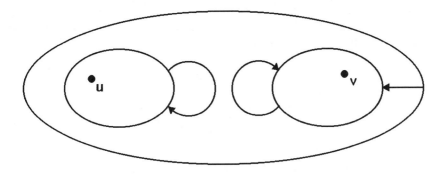

Fig. 1.

are not centered: u is not centered since $u \notin *(u, \{u, v\})$. Together with suitable $\mathcal{R}_B$ and $\mathcal{R}_\circ$ these structures form modal frames. In the coming examples these functions will simply be the identity functions. That is, for each $x \in \{u, v\}, \mathcal{R}_B(x) = \{x\}$, and similarly for $\mathcal{R}_\circ$.

A modal frame becomes a model on adding an interpretation function I, which assigns appropriate intensions to the atomic sentences of $L_\triangleright$. Sentences of $L_\triangleright$ have truth conditions relative to possible worlds $w \in \mathcal{W}$ of models $M = \langle \mathcal{W}, \mathcal{R}_B, \mathcal{R}_\circ, *, I \rangle$. The clauses of the truth definition which deal with atomic sentences and sentential connectives apart from $\triangleright$ are quite familiar. The clauses for B and $\bigcirc$ too are standard:

$$M, w \models B(\phi) \text{ if and only if } \mathcal{R}_B(w) \subseteq \|\phi\|_M, \text{ and}$$
$$M, w \models \bigcirc(\phi) \text{ if and only if } \mathcal{R}_\circ(w) \subseteq \|\phi\|_M.$$

Here $\|\phi\|_M$, the proposition expressed by ϕ in M, is just $\{v \in \mathcal{W} : M, v \models \phi\}$. The clause of the truth definition which deals with $\triangleright$ is

$$M, w \models \phi \triangleright \psi \text{ if and only if } *(w, \|\phi\|_M) \subseteq \|\psi\|_M.$$

According to this truth definition, for a sentence $\phi \triangleright \psi$ to be true it is required that ψ holds in every world where things are as they will be, other things being equal, if ϕ. The following examples illustrate the truth conditions of reason sentences in possible worlds.

3.2. Some Examples

The simplest case is one we started out with.

Example 1 The symptom and the condition: S & (S ▷ B(C)) expresses the evidential relation between symptom and condition. This sentence is satisfied at world u of the following model:

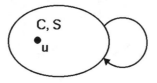

Fig. 2.

An analogous construction shows that P & (P ▷ ◯(M)), the reason sentence concerning your promise to meet me, is satisfiable.

Example 2 Embedded Reasons: The embedded reason sentence

$$(L\&(L \triangleright \bigcirc(D)))\&((L\&(L \triangleright \bigcirc(D))) \triangleright \bigcirc(A)).$$

expresses that it is a reason for Jones to get to work earlier that his lateness is a reason to dismiss him. This sentence is satisfied at world u of the following model:

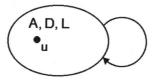

Fig. 3.

Notice that in both of the previous cases the reason sentences are satisfiable in a centered world. It is an immediate consequence of the truth conditions of ▷ that every sentence of the form $(\phi \triangleright \psi) \rightarrow (\phi \rightarrow \psi)$ holds true in such a world. So both reason sentences are satisfiable together with every sentence of this form. This fact will come in useful in the corresponding examples of section 4.1.

Example 3 Conflicting Duties: You are too busy so you have invested two secretaries with the authority to make appointments on your behalf. Now the one secretary makes an appointment for you to meet someone. At the same time however, through a coordination problem, the other secretary agrees with someone else that you will not meet the person in question. Let P_1 be "you have promised to meet the person in question". Let P_2 be "you have promised not to meet this person". And let M be "you meet this person". The reason sentences P_1 & $(P_1 \triangleright \bigcirc(M))$ and P_2 & $(P_2 \triangleright \bigcirc(\neg M))$ express that the promises made on your behalf are reasons for you to do incompatible things. They are satisfied at world u of the model of figure 4.

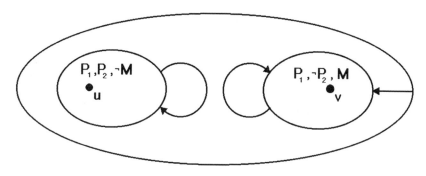

Fig. 4.

Notice that along with P_1 & $(P_1 \rhd \bigcirc(M))$, the sentence $\neg \bigcirc (M)$ holds at u. So this example shows that for some ϕ and ψ, $(\phi \rhd \psi) \rightarrow (\phi \rightarrow \psi)$ is false at some world. In fact $\bigcirc(\neg M)$ holds at u. So this example also shows that $(P_2 \rhd \bigcirc(\neg M)) \rightarrow (P_2 \rightarrow \bigcirc(\neg M))$ is satisfiable together with the two reason sentences. An analogous model shows that $(P_1 \rhd \bigcirc(M)) \rightarrow (P_1 \rightarrow \bigcirc(M))$ too is satisfiable together with the reason sentences. These facts will be used in later sections.

Example 4 Rebutting defeaters: In (1986) John Pollock introduced the notion of *rebutting defeaters* into his discussion of *prima facie* evidence. Where A is a *prima facie* reason to suppose C, a rebutting defeater is a proposition B such that A & B not only fails to be a reason to suppose C, but is a reason to suppose ¬C. Consider again the medical condition, and suppose that while its symptom is a fairly good indicator, it is not a perfect one. There is however a reliable test: a patient will invariably test positive if he has the condition, and negative if he does not. Then while his having the symptom is a reason to think a patient has the condition, a negative test result, even in conjunction with his having the symptom, is a reason to think he does not have the condition. The proposition that the test result is negative is a rebutting defeater in the sense of Pollock.

Let S stand for "the patient has the symptom", let C stand for "the patient has the condition" and let T stand for "the test result is positive". Then, as before, S & (S $\rhd B(C)$) expresses the evidential relation between symptom and condition. Further ¬((S&¬T)&((S&¬T) $\rhd B(C)$)) expresses that having the symptom along with a negative test result is not a reason to suppose the patient has the condition. Finally, (S&¬T)&((S&¬T) $\rhd B(\neg C)$) expresses that this is a reason to suppose the patient does not have the condition. All three sentences are satisfied at world u of the model of figure 5.

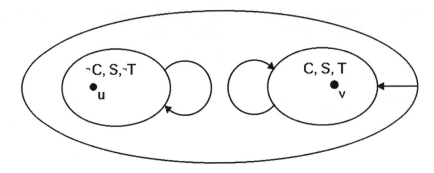

Fig. 5.

3.3. *The Logic of Fainthearted Conditionals*

The interpretation of the previous section gives rise to a notion of logical entailment. A set Γ of sentences entails a sentence ϕ, written $\Gamma \models \phi$, just in case for each model M, and for each world w of M, if $M, w \models \Gamma$ then $M, w \models \phi$. Where Γ is the empty set, write $\models \phi$ instead of $\Gamma \models \phi$ and say that ϕ is *valid*. Example 3 of the previous section brings out a formal characteristic of fainthearted conditionals: *modus ponens* is not valid. That is, for some ϕ and ψ, $\not\models (\phi \triangleright \psi) \rightarrow (\phi \rightarrow \psi)$.

Entailment has a sound and complete syntactic characterization. I will start with a notion of derivability without premises, which characterizes validity. Let " $\vdash \phi$ " mean that ϕ can be derived using the following axioms and rules:

A1. All truth-functional tautologies of $L_{\triangleright}$,
A2. $\phi \triangleright \phi$,
A3. $\neg B(\bot)$,
A4. $\neg \bigcirc (\bot)$,
R1. If $\vdash \phi$ and $\vdash \phi \rightarrow \psi$ then $\vdash \psi$,
R2. If $\vdash (\psi_1 \wedge \psi_2 \ldots \wedge \psi_n) \rightarrow \psi$
    then $\vdash (\phi \triangleright \psi_1 \wedge \phi \triangleright \psi_2 \ldots \wedge \phi \triangleright \psi_n) \rightarrow (\phi \triangleright \psi)$,
R3. If $\vdash (\psi_1 \wedge \psi_2 \ldots \wedge \psi_n) \rightarrow \psi$
    then $\vdash (B(\psi_1) \wedge B(\psi_2) \ldots \wedge B(\psi_n)) \rightarrow B(\psi)$,
R4. If $\vdash (\psi_1 \wedge \psi_2 \ldots \wedge \psi_n) \rightarrow \psi$
    then $\vdash (\bigcirc(\psi_1) \wedge \bigcirc(\psi_2) \ldots \wedge \bigcirc (\psi_n)) \rightarrow \bigcirc(\psi)$,
R5. If $\vdash \phi \leftrightarrow \psi$ then $\vdash (\phi/\psi)\chi \leftrightarrow \chi$.

In this last rule $(\phi/\psi)\chi$ is the result of replacing, within χ, an occurrence of ψ by an occurrence of ϕ.

$\Gamma \vdash \phi$, or ϕ is *derivable from premises* Γ, can be defined in terms of the above notion. It means that for some finite $\Gamma^* \subseteq \Gamma$, $\vdash \wedge \Gamma^* \rightarrow \phi$. Compactness and the deduction theorem involving $\rightarrow$ are close to self evident.

Finally, a standard, Henkin-style construction of a canonical model proves the completeness theorem: $\Gamma \vdash \phi$ if and only if $\Gamma \models \phi$. The proof is a variation on results in (Chellas, 1980).

4. REASONS, SUPPOSITIONS AND WHAT TO DO

We agree that a patient's having a symptom is a reason to think he has the corresponding condition. Now we are wondering what is wrong with him. No test result suggests he does not have the condition. We have no other reason to think he does not. And so it seems we can suppose he has the condition.

We agree that your having promised to do so is a reason to meet me at the time and place arranged. And now you are deciding what to do. You have nothing else to do at that time. You can easily be there. We have not made alternative plans. You have no other more pressing duty. And so it seems you ought to meet me.

Simple cases like these are the easy ones in everyday life. From a theoretical standpoint, though, it is not clear what kind of inference can lead us from reason sentences to claims about the suppositions it seems we can make, and the duties it seems we have. Such inference – if that is what it is – has properties which set it apart from entailment and other familiar forms of inference. For one thing it is *invalid*. It is in the nature of seeming that something can seem to be the case, and yet not be. For another thing, the inference is *defeasible*. What once seemed to be the case can turn out not to be, and when that happens it no longer seems to be the case.

Characteristically, too, this inference is *perplexing*. Each of two incompatible things can seem to be the case. That happens, for example, if there are two different reasons to think or do incompatible things, but neither outweighs the other. His having a characteristic symptom is a reason to suppose the patient has the condition. But his lacking another symptom is a reason to suppose he doesn't. Now in view of the first reason it seems we can suppose the patient has the condition. At the same time however, in view of the second reason, it seems we can suppose he doesn't have it. Again, to take the earlier example, a promise has been made on your behalf that you will do something. But another promise has been made that you won't do it. In view of the first promise it seems you ought to do it. But at the same time, in view of the second promise, it seems you ought not to do it.

I will now begin on a reconstruction of inferences leading from reasons to seemingly justified conclusions and seeming duties. The inference notion which I will develop for this purpose, *allowed consequence*, is invalid, defeasible and perplexing.[4]

---

[4]The technical presentation follows closely that of (Morreau, 1995). In fact this inference notion is a "credulous" version of the notion of allowed argument presented there.

The main idea is to augment the logic of fainthearted conditionals, discussed in section 3.3, by allowing *modus ponens* to detach the consequents of fainthearted conditionals. Speaking figuratively, we assume that "other things" *are* "equal". We will not always assume this however – only when it doesn't introduce inconsistencies. We will assume that "other things" are "equal" only if we do not already know better.

Technically, this effect can be had by adding to the premises of an argument as much of the axiom scheme $(\phi \rhd \psi) \rightarrow (\phi \rightarrow \psi)$ as is consistent with them. Let MP be the set of all sentences of this form. The following definition concerns subsets Ω of MP which can consistently be added to the premises Γ of an argument, and than which no such sets are more inclusive:

Definition 3 Ω is *maximal Γ-consistent within* MP iff
  (i) $\Omega \subseteq$ MP, and
  (ii) $\Gamma \cup \Omega \nvdash \bot$,
while for every Ω^*, if $\Omega \subseteq \Omega^* \subseteq$ MP and $\Gamma \cup \Omega^* \nvdash \bot$, then $\Omega = \Omega^*$.

Observe that for each $\vdash$ consistent set Γ there is some set Ω which is maximal Γ-consistent within MP. This is a consequence of the compactness of $\vdash$ and the deduction theorem involving $\rightarrow$.

In general, of course, there will be more than one such Ω. Letting Γ be $\{P_1 \& (P_1 \rhd \bigcirc(M)), P_2 \& (P_2 \rhd \bigcirc(\neg M))\}$ for example, the premise set arising from the conflicting promises, at least two sets are maximal Γ-consistent within MP. One includes $(P_1 \rhd \bigcirc(M)) \rightarrow (P_1 \rightarrow \bigcirc(M))$, the other $(P_2 \rhd \bigcirc(\neg M)) \rightarrow (P_2 \rightarrow \bigcirc(\neg M))$.

To see that some such set includes $(P_2 \rhd \bigcirc(\neg M)) \rightarrow (P_2 \rightarrow \bigcirc(\neg M))$, remember that this sentence is satisfied at the world u which, in example 3 of section 3.2, showed Γ to be satisfiable. So this sentence is consistent with Γ. The existence of a suitable set now follows directly with the earlier observation that for each consistent set a suitable Ω can be found. By analogous reasoning some maximal Γ-consistent set within MP includes $(P_1 \rhd \bigcirc(M)) \rightarrow (P_1 \rightarrow \bigcirc(M))$. Finally, these sets are distinct since, considering the logic of $\bigcirc$, no set consistent with Γ can include both $(P_1 \rhd \bigcirc(M)) \rightarrow (P_1 \rightarrow \bigcirc(M))$ and $(P_2 \rhd \bigcirc(\neg M)) \rightarrow (P_2 \rightarrow \bigcirc(\neg M))$.

Now the following inference notion augments the logic of $\rhd$ by adding, to premises Γ, as much of MP as is consistent with them.

Definition 4 Allowed Consequence: $\Gamma \vdash_{MP} \phi$ if and only if for some Ω which is maximal Γ-consistent within MP, $\Gamma \cup \Omega \vdash \phi$.

Notice that, provided Γ is consistent, if $\Gamma \vdash \phi$, then $\Gamma \vdash_{MP} \phi$. This follows with the above observation that for each consistent set Γ, some Ω is maximal Γ-consistent within MP. Notice also that $\vdash_{MP}$ has properties quite different from those of logical consequence. For one thing, for no Γ do we have $\Gamma \vdash_{MP} \bot$. Even so, since in general more than one set is maximal Γ-consistent within MP, it can happen that both $\Gamma \vdash_{MP} \phi$ and $\Gamma \vdash_{MP} \neg \phi$. Where $\Gamma \vdash_{MP} \phi$ I will say that Γ *allows* the conclusion ϕ. I take this to have the following significance: on the basis of Γ it seems that ϕ holds true. The observations just made amount to this: a contradiction never seems to hold true. But it can happen that, taken individually, each of two incompatible things seems to hold true.

4.1. *The Examples Again*

Apart from any plausibility it has, one justification for an analysis such as this is that it accords with informal judgments in relatively simple cases. Now I will return to the earlier examples, showing how allowed consequence can be used to reconstruct the relation between reasons, seemingly justified conclusions, and seeming duties.

Example 1 The Symptom and the Condition: The reason sentence S & (S ▷ $B(C)$) expresses that the patient's having the symptom is a reason to suppose he has the condition. Here we will see that

S & (S ▷ $B(C)$)
$\vdash$ MP
$B(C)$.

Given that his having the symptom is a reason to suppose the patient has the condition, it seems we can suppose he has the condition. Also,

S & (S ▷ $B(C)$)
$\nvdash$ MP
$B(\neg C)$.

It *unambiguously* seems we can suppose the patient has the condition, insofar as it doesn't also seem we can suppose he doesn't have it.

These results follow immediately from the observation, in section 3.2, that S & (S ▷ $B(C)$) is satisfiable in a centered world, and is therefore satisfiable with all of MP. There is therefore a unique maximal premise-consistent set within MP, and that is MP itself. Now clearly S & (S ▷ $B(C)$), MP $\vdash B(C)$. Also, by the logic of B and the satisfiability of the premises, S & (S ▷ $B(C)$), MP $\nvdash B(\neg C)$.

Of course, once it becomes clear that we cannot suppose the patient has the condition – say, because it becomes clear that he doesn't have it – it will no longer seem we can suppose he does. These inference notions reflect this defeasibility of seeming: by adding to the premises we can lose conclusions. Specifically, on adding the premise $\neg B(C)$ to the premise of the previous argument the conclusion $B(C)$ will no longer follow.

$\neg B(C),$
$S\&(S \rhd B(C))$
$\nvdash_{MP}$
$B(C).$

The proof of this is trivial: clearly no maximal premise-consistent set within MP will, in conjunction with the premises, entail $B(C)$. Any set which in conjunction with the premises entails $B(C)$ is inconsistent with them.

Example 2 Embedded Reasons: The embedded reason sentence

$$(L\&(L \rhd \bigcirc(D)))\&((L\&(L \rhd \bigcirc(D))) \rhd \bigcirc(A))$$

expresses the following thing: it is a reason for Jones to get to work earlier that his lateness is a reason to dismiss him. Here we see that

$(L\&(L \rhd \bigcirc(D)))\&((L\&(L \rhd \bigcirc(D))) \rhd \bigcirc(A))$
$\vdash_{MP}$
$\bigcirc(A).$

It seems Jones ought to try to arrive on time. Also,

$(L\&(L \rhd \bigcirc(D)))\&((L\&(L \rhd \bigcirc(D))) \rhd \bigcirc(A))$
$\nvdash_{MP}$
$\bigcirc(\neg A).$

It unambiguously seems Jones ought to try to arrive on time. The proofs are analogous to those in the discussion of the previous example. The premise is satisfiable in a centered world, so MP is the unique maximal premise-consistent set within MP.

Example 3 Conflicting Duties: That one secretary has promised you will meet with someone is a reason for you to do so. This we expressed $P_1 \& (P_1 \rhd \bigcirc(M))$. And that the other secretary has promised you will not do so is a reason not to. This we expressed $P_2 \& (P_2 \rhd \bigcirc(\neg M))$. Now the following two facts give a precise sense to the earlier observation that inference towards seeming duties is perplexing. We have

$P_1 \& (P_1 \rhd \bigcirc(M)),$
$P_2 \& (P_2 \rhd \bigcirc(\neg M))$
$\vdash_{MP}$
$\bigcirc(M).$

And we also have

$P_1 \& (P_1 \rhd \bigcirc(M)),$
$P_2 \& (P_2 \rhd \bigcirc(\neg M))$
$\vdash_{MP}$
$\bigcirc(\neg M).$

That is, on the basis of these premises it seems that you ought to meet with the person in question, expressed $\bigcirc(M)$. And it seems that you ought not to, $\bigcirc(\neg M)$. Consequently, neither thing seems unambiguously to be the case. That is your seeming dilemma. These two facts follow directly from the earlier observation, in the discussion of definition 3, that there are two maximal premise-consistent sets, one including $(P_1 \vartriangleright \bigcirc(M)) \rightarrow (P_1 \rightarrow \bigcirc(M))$, the other including $(P_2 \vartriangleright \bigcirc(\neg M)) \rightarrow (P_2 \rightarrow \bigcirc(\neg M))$.

4.2. Setting Priorities: the focus of attention and exclusionary reasons

In this section I will generalize slightly the notion of allowed consequence. Let $\mathcal{F}$ be a set of sentences, the *focus of attention*. Now redefine allowed consequence relative to $\mathcal{F}$, by substituting $\mathcal{F}$ for MP in all of the definitions. The resulting inference notion $\vdash_{\mathcal{F}}$ is a generalization of $\vdash_{MP}$, since choosing $\mathcal{F}$ as MP, they coincide. Intuitively speaking the focus of attention is a parameter which can reflect some of the reasoning agent's relative concerns: to include a conditional $(\phi \vartriangleright \psi) \rightarrow (\phi \rightarrow \psi)$ in $\mathcal{F}$ is to let it matter that other things being equal ψ, if ϕ. Thus the focus of attention is a crude way of dividing reason sentences into two classes: those reflected in $\mathcal{F}$ are alike in being allowed to influence what seems to be, while those not reflected in $\mathcal{F}$ are alike in having no such influence.[5] Unless otherwise specified, in the examples $\mathcal{F}$ will be the set of all sentences $(\phi \vartriangleright \psi) \rightarrow (\phi \rightarrow \psi)$ such that $\phi \& (\phi \vartriangleright \psi)$ is among the premises. That is, all and only those reason sentences which appear in the premises will be reflected in $\mathcal{F}$.

Now I will return to the example concerning rebutting defeaters. And I will show how the focus of attention can be used to reconstruct the inferential role of "exclusionary" reasons, discussed by Joseph Raz (1990).

Example 4 Rebutting defeaters: So long as we know only that the patient has the symptom, it seems we can suppose he has the condition. Earlier we saw that

$$S\&(S \vartriangleright B(C))$$
$$\vdash_{\mathcal{F}}$$
$$B(C).$$

Now suppose a reliable test has been carried out with negative result, expressed $\neg T$. And consider premises registering this result, along with the earlier sentences expressing that it is a rebutting defeater:

---

[5]A reason sentence $\phi \& (\phi \vartriangleright \psi)$ is *reflected in* $\mathcal{F}$ if $\mathcal{F}$ includes $(\phi \vartriangleright \psi) \rightarrow (\phi \rightarrow \psi)$.

$\neg$T
S&(S $\triangleright$ B(C)),
$\quad \neg$((S&$\neg$T)&((S&$\neg$T) $\triangleright$ B(C))),
(S&$\neg$T)&((S&$\neg$T) $\triangleright$ B($\neg$C)).

Now it no longer seems we can suppose the patient has the condition. It unambiguously seems we can suppose that he doesn't have it. Allowed consequence doesn't obviously account for this however. It can be shown that as they stand, these premises allow both the conclusion $B(C)$ and the conclusion $B(\neg C)$.

I suggest that we add a sentence expressing that we can suppose the test result is negative, $B(\neg T)$, along with another sentence supported by the reliability of the test: $B(\neg T) \to \neg B(C)$, or

> If we can suppose the test result is negative, then we cannot suppose the patient has the condition.[6]

With these additions we can show

$\neg$T,
$B(\neg T)$,
$B(\neg T) \to \neg B(C)$,
S&(S $\triangleright$ B(C)),
$\quad \neg$((S&$\neg$T)&((S&$\neg$T) $\triangleright$ B(C))),
(S&$\neg$T)&((S&$\neg$T) $\triangleright$ B($\neg$C))
$\vdash_{\mathcal{F}} B(\neg C)$ and $\not\vdash_{\mathcal{F}} B(C)$.

To verify this, notice that $\mathcal{F}$ includes just the following two sentences:

(S $\triangleright$ B(C)) $\to$ (S $\to$ B(C)),
((S&$\neg$T) $\triangleright$ B($\neg$C)) $\to$ ((S&$\neg$T) $\to$ B($\neg$C)).

The first of these sentences is clearly not consistent with the premises, once the two hidden premises $B(\neg T)$ and $B(\neg T) \to \neg B(C)$ have been added. But the second sentence is consistent with them. (Along with the hidden premises, it holds true in the possible world which, in that part of section 3.2 dealing with rebutting defeaters, demonstrates the satisfiability of the rest of the premises.) Therefore $\{((S\&\neg T) \triangleright B(\neg C)) \to ((S\&\neg T) \to B(\neg C))\}$ is the sole maximal premise-consistent set within $\mathcal{F}$. Finally, the premises together with this set entail $B(\neg C)$, and they do not entail $B(C)$.

Example 5 What to do about your Taxes: That the law requires it is a reason to pay your taxes. And that you stand to gain from cheating is a reason not to do so. Let L stand for "the law requires you to pay your taxes", let P stand for "you pay your taxes in full" and let G stand for "you stand to

---

[6]In a language with an appropriate nomic conditional, $\Rightarrow$, we could write $B(\neg T) \Rightarrow \neg B(C)$ instead. My argument requires that $\Rightarrow$ be stronger than $\to$.

gain from not paying your taxes in full". The two reason sentences which will inform your decision about what to do can be written L & (L ▷ ◯(P)) and G & (G ▷ ◯(¬P)). So far things are analogous to the case involving conflicting promises. There are reasons to do incompatible things. Other than in that case, however, there is no seeming conflict, because the legal reason keeps the merely prudential reason from entering into things. It is, in the sense of Raz (1990), an "exclusionary" reason. This can be taken into account by allowing the legal reason to exclude the reflection of the prudential reason from the focus of attention. In deriving your seeming duties we will choose $\mathcal{F}$ so that it includes (L ▷ ◯(P)) → (L → ◯(P)) but not (G ▷ ◯(¬P)) → (G → ◯(¬P)). Arguing as in the previous example we then can then show that

$$L \text{ \& } (L \rhd \bigcirc(P)),$$
$$G \text{ \& } (G \rhd \bigcirc(\neg P))$$
$$\vdash_{\mathcal{F}} \bigcirc (P) \text{ and } \nvdash_{\mathcal{F}} \bigcirc (\neg P).$$

Your seeming duty is unambiguous: you ought to pay up.

Priority Orders

The device of a focus of attention allows us to take into account the fact that some reasons weigh more heavily than others. It does so too crudely, however. That legal reasons weigh more heavily than prudential reasons does not require that the latter be excluded altogether from decision-making when legal reasons are brought to bear. Rather it requires that legal reasons be brought to bear first, before prudential reasons, so that prudential reasons will sway us only where they do not conflict with legal reasons.

Accordingly I will now generalize allowed consequence to take into account finite linear priorities among reasons. This generalization will take us well beyond the needs of the examples I have considered here, but I have no doubt that more realistic analyses will make full use of its resources. Indeed I expect that further generalization to hierarchies of reasons may be called for. Meanwhile, the first step is to generalize the focus of attention from a single set to a linearly ordered finite set of such sets, or a focal vector.

Definition 5 $\vec{\mathcal{G}} = \langle \mathcal{G}_1, \mathcal{G}_2, \ldots \mathcal{G}_k \rangle$ is a *focal vector* just in case each $\mathcal{G}_i$ is a focus of attention in the earlier sense.

The idea is that reasons reflected in $\mathcal{G}_1$ will be brought to bear first, so that they will take precedence in conflicts with reasons in $\mathcal{G}_2, \mathcal{G}_3, \ldots$; reasons reflected in $\mathcal{G}_2$ will be brought to bear second, so that they take precedence in conflicts with those in $\mathcal{G}_3, \mathcal{G}_4, \ldots$ and so on. Letting $\vec{\mathcal{G}} = \langle \mathcal{G}_1, \mathcal{G}_2, \ldots \mathcal{G}_k \rangle$ be a focal vector and letting $\mathcal{H}$ be a set of sentences, $\vec{\mathcal{G}}|\mathcal{H}$ is a useful notation for the focal vector $\langle \mathcal{G}_1, \mathcal{G}_2, \ldots \mathcal{G}_k, \mathcal{H} \rangle$. Using this notation, definitions and proofs can proceed by induction on the length of focal vectors. For a trivial start, $\vec{\mathcal{G}}$ can be "flattened" into a set $\cup \vec{\mathcal{G}}$ of sentences as follows: $\cup \langle \rangle = \{\}$; and $\cup \vec{\mathcal{G}} | \mathcal{H} = \cup \vec{\mathcal{G}} \cup \mathcal{H}$. The following notion generalizes to the case of focal vectors the earlier notion of maximal Γ-consistency within $\mathcal{F}$:

Definition 6 Ω is *maximal Γ-consistent within $\vec{\mathcal{F}}$* is defined by induction on the length of $\vec{\mathcal{F}}$:
base step: $\{\}$ is maximal Γ-consistent within $\langle \rangle$;
induction step: Ω is maximal Γ-consistent within $\vec{\mathcal{G}} | \mathcal{H}$ if
(i) $\Omega \subseteq \cup \vec{\mathcal{G}} | \mathcal{H}$;
(ii) $\Omega \cap \cup \vec{\mathcal{G}}$ is maximal Γ-consistent within $\vec{\mathcal{G}}$; and
(iii) $\Gamma \cup \Omega \not\vdash \bot$. And if $\Omega \subseteq \Omega^* \subseteq \cup \vec{\mathcal{G}} | \mathcal{H}$ and $\Gamma \cup \Omega^* \not\vdash \bot$, then $\Omega = \Omega^*$.

Now the following definition generalizes allowed consequence, replacing the simple focus of attention with a focal vector.

Definition 7 Allowed Consequence: $\Gamma \vdash_{\vec{\mathcal{F}}} \phi$ if and only if for some Ω which is maximal Γ-consistent within $\vec{\mathcal{F}}$, $\Gamma, \Omega \vdash \phi$.

Clearly this notion reduces to $\vdash_{\mathcal{F}}$ if we choose $\langle \mathcal{F} \rangle$ as the focal vector.

5.   A SEMANTICAL COMPANION TO ALLOWED CONSEQUENCE

Now I will provide allowed argument, which I have treated so far in purely syntactical terms, with a model-theoretic characterization. Another such result can be found in (Morreau, 1995), where a closely related notion of allowed consequence – it can be defined in terms of this one – is provided with such a characterization. Lemmas and facts demonstrated there can be used to prove a claim made here without proof.

Here is a preference relation on possible worlds, which I will use to characterize allowed consequence.

Definition 8 $L, v \leq_{\mathcal{F}} M, w$ means $(Th(M, w) \cap \mathcal{F}) \subseteq Th(L, v)$.

Here $Th(M, w)$ is the theory, $\{\phi : M, w \models \phi\}$, of w in M. One world lies underneath another in the sense of this relation if it "gets more of $\mathcal{F}$ right". With $\mathcal{F}$ chosen within MP, however, more can be said about $\leq_{\mathcal{F}}$. Consider any given sentence $(\phi \triangleright \psi) \to (\phi \to \psi)$ in $\mathcal{F}$. We can say that w is *irregular in regard to $\phi \triangleright \psi$ in M* if $M, w \models \phi$ and $M, w \models \phi \triangleright \psi$, but $M, w \not\models \psi$. Equivalently, of course, w is irregular in regard to $\phi \triangleright \psi$ if $M, w \not\models (\phi \triangleright \psi) \to (\phi \to \psi)$. So $L, v \leq_{\mathcal{F}} M, w$ just means that w is at least as irregular as v, as far as the reasons we are focusing on are concerned.

Now we can generalize this relation to an order $\leq_{\vec{\mathcal{F}}}$ relative to a focal vector. Intuitively it is clear what needs to be done in order to define $\leq_{\vec{\mathcal{F}}}$, for any given focal vector $\vec{\mathcal{F}} = \langle \mathcal{F}_1, \mathcal{F}_2, \ldots \mathcal{F}_k \rangle$. It is necessary to combine the different orders $\leq_{\mathcal{F}_1}, \leq_{\mathcal{F}_2}, \ldots \leq_{\mathcal{F}_k}$ appropriately, allowing $\leq_{\mathcal{F}_1}$ to order worlds first, then allowing $\leq_{\mathcal{F}_2}$ to further discriminate between worlds which as far as $\leq_{\mathcal{F}_1}$ is concerned are indiscriminable, and so on. Such combinations of partial orders are the subject of the following definition, in which v is a finite vector of partial linear orders, each defined on the same domain, D:

Definition 9 The *alphabetic composition* $\leq_v$ of v is defined by induction on the length of v:
base step: $\leq_{\langle\rangle} = D^2$;
induction step: $\leq_{v\underline{k}} = \{(d_1, d_2) : d_1 \leq_v d_2$ and if $d_1 \approx_v d_2$, then $d_1 \leq d_2\}$.

A straightforward induction on the length of v shows that $\leq_v$ is a partial linear order on D. The familiar alphabetic order of words in a dictionary can be construed as such an alphabetic composition.

   Further, let us define a notion of minimal satisfaction analogous to a notion of John McCarthy (1980). Informally speaking, a world minimally satisfies Γ if no world satisfies Γ that lies under it in the sense of $\leq_{\vec{\mathcal{F}}}$. Letting "$L, v \approx_{\vec{\mathcal{F}}} M, w$" mean that both $L, v \leq_{\vec{\mathcal{F}}} M, w$ and $M, w \leq_{\vec{\mathcal{F}}} L, v$, we have the following

Definition 10 Minimal Satisfaction: $M, w \models_{\vec{\mathcal{F}}} \Gamma$ means:
$M, w \models \Gamma$; and
for all L, v, if $L, v \models \Gamma$ and $L, v \leq_{\vec{\mathcal{F}}} M, w$, then $L, v \approx_{\vec{\mathcal{F}}} M, w$.

This notion can now be used to give a sound and complete model-theoretic characterization of allowed consequence.

Definition 11 Allowed Entailment: $\Gamma \models_{\vec{\mathcal{F}}} \phi$ if and only if there is some $M, w \models_{\vec{\mathcal{F}}} \Gamma$ such that for each $L, v \approx_{\vec{\mathcal{F}}} M, w$, if $L, v \models \Gamma$ then $L, v \models \phi$.

Now the following claim ties allowed consequence and allowed entailment together:

Claim: $\Gamma \vdash_{\vec{\mathcal{F}}} \phi$ just in case $\Gamma \models_{\vec{\mathcal{F}}} \phi$.

This claim can be proved using the lemmas of (Morreau, 1995).

Michael Morreau
Philosophy Department and Institute for Advanced Computer Studies
University of Maryland

REFERENCES

Chellas, B. (1980). *Modal Logic, an Introduction.* Cambridge University Press.
Fodor, J. (1991). You can fool some of the people all of the time, everything else being equal; hedged laws and psychological explanations. *Mind* 100:19-34.

Goodman, N (1947). The problem of counterfactual conditionals. *The Journal of Philosophy,* 44:113-128. Appears also in Nelson Goodman. *Fact, Fiction and Forecast,* Fourth Edition. Harvard University Press, 1983.

Hempel, C (1988). Provisos: A problem concerning the inferential function of scientific theories. *Erkenntnis* 28:147-164.

Lewis, D (1973). *Counterfactuals.* Harvard University Press.

McCarthy, J (1980). Circumscription – a form of nonmonotonic reasoning. *Artificial Intelligence* 13:27-39.

Morreau, M (1995). Allowed arguments. In C. Mellish, (ed.), *Proceedings of the Fourteenth International Joint Conference on Artificial Intelligence,* Morgan Kaufmann Publishers, San Mateo Ca., Vol. 2, pages 1466-1472.

Morreau, M (1996). *Prima facie* and seeming duties. Forthcoming in *Studia Logica,* 57.

Pietroski, P. and G. Rey (1995). When other things aren't equal: saving ceteris paribus laws from vacuity. *The British Journal for the Philosophy of Science* 46:81-110.

Pollock, J (1986, *Contemporary Theories of Knowledge.* Rowman and Littlefield, Totawa, NJ..

Schiffer, S (1991). Ceteris paribus laws. *Mind* 100:1-17.

Raz, J (1990). *Practical Reason and Norms.* 2nd edition, Princeton University Press.

Ross, D (1963). *Foundations of Ethics.* Clarendon Press, Oxford.

Ross, D (1930). *The Right and the Good.* Oxford University Press.

Stalnaker R. and R. H. Thomason (1970). A semantic analysis of conditional logic. *Theoria* 36:23-42.

NICHOLAS ASHER AND DANIEL BONEVAC

COMMON SENSE OBLIGATION*

To attack the sophists' conception of weakness of will, Aristotle cites Sophocles' (Aristotle, 335B.C., *Philoctetes* VII, 2, 1146a19). Philoctetes had wandered into a forbidden garden, through no fault of his own, and had been punished by the gods with a disfiguring disease. Banishing him to a remote island, they had taken everything from him but his bow. As the play opens, the gods reveal to Odysseus that only that bow can win the Trojan War. So, Odysseus orders Neoptolemus to trick Philoctetes out of his bow.

Neoptolemus obeys. Overcome with regret, however, he decides to return the bow:

Odysseus:	You have turned back, there is hurry in your step. Will you not tell me why?
Neoptolemus:	I go to undo the wrong that I have done.
Odysseus:	A strange thing to say! What wrong was that?
Neoptolemus:	I did wrong when I obeyed you and the Greeks.
Odysseus:	What did we make you do that was unworthy?
Neoptolemus:	I practiced craft and treachery with success.
Odysseus:	On whom? Would you do something rash now?
Neoptolemus:	Nothing rash. I am going to give something back.

(1222-30)

Neoptolemus tricks Philoctetes for serious reasons: to obey Odysseus, his commander, and to win the Trojan War. But those reasons, he concludes, cannot justify his cruelty to the anguished Philoctetes.

Philosophers have tended to analyze situations of moral conflict like that of Neoptolemus in terms of *prima facie* duties. W. D. Ross defined a *prima facie* duty as a "characteristic (quite distinct from that of being a duty proper) which an act has, in virtue of being of a certain kind (e.g. the keeping of a promise), of being an act which would be a duty proper if it were not at the same time of another kind which is morally significant" (Ross, 1930, p.19).

---

*This paper was presented at the 1993 meeting of the Society for Exact Philosophy at York University. We would like to thank Marvin Belzer, Robert Koons, Barry Loewer, Paul McNamara, Michael Morreau, Donald Nute, and the rest of the audience for their helpful criticisms and remarks. We owe added and special thanks to Michael Morreau, who has taught us much in discussions over the past several years, and to several anonymous referees.

D. Nute (ed.), Defeasible Deontic Logic, 159–203.

A prime facie obligation, that is, holds under normal circumstances; it holds all other things being equal, becoming actual ("a duty proper") unless some other moral consideration intervenes (Frankena, 1973, p. 26).

Neoptolemus' situation intrigues us because other moral considerations do intervene. In general, a soldier should obey his commanding officer. Moreover, a soldier should strive for victory. These might come into conflict. In Neoptolemus' case, they work together. But they clash with honesty, kindness, and justice. In general, one shouldn't practice deception, and one shouldn't injure someone already suffering, as Philoctetes is, by taking away the only thing he has left. All these principles–concerning obedience, victory, honesty, cruelty, and justice–are correct, in general. But, as their conflict demonstrates, they have exceptions.

Indeed, the primary motivation for speaking of *prima facie* obligation is that, in many domains, conflicts can happen, and rules have exceptions. Domains that have a high degree of complexity–that are, in the terms of (Bonevac, 1991), *unruly*–may be immune from even partial characterization by rules. *Prima facie* obligations offer a way to explain the force of rules while allowing for exceptions. The idea, in essence, is that a *prima facie* rule applies unless some other rule conflicts with it. John Stuart Mill's secondary principles are paradigms of *prima facie* principles: they dictate obligations unless they come into conflict (Mill, 1861). In that case, Mill stipulates, the principle of utility, the sole rule in his system that has an absolute rather than *prima facie* character, resolves the conflict. This indicates a key difference between actual and *prima facie* obligation: *Prima facie* obligations can conflict, while actual obligations cannot. (See (von Wright, 1951; Conee, 1982; Pietroski, 1993) for arguments.) Neoptolemus, for example, has a *prima facie* obligation to trick Philoctetes, and another *prima facie* obligation not to trick him. At most one of these obligations can be actual. Neoptolemus, returning the bow, decides that his obligation not to trick Philoctetes takes precedence.

Throughout this paper, we shall treat *prima facie* principles of the form if A, then it ought to be the case that B or the analogous quantified form Fs should G. We may put the above considerations in the form of criteria that an adequate account of obligation should satisfy.

(I) *Default Detachment*: Inferences of the form

(1)

Fs should G	If A, then it ought to be the case that B
a is an F	A
—	—
a should G	It ought to be the case that B

should count as acceptable if no other moral considerations apply. They are not valid, but they are legitimate default inferences; we may draw the conclusion if no other rules intervene. If Neoptolemus knows only that Odysseus has commanded him to get Philoctetes' bow, and that Odysseus's commands should be obeyed, it is reasonable for him to conclude that he should get the bow.

(II) *Conditional Conflict*: In cases where conditional *prima facie* principles conflict, we should be able in general to draw no conclusions:

(2)

Fs should G	If A, then it ought to be the case that C
Hs should not G	If B, then it ought not to be the case that C
a is an F and an H	A and B
———————	———————
?	?

Given that Neoptolemus has both *prima facie* obligations, logic alone should not decide between them.

(III) *Deontic Specificity*: More specific *prima facie* obligations should take precedence over less specific ones. So, we should be able to draw conclusions when the antecedents of the conditionals expressing *prima facie* obligations relate in the right way:

(3)

Fs should G	If A, then it ought to be the case that C
Hs should not G	If B, then it ought not to be the case that C
All Fs are Hs	If A, then B
a is an F and an H	A and B
———————	———————
a should G	It ought to be the case that C

Given that commands should be obeyed, that unjust commands should not be obeyed, and that Odysseus' command is unjust, we should be able to conclude, unless other considerations intervene, that it should not be obeyed.

(IV) *Unwanted Implications*: Any system of deontic logic should avoid unwanted implications. In particular, any system should be able to handle various paradoxes of deontic logic. The robber and victim paradoxes, for example, lead from seemingly innocuous premises to troubling conclusions:

(4)

> Neoptolemus is a robber.
> Robbers should repent.
> One can repent only if one has done wrong.
> ———————
> Neoptolemus should have done wrong.

The more recent gentle murder paradox (Forrester, 1984; Castañeda, 1985; Castañeda, 1986; Sinnott, 1985; Loewer, 1986; Goble, 1990; Goble, 1990; Goble, 1990) has a similar form:

(5)

> If you murder Jones, you should murder him gently.
> You murder Jones.
> If you murder Jones gently, you murder him.

> You should murder Jones.

An adequate deontic logic should avoid, or at least explain away, such conclusions.

(V) *Unconditional Actual Obligation*: Unconditional statements of actual obligation should be expressible, and should not be able to conflict. This pair should be inconsistent:

(6)

> a has an actual obligation to F
> a has an actual obligation not to F

Neoptolemus' decision that his obligation not to trick Philoctetes is actual is incompatible with a conclusion that his obligation to trick him is actual.

(VI) *Unconditional* Prima Facie *Obligation*: It should be possible to express unconditional *prima facie* obligations, and it should be possible for them to conflict. This pair of statements should be consistent:

(7)

> a has a *prima facie* obligation to F
> a has a *prima facie* obligation not to F

We want to be able to say that Neoptolemus has, at the same time, *prima facie* obligations to trick Philoctetes and not to trick him.

There is a natural model for the behavior of conditional obligation found in (1) and (2): nonmonotonic inference. As (Chisholm, 1964) and (Horty, 1993; Horty, 1994) have argued, *prima facie* principles license conclusions that might have to be withdrawn in the face of further information. Traditional analyses of *prima facie* principles use modal logic and a standard, monotonic conception of validity incapable of analyzing the acceptable but defeasible nature of these obligations. Like Horty, we shall use nonmonotonic logic to elucidate *prima facie* obligation. We shall, however, choose a different nonmonotonic system of reasoning: commonsense entailment, a modal theory of nonmonotonic reasoning developed by Asher and Morreau (1991; 1995).

In this paper we offer two treatments of *prima facie* obligation in terms of commonsense entailment. Our first approach analyzes *prima facie* obligations as holding under normal circumstances. Our second treats them as holding *ceteris paribus*. As we shall see, these approaches differ in some subtle but important ways.

Our theory offers at least four advantages. First, it preserves a principle of closure under logical consequence:

(8)

Fs should G	If A, then it ought to be the case that B
G entails H	B entails C

Fs should H	If A, then it ought to be the case that C

This principle seems to us central to understanding *prima facie* obligation: A *prima facie* duty to B surely entails a *prima facie* duty to any logical consequence of B. This is implicit in Ross's characterization of *prima facie* duties as following from some feature of an act or circumstance. If B follows from that feature, say, A, and C follows logically from B, then C follows from A. This is also implicit in most rule-based treatments of moral obligation. Obligations, in a rule- based theory, follow from the rules. But if B follows from the rules, and C follows from B, then C follows from the rules as well. More broadly, without closure under logical consequence, it is hard to preserve a notion of moral argument.

Second, our theory allows the embedding of *prima facie* obligations, or other forms of genericity, within others. Sentences such as *Students who should take physics should also take mathematics* and *People often don't know when they should call a doctor* are difficult to accommodate within an inference-ticket theory such as Horty's.

Third, unlike (van Fraassen, 1972; van Fraassen, 1973) or (Bonevac and Seung, 1988), our theory does not assume any underlying system of multiple values, imperatives, or other sources of obligation. We do not wish to deny that such a system may be important to understanding ethics or practical reasoning in a broad sense. In fact, a natural way of introducing a unary *prima facie* obligation operator into our approach is easily interpreted as reflecting one. A system of multiple values is not presupposed by our account of the characteristic logical features of *prima facie* duties, but turns out to be generated by it.

Finally, our theory successfully predicts valid inference patterns involving *prima facie* obligation. Many systems count inferences valid that hold, if at all, only in certain contexts. In particular, they assume a principle that whatever is, is right. We therefore call them *Pope* systems. The assumption and consequent overgenerosity in counting inferences valid afflicts any approach that views conditional obligation statements as defaults. *Prima facie* principles link *is* to *ought*; they do not license inferences on a single set of sentences as default rules do.

1. TRUTH AND MONOTONIC CONSEQUENCE

Our approaches use the same nonmonotonic framework. One, however, uses only a unary obligation operator $\bigcirc$ and a defeasible conditional, $>$, appropriate for reasoning about generics (Asher and Morreau, 1991; Asher and Morreau, 1995). The other introduces a new conditional obligation operator $>_o$. The approaches agree on the inference patterns to be discussed in later sections. But they are different; the second has greater expressive power. Because they use the same framework, we will develop them in tandem.

The first approach symbolizes formulas expressing conditional obligation as follows:

$$A > \bigcirc B$$

or

$$\forall x (F(x) > \bigcirc G(x)).$$

The second approach offers two possible symbolizations: as above, or as

$$A >_o B$$

or

$$\forall x (F(x) >_o G(x)).$$

Because the only quantification that interests us in this paper is initial universal quantification, we shall generally discuss only the simpler, sentential forms. Everything we shall say applies, *mutatis mutandis*, to the related quantificational forms.

Assume that $\bigcirc$ is a unary operator expressing actual obligation. Then inferences of pattern (1) are of the forms

(9)

$$
\begin{array}{cc}
A > \bigcirc B & A >_o B \\
A & A \\
\hline
\bigcirc B & \bigcirc B
\end{array}
$$

while those of pattern (4) look like:

(10)

$$A > \bigcirc C \qquad A >_o C$$
$$B > \bigcirc \neg C \qquad B >_o \neg C$$
$$A \ \& \ B \qquad\quad A \ \& \ B$$

$$\overline{} \qquad \overline{}$$

$$? \qquad\qquad ?$$

Our base language is a first-order language L with $\top$ and $\perp$, a unary obligation operator $\bigcirc$, and a binary connective, $>$; the second approach extends L to L_o, which contains in addition a binary connective $>_o$. We interpret $\bigcirc$ in the standard way: $\bigcirc A$ holds at a world w if and only if A holds in all of w's "ideal" worlds. The connective $>$ is a doxastic, nonmoral, generic conditional: $A > B$ means that, where A holds, B normally holds too. The connective $>_o$ is a generic deontic conditional: $A >_o B$ means that, where A holds, then, other things being equal, B should hold.

Morally normal circumstances are those where other things are equal, morally speaking. They are morally pure or uncomplicated in the sense that only one kind of moral consideration pertains to them; conflicts involving A do not arise. In ideal worlds, all actual obligations are fulfilled; in morally normal worlds, all *prima facie* obligations become actual. Asher and Morreau construe normality in generic contexts in terms of an accessibility relation *; we introduce another accessibility relation, •, which assigns to each world w and proposition p a set •(w, p) of "good-and-simple" worlds.

Our first approach is to characterize *prima facie* conditional obligation sentences as generic conditionals with actual obligation sentences as consequents. A sentence of the form *If A, it should be the case that B* holds in a world w iff in all normal w-A-worlds it ought to be the case that B. It holds, in other words, iff B holds in all ideals of the normal w-A-worlds.

The central idea behind our second approach is that a statement of *prima facie* obligation $A >_o B$ holds in a world w if B is true in all w-A-good-and-simple worlds. These may or may not be worlds in which A is true. But they are worlds that, from the perspective of w, and with respect to A, are both good and simple. They are simple in that moral issues in them are, in a sense, one-dimensional. No moral complications arise; there are no conflicting obligations. And they are good in that obligations arising from the truth of A in w are fulfilled.

Consider a simple conditional expressing *prima facie* obligation:

(11)

> If Neoptolemus promised to obey, he should obey.

This is true, according to our second approach, if Neoptolemus obeys in all worlds that are good-and-simple with respect to his promising to obey. Similarly, a deontic generic such as

(12)

Soldiers should obey.

is true if each soldier obeys in all soldier-good-and-simple worlds.

The dependence on both w and A here is important. The relevant class of worlds must depend on w, for many obligations are contingent; they hold in some worlds but not in others. Neoptolemus' obligation to obey, for example, might have force only in those worlds in which his obedience has good consequences or in which various other conditions are met. The relevant class of worlds must also depend on A, for A expresses the condition of the conditional obligation.

1.1. *Constitutive and epistemic principles*

Our second approach distinguishes two kinds of *prima facie* obligation. In L_0, $A > \bigcirc B$ and $A >_0 B$ are both available. They have essentially the same logic, but mean different things. Sentences of the form $A >_0 B$ are *ceteris paribus* principles. They say that, if A, then, all other things being equal, B is obligatory. They are thus *constitutive*: $A >_0 B$ implies that the truth of A is a reason for doing B. *Promises ought to be kept*, for example, is ordinarily constitutive, for something's being a promise is a reason for its being kept.

Sentences of the form $A > \bigcirc B$, in contrast, generalize about circumstances in which A is true, saying that, generally, where A is true, then B is obligatory. They are thus *epistemic*: they imply that the truth of A is a good indicator that B is obligatory. *Promises ought to be ignored*, for example, would ordinarily be interpreted as epistemic, as resting on a cynical view of human nature rather than on the nature of promises *per se*.

To put the distinction another way, sentences of the form $A >_0 B$ say what is true *ceteris paribus*, all other things being equal; those of the form $A > \bigcirc B$ say what is true normally. If other things are normally not equal, then sentences of these forms convey different information. Our second approach has the advantage of incorporating both.

The distinction between constitutive and epistemic generics is not limited to deontic contexts; it extends to all generics. Philosophical recognition of the distinction goes back at least as far as Aristotle's discussion of *qua* phrases. The account we offer here is a special case of a more general theory.

Constitutive principles are nonmonotonically stronger than epistemic principles. If the truth of A is a reason for B's being obligatory, then, normally, the truth of A is a good indicator that B is obligatory. Nevertheless, constitutive and epistemic principles have the same logic, as we might expect from their sharing the same forms of expression in natural language. Truth conditionally, however, they are distinct in philosophically important ways.

Most writers on moral reasoning identify *prima facie* and *ceteris paribus* principles. (Pietroski, 1993, 497), for example, proposes the schema:

(13)

> 'M ought (*prima facie*) to do X' is true iff, *ceteris paribus*,
> M ought actually to do X.

This is a constitutive notion of *prima facie* obligation, captured in our connective $>_o$. But it is arguably not the only notion of *prima facie* obligation. Certainly it is not the only notion of defeasibility relevant to understanding defeasible moral principles. Treating all such principles as constitutive leads one to miss some important distinctions and, in the context of certain moral theories, most notably utilitarianism, misconstrue the nature and force of those principles.

Illustrations of the difference between constitutive and epistemic principles are easy to find.

(i) Kantians and utilitarians both defend many traditional moral principles. They not only argue for them on different grounds, however; they read the principles themselves differently. Traditional moral rules find support in utilitarian theory, Mill argues, because they are generalizations, based on a vast range of experience, about good action, good character, and the good life. In short, they are generalizations about actual obligation. A utilitarian such as Mill thinks of a moral rule as generalizing about actual obligations in a wide array of circumstances. A principle of the form

> If A, then it ought to be the case that B

from this perspective asserts that, where A holds, there is normally an actual obligation that B. This is well-represented by $A > \bigcirc B$.

This is very different from a Kantian conception of moral rules, which subjects rules to tests of rationality. Kantians see such a principle as a hypothetical imperative or maxim justified by the categorical imperative, "on grounds valid for every rational being as such" (Kant, 1785). They may interpret it as strictly universal or as nonmonotonic: in conflicts between reason and inclination, "the universality of the principle is changed into mere generality, whereby the practical principle of reason meets the maxim halfway" (Kant, 1785). Even in the latter case, however, a situation's being such that A itself provides a reason for an obligation that B. This corresponds to a constitutive *ceteris paribus* principle, and is well-represent ed by $A >_o B$.

The Kantian reading of moral principles tends to imply the utilitarian reading. If promises ought to be kept in the sense that a promise itself creates, *ceteris paribus*, an obligation to keep it, then we can expect that, if an agent makes a promise, he or she generally has an actual obligation to keep it. The implication, however, is nonmonotonic. There may be unusual worlds in which promises, while still having real moral force, are generally outweighed by other moral factors.

(ii) Mill argues for the importance of traditional moral rules in defending utilitarianism against common objections. There is not enough time, a hypothetical opponent objects, to perform all the calculations that utilitarianism requires. Not so, Mill replies; "there has been ample time, namely, the whole past duration of the human species. During all that time mankind have been learning by experience the tendencies of actions" (Mill, 1861). We ought to obey traditional moral rules, in general, because they are products of experience, experimentation, and reasoned choice. In our terms, then, Mill advocates a principle of the form $\forall x$ (traditional-rule(x) $>$ $\bigcirc$follow(x)): traditional rules generally ought to be followed. Being traditional is not itself a right-making property; it is merely a good indicator of such properties.

Edmund Burke, in contrast, holds the generally stronger position that traditional rules ought to be followed precisely because they are traditional. He maintains, in other words, that being traditional is itself right-making, in the sense that traditional rules, *ceteris paribus*, ought to be followed: $\forall x$ (traditional-rule(x) $>_o$ follow(x)). Not only do traditional rules issue from a history of reasoned choice; respect for them engenders critical virtues. Once again, this constitutive position is stronger, but only nonmonotonically. The tradition could be so corrupt that other defects generally outweigh the benefits of tradition.

(iii) Many writers argue for affirmative action programs as compensating for prior injustice. Some (e.g., (Nickle, 1975)) defend the use of racial criteria as an administrative convenience: blacks, for example, are generally worse off than they might have been had there been no racial discrimination. Some blacks may not be, however; their inclusion is justified only by the headaches it would require to identify them. On this view, we should, *prima facie*, compensate blacks for discrimination, in the sense that blacks generally ought to be compensated. This is precisely what we would represent as $\forall x$ (black(x) $>$ $\bigcirc$compensated(x)). Other writers (e.g., (Taylor, 1973; Duncan, 1982)) defend the use of racial criteria differently. They contend that, because discrimination was directed at blacks as a group, blacks deserve compensation as a group. They contend, in other words, that being black is itself a reason for compensation, not merely a convenient proxy for the reason. All other things being equal, they maintain, blacks ought to be compensated. This we represent as the constitutive$\forall x$ (black(x) $>_o$ compensated(x)).

These two positions are not equivalent. Ordinarily, the latter is stronger; to say that being black itself justifies receiving compensation implies, but is not implied by, the assertion that blacks generally ought to be compensated. The implication is nonmonotonic, however, for it is possible to imagine a situation in which blacks ought, *ceteris paribus*, to be compensated, but in which, due to grave budget problems, for example, it is not true that blacks generally ought to be compensated.

(iv) Nominalists have sometimes wanted to understand a sentence such as (14)a by translating it into the putatively equivalent (14)b or, to simplify somewhat, (14)c:

(14)

        a. Honesty is a virtue

        b. Honest acts are virtuous

        c. Honest acts ought to be done.

Those with other motives have sometimes agreed, arguing that there must be some logical relation between talk of honesty and talk of honest actions, or we could never apply abstract sentences to concrete situations (Ryle, 1931). Platonists have objected that honesty is only one of the virtues; not all honest actions ought to be performed. Clearly, the nominalist needs to say that *Honesty is a virtue* is equivalent to *Honest acts, other things being equal, ought to be done*. This we might represent as $\forall x \, (\text{honest}(x) >_o \text{do}(x))$. It would not do to translate the sentence as the epistemic $\forall x \, (\text{honest}(x) > \bigcirc \text{do}(x))$, for this says something nonmonotonically weaker– that honest acts normally ought to be done. It might be contingently true, for example, that acts done with a smile normally ought to be done, but that would not make *Smiling is a virtue* true. That an act is honest is itself a reason for doing it, but that it is done with a smile is not.

(v) The distinction between constitutive and epistemic principles is crucial to understanding the consequences of moral conflict. (Pietroski, 1993), following (Williams, 1973), contends that regret is justified if and only if an agent has and fails to fulfill a *prima facie* obligation. Such obligations carry moral cost even when overridden by other considerations. So, Neoptolemus should regret his deception of Philoctetes, whether or not that deception is ultimately justified. And, after returning the bow, he should regret disobeying Odysseus, even if his decision is correct. It is thus plausible to hold that *prima facie* obligations understood as stemming from *ceteris paribus* principles, having the form $A >_o B$, justify regret. But the same does not hold of such obligations understood as stemming from generalizations having the form $A > \bigcirc B$. Suppose acts performed with a smile generally ought to be done. It does not follow that one ought to regret failures to smile.

We draw two morals from these examples. First, there are at least two kinds of *prima facie* obligation. One is constitutive, well-expressed by *ceteris paribus* principles; the other is epistemic, well-expressed by generalizations. Second, constitutive principles are nonmonotonically stronger than epistemic principles. If the truth of A is a reason for B's being obligatory, then, normally, the truth of A is a good indicator that B is obligatory.

1.2. *Frames*

We now express these ideas more formally. Throughout the following we take w, w', etc. to be arbitrary worlds in W and p, q, etc. to be arbitrary subsets of W. (We identify propositions with sets of worlds.) $\oplus$w is the set of w's ideal worlds; $\oplus$(X), where X is a set of worlds, is $\cup\oplus$(w) for w$\in$X; *(w, p) is the set of w-p-normal worlds, and •(w, p) is the set of w-p-good-and-simple worlds. To preview our truth conditions for constitutive and epistemic principle s: A $>_o$ B is true in world w if B is true in all good-and-simple worlds relative to A and w; that is, if (suppressing references to models and assignments) •(w, $\|A\|$) $\subseteq$ $\|B\|$. A generic A>B is true in w if B is true in all normal worlds relative to A and w; if, in other words, *(w, $\|A\|$)$\subseteq$$\|B\|$. A unary obligation statement $\bigcirc$A is true in w if A holds in all ideal worlds, i.e., if $\oplus$(w)$\subseteq$$\|A\|$. It follows that an epistemic principle A $>$ $\bigcirc$B is true in w if $\oplus$*(w, $\|A\|$) $\subseteq$ $\|B\|$.

Definition 1 An L *frame* $\Im$ is a quadruple $\langle$W, D, $\oplus$, *$\rangle$, where W is a nonempty set of worlds, D is a nonempty set of individuals, $\oplus$ is a function from W to $\wp$(W), and * is a function from W X $\wp$(W) to $\wp$(W).

Definition 2 L$_o$ *frames* are pairs $\langle\Im$, •$\rangle$, where $\Im$ is an L frame and • is a function from W $\times\wp$(W) to $\wp$(W).

Definition 3 Proper L frames are frames obeying:

(a)   the SERIALITY constraint: $\oplus$(w) $\neq$ $\emptyset$;
(b)   the FACTICITY constraint: *(w,p)$\subseteq$p; and
(c)   the DISJUNCTION constraint: *(w,p$\cup$q)$\subseteq$*(w,p)$\cup$*(w,q).

The seriality constraint guarantees that $\bigcirc$ is an actual obligation operator, admitting no moral dilemmas. The facticity constraint stipulates that p is one of the things that normally hold when p holds. Facticity thus makes sentences such as *Criminals are criminals* valid. The Disjunction constraint guarantees the validity in L of inferences such as

(15)

> If Dudley loves Nell, he should marry Nell
> If Dudley loves his horse, he should marry Nell
> _____
> If Dudley loves either Nell or his horse, he should marry Nell

As (Morreau, 1992) shows, facticity and the Disjunction schema entail generic specificity:

Fact 1 : [p$\subseteq$q & *(w, p)$\cap$*(w, q) = $\emptyset$] $\Rightarrow$*(w, q) $\cap$p = $\emptyset$.

Proof: Assume facticity and Disjunction. Assume further that p⊆q & *(w, p)∩*(w, q) = ∅. Since p⊆q, p∩q = p. So, q = p∪(q - p). By Disjunction, *(s, q)⊆*(s, p)∪*(s, q - p). Since *(s, q)∩*(s, p) = ∅, *(s, q)⊆*(s, q - p). But, by facticity, *(s, q - p)⊆q - p⊆-p. It follows that *(s, q)∩p = ∅. Facticity and the Disjunction schema entail both generic specificity, validating Penguin Principle inferences such as

(16)

> Birds fly
> Penguins are birds
> Penguins don't fly
> Tweety is a penguin
> _____
> Tweety doesn't fly

We cannot yet show formally that this is nonmonotonically valid, for we have not yet defined nonmonotonic validity. But the central idea is easy to explain. Since birds fly, and penguins do not, normal penguins are not normal birds. But all penguins are birds. It follows, by Fact 1, that no penguins are normal birds. Thus, Tweety is not a normal bird. In evaluating (16) for nonmonotonic validity, to anticipate, we assume as much normality as possible, given the premises. We cannot consistently assume Tweety to be a normal bird. But we can assume Tweety to be a normal penguin, and normal penguins do not fly. So, we can conclude, nonmonotonically, that Tweety does not fly.

The validity of arguments of the form (16) above thus follows from Fact 1 and seriality on the first approach. These constraints imply that unjust commands are abnormal commands, for example, forcing the more specific obligation to take precedence. So, the first approach satisfies the Deontic Specificity condition (III).

On our first approach, A's *should* B holds in a world w if B holds in all ideals of the normal w-A-worlds. On the second, it holds in w if B is true in all w-A-good-and-simple worlds. We adopt constraints requiring that ideals of normal worlds are good-and-simple and that Disjunction inferences hold in L_o.

Definition 4 A world w is normal (written Nw) iff $\exists w'$ w ∈ *(w', W).

(d) the Ideals are good-and-simple constraint: Nw→ ⊕*(w, p)⊆ •(w, p)
(e) the Deontic Disjunction constraint: •(w, p∪q)⊆ •(w, p)∪•(w, q).

The first verifies an axiom, which appears below as (A13), permitting the monotonic inference from A $>_o$ B to⊤ $>$(A$>$ ◯B). This is crucial to getting our second approach to satisfy Default Detachment and Deontic Specificity. It also reflects the philosophical thesis that *ceteris paribus* principles are nonmonotonically stronger than generalizations about actual obligation. The second validates arguments such as (14) in L_o.

We note the following about $\oplus$ and $\bullet$:

Fact 2 : $\oplus$ and $\bullet$ obey the following:

> a. $p \subseteq q \rightarrow \oplus p \subseteq \oplus q$
> b. $\oplus(p \cup q) = \oplus p \cup \oplus q$
> c. $\oplus(p \cap q) \subseteq \oplus p \cap \oplus q$
> d. $p \neq \emptyset \rightarrow \oplus p \neq \emptyset$
> e. $Nw \rightarrow (*(w, p) \neq \emptyset \rightarrow \bullet(w, p) \neq \emptyset)$

Definition 5 Proper L_o frames have proper L frames whose ideals are good-and-simple and that satisfy the Deontic Disjunction constraint.

Proper L_o *frames* verify a deontic principle analogous to generic specificity, which enables the second approach to satisfy Deontic Specificity in normal worlds. If p is more specific than q, but the two give rise to conflicting obligations, then p is not a normal q:

Fact 3 : $Nw \rightarrow [(p \subseteq q \& \bullet(w, p) \cap \bullet(w, q) = \emptyset) \Rightarrow *(w, q) \cap p = \emptyset]$.

Proof: Suppose Nw, $p \subseteq q$ and $\bullet(w, p) \cap \bullet(w, q) = \emptyset$. By the "ideals are good-and-simple" constraint, $\oplus *(w, p) \oplus *(w, q) = \emptyset$. Fact 2c allows us to deduce $\oplus(*(w, p) \cap *(w, q)) = \emptyset$. Applying fact 2d, we obtain $*(w, p) \cap *(w, q) = \emptyset$. This, and fact 1, yield $*(w, q) \cap p = \emptyset$.

1.3. *Models*

We shall present the model theory and axiomatization of L_o; those for L are obvious variants of these. But we shall indicate which features, axioms, etc. are special to L_o.

Definition 6 A *base model* is a tuple $\langle W, D, \oplus, *, \bullet, \| \ \| \rangle$, where $\langle W, D, \oplus, *, \bullet \rangle$ is a proper L_o frame and $\| \ \|$ is a function from nonlogical constants of L_o to intensions (which, in turn, are functions from worlds to extensions).

A variable assignment α is a function from variables into D, the domain of a base model; all worlds have the same domain. It would be more appropriate to let domains vary from world to world, but the additional complication this requires yields no benefits for our purposes in this paper. Similarly, for the sake of simplicity, we assume that all objects in D have names in L, and we assume bivalence. We define satisfaction on everything but the connectives $>$ and $>_o$ in the standard way. Truth is satisfaction under all assignments: $M, w \models A$ iff $\forall \alpha \ M, w, \alpha \models A$. Where Γ is a set of formulas, $M, w, \alpha \models \Gamma$ iff $M, w, \alpha \models A$ for all $A \in \Gamma$. We extend the interpretation function $\| \ \|$ to formulas with the following definitions. $\|A\|$ M, α, the proposition A expresses under α in M, is the set of worlds in which α satisfies A: w $\in$ W: M, w, $\alpha \models$ A. If A is a sentence, and Γ a set thereof, we write $\|A\|$ M for w $\in$ W: M, w$\models$A and $\|\Gamma\|$ M for $\cap\|A\|$M : A $\in \Gamma$.

Definition 7 $\delta(t) = \|t\|$, if t is a constant, and $\alpha(t)$, if t is a variable

$$M, w, \alpha \models Rx_1\ldots x_n \text{ iff } \langle\delta(x_1),\ldots,\delta(x_n)\rangle \in \|R\|$$
$$M, w, \alpha \models \neg A \text{ iff not } M, w, \alpha \models A$$
$$M, w, \alpha \models A \& B \text{ iff } M, w, \alpha \models A \text{ and } M, w, \alpha \models B$$
$$M, w, \alpha \models \forall x\, A \text{ iff } M, w, \alpha' \models A, \text{ for all } \alpha' \text{ such that,}$$
$$\text{for all } v \neq x, \alpha(v) = \alpha'(v)$$
$$M, w, \alpha \models \bigcirc A \text{ iff } \oplus(w) \subseteq \|A\| M, \alpha$$
$$M, w, \alpha \models A > B \text{ iff } *(w, \|A\| M, \alpha) \subseteq \|B\| M, \alpha$$
$$M, w, \alpha \models A >_o B \text{ iff } \bullet(w, \|A\| M, \alpha) \subseteq \|B\| M, \alpha.$$

A generic conditional A>B holds in w if B holds in all worlds normal with respect to w and A. Abbreviating, B must hold in all the w-A-normal worlds. A statement of *prima facie* obligation in L_o, $A >_o B$, holds in w if B holds in all w-A-good-and-simple worlds.

Definition 8 If A is an L_o formula, and Γ a set thereof, then $\Gamma \models A$ iff, for all M, w, and α, if M, w, $\alpha \models \Gamma$, then M, w, $\alpha \models A$. A is valid,$\models A$, iff $\emptyset \models A$.

It is easy to verify that A>A is valid but A $>_o$ A is not. W-A-normal worlds are A-worlds in proper L_o frames. But w-A-good-and-simple worlds are not necessarily A-worlds; there may be nothing good and simple about A.

1.4. *Axiomatization*

We define derivability using the axioms and rules:

(A1) Truth-functional L-tautologies
(A2) $\forall x A \rightarrow A(t/x)$ for any term t
(A3) $\forall x A \leftrightarrow \neg\exists\neg Ax$
(A4) $\forall x(A \rightarrow B) \rightarrow (\exists A \rightarrow B)$ for x not free in B.
(A5) $\forall x(A > B) \rightarrow (A > \forall x B)$, for x not free in A.
(A6) $A > A$
(A7) $((A > C)\&(B > C)) \rightarrow ((A \vee B) > C)$
(A8) $\neg \bigcirc \bot$
(A9) $\bigcirc(A \rightarrow B) \rightarrow (\bigcirc A \rightarrow \bigcirc B)$
(A10) $A >_o \top$
(A11) $\forall x\,(A >_o B) \rightarrow (A >_o \forall x\,B)$, for x not free in A.
(A12) $((A >_o C)\&(B >_o C)) \rightarrow ((A \vee B) >_o C)$
(A13) $(A >_o B) \rightarrow (\top > (A > \bigcirc B))$
(R1) $\vdash A$ and $\vdash A \rightarrow B \Rightarrow \vdash B$
(R2) $\vdash (B_1\& \ldots \&B_i) \rightarrow B \Rightarrow \vdash (A > B_1\& \ldots \&A > B_i) \rightarrow A > B$

(R3) $\vdash A \to B(t/x) \Rightarrow \vdash A \to \forall x\ B$, where t is a constant not in A or B

(R4) $\vdash A \Rightarrow \vdash A(t/x)$ where t is a term not in A

(R5) $\vdash A \leftrightarrow B$ and A a subformula of $C \Rightarrow \vdash C \leftrightarrow C(B/A)$

(R6) $\vdash A \Rightarrow \vdash \bigcirc A$

(R7) $\vdash (B_1 \& \ldots \& B_i) \to B \Rightarrow \vdash (A >_o B_1 \& \ldots \& A >_o B_i) \to A >_o B$

(R8) $\vdash A \leftrightarrow B \Rightarrow \vdash A > C \leftrightarrow B > C$

(R9) $\vdash A \leftrightarrow B \Rightarrow \vdash A >_o C \leftrightarrow B >_o C$

(A10)-(A14), (R7), and (R9) are special to L_o.

A *derivation* is a finite sequence of formulas, each of which instantiates an axiom or follows by means of a rule from earlier formulas. A is derivable, $\vdash A$, iff some derivation ends with A. Derivability generalizes as usual to allow premises. Following standard methods, we obtain:

COMPLETENESS THEOREM: $\Sigma \vdash A$ iff $\Sigma \models A$.

1.5. *Monotonic Inferences*

The truth conditions we assign to *prima facie* obligation statements under either approach suffice to explain the monotonic validity of closure under logical consequence:

(17)

Fs should G	If A, then it ought to be the case that B
G entails H	B entails C
---	---
Fs should H	If A, then it ought to be the case that C

On our first approach, this follows from the closure of each of $\bigcirc$ and $>$ under logical consequence. On our second, the first premise, $A >_o B$, holds in w if B is true in all w-A-good-and-simple worlds. But, wherever B is true, C is true also, according to the second premise. So, C must hold in all w-A-good-and-simple worlds. And this is just the truth condition for the conclusion. To take an example: if machines should work, and, to work, a thing must change, then machines should change. Suppose that each machine works in all machine-good-and-simple worlds. Anything that works in a world changes in that world. It follows that each machine changes in every machine-good-and-simple world.

Another monotonic validity resulting from our truth definition is a conditional variant of a controversial principle that (Williams, 1973) calls agglomeration and that (Marcus, 1980) calls factoring:

(18)

Fs should G	If A, then it should be the case that B
Fs should H	If A, then it should be the case that C
---	---
Fs should G and H	If A, then it should be the case that B and C

Clearly, this follows from both analyses. If both B and C are true in all w-A-normal-ideal worlds, so is their conjunction. Similarly with w-A-good-and-simple worlds.

2. NONMONOTONIC CONSEQUENCE

The chief advantages of our theory stem from our use of nonmonotonic logic. To explain them, therefore, we need to explain our account of nonmonotonic inference.

Our truth conditions for generics and for *prima facie* obligation evaluate them by considering certain classes of worlds: for generics, w-A-normal worlds, and, for conditional obligation sentences, w-A-good-and-simple worlds. These classes of worlds indicate what is normal, doxastically or deontically, in a given world. Within L, we need to worry only about doxastic normality. This allows a straightforward approach to nonmonotonic consequence.

To determine the nonmonotonic consequences of a set of premises,

> Assume everything to be as normal as possible,
> given the premises (and only the premises);
> ask what follows.

Assume, initially, that we have no information. We are ideal logical reasoners, but know nothing about the actual world. If we think of our information state as a set of worlds compatible with the information we have, then the information state is simply W. Each premise gives us information. In monotonic logic, the first premise, say A_1, restricts the information state to $\|A_1\|$; each A_{n+1} changes the state s_i obtained by processing the first n premises to $s_i \cap \|A_{n+1}\|$. In nonmonotonic inference, each premise also restricts s_i so that everything is as doxastically or deontically normal as possible. That is, it restricts the state to the subset of w-$\|A_{n+1}\|$ -normal (or w-$\|A_{n+1}\|$ -good-and-simple) worlds, unless the result of this further restriction would be an empty set of worlds. So, we assume that everything is as normal as can be, given the information we have; we do not assume blithely that everything is normal, for we may already know that to be false.

The function * specifies what is generically normal in each world. We use it to characterize a normalization function on information states. First, we generalize * from worlds to information states:

Definition 9 $*(s, p) = \cup_{w \in s} *(w, p)$; $\bullet(s, p) = \cup_{w \in s} \bullet(w, p)$

We then define normalization:

Definition 10

$$N(s, p) = \begin{cases} (s \cap W\text{-}p) \cup (s \cap *(s, p)); & \text{if } s \cap *(s, p) \neq \emptyset \\ s & \text{otherwise.} \end{cases}$$

Normalizing information state s with respect to proposition p restricts s to worlds that are not p-abnormal. If s⊆p, normalization yields s∩*(s, p), so long as this set is nonempty.

Requiring that s∩*(s, p) ≠ ∅ and letting N(s, p) be s otherwise strengthens s with an assumption of normality only if that does not contradict s. If it does, the normalization function does nothing.

2.1. Deontic Normalization

If we stay with L's analysis of conditional obligation, this sort of normalization suffices. In L_o, however, practical reasoning requires a complication of information states and, correspondingly, of normalization. Because we frequently reason using both doxastic generics (such as *People are selfish*) and deontic generics (such as *People ought to be altruistic*), we must keep careful track of two different kinds of information. An agent will typically have information about the way the w orld is and about the way it ought to be. We must treat these two aspects separately. We begin by defining deontic normalization and nonmonotonic consequence for arguments without nested deontic operators, to keep the intuitive picture clearer; a small change extends the scheme to arguments with nesting of arbitrary finite depth.

Formally, we begin by representing information states as pairs of sets of worlds. One is factual, the other normative. We reason about deontic matters in L_o in terms of good-and-simple worlds. We draw conclusions about actual obligation from the normative set. But the truth of actual obligation sentences is defined in terms of ideal worlds. We are justified in using the normative set and its conclusions about good-and-simple worlds to make defeasible inferences about ideal worlds because of our constraint stating that ideals of normal worlds are good-and-simple.

So, updating an information state involves adding to its information about the way the world is, or to its information about the way the world ought to be, or both. Normalizing an information state, similarly, involves

(a) assuming that the world is as doxastically normal as possible, given the state's picture of how the world is,
(b) assuming that everything is as deontically normal as possible in ideal worlds, given the state's picture of how the world is and ought to be, and
(c) assuming that everything is as doxastically normal as possible in ideal worlds.

Part (a) proceeds just as above. To effect (b), we assume that circumstances are good-and-simple whenever possible. The set t is the set of "normative" worlds–the worlds, that is, that determine obligations–and s is the set of "doxastic" wor lds of the information state in which the nonmoral statements are true.

Definition 11

$$
\Omega(s,t,p) = \left\{
\begin{array}{cl}
w \in t : w \in \bullet(s,p) & \text{if } \bullet(s,p) \cap t \neq \emptyset, *(s,p) \cap s \neq \emptyset, \\
& \text{and } p \subseteq s \\
t & \text{otherwise.}
\end{array}
\right.
$$

The effect of updating a set t of normative worlds deontically with respect to p, given an information state s, then, is to restrict t to worlds that are morally normal with respect to p. Like doxastic normalization, the update occurs only if certain conditions are satisfied. First, the update must not result in absurdity. This makes the obligation *prima facie*. Second, it must be doxastically possible that we are dealing with a normal p situation. If we are not, then *prima facie* obligations conditional on p are moot. Finally, the information state s must contain p. Conditional obligations apply only when their antecedents hold. To effect (c), we apply doxastic normalization, as defined above, to the result of (b). Ordinary reasoning about generics takes place with respect to ideal worlds as well as the actual world. This step is necessary to capture the nonmonotonic validity, for example, of the inference from $\bigcirc A$ and $\bigcirc(A{>}B)$ to $\bigcirc B$.

2.2. *Information Models*

In both L and L_o, we need to define iterative normalization. In L_o, to normalize iteratively an information state using a set of propositions, we have to combine both doxastic and deontic normalization in a single procedure.

We begin by defining support in L. To define iterative normalization, we need to know which formulas an information state supports or rejects.

Definition 12 The *update function* +: $\wp(W) \times \wp(L) \to \wp(W)$ for M = $\langle W, D, \oplus, *, \bullet, \| \| \rangle$ is such that, for all information states s $\in \wp(W)$, and for all sets Γ of L sentences: s + Γ = s$\cap \| \Gamma \|$ M.

Definition 13 A model M and information state s *support* an L-sentence A (written M, s$\models$A) if and only if s$\subseteq \|A\|$ M.

Thus s supports A in M just in case A is true in M at each world of s.

In L_o, we need to extend this to an additional support relation, $\approx$, since information states are pairs of sets. To keep our monotonic logic classical, we define this relation in terms of supervaluations over conforming assignments.

Definition 14 An assignment v of truth values to L_o-sentences *conforms* to M and $\langle s, t \rangle$ iff

If A is atomic or of the form B>C or of the form B $>_o$ C:

    $v(A) = 1$ iff M, s$\models$A

    $v(A) = 0$ iff M, s$\models$ ¬A

If A is of the form $\bigcirc$B:

    $v(A) = 1$ iff t$\models$B

    $v(A) = 0$ iff not t$\models$B

If A is of the form B & C:

    $v(A) = 1$ iff $v(A) = v(B) = 1$

    $v(A) = 0$ iff $v(A) = 0$ or $v(B) = 0$

If A is of the form ¬B

    $v(A) = 1$ iff $v(B) = 0$

    $v(A) = 0$ iff $v(B) = 1$

If A is of the form $\forall x$ B:

    $v(A) = 1$ iff $v(Ac/x) = 1$ for all $c \in L_o$

    $v(A) = 0$ iff $v(Ac/x) = 0$ for some $c \in L_o$

Definition 15 A model M and information state (s, t) support an L_o-sentence A (M, $\langle s, t \rangle \models$ A) iff A is true on every assignment of truth values to L_o-sentences conforming to M and $\langle s, t \rangle$.

Let Γ be a set of sentences, P an enumerable set of propositions, and ν any one-to-one correspondence between P and N, or some initial segment thereof. The recursion we describe cycles through P as enumerated by ν, starting over again when P is exhausted and after each limit ordinal. Let p^α be the αth proposition in the cycle determined by ν, and let 1st and 2nd map ordered pairs into their first and second constituents, respectively.

Definition 16 The *P-normalization chain with respect to ν that begins from s* is the sequence:

$$s_\nu^0 = \langle s, W^* \rangle$$
$$s_\nu^{\alpha+1} = \langle N (1st(s_\nu^\alpha), p^\alpha), N(\Omega(2nd(s_\nu^\alpha), p^\alpha), p^\alpha) \rangle$$
$$s_\nu^\lambda = \langle \cap_\mu \in \lambda \; 1st(s_\nu^\mu), \cap_\mu \in \lambda \; 2nd(s_\nu^\mu) \rangle$$

Each state has a successor obtained by normalizing with the next proposition. At limit ordinals, we take the intersection of all preceding states.

The idea of assuming nothing but the premises of an argument underlies nonmonotonic reasoning. In monotonic systems, additional information cannot disrupt a conclusion. In nonmonotonic systems, however, added assumptions can invalidate arguments. To model nonmonotonic inference, therefore, we must capture the intuitive notion of assuming just the premises of an argument.

To do this, begin with a state of complete ignorance, in other words, with the set W* of all possible worlds in the canonical model M*. It supports only logical validities. To evaluate an argument, update it with the argument's premises. Then, normalize with a unified procedure. The P-normalization chain with respect to $\sim$ that begins from a state that assumes nothing but the premises Γ is the sequence with $\langle W^* + \Gamma, W^* \rangle$ as its first element.

Each state and enumeration ν of P determines a P-normalization chain beginning with $\langle W^* + \Gamma, W^* \rangle$ for Γ. Since normalization monotonically depletes sets of possible worlds, every chain C reaches a fixed point C^*: for each s and ν, there is an ordinal α such that, for all larger ordinals β, $s_\nu^\beta = s_\nu^\alpha$. We define nonmonotonic consequence:

Definition 17 $\Gamma \mathrel{\vertbar\approx}_P A$ iff, for any P-normalization chain C beginning from $W^* + \Gamma$, M^*, $C^* \not\models A$.

We are interested, specifically, in the case where P is the set of all instantiations of antecedents of $>$- and $>_o$-conditionals in formulas or subformulas in Γ to those individual constants appearing in the premises and new constants serving as witnesses for existential premises. Call this set of instantiations Prop(Γ). We define:

Definition 18 $\Gamma \mathrel{\vertbar\approx} A$ iff $\Gamma \mathrel{\vertbar\approx}_{Prop(\Gamma)} A$.

In L_o, this means that we reach practical conclusions nonmonotonically from information about good-and-simple worlds. We define nonmonotonic validity in terms of fixed points. A set of premises Σ nonmonotonically entails a conclusion A if and only if every normalization of Σ reaches a fixed point that supports the truth of A. If A contains no deontic operators, it speaks solely of the way the world is; we look only at that aspect of the information state at each fixed point, and evaluate A in the usual way. If A does contain deontic operators, however, it speaks of the way the world ought to be, as well as, perhaps, the way it is. Evaluating A then requires us to examine what the information state tells us about the way the world ought to be. A statement of the form $\bigcirc B$, in particular, gains support at a state if B is true at every world in the set containing the state's information about how the world ought to be.

2.3. *Nested Deontic Operators*

The scheme we have developed handles arguments without nested deontic operators. It is adequate for almost all the arguments discussed in the literature on deontic logic or practical reasoning. Some arguments, however, do contain nested operators: inferences, for example, from A $>_o$ (B $>_o$ C) and A & $\bigcirc$B to $\bigcirc\bigcirc$C. To extend our definitions to arguments with nesting of arbitrary finite depth, however, we need to alter our characterization of information states and our definition of deontic normalization.

Let Σ be a set of sentences with deontic operators nested to a depth of at most n. We may represent an information state as an n+1-tuple $\langle s_o, s_1, \ldots, s_i \rangle$ of sets of worlds. The first, s_o, is factual; the others are normative. We define normalization procedures as above, but combine them in a more complex transfinite recursion. Each stage of the recursion is an n-step process. In step one, we normalize as before with s_0 and s_1. In step two, we normalize with the resulting s_1' and s_2. We continue taking pairs in this way until we reach s_{n-1}' and s_i.

Definition 19 The *P-normalization chain with respect to ν that begins from s* is the sequence:

$$s_\nu^0 = \langle s_0^0, s_1^0, \ldots, s_i^0 \rangle = \langle s, W^*, \ldots, W^* \rangle$$

$s^{\alpha+1}\nu$ = the result of an n-step procedure, where, at each step i:

$$s_j^{\alpha+1,0_\nu} = s_j^\alpha$$
$$s_j^{\alpha+1,i_\nu} = s_j^{\alpha+1,(i-1)_\nu} \text{ for all } j < i;$$
$$s_j^{\alpha+1,i_\nu} = s_j^{\alpha,i_\nu} \text{ for all } j > i+1;$$
$$s_i^{\alpha+1,i_\nu} = N(s_i^{\alpha,i_\nu}, p^\alpha);$$
$$s_{i+1}^{\alpha+1,i_\nu} = N(\Omega(s_i^{\alpha,i_\nu}, s_{i+1}^{\alpha,i_\nu}, p^\alpha), p^\alpha).$$

$s^{\lambda_\nu} = \langle s_0^{\lambda_\nu}, \ldots, s_i^{\lambda_\nu} \rangle$, where $s_i^{\lambda_\nu} = \cap_\mu \in \lambda \, s_i^{\mu_\nu}$

At each stage, we proceed through the n+1-tuple, taking pairs of sets. The first set of the n+1-tuple is the factual set. The second is a normative set, saying how things ought to be from the perspective of the first, factual set. The third is another normative set, saying how things ought to be from the perspective of the second set. At each step of the n-step procedure for successor ordinals, we normalize on a pair of successive sets in the sequence, treating the first as if it were factual and the second as if it were normative for the sake of that step.

We may define nonmonotonic consequence as above by expanding the notion of support once again:

Definition 20 A model M and information state $s = \langle s_0, \ldots, s_i \rangle$ support an L_0-sentence A at s_j ($M, s, s_j \Vdash A$) iff s_j is among $s_0, \ldots, s_i$ and A is true on every assignment of truth values to L_0-sentences conforming to M and $\langle s_j, s_{j+1} \rangle$.

Definition 21 A model M and information state $s = \langle s_0, \ldots, s_i \rangle$ support an L_0-sentence A ($M, s \Vdash A$) iff M and s support A at s_0.

The consequence definition is now adequate to handle nesting to any finite depth.

3. NONMONOTONIC INFERENCES

The implications of this account for generics are spelled out in (Asher and Morreau, 1991; Asher and Morreau, 1995). All the practical inferences, on our first approach, collapse into the inference patterns for generics detailed there. Here we focus solely on deontic inferences in L_o. Our two approaches agree on all the inference patterns we discuss, unless we note otherwise. Despite the complexity of its definition, the nonmonotonic validity of most arguments can be decided by a simple finite procedure.

First, our approaches satisfy criterion (I). Default detachment, the inference from $A >_o B$ and A to $\bigcirc B$, is nonmonotonically valid. The conclusion is defeasible; it may be defeated by further information. Consider these examples:

(19)

> Neoptolemus is a person
> People should be kind
>
> _____
>
> Neoptolemus should be kind

(20)

> Neoptolemus is a person
> Neoptolemus should not be kind
> People should be kind
>
> _____
>
> Neoptolemus should be kind*

(We use '*' to indicate a conclusion that does not follow.) (18) is acceptable, but (19) fails. *Prima facie* principles that apply to people in general may not apply to people in unusual circumstances. (As Odysseus stresses, "His [Philoctetes'] weapons alone are destined to take Troy" (113).)

Our theory predicts this correctly. As in Asher and Morreau, a formal proof of this involves the construction of a survivor world that is an element of the initial moral state and belongs to every fixed point. But the idea is straightforward. For simplicity, begin with the premise that Neoptolemus is a person. We restrict the factual set of all worlds to those in which Neoptolemus is a person. We know nothing yet about normalcy, deontic or otherwise, so this is all we do. We then process the premise that people should be kind. This does not affect the factual set of worlds, but it restricts the normative set to those in which everyone who is a person, according to the factual set, is kind. In particular, Neoptolemus is kind in all such worlds.

Factual Set	Normative Set
Neoptolemus is a person	People (in the factual set) are kind
	Neoptolemus is kind

So, the result of normalizing is a state that supports the conclusion, *Neoptolemus should be kind*–Neoptolemus is kind in every world in the state's normative set. This explains the validity of (18).

To see why (19) fails, again assume that we begin with a state of total ignorance. The premise that Neoptolemus is a person restricts the factual set to worlds in which Neoptolemus is a person. The premise that Neoptolemus should not be kind restricts the normative set to worlds in which Neoptolemus is not kind.

Factual Set	Normative Set
Neoptolemus is a person	Neoptolemus is not kind

Now, the premise that people should be kind restricts the normative set, for each entity that is a person according to the factual set, to worlds in which that person is kind–except where the result of the restriction would be absurdity, that is, the empty set of worlds. Neoptolemus is just such an exception. So, the result of normalizing supports, not the conclusion that Neoptolemus should be kind, but the opposite conclusion that he should not be.

Reasoning similar to that showing that (18) is valid also demonstrates the validity of (20), an inference involving irrelevant information:

(21)

> People should be kind
> Neoptolemus is a person
> Neoptolemus watches a lot of television
> ———————————————————
> Neoptolemus should be kind

Updating the factual set with the information that Neoptolemus is a couch potato does nothing to interfere with support for the conclusion at each fixed point.

Our approaches also satisfy criterion (II), Conditional Conflict. The reasoning showing the invalidity of (19) extends easily to show the invalidity of the following arguments, which are deontic versions of the Nixon diamond:

(22)

> Judges should be partial to no one
> Fathers should be partial to their children
> Sam is a judge and a father
> ———————————————————
> Sam should be partial to no one*

(23)

> Judges should be partial to no one
> Fathers should be partial to their children
> Sam is a judge and a father
> ———————————————————
> Sam should be partial to his children*

These cases reflect moral conflicts. We have already seen that moral conflicts arise from *prima facie* principles with different antecedents that both happen to be true. To what extent should logic determine which principle takes precedence? When there is no logical relation between the antecedents, the answer is surely that logic should determine nothing. Whether the obligations of judges or fathers take precedence in a particular case is a substantive moral issue. Logically, then, neither (21) nor (22) is acceptable.

That is precisely what we predict. Begin with a state of ignorance and update with the premise that Sam is a judge and a father. This restricts the worlds in the factual set to those in which the premise is true. Then update with the premise that judges should be partial to no one. Next, update with the premise that fathers should be partial to their children. Now, begin the process of normalization. Suppose we normalize first with the impartiality premise. This restricts the normative set to worlds in which those who are judges according to the factual set are impartial. In particular, Sam is now impartial in all the normative worlds.

Factual Set	Normative Set
Sam is a judge	Judges (in factual set) are impartial
Sam is a father	Sam is impartial

We then normalize with the partiality premise. Where possible, we restrict the normative set to worlds in which those who are fathers according to the factual set are partial to their children. Such a restriction is impossible for Sam, since he is already impartial toward everyone in all normative worlds. So, taking the impartiality premise first yields a fixed point in which Sam should be partial to no one. It should be clear from the procedure just outlined, however, that taking the partiality premise first would give the opposite result, a fixed point in which Sam should be partial to his children.

Factual Set	Normative Set
Sam is a judge	Fathers (in factual set) are partial to
Sam is a father	their children
	Sam is partial to his children

Neither conclusion gains support in every fixed point, so both arguments are invalid.

Note, however, that, in each fixed point, Sam is either partial to no one or partial to his children. This establishes the nonmonotonic validity of the following argument:

(24)

>Judges should be partial to no one
>Fathers should be partial to their children
>Sam is a judge and a father

>Sam should be partial to his children or to no one

Our approaches also satisfy criterion (III), Deontic Specificity. Consider:

(25)

>Commands should be obeyed
>Unjust commands are commands
>Unjust commands should not be obeyed
>Odysseus' command is unjust

>Odysseus' command should not be obeyed

We begin in ignorance and update with the premises, restricting the factual set to worlds in which Odysseus' command is unjust. Because commands should be obeyed, but unjust commands should not be obeyed, we encounter a conflict. By fact 3 above, however, we can conclude from this that normal commands are not unjust; this in turn implies that Odysseus' command is not a normal command. We then normalize, assuming things to be as normal, generically and deontically, as possible. Although we know that Odysseus' command is an abnormal command, we may still assume that it is a normal unjust command. So, we restrict the normative set to worlds in which unjust commands are not obeyed.

Factual Set	Normative Set
O's command is unjust	Unjust commands (in factual set) are not obeyed
	O's command is not obeyed

In no world of the normative set, therefore, is Odysseus' command obeyed.

Finally, our approaches satisfy criterion (IV), Unwanted Implications. We follow (Loewer, 1983; Loewer, 1986) in holding that the robber and gentle murder paradoxes revolve around issues of judgment and deliberation, rather than around closure of logical consequence (as in (Goble, 1990; Goble, 1990; Goble, 1990)). But we have a rather different view of that contrast. (Thomason, 1981; Thomason, 1981) distinguishes the context of deliberation, in which one must decide what to do and takes the facts simply as given, from the context of judgment, in which one can reflect on the moral status of the facts themselves. According to Thomason, Belzer, and Loewer, the paradoxes reveal that the context of deliberation presupposes that whatever is, is right: robbers should rob and murderers should murder. This happens because, in deliberation, we restrict our attention to possible courses of events that share our history.

It is harmless because we are not deliberating about the present or matters otherwise already settled; the context of judgment is available for doing that. The essential contrast between judgment and deliberation is, on this view, a difference in what we take as settled.

From our perspective, however, the contrast is one of including or suppressing information about the moral status of certain facts, whether they are in the present or the past, whether they are settled or unsettled. The robber and gentle murder paradoxes have similar forms. For both, let B monotonically imply A:

(26)

	Robber:		Gentle murder:	
	C			A
	$C >_o B$			$A >_o B$
	$\bigcirc A$			$\bigcirc A$

The gentle murder paradox is just the special case of the robber paradox in which C = A. The conclusions follow nonmonotonically. To take just the robber paradox:

Factual Set	Normative Set
C	B, A

The first premise restricts the factual set to worlds in which C is true. The second restricts the normative set to those in which B is true. But, since B monotonically implies A, A is also true in every world in the normative set. This certainly seems counterintuitive. In the context of deliberation, however, we ignore the moral status of the facts as they are now; we simply take them for granted and ask what ought to be done about them. We assume that the robber has robbed, and you will murder Jones. We ask what ought to be done given that information.

In the context of judgment, however, we consider the moral status of the facts. Making this explicit requires adding a moral premise to each argument form (where, again, B monotonically implies A):

(27)

	$\bigcirc \neg A$		$\bigcirc \neg A$
	C		A
	$C >_o B$		$A >_o B$
	$\bigcirc A^*$		$\bigcirc A^*$

Now, neither $\bigcirc A$ nor $\bigcirc B$ follow, even nonmonotonically. Normalization with A fails to yield anything new, because every world in the normative set already verifies something incompatible with the result of normalizing. For the robber paradox:

Factual Set   Normative Set
C   ¬A

In the context of deliberation, then, the robber should repent, and you should murder Jones gently. The question of whether the robber should have become a robber and whether you should murder Jones does not arise. In the context of judgment, however, the robber should not have been in a position to repent, and you should not murder Jones, gently or otherwise. This conclusion does not depend on ignoring the fact that the robber is a robber, or treating it as unsettled whether or not you will murder Jones. It does not involve a thought experiment of going back in time to a point before the truth of C or A above. It simply depends on recognizing that, although they are true, they should not be.

The most distinctive features of our approach emerge in its solution to Roderick Chisolm's contrary-to-duty paradox (Chisholm, 1963).

(28)

Arabella ought to visit her grandmother.
It ought to be the case that, if she visits, she calls to say she's coming.
Arabella doesn't visit her grandmother.
If she doesn't visit, she shouldn't call to say she's coming.

(29)

$$\bigcirc A$$
$$\bigcirc (A > B)$$
$$\neg A$$
$$\neg A >_o \neg B \quad (\text{or } \neg A > \bigcirc \neg B)$$

In standard deontic logic, these assertions are inconsistent. (Treating the conditionals differently has struck many as artificial, but the technical point remains.) The first two, in an instance of deontic detachment, imply $\bigcirc B$, while the last two, in an instance of factual detachment, imply $\bigcirc \neg B$ (Greenspan, 1975; Loewer, 1983). Yet the English sentences in (28) are not only consistent but commonplace. Many have drawn the moral that one must choose between these two modes of detachment.

Our nonmonotonic logic allows us to have both factual and deontic detachment without inconsistency. It is easy to verify that both are nonmonotonically valid:

(30)

    a. $\bigcirc$A

        $\bigcirc(A > B)$

        ———————

        $\bigcirc$B

    b. ¬A

        ¬$A >_o$ ¬B   (or ¬$A > \bigcirc$¬B)

        ———————

        $\bigcirc$¬B

(30)b is analogous to (18) above. The premises of (30)a restrict the normative set to worlds in which A, A>B, and– because we normalize the normative set as well as the factual set– B are true.

Nevertheless, the assertions in (20) are not inconsistent. Only the second of these is valid:

(31)

    a. $\bigcirc$A

        $\bigcirc(A > B)$

        ¬A

        ¬$A >_o$ ¬B   (or ¬$A > \bigcirc$¬B)

        ———————

        $\bigcirc$B

    b. $\bigcirc$A

        $\bigcirc(A > B)$

        ¬A

        ¬$A >_o$ ¬B   (or ¬$A > \bigcirc$¬B)

        ———————

        $\bigcirc$¬B

We may begin by restricting the normative set to worlds in which A and A>B are true, as the first two premises demand, and then restricting the factual set to worlds in which ¬A holds by processing the third premise. We must apply deontic normalization to the factual set before normalizing the normative set. So, we must next process the fourth premise, restricting the normative set to worlds satisfying ¬B. We cannot then normalize that set by restricting it to worlds satisfying B, for the result would be empty.

Our theory, then, extends standard deontic logic, employing both deontic and factual detachment, without encountering contradiction. Notably, we do not need tense or even an irreducible conditional obligation operator to accomplish this. Our resolution of the paradox depends only on making detachment defeasible.

4. POPE SYSTEMS

A simple but important difference between our account and those of Thomason, Horty, Lewis, Loewer, Belzer, and Goble concerns statements of the form $A >_o A$ (in their language, $\bigcirc(A/A)$). They take them to be valid. This makes sentences such as the following valid:

(32)

        a. If Jackie cheats, then Jackie ought to cheat
        b. Those who commit murders should commit murders.

Used in a defeasible detachment inference, moreover, such sentences seem to permit the derivation of ought from is:

(33)

        Max commits murders.
        Those who commit murders should commit murders.

        ―――――――――――――――――――――――――――――――――

        Max should commit murders.

These systems thus seem committed to a *prima facie* principle that whatever is, is right. For that reason, we call them Pope systems. From one point of view, their commitment threatens to trivialize moral and practical reasoning. More generally, it restricts their theories to deliberative contexts. As we have seen in discussing the gentle murder paradox, our own system can yield $\bigcirc A$ from the premise A under certain conditions. This may be harmless in deliberative contexts, but it surely wreaks havoc with contexts of judgment. Our theory avoids the conclusion in those contexts. Most fundamentally, validities such as (32)a and b, and arguments such as (33), are out of place in logical systems devised for analyzing moral conflict, a point Alexander Pope himself would surely have recognized (Pope, 1733):

        All Nature is but art, unknown to thee;
        All chance, direction, which thou canst not see;
        All discord, harmony not understood;
        All partial evil, universal good;
        And, spite of pride, in erring reason's spite,
        One truth is clear: Whatever is, is right.

Pope, interestingly, maintains that all conflict is merely epistemic. Our systems, designed for discord and partial evil, constitutive as well as epistemic, are not Pope systems.

    Horty's nonmonotonic deontic logic, founded on default logic, is a Pope system. Horty shows that, where Θ is the default theory associated with an imperative set I, $A >_o B$ is true with respect to I if and only if B belongs to an extension of $\Theta(A)$. Clearly, $A >_o A$ holds with respect to every imperative set I, for A by definition belongs to every extension of $\Theta(A)$. We think that a moral theory cannot avoid the conclusion that what is necessary is morally obligatory, but contingent matters of fact should not automatically count as morally obligatory, at least in contexts of judgment. Since default logic defines nonmonotonic validity in terms of extensions, this consequence seems difficult to avoid.

A modal cousin of Horty's approach is to define the truth of conditional obligation statements modally: $A >_o B$ is true in w if and only if B is true in the best A-world(s) relative to w (or, the AB worlds are better, relative to w, than the A¬B worlds) (Lewis, 1973; Lewis, 1974; Loewer, 1983; Loewer, 1986; Goble, 1990). Some intuitions support such an approach. We might think that, to evaluate a conditional obligation statement $A >_o B$, we must first find worlds in which A holds and then see whether B holds in the best of those worlds (or whether the AB-worlds are better than the A¬B-worlds). But the result is a Pope system: it validates $A >_o A$ and so holds at best for deliberative contexts.

Our approaches treat judgmental contexts very naturally. In deliberative contexts, we ignore the moral status of the facts themselves; in judgmental contexts, we consider the moral status of the facts. In a nonmonotonic setting, that means that conclusions available in deliberative contexts may not be available in related judgmental contexts. The troubling conclusions of the robber and gentle murder paradoxes are good examples. Pope systems, however, cannot adopt our straightforward account of the deliberative/judgmental distinction. All the above philosophers follow Thomason in trying to extend their accounts to judgmental contexts by defining them in terms of deliberative contexts at an earlier time: It ought to be the case that A, in a judgmental context at a time, if and only if, at some earlier deliberative context before A's truth value was settled, it ought to have been the case that A. This is plausible at first glance. But it follows that whenever the world is not what it ought to be, in the judgmental sense, it is because of some earlier moral mistake, some swerving from the proper moral path, by an agent or by the unthinking course of events. But when Jimmy Carter announced that life is unfair, for example, he did not commit himself to the existence of some earlier moral swerving that brought about the unfairness.

There is a link between judgmental contexts and earlier deliberative contexts. Pace Thomason, however, it is nonmonotonic. In fact, it is just an instance of a general principle of causality. Judgmental contexts can no more be defined in terms of deliberative ones than effects can be defined in terms of their usual causes.

What is right in default logic and other Pope systems is that we must evaluate the antecedent in the actual world, and the consequent relative to the antecedent. As we have put it, $A >_o B$ is true in w if and only if B holds in all the w-A-good-and-simple worlds. These worlds are usually A-worlds, but they need not be. In particular, they are likely not to be if there is nothing good or simple about A. In updating with something of the form $A >_o B$, similarly, we restrict the normative set to worlds in which B holds of as many things that are A in the factual set as we can while avoiding absurdity. The antecedent is thereby evaluated in the actual world–in the factual set of the information state–and the consequent is evaluated relative to the antecedent, for we consider only w-A-good-and-simple worlds. We do not, however, assume that such worlds are A worlds, or, what would be the same thing, restrict the normative set to A-worlds. Consequently, arguments such as (33), having the form

(34)

$$A >_o A$$
$$A$$
$$\overline{}$$
$$\bigcirc A$$

fail in our theories, not only because, in cases such as the gentle murder paradox, one needs to make explicit the moral status of the facts–by, for example, adding the premise $\bigcirc \neg A$–but also because the premise $A >_o A$ is not valid. Our approach thus handles judgmental as well as deliberative contexts.

Our account of judgmental contexts would allow us to accept $A >_o A$ as valid without making (34) valid. But $A >_o A$ has other deplorable consequences. Accepting it commits one to an unacceptable principle, deontic cut:

(35)

> Rich people should give all they have to the poor
> Rich people who give all they have to the poor should be canonized
> _____
> Rich people should be canonized*

Plainly, deontic cut does not hold in our system, because we keep the factual and normative aspects of information states distinct. Say Scrooge is a rich person. Updating with the first premise, we restrict the normative set to worlds in which he gives everything to the poor. Updating with the second premise, we restrict the normative set to worlds in which those who give everything to the poor in the factual set are canonized. We have no reason to count Scrooge among such saints.

Factual Set (F)	Normative Set
Scrooge is a rich person	The rich-in-F give all they have to poor-in-F
	Scrooge gives all to the poor-in-F
	Rich-persons-in-F who give-in-F all they have-in-F to the poor-in-F are canonized

Any Pope system with something like the logic we have developed accepts the inference, however. If Scrooge is rich, and rich people should give all they have to the poor, then Scrooge should give all he has to the poor. All who do so should be canonized. Applying $A >_o A$ to this very principle, we conclude that it ought to be the case that all who do so should be canonized. And this yields the conclusion that Scrooge should be canonized.

The inference underlying this example, on which our system differs from Pope systems, is (36)a. It allows one to apply conditional moral rules, not only when the condition of the rule is met, but when it ought to be met. Pope systems accept it because they license the inference from $A >_o B$ to $\bigcirc(A >_o B)$. But (36)a not only has the silly instance (36)b; it underlies what we call deontic defeasible chaining inferences, (36)c-e. All the following are valid in Pope systems:

(36)

a. $\bigcirc A$
         $A >_o B$

         $\bigcirc B*$

b.   I should never do anything immoral.
         If I never do anything immoral, I should be revered.

         I should be revered.*

c.   Those who remain alert should be rewarded
         Police officers should remain alert
         Pat is a police officer

         Pat should be rewarded *

d.   Those who remain alert don't work the night shift
         Police officers should remain alert
         Pat is a police officer

         Pat shouldn't work the night shift *

(36)

    e.   Those who remain alert should be rewarded
             Good police officers remain alert
             Pat is a good police officer

             Pat should be rewarded

In our theory, only (36)e holds. Updating with its third premise, we restrict the factual set to worlds in which Pat is a good police officer. The second premise restricts the factual set to one in which good police officers and, so, Pat remain alert.

The first premise restricts the normative set to worlds in which those who remain alert in the factual set are rewarded. Thus, Pat is rewarded in every world in the normative set.

Factual Set (F)	Normative Set
Pat is a good police officer	All who remain-alert-in-F
Good police officers remain alert	are rewarded
Pat remains alert	Pat is rewarded

Argument (36)c fails for the same reasons that deontic cut fails. In argument (36)d, which is more intuitively appealing, the factual and normative sets also fail to interact in the right way. The third premise restricts the factual set to worlds in which Pat is a police officer. The second restricts the normative set to worlds in which all who are police officers in the factual set, including Pat, remain alert. The first restricts the factual set to worlds in which nobody works nights and remains alert. It has no effect at all on the normative worlds. Consequently, we can draw no conclusion about Pat's working hours in the normative worlds.

Factual Set (F)	Normative Set
Pat is a police officer	All police-officers-in-F remain alert
Nobody working nights	Pat remains alert
remains alert	

If (36)d is a good inference, it is only because its first premise has modal force. That is, the plausibility of (36)d and similar inferences depends on the plausibility of taking the doxastic conditional premise as true beyond the actual world. The situation is similar with defeasible transitivity inferences:

(37)

    a.   Rover is an Airedale
            Dogs should be well cared-for
            Airedales are dogs

            Rover should be well cared-for

    b.   Fido is a dog
            Dogs should be obedient
            Obedient animals are smart

            Fido should be smart*

    c.   Midas is a person
            People should be generous
            Generous people should be thanked

            Midas should be thanked*

Pope systems accept all three. But only (37)a emerges as valid on our account.

The key to predicting the above inference patterns correctly appears to be to divide factual and normative issues clearly. Just as we have taken information states to be pairs of sets of worlds, a default logician might use pairs of extensions in defining validity. So, we might define an information state as a pair $\langle \Theta_1, \Theta_2 \rangle$ of default theories, where each $\Theta_j = \langle W_j, D_j \rangle$ is a pair consisting of a set of sentences and a set of defaults. In updating with a *prima facie* principle $A >_o B$, we would add A to W_1 and B to W_2 for every object d such that $A(d) \in W_1$. D_1 would serve as a repository for doxastic defaults, which would function normally within Θ_1. This version of a default theory, however, gives D_2 nothing to do. We cannot use it as a repository for deontic defaults, because they would then look for their antecedents in W_2 rather than W_1. D_2 must look at both W_1 and W_2. But then Θ_2 is not a default theory in the usual sense of the term. The theory would more perspicuously represent information states as pairs consisting of a default theory and a set of sentences. This reveals the problem: according to the revised theory, statements of *prima facie* obligation are not defaults at all. They link two sets of sentences; they cannot be understood as licensing inferences on a single set. But if *prima facie* principles are not defaults, much of the motivation for using default logic as a logic of *prima facie* obligation disappears.

5. UNCONDITIONAL OBLIGATIONS

We must still examine criteria (V) and (VI) concerning unconditional obligation. Unconditional *prima facie* obligations should be able to conflict, while
unconditional actual obligations should not. In fact, we would go further. Say
that a logic of unconditional obligation is *classical* iff it satisfies the following:

(i)	$\bigcirc A, A \models B \Rightarrow \bigcirc B$	closure under logical consequence
(ii)	$(\bigcirc A \& \bigcirc B) \to \bigcirc(A \& B)$	agglomeration
(iii)	$\bigcirc \top$	logical truth
(iv)	$\neg \bigcirc \perp$	*ought*-implies-*can* (no conflicts)

A logic of actual obligation, as Pietroski (1993) argues, should be classical,
while a logic of *prima facie* obligation should not be.

Our approaches clearly satisfy criterion (V), Unconditional Actual Obliga-
tion, for seriality guarantees that $\bigcirc A$ and $\bigcirc \neg A$ are inconsistent. Indeed, our
theory of $\bigcirc$ is classical. So far, however, we have no unconditional *prima facie* obligation operator. Can we define a unary operator expressing *prima facie*
obligation that fulfills criterion (VI), Unconditional *Prima Facie* Obligation?

Yes; in fact, we can have several, with different meanings. There are at least
two kinds of unconditional obligation sentences: categorical imperatives such
as *Thou shalt not kill* and *prima facie* obligation sentences with a nonclassical
logic.

Categorical imperatives such as Thou shalt not kill or Treat people as
ends-in-themselves, not as means only might be construed as universals or as
deontic generics, i.e., *prima facie* principles. Even in the latter sense, they have
a natural representation in our system; we can render "It ought (categorically)
to be the case that A" ($\bigcirc_c A$) as

(38)

$$\top >_o A \quad (\text{in } L_o) \quad \top > \bigcirc A \quad (\text{in } L)$$

Applying such a generic categorical imperative involves a nonmonotonic
inference: $\top >_o A \mathrel{\vert\approx} \bigcirc A (or \top > \bigcirc A \mathrel{\vert\approx} \bigcirc A)$. These are not valid
monotonically. Categorical imperatives, so interpreted, can have exceptions.
They satisfy the classical schemata (i)-(iii). If we adopt a global seriality
constraint, furthermore, requiring that there are normal things ($*(w, W) \neq \emptyset$),
then categorical obligation in L_o also satisfies (iv): If $*(w, W) \neq \emptyset$, then, by
fact 2e, $\bullet(w, W) \neq \emptyset$, so $\neg(\top >_o \perp)$. The L representation, $\neg(\top > \bigcirc \perp)$,
already follows from the seriality of $\oplus$.

The ought-implies-can principle precludes conflict among categorical imperatives:

(39)

$$\neg(\bigcirc_c A \,\&\, \bigcirc_c \neg A)$$

This seems plausible to us; Thou shalt not kill and Thou shalt kill seem incompatible. But our intuitions are weak enough that we will not insist on it. Perhaps there are worlds where practical reasoning breaks down entirely.

Additionally, there are obligation sentences that are both unconditional and *prima facie* without having general, categorical force. Recall that (18) is only nonmonotonically valid:

(18)

> Neoptolemus is a person
> People should be kind
> _____
> Neoptolemus should be kind

This seems right if we read the conclusion as a statement of actual obligation. We might, however, read it as *prima facie*, taking the premises to imply monotonically that Neoptolemus has a *prima facie* obligation to be kind. This seems to accord with the usage of Ross and Frankena. If Odysseus has ordered Neoptolemus to trick Philoctetes, Neoptolemus may have a *prima facie* obligation to obey:

(40)

> Odysseus ordered Neoptolemus to trick Philoctetes.
> If so, Neoptolemus should trick Philoctetes.
> _____
> Neoptolemus should trick Philoctetes.

Reading the conclusion as a *prima facie ought*, the inference appears monotonically valid.

Loewer and Belzer, Pietroski, and others understand this sort of unconditional *prima facie* obligation by defining it as an obligation following from an applicable rule. There is a *prima facie* obligation to A, then, if and only if there is a true B such that $B >_o A$:

(41)

$$\bigcirc_{cp} A \Leftrightarrow \text{There is a } B \text{ such that } B >_o A, \text{ and } B.$$

This is close to Ross's definition; there is a *prima facie* obligation to A in virtue of a feature the world has, namely, B. Various authors, including (van Fraassen, 1973; Nagel, 1979) and (Bonevac and Seung, 1988), treat conflict as arising from different imperatives, value measures, or other sources of value. Understanding *prima facie* obligation in terms of (41) explains this; the Bs are the sources of value. Our theory, together with (41), thus generates an account of value sources and the logical relations between them automatically.

With our nonmonotonically weaker notion of conditional obligation, we can generate a similar concept of *prima facie* obligation based on moral generalizations:

(42)

$$\bigcirc_g A \Leftrightarrow \text{There is a } B \text{ such that } B > \bigcirc A, \text{ and } B,$$

and identify *prima facie* obligation with one or the other of these concepts:

(43)

$$\bigcirc_{pf} A \Leftrightarrow (\bigcirc_{cp} A \vee \bigcirc_g A).$$

Whether we should adopt (42) and (43), or rest content with (41), as Pietroski does, depends on whether unconditional *prima facie* obligation is ever purely epistemic rather than constitutive. Utilitarians such as Mill could surely speak of some obligations as *prima facie*, we think. If so, then such obligations can be generated from epistemic as well as constitutive principles.

As we might expect, *prima facie* obligation in the sense of (41), or (41)-(43), satisfies only some of the classical deontic axioms. Closure under logical consequence holds, because it holds for $>_o$ and $>$. And we have a *prima facie* obligation to the laws of logic. Agglomeration, in contrast, plainly fails; that there is a B such that $B >_o A$ and a D such that $D >_o C$, where both B and D hold, does nothing to show that there is a single E such that $E >_o (A \& C)$. (The facts are similar for $>$ or a mixture of the two connectives.) The status of ought-implies-can depends on whether one adopts GENERIC SERIALITY: $*(w, p) = \emptyset \rightarrow p = \emptyset$.

Prima facie obligations defined in terms of (41), (42), or (43) can conflict. Our theories thus satisfy criterion (VI). This situation, for example, gives rise to moral conflict:

(44)

Odysseus ordered Neoptolemus to trick Philoctetes.
Doing so would be cruel.
If Odysseus ordered Neoptolemus to trick Philoctetes, he should.
If tricking Philoctetes would be cruel, Neoptolemus shouldn't do it.

Neoptolemus has a *prima facie* obligation to trick Philoctetes,
and a *prima facie* obligation not to trick him.

(45)

$$B$$
$$C$$
$$B >_o A \qquad (or B > \bigcirc A)$$
$$C >_o \neg A \qquad (or C > \bigcirc \neg A)$$

$$\overline{\bigcirc_{pf} A \,\&\, \bigcirc_{pf} \neg A}$$

When the conclusion has *prima facie* force, it follows monotonically from the premises. When the obligations alleged are actual, in contrast, the argument is a deontic Nixon diamond; nothing of interest follows, monotonically or nonmonotonically.

Characterizing *prima facie* obligations in terms of (41)-(43), however, gives rise to too many of them. In particular, it generates *prima facie* obligations in cases where there are none. For example, suppose Odysseus were to have a change of heart:

(46)

Odysseus ordered Neoptolemus to trick Philoctetes.
If Odysseus ordered Neoptolemus to trick Philoctetes, he should.
If Odysseus ordered Neoptolemus to trick Philoctetes,
    but rescinded the order, Neoptolemus shouldn't trick Philoctetes.
Odysseus rescinded the order.

Neoptolemus has a *prima facie* obligation to trick Philoctetes.*

Given these premises, our theory holds, Neoptolemus has an actual obligation not to trick Philoctetes. It seems plausible to hold that he does not have even a *prima facie* obligation to trick him. Rescinding the order removes the source of the obligation to trick him without remainder; Neoptolemus has no reason for regret. Yet interpreting *prima facie* obligation by means of (41)-(43) forces one to recognize an overridden but still surviving *prima facie* obligation.

Our semantics suggests yet another way to construe *prima facie* obligations that avoids this problem. As we define nonmonotonic consequence, $\Gamma \mathrel{\approx\!\!\!/} \bigcirc A$ iff, for any Prop(Γ)-normalization chain C beginning from $W^* + \Gamma, M^*, C^* \models \bigcirc A$. Actual obligations, in other words, hold at every fixed point. $\bigcirc A$ follows nonmonotonically from Γ iff A holds in the normative set of every fixed point generated by the canonical model. We can define conclusions of *prima facie* obligations analogously:

(47)

$\Gamma \mathrel{\approx\!\!\!/} \bigcirc_{pf} A \Leftrightarrow$ for some Prop(Γ) -normalization chain C beginning from $W * + \Gamma, M *, C * \models \bigcirc A$.

In cases of conflict, such as (21) and (22), this yields the correct *prima facie* obligations, as do (41)-(43). Sam has a *prima facie* obligation to be partial to his children, and another such obligation to be impartial. In specificity cases such as (46), however, the approaches disagree. (47) generates no undesired obligations, for Neoptolemus has an obligation not to trick Philoctetes at every fixed point. The logic of *prima facie* obligation defined by (47) is nonclassical, respecting only (i) and (iii). It is also fragmentary, since (47) specifies the meaning of Opf only in the conclusions of arguments.

Deciding between (41)-(43) and (47) is not as simple as it seems. Specificity inferences such as (24) appear to leave a moral remainder:

(24)

> Commands should be obeyed
> Unjust commands are commands
> Unjust commands should not be obeyed
> Odysseus' command is unjust
>
> ---
>
> Odysseus' command should not be obeyed

Is there a *prima facie* obligation to obey Odysseus' command? Plausibly, yes. This accords with (41)-(43) but not (47). Overridden considerations sometimes, but only sometimes, continue to exert moral force. One may either assume that they do, as with (41)-(43), and seek to explain exceptions such as (46), or assume that they do not, as with (47), and seek to explain exceptions such as (24).

6. OTHER INFERENCES

We have concentrated on describing two conceptions of *prima facie* obligation. One sees such obligations as arising from moral generalizations; another sees them as arising from *ceteris paribus* rules. We conclude by mentioning some inferences, mostly involving disjunction, excluded from these conceptions but with some plausibility.

First, Loewer and Belzer have proposed a principle concerning disjunction which, when coupled with Disjunction, generates a partial order on worlds:

(48)

$$((A \vee B) >_o C) \rightarrow ((A >_o C) \vee (B >_o C)).$$

We do not want to validate this principle, because it would yield $A >_o A$ monotonically for a wide range of formulas A: specifically, for all A that are forbidden but but better than some other option. Neoptolemus, for example, tricks Philoctetes, which is bad. But at least he doesn't kill him. We seem to have, by virtue of (49):

(49)

> If Neoptolemus is going to trick Philoctetes or kill him,
>   he should trick him.
> It's false that if Neoptolemus is going to kill Philoctetes,
>   he should trick him.

> If Neoptolemus is going to trick Philoctetes, he should trick him.

This does not worry Loewer and Belzer, who are willing to count $A >_o A$ monotonically valid in any case. For reasons we outline above, however, we do not follow suit.

Second, von Wright, Loewer, and Belzer advocate a principle of conservative strengthening of the antecedent, which, with deontic Disjunction and (49), can generate a total order on worlds. Defining P(B/A) as $\neg(A >_o \neg B)$:

(50)

$$((A >_o C)\&P(B/A)) \to ((A\&B) >_o C).$$

Strengthening the antecedent fails with $>$, $>_o$, and other conditional operators such as counterfactuals that exhibit a kind of nonmonotonic behavior. (51), analogous to Lewis's $((A\square\!\!\rightarrow C)\&(A\diamond\!\!\rightarrow B)) \to ((A\&B)\square\!\!\rightarrow C)$, retrieves some of the power of strengthening the antecedent without violating the spirit of those connectives.

Like $A >_o A$, (51) points toward a fundamental difference between our approach and those of von Wright, Loewer, and Belzer. (51) assumes that conflict results from moral or practical mistakes. It is equivalent to:

(51)

$$((A >_o C)\&\neg((A\&B) >_o C)) \to (A >_o \neg B).$$

This says that, if A, then you should not do anything that would undercut an obligation conditional on A. To encounter a conflict, according to (52), you must perform a forbidden act. In our view, this is wrong. Some conflicts are natural; they have no artificial ingredients resulting from moral mistakes. From a semantic point of view, the deontic ordering on worlds should not be total; some worlds may be morally incomparable. For example, (52) makes the following monotonically valid:

(52)

> If you want to be rich, you should work as hard as you can.
> It's not true that, if you want to be rich and want to be a good parent,
> you should work as hard as you can.

> If you want to be rich, you shouldn't want to be a good parent.

Other examples involve releases from promises. Loewer and Belzer themselves provide a good example without recognizing it as such:

(53)

> If the editor set September as the deadline,
>   I should write the paper by September.
> If the editor set September as the deadline,
>   but then moved it to November,
> I shouldn't write the paper by September. (Too much else to do!)
>
> ---
>
> If the editor set September as the deadline,
>   he or she shouldn't move it to November.

Generalizing, the principle entails that no one should release anyone from a promise or other obligation, which is absurd.

Another example: Robert Koons and Thomas Seung have drawn our attention to McLoughlin v. O'Brian (1989), which uses the following principles:

(54)

   a. If you injure someone, you are liable.
   b. If you injure someone nonphysically, you are not liable.
   c. If you injure someone nonphysically, but should have foreseen
      the injury, then you are liable.

From these principles, using (52), we can monotonically infer

(55)

   a. If you injure someone, you should injure them physically.
   b. If you injure someone nonphysically,
      you shouldn't have foreseen the injury.

(56)a, especially, seems absurd. To put the problem in a slightly different way: it is plausible to say that, if you hurt someone, you should compensate them. If you hurt them, but not very badly, however, you shouldn't compensate them. (It's not worth the effort, say.) (52) allows you to infer that, if you hurt someone, you should hurt them very badly.

Finally, is L_o redundant in that O, the unary obligation operator, can be defined in terms of $>$ and $>_o$? (Chisholm, 1964) proposes a definition of unconditional, actual obligation to A in terms of conditional and defeasible obligation. One interpretation in the metalanguage of L_o is:

(56)

   (i)   There is a B such that $B >_o A$, and B, and
   (ii) there is no C such that C and $\neg((B\&C) >_o A)$.

An actual obligation, then, follows from an applicable *prima facie* principle and conflicts with no other applicable and more specific *prima facie* principle. Specificity guarantees that more specific principles override less specific principles. This definition, in Chisholm's words, says that "there is a requirement for (A) which has not been overridden" (Chisholm, 1964, p. 149).

Is the logic of this sort of unconditional obligation classical? It satisfies closure under logical consequence and satisfies $\bigcirc \top$ and $\neg \bigcirc \bot$ on the assumption of generic seriality. On the same assumption, it does not allow conflict. If both $\bigcirc A$ and $\bigcirc \neg A$ were to hold, there would be a pair of sentences B and C, both of which hold, such that $B >_o A$ and $C >_o \neg A$. Moreover, every D would be such that $(B \& D) >_o A$ and $(C \& D) >_o \neg A$. Thus, $(B \& C) >_o (A \& \neg A)$, which, if we assume generic seriality, is absurd.

Chisholm's definition, then, gives $\bigcirc$ the logic appropriate to an actual obligation operator, if we adopt a generic seriality constraint. Its higher-order character, of course, means that $\bigcirc$ is still not eliminable in a first-order theory of the kind we have presented here. But there is a more serious problem: Chisholm's criterion is not necessary for actual obligation. Chisholm himself notes that overridings may be overridden. If there are infinitely complex moral circumstances, however, this means that we may have an actual obligation without having any principle that is not overridden in the sense expressed by (57). Suppose that B and C both hold and that $B >_o A$, $C >_o \neg A$, and neither $(B \& C) >_o A$ nor $(B \& C) >_o \neg A$. It may be that whether A or $\neg A$ is obligatory depends on infinitely many features $D_1, \dots, D_n, \dots$ of the circumstances. So, there could be a circumstance in which

$$(B \& C \& D_1) >_o A$$
$$(B \& C \& D_1 \& D_2) >_o \neg A$$
$$(B \& C \& D_1 \& D_2 \& D_3) >_o A$$
$$(B \& C \& D_1 \& D_2 \& D_3 \& D_4) >_o \neg A$$

and so on. This means that Chisholm's definition is adequate only if no moral circumstances are infinitely complex. In such a circumstance, there could be an actual obligation without any expressible undefeated conditions. Consider, for example, the sequence of principles about liability in (55). It is not difficult to imagine continuing it on the same pattern. Do we have any reason to believe that it cannot be continued indefinitely?

Nicholas Asher
Department of Philosophy
University of Texas at Austin

Daniel Bonevac
Department of Philosophy
University of Texas at Austin

REFERENCES

Aristotle (1962) *Nicomachean Ethics*, Translated by Martin Ostwald, New York: Macmillian Publishing Company.

Asher N., and Morreau, M. (1991). Common sense entailment: A modal theory of nonmonotonic reasoning, *Proceedings of the 12th IJCAI*. San Mateo, Morgan Kaufmann, 387–392.

Asher N., and Morreau, M. (1995) What some generic sentences mean, In J. Pelletier (ed.), *The Generic Book*. University of Chicago Press, Chicago, pages 300–338.

Bonevac, D. (1991). Ethical impressionism: A response to Braybrooke. *Social Theory and Practice* 17:157–173.

Bonevac, D., and Seung, T.K. (1988). Conflict in Practical Reasoning. *Philosophical Studies* 53:315–345.

Castañeda, H.N. (1985). Aspectual Actions and Davidson's Theory of Events. In LePore, E., and McLaughlin, B.P. (eds.), *Aspects and Events,* Blackwell, Oxford.

Castañeda, H.N. (1986). Obligations, aspectual actions, and circumstances. *Philosophical Papers* 15:155–170.

Chisholm, R. (1963). Contrary-to-duty imperatives and deontic logic. *Analysis* 24:33–36.

Chisholm, R. (1964). The Ethics of requirement. *American Philosophical Quarterly* 1:147–153.

Conee, E. (1982). Against moral dilemmas. *Philosophical Review* 91:87–97.

Duncan, M.L. (1982). The future of affirmative action: A jurisprudential/legal critique. *Harvard Civil Rights - Civil Liberties Law Review* 17.

Foot, P. (1983). Moral realism and moral dilemmas. *Journal of Philosophy* 80:379–398.

Forrester, J. (1984). Gentle murder, or the adverbial samaritan. *The Journal of Philosophy* 81:193–197.

Frankena, W. (1973). *Ethics.* Prentice-Hall, Englewood Cliffs.

Goble, L. (1990). A logic of good, should and would, part I. *Journal of Philosophical Logic* 19:169–200.

Goble, L. (1990). A logic of good, should and would, part II. *Journal of Philosophical Logic* 19:253–276.

Goble, L. (1990). Murder most gentile: The paradox deepens. *Philosophical Studies* 64:217–227.

Greenspan, P. (1975). Conditional ought and hypothetical imperatives. *The Journal of Philosophy* 72:259–276.

Horty, J. (1994). Moral dilemmas and nonmonotonic logic. *Journal of Philosophical Logic* 23:35–65.

Horty, J. (1993). Deontic logic as founded on nonmonotonic logic. *Annals of Mathematics and Artificial Intelligence* 9:69–91.

Jones, A. J. I. (1991). On the Logic of Deontic Conditionals. *Ratio Juris* 4:355–66.

Kant, I. (1785). *Foundations of the Metaphysics of Morals*. Translated by Lewis White Beck, Bobbs-Merrill, Indianaplolis, (1959).

Lewis, D. (1973). *Counterfactuals*. Harvard University Press.

Lewis, D. (1974). Semantical analysis for dyadic deontic logic. In Stenlund, S. (ed.), *Logical Theory and Semantic Analysis*. K. Reidel, Dordrecht, pages 1–14.

Loewer, B., and Belzer, M. (1983). Dyadic deontic detachment. *Synthese* 54:295–318.

Loewer, B., and Belzer, M. (1986). Help for the good samaritan paradox. *Philosophical Studies* 50:117–28.

Marcus, R. B. (1966). Iterated deontic modalities. *Mind* 75:580–81.

Marcus, R. B. (1980). Moral dilemmas and consistency. *Journal of Philosophy* 77:121–136.

Mill, J. S. (1861). *Utilitarianism*. Hackett Publishing Company, Indianapolis, (1979).

Morreau, M. (1992). *Conditionals in Philosophy and Artificial Intelligence*. PhD dissertation, University of Amsterdam.

Nagel, T. (1979). The frangmentation of value. In *Mortal Questions*. Cambridge University Press.

Nickle, J. (1975). Preferential policies in hiring and admissions: A jurisprudential approach. *Columbia Law Review* 75:534.

Pietroski, P. (1993). Prima facie obligations, ceteris paribus laws in moral theory. *Ethics* 103:489–515.

Pope, A. (1733). An essay on man. *The Norton Anthology of Poetry*, W. W. Norton & Co., New York, (1970).

Reiter, R. (1980). A logic for default reasoning. *Artificial Intelligence* 13:81–132.

Ryle, G. (1931). Systematically misleading expressions. *Proceedings of the Aristotelian Society* 32:139–170.

Ross, W. D. (1930). *The Right and the Good*. Oxford University Press.

Sinnott-Armstrong, W. (1985). A solution to forrester's paradox of gentle murder. *Journal of Philosophy* 82.

Taylor, P. (1973). Reverse discriminiation and compensatory justice. *Analysis* 33:177.

Thomason, F. (1981). Deontic logic as founded on tense logic. In Hilpinen, R. (ed.), *New Studies in Deontic Logic*. D. Reidel, Dordrecht.

Thomason, F. (1981). Deontic logic and the role of freedom in moral deliberation. In Hilpinen, R. (ed.), *New Studies in Deontic Logic*. D. Reidel, Dordrecht.

van Frassen, B. C. (1972). The logic of conditional obligation. *The Journal of Philosophical Logic* 1:417–438.

van Frassen, B. C. (1973). Values and the heart's command. *Jorunal of Philosophy* 70:5–19.

von Wright, G. H. (1951). Deontic logic. *Mind* 60:1–15.

Williams, B. (1973). Ethical consistency. In *Problems of the Self*, Cambridge University Press, New York, 199–186.

ROBERT C. KOONS AND T. K. SEUNG

DEFEASIBLE REASONING AND MORAL DILEMMAS

The Divorce of Ethics from Classical Logic

1. INTRODUCTION

Since Aristotle, ethical theory has been tied to what we call the Classical Deductivist Model. Classical deductivism consists of two tenets: (1) ethical truth is consistent and completely determinate, (2) all particular ethical truths are deducible from a set of exceptionless general principles. Ethical theorists as diverse as Aristotelian naturalists, ethical hedonists, utilitarians, Moorean intuitionists, Kantians, relativists and subjectivists share this common logical framework. The only exceptions are those, like emotivists and prescriptivists, who deny that ethical statements have any truth-values. Yet even these theorists have typically embraced tenets analogous to those of the Classical Deductivist Model. For example, the prescriptivist Hare insists that our moral prescriptions consist of a set of logically consistent, fully general principles.

Nonetheless, we are convinced that this broad consensus is profoundly mistaken, and that it has distorted ethical theory in several important respects. We defend a model of ethics in which all principles are defeasible (admit exceptions) and in which the totality of ethical truths is not classically consistent. We will show that the rejection of the Classical Model does not lead to logical chaos or irrationalism, nor does it force us to embrace extreme forms of existentialism in which particular ethical commitments are created by *fiat ex nihilo* in each concrete situation. Particular ethical judgments must be derivable from general principles, but they need not be derivable from those principles in classical, deductive logic, nor do the principles need to be exceptionless, nor do the resulting judgments need to be classically consistent.

We will use a logical framework that deviates from classical logic in two ways: by permitting partial inconsistency and by sacrificing the monotonicity of logical implication. Classical logic is monotonic: if additional premises are added to a valid argument, the resulting argument is still valid. In a nonmonotonic logic, adding premises to a correct or reasonable argument may result in an unreasonable one. The conclusions of correct nonmonotonic arguments are tentative or defeasible in a way that is never found in classical deductions. To use the hackneyed example, from the premise {Tweety is a bird}, we may reasonably conclude that Tweety flies, but this conclusion cannot reasonably be drawn from the larger set of premises {Tweety is a bird, Tweety is a penguin}.

205

D. Nute (ed.), Defeasible Deontic Logic, 205–222.
© 1997 *Kluwer Academic Publishers. Printed in the Netherlands.*

Nonmonotonic logics have been developed by researchers in the area of artificial intelligence over the last fifteen years. To date these developments have largely been ignored by philosophers (and *a fortiori* by ethicists), and the AI researchers have not been concerned with the implications of these developments for traditional metaphysical and ethical issues.

Researchers in AI have been driven to develop nonmonotonic logics because, as they soon discovered, classical, monotonic logic is extremely limited in its usefulness in solving real-life problems. Of course, the vacuity of classical logic has from antiquity been a common complaint. For example, the Aristolean syllogistic forms, like Barbara – All men are mortal. Socrates is a man. So, Socrates is mortal – are of very limited usefulness, as Francis Bacon, Locke and Kant long ago observed. Recent developments in AI support the justice of this complaint. Anyone who attempts to use classical logic to illuminate real-life cases of ethical reasoning is quickly stymied. If one tries to represent moral inferences as classical, syllogistic enthymemes, one is confronted with the impossibility of formulating the exceptionless general principle that the reasoner is supposed to be invoking tacitly. The early Socratic dialogues of Plato are consumed with exactly this futile quest, as Socrates vainly attempts to discover the definitions from which particular instances of virtue are syllogistically derived.

These general principles of the Classical Deductivist Model do not correspond to our ordinary moral rules, which do admit of exceptions. Instead, the rules hypothesized by the model are the result of adding to these ordinary moral rules explicit conditions which carve out exactly the exceptional cases. No one has succeeded in producing a plausible example of even one such ethical principle, much less a complete, consistent set from which all ethical truths can be derived, but many believe nonetheless that ethical realism entails the existence of such a set. Some, like Augustine and, in some moods, Kant, have defended exceptionless rules – such as Always tell the truth – , but only at the cost of maintaining insane ethical judgments in particular cases, such as that it is simply and without qualification wrong to lie to a would-be murderer about the whereabouts of the intended victim.

We maintain that all ethical principles admit exceptions, and that all ethical inferences are defeasible. Particular ethical judgments are not logically deducible from exceptionless principles, since there are not such things. At the same time, there is an element of truth to the Principle Principle. We reject those extreme forms of existentialism according to which particular ethical judgments are created ex nihilo in each immediate situation. Particular ethical judgments are always derivable (in some sense) from ethical principles. Since these principles admit exceptions, and an exhaustive list of the exceptions (and of the exceptions to the exceptions, and so on) is impossible (as Socrates discovers in the early dialogues), the form of derivation involved is not classical logic. Instead, it must be a form of nonmonotonic inference.

As we stated above, classical deductivism consists of the following two theses: (1) all particular ethical facts are logically deducible from some set of exceptionless universal principles, (2) ethical facts are mutually consistent, and no ethical claim is both true and false. The second thesis entail the total determinacy of ethical fact. The denial of either of these theses amounts to the acceptance of indeterminacy in ethics. Our second source of dissatisfaction with classical logic is its inability to handle indeterminacy.

It is vitally important to distinguish between partial and total indeterminacy. Meta-ethics has often been led astray by the acceptance of the false dilemma: total determinacy/total indeterminacy. One can affirm that many ethical judgments have just one classical truth-value without being forced to maintain that they all do. In classical logic, everything follows from a contradiction. Hence, classical logic is unable to countenance the existence of a partially inconsistent theory. However, it is possible to develop formal logics (paraconsistent logics) which can tolerate partial inconsistency without absolute inconsistency. Many ethicists, concerned with defending the objectivity of ethics, have felt constrained to deny the existence of even partial indeterminacy. Some have quite reasonably pointed out that simply because we do not know how to settle a particular ethical dispute, it does not follow that there is no fact of the matter as to which side is right. However, there are cases which are even worse than cases of invincible ignorance: there are cases in which we know perfectly well what are the correct ethical judgments to make; unfortunately, these ethical judgments are mutually inconsistent. There are cases, of which many occur in Attic tragedy, in which an action is both right and not right. There are agents who are both just and not just. Of course, we are not the first to suggest that there are real inconsistencies in the ethical world. Heraclitus, Plato, Hegel, Kierkegaard, and the school of contemporary paraconsistent logicians (Belnap, Rescher, Brandom, Priest, Routley) have held various versions of this thesis. Aristotle was the first to explicitly reject the thesis, and the philosophical mainstream has followed him. The time has come for a reconsideration of the Aristotelean dogma of logical consistency, and of the underlying ontological assumption of total determinacy.

Many paraconsistent logicians have worked within the framework of relevance logics These logics were not initially designed with the tolerance of paraconsistency in mind. The motive behind the development of relevance logic was the avoidance of the so-called "paradoxes of material implication". The motivation was primarily proof-theoretic: to accept a conditional proof of '$p \rightarrow q$' only if the assumption of 'p' is actually used in the derivation of 'q' (thereby demonstrating the "relevance" of 'p' to 'q'). The semantics for the language of relevance of logic is, despite recent advances, still somewhat unintuitive and under-motivated. Paraconsistent logicians have, up to the present, followed classical logic in maintaining monotonicity. We advocate a new approach to paraconsistency, one which extends Van Fraassen's supervaluational semantics for three-valued logic and which builds on a new foundation of nonmonotonic logic.

2. THE CLASSICAL MODEL

2.1. Bivalent supervenience

According to the Classical Model, all the truth-value of every ethical proposition is wholly determined by the set of non-moral facts, and this determination guarantees that every ethical proposition receives exactly one classical truth-value (true or false). More formally, let $\mathcal{L}_0$ be a formal language containing only descriptive, ethically neutral vocabulary, and let $\mathcal{L}$ be the result of adding the vocabulary of ethics to $\mathcal{L}_0$. The Classical Deductivist contends that there is a set $\mathcal{R}$ of conceptually necessary moral truths (expressible in $\mathcal{L}$) such that:

1. For any consistent set $\mathcal{F}$ of non-moral truths (in $\mathcal{L}_0$) $\mathcal{R} \cup \mathcal{F}$ is a conservative extension (in relation to $\mathcal{L}_0$) of $\mathcal{F}$.
2. For any consistent and $\mathcal{L}_0$-complete $\mathcal{F}$, $\mathcal{R} \cup \mathcal{F}$ is $\mathcal{L}$-complete.

Moral philosophers (including Hume, Kant, Mill, Ross, Rawls and many others) assume tacitly that this $\mathcal{R}$ is a set of finitary, first-order formulas, and that these formulas contain no proper names or indexicals, and none of the vocabulary of mathematics or set theory. Most ethicists have also tacitly assumed that $\mathcal{R}$ has a recursively axiomatizable basis. For example, for the utilitarian, this basis consists of the single axiom, 'Acts are right if and only if they maximize expected utility', and for the Kantian, the basis consists of the axiom 'Acts are right if and only if they conform to a universalizable maxim'. For an intuitionist like Ross, the basis consists of a set of axioms defining the extent of *prima facie* duties, plus another set defining all-out duties by reference to *prima facie* duties and the conditions under which some of these outweigh the others.

These assumptions guarantee that the moral implications of a finite situation are always computable. One simply enumerates the logical consequences of the first-order, axiomatizable theory consisting of $\mathcal{R}$ together with a finite set of concrete, non-moral facts.

2.2. Problems with the Classical Model

No such thing as finitary, exceptionless generalizations.

The Classical Deductivist faces a dilemma: either the theory of morality is recursively axiomatizable in classical, first-order logic, or the demands of morality can in some cases fail to be perspicuous. Each of these alternatives leads to unacceptable consequences for ethics. Embracing the first alternative leads to a fanatical form of rigorism, of the kind exemplified by Augustine,

Kant, or (in a somewhat different way) by pure consequentialists (like utilitarians). In fact, it is clear that any finitary, first-order generalization admits of exceptions, or at the very least, moral theory cannot be exhaustively axiomatized by such exceptionless generalizations. Every moral rule is applied under the proviso, "assuming that these are all the relevant factors". It is impossible, however, to anticipate and enumerate (in finitary, first-order logic) all the relevant conditions that may arise in the application of any moral rule. (In infinitary logic, it may be possible to exhaust all possible exceptions, and in higher-order logic we may define such notions as 'exception to the rule' or 'relevant to the rule' and thus we may explicitly exclude exceptional cases.)

However, the second alternative is also unacceptable. If the basis of morality cannot be recursively axiomatized, or if it can be axiomatized only by incorporating infinitary formulas or second-order logic or set theory, then the ethical consequences of a given situation might not be effectively enumerable. It is inconceivable that something so opaque to our consciousness could nonetheless constitute a genuine moral demand upon us.

Problem of moral residue (B. Williams)

A second major difficulty with the Classical Model has been articulated by Bernard Williams in a number of papers dealing with the problem of 'moral residues' of dilemmas. According to the Classical Model, conflicts can occur only with respect to *prima facie* duties or evaluations. The rightness (or justice or wisdom or whatever) of a given action must be decided uniquely by the true moral theory, together with the non-moral facts. Principles cannot really conflict, according to the Classical Deductivist: the most that can happen is for a situation to fall within an unusual exception to an important and widely-applicable rule. This makes it difficult for the Classical Deductivist to explain the occurrence of 'moral residue' – guilt, compunction, blame, secondary obligations and liabilities, for example – that are generated in such exceptional cases by the supposedly inapplicable, overridden general rule.

For example, if I violate your property or privacy rights in order to save an innocent life, how is it that I owe you an apology, an explanation, perhaps some form of reparation, and why should I feel some compunction, even a kind of guilt, for my action? According to the Classical Deductivist, I did nothing wrong (assuming for the sake of argument that the property or privacy principle is overridden in this case, which means, for the Deductivist, that some exception to this principle is activated). The Deductivist must resort to *ad hoc* measures, adding perhaps special duties to feel quasi-guilt or quasi-compunction even in cases in which no wrong was done, no right violated, or he must simply dismiss such moral residue as an illusion, based on our tendency to embrace inconsistent evaluations in these exceptional cases.

3. ALTERNATIVES TO THE CLASSICAL MODEL

3.1. *Weak classical model – 3-valued*

One alternative to the Classical Model is to give up the claim of moral completeness, without sacrificing consistency. This could be done by means of a three-valued models, either using van Fraassen's method of super valuations or Kleene's three-valued truth tables. A moral dilemma could be modeled as a situation in which moral theory and non-moral facts fail to assign either classical truth value to a given ethical proposition.

There are two defects of such an account.

1. This model cannot distinguish between cases of moral underdetermination and cases of moral overdetermination. In some cases, we simply cannot apply some moral standard to a given situation: for example, we cannot say whether an isolated Robinson Crusoe is acting fairly or not. The facts under-determine this ethical evaluation. However, a moral dilemma is a case of over-determination. Two conflicting evaluations are well (even conclusively) supported by the facts. An adequate meta-ethical theory ought to be able to draw this distinction.
2. This model provides no solution of the problem of moral residue. It might be clear, for example, that my response to a moral dilemma obligates me to make reparations to an injured party, the very reparations I would have owed had I violated that person's rights in a straightforward, non-dilemmatic act of wrongdoing. However, on the three-valued model, all such residual obligations would be underdetermined, as is the evaluation from which they flow.

3.2. *Relevance logic*

An obvious alternative to the Classical Model is that provided by relevance logic. Relevance logics allow propositions to be given any one of four truth-values: true only, false only, neither and both. However, there are two principal drawbacks to the use of relevance logic in ethics:

1. Using relevance logic involves the loss of plausible principles of classical logic, such as the disjunctive syllogism. Such principles are quite naturally used in ethical reasoning, and their loss is a very high price to pay.
2. Relevance logic does not handle genuine exceptions well. We ought to be able to distinguish between cases in which one ethical principle is overridden by another, more specific rule that carves out an exception and cases in which two ethical principles come into irresolvable conflict. However, relevance logic would treat these two kinds of cases in the same way, as cases giving rise to ethical paradox.

3.3. *Sectoring strategy*

Another approach to handling inconsistency is the sectoring strategy, developed by Brandom and Rescher (1979). In this case, the set of moral facts is divided into a number of separate sources or domains, and severe limits are placed on the combination of information from disparate sources or domains. Consequently, one can accept A (from source 1) and not-A (from source 2), but reject (A & not-A), since the two pieces of information cannot be combined by means of adjunction.

On such an approach, we would divide the set $\{\mathcal{R}\}$ into a family of disjoint sets of moral rules: $\{\mathcal{R}_0, \mathcal{R}_1, ..., \mathcal{R}_i, ...\}$. The Classical model then applies to each R_i, but not to their union, $\bigcup \mathcal{R}$.

This approach suffers from three defects:

1. The prohibition on combining information from disparate ethical sources is drastic and untenable. There are many cases in which our ethical judgments combine information about justice and virtue, or intentions and consequences.
2. Moral dilemmas can arise from a single source, rule, or imperative. For example, if I make two promises that come into conflict, then a single source of moral obligations, the promise-keeping rule, comes into conflict with itself.
3. This approach, like those mentioned above, cannot distinguish between exceptions and genuine dilemmas.

4.   NONMONOTONIC LOGICS AND SOLUTION-MULTIPLICITY

Jeff Horty (1994) has made a novel and promising suggestion: to turn to recent work in AI on nonmonotonic reasoning in order to create a new model for ethical dilemmas. In that paper, Horty uses one particular nonmonotonic formalism, Reiter's default logic. In this paper, we will generalize Horty's suggestion.

4.1. *Varieties of NML*

Existing systems of nonmonotonic logic can be classified into the following three types:

1. Fixed-point theories, such as default logic, autoepistemic logic, and logic programming.
2. Minimization theories, such as circumscription, Pearl's System Z, and a new version of Asher and Morreau's theory of commonsense entailment.
3. Algorithmic theories, such as inheritance networks, and the original version of Asher and Morreau's commonsense entailment.

Systems of all of these types share a common feature: the existence of multiple solutions, extensions, or answer sets. This suggests a simple proposal: a moral dilemma exists whenever the theory $\mathcal{F} \cup \{\mathcal{R}\}$ has multiple extensions or solutions. Horty suggests exactly this by reference to the multiple extensions of default theories in his 1994 paper. This proposal has a number of advantages.

- It involves taking moral dilemmas seriously. Moral dilemmas are not treated as mere cases of indifference, like that of Buridan's ass.
- It enable us to distinguish between under- and over-determination.

How well does this proposal handle the problem of exceptions, and the distinction between dilemmas and mere exceptions?

It depends.

As Horty noted, default theory does not handle exceptions well. Any genuine exceptions to a moral principle or imperative must be explicitly incorporated in that principle. Thus, the possibility of an endless series of exceptions to exceptions cannot be represented in a finitary language. In fact, autoepistemic logic and logic programming suffer from the same defect.

Circumscription does much better. We can add a placeholder predicate, like ab_{37} to moral rule 37, and then we can add new exceptions to this rule as necessary by adding new sufficient conditions for the truth of ab_{37}:

(37)

$$\phi \,\&\, \neg ab_{37} \rightarrow \psi$$

$$\gamma_1 \rightarrow ab_{37}$$

$$\gamma_2 \rightarrow ab_{37}$$

There are two drawbacks to circumscription:

- Problems with computational tractability. Circumscription is not r.e., since it is in effect a form of second-order logic. Consequently, circumscription runs afoul of the requirement of the perspicuity of the moral.
- Circumscription does not provide for the automatic generation of exceptions. For example, it seems plausible that whenever a rule with a more specific antecedent comes into conflict with a less specific rule, the first rule should carve out an exception to the second (this is known as the Principle of Specificity).

Some systems of nonmonotonic logic do still better than circumscription in regard to the *second* of these points. For example, both Pearl's System Z and Asher and Morreau's Commonsense Entailment, automatically respect the Principle of Specificity. In fact, we can distinguish between strong and weak specificity:

Weak specificity:

$$\phi, \psi, (\phi \Rightarrow \gamma), (\phi \& \psi \Rightarrow \neg\gamma) \hspace{1mm}\mid\approx\neg\gamma$$

Strong specificity:

$$\phi, \psi, (\psi \Rightarrow \phi), (\phi \Rightarrow \gamma), (\psi \Rightarrow \neg\gamma) \hspace{1mm}\mid\approx\neg\gamma$$

Commonsense Entailment respects weak specificity, and System Z and certain variants of CE respect strong specificity as well. Unfortunately, in both cases the consequence relation is still not r.e. Producing effectively computable and tractable versions of these theories remains an unfinished task.

Nonetheless, for certain restricted sets of formulas, nonmonotonic logics like Z and CE are r. e. For example, if we restrict the conditions of moral rules to the monadic predicate calculus, a not implausible restriction, the nonmonotonic consequences of any finite set of facts will be effectively computable. (See Pearl 1988 and Asher and Morreau 1991 for more details.)

5. ACCOUNTING FOR MORAL RESIDUES: HYPERVALUATIONS

Van Fraassen's method of supervaluations (1968) is a very attractive way of dealing with undetermination, primarily because it is so conservative, preserving all of classical logic. In this paper, we extend van Fraassen's idea to the problem of semantic overdetermination.

A single extension of a nonmonotonic theory is consistent, but typically not complete. Thus, an extension induces a 3-valued supervaluation. Let $\mathcal{M}_0$ be a classical model of $\mathcal{L}_0$. Let $\mathcal{R}$ be the collection of general moral truths (including default rules). Suppose $\mathcal{A}$ is a nonmonotonic extension of $Th(\mathcal{M}_0) \cup \mathcal{R}$. Corresponding to $\mathcal{A}$ is a supervaluation $\Sigma(\mathcal{A})$:

$$\Sigma(\mathcal{A}) = \{\mathcal{M} : \mathcal{M} \text{ is a model of } \mathcal{L} \ \& \ \mathcal{M} \models \mathcal{A}\}$$

$$\Sigma(\mathcal{A})(\phi) = t \Leftrightarrow \forall \mathcal{M} \in \Sigma(\mathcal{A}) \ \mathcal{M} \models \phi$$

$$\Sigma(\mathcal{A})(\phi) = f \Leftrightarrow \forall \mathcal{M} \in \Sigma(\mathcal{A}) \ \mathcal{M} \models \neg\phi$$

$$\Sigma(\mathcal{A})(\phi) = u \ \text{otherwise}$$

Since there can be multiple extensions, this procedure must be iterated, producing "hypervaluations". Corresponding to $\langle \mathcal{M}_0, \mathcal{R} \rangle$ is a hypervaluation Ω:

$$\Omega = \{\Sigma(\mathcal{A}) : \mathcal{A} \text{ is an extension of } Th(\mathcal{M}) \cup \mathcal{R}\}$$

Just as van Fraassen's method of supervaluations results in three supervalues, true in all models, false in all models, and true in some, false in others, so our method of hypervaluations gives rise to seven hypervalues:

$$\{t\}$$

$$\{f\}$$

$$\{u\}$$

$$\{t, u\}$$

$$\{f, u\}$$

$$\{t, f\}$$

$$\{t, f, u\}$$

The first two of these values correspond to the case of pure, simple truth values. The third corresponds to a situation of moral undetermination. The sixth and seventh hypervalues arise in cases of genuine moral dilemmas. The fourth and fifth constitute what we call 'residual' values. In these cases, there is no real conflict, since a definite value is opposed only by the undefined value. These residual values arise out of moral dilemmas, and the ambiguity of the underlying situation is reflected in the inclusion of the 'u' value.

6. ILLUSTRATIONS

6.1. *Churchill & Coventry*

There are a number of historical cases, especially cases involving choices in the political sphere, that illustrate the usefulness of this theoretical framework. For example, during the Battle of Britain, Churchill was faced with the following choice. Thanks to the British government's access to Germany's secret codes, he was informed in advance of many planned German air raids on populated areas. He could evacuate those areas, sparing many innocent lives, but doing so would, with a significant degree of probability, reveal to the Germans that their codes had been broken, seriously impairing the British war effort. He decided not to evacuate these areas. Churchill's analysis of the situation might be represented by the following rules and assertions (where '$\Rightarrow$' represents the defeasible conditional connective):

C 1 *Spares innocent lives & Agent is commander* $\Rightarrow$ *Right*

C 2 *Seriously impairs war effort & Agent is commander* $\Rightarrow$ *Not Right*

C 3 *Evacuation spares innocent lives & Agent of evacuation is commander
& Evacuation seriously impairs war effort*

In this case, since defeasible *modus ponens* applies both to C1 and to C2, the default theory has two extensions: one in which evacuation is right and one in which it is not right. The proposition that evacuation is right receives the paradoxical value $\{t, f\}$. Such a situation we call a dilemma in the strict sense. In a strict dilemma, morality gives no clear guidance as to the best course of action. Thus, in encountering a strict dilemma, one must bear the moral cost oneself — one cannot shift the burden onto morality itself by attributing the decision to some abstract ethical mechanism. Dilemmas in the strict sense are classified by our account as paradoxical relative to the facts of the situation.

Paradoxical situations can leave non-paradoxical moral residue. For example, those whose loved ones died in the German air raid have legitimate grounds for demanding compensation – at the very least, an apology. If Churchill had acted without any compunction whatsoever, complacent in the conviction that he had acted for the best, we would judge this to be a serious moral flaw. Suppose we represent this fact by adding the following rule:

C 4 *Right & No evacuation* ⇒ *Agent owes compensation*

The default theory still has two extensions: in one, evacuation is right and compensation is owed (due to rule C3), and in the other, evacuation is not right and the status of the proposition that compensation is owed is undecided. Consequently, the proposition that the evacuation was right still has the paradoxical value $\{t, f\}$, while the proposition that compensation is owed has the residual value $\{t, u\}$. Although the situation is ambiguous, the moral rules clearly direct Churchill to compensate those who were harmed by his decision.

6.2. Antigone

Our second set of examples comes from Sophocles' *Antigone*. Acute moral dilemmas confront Antigone and Creon. First of all, Antigone and her sister Ismene must decide whether there is virtue (arete) in burying their brother Polyneices, who was killed leading an unsuccessful rebellion. The decent burial of a brother is commanded by the gods, and is therefore an act of virtue:

> *Decent burial & Of a brother* ⇒ *Commanded by gods*
> *Commanded by gods* ⇒ *Virtuous.*

At the same time, Antigone concedes that it is not virtuous to bury a traitor, and Ismene forcefully argues that any act of knowingly breaking laws that were made for the public good is not virtuous.

A 1 *Decent burial & Of a traitor* ⇒ *Not virtuous.*

A 2 *Knowingly breaks human law & Law made for public good* ⇒ *Not virtuous*

Antigone questions the applicability of the first principle. She denies that it is possible to know who is wicked and who is just. Given the complexities of the situation, Polyneices's status as a traitor is itself in a state of ambiguity. On the question of the applicability of the second principle, Antigone insists that divine law overrides human law. She embraces a principle of the form:

A 3 *Commanded by gods & Knowingly breaks human law & Law made for public good ⇒ Virtuous.*

If such a principle is true, then it overrides A2, the principle to which Ismene appeals, just as C2 overrode C1, since its conditions are of greater specificity. It is not clear that Sophocles himself endorsed Antigone's position. He has the chorus explain that Antigone dies not without praise and with a kind of honor or virtue. The chorus admits that piety to the gods is a virtue, but counters that "strength lives in established laws that must prevail." [1]

Creon also faces several moral dilemmas in the play. Creon insists that he must punish Antigone for knowingly breaking his law. In contrast, his son Haimon argues that this consequence does not follow, since Creon's law was itself invalid, violating divine right.

A 4 *Treats lawbreaker with impunity & Agent is the king ⇒ Not virtuous.*

A 5 *Treats lawbreaker with impunity & Agent is the king & Law is unjust ⇒ Virtuous.*

Haimon in effect endorses A5 which would override A4 in the situation at hand.

Creon resorts to a second argument: the king must not harm the public good, and the king's appearing weak (by not punishing Antigone) would harm the public good. Haimon rebuts this claim by arguing that apparent weakness on the king's part does not harm the public good if it is necessitated by a decent respect for public opinion.

A 6 *Harms public good & Agent is the king ⇒ Not virtuous*

A 7 *Displays weakness & Agent is the king ⇒ Harms the public good*

A 8 *Respects public opinion & Displays weakness & Agent is the king ⇒ No harm to public good*

Conditionals A7 and A8 are perhaps causal rules rather than simple ethical ones. In fact, the structure of causal and ethical reasoning is quite similar, and it is a virtue of our system that the two can take place in a homogeneous environment.

6.3. Sophie's Choice

Another example comes from William Styron's novel *Sophie's Choice*. Sophie is forced by a Nazi death camp commandant to choose between her two

---

[1] Fitts and Fitzgerald (1939), pages 59-60 (Scene IV)

children. She chooses her daughter, thereby consigning her son to certain death. Of course, she acted so as to save as many of her children as possible: if she had refused to make a choice, both children would have been killed. Nonetheless, she faced an irresolvable moral dilemma, since she was forced to act from an illegitimate favoritism toward one child over the other (she didn't have the opportunity to flip a coin, and even if she had, she would still have had to decide whether to carry out its "decision"). We can represent Sophie's dilemma by the following set of rules:

S 1 *Causes child's death & Agent is mother* ⇒ *Wrong*

S 2 *Causes child's death & Agent is mother & Saves as many of her children as possible* ⇒ *Not wrong*

S 3 *Favors one child over another & Agent is mother of both* ⇒ *Wrong*

The applicability of rule S1 is overridden in this case by the presence of S2. The mere fact that Sophie cannot save both children, together with her *prima facie* duty to save each child, poses a dilemma only in the weakest sense, as in the case of Buridan's ass. In the absence of other considerations, to save either child would appear to be simply right. However, there is at least one additional factor to consider. Among a parent's duties is the avoidance of undue favoritism of one child over another. To sacrifice one child's life to save another's is an extreme case of such favoritism. An act-utilitarian would presumably argue that the need to save as many children as possible takes precedence over such considerations. However, from a deontological point of view, it is not obvious that refusing to make such a choice would have been (simply) wrong.

Even if we grant the utilitarian claim that Sophie was morally constrained to make her choice, there is still plenty of room in such a case for ethical indeterminacy. Such cases are of course never instances of the Buridan's ass dilemma: there are always some relevant factors that differentiate the two choices. One child might have a better chance of surviving the rigors of camp life than the other, or one might be older and thus have already enjoyed more of life, as well as being perhaps better able to face death. In many cases, including Sophie's, some of these factors pull in one direction, and some in the other. Applying one set of moral rules would give the answer that it is wrong to sacrifice child A but permissible to sacrifice child B, while applying another set of rules might give the opposite answer, and a third set might imply that either act of sacrifice is permissible. In many such cases, there simply are no all-encompassing rules or meta-rules that can settle the issue. The most one can say is that these contradictory conclusions are all residual consequences of the description of the case, and that the choice is therefore a paradoxical one.

6.4. *Riggs v. Palmer (1889)*

Legal reasoning can provide a number of rich examples of defeasible ethical reasoning. We will consider two cases discussed by Ronald Dworkin in *Law's Empire*.[2] This first is Riggs v. Palmer 115 NY 506, 22 NE 188 (1889), in which the validity of a will was disputed. Elmer had murdered his grandfather (for which crime he was convicted). The grandfather's will bequeathed a substantial sum to Elmer. The grandfather's will violated none of the explicit provision of estate law in New York, and no statute explicitly justified withholding the inheritance from Elmer. Nonetheless, the court ruled the bequest invalid, appealing to the real but unstated intentions of the lawmakers. The relevant rules applied in this case were:

R 1 *Will valid* ⇒ *Entitled*

R 2 *Conforms to explicit provisions of law* ⇒ *Will valid*

R 3 *Violates intentions of lawmakers & Conforms to explicit provisions of law* ⇒ *Will not valid*

This is the sort of case which the classical deductivist model does not handle well. We cannot replace the second rule above with the supposedly universal principle: if the will conforms to the explicit provisions of the law and does not violate the intentions of the lawmakers, then it is valid. If we try to make the possible exceptions explicit, we make the rule unusable in a wide range of cases. There are many cases where the intentions of the lawmakers were themselves unclear, ambivalent, or otherwise indeterminate. In these cases, we want the simpler but defeasible rule to apply and to enable us to decide for the validity of the will.

6.5. *McLoughlin v. O'Brian (1989)*

Another interesting case discussed by Dworkin is the British case McLoughlin v. O'Brian [1983] 1 AC 410.[3] This case concerns the conditions under which one is liable for emotional damage caused to others. There are a number of defeasible rules which can be extracted from the arguments in this case:

M 1 *Injury* ⇒ *Liable*

M 2 *Injury & Not physical* ⇒ *Not liable*

M 3 *Injury & Not physical & Caused by carelessness* ⇒ *Liable*

M 4 *Injury & Not physical & Caused by carelessness & Unforeseeable* ⇒ *Not liable*

---

[2]Dworkin (1986), pages 15-20.
[3]Ibid., pp. 23-29.

M 5 *Injury & Not physical & Caused by carelessness & Compensation would impose morally disproportionate financial burden ⇒ Not liable*

In this situation, we have a hierarchy of exceptions, exceptions to exceptions, etc. This kind of series can be extended indefinitely far.

7. VAN FRAASSEN'S ACCOUNT

We anticipate the following objection. Do the examples of dilemmas really necessitate the abandonment of classical logic? Couldn't one instead use some sort of deontic operator, like 'O' for obligatory, and represent cases of moral conflict as cases in which something like $Op \& O\neg p$ holds? In standard deontic logics, '$O\neg p$' entails '$\neg Op$', so this sort of alternative would require a substantial deviation from standard modal semantics for the deontic operator. Nonetheless, some, including van Fraassen, have advocated such deviant deontic logics.[4]

A van Fraassen modal logic for moral conflict is fully classical and two-valued. The proposition 'Op' is interpreted as meaning this: According to some source of moral imperatives, it is obligatory to bring it about that p. If there are more than one source of moral imperatives (such as Justice and Loyalty), then it is possible for both Op and $O\neg p$ to be true, p being obligatory according to one source and $\neg p$ being obligatory according to another.

There are a number of difficulties with this alternative. First of all, there are cases of ethical overdeterminacy involving the classification of a situation or a person in terms of virtues or entitlements that are not easily translatable into deontic logic. For the virtue theorist, ethics is primarily a matter of correctly characterizing reality, not simply one of generating a set of imperatives or 'oughts'. For example, in the Riggs case, the central issue was the validity of the will. Validity is not identical to that which ought to be carried out: there are valid wills that ought not to be carried out, and invalid wills that ought to be carried out.

Secondly, the deontic account of moral conflict wrongly seeks to minimize the kind of cognitive dissonance that these cases involve. The assumption of the adequacy of classical logic depends on an assumption of total semantic determinacy in ethics. The classical deductivist imagines the phenomenal world to be carved up in ready-made ethical categories, to which the predicates of our ethical language can be mapped one-for-one. A thesis of partial semantic indeterminacy, as defended by Plato in his mature dialogues (including the *Cratylus*, *Phaedrus*, and *Sophist*) seems more plausible. Only a hypothetical instance of perfect or paradigmatic justice is determinately just, prior to all conventions. The postulation of defeasible rules establish conventional benchmarks that more and more precisely define the boundaries

---

[4]Van Fraassen (1973); compare also Bonevac and Seung (1988).

between ethical categories. Nonetheless, this project of precisification cannot be completed: semantic indeterminacy remains.

Thirdly, the deontic account suffers from a lack of flexibility in representing situations of moral conflict. Suppose, for example, that I am bound by a debt of gratitude to be loyal to a given political party. At the same time suppose that I am permitted not to support party A, because I have become aware of malfeasance and corruption on the part of the party's current leadership. Finally, suppose that I have made a conditional promise to support party B, if I am not obliged to support party A. We might represent the situation by the following premises:

P 1 *Owe debt to party A* $\Rightarrow$ *Obliged to support party A*

P 2 *Know of corruption in party A* $\Rightarrow$ *Obliged not to support party A*

P 3 *Not obliged to support party A, Made conditional promise* $\Rightarrow$ *Obliged to support party B*

P 4 *Obliged to support party B & Didn't support party B* $\Rightarrow$ *Obliged to make restitution to party B*

P 5 *Obliged to support party B* $\rightarrow$ *Obliged not to support party A*

P 6 *Obliged to support party A* $\rightarrow$ *Obliged not to support party B*

P 7 *Owe debt to party A & Know of corruption in party A & Made conditional promise & Didn't support party B*

In our theory, we can accept the intuitively correct axiom schema: if one is obliged not to A, then one is not obliged to A. Given this axiom, rules P1 and P2 come into conflict in this case. The evaluative propositions receive the following hypervalues in this situation:

Obliged to support party A	$\{t, f\}$
Obliged to support party B	$\{t, f\}$
Obliged to make restitution to party B	$\{t, u\}$

Neither the obligation to support party A nor the obligation to support party B are assigned unique classical values, since premises P5 and P6 force every model to choose between the obligations. It is a residual consequence that one is obliged to make restitution to party B, since this is entailed by the obligation to support party B and consistent with the obligation to support party A.

On the deontic alternative, the premises do indeed entail the existence of a dilemma of obligation: one is obliged to support party A and not to support it. However, this alternative cannot explain the existence of any sort of obligation to party B, *not even a residual one*. Consequently, there was no failure to fulfill an obligation to party B, and no obligation to make restitution to party B. This seems to be the wrong answer. On one way of weighing the situation, I have an obligation to party A and none to party B, while on another way, I have no obligation to party A but I do have one to party B. The situation is indeterminate: neither assessment clearly takes priority. Hence, if I do not support party B, I incur thereby some kind of moral cost, which the deontic alternative cannot recognize.

8. CONCLUSION

Another alternative to paraconsistency would be to interpret negation as we use it to be some operator other than logical negation. For example, in a case in which it is derivable that the action in question is both just and not just, we might re-interpret the word 'not' in this context as an operator which generates a new predicate, i.e., by 'not just' we mean 'unjust', where 'just and unjust' is not a logical contradiction. Again, this strikes us as an ill-advised attempt to minimize the severity of the conflict. It is not enough to show that some verbal trick can be used to restore consistency: some reason must be given for thinking that 'not' or the prefix 'un-' does not have its usual meaning in these contexts.

Our theory has another advantage. Our framework enables us to clarify a central doctrine of Platonic ethics: that of the unity of the virtues. The Platonist asserts that each of the virtues is a necessary condition of all of the others. If one tries to account for this doctrine in the traditional deductivist framework, in which one must provide necessary and sufficient conditions for each of the virtues which are mutually consistent, one must either define each of the virtues in terms of the others, which renders the whole system viciously circular, or one must assign logically equivalent conditions to all of the virtues, in which case one is unable to distinguish one virtue from the other.

In our framework, it is possible to give unique positive conditions to each of the virtues, while also adding rules making any given virtue a necessary condition of all of the others. For example, suppose there are three virtues, A, B and C. We can have three distinct sets of conditions, Σ_1, Σ_2, and Σ_3, corresponding to positive rules for the virtues: $(\Sigma_1 \Rightarrow A)$, $(\Sigma_2 \Rightarrow B)$, and $(\Sigma_3 \Rightarrow C)$. At the same time, the following six negative rules establish the unity of the virtues: $(\neg A \Rightarrow \neg B)$, $(\neg A \Rightarrow \neg C)$, $(\neg B \Rightarrow \neg A)$, $(\neg B \Rightarrow \neg C)$, $(\neg C \Rightarrow \neg A)$, $(\neg C \Rightarrow \neg B)$. The three virtues are distinct, since they can have different hyper-values. For example, A might be have the value $\{t, f\}$, and B and C have the value $\{f, u\}$. Yet, there is a unity of the virtues, since if any one of the three has a hypervalue including f, then so must the other two.

Robert C. Koons
Department of Philosophy
University of Texas at Austin

T. K. Seung
Department of Philosophy
University of Texas at Austin

REFERENCES

Asher, N. and Morreau, M. (1991). Commonsense entailment: a modal theory of nonmonotonic reasoning. *Proceedings of the International Joint Committee on Artificial Intelligence,* Morgan Kaufmann, Los Altos, Ca..

Bonevac, D. and Seung, T. K. (1988). Conflict in practical reasoning. *Philosophical Studies* 53:315–345.

Dworkin, R. (1986). *Law's Empire.* Harvard University Press, pages 15–20, 23–29.

Fitts, D. and Fitzgerald, R. (trans.) (1939). *The Antigone of Sophocles.* Harcourt, Brace and Company, New York, pages 59–60 (Scene IV).

Horty, J. F. (1994). Moral dilemmas and nonmonotonic logic. *Journal of Philosophical Logic* 23(1):35–66.

Pearl, Judea (1988). *Probabilistic Reasoning in Intelligent Systems: Networks of Plausible Inference.* Morgan Kaufmann, Los Altos, Ca..

Rescher, N. and Brandom, R. (1979). *The Logic of Inconsistency: A study in non-standard possible-world semantics and ontology.* Rowman and Littlefield, Totowa, NJ..

van Fraassen, B. (1969). Presuppositions, supervaluations and free logic. In Lambert, K. (ed.), *The Logical Way of Doing Things,* Yale University Press.

van Fraassen, B. (1973). Values and the heart's command. *Journal of Philosophy* 70:5–19.

Williams, B. (1973). *Problems of the Self: Philosophical Papers, 1956-1972.* Cambridge University Press, pages 37, 74.

HENRY PRAKKEN AND MAREK SERGOT

DYADIC DEONTIC LOGIC AND CONTRARY-TO-DUTY OBLIGATIONS

1. INTRODUCTION

One of the main issues in the discussion on standard deontic logic (SDL) is the representation of contrary-to-duty (CTD) obligations. A well-known example is Forrester's (1984) paradox of the gentle murderer: it is forbidden to kill, but if one kills, one ought to kill gently. Intuitively, one would feel that these sentences are consistent, but in SDL no (obvious) consistent formalisation is available: assuming that *kill-gently* logically implies *kill*, the formalisation

(1) $\bigcirc \neg kill$
(2) $\bigcirc kill\text{-}gently$

is inconsistent, since SDL contains the inference rule of consequential closure:

$$\text{ROM.} \qquad \frac{A \to B}{\bigcirc A \to \bigcirc B}$$

and the valid scheme[1]

D. $\qquad \neg(\bigcirc A \wedge \bigcirc \neg A)$

The reason why this paradox is so challenging is that some well-studied approaches that work for other paradoxes fail here. It does not help to distinguish between the times of violating an obligation and fulfilling its associated contrary-to-duty obligation (cf. (Åqvist and Hoepelman, 1981; van Eck, 1982)), since here these times are equal. Neither do solutions apply where the condition of a conditional obligation is regarded as a state of affairs and the content of an obligation as an act ((Castañeda, 1981; Meyer, 1988)). Clearly, in the gentle murderer both the condition and the content of the CTD obligation are acts. Moreover, there are variants of the example where both are states of affairs; a holiday cottage regulation could say: there must be no fence around the cottage, but if there is a fence, it must be a white fence (Prakken and Sergot, 1994, 1996).

Another option is to reject the rule ROM. Reasons for giving up this principle have been put forward independently of CTD reasoning, notably in connection with Ross's paradox 'You ought to mail this letter, so you ought to mail it or burn it'. However, we feel that this solution is not adequate. As we

---

[1]The names of the schemes in this article are based on those of (Chellas, 1980).

D. Nute (ed.), Defeasible Deontic Logic, 223–262.
© 1997 *Kluwer Academic Publishers. Printed in the Netherlands.*

remarked earlier in (Prakken and Sergot, 1994, 1996), there are also strong reasons to believe that ROM should be retained, at least in some restricted form: someone who is told not to kill must surely be able to infer that he or she ought not to kill by strangling, say.

Yet another option is to reject the D scheme, a move which has also been suggested for other reasons, viz. as a way to represent moral dilemmas in a meaningful way (cf. e.g. (Horty, 1994)). However, as one of us has defended in (Prakken, 1996), we feel that that aim is better served by embedding a deontic logic validating the D scheme in some suitable non-monotonic logic. In such a logic contradictions do not necessarily trivialise the premises, and thus they provide a way to unify a realistic view on moral dilemmas with a rationality requirement for normative systems that obligations do not conflict.

Contextual obligations

In accord with e.g. (Lewis, 1974), (Jones and Pörn, 1985) and (Tan and van der Torre, 1994) we feel that the cause of SDL's failure to deal with the gentle murderer is different. SDL cannot distinguish between various grades or levels of non-ideality; in the semantics of SDL worlds are either ideal or non-ideal. Yet the expression 'if you kill, kill gently' says that some non-ideal worlds are more ideal than other non-ideal worlds; it says: presupposing that one kills, then in those non-ideal worlds that best measure up to the deontically perfect worlds, one kills gently. In formalising CTD reasoning the key problem is formalisation of what is meant by 'best measure up'.

In (Prakken and Sergot, 1994) and its extended version (Prakken and Sergot, 1996) we gave a first formalisation of our intuitions. The key idea was to interpret obligations as being relative to a *context*. For instance, the obligation to kill gently should be taken to pertain to the context where the killing is taking place. We formalised this by making the deontic modalities dyadic: $\bigcirc_B A$ says that A is obligatory given, or pre-supposing, or from the point of view of, the context B. $\bigcirc_B A$ and $\bigcirc_C \neg A$ can both hold at the same time, since they pertain to different contexts, or points of view, and one context can be more or less close to ideal than another.

As formulated in (Hilpinen, 1993, p. 96), a context stands for a constellation of acts or situations that agents regard as being settled in determining what they should do. In deciding how to kill, a person takes it for granted that he or she kills. Normgivers, in stating contrary-to-duty obligations, anticipate the choices of context that agents can make. However, it is important to see that the settledness of contexts is subjective, since a normgiver is in no way required to respect a person's choice of context; anything within a context can be designated as forbidden, and anything outside the context as obligatory. This is why a moral code can consistently say: you should not kill, but if you kill, kill gently.

Although we were and still are convinced that the introduction of contexts is the right way to analyse CTD reasoning, the system presented in our earlier paper contained a flaw, and we concluded that further research is needed. The present paper reports on an aspect of that further research. The following section outlines the general idea, after recapturing the basics of our earlier proposal.

2. GENERAL CONSIDERATIONS

In this paper we employ the following notational conventions: capitals A, B and C are metavariables for arbitrary formulas, lower case letters w, v, ..., possibly subscripted, represent worlds, capitals P, Q, R, W stand for propositions in the sense of sets of worlds, and X, Y, Z stand for sets generally. $\|A\|^{\mathcal{M}}$ denotes the set of worlds (of a model $\mathcal{M}$) in which A is true. We leave the model $\mathcal{M}$ implicit where it is obvious from context. Finally, we assume the basic definitions of SDL to be known.

As for terminology, in examples of CTD structures we will often call an obligation and its associated CTD obligation, the 'primary' and 'secondary' obligation, respectively.

Our earlier approach

In making obligations relative to contexts, the main idea of (Prakken and Sergot, 1994, 1996) was to represent a context as a proposition, i.e. as a set of possible worlds, and then to pick out the ideal worlds not only relative to a world but also relative to a set of worlds. To this end we augmented the language of SDL with, for every formula B, a modal operator $\bigcirc_B$, standing for 'obligatory from the point of view of the (sub-ideal) context B'. To capture the semantics we defined a function dc of contextual deontic ideality: for any world w and set of worlds Q, $dc(Q, w)$ picks out those worlds that are the best alternatives of w as assessed from the context Q. The truth conditions of $\bigcirc_B A$ were defined as:

$$w \models \bigcirc_B A \text{ iff } dc(\|B\|, w) \subseteq \|A\|$$

$\mathcal{P}_B A$ was defined as $\neg \bigcirc_B \neg A$ and $\bigcirc A$ as $\bigcirc_\top A$.

Thus the gentle murderer can be expressed consistently as follows.

(1) $\bigcirc \neg kill$

(2) $\bigcirc_{kill} kill\text{-}gently$

Apart from finding a consistent representation of such examples, another main concern was to state conditions on dc that would make the B-best worlds resemble the best worlds as closely as possible, given that B. Firstly, we wanted to prevent that a CTD context could contain new obligations for no reason: if a CTD context introduces a new obligation it should be to regulate the violation of a 'higher' obligation. The model conditions that imposed bounds on dc validated the following 'Up' principle

Up. $\mathcal{P}_B C \rightarrow (\bigcirc_{(B \wedge C)} A \rightarrow \bigcirc_B A)$

More importantly, we also wanted to formulate conditions on dc under which conflicting primary and secondary obligations are consistent. Here it becomes important how exactly we read a contextual CTD obligation, such as 'Given that you kill, offer a cigarette first'. If we read this as saying that in the best of worlds in which you kill, you offer a cigarette first, then intuitively this seems consistent with a primary obligation not to offer cigarettes. The worlds in which you kill are, after all, already non-ideal. But in certain other readings this seems wrong. If the CTD obligation is read as saying 'of the worlds where you kill, in those that resemble as closely as possible the ideal worlds, you offer a cigarette first', this conflicts with a primary obligation not to offer cigarettes. On this reading, a legislator who wants to regulate violation of the obligation not to kill must take account of the primary obligation not to offer cigarettes, since this is also intended to regulate killing contexts. Regulation of norm-violation must still respect other norms that are in force. On the other hand, not all primary obligations have to be taken into account in this way: the primary obligation not to kill can be ignored by the legislator, since the CTD context where you kill already covers its violation. In other words, the context where you kill is *related* to the obligation not to kill.

Accordingly, we let the logic of our earlier paper validate a scheme according to which primary obligations are 'downwards inherited' by unrelated contexts.

Down. $\varepsilon \rightarrow (\bigcirc_B A \rightarrow \bigcirc_{(B \wedge C)} A)$

The actual form of ε is shown later, in section 6.1. For now, the point is that it captured, or so we thought, the notion of relatedness of an obligation to a context. However, we ended our paper with the observation that our system validated some undesirable inferences. And although we were able to pinpoint a number of ways these problems could be removed, we could not see how finding the right version of Down could be solved by adjusting the conditions on the function dc without further guidance. We need some way of building it up from more basic, simpler, components.

We therefore suggested a different semantical perspective, viz. that of preference orderings on worlds. The idea here is to define an ordering on the set of possible worlds in such a way that, roughly speaking, the more obligations a world satisfies, the better it is. Then the truth of a contextual obligation $\bigcirc_B A$ can be defined as: A holds in the best of the worlds where B is the case. Our hope was that this view would reflect our intuitions on down inheritance. In this paper we develop this approach, and we will investigate whether our hope was justified.

The relation with dyadic deontic logic

The reader will have noticed the formal similarities between our approaches to contextual obligation and well-known systems of dyadic deontic logic. In particular, 'best of the worlds where B is the case' is the basis for the logics developed by David Lewis (1974), which in turn resemble and generalise the system of Bengt Hansson (1969). We therefore want to develop our new account as a variant of the Hansson-Lewis systems. In doing so, we want to address two main points. The first is of a philosophical nature, viz. an examination of dyadic deontic logics of the Hansson-Lewis type as systems of contextual rather than conditional obligation. This will also help to clarify what we mean by 'context' and the difference between what we are calling 'contextual obligations' and conditional obligations as ordinarily understood. The second point is to make a technical contribution, by investigating how dyadic deontic logics of this type can be augmented to capture our intuitions on upward and downward inheritance of contextual obligations.

The relation with defeasible deontic logic

We should also motivate why this paper appears in a volume on *defeasible* deontic logics. This is for three reasons.

First, some authors, e.g. (Loewer and Belzer, 1983; Alchourrón, 1993), have interpreted Hansson-Lewis systems as candidates for logics of *prima facie*, or defeasible conditional obligations. They have done so since these logics exhibit some of the kinds of properties one would expect of defeasible conditionals. They invalidate, in particular, the principle of strengthening of the antecedent for the dyadic operators: from 'promises ought to be kept' it does not follow that 'promises to do immoral things ought to be kept'. Thus, so it is argued, they seem to capture the idea that *prima facie* obligations can be defeated in exceptional circumstances. We will argue that this view on these systems, although understandable, is mistaken; it is not *prima facie* obligations that these logics represent.

The second issue concerns a proposal of some to formalise timeless CTD structures using non-monotonic techniques (e.g. (McCarty, 1994; Ryu and Lee, 1996)). In these proposals, in circumstances where a primary obligation is violated, consistency is maintained by regarding the derivation of the primary obligation as somehow blocked by the derivation of the secondary obligation that comes into force.

We here briefly summarise our arguments in (Prakken and Sergot, 1994, 1996) as to why we think this view is incorrect. What it fails to capture is that when the secondary obligation, say to kill gently, is being fulfilled, at the same time the primary obligation not to kill is being violated: violating an obligation in a situation does not make it inapplicable to that situation.

In (Prakken and Sergot, 1994, 1996) we illustrated this with the following example.

(1) There must be no fence.
(2) If there is a fence, it must be a white fence.
(3) If the cottage is by the sea, there may be a fence.

(2) is intended as a CTD obligation of (1) and (3) as an exception to (1).

A person who has a cottage by the sea with a fence does not violate (1), since (1) is defeated by (3): (1) does not apply when the cottage is by the sea. Someone whose cottage is not by the sea and who has a white fence complies with (2) but still violates (1): any fine imposed for violating (1) will have to be paid. A logic that in these circumstances regards (1) as being defeated by (2) cannot express this.

The third connection with defeasibility is that in later sections of the paper we shall argue, not only that the Hansson-Lewis systems must be extended if they are to deal with contrary-to-duty reasoning, but that these extensions apparently cannot be undertaken using standard model-theoretic devices. We shall sketch the outline of a solution which yields a non-monotonic consequence relation, of a kind not unlike those studied in the field of defeasible reasoning, but respecting that secondary obligations do not defeat primary ones.

The structure of this paper

We will develop the discussion as follows. To make the link with the Hansson-Lewis logics, section 3 will present a representative system, a modified version which includes an additional operator for alethic necessity. Consideration of how to interpret this logic leads to a discussion in section 4 of various notions of obligation that have appeared in the literature. In section 5 we re-assess the system in the light of the preceding discussion, with the aim of providing a more detailed conceptual analysis of contextual obligations and CTD reasoning. Section 6 presents a possible extension of the Hansson-Lewis logic intended to provide some form of up and down 'inheritance'; section 7 identifies its shortcomings and sketches a solution. In section 8 we will assess what we have achieved.

3. HANSSON-LEWIS CONDITIONALS

The basic idea in the Hansson-Lewis account of obligation is that expressions 'Given that B, it ought to be that A' are interpreted as saying that A holds in a chosen subset of the (accessible) B-worlds: these are the 'best' (accessible) B-worlds, as determined by an ordering on worlds representing preferences or the relative 'goodness' of worlds. The idea originates in (Hansson, 1969) and was subsequently developed by several authors, notably Lewis (1974) presents several different value structures, in addition to orderings on worlds, and also provides a useful comparison with other proposals, including Hansson's.

In this section we present a representative system of the Hansson-Lewis family. Most of the details can be found in (Lewis, 1974), although our version will also be different in several respects. We focus only on preference orderings, and not on the other kinds of value structures considered by Lewis; we make a notational change designed to make the intended reading of the deontic operators more perspicuous; and we isolate and discard some assumptions that are made by Lewis about preference orderings. We also add a new component, viz. an alethic accessibility relation. This is not present in the systems studied in (Lewis, 1974) but it is a standard feature in counterfactual conditionals, which formally are constructed in exactly the same way.

The language is that of propositional logic, augmented with two dyadic deontic operators $\bigcirc[B]A$ and $\mathcal{P}[B]A$, meant to be interdefinable as usual: $\mathcal{P}[B]A =_{def} \neg\bigcirc[B]\neg A$. (Lewis's notation is $\bigcirc(A/B)$ and $\mathcal{P}(A/B)$.) The intended reading of $\bigcirc[B]A$ is 'Given that B, it ought to be that A' *in the sense that* A holds in all of the best (accessible) B-worlds. Notice that $\bigcirc[\top]A$ ($\top$ any tautology) then says that A holds in all of the best of all worlds, a reading which coincides with that of Standard Deontic Logic (SDL). Accordingly, the expression $\bigcirc A$ is used as an abbreviation for $\bigcirc[\top]A$. As in (Prakken and Sergot, 1994, 1996), we add to the language two more operators $\square$ and $\diamond$, standing for 'necessary' and 'possible' respectively.

Models are structures

$$\mathcal{M} = \langle W, f, \geq^W, V \rangle$$

W is a set of possible worlds and V is a valuation function for atomic sentences in each of the possible worlds. f is a function from W into $\wp(W)$ representing the alethic accessibility relation: $f(w)$ is the set of worlds in W accessible from w. The relevant truth conditions are

$$\mathcal{M}, w \models \square A \text{ iff } f(w) \subseteq \|A\|$$

$\diamond A$ is defined as $\neg\square\neg A$. We make no further assumptions about the nature of f at this stage.

A formula A is *true in a model* $\mathcal{M}$ iff $\mathcal{M}, w \models A$ for all w. And A is *valid* iff A is true in all models. Furthermore, for any set Γ of sentences $\mathcal{M}, w \models \Gamma$ iff $\mathcal{M}, w \models B$ for all $B \in \Gamma$. Finally, we will use the following notion of entailment: A set Γ of sentences *entails* a sentence A iff $\mathcal{M}, w \models A$ for all models $\mathcal{M}$ and worlds w such that $\mathcal{M}, w \models \Gamma$.

The main semantical device is $\geq^W$, which is a *preference frame* over W: for each w in W it assigns an ordering $\langle K_w, \geq_w \rangle$ where K_w is a (possibly empty) subset of W and $\geq_w$ is a pre-order (a reflexive and transitive relation) on K_w. In (Lewis, 1974) it is further assumed that each $\geq_w$ is a total ('strongly connected') pre-order, i.e. that, for all w_1 and w_2 in K_w, either $w_1 \geq_w$ w_2 or $w_2 \geq_w w_1$. We do not make this assumption. We comment on its significance, and on other features of Lewis's systems, in later discussions. The K_w component provides an extra degree of flexibility but for present purposes it can be discarded; it is sufficient to restrict attention to the case where all accessible worlds are evaluable, i.e. to frames in which $f(w) \subseteq K_w$ for all worlds w in W.

The intended reading of $w_1 \geq_w w_2$ is that world w_1 is *at least as good as* w_2 according to some valuation of worlds, as measured from w. The orderings are indexed by worlds w to allow for the possibility that preferences or measures of goodness may differ from one world to another.

As already indicated, the idea now is that $\bigcirc[B]A$ will hold at a world w just in case A holds at all the $\geq_w$-best B-worlds. However, there are alternative ways of formalising this idea, depending on the level of generality required.

Terminology and notation   For any pre-order $\geq_w$ on K_w, $>_w$ is the associated strict (irreflexive and transitive) ordering. w_m will be said to be *maximal* under $\geq_w$ in a subset X of K_w iff it is maximal in X under the associated ordering $>_w$, i.e., iff $w_m \in X$ and there is no $w' \in X$ such that $w' >_w w_m$. We use the notation $\max_w(X)$ for the set of elements of X ($X \subseteq K_w$) that are maximal under $\geq_w$.

The truth conditions for $\bigcirc[B]A$ are required to capture the idea that the best of the (accessible) B-worlds in which A holds are strictly better than the best of the (accessible) B-worlds in which A does not hold. One way of formalising this is as follows:

(obl) $w \models \bigcirc[B]A$ iff there exists some world $w_m \in f(w) \cap \|B \wedge A\|$ such that $w_m >_w w'$ for all $w' \in f(w) \cap \|B \wedge \neg A\|$

(An alternative, that $\bigcirc[B]A$ should hold at world w iff *all* worlds in $f(w) \cap \|B \wedge A\|$ are strictly preferable ($>_w$) to all worlds in $f(w) \cap \|B \wedge \neg A\|$ is much too strong a requirement to be useful.)

The truth definition (obl) caters for the possibility that there are infinite sequences of better and better and better worlds. If attention is restricted to frames satisfying the *limit assumption*, in conditional logics also referred to as *stoppering* — frames in which there are no infinite sequences of better and better worlds — or to the slightly more restrictive class of *well-founded* orderings — frames in which $\max_w(X)$ is non-empty for every non-empty subset X of K_w — then the truth conditions may be stated equivalently as follows:

(obl$_{\max}$) $w \models \bigcirc[B]A$ iff $\max_w(f(w) \cap \|B\|) \neq \emptyset$ and $\max_w(f(w) \cap \|B\|) \subseteq \|A\|$

The condition $\max_w(f(w) \cap \|B\|) \neq \emptyset$ appears here, as in (Lewis, 1974), because then the truth definitions (obl) and (obl$_{max}$) coincide under the limit/well-foundedness assumption. This makes $\bigcirc[B]A$ false for the degenerate case where B is inconsistent ($\|B\|$ is empty) or not 'possible' ($f(w) \cap \|B\|$ is empty).

In what follows we shall tend to refer to the truth definition (obl$_{max}$), but this is just to simplify the presentation. The logic of $\bigcirc[B]A$ does not change if the limit/well- foundedness assumption is removed, as long as the truth conditions are then stated in the form (obl) to compensate.

With these truth conditions the logic of each $\bigcirc[B]$ (for consistent, 'possible' B) is that of SDL. More precisely, $\bigcirc[B]A$ is (almost) a 'normal conditional logic' in the terminology of (Chellas, 1980, Ch10). It contains the following rules:

RCOEA.
$$\frac{B \leftrightarrow B'}{\bigcirc[B]A \leftrightarrow \bigcirc[B']A}$$

RCOK.
$$\frac{A_1 \wedge \ldots \wedge A_n \rightarrow A}{\bigcirc[B]A_1 \wedge \ldots \wedge \bigcirc[B]A_n \rightarrow \bigcirc[B]A} \qquad (n > 0)$$

Because B can be inconsistent/'impossible' the rule RCOK does not hold for $n = 0$; it holds in a restricted form:

RCON.
$$\frac{A}{\Diamond B \rightarrow \bigcirc[B]A} \qquad \text{i.e.} \qquad \text{ON.} \quad \Diamond B \rightarrow \bigcirc[B]\top$$

Validity of the scheme

OD. $\bigcirc[B]A \rightarrow \mathcal{P}[B]A$

follows from the evaluation rule for $\bigcirc[B]A$ (without any assumptions about f). Seriality of f (i.e. $f(w)$ is non-empty for all w in W) validates:

P. $\bigcirc[\top]\top$ i.e. $\Diamond\top$

(This may seem a little surprising at first sight but it is really a consequence of the way the truth conditions are defined. A variant of SDL could be constructed in similar style. Define $w \models \bigcirc A$ iff $d(w) \neq \emptyset$ and $d(w) \subseteq \|A\|$ where d is the usual deontic accessibility relation of SDL. Validity of $\bigcirc A \rightarrow \mathcal{P}A$ follows without any assumption about seriality of d. But then $\bigcirc\top$ is not valid: it is validated by adding the assumption that d is serial.)

It can be seen that this Hansson-Lewis system is a generalisation of SDL. Semantically, notice that the deontic accessibility relation $d(w)$ of SDL can be defined as $d(w) =_{def} \max_w(f(w))$; then $d(w) \subseteq f(w)$ for all w in W, and d will be serial if f is serial. (Furthermore, every deontic accessibility relation can be so characterised.)

Some further properties of $\bigcirc[B]A$ are forthcoming without any further assumptions about the orderings $\geq_w$ or the nature of f. For instance, the following, named as in (Chellas, 1980), is valid in all models

ODIL. $\bigcirc[B]A \wedge \bigcirc[C]A. \rightarrow \bigcirc[B \vee C]A$

ODIL will be referred to later in connection with 'Up inheritance' principles.

Since $w \models \Box(B \to C)$ iff $f(w) \cap \|B\| \subseteq f(w) \cap \|C\|$, it is easy to verify that the logic contains the valid scheme:

O□A. $\Box(B \to C) \to (\bigcirc[B]A \to \bigcirc[B \wedge C]A)$

and also:

□ON. $\Box A \to (\Diamond B \to \bigcirc[B]A)$

which implies, for instance:

□OCK. $\Box(A \to C) \to (\bigcirc[B]A \to \bigcirc[B]C)$

□ON together with OD gives:

$$\bigcirc[B]A \to \Diamond(B \wedge A)$$

which we shall refer to as the 'ought implies can' property.

Of particular importance for the interpretation of the Hansson-Lewis family of dyadic deontic logics are the following properties.

Since $\max_w(f(w) \cap \|B\|) \subseteq \|B\|$, $\bigcirc[B]B$ holds for every 'possible' B, i.e. the following scheme is valid:

OI. $\Diamond B \to \bigcirc[B]B$

and also, more generally:

□OI. $\Box(B \to A) \to (\Diamond B \to \bigcirc[B]A)$

And since $f(w) \subseteq \|B\|$ implies that $f(w) \cap \|B\| \cap \|C\| = f(w) \cap \|C\|$, we get:

SFD. $\Box B \to (\bigcirc[B \wedge C]A \to \bigcirc[C]A)$

of which a special case is:

$$\Box B \to (\bigcirc[B]A \to \bigcirc A)$$

The significance of these two properties for the interpretation of $\bigcirc[B]A$ will be discussed separately, in section 5.

Further properties

The reader familiar with the logics presented in (Lewis, 1974) will recall that all the systems presented there contain three valid schemes which are of interest in that they already begin to resemble the 'Up' and 'Down' inheritance principles we are seeking. The schemes are (with the numbering of (Lewis, 1974), but employing the □ and ◇ operators):

A6. $\bigcirc[B]A \wedge \bigcirc[C]A. \to \bigcirc[B \vee C]A$

A7. $\neg\Diamond C \wedge \bigcirc[B \vee C]A. \to \bigcirc[B]A$

A8. $\mathcal{P}[B \vee C]B \wedge \bigcirc[B \vee C]A. \to \bigcirc[B]A$

A6 can be regarded as a form of 'upward inheritance'. It is the scheme we referred to as ODIL earlier, valid in all models without any further assumptions about the preference orderings. It will be discussed in connection with deontic detachment presently.

A7 and A8 are special cases of 'downward inheritance'. A7 is equivalent to the scheme O□A above, valid in all models. Since $\Box(B \rightarrow C) \rightarrow \Box(B \leftrightarrow (B \wedge C))$, A7/O□A just says that a contextual obligation is inherited by necessarily equivalent contexts. A8 is validated by the further assumption that preference orderings on worlds are strongly connected (i.e. 'total' or 'linear'). A8 can be written equivalently as:

A8′. $\quad \mathcal{P}[B]C \rightarrow (\bigcirc[B]A \rightarrow \bigcirc[B \wedge C]A)$

of which the following is a special case:

$$\mathcal{P}B \rightarrow (\bigcirc A \rightarrow \bigcirc[B]A)$$

Both of A7/O□A and A8′ provide a kind of 'Down', except that, of course, they do not cover CTD contexts: A7/O□A is the boundary case in which contextual obligations are inherited by the same context, and in A8′ the more specific context $B \wedge C$ does not violate any obligation of the more general context B.[2]

This last observation is the reason why we want to go beyond the Hansson-Lewis systems. For our purposes $\bigcirc[B]A$ as defined so far is too weak. A8 depends on the very strong, and in our view inappropriate, assumption that preference orderings are linear. But in any case it is too weak. It states logical relations between obligations for different contexts but does not cover the case where one context is a CTD context of the other. In the Hansson-Lewis framework, such obligations are mutually consistent, regardless of whether they are conflicting. We, by contrast, want to analyse what kind of consistency relations hold between obligations pertaining to contexts which stand in a CTD relation to one another.

Upward inheritance and deontic detachment

Let us now investigate what forms of Up principle are available. A version analogous to that of Up in (Prakken and Sergot, 1994, 1996) would take the form:

$$\mathcal{P}[B \vee C]B \rightarrow (\bigcirc[B]A \rightarrow \bigcirc[B \vee C]A)$$

It is not valid. The following, weaker version of the original Up is valid:

$$\mathcal{P}[B \vee C]B \rightarrow (\bigcirc[B]A \rightarrow \mathcal{P}[B \vee C]A)$$

However, we can already derive a stronger property, a generalised form of deontic detachment, derivable from ODIL (which is not exclusive to the Hansson-Lewis family) and OI ($\Diamond A \rightarrow \bigcirc[A]A$) which is characteristic of Hansson-Lewis.

---

[2]Where there is no danger of confusion we often refer to a context by a formula B rather than set of worlds $\|B\|$.

The derivation is as follows. First observe that $\bigcirc[B]A \to \bigcirc[B](B \to A)$. And from $\Diamond\neg B \to \bigcirc[\neg B]\neg B$ (OI), we have also $\Diamond\neg B \to \bigcirc[\neg B](B \to A)$. Putting these together, using ODIL, we obtain $\Diamond\neg B \to (\bigcirc[B]A \to \bigcirc[B](B \to A))$. Note finally that $\neg\Diamond\neg B \to (\bigcirc[B]A \to \bigcirc[B](B \to A))$ is a special case of the valid scheme SFD. So then we have:

DK. $\bigcirc[B]A \to \bigcirc(B \to A)$

Deontic detachment (DD) follows from DK and $\bigcirc(B \to A) \to (\bigcirc B \to \bigcirc A)$:

DD. $\bigcirc[B]A \to (\bigcirc B \to \bigcirc A)$

Note that from DD and OD we obtain a weak form of 'Up':

WeakUp'. $\mathcal{P}B \to (\bigcirc[B]A \to \mathcal{P}A)$

This in turn can be re-written in equivalent form as:

Ctd'. $\bigcirc[B]A \land \bigcirc\neg A. \to \bigcirc\neg B$

The derivation of DK and DD may be generalised easily. We obtain:

GDK. $\bigcirc[B \land C]A \to \bigcirc[C](B \to A)$

From GDK follows the generalised form of deontic detachment:

GDD. $\bigcirc[B \land C]A \to (\bigcirc[C]B \to \bigcirc[C]A)$

and weak 'Up':

WeakUp. $\mathcal{P}[C]B \to (\bigcirc[B \land C]A \to \mathcal{P}[C]A)$

and its equivalent form:

Ctd. $\bigcirc[B \land C]A \land \bigcirc[B]\neg A. \to \bigcirc[C]\neg B$

Other dyadic deontic logics

We conclude this presentation by remarking that there are of course other families of dyadic deontic logics besides the Hansson-Lewis kind. (See e.g. the discussion in (Loewer and Belzer, 1983).) Many of these logics are candidates for representing (defeasible) conditional obligations, and perhaps even contextual obligations. Sorting out their various claims can be difficult because, given the way they are typically constructed, the resulting systems are inevitably almost identical. A detailed discussion is well beyond the scope of this paper, but it is instructive to refer again to the dyadic deontic logic $\bigcirc_B A$ in our earlier work (Prakken and Sergot, 1994, 1996).

The truth conditions of $\bigcirc_B A$ were defined as:

$$w \models \bigcirc_B A \text{ iff } dc(\|B\|, w) \subseteq \|A\|$$

The form of these truth conditionals is very common: it is just that of a normal conditional logic. And if there is another (alethic) accessibility relation f, then imposing $dc(Q, w) \subseteq f(w)$ as a model condition yields almost all of the rules and valid schemes identified earlier in this section. What is critical is what further conditions are imposed on the function dc.

The characteristic feature of Hansson-Lewis systems is that $dc(Q, w) \subseteq Q$, which here would validate $\bigcirc_A A$. From this flows deontic detachment. But this is not a feature of our earlier (Prakken and Sergot, 1994, 1996) system, not because of an oversight but because we were there not thinking of $dc(Q, w)$ as necessarily picking out some 'best' subset of the Q worlds. In the present paper we have chosen the Hansson- Lewis framework as a starting point, because it fits the kind of semantic structure we want to investigate in later sections. But there are also other possibilities we want to explore; they will not be discussed further in this paper.

4. SOME NOTIONS CONCERNING OBLIGATION

We have said that dyadic deontic logics of the Hansson-Lewis type are good starting points for the analysis of CTD structures. This seems to agree with the positions of Hansson and Lewis themselves. Hansson says explicitly that "... dyadic obligations are secondary, reparational obligations, telling someone what he should do if he has violated (...) a primary obligation" (Hansson, 1969, p.142). Although (Lewis, 1974) does not discuss this issue at length (the paper is mainly concerned with technical aspects of the logics), the only informal example is of a CTD structure, viz. the well-known Good Samaritan: it ought to be that you are not robbed, but given that you have been robbed you ought to be helped. This again fits the suggestion to regard Lewis's system as a candidate logic for CTD structures.

However other authors have interpreted the Hansson-Lewis systems in other ways. For instance, Loewer and Belzer (1983) have argued that these systems should be interpreted as logics for *prima facie*, or *ideal* obligation, as opposed to a logic for *all-things-considered*, or *actual* obligation. Sometimes they even seem to use the terms 'conditional' and 'unconditional' obligations to denote this distinction. And as mentioned above, others have interpreted the Hansson-Lewis family as candidate logics for defeasible conditional obligations.

So what are we analysing in this paper? What is the relation between CTD structures and the various distinctions that have appeared in the literature? This section attempts to answer these questions. A secondary aim is to compare some of the different senses in which the various notions are used in the literature, with the aim of preventing terminological confusion.

Conditional vs. unconditional obligations

Since we propose to formalise CTD obligations with dyadic modalities, the question naturally arises whether we regard CTD obligations as a kind of conditional obligation. In particular, does the obligatoriness of A in the context B mean that A is obligatory on the condition that B holds? Our discussion in section 2 of the gentle murderer and the white fence is intended to indicate that this is not the case. Recall that we have described CTD obligations as obligations that are relative to a certain context, or certain circumstances. They may give cues for action for persons who regard the context as settled, but, and this is critical, regarding something *subjectively* as settled does not make obligations that hold outside the context go away. Even if I regard it as settled that I kill, the obligation not to kill is still binding upon me. The key to a consistent representation of timeless CTD structures is that the context is an essential part of the obligation: the obligation to kill gently pertains to the context where you kill: placing yourself outside the context, even if it is the case that you kill, makes the obligation cease to be a cue for action. This is one reason why we regard Hansson-Lewis systems as a basis for contextual rather than conditional obligations: they fail to satisfy factual detachment: $\bigcirc[B]A, B \not\models \bigcirc A$.

But perhaps this inference holds in a weaker sense? Perhaps it is only defeasibly valid, since contextual obligations are *prima facie* obligations? To answer this, we have to discuss what could be meant by the term *prima facie* obligation.

Prima facie vs. all-things-considered obligation

The term *prima facie* obligation originates from (Ross, 1930). According to Ross an act is *prima facie* obligatory if it has a characteristic that makes the act (by virtue of an underlying moral principle) *tend* to be a 'duty proper'. Fulfilling a promise is a *prima facie* duty because it is the fulfillment of a promise, i.e. because of the moral principle that you should do what you have promised. But the act may also have other characteristics which make the act tend to be forbidden. For instance, if I have promised a friend to visit him for a cup of tea, and then my mother suddenly falls ill, then I also have a *prima facie* duty to do my mother's shopping, based, say, on the principle that we ought to help our parents when they need it. To find out what one's duty proper is, one should 'consider all things', i.e. compare all *prima facie* duties that can be based on any aspect of the factual circumstances and find which one is 'more incumbent' than any conflicting one.

To see how *prima facie* obligations might be formalised, we have to discuss the notion of 'defeasible' obligation.

Defeasible vs. non-defeasible obligations

Following Ross (1930), Loewer and Belzer (1983) say that *prima facie* duties are defeasible, or subject to exceptions. What can they mean by this? As we have just seen, *prima facie* duties tend to be duties by virtue of an underlying moral principle, that stresses only some of the characteristics of an act. Now *normally* such a principle can be applied to a situation without conflicting with other principles, but there can be exceptional circumstances in which conflicting principles also apply and perhaps even prevail. What happens in such a situation is that an argument, or inference, using such a moral principle is overridden, or defeated by another argument, using a stronger principle. To go back to the example, if in the circumstances I regard the principle concerning helping one's parents as more incumbent than the principle concerning keeping promises, then the argument for the obligation to help my mother defeats the argument for the obligation to have a cup of tea with my friend.

Arguments for conclusions that can be overridden are usually called 'defeasible'. More precisely, an argument is called defeasible if, although valid on the basis of a certain set of premises, it might be invalidated if new premises are added.

Note that defined in this way defeasibility is a property of an argument and not of a conditional. This is because one can have strengthening of the antecedent with or without the validity of modus ponens, and modus ponens with or without strengthening of the antecedent, and all these inferences can be both defeasible and deductive: so strengthening properties of a conditional have no bearing on the nature of arguments that use the conditional (see also (Makinson, 1993)). The often-used phrase 'defeasible conditional' is on this account elliptical for 'a conditional which, when used in an argument, makes the argument defeasible'.

The study of defeasible arguments is the field of so-called non-monotonic logic, a subfield of Artificial Intelligence. This, then, is the area where tools can be found for formalising reasoning about *prima facie* obligations. Reasoning about such obligations is reasoning with defeasible moral principles. Such principles can be formalised as defeasible conditionals; the antecedents of such conditionals stand for the aspect of a situation on which the *prima facie* obligation is based. More specifically, an obligation is *prima facie* if it is the conclusion of an argument that is (non-monotonically) valid under a subset of the actual circumstances, although under the totality of the circumstances it may be invalidated. Only if the latter is not the case, is the *prima facie* duty also an all-things-considered duty (although still defeasibly derived, since we might come to know even more about the situation: 'all things considered' means 'all things considered that are known').

As a terminological matter it should be noted that in our terms (as in (Morreau, 1994)), it is not a *prima facie* obligation that is defeasible, but the argument from something being a *prima facie* obligation to its being an all-things-considered obligation. Defeat of such an argument does not mean that the conclusion ceases to be a *prima facie* obligation; a reason to act remains a reason to act, even if in the circumstances other reasons prevail.

It should be noted that earlier discussions of *prima facie* obligations, of e.g. (Hintikka, 1971; Loewer and Belzer, 1983; Jones and Pörn, 1985), do not use non-monotonic techniques. However, this is perhaps because at the time non-monotonic logics were not yet (widely) available. Since this has changed, the view that reasoning with *prima facie* obligations is non-monotonic has become increasingly popular; see e.g. (Horty, 1994; Morreau, 1994; Prakken, 1996).

Are contextual obligations prima facie obligations?

So then, are contextual obligations *prima facie* obligations? From our discussion it follows that if they are, then they should satisfy some form of defeasible factual detachment: from it ought to be that A given context B, and the truth of B, it should follow defeasibly that it ought to be that A. But this cannot be, since then in the gentle murderer and the white fence examples we would end up with a normative conflict between the primary and secondary obligation, which runs counter to our intuitions about these examples. As we explained in section 2, the primary obligation not to kill and the secondary one to kill gently need not in any sense be weighed to see which one should prevail in the situation: they both apply to the situation. There is no need for conflict resolution: if someone complies with the CTD obligation to kill gently, the sanction for killing can still be applied. As we argued at length in (Prakken and Sergot, 1994, 1996) and have repeated above in section 2, this is the key difference between contrary-to-duty and *prima facie* obligations.

Of course, a different matter is that primary or CTD obligations can be based on *prima facie* principles, just as any other type of obligation can. But what is essential is that defeasibly derived contrary-to-duty obligations still have a context attached. To give an example, imagine I have a friend who has some kind of personal problem. In conversations where he is present I should not mention this problem; in the context where I do mention it, there can be reasons why I should apologise for mentioning it and reasons why I should not apologise and let the matter rest. Weighing these two *prima-facie* CTD-obligations might result in an all-things-considered, but still contextual, obligation to apologise or not to apologise.

Hansson-Lewis systems and prima facie obligations

Let us now return to the interpretation of Hansson-Lewis dyadic deontic logics as logics for *prima facie* obligations. If this interpretation is correct, then what we have just said implies that we cannot use such systems for representing contextual obligations. At first sight, it would seem that the way these systems define dyadic obligations indeed fits our description of *prima facie* obligations: being dyadic, the obligations depend only on certain aspects of a situation; moreover, conflicting obligations with different antecedents are consistent, which seems to capture that *prima facie* obligations remain a reason to act, even if in a given situation they do not become all-things-considered obligations.

Yet this interpretation is not appropriate. Recall that if the aspect on which a *prima facie* obligation is based is present in a situation, the *prima facie* obligation defeasibly implies an all-things-considered obligation. Now if Hansson-Lewis logics are regarded as logics for *prima facie* obligations, then such inferences should be captured in a non-monotonic extension of these systems: $B \wedge \bigcirc[B]A$ should defeasibly imply $\bigcirc A$. But how can this inference be formalised given the semantic interpretation of these logics? The only way seems to be to formalise an assumption to the effect that any world is as good as is consistent with the premises. However, apart from the question whether this assumption is realistic, it does not work: suppose that in our example it warrants that the actual world is among the best B worlds; all we can then derive is that in the actual world A is the case, not that in the actual world A is obligatory. Thus it seems that the attempt to interpret dyadic deontic logics of the Hansson-Lewis type as logics for *prima facie* obligations is fundamentally flawed.

Yet these attempts are understandable. As pointed out by Makinson (1993), $\bigcirc[B]A$ as interpreted in a Hansson-Lewis semantics can very well be read as 'A holds in all the most normal B worlds'. The $\bigcirc$ then stands for 'normally', which makes the dyadic formula express a defeasible conditional. However, the point is that it then expresses a conditional fact, not a conditional obligation.

Ideal vs. actual obligations

In discussing Lewis's logic, Loewer and Belzer (1983) sometimes use the terms 'ideal' and 'actual' obligation. Others have also linked these terms with CTD structures, e.g. (Jones and Pörn, 1985). How do these terms relate to the notion of contextual obligation? An answer is not straightforward, since it seems that in the literature this distinction has been used in several different ways. It seems useful to point out these differences.

A common element in all analyses is that 'ideally it ought to be that A' at least implies that in a world where nothing has gone wrong A is the case. Now there are several ways in which things can go wrong. Sometimes the undesirable event is something unusual, motivating an exception to an obligation, as the obligation for soldiers to kill in war is an exception to the prohibition to kill. If used to describe such situations, as Loewer and Belzer (1983) seem to do, the distinction ideal/actual seems to stand for *prima facie*/all-things-considered.

Another usage of the terms is that of Jones and Pörn (1985), who also discuss CTD structures, but of a different form. We can illustrate it by reference to a timeless version of the Chisholm (1963) scenario, as in (Prakken and Sergot, 1994, 1996). Suppose that: there must be no dog around the house, and if there is no dog, there must be no warning sign, but if there is a dog, there must be a warning sign. Obviously, if there is a dog, the conditional obligation that there must be no sign does not become unconditional, since its condition is not fulfilled. On the other hand, it can also be inferred that if no obligations are violated, there will be no sign (modulo exceptions, of course). Jones and Pörn (1985) have argued that this is an inference of an ideal but not actual obligation not to have a sign, and they formalise it as a deontic detachment inference, maintaining consistency by introducing distinct modal operators for ideal and actual obligation.

Finally, the terms ideal/actual are sometimes used in a different sense again, especially in connection with CTD structures like the gentle murderer and the white fence. Here the intended point seems to be that, while several conflicting contextual obligations can apply to a situation, the job of actual obligations is to tell us what in the end we must do. And on this reading there can be at most one actual obligation: either don't kill, or kill gently; either tear down the fence, or paint it white. So further, if one regards the violation of the primary obligation as settled, the actual obligation is the secondary one, but if one regards the violation as still avoidable, the actual obligation is the primary one. This seems to be the sense motivating a recent proposal by Carmo and Jones (1996).

Can we describe primary obligations as ideal obligations and contrary-to-duty obligations as actual ones? If the distinction ideal/actual stands for *prima facie*/all-things-considered then, as explained, it is independent of primary/CTD. The sense in which Jones and Pörn (1985) make the distinction is meaningful, but it does not apply to the CTD examples we are studying. In the dog example where there is a dog, having a sign does not violate an obligation that applies to the situation: no fine is due for having a warning sign, only for having a dog. By contrast, the primary obligations not to kill, or not to have a fence, do apply to the situation where a killing is taking place, or where there is a fence. The sanctions for violating them can be executed.

Finally, what of the last interpretation? An answer to this question requires a study of the detachment properties of contextual obligations. We now examine the properties of the Hansson-Lewis systems from that point of view.

5. HANSSON-LEWIS CONDITIONALS AS CONTEXTUAL OBLIGATIONS

In section 3 we presented a Hansson-Lewis logic extended with an operator for alethic necessity. Technically this is a simple addition, but it is a significant one. It enables us to clarify the sense in which contextual obligations are conditional, and to comment on the link between this system and the commonly accepted approach to temporal CTD structures in deontic logics with time.

5.1. *Detachment properties of contextual obligations*

We have said that contextual obligations are not to be confused with conditional obligations, that is, obligations which apply in certain circumstances but not in others. Yet there is a relationship between contextual and conditional obligations. Although contextual obligations do not satisfy modus ponens or any form of (possibly defeasible) factual detachment, they do satisfy another form of detachment which makes them conditional obligations of a sort. The point is that they are conditional in a special sense. The valid formula SFD of section 3 implies that contextual obligations, at least those of the Hansson-Lewis kind, satisfy a kind of 'strong-factual' detachment:

$$\models (\bigcirc[B]A \land \Box B) \to \bigcirc A$$

Contextual obligations are conditional, not upon the mere truth of the context, but upon the fact that the context is necessarily true, or 'objectively settled' as we shall also say.

For CTD obligations this form of strong factual detachment seems very appropriate, but it must be read with extreme care. As long as it is possible to avoid violation of a primary obligation $\bigcirc\neg B$ a CTD obligation $\bigcirc[B]A$ remains restricted to the context; it is only if the violation of $\bigcirc\neg B$ is unavoidable, if $\Box B$ holds, that the CTD obligation comes into full effect, pertains to the context $\top$. But it is important to note that the kind of necessity expressed by the $\Box$ operator is objective necessity, rather than some kind of subjective necessity, such as when an agent decides to regard it as settled *for him* that there will be a fence. It may be that a given agent is determined or becomes convinced that there is going to be a fence, come what may, but this does not make the obligation to have no fence go away. By contrast, 'it is *objectively* settled that B', $\Box B$, is much stronger: $\Box B$ implies $\bigcirc B$ and is inconsistent with $\bigcirc\neg B$. By SFD, $\bigcirc[B]A$ implies $\Box B \to \bigcirc A$, but it is not equivalent to the latter.

5.2. *Temporal necessity*

In (Prakken and Sergot, 1994, 1996), we presented a series of examples to draw parallels between temporal and timeless CTD structures. In temporal CTD structures, that is to say, in CTD structures where there is a difference between the times of the primary and secondary (CTD) obligations, the objective necessity will often be of a temporal kind, i.e. of the kind whereby it is settled now that yesterday I violated an obligation to keep a certain promise.

Whatever course the world will take from now on, the past cannot be undone. If I have an obligation to apologize for not keeping my promise, it pertains to a context that has been settled: I cannot undo the not keeping of my promise; all I can do now is apologize. This is the kind of inference that is captured by strong factual detachment. Perhaps we should call it 'contextual detachment'?

The temporal effect is a little awkward to demonstrate using the timeless system of section 3 since that logic is expressively restricted. We are forced to choose whether to represent the situation before the violation, at the time of the violation, or after the violation. Before the violation:

(1) $\bigcirc keep$

(2) $\bigcirc[\neg keep]apologize$

At the moment of breaking the promise the following can be added:

(3) $\neg keep$

To represent the situation after the violation, (3) can be strengthened. We then have:

(2) $\bigcirc[\neg keep]apologize$

(3*) $\Box \neg keep$

From (3*) and (2) follows the obligation $\bigcirc apologize$. The sentence (1) cannot be included, however, because it is inconsistent with (3*): once it is (objectively) settled that the promise is broken, there can be no obligation to keep it.

The effect is most clearly illustrated in temporal deontic logics that allow time to be expressed in the object language. Then it is not necessary to choose which of the three situations to represent because obligations pertaining to different times can be conjoined. For instance, in the system of van Eck (1982), we can say consistently:

(1') $\bigcirc_{t_1} keep_{t_1}$

(2') $\bigcirc_{t_2}[\neg keep_{t_1}] apologize_{t_3}$

(3') $\neg keep_{t_1}$

Here time t_1 is before time t_2 is before time t_3. Expression (1') says that at time t_1 it is obligatory that the promise is kept at t_1, and so on. The use of our notation for contextual obligations at (2') is justifiable because van Eck (1982) also employs a dyadic deontic operator (but relativised to time points) and adopts the Hansson-Lewis 'best of accessible worlds' interpretation of obligation; indeed the logic of each temporal obligation operator $\bigcirc_t[B]A$ is that of $\bigcirc[B]A$ in section 3.

It is beyond the scope of this paper to give a detailed account of the temporal semantics but a general sketch is in order to illustrate the extent of the similarities with the timeless case. Typically (see e.g. (van Eck, 1982; Åqvist and Hoepelman, 1981)) the set of possible worlds has the form of a tree. Each branch represents a possible world, or better: a possible course of events through time, and each node in a branch is a point in time. The notion of temporal necessity is captured in the following way. At any node in the tree, i.e. at any given point of time t in a given world w, the worlds accessible for w are those worlds that up to but not including t have the same past as w, i.e. that so far are indistinguishable from w. Those worlds that branched off in the past have become inaccessible: if yesterday I did not keep my promise, worlds in which I did keep it are today inaccessible. The deontic modalites are interpreted as follows: some of the possible futures of w at t will be marked as the ideal ones; what holds in all of them are the obligations at t, what holds in some of them is permissible at t.

Now it follows immediately from this that, for t_1 before t_2, (3′) $\neg keep_{t_1}$ implies

(3*′) $\Box_{t_2} \neg keep_{t_1}$

When t_2 is after t_1, it is settled at t_2 that the promise was not kept at t_1. (3*′) and (2′) imply $\bigcirc_{t_2} apologize_{t_3}$ by strong factual detachment, exactly as in the timeless case. To complete the comparison with the timeless representation, note that (3*′) implies $\bigcirc_{t_2} \neg keep_{t_1}$, but this does not contradict (1′). Violation of (1′) can be expressed by conjoining it with (3′).

The reader may be wondering why the contextual obligation at (2′) could not have been represented instead as a conditional obligation, of the form:

(2*′) $\neg keep_{t_1} \rightarrow \bigcirc_{t_2} apologize_{t_3}$

The answer is that in van Eck's system, (2′) and (2*′) are equivalent; where t_1 is before t_2, the following is valid (van Eck, 1982, Thm. 17):

$$\bigcirc_{t_2}[B_{t_1}]A \leftrightarrow (B_{t_1} \rightarrow \bigcirc_{t_2} A)$$

van Eck does not identify what we have been calling 'strong factual detachment'; his Thm. 17 serves much the same purpose.

One can see a corresponding feature in the timeless logic of section 3. In that system the following is valid:

$$\Box B \rightarrow (\bigcirc[B]A \leftrightarrow (B \rightarrow \bigcirc A))$$

One half is an instance of the 'strong factual detachment' property SFD. The other half, $\Box B \rightarrow ((B \rightarrow \bigcirc A) \rightarrow \bigcirc[B]A)$, is a special case of the scheme O□A (A7 in Lewis's numbering) that relates necessarily equivalent contexts. Here again one can see the essential point we are striving to make: contextual obligations and conditional obligations are indistinguishable when the context is necessarily true, but not otherwise.

In (Prakken and Sergot, 1994, 1996) we gave temporal CTD examples no detailed discussion because we thought they were not problematic; we thought that where fulfilling the secondary obligation comes after violating the primary one, the problems of the timeless examples do not occur, and that use of existing temporal deontic logics gives an adequate representation. We see now that this is not so. Suppose that at time t_1 I have the following two obligations, one to visit my neighbour's birthday party at t_2, and one to pay my taxes at t_4. Suppose that I do not visit my neighbour's party. Then at t_3, after t_2 but before t_4, what were the best futures of w at t_1 are not accessible any more; at t_3 there will be a completely different set of ideal futures. But how should these new ideal futures of w at t_3 be picked out? Surely in such a way that in all of them I still pay my taxes at t_4; the obligation to pay my taxes cannot disappear simply because I have violated another obligation. So the ideal futures at t_3, although disjoint from those at t_1, should still measure up to the old t_1-ideals as much as possible. Here we have a problem intimately related to the problem we want to study in a timeless setting in the present paper; the relevance of our discussions is not restricted to timeless CTD structures. However, since temporal notions introduce a host of further complications of their own, we confine ourselves here to the simpler, timeless case.

5.3. *The conditional nature of timeless CTD obligations*

For timeless CTD structures, such as the gentle murderer and the white fence, the use of temporal deontic logics does not help, since all statements pertain to the same point of time. Our earlier formulation of the gentle murderer re-written in the system of van Eck would look like this:

(1) $\bigcirc_t \neg kill_t$
(2) $\bigcirc_t [kill_t] kill\text{-}gently_t$

Adding

(3) $kill_t$

changes nothing. At the time of the killing this event is not yet unavoidable: in van Eck's system $kill_t$ does not imply $\Box_t kill_t$. This is how it should be, otherwise there could be no obligation at time t not to kill.

This is the key to the consistent representation of the gentle murderer, the white fence, and similar timeless examples. Since contextual CTD obligations do not satisfy (ordinary) factual detachment, we never derive two conflicting obligations that pertain to the same context; and although we have strong factual detachment, violation of the primary obligation cannot be (objectively) settled, since this makes the primary obligation inconsistent. Of course in timeless CTD structures we usually do not judge the situation from the point of view where violation of the primary obligation is (temporally) settled, since then it will also be settled either that the secondary obligation is fulfilled, or that it is violated.

We feel that we should remark also on the validity in the Hansson-Lewis family of the formula

$$\bigcirc[A]A$$

(for consistent, 'possible' A), since this is often cited as a fundamental flaw of these systems. When interpreted as expressing a standard conditional obligation to the effect that 'if A then it ought to be the case that A' then of course the criticisms cannot be disputed. But this is not the reading that is ascribed to the $\bigcirc$ operator. $\bigcirc[A]A$ says only that A holds in all of the best accessible A worlds, which is no more (or less) unacceptable than the validity of $\bigcirc\top$ in standard deontic logic. Nor is there anything problematic about the reading of $\bigcirc[A]A$ as a special kind of conditional: if the context A is objectively settled, the truth of A is unalterable; again there seems nothing particularly odd about saying that what is unalterably true is also obligatory. Notice finally that to violate $\bigcirc[A]A$, a world would have to satisfy $A \wedge \neg A$. Our conclusion is that the Hansson-Lewis systems are not philosophically flawed, as long as they are not interpreted as systems for 'ordinary' conditional obligations. Their characteristic feature is the validity of $\bigcirc[A]A$, from which stems deontic detachment.

Finally, we are able to comment on one use of the distinction between ideal/actual obligations, viz. the use in which just one of the conflicting primary and secondary obligations in CTD examples is taken to be the 'actual' obligation, depending on circumstances. For temporal CTD examples what is actual is clear-cut (though superfluous) since what is obligatory changes with time and the primary and secondary obligations do not hold simultaneously. For timeless CTD examples, we cannot see that the ideal/actual distinction is useful. It is only meaningful to consider the case where violation of the primary obligation is not settled (for otherwise violation or fulfillment of the secondary obligation is also settled). In that case both primary and secondary obligations apply to the situation. Why should we single out one of them as 'actual' and the other as merely ideal? The situation is different if $\Box$ is interpreted as some other kind of settledness, such as the *subjective* notion whereby an agent is determined that violation of the primary obligation will take place (cf. (Carmo and Jones, 1996)), in which case it can be that violation of the primary obligation is 'settled' while violation/fulfillment of the secondary obligation is not. This is not the kind of 'settledness' that we have been discussing.

5.4. A timeless Chisholm scenario

Let us now look at a timeless version of the Chisholm scenario, and ask how it can be represented in the modified Hansson-Lewis system of section 3. The example is taken from our earlier work:

(1)   There must be no dog.
(2)   If there is no dog there must be no sign.
(3)   If there is a dog, there must be a sign.

Let us consider the following partial representation, where the proper formalisation of (2) is left open for now:

(1') $\bigcirc\neg dog$
(2')
(3') $\bigcirc[dog]sign$

Clearly (3), being a CTD obligation, should be formalised as a contextual obligation. But how must (2) be formalised? The view is sometimes expressed that it should have the same conditional form as (3), i.e.

(2'') $\bigcirc[\neg dog]\neg sign$

But is this really what the statement (2) says? This is, of course, a matter of interpretation, but we think that on a very plausible reading of (2) the obligation not to have a sign is conditional upon the mere fact that there is no dog, not on the stronger condition that non-violation of (1) has been settled. And in this reading, (2) is not adequately formalised by (2'').

In our reading, (2) just says that if a world is such that there happens to be no dog, then there must be no sign. And on this reading, if we combine (2) with (1), they surely do not imply that in this world there *is* an obligation to have no sign; it just depends on how good this world is. Accordingly, it seems natural to regard (2) not as a CTD obligation but as a primary obligation conditional upon the (mere) fact that there is no dog. This reading is captured by the following representation:

(2') $\neg dog \Rightarrow \bigcirc\neg sign$

where $\Rightarrow$ is any suitable conditional satisfying factual detachment. (We put to one side questions of defeasibility and the possibility of implicit exceptions.)

Let us now examine how well this representation satisfies the usual requirements for formalisations of the Chisholm set. As just observed, the conditional statements (2) and (3) have received different representations, but we think that because (2) is a primary and (3) is a secondary obligation, this is how it should be: primary obligations satisfy weak factual detachment but CTD obligations, by their very nature, only satisfy strong factual detachment. Interestingly, in the temporal deontic logics of (Åqvist and Hoepelman, 1981) and (van Eck, 1982) these two statements of the Chisholm set also receive different formalisations (although naturally there a temporal variant of (2') is chosen).

Another requirement is that from (2) and the (mere) fact that there is no dog, it should follow unconditionally that there must be no sign. (2') satisfies this condition; (2'') does not.

Chisholm's own requirements are consistency and logical independence of the statements (1)–(3) and the further assertion that (4) there is a dog. Logical independence is determined by the choice of the conditional $\Rightarrow$ in (2'). As regards consistency, the sentences (1')–(3') are consistent. Adding

(4') *dog*

does not make the formalisation inconsistent. But then another commonly stated requirement is not satisfied, viz. that (3') and (4') allow detachment of an obligation $\bigcirc sign$ that there should be a sign. For us this is not problematic. We have just discussed at length why factual detachment is not valid for contextual obligations. However, there are other problems with the formalisation, to which we now turn.

5.5. *Inadequacies*

Consider now the following fragment of the previous example, taken, let us suppose, from regulations governing the use of holiday cottages.

(1)   There must be no dog.
(2)   If there is a dog, there must be a sign.

Suppose that to these requirements is added a further regulation:

(3)   There must be no sign.

And suppose that the relevant authorities have explicitly declared that these three statements are not to be understood defeasibly: there are no exceptions. Are regulations (1)–(3) consistent? Is it logically possible, given (1)–(3), that there is a dog?

Much of our earlier work has been motivated by the very strong intuition that these regulations, and other examples discussed in (Prakken and Sergot, 1994, 1996), are inconsistent when given a particular, rather natural reading.[3] The Hansson-Lewis framework does not capture this reading. On the Hansson-Lewis account of obligation, (1) says that in the best of all worlds there is no dog, (2) that in the best of dog worlds there is a sign, and (3) that in the best of all worlds there is no sign. There is nothing contradictory about that: (2) and (3) say that there is no dog in any ideal world, which is also what (1) says. Although the Hansson-Lewis systems do include principles that relate what is best in B-worlds with what is best in C-worlds for certain contexts B and C, these principles do not cover the case, essential for contrary-to-duty reasoning, where one context B is sub-ideal with respect to, contains a violation of, what is obligatory in context C. What these systems do not capture is that sub-ideal worlds should still measure up to the ideal worlds as much as possible.

---

[3]When we say that a set of regulations or set of (contextual) obligations such as (1)–(3) is inconsistent, we mean by this that the set is logically inconsistent with some further assumptions, in this case that it is logically possible there is a dog. In presenting examples we tend to leave these further assumptions unstated. Wherever the point of the example depends on it, we will state the assumptions explicitly.

In (Prakken and Sergot, 1994, 1996) our aim was to capture this aspect of CTD structures. At the very least we wanted to derive consistency requirements which would detect examples such as (1)–(3), an instance of what we called 'the considerate assassin', as inconsistent. Preferably we would like to obtain stronger 'down inheritance' principles, i.e. 'strengthening of the antecedent' principles in the terminology of conditional logics, allowing the inference from $\bigcirc[B]A$ to $\bigcirc[B \wedge C]A$, for certain combinations of A, B and C. So in the example, it seems to us that in at least one reading, we should be able to infer from (3) that even in dog worlds there should be no sign: in dog worlds that are as close as possible to ideal there is no sign. This inference would contradict (2), making the regulations inconsistent, which is what we want to infer in this example.

There is nothing wrong or incoherent about the Hansson-Lewis reading of (1)–(3). It is just that it does not capture adequately the notion of 'obligation' which makes us think that (1)–(3) are contradictory. What we want to investigate next is whether that notion of obligation can be captured without abandoning the Hansson-Lewis framework altogether.

Before moving on to that question, there is one further remark to make. If we have 'down inheritance' of contextual obligations, *no matter how it is obtained*, then the formalisation of the Chisholm set discussed in the previous section must be adjusted. The reason is that, in the case where there is no dog, the sentences

(1′) $\bigcirc\neg dog$
(2′) $\neg dog \Rightarrow \bigcirc\neg sign$
(3′) $\bigcirc[dog]sign$

are inconsistent: (2′) and factual detachment gives $\bigcirc\neg sign$, 'down inheritance' of this obligation gives $\bigcirc[dog]\neg sign$, and this contradicts (3′). Since we want down inheritance, it seems that we must adopt the formalisation used in (Prakken and Sergot, 1994, 1996) and replace (3′) by a conditional contextual obligation of the form:

(3″) $dog \Rightarrow \bigcirc[dog]sign$

The alternative is to find a 'down inheritance' principle which blocks this instance of inheritance but not others, a task that is not straightforward.

6.   ON FORMALISING DOWN INHERITANCE

6.1. *Our earlier attempts*

As just explained, in the Hansson-Lewis framework obligations from different contexts are logically related only if none of the obligations are violated. It seems to us that for the analysis of contrary-to-duty structures it is essential that some logical relations hold also between obligations in contexts where one is a CTD context of another. In the present section we will investigate how this can be achieved.

What we were seeking in (Prakken and Sergot, 1994, 1996) was a principle of 'downward inheritance' of obligations, of the following form:

Down. $\varepsilon \to (\bigcirc[B]A \to \bigcirc[B \wedge C]A)$

ε was intended to capture the notion of relatedness of an obligation to a context: it had the form

$$\Diamond(A \wedge B \wedge C) \wedge \neg\Box((B \wedge \neg A) \to C)$$

The first conjunct says that the context $B \wedge C$ leaves compliance with the B-context obligation open, i.e. the context $B \wedge C$ does not imply a violation, $\neg A$, of the B-context obligation that A. The second conjunct states that violation of the B-context obligation does not necessarily put us into the $B \wedge C$ context, i.e. the context $B \wedge C$ does not already cover violation of the B-context obligation. The intended effect of these conditions is perhaps most easily illustrated with some examples.

The 'gentle murderer':

(1) $\bigcirc\neg kill$
(2) $\bigcirc[kill]kill\text{-}gently$

should be consistent with the further assumptions that $\Box(kill\text{-}gently \to kill)$ and $\Diamond(kill \wedge \neg kill\text{-}gently)$. Since the first of these assumptions contradicts the first conjunct of ε, $\bigcirc\neg kill$ is not 'downwards inherited' to $\bigcirc[kill]\neg kill$. Furthermore, the derived primary obligation $\bigcirc\neg kill\text{-}gently$ is not 'downwards inherited' to $\bigcirc[kill]\neg kill\text{-}gently$ since the second assumption contradicts the second conjunct of ε.

On the other hand, the 'considerate assassin' (Prakken and Sergot, 1994, 1996):

(1) $\bigcirc\neg kill$
(2) $\bigcirc[kill]offer\text{-}cigarettes$
(3) $\bigcirc\neg offer\text{-}cigarettes$

should come out inconsistent with the assumptions that $\Diamond(kill \wedge \neg offer\text{-}cigarettes)$ and $\Diamond(offer\text{-}cigarettes \wedge \neg kill)$. These assumptions satisfy the ε conditions, and so the primary obligation $\bigcirc\neg offer\text{-}cigarettes$ is 'down inherited' to $\bigcirc[kill]\neg offer\text{-}cigarettes$, which is inconsistent with (2).

However, as pointed out by Leon van der Torre and further discussed in (Prakken and Sergot, 1994, 1996), there are examples in which these ε conditions give unacceptable results. Rather than repeat that discussion here, we now give a general argument why a down inheritance principle of the form Down cannot be acceptable in any Hansson-Lewis system. For simplicity we shall just show the details for the special case where one context is $\top$. The ε conditions are then $\Diamond(A \wedge C) \wedge \neg\Box(\neg A \to C)$, i.e. $\Diamond(A \wedge C) \wedge \Diamond(\neg A \wedge \neg C)$.

Suppose that the following is valid in some class of Hansson-Lewis models:

Down'. $\diamond(A \wedge C) \wedge \diamond(\neg A \wedge \neg C). \rightarrow (\bigcirc A \rightarrow \bigcirc[C]A)$

Now consider any two (unrelated) obligations $\bigcirc A$ and $\bigcirc B$, and the context $C = (A \wedge \neg B) \vee (\neg A \wedge B)$. It is easy to check that the conditions for Down' inheritance of obligation $\bigcirc A$ to the context C are $\diamond(A \wedge \neg B) \wedge \diamond(\neg A \wedge \neg B)$. Similarly, the conditions for Down' inheritance of obligation $\bigcirc B$ to the context C are $\diamond(B \wedge \neg A) \wedge \diamond(\neg B \wedge \neg A)$. So, if all three conditions $\diamond(A \wedge \neg B)$, $\diamond(\neg A \wedge B)$, and $\diamond(\neg A \wedge \neg B)$ hold, we have both $\bigcirc A \rightarrow \bigcirc[C]A$ and $\bigcirc B \rightarrow \bigcirc[C]B$.

Suppose $\diamond(A \wedge \neg B)$, $\diamond(\neg A \wedge B)$, and $\diamond(\neg A \wedge \neg B)$, and $\bigcirc A$ and $\bigcirc B$. Then both $\bigcirc[C]A$ and $\bigcirc[C]B$, from which $\bigcirc[C](A \wedge B)$ follows by RCOK. But for $C = (A \wedge \neg B) \vee (\neg A \wedge B)$, $\bigcirc[C](A \wedge B)$ must be false in any Hansson-Lewis system, by 'ought implies can': $\bigcirc[C](A \wedge B) \rightarrow \diamond(C \wedge (A \wedge B))$, but $\diamond(C \wedge (A \wedge B)) = \diamond(((A \wedge \neg B) \vee (\neg A \wedge B)) \wedge (A \wedge B))$, which is logically equivalent to $\diamond\bot$, which is false.

We must conclude that if $\bigcirc A$ and $\bigcirc B$, then either $\neg\diamond(A \wedge \neg B)$, or $\neg\diamond(\neg A \wedge B)$, or $\neg\diamond(\neg A \wedge \neg B)$. If Down' is valid then the following is valid also:

$$\bigcirc A \wedge \bigcirc B. \rightarrow (\Box(A \rightarrow B) \vee \Box(B \rightarrow A) \vee \Box(\neg A \rightarrow B) \vee \Box(\neg B \rightarrow A))$$

Proposition 6.1 If Down is valid in any class of Hansson-Lewis models then, for any A, B and C, the following is valid also:

$$\bigcirc[C]A \wedge \bigcirc[C]B \rightarrow \Box(C \wedge A. \rightarrow B) \vee \Box(C \wedge B. \rightarrow A) \vee$$
$$\Box(C \wedge \neg A. \rightarrow B) \vee \Box(C \wedge \neg B. \rightarrow A)$$

Proof Generalise the derivation shown above. $\Box$

It follows that in any Hansson-Lewis system in which Down is valid, there can be no logically independent obligations.

This is a general argument. It does not depend on any particular orderings. It does not even depend on the exact form of ε. Since it uses only 'ought implies can' and the scheme

OC. $\bigcirc[C]A \wedge \bigcirc[C]B. \rightarrow \bigcirc[C](A \wedge B)$

proposition 6.1 can easily be generalised to argue that ε conditions for any strong down inheritance principle of the form Down cannot be axiomatised.

But this does not imply that there are no acceptable down inheritance principles at all. Does the present setting, where contextual obligations are interpreted in terms of a preference relation on worlds, enable us to find a suitable version of down inheritance? This is what we now want to investigate. The essence of the problem is that the Hansson-Lewis framework allows for the possibility of sub-ideal worlds but has very little to say about what they are like and nothing to say about how they compare with ideal worlds. Somehow we have to find a way of relating, for any pair of contexts $Q \subset Q'$, the best of Q-worlds with the best of Q'-worlds. The idea is that this can be done by putting more structure on the preference orderings $\geq_w$ to reflect the requirement that sub-ideal contexts should still measure up to the standards of more ideal contexts as much as possible. After formalising this idea, we return to our intuitions concerning downwards (and upwards) inheritance, and check to what extent these intuitions are captured by this approach.

6.2. *The general idea*

The general idea can be explained by simple diagrams, of a kind not uncommon in both non-monotonic logic and some recent presentations of deontic logic.

For simplicity consider a language with just two atomic propositions p and q. Suppose that $\bigcirc p$ holds. In a model structure with four distinct worlds, one would feel intuitively that they are ordered according to their relative goodness as in figure 1. (Worlds within circles are equally good, and if two circles are connected by a line, those on the left are strictly better than those on the right.)

Fig. 1. A model for $\bigcirc p$

In terms of Hansson-Lewis models, the picture can be seen as depicting a fragment of a model where the worlds w_1–w_4 are those that are accessible from some world w and the ordering shown is $\geq_w$.

Adding an extra obligation $\bigcirc q$ would give the ordering shown in figure 2. It is easy to see that in the best $\neg p$ worlds q is true, for which reason we like to say that $\bigcirc q$ is inherited by, or transported down, to context $\neg p$.

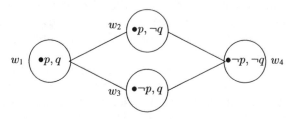

Fig. 2. A model for $\bigcirc p, \bigcirc q$

A further element of the idea, the key feature, is that contextual obligations refine the ordering within the context to which they pertain. Thus, to construct a model for $\bigcirc p, \mathcal{P}q, \mathcal{P}\neg q$ and $\bigcirc[\neg p]q$ we first order the worlds as to how well they fulfill the primary obligation $\bigcirc p$, and then refine the ordering within the set $\|\neg p\|$ with respect to $\bigcirc[\neg p]q$. This is illustrated in figure 3, where the box focusses on $\|\neg p\|$.

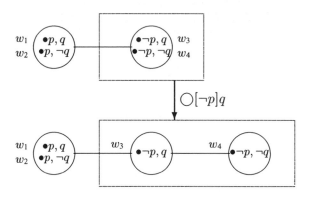

Fig. 3. A model for $\bigcirc p, \bigcirc[\neg p]q$

6.3. *The ordering on the set of worlds*

We now investigate a way to formalise the ideas behind these pictures. We will do this by adapting a technique used by Ryan in the study of non-monotonic reasoning. (Ryan, 1992) investigates the problem of ordering models of sets of defaults according to how well each model satisfies the defaults, while taking into account a further priority ordering on defaults. We will use his technique to order, not models, but worlds within models. Worlds will be ordered according to how well they satisfy various obligations, but allowing for the fact that not all obligations are equally important. The key idea, illustrated by figure 3, is that it is better to fulfill an obligation from a more ideal context and violate one from a less ideal context than the other way around. Obligations from 'better' contexts dominate over obligations from worse contexts. If our intuitions on down inheritance are validated at all, it will be because of this idea.

The general strategy, adapted from (Ryan, 1992), is to employ a generalised form of lexicographic ordering constructed from a number of intermediate orderings. First, we want to determine the relative goodness of worlds by comparing which of the obligations in force they fulfill and which they violate. But what are the obligations 'in force' whose violation or fulfillment is to be checked? As a first shot we will say that they are all the contextual obligations that are true in the model. We shall have reason to change this decision later, in section 7.

We define for each $v \in W$ the *violation set* of v relative to any context C, i.e. the set of all C-obligations violated by v.

Definition 6.2 (Violation sets) *For all $w, v \in W$ and $Q \subseteq W$ the violation set $V_{w,Q}(v)$ is defined as $\{P \subseteq W \mid \max_w(f(w) \cap Q) \subseteq P \ \& \ v \notin P\}$.*

Violation sets can be used to determine, for each context Q, how well worlds w_1 and w_2 fulfill the obligations that pertain to context Q: let this be represented by an ordering $\sqsupseteq_w^Q$ (all orderings are also relativised to worlds w, as usual). Specifically, we define the intermediate orderings $w_1 \sqsupseteq_w^Q w_2$ iff $V_{w,Q}(w_1) \subseteq V_{w,Q}(w_2)$.

Now, the main technical problem is to combine these intermediate orderings into an ordering $\sqsupseteq_w$ to reflect the relative 'ideality' or importance of contexts. Given the truth conditions for $\bigcirc[B]A$, it is natural to say that a context Q_1 is more 'ideal', more important, than a context Q_2 when $Q_1 \supset Q_2$. So, given two intermediate orderings $\sqsupseteq_w^{Q_1}$ and $\sqsupseteq_w^{Q_2}$ such that $Q_1 \supset Q_2$, their combined effect can be captured by the standard lexicographic construction in which $\sqsupseteq_w^{Q_1}$ takes precedence and $\sqsupseteq_w^{Q_2}$ just refines the ordering of the $\sqsupseteq_w^{Q_1}$-equivalent worlds. This is the basic step. It has to be generalised to combine the effects of orderings $\sqsupseteq_w^Q$ for all contexts $\emptyset \subset Q \subseteq W$, not just two of them. This can be done by employing a generalisation of the lexicographic ordering, as used in (Ryan, 1992) and further studied in (Ryan and Schobbens, 1993). We state the definition directly in terms of violation sets, without explicit reference to intermediate orderings.

Definition 6.3 ('Layered ordering') *For any triple of worlds w, w_1 and w_2 in W it holds that*

- $w_1 \sqsupseteq_w w_2$ *iff* $\forall Q \subseteq W$ *such that* $Q \neq \emptyset$:

    1. $V_{w,Q}(w_1) \subseteq V_{w,Q}(w_2)$ or

    2. $\exists Q' \subseteq W. (Q' \supset Q$ and $V_{w,Q'}(w_1) \subset V_{w,Q'}(w_2))$

The effect of the definition is to generalise the lexicographic construction to a set of orderings which is itself partially ordered. Results of (Ryan and Schobbens, 1993) ensure that $\sqsupseteq_w$ is a pre-order when W is finite. (The restriction to finite W can be removed by complicating the truth conditions for $\bigcirc[B]A$ but we will not discuss that here.)

The definition says that w_1 is as good as w_2 ($w_1 \sqsupseteq_w w_2$) if w_1 is as good as w_2 at all contexts, except possibly those at which there is a higher context at which w_1 is strictly better than w_2. And $w_1 \sqsupseteq_w w_2$ means that all (maximal) chains $Q_1 \subset Q_2 \subset \ldots \subset W$ end with first a context Q_i such that $V_{w,Q_i}(w_1) \subset V_{w,Q_i}(w_2)$ and then zero or more contexts $Q_j \supset Q_i$ such that $V_{w,Q_j}(w_1) \subseteq V_{w,Q_j}(w_2)$. Note that the last element of every such chain is W. In terms of obligations, $w \models \bigcirc[B]A$ means that all (maximal) chains $\|B\| \subset Q_1 \subset \ldots \subset W$ end with first a Q_i such that $\max_w(f(w) \cap Q_i) \subseteq \|A\|$, and then a sequence of zero or more $Q_j \supset Q_i$ such that $\|A\| \cap \max_w(f(w) \cap Q_j) \neq \emptyset$.

So in summary: the (contextual) obligations that are true at a world w in a model $\mathcal{M}$ are determined by the orderings $\sqsupseteq_w$; these orderings are defined in terms of violation sets; violation sets are determined by the (contextual) obligations that are true at w in model $\mathcal{M}$. This construction generates a set of constraints on $\sqsupseteq_w$: any model whose orderings $\sqsupseteq_w$ satisfy these constraints will be said to be a 'Layered ordering' model. We now want to know what additional formulas are valid in the class of such models.

6.4. *Valid and invalid formulas*

We now investigate to what extent these semantic ideas capture our intuitions concerning up and down inheritance. First, we observe that the analogue of the strong 'Up' principle in (Prakken and Sergot, 1994, 1996)

  StrongUp. $P[B]C \rightarrow (\bigcirc[B \wedge C]A \rightarrow \bigcirc[B]A)$

is invalid. Figure 4 shows a counterexample, already for the special case where $B = \top$. It depicts a model of $\bigcirc[p]q$ (and $\bigcirc[\neg p]\neg q$) which does not satisfy $\bigcirc q$ (and $\bigcirc\neg q$).

Fig. 4. A counterexample to Up

We still have the weaker 'Up' principle valid in all Hansson-Lewis systems:

  WeakUp. $P[B]C \rightarrow (\bigcirc[B \wedge C]A \rightarrow P[B]A)$

As shown in section 3 this follows from deontic detachment (DD) and the scheme OD, and does not depend on any particular way of obtaining the orderings $\sqsupseteq_w$. The following, equivalent formulation clearly shows that WeakUp formulates a consistency condition on conflicting obligations from different contexts.

$$\bigcirc[B]A \wedge \bigcirc[B \wedge C]\neg A. \rightarrow \bigcirc[B]\neg C$$

We next turn to our main concern in this paper, down inheritance. First we check that this semantics does not validate the strong Down principle we were originally seeking in (Prakken and Sergot, 1994, 1996). By Proposition 6.1 we simply need to construct a model for any two obligations $\bigcirc A$ and $\bigcirc B$ where $\Diamond(A \wedge \neg B)$ and $\Diamond(B \wedge \neg A)$ and $\Diamond(\neg A \wedge \neg B)$, such that the requirements of the 'Layered ordering' (definition 6.3) are satisfied. This is easily done. (Figure 2 already shows an example.)

We can also see semantically why there are no prospects for finding a sensible condition ε under which an obligation in a certain context transports down to a more specific context. The reason is that this condition will have to depend on all other obligations that possibly transport downwards. For every obligation a model can always be constructed with yet another interfering candidate. We cannot block all of them: ε cannot be axiomatised.

We turn now to the more modest goal of finding consistency conditions for obligations from different contexts. On what conditions are the formulas $\bigcirc[B]A$ and $\bigcirc[B \wedge C]\neg A$ inconsistent? For which formulas φ, if any, is the following scheme valid?

WeakDown. $\varphi \rightarrow (\bigcirc[B]A \rightarrow \neg\bigcirc[B \wedge C]\neg A)$

We have been able to find such a valid scheme for the special case where $B = \top$.

Proposition 6.4 The following scheme is valid in the class of 'Layered ordering' models, for any A and C:

WeakDown'. $\Diamond(A \wedge C) \rightarrow (\bigcirc A \rightarrow \neg\bigcirc[C]\neg A)$

Proof The most concise statement uses the more general form (obl) of truth conditions for $\bigcirc[B]A$ (see section 3). The proof works just as well with conditions (obl$_{\max}$), as is easily checked.

Consider any w satisfying (i) $\Diamond(A \wedge C)$, (ii) $\bigcirc A$ and (iii) $\bigcirc[C]\neg A$. By (i) there exists a w_1 in $f(w) \cap \|A \wedge C\|$. By (iii) there is a w_2 in $f(w) \cap \|C \wedge \neg A\|$ which is strictly better than any world in $f(w) \cap \|C \wedge A\|$: so $w_2 \sqsupset_w w_1$.

Now, by (ii), $w \models \bigcirc A$. Since $w_1 \models A$ and $w_2 \not\models A$, $V_{w,W}(w_2) \not\subseteq V_{w,W}(w_1)$. So condition (1) of definition 6.3 is not satisfied. Then, to have even $w_2 \sqsupset_w w_1$, we must find a $Q \supset W$ such that $V_{w,Q}(w_2) \subset V_{w,Q}(w_1)$. Clearly such a Q does not exist. $\square$

This result is surprising. The antecedent of this WeakDown' seems too weak. It contains only the first conjunct of the ε condition of Down in section 6.1, while there we saw that for consistent representation of the gentle murderer the second conjunct of ε is needed also. The validity of WeakDown' causes us to question some of our fundamental assumptions, as we discuss next.

7. A CASE FOR EXPLICIT OBLIGATIONS

As we have just seen, the 'Layered ordering' of section 6 does not fully capture our intuitions. Yet still it seems that the general idea of the previous section is a reasonable one; in this section we discuss how it can be modified to yield something more promising.

Consider first the following example, which is the one used in section 5.5 to motivate the need for 'down inheritance' (strengthening of the antecedent) for contextual obligations.

(1) There must be no dog.
(2) If there is a dog, there must be a sign.

(3)   There must be no sign.

As we indicated earlier, our view is that on a particular, rather natural reading, these statements are inconsistent. The basic reason is this: CTD obligations are intended to regulate norm violation but they cannot just ignore all other norms. Here, the CTD obligation (2) regulating the violation of (1) does not respect another primary obligation, (3). We want to say that for this reason, (2) and (3) are inconsistent.

Consider now the following variant, which is a version of the gentle murderer:

(1a)   There must be no dog.
(2a)   If there is a dog, it must be a poodle.

Since poodles are dogs, one can see that this is indeed a version of the gentle murderer. Intuitively this should be consistent. But suppose now that we add another primary obligation, to the effect that:

(3a)   There must be no poodle.

What we want to suggest is that (1a)–(3a) are inconsistent in precisely the same way that (1)–(3) are. (2a) regulates the violation of (1a) but it does not respect another primary obligation, (3a): (2a) and (3a) are inconsistent. The new feature of the poodle example, of course, is that (3a) is implied by (1a). Thus, we want to say that (1a)–(3a) are inconsistent, *even though* (1a)–(2a) are consistent and (3a) is implied by (1a).[4]

How can we formalise these intuitions? At first sight it would seem that we must abandon consequential closure (i.e. □OCK of section 3). This is the route taken by e.g. Tan and van der Torre (1996) who have also discussed the validity of what we call 'down inheritance' in connection with one of their dyadic deontic logics. We do not think this is the right solution. As we have said earlier, if a normgiver forbids having dogs he surely also implicitly forbids having any particular kind of dog. Our view is that consequential closure should not be disregarded when determining what is *obligatory* but only when determining how good sub-ideal worlds are.

If we look more closely at these examples, the difference between what appears consistent and inconsistent seems to depend critically on what is stated explicitly. In (1a)–(2a) the obligation not to have a poodle is only implicit whereas (3a) states this obligation explicitly. Suppose we take this difference seriously. We now sketch the development of an entailment relation $\Gamma \mathrel{|\!\!\!|\!\!\sim} A$ in which designated *explicit obligations* in premises Γ will be given special status. (Some traces of this idea can also be found in (Tan and van der Torre, 1994) though the details are different. Also the 'Type 2 obligation' of

---

[4]Or consider: (1b) the door must be painted red; (2b) if the door is not painted red, it must be left unpainted; (3b) the door must not be left unpainted. Again we want to say that (1b)-(3b) are inconsistent, even though (1b)-(2b) are consistent, and (1b) implies (3b).

(Brown, 1996) seems to be related.) Given a set S of designated explicit (contextual) obligations, we restrict attention to models where the orderings $\sqsupseteq_w$ are obtained as in definition 6.3 but where the violations sets are determined only by the *explicit* obligations S. We thereby obtain an entailment relation parametrised by a set of explicit obligations, as designated in the premises.

In the poodle example it will be obvious what the designated explicit obligations are, but in general this will not be so, since the premises can be of any form. Therefore, we will assume a function D that assigns to each set Γ of sentences the set of explicit obligations that are designated by Γ. We leave it to future research to investigate in general the properties of the function D; in this paper we will employ a simple notational device to specify what is in $D(\Gamma)$. We write $\widehat{O}[B]A$ to indicate when $O[B]A$ is one of the explicit obligations of a set of premises: $\widehat{O}[B]A$ in premises Γ signifies that $O[B]A \in D(\Gamma)$; moreover, no other obligations are designated as members of $D(\Gamma)$ beyond those written as $\widehat{O}$–obligations.

Next we define the entailment relation, in terms of the standard notion of validity in a class of models (cf. e.g. (Chellas, 1980, p. 36)), which is that A is valid in a class C of models ($\models_\mathsf{C} A$) iff A is true in all models $\mathcal{M}$ in C. Then as usual, for any set Γ of sentences, $\Gamma \models_\mathsf{C} A$ iff $\mathcal{M}, w \models A$ for all models $\mathcal{M} \in \mathsf{C}$ and worlds w such that $\mathcal{M}, w \models \Gamma$.

For any set Γ of sentences, let the set $\mathsf{C}(\Gamma)$ of Γ–*ordered models* be the set of all 'Layered ordering' models where the violation sets inducing the ordering $\sqsupseteq_w$ are determined by the explicit obligations $D(\Gamma)$. Then the entailment relation $\models$ is defined as follows:

$$\Gamma \models A \quad \text{iff} \quad \Gamma \models_{\mathsf{C}(\Gamma)} A$$

What does this framework have to say about the logic of explicit obligations? By imposing some (modest) restrictions in the definition of violation sets it is easy to arrange that, for any Γ, if $\widehat{O}[B]A$ is an explicit obligation of Γ then $\models_{\mathsf{C}(\Gamma)} O[B]A$, i.e.

$$\widehat{O}[B]A, \ \Delta \models O[B]A$$

for any set of additional premises Δ. This in turn induces some constraints on sets of premises Γ: in particular any set of premises Γ designating both $\widehat{O}[B]A$ and $\widehat{O}[B]\neg A$ is inconsistent, in the sense that the set of Γ-ordered models is empty.

In the example, the following set of premises Γ_1:

  (1') $\widehat{O}\neg dog$
  (2') $\widehat{O}[dog]poodle$

has, e.g., $\Gamma_1 \models \bigcirc\neg dog$ and $\Gamma_1 \models \square(poodle \rightarrow dog) \rightarrow \bigcirc\neg poodle$. It is important to note that what is obligatory, represented by expressions of the form $\bigcirc[B]A$, is closed under consequence ($\square$OCK of section 3 is valid in the class of all Γ–ordered models). Explicit obligations, by contrast, are not closed under consequence: premises Γ_1 do not entail the *explicit* obligation $\widehat{\bigcirc}\neg poodle$.

Another property of sets of explicit obligations can be obtained from the derivation of the WeakDown′ principle of Proposition 6.4. When violation sets are defined in terms of designated explicit obligations only, WeakDown′ does not hold for $\bigcirc[B]A$ but for $\widehat{\bigcirc}[B]A$; more precisely, the same derivation as for Proposition 6.4 now yields a weak down principle according to which, if $\widehat{\bigcirc}A$ and $\widehat{\bigcirc}[B]\neg A$ are both in Γ, then $\models_{C(\Gamma)} \neg\Diamond(A \wedge B)$, i.e.

$$\widehat{\bigcirc}A, \ \widehat{\bigcirc}[B]\neg A, \ \Delta \models \neg\Diamond(A \wedge B)$$

We shall refer to this principle as WeakDown*.

In the example, with the further assumptions that

(4′) $\square(poodle \rightarrow dog)$
(5′) $\Diamond(dog \wedge \neg poodle)$

the difference is between the set of premises Γ_1 which satisfies WeakDown*, and the following set of premises Γ_2

(1′) $\widehat{\bigcirc}\neg dog$
(2′) $\widehat{\bigcirc}[dog]poodle$
(3′) $\widehat{\bigcirc}\neg poodle$

which is inconsistent, in the sense that, by WeakDown*, there are no Γ_2-ordered models of (4′) and (5′).

What then of strong 'down'? Our earlier argument for the unacceptability of strong 'down' depended on the observation that all other obligations that are true have to be considered; and since for every obligation a model can always be constructed with yet another interfering candidate, we concluded that down inheritance cannot be axiomatised. However, this argument does not hold if it is only explicitly stated obligations that are taken into account when determining violation sets. Assume that we have as premises

(1) $\widehat{\bigcirc}A$
(2) $\widehat{\bigcirc}B$

In verifying down inheritance we need to consider models where the ordering is determined by (1) and (2) only; other obligations, whether implied by (1) and (2) or not, can be ignored since they do not appear explicitly in the premises. In all such models any $\neg A \wedge \neg B$ worlds will be worse than the best $A \wedge \neg B$ worlds; so then in all those models $\bigcirc A$ is downwards inherited by the context $\neg B$ (assuming of course that there are $A \wedge \neg B$ worlds). We get:

$$\widehat{O}A, \widehat{O}B \models \Diamond(A \wedge \neg B) \to O[\neg B]A$$

Suppose that we add as another premise

(3) $\widehat{O}C$

Now (3) is also relevant to construction of the ordering, and if $\Diamond(C \wedge \neg B)$, then not all best $\neg B$ worlds will contain A; some may contain $C \wedge \neg A$. So:

$$\widehat{O}A, \widehat{O}B, \widehat{O}C \not\models \Diamond(A \wedge \neg B) \to O[\neg B]A$$

So the consequence relation $\models$ is non-monotonic (although each individual $\models_{C(\Gamma)}$ is not).

Clearly, much work remains to be done to refine these ideas. The main aim of this part of the paper has been to show that this work is needed; that the Hansson-Lewis account of obligation must be extended to capture even the most basic features of contrary-to-duty reasoning; that these extensions cannot be undertaken using standard model-theoretic devices; but that there are nevertheless promising avenues to explore.

We do not expect that finalising these details will be easy. Similar reasoning patterns have been studied in non-monotonic reasoning, where they have proved notoriously hard to formalise. In particular, down inheritance of contextual obligations, even with explicitly designated obligations, raises similar problems to the problem of irrelevance in possible-worlds accounts of defeasible conditionals: from 'birds fly', 'penguins do not fly' and 'birds are small' we want to infer for Frank the penguin that he does not fly but that he is small; if we know that birds fly and we know that Gloria is a black bird, we should be able to conclude that Gloria can fly given that she is black.

Another area where similar problems have arisen is temporal reasoning. A main problem here is the frame problem: how to formalise the persistence of facts through time and the ramifications of change. Likewise, as we discussed in section 5, temporal deontic logics must account for the persistence of obligations through time. In systems such as those of (van Eck, 1982; Åqvist and Hoepelman, 1981) the best futures at t in w must be related somehow to the best futures at $t + 1$ in w; otherwise we can lose obligations in the future simply by violating an unrelated obligation now. It is not that persistence is the same problem as 'down inheritance', but that the same problems, of irrelevance, have to be confronted. How close these resemblances actually are is also a topic of our current investigations. One point we might make, however, is this: if, as we now believe, CTD reasoning depends on what obligations are stated explicitly as premises, then the temporal persistence problem might not be too difficult; perhaps it is sufficient to account for how explicitly designated obligations persist through time, without having to worry about all the obligations that can be derived from them as consequences. This remains to be seen.

8. CONCLUSION

In this paper we have tried to improve on our earlier analysis of CTD reasoning by interpreting obligations in terms of preference structures, that is, orderings on the relative 'goodness' of worlds. We presented our attempts as a modification of the well-known systems of dyadic deontic logics of (Hansson, 1969) and (Lewis, 1974). Let us recapitulate.

First of all, we have argued that dyadic deontic logics validating the principle $\bigcirc[A]A$ are not flawed, as long as they are regarded as candidates for representing contextual rather than 'ordinary' (defeasible or non-defeasible) conditional obligations. To argue for this, it was necessary to clarify several distinctions of kinds of obligations that have appeared in the literature.

A main ingredient of our argument was the addition of a notion of alethic necessity to the systems of Hansson and Lewis. Thus we were able to formalise the idea that contextual obligations do not satisfy factual detachment, as ordinary conditionals do, but only a stronger form, whereby the obligation becomes unrestricted to context when its antecedent is necessarily true.

The introduction of alethic necessity has also clarified the link between contextual obligations and generally accepted treatments of temporal CTD structures, to which we were previously able to allude only implicitly. The problems we have studied in a timeless setting do not disappear when time is introduced. This is not only because there are examples of CTD structures where all obligations pertain to the same point of time, so that the greater expressive power of temporal deontic logics remains unused; it is also because there are some outstanding problems concerning the persistence of obligations in time that seem to have been overlooked in the literature on temporal CTD structures. We have suggested that there are close parallels between the formalisation of down inheritance (strengthening of the antecedent) in contextual obligations and persistence in temporal deontic reasoning. It remains to be seen if this is borne out by future investigations.

The last part of the paper was concerned with an investigation of how the Hansson-Lewis framework could be augmented if it is to deal with the analysis of CTD structures. According to our diagnosis, the weakness of the Hansson-Lewis account of obligation is that, although it allows for the possibility of non-ideal worlds, it has nothing to say about them. We therefore focussed on a class of models in which the orderings on the relative goodness of worlds are given additional structure: we adapted a technique from the study of default reasoning to construct orderings which rank non-ideal worlds according to how well they measure up to the ideal ones.

Perhaps the most significant result of these technical investigations is the emergence of CTD examples whose consistency seems to depend critically on whether an obligation is stated explicitly or is simply implied by other statements. This has led us to construct a non-monotonic consequence relation parametrised by a set of explicitly designated obligations. We obtain thereby a logic of explicit obligations, which is not closed under logical consequence, and a separate logic of what is obligatory, which is closed under consequence. Although the construction is quite natural, it is not something we undertake lightly. We have avoided it for as long as possible; we now feel the evidence is irresistible.

ACKNOWLEDGEMENTS

The authors wish to thank Andrew Jones, Donald Nute, Mark Ryan and Leon van der Torre for valuable discussions on the topic of this paper.

Henry Prakken
Amsterdam, The Netherlands

Marek Sergot
Department of Computing
Imperial College
London, UK

REFERENCES

Alchourrón, C. E. (1993). Philosophical foundations of deontic logic and the logic of defeasible conditionals. In J.-J. Ch. Meyer and R. J. Wieringa (eds.), *Deontic logic in Computer Science: Normative System Specification.* John Wiley & Sons, Chichester, pages 43–84.

Åqvist, L. and Hoepelman, J. (1981). Some theorems about a "tree" system of deontic tense logic. In R. Hilpinen (ed.): *New Studies in Deontic Logic.* Reidel, Dordrecht, pages 187–221.

Brown, C.E. (1996). Doing as we ought: towards a logic of simply dischargeable obligations. In M. A. Brown and J. Carmo (eds.), *Deontic Logic, Agency and Normative Systems.* Workshops in Computing, Springer, London, pages 50–65.

Carmo, C.E. and Jones, A. J. I. (1997). A new approach to contrary-to-duty obligations. *This volume.*

Castañeda, H.-N. (1981). The paradoxes of deontic logic: the solution to all of them in one fell swoop. In R. Hilpinen (ed.), *New Studies in Deontic Logic.* Reidel, Dordrecht, pages 37–85.

Chellas, B. (1980). *Modal logic: An introduction.* Cambridge University Press.

Chisholm, R. M. (1963). Contrary-to-duty imperatives and deontic logic. *Analysis* 24:33–36.

van Eck, J. A. (1982). A system of temporally relative modal and deontic predicate logic and its philosophical applications. *Logique ét Analyse* 100:249–381.

Forrester, J. W. (1984). Gentle murder, or the adverbial Samaritan. *Journal of Philosophy* 81(4):193–197.

Hansson, B. (1969). An analysis of some deontic logics. *Nôus* 3:373–398. Reprinted in R. Hilpinen (ed.): *Deontic Logic: Introductory and Systematic Readings.* Reidel, Dordrecht, pages 121–147, (1971).

Hilpinen, R. (1993). Actions in deontic logic. In J.-J. Ch. Meyer and R. J. Wieringa (eds.), *Deontic Logic in Computer Science: Normative System Specification.* John Wiley & Sons, Chichester, pages 85–100.

Hintikka, J. (1971). Some main problems of deontic logic. In R. Hilpinen (ed.), *Deontic Logic: Introductory and Systematic Readings.* Reidel, Dordrecht, pages 59–104.

Horty, J. F. (1994). Moral dilemmas and non-monotonic logic. *Journal of Philosophical Logic* 23:35–65.

Jones, A. J. I. and Pörn, I. (1985). Ideality, sub-ideality and deontic logic. *Synthese* 65:275–290.

Lewis, D. (1974). Semantic analyses for dyadic deontic logic. In S. Stendlund (ed.), *Logical Theory and Semantic Analysis.* Reidel, Dordrecht, pages 1–14.

Loewer, B. and Belzer, M. (1983). Dyadic deontic detachment. *Synthese* 54:295–318.

McCarty, L. T. (1994). Defeasible deontic reasoning. *Fundamenta Informaticae* 21:125–148.

Makinson, D. (1993). Five faces of minimality. *Studia Logica* 52(3):339–379.

Meyer, J.-J. Ch. (1988). A different approach to deontic logic: Deontic logic viewed as a variant of dynamic logic. *Notre Dame Journal of Formal Logic* 29(1):109–136.

Morreau, M. (1994). Prima facie and Seeming Duties. In A. J. I. Jones and M. J. Sergot (eds.), *Proc. Second International Workshop on Deontic Logic and Computer Science,* Oslo, Tano Publishers, Norway, pages 221–251.

Prakken, H. (1996). Two approaches to the formalisation of defeasible deontic reasoning. *Studia Logica* 57(1):73–90.

Prakken, H. and Sergot, M. J. (1994). Contrary-to-duty imperatives, defeasibility and violability. In A. J. I. Jones and M. J. Sergot (eds.): *Proc. Second International Workshop on Deontic Logic in Computer Science,* Oslo, Tano Publishers, Norway, pages 296–318.

Prakken, H. and Sergot, M. J. (1996). Contrary-to-duty obligations. *Studia Logica* 57(1):91–115.

Ross, W. D. (1930). *The Right and the Good.* Oxford University Press.

Ryan, M. D. (1992). Representing defaults as sentences with reduced priority. *Proc. Third International Conference on Principles of Knowledge Representation and Reasoning,* Morgan Kaufman.

Ryan, M. D. and Schobbens, P.-Y. (1993). The lexicographic combination of preferences. Working notes from the the Dutch/German workshop on non-monotonic reasoning techniques and their applications, Aachen.

Ryu, Y.-H. and Lee, R. M. (1997). Deontic logic viewed as defeasible reasoning. *This volume.*

Tan, Y.-H. and van der Torre, L. W. N. (1994). Multi preference semantics for a defeasible deontic logic. In H. Prakken, A. J. Muntjewerff, A. Soeteman (eds.), *Legal knowledge based systems. The relation with legal theory,* Koninklijke Vermande BV, Lelystad, pages 115–126.

Tan, Y.-H. and van der Torre, L. W. N. (1996). How to combine ordering and minimizing in a deontic logic based on preferences. In M. A. Brown and J. Carmo (eds.), *Deontic Logic, Agency and Normative Systems.* Workshops in Computing, Springer, London, pages 216–232.

LAMBÈR ROYAKKERS AND FRANK DIGNUM

DEFEASIBLE REASONING WITH LEGAL RULES

1. INTRODUCTION

Logical analysis of reasoning with inconsistent rules is a very relevant area
for AI-and-Law research, since rules used in the legal domain are often
conflicting. 'Prioritised' rules received attention in the research on the formalisation of nonmonotonic reasoning, particularly as a way of modeling
the choice criterion in dealing with exceptions (cf. (Poole, 1988); (Shoham,
1988); (Brewka, 1991); (Prakken, 1993)).

To deal with the inconsistencies, various sorts of consistency-based approaches have been developed, such as McDermott and Doyle's (1980) nonmonotonic logic and Reiter's (1980) default logic. But these approaches fail to
reason about conflicting norms since they are all based on non-modal logics.
As a way of solving the problems of deontic conflicts, forms of defeasible reasoning (cf. (Pollock, 1987)) have been adopted, which provide a mechanism
to establish preference hierarchies of norms and to select a more applicable
norm from among conflicting ones in a specific situation (cf. (Alchourrón and
Makinson, 1981); (Royakkers and Dignum, 1994)). The existing formalisations of defeasible deontic reasoning approaches (Horty, 1994); (Tan and van
der Torre, 1994); (Ryu, 1992) cannot deal with several highly common forms
of deontic logic (cf. (Prakken, 1993)).

A first problem is *the absence of the notion of permission* in certain approaches (Horty, 1994); (Tan and van der Torre, 1994). In these approaches,
the conditional obligation is represented as $\bigcirc(p/q)$: 'p is obligatory in case
of q', and is treated as a normal default; it can be read as a Reiter default
$q : p/p$: a non-deontic Reiter default. Inherent in this treatment is the absence
of a reasonable Reiter default for the *negated obligation* (permission).

Another problem is *the defeasibility of only a single opposing statement*
in some approaches (Horty, 1994); (Tan and van der Torre, 1994); (Prakken,
1996). In these approaches, only couples of statements are considered to check
inconsistencies. For instance, take the three statements $\bigcirc(a)$, $\bigcirc(\neg a \vee b)$ and
$\neg \bigcirc (b)$. No single statement is in conflict with the other single statements.
However, the group of statements $\bigcirc(a)$ and $\bigcirc(\neg a \vee b)$ implies $\bigcirc(b)$ in
standard deontic logic, which is in conflict with statement $\neg \bigcirc (b)$.

The third problem is that most approaches (Horty, 1994); (Tan and van
der Torre, 1994); (Ryu, 1992) can only deal with defeasible conditionals that
are deontic. But deontic defaults are not the only defaults in legal reasoning.
Consider the deontic default $a : \bigcirc(b)/ \bigcirc (b)$. With this default, it is very

D. Nute (ed.), Defeasible Deontic Logic, 263–286.

often the case that a is derived by another default rule, e.g. $c : a/a$, which is called a 'classification rule' or an 'interpretation rule'. In the legal domain, it is accepted that these rules are also defeasible (cf. (Hart, 1961)). Prakken showed this by extending Hart's standard example on a park regulation that forbids vehicles to enter the park:

> Not only this rule itself may turn out to be defeasible, for example, if the vehicle is an ambulance, but also rules on when something counts as a vehicle may be defeasible: imagine that a court says that objects on wheels that are meant for normal transport are vehicles: then roller skates used by people on their way to the office might be recognisèd as an exception. (Prakken, 1996)

In this paper, we develop a theory of defeasible deontic reasoning which adequately deals with the above-mentioned problems. The theory is an extension and modification of the argumentation framework in default logic developed by Prakken (1993), and Prakken and Sartor (1995). Further, our theory is an extension of Dung's (1993) theory, which only considers argumentation frameworks with one kind of conflict between arguments. Our theory shows similarity to (Prakken and Sartor, 1996), which is based on dialectic logic (cf. (Loui and Norman, 1995)), however, the elaboration differs.

The structure of this paper is as follows. In section 2, we give the representation of legal rules, which we subdivide into rules and conditional norms. Section 3 discusses the argumentation framework for rules. The argumentation framework for norms depending on rules selected from the argumentation framework for rules is discussed in section 4. Here, we concentrate on defeasibility and violation. We end this paper with some conclusions.

2. LEGAL RULES: RULES AND CONDITIONAL NORMS

The fundamental logical structure of legal knowledge gives rise to the nonmonotonicity of legal reasoning (Reiter, 1980); (Delgrande, 1988): the consequences that may follow from a set of legal and factual premises can be invalidated by further information. This means that rules can be 'defeated' by other or new rules and facts. The principal idea of this paper, which goes back to Rescher (1964), is to allow the rules to be ordered and to use this ordering in such a way that conflicts can be solved in a logical argumentation framework using nonmonotonic logic. Such an ordering can often be discerned when considering the rules in a legal code. The 'Lex Superior' principle, for instance, is based on the general hierarchy of a legal system; the rules are divided along the lines of the hierarchical structure of the normative system. Rules with a lower rank of priority have to respect the consequences that follow from a higher ranked rule. To describe the ordering between the formulas, we use the following notation. Let x and y be legal rules, then '$x \preceq y$' means that y is preferred to x; '$x \sim y$' is an abbreviation of '$x \preceq y$ and $y \preceq x$'; and

'$x \prec y$' is an abbreviation of '$x \preceq y$ and $y \npreceq x$'. The ordering relation $\preceq$ is reflexive and transitive.

Legal rules, or in any case most of them, subordinate a legal effect to a legal condition. By legal effect we mean every qualification generated by a legal norm: the ascription of deontic or normative modalities, status, professional titles, other legal qualities of persons and things. By legal condition we mean every condition to which a legal effect is subordinated. The legal rules are represented as conditional statements of the type

$$a_1 \wedge a_2 \wedge \ldots \wedge a_n \Rightarrow \theta,$$

where θ is the legal effect and $a_1, a_2, \ldots, a_n$ are the elements of the antecedent: the conjunction of literals,[1] representing the legal condition. If θ is a norm: an obligation ($\bigcirc(\phi)$) or a permission ($P(\phi)$), with ϕ a formula of the propositional logic, then the conditional statement is called a *conditional norm*. Thus, the conditional obligation is represented as $a_1 \wedge a_2 \wedge \ldots \wedge a_n \Rightarrow \bigcirc(p)$, instead of $\bigcirc(p/a_1 \wedge a_2 \ldots \wedge a_n)$ as in (Horty, 1994) and (Tan and van der Torre, 1994).[2] If θ is a literal, then the statement is called a *rule*.

The statement $A \Rightarrow B$ has to be interpreted as a *normal default* according to Reiter's (1980; 1987) theory, $A : B/B$: 'If A, and it can be consistently assumed B, then we can infer B.' This means that $\Rightarrow$ is *not* interpreted as the material implication, but as an inference rule that can be defeated. From A and $A \Rightarrow B$, we can infer B unless $\neg B$ can be proven. This representation corresponds to the formalisations usually proposed by legal theory and legal logic (cf. (Sartor, 1993)).

In our theory, we distinguish between rules and norms for the following reasons:

- Rules cannot be violated.
- The defeasibility of rules is different from the defeasibility of norms (cf. definition 3.5 and definition 4.8), which is the most important difference.

The most important thing about the difference between rules and norms is not *what* differences there are, but simply *that* there are differences. This is why we discuss our theory on different levels: first, on the level of rules (section 3), and second, on the level of norms based on a given set of rules (section 4).

The set of rules is denoted by W and the set of conditional norms by Δ. Furthermore, we have a factual sentence F representing the factual situation, which consists of background knowledge and contingent facts. The background knowledge consists of necessary conditions, for example, a human being is mortal. A set of conditional norms, a set of rules and a factual sentence is called a deontic context.

---

[1] A literal is any atomic propositional formula and any negation of an atomic propositional formula.

[2] For a discussion of the problems of the formalisation of the conditional norms, we refer to (Alchourrón, 1986).

Definition 2.1 A deontic context $T = (\Delta, W, F, \preceq)$ consists of a set Δ of conditional norms, a set W of rules, a factual propositional sentence F: the conjunction of background knowledge F_b and contingent facts F_c, and an ordering $\preceq$ over rules and conditional norms.

3.   RULES

Facts (formalised by the sentence F) can contain material implications. Rules, however, are represented by normal defaults written as a conditional statement of the type $a_1 \wedge a_2 \wedge \ldots \wedge a_n \Rightarrow \theta$, with θ the legal effect formalised by a literal. Our theory of defeasible reasoning for rules is based on four notions:

- the notion of *argument* (definition 3.4);
- the notion of *defeating* (definition 3.5);
- the notion of *defeasibility chain* (definition 3.7);
- the notion of *justified, defensible and overruled arguments* (definition 3.9).

At the end of this section, we define *maximal-coherent argument sets* of rules that we use for the notion of the applicability of norms and the violation of obligations in section 4.

Before we discuss the notion of argument, we give three definitions which we will use in the sequel.

Definition 3.1 Let F be the factual propositional sentence, V be a set of rules and r a literal, then V explains r ($V \cup \{F\} \models r$) iff

$$r \in \cup_{i=0}^{\infty} G_i,$$

with

$$G_0 = \{r \mid \{F\} \vdash r\} \text{ and}$$

$$G_{i+1} = G_i \cup \{r \mid \exists_{a_1 \wedge a_2 \wedge \ldots \wedge a_n \Rightarrow r \in V}(G_i \cup \{F\} \models a_i)\},$$

$$\text{for all } i \in \{0, 1, 2, \ldots\}.$$

Intuitively, *explaining* is the same as logical consequence, except that now we deal with defaults and not with implications.

Definition 3.2 Let V be a set of rules, then the consequences of $V \cup \{F\}$ ($Cons(V \cup \{F\})$) is defined as

$$Cons(V \cup \{F\}) := \{r \mid r \text{ is a literal and } V \cup \{F\} \models r\}.$$

Thus, the *Cons* relation is a transitive closure of the *explaining*. It gives the set of all the literals that can be consistently derived from V and $\{F\}$.

Definition 3.3 Let V be a set of rules. Then $V \cup \{F\}$ is coherent iff

$$\neg \exists_{r \text{ is a literal}}(r \in Cons(V \cup \{F\}) \wedge \neg r \in Cons(V \cup \{F\})).$$

The notion of argument can now be defined as follows:

Definition 3.4 Let $M \subseteq W$, ϕ a literal and $M \cup \{F\}$ coherent. Then M explains ϕ minimally iff

- $\{F\} \cup M \models \phi$ and
- $\neg \exists_{\phi_1 \in M}(\{F\} \cup M \setminus \{\phi_1\}) \models \phi$.

We call M a minimally explaining set or an argument. The set of all arguments is denoted as $\mathcal{M}$. The ϕ-relevant set of W, denoted by $[\phi]\mathcal{M}$, is the set of all arguments in $\mathcal{M}$ that explain ϕ minimally. M_1 is a subargument of M iff $M_1 \subset M$ and M_1 is an argument. If there is an argument for ϕ, thus $[\phi]\mathcal{M} \neq \emptyset$, then ϕ is called an outcome.

Our definition of 'defeat' is based on the idea that, in order to defeat an argument, a counterargument can point its attack at the argument itself, but also at one of its proper subarguments, since an argument cannot be stronger than its *weakest link* (cf. (Prakken and Sartor, 1995)).

Definition 3.5 Let $M_1 \in [\phi]\mathcal{M}$ and $M_2 \in [\phi']\mathcal{M}$. Then M_1 is defeated by M_2 ($M_1 \prec^* M_2$) iff

$$\exists_{\phi_1 \Rightarrow \phi_2 \in M_1} \exists_{\phi_3 \Rightarrow \phi_4 \in M_2} \{\phi_3 \Rightarrow \phi_4 \succeq \phi_1 \Rightarrow \phi_2\} \text{ and}$$

$$\{\phi_2\} \cup \{\phi_4\} \cup \{F\} \text{ is inconsistent.}$$

Thus, an argument M_2 defeats an argument M_1 iff M_1 and M_2 have contradictory conclusions ϕ_2 and ϕ_4 with respect to the factual sentence F, and the rule $\phi_3 \Rightarrow \phi_4 \in M_2$ (responsible for the conflict) does not have a lower priority than the rule $\phi_1 \Rightarrow \phi_2 \in M_1$. Note that $\{\phi_2\} \cup \{F\}$ and $\{\phi_4\} \cup \{F\}$ are consistent, which directly follows from definition 3.4.

Relation $\prec^*$ is not transitive and not asymmetric. It is possible that $M_1 \prec^* M_2$ and $M_2 \prec^* M_1$ both hold. The following example illustrates this point:

Example 3.6

$$
\begin{array}{lll}
(1) & a \Rightarrow b & \\
(2) & & c \Rightarrow \neg a \\
(3) & d \Rightarrow a & \\
(4) & b \Rightarrow \neg c & \\
(5) & & e \Rightarrow c
\end{array}
$$

F: $f \wedge (f \to d) \wedge e$

with $(5) \prec (4) \prec (3) \prec (2) \prec (1)$.

Let $M_1 = \{e \Rightarrow c, c \Rightarrow \neg a\}$ and $M_2 = \{d \Rightarrow a, a \Rightarrow b, b \Rightarrow \neg c\}$. Then $M_1 \prec^* M_2$, since $e \Rightarrow c \prec b \Rightarrow \neg c$, and $M_2 \prec^* M_1$, since $d \Rightarrow a \prec c \Rightarrow \neg a$.

Definition 3.7 A defeasibility chain is a sequence of arguments in $\mathcal{M}$:

$$M_1 \prec^* M_2 \prec^* \ldots \prec^* M_n$$

with the following conditions:

- $\forall_{k,l=1,2,\ldots,n \wedge k<l} M_k \nsubseteq M_l$;

- $\neg \exists_{M_{n+1} \in \mathcal{M}} \{(M_1, \ldots, M_n \not\subseteq M_{n+1}) \wedge (M_n \prec^* M_{n+1})\}$.

We define $Ch(\mathcal{M})$ as the set of all defeasibility chains of arguments in $\mathcal{M}$.

The first condition ensures that cycles in defeasibility chains are avoided. Suppose that $M_1 \prec^* M_2$ and $M_2 \prec^* M_3$, with $M_1 \subset M_3$. We would thus end up with the endless chain $M_1 \prec^* M_2 \prec^* M_3 \prec^* M_2 \prec^* M_3 \ldots$. This would also be accomplished by '$\neq$' instead of '$\not\subseteq$'. The reason why indeed we need '$\not\subseteq$' is to satisfy the *weakest link principle*, which will become clear in example 3.17.

The second condition provides that a chain stops if there is no 'stronger' argument than the last argument in the chain.

Take the example above, then

$$Ch(\mathcal{M}) = \{\{d \Rightarrow a, a \Rightarrow b\} \prec^* \{e \Rightarrow c, c \Rightarrow \neg a\},$$

$$\{d \Rightarrow a, a \Rightarrow b, b \Rightarrow \neg c\} \prec^* \{e \Rightarrow c, c \Rightarrow \neg a\},$$

$$\{e \Rightarrow c\} \prec^* \{d \Rightarrow a, a \Rightarrow b, b \Rightarrow \neg c\},$$

$$\{d \Rightarrow a\} \prec^* \{e \Rightarrow c, c \Rightarrow \neg a\},$$

$$\{e \Rightarrow c, c \Rightarrow \neg a\} \prec^* \{d \Rightarrow a, a \Rightarrow b, b \Rightarrow \neg c\}\}.$$

Definition 3.8 $Ch(M)$ is the set of all defeasibility chains in $Ch(\mathcal{M})$ starting with M.

The defeasibility chains in $Ch(\mathcal{M})$ take the set of all possible arguments and their mutual relations of defeat as inputs. They produce a distinction between in three types of argument:[3]

1. *justified* arguments;
2. *overruled* arguments;
3. *defensible* arguments.

A justified argument is a 'winning' argument. Such an argument can be defeated by another argument, but that argument will be overruled. An overruled argument is a 'losing' argument. A defensible argument is an argument that is neither justified nor overruled. In other words, an 'undeciding' argument.

Definition 3.9 Let $M \in \mathcal{M}$. Then

- M is a justified argument iff $Ch(M) = \{M\}$ or for all chains $M \prec^* M_1 \prec^* \ldots \prec^* M_n \in Ch(\mathcal{M})$ it holds that

  n is even $\wedge \neg \exists_{M' \in \mathcal{M}} M_n \prec^* M' \wedge \forall_k$ is even

  (M_k is a justified argument assuming M is a justified argument).
- M is an overruled argument iff there is a chain $M \prec^* M_1 \prec^* \ldots \prec^* M_n \in Ch(\mathcal{M})$ with

  n is odd $\wedge \neg \exists_{M' \in \mathcal{M}} M_n \prec^* M'$.

---

[3]The terms justified, overruled and defensible arguments were introduced by Prakken and Sartor (1995).

- M is a defensible argument iff M is neither a justified argument nor an overruled argument.

Note that M_n in the chains of definition 3.9 is a justified argument, since $Ch(M_n) = \{M_n\}$, which is equivalent to $\neg \exists_{M' \in \mathcal{M}} M_n \prec^* M'$. The condition in the definition of a justified argument M that all arguments M_k with k is even are justified *assuming M is a justified argument* is necessary, since the justification of M_k can depend on M (see example 3.11). In other words, 'if it cannot be proven whether M_k is justified or not, then M_k should be justified assuming that M is justified.'

Let $M \prec^* M_1 \prec^* \ldots \prec^* M_n$ be a chain in $Ch(\mathcal{M})$, then we call the arguments M_i with i is odd *odd arguments*, and the arguments M and M_i with i is even *even arguments*.

In a defeasibility chain $M \prec^* M_1 \prec^* \ldots \prec^* M_n$ with n is even (odd) and $Ch(M_n) = \{M_n\}$, we stipulate that the odd (even) arguments are the *attacked* arguments and the even (odd) arguments the *non-attacked* arguments. The chain ends with M_n, so M_{n-1} is an attacked argument, because it is defeated by a non-attacked argument. M_{n-2} is not attacked, because it is defeated by an attacked argument (M_{n-1}), and so on. For example, M is overruled if M_1 is a non-attacked argument and this follows if n is odd. The following example clarifies the above definition:

Example 3.10

(1)	$a \Rightarrow b$
(2)	$c \Rightarrow \neg b$
(3)	$d \Rightarrow \neg e$
(4)	$e \Rightarrow \neg f$
(5)	$b \Rightarrow e$
(6)	$h \Rightarrow b$
(7)	$f \Rightarrow \neg d$
(8)	$i \Rightarrow f$
(9)	$j \Rightarrow d$

$F: a \wedge c \wedge h \wedge i \wedge j$
with $(9) \prec (8) \prec \ldots \prec (1)$.

Let
$M_1 = \{a \Rightarrow b\}$
$M_2 = \{c \Rightarrow \neg b\}$
$M_3 = \{d \Rightarrow \neg e, j \Rightarrow d\}$
$M_4 = \{e \Rightarrow \neg f, b \Rightarrow e, h \Rightarrow b\}$
$M_5 = \{f \Rightarrow \neg d, i \Rightarrow f\}$

1. $Ch(M_1) = \{M_1\}$, thus M_1 is a justified argument.
2. $Ch(M_2) = \{M_2 \prec^* M_1\}$, thus M_2 is an overruled argument, since the chain contains an even number of arguments and $Ch(M_1) = \{M_1\}$.

3. $Ch(M_3) = \{M_3 \prec^* M_5 \prec^* M_4 \prec^* M_2 \prec^* M_1\}$. M_3 is not overruled, since otherwise the chain contains an even number of arguments. It depends on argument M_4 whether M_3 is justified or defensible.
4. $Ch(M_4) = \{M_4 \prec^* M_2 \prec^* M_1, M_4 \prec^* M_3 \prec^* M_5\}$. M_4 is not a justified argument, since $Ch(M_5) \neq \{M_5\}$. M_4 is not an overruled argument, since there is no chain in $Ch(M_4)$ with an even number of arguments. Thus, M_4 is a defensible argument. Hence, from the chain in $Ch(M_3)$ it also follows that M_3 is a defensible argument.
5. $Ch(M_5) = \{M_5 \prec^* M_4 \prec^* M_2 \prec^* M_1, M_5 \prec^* M_4 \prec^* M_3\}$. M_5 is an overruled argument, since the chain $M_5 \prec^* M_4 \prec M_2 \prec^* M_1$ contains an even number of arguments and $Ch(M_1) = \{M_1\}$.

In definition 3.9 of a justified argument M, the even arguments have to be justified assuming M is justified. The condition 'assuming M is justified' is necessary since otherwise we cannot determine whether an argument is justified or defensible in certain cases. Consider the next example.

Example 3.11

(1) $i \Rightarrow \neg d$
(2) $b \Rightarrow \neg h$
(3) $d \Rightarrow \neg b$
(4) $f \Rightarrow \neg d$
(5) $a \Rightarrow b$
(6) $c \Rightarrow d$
(7) $j \Rightarrow \neg h$
(8) $h \Rightarrow \neg f$
(9) $e \Rightarrow f$
(10) $g \Rightarrow h$

$F: a \wedge c \wedge e \wedge g \wedge i \wedge j$
with $(10) \prec (9) \prec \ldots \prec (1)$.

Let
$M_1 = \{c \Rightarrow d, d \Rightarrow \neg b\}$;
$M_2 = \{e \Rightarrow f, f \Rightarrow \neg d\}$;
$M_3 = \{g \Rightarrow h, h \Rightarrow \neg f\}$;
$M_4 = \{a \Rightarrow b, b \Rightarrow \neg h\}$;
$M_5 = \{i \Rightarrow \neg d\}$;
$M_6 = \{j \Rightarrow \neg h\}$.
Suppose that we state that the even arguments have to be justified instead of the even arguments have to be justified assuming M is justified in the definition 3.9 of a justified argument M. Then, we cannot determine whether M_2 and M_4 are justified or defensible arguments. The set of defeasibility chains starting with M_4 is

$$Ch(M_4) = \{M_4 \prec^* M_1 \prec^* M_2 \prec^* M_3 \prec^* M_6, M_4 \prec^* M_1 \prec^* M_5\}.$$

M_4 is not an overruled argument, since both chains contain an odd number of arguments. Suppose M_4 is a justified argument, then the following three conditions have to be satisfied:

1. $Ch(M_5) = \{M_5\}$;
2. $Ch(M_6) = \{M_6\}$;
3. M_2 is a justified argument.

The first two conditions are satisfied. For the third condition, we have to analyse the set of defeasibility chains starting with M_2:

$$Ch(M_2) = \{M_2 \prec^* M_3 \prec^* M_4 \prec^* M_1 \prec^* M_5, M_2 \prec^* M_3 \prec^* M_6\}.$$

M_2 is not an overruled argument, since both chains contain an odd number of arguments. Suppose M_2 is a justified argument, then the following three conditions have to be satisfied:

1. $Ch(M_5) = \{M_5\}$;
2. $Ch(M_6) = \{M_6\}$;
3. M_4 is a justified argument.

Again, the first two conditions are satisfied. Thus, whether M_2 is a justified argument or not, depends on the 'status' of argument M_4, and vice versa. Hence, we cannot find out whether M_2 and M_4 are justified or defensible arguments. To overcome this problem, we have set the condition that the even arguments in the chains are justified assuming M is justified:

According to definition 3.9, argument M_4 is justified if

1. $Ch(M_5) = \{M_5\}$;
2. $Ch(M_6) = \{M_6\}$;
3. M_2 is justified assuming that M_4 is justified.

Argument M_2 is justified assuming M_4 is justified, since the three conditions mentioned above, i.e., $Ch(M_5) = \{M_5\}$, $Ch(M_6) = \{M_6\}$ and M_4 is a justified argument, are now satisfied. Thus, M_2 is a justified argument assuming that M_4 is justified. Hence, M_4 is a justified argument.

Analogously, we can show that M_2 is also a justified argument. Intuitively, this is correct: argument M_4 (M_2) is only defeated by argument M_1 (M_3), and, in turn, M_1 (M_3) is defeated by argument M_5 (M_6), which is not defeated. Thus, M_1 (M_3) is an overruled argument, and cannot invalidate an argument.

Proposition 3.12

1. Let M be a justified argument. Then all odd arguments in the chains of $Ch(M)$ are overruled arguments.
2. Let M be an overruled argument. Then there is a chain in $Ch(M)$ where all even arguments are overruled or defensible.

Proof

1. Let M be a justified argument. Then for all chains $M \prec^* M_1 \prec^* \ldots \prec^* M_n$ in $Ch(M)$, it holds that n is even and $\neg \exists_{M' \in \mathcal{M}} M_n \prec^* M'$. Let

M_k with k is odd be an argument of a chain $M \prec^* M_1 \prec^* \ldots \prec^* M_n$ in $Ch(M)$. Then this chain without the first k arguments, thus $M_k \prec^* M_{k+1} \prec^* \ldots \prec^* M_n$, is a chain in $Ch(M_k)$ which satisfies the conditions of an overruled argument M_k, since the chain contains an even number of arguments and $Ch(M_n) = M_n$. Thus, all odd arguments are overruled arguments.

2. Let M be an overruled argument. Then there is a chain $M \prec^* M_1 \prec^* \ldots \prec^* M_n$ with n is odd and $\neg\exists_{M' \in \mathcal{M}} M_n \prec^* M'$. Suppose an even argument M_k is justified, then the chain $M \prec^* M_1 \prec^* \ldots \prec^* M_n$ without the first k arguments, i.e., $M_k \prec^* M_{k+1} \prec^* \ldots \prec^* M_n$ is a chain in $Ch(M_k)$ and does not satisfy the conditions for a justified argument M_k, since the chain contains an even number of arguments. Thus, the even arguments in such chains in $Ch(M)$ are overruled or defensible.

The condition that all even arguments in the chains of $Ch(M)$ with M being a justified argument have to be justified arguments, is necessary, since otherwise we obtain some undesirable results:

Example 3.13

(1)	$a \Rightarrow \neg b$		
(2)	$c \Rightarrow a$		
(3)		$b \Rightarrow \neg d$	
(4)		$e \Rightarrow b$	
(5)			$\neg g \Rightarrow \neg f$
(6)			$d \Rightarrow \neg h$
(7)			$f \Rightarrow d$
(8)			$i \Rightarrow f$
(9)				$h \Rightarrow \neg j$
(10)				$k \Rightarrow h$
(11)			$j \Rightarrow \neg g$
(12)			$l \Rightarrow j$

$F: c \wedge e \wedge i \wedge k \wedge l$

with $(12) \prec (11) \prec \ldots \prec (1)$.

Let $M_1 = \{a \Rightarrow \neg b, c \Rightarrow a\}$;
$M_2 = \{b \Rightarrow \neg d, e \Rightarrow b\}$;
$M_3 = \{\neg g \Rightarrow \neg f, j \Rightarrow \neg g, l \Rightarrow j\}$;
$M_4 = \{d \Rightarrow \neg h, f \Rightarrow d, i \Rightarrow f\}$;
$M_5 = \{h \Rightarrow \neg j, k \Rightarrow h\}$.
$Ch(M_3) = \{M_3 \prec^* M_5 \prec^* M_4 \prec^* M_2 \prec^* M_1\}$ and $Ch(M_1) = \{M_1\}$, thus without the condition that all even arguments have to be justified arguments, M_3 would be a justified argument instead of a defensible argument, since M_4 is not a justified argument, but defensible.[4] Suppose M_3 is justified.

---

[4] Argument M_4 is defensible: the set of defeasibility chains starting with M_4 is $Ch(M_4) = \{M_4 \prec^* M_2 \prec^* M_1, M_4 \prec^* M_3 \prec M_5\}$. Since M_5 is an overruled argument (the chain

The outcomes of argument M_4 and its subarguments are $\neg h$, d and f, and the outcome of M_3 is $\neg f$. Thus, if we decide to use argument M_4, there is a conflict with the 'winning' (justified) argument M_3; we cannot use M_4, since we need the outcome f to derive $\neg h$ (the outcome of M_4), which is in conflict with f, the outcome of the justified argument M_3. Thus, it is counter-intuitive to call M_4 defensible and M_3 justified. However, M_3 is a defensible argument. Now we have to decide which of the two arguments will be used: both arguments are defensible.

Corollary 3.14

1. A justified argument can only be defeated by an overruled argument.
2. If there is no justified argument, then there is no overruled argument.
3. There is no justified argument iff all arguments are defensible.
4. There is a justified argument iff there is a defeasibility chain with one argument.

Proof

1. Let M be a justified argument, and defeated by M_1. We have to prove that M_1 is an overruled argument. For all chains $M \prec^* M_1 \ldots \prec^* M_n$ in $Ch(M)$ it holds that n is even and $Ch(M_n) = \{M_n\}$. For all these chains without the first argument M, i.e., $M_1 \prec^* \ldots \prec^* M_n$, it holds that they are elements of $Ch(\mathcal{M})$ and satisfy the conditions of an overruled argument. Thus, M_1 is an overruled argument.
2. Suppose that there is no justified argument. Then there is no chain $M \prec^* M_1 \prec^* \ldots \prec^* M_n$ in $Ch(\mathcal{M})$ with $Ch(M_n) = \{M_n\}$. Hence, there is no overruled argument.
   The converse does not hold. For example, let $W = \{a \Rightarrow b\}$ and a a fact. Then the only argument is $\{a \Rightarrow b\}$, which is justified.
3. Suppose that there is no justified argument. Then there is no overruled argument, thus all arguments are defensible.
   Evidently, if all arguments are defensible, then there are no justified arguments.
4. Suppose M is a justified argument. Then for all chains $M \prec^* M_1 \prec^* \ldots \prec^* M_n$ in $Ch(M)$ it holds that $Ch(M_n) = \{M_n\}$. Thus, there is a defeasibility chain with one argument.
   If there is a chain with one argument, say M, then M is a justified argument. Hence, there is a justified argument.

The converse of 3.14.1 does not hold: an overruled argument need not be defeated by a justified argument.

$M_5 \prec^* M_4 \prec^* M_2 \prec^* M_1$ satisfies the conditions for the overruled argument M_5), the chain $M_4 \prec^* M_3 \prec^* M_5$ does not satisfy the conditions for a justified argument M_4. Thus, M_4 is not a justified argument. M_4 is not an overruled argument either, since neither of the two chains in $Ch(M_4)$ satisfies the conditions for an overruled argument M_4. Thus, M_4 is a defensible argument.

Example 3.15

(1) $a \Rightarrow b$

(2) $c \Rightarrow d$

(3) $\neg b \Rightarrow \neg e$

(4) $f \Rightarrow \neg b$

(5) $e \Rightarrow \neg d$

(6) $g \Rightarrow e$

(7) $h \Rightarrow d$

$F: a \wedge c \wedge f \wedge g \wedge h$

with $(7) \prec (6) \prec \ldots \prec (1)$.

Let $M_1 = \{a \Rightarrow b\}$;

$M_2 = \{c \Rightarrow d\}$;

$M_3 = \{\neg b \Rightarrow \neg e, f \Rightarrow \neg b\}$;

$M_4 = \{g \Rightarrow e, e \Rightarrow \neg d\}$;

$M_5 = \{h \Rightarrow d\}$.

Then $Ch(M_5) = \{M_5 \prec^* M_4 \prec^* M_3 \prec^* M_1, M_5 \prec^* M_4 \prec^* M_2\}$. M_5 is an overruled argument, since chain $M_5 \prec^* M_4 \prec^* M_3 \prec^* M_1$ contains an even number of arguments and $Ch(M_1) = \{M_1\}$. Further, M_5 is only defeated by argument M_4, which is an overruled argument, since $M_4 \prec^* M_2 \in Ch(M_4)$ and $Ch(M_2) = \{M_2\}$. Thus, an overruled argument can be defeated by an overruled argument.

The following proposition shows that definition 3.9 satisfies the *weakest link principle*.

Proposition 3.16 All subarguments of a justified argument are justified arguments.

Proof. Suppose that M is a justified argument and M' is a subargument of M. We have to prove that M' is a justified argument, and without loss of generality we assume that M' is a 'largest' subargument of M, i.e., $\neg \exists_{M'' \in \mathcal{M}} M' \subset M'' \subset M$. For if this argument is justified, we can repeat this process for M' to prove that all subarguments of M' are justified. Suppose that M' is not a justified argument, then M' is an overruled or a defensible argument.

- Suppose that M' is an overruled argument. Then there is a chain $M' \prec^* M_1 \prec^* \ldots \prec^* M_n$ with $Ch(M_n) = \{M_n\}$, and n is odd. However, then the chain $M \prec^* M_1 \prec^* \ldots \prec^* M_n$ is a chain of $Ch(M)$, which is in contradiction with the assumption that M is a justified argument.

- Suppose now that M' is a defensible argument. Then there is a chain $M' \prec^* M_1 \prec^* \ldots \prec^* M_n$ and $Ch(M_n) \neq \{M_n\}$. Now, the chain $M \prec^* M_1 \prec^* \ldots \prec^* M_n$ is not an element of $Ch(M)$, but part of a chain in $Ch(M)$. M_n can only be followed by M', thus $M \prec^* M_1 \prec^* \ldots \prec^* M_n \prec^* M' \prec^* M'_1 \prec^* \ldots \prec^* M'_l$, with $Ch(M'_l) = \{M'_l\}$. However, now it follows that M' is an overruled argument (if it is an odd argument in the chain (proposition 3.12.1)) or a justified argument (if it is an even argument (definition 3.9)), which is in contradiction with the assumption that M' is defensible.

Thus, M' is a justified argument.

In definition 3.7, we chose operator '$\not\subseteq$' instead of '$\neq$', otherwise the *weakest link principle* is not satisfied. The following example illustrates this point:

Example 3.17

(1) $d \Rightarrow \neg e$
(2) $e \Rightarrow \neg b$
(3) $a \Rightarrow b$
(4) $b \Rightarrow \neg c$
(5) $c \Rightarrow e$
(6) $f \Rightarrow c$

$F: a \wedge d \wedge f$
with $(6) \prec (5) \prec \ldots \prec (1)$.

Let $M_1 = \{d \Rightarrow \neg e\}$;
$M_2 = \{e \Rightarrow \neg b, c \Rightarrow e, f \Rightarrow c\}$;
$M_3 = \{a \Rightarrow b, b \Rightarrow \neg c\}$;
$M_4 = \{a \Rightarrow b\}$.
Then, $Ch(M_3) = \{M_3 \prec^* M_2 \prec^* M_1\}$ and $Ch(M_1) = \{M_1\}$, thus M_1 and M_3 are justified arguments. M_4 is a subset of the justified argument M_3, thus also justified (proposition 3.16).

Suppose now that we use operator '$\neq$' instead of '$\not\subseteq$', then subargument M_4 of M_3 is not justified, since the chain $M_4 \prec^* M_2 \prec^* M_3$ would be an element of $Ch(M_4)$ and $Ch(M_3) \neq \{M_3\}$. Thus, the weakest link principle is not satisfied if we use operator '$\neq$'.

The following three problems form the main problems in the literature on defeasible arguments. We will show that these problems can be adequately dealt with in the theory as it follows from definition 3.9.

Example 3.18 The intermediate conclusion

(1) $a \Rightarrow b$
(2) $c \Rightarrow \neg b$
(3) $d \Rightarrow a$

$F: c \wedge d$
with $(3) \prec (2) \prec (1)$.

Here, a conflict arises between rules (1) and (2). By definition 3.5, the choice is made between the rules which are certain to be in conflict with each other. Rule (3) with *intermediate conclusion* a, necessary to derive outcome b, is irrelevant to the conflict.

The minimally explaining sets (arguments) are $M_1 = \{d \Rightarrow a, a \Rightarrow b\}$, $M_2 = \{c \Rightarrow \neg b\}$ and $M_3 = \{d \Rightarrow a\}$. The sets of defeasibility chains are $Ch(M_1) = \{M_1\}$, $Ch(M_2) = \{M_2 \prec^* M_1\}$ and $Ch(M_3) = \{M_3\}$. M_1 and M_3 are justified, since they are not defeated by any argument. M_2 is overruled, because it is defeated by justified argument M_1. Thus, a and b are the outcomes.

Example 3.19 Iterated conflicts

    (1) $c \Rightarrow a$

    (2) $d \Rightarrow \neg a$

    (3) $\neg a \Rightarrow \neg b$

    (4) $a \Rightarrow b$

$F: c \wedge d$

with $(4) \prec (3) \prec (2) \prec (1)$.

Here, a conflict arises between rules (1) and (2) and between rules (3) and (4). Rules (1) and (2) have intermediate conclusions a and $\neg a$ for their final conclusions $\neg b$ and b. This type of problem is called *iterated conflicts*: conflicts on both intermediate and final conclusions.

The minimally explaining sets are $M_1 = \{c \Rightarrow a\}$, $M_2 = \{d \Rightarrow \neg a\}$, $M_3 = \{d \Rightarrow \neg a, \neg a \Rightarrow \neg b\}$ and $M_4 = \{c \Rightarrow a, a \Rightarrow b\}$. The sets of defeasibility chains are $Ch(M_1) = \{M_1\}$, $Ch(M_2) = \{M_2 \prec^* M_1\}$, $Ch(M_3) = \{M_3 \prec^* M_1\}$ and $Ch(M_4) = \{M_4 \prec^* M_3 \prec^* M_1\}$. M_1 and M_4 are justified arguments. M_2 and M_3 are overruled arguments, because they are defeated by justified argument M_1: a and b are the outcomes. Note that M_4 is defeated by M_3, though not overruled, since M_3 is an overruled argument (defeated by M_1).

Example 3.20 Circular conflicts

    (1) $a \Rightarrow b$

    (2) $c \Rightarrow \neg b$

    (3) $b \Rightarrow \neg a$

    (4) $d \Rightarrow a$

    (5) $d \Rightarrow b$

$F: c \wedge d$

with $(5) \prec (4) \prec (3) \prec (2) \prec (1)$.

Here, we have conflicts between rules (1) and (2), rules (3) and (4) and rules (2) and (5). The applicability of rule (1) depends on rule (4) with intermediate conclusion a. Rule (4) is in conflict with a higher rule, (3), (iterated conflict), and the applicability of (3) depends on (5), which is in conflict with (2). Rule (2) is in conflict with rule (1), and the applicability of (1) depends on rule (4), and so on. This will never stop, therefore we call this *the problem of circular conflicts*.

The minimally explaining sets are $M_1 = \{d \Rightarrow a, a \Rightarrow b\}$, mbox$M_2 = \{c \Rightarrow \neg b\}$, $M_3 = \{d \Rightarrow b, b \Rightarrow \neg a\}$, $M_4 = \{d \Rightarrow a\}$ and $M_5 = \{d \Rightarrow b\}$.

The sets of defeasibility chains are $Ch(M_1) = \{M_1 \prec^* M_3 \prec^* M_2\}$, $Ch(M_2) = \{M_2 \prec^* M_1 \prec^* M_3\}$, $Ch(M_3) = \{M_3 \prec^* M_2 \prec^* M_1\}$, $Ch(M_4) = \{M_4 \prec^* M_3 \prec^* M_2\}$ and $Ch(M_5) = \{M_5 \prec^* M_2 \prec^* M_1\}$. All the arguments are defensible since there is no justified argument. Thus, b, $\neg b$, $\neg a$ and a are the outcomes.

Definition 3.21 Let $\mathcal{M}^*$ be the set of all defensible and justified arguments in $\mathcal{M}$. Then w is a maximal-coherent argument set iff w is the set $\{M_1, M_2, \ldots, M_n\}$ of arguments in $\mathcal{M}^*$, such that

- $Cons(M_1 \cup M_2 \cup \ldots \cup M_n \cup \{F\})$ is consistent and
- $\neg \exists_{M \in \mathcal{M}^* \setminus w}(Cons(M_1 \cup M_2 \cup \ldots \cup M_n \cup \{F\} \cup M)$ is consistent).

W is defined as the set of all maximal-coherent argument sets $w \subseteq \mathcal{M}$. $Out(w)$ is defined as the set of all outcomes of the arguments $M \in w$.

Consider example 3.20. Then $W = \{w_1, w_2, w_3\}$ with $w_1 = \{M_1, M_4, M_5\}$, $w_2 = \{M_2, M_4\}$ and $w_3 = \{M_3, M_5\}$. It follows that $Out(w_1) = \{a, b\}$, $Out(w_2) = \{a, \neg b\}$ and $Out(w_3) = \{\neg a, b\}$. There is no $w \in W$ with $Out(w) = \{\neg a, \neg b\}$, since M_3 is the argument for $\neg a$ and $M_3 \cup \{F\} \models b$. Thus, if $\neg a \in Out(w)$, then b must also be an element in $Out(w)$, since otherwise we cannot derive $\neg a$: the literal b is necessary to derive $\neg a$. In other words, if an argument M is a subset of a maximal-coherent argument set w, then all outcomes of the subarguments of M are elements of the set $Out(w)$.

Corollary 3.22 Let $w \in W$. Then for all justified arguments M in $\mathcal{M}$ it holds that $M \in w$.

The following definition is needed for the definition of arguments of norms in the next section.

Definition 3.23 Let W be the set of rules, $w \in W$ and $w = \{M_1, M_2, \ldots, M_n\}$, then $W(w)$ is defined as the maximal-coherent set of rules in W with respect to w and F. Let $\phi \Rightarrow \phi_1 \in W$, then

$$\phi \Rightarrow \phi_1 \in W(w) \text{ iff } \{\phi \Rightarrow \phi_1\} \cup M_1 \cup M_2 \cup \ldots \cup M_n \cup \{F\} \text{ is coherent.}$$

Note that all rules in the arguments in w are in $W(w)$.

Example 3.24
    (1) $c \Rightarrow a$
    (2) $d \Rightarrow \neg a$
    (3) $d \Rightarrow b$
    (4) $\neg c \Rightarrow \neg b$
$F \colon c \wedge d$
with $(4) \prec (3) \prec (2) \prec (1)$.

Then $w = \{\{c \Rightarrow a\}, \{d \Rightarrow b\}\}$ and $W(w) = \{c \Rightarrow a, \neg c \Rightarrow \neg b, d \Rightarrow b\}$. Rule $d \Rightarrow \neg a$ is not an element of $W(w)$, since the rule is incoherent with

$\{c \Rightarrow a\} \cup \{d \Rightarrow b\} \cup \{F\}$. Furthermore, note that $\neg c \Rightarrow \neg b$ is an element of $W(w)$, though not of an argument in w. We will see in the following section that such a rule can be applicable for the derivation of a certain norm.

4. NORMS

Defeasible deontic reasoning is based on five notions: the notion of *applicable norms* based on a set $w \in \mathcal{W}$ (definition 4.1) and the same four notions of defeasible reasoning for rules (definitions 4.3, 4.8, 4.10 and 4.12).

We also define *maximal-coherent argument sets* for norms that we will use for the definition of violated obligations in subsection 4.2. At the end of this section, we give an example of defeasible deontic reasoning with violated norms.

Definition 4.1 Let $w \in \mathcal{W}$, $w = \{M_1, M_2, \ldots, M_n\}$ and $a_1 \wedge a_2 \wedge \ldots \wedge a_n \Rightarrow \psi$ be a conditional norm in Δ. Then

$$\psi \in \Delta(w, F) \text{ iff } \forall_{i \in \{1,2,\ldots,n\}} M_1 \cup M_2 \cup \ldots \cup M_n \cup \{F\} \models a_i.$$

ψ is called an applicable norm in Δ with respect to w and F. Thus, $\Delta(w, F)$ is the set of all applicable norms in Δ with respect to w and F.

Example 4.2

W:	(1) $a \Rightarrow b$	Δ: (1') $b \Rightarrow \bigcirc(\neg a)$
	(2) $b \Rightarrow c$	(2') $d \wedge h \Rightarrow \bigcirc(i \vee l)$
	(3) $e \Rightarrow d$	(3') $g \Rightarrow \bigcirc(b)$
	(4) $f \Rightarrow g$	
	(5) $h \Rightarrow \neg c$	

$F: a \wedge e \wedge h$

with $(5) \prec (4) \prec (3) \prec (2) \prec (1)$ and $(3') \prec (2') \prec (1')$.

The arguments are:
$M_1 = \{a \Rightarrow b\}$;
$M_2 = \{a \Rightarrow b, b \Rightarrow c\}$;
$M_3 = \{e \Rightarrow d\}$;
$M_4 = \{h \Rightarrow \neg c\}$.

It is easy to see that M_1, M_2 and M_3 are justified arguments, since they are not defeated by an argument. M_4 is defeated by M_2, thus M_4 is an overruled argument. There is one maximal-coherent argument set w: $\{M_1, M_2, M_3\}$. Now we can give the applicable norms:

1. $\bigcirc(\neg a) \in \Delta(w, F)$, since $M_1 \cup M_2 \cup M_3 \cup \{F\} \models b$;
2. $\bigcirc(i \vee l) \in \Delta(w, F)$, since $M_1 \cup M_2 \cup M_3 \cup \{F\} \models d$ and $M_1 \cup M_2 \cup M_3 \cup \{F\} \models h$;
3. $\bigcirc(b) \notin \Delta(w, F)$, since $M_1 \cup M_2 \cup M_3 \cup \{F\} \not\models g$.

Thus, $\Delta(w, F) = \{\bigcirc(\neg a), \bigcirc(i \vee l)\}$.

For $\Delta(w, F)$, we use standard deontic logic (SDL). By standard deontic logic, a modal (Kripke-style) version of the now so-called 'Old System' of

Von Wright (1951), we mean the system D^{*5} based on propositional logic
and axiomatised by the rule of inference:

(ROM) $\dfrac{p \rightarrow q}{\bigcirc(p) \rightarrow \bigcirc(q)}$,

together with the following axiom schemata:[6]

(OC) $\quad (\bigcirc(p) \wedge \bigcirc(q)) \rightarrow \bigcirc(p \wedge q)$

(ON) $\quad \bigcirc(p \vee \neg p)$

(OD) $\quad \neg \bigcirc(p \wedge \neg p)$

$(Df.P)$ $\quad P(p) \equiv \neg \bigcirc(\neg p)$

Furthermore, we add the following inference rule to SDL:[7]

$(ROM2)$ $\quad \dfrac{\bigcirc(p_1), \bigcirc(p_2), ..., \bigcirc(p_n), p_1 \wedge p_2 \wedge ... \wedge p_n \Rightarrow q}{\bigcirc(q)}$

Analogous with the definition of arguments for rules, we define arguments
for norms.

Definition 4.3 Let $N \subseteq \Delta(w, F)$, ψ a norm and $N \cup \{F_b\} \cup W(w)$ consistent.
Then N explains ψ minimally iff

- $\{F_b\} \cup W(w) \cup N \vdash \psi$ and
- $\neg \exists_{\psi_1 \in N} \{F_b\} \cup W(w) \cup N \setminus \{\psi_1\} \vdash \psi$.

We call N a minimally explaining set or an argument. The set of all arguments
will be denoted as $\mathcal{N}(w, F)$. The ψ-relevant set of $\Delta(w, F)$, denoted by
$[\psi]\mathcal{N}(w, F)$ is the set of all arguments that explain ψ minimally.
Let $\mathcal{N} \subseteq \mathcal{N}(w, F)$. If there is an argument for ψ, thus $[\psi]\mathcal{N} \neq \emptyset$, then ψ is
called an outcome.

We do not use F, but F_b in this definition, because otherwise we would derive
ridiculous conclusions. Consider the following example.

Example 4.4

(1) $\quad \bigcirc(a)$: It is obligatory to go to school.

(2) $\quad \bigcirc(b)$: It is obligatory to behave.

$F = F_c$: $a \wedge \neg b$: You go to school and you do not behave,
with $(2) \prec (1)$.

Now we can derive $\bigcirc(\neg b)$ from $\bigcirc(a)$ and F_c, because $\{F_c\} \vdash a \rightarrow \neg b$ and
by (ROM) $\bigcirc(a) \rightarrow \bigcirc(\neg b)$. Thus, if we use F instead of F_b, then $\{\bigcirc(a)\}$
would be an argument for the outcome $\bigcirc(\neg b)$, which is not a desirable result.

Definition 4.5 Let $\mathcal{N} \subseteq \mathcal{N}(w, F)$ and $N_1, N_2 \in \mathcal{N}$. Then N_1 and N_2 are in
conflict iff

$$\{F_b\} \cup W(w) \cup N_1 \vdash \psi \text{ and } \{F_b\} \cup W(w) \cup N_2 \vdash \neg \psi.$$

---

[5] System D^* is the smallest normal KD-system of modal logic (cf. (Chellas, 1980)).

[6] This axiom was rejected by Von Wright (1951, p.11), since he developed the *principle of deontic contingency*: 'A tautologous act is not necessarily obligatory, and a contradictory act is not necessarily forbidden'. We have to commit ourselves to this axiom, since otherwise we cannot view deontic logic as a branch of Kripke-style normal modal logic.

[7] For a brief discussion of this rule, see section 5.

Example 4.6

$\quad$ (1) $\quad \bigcirc(a \vee b)$
$\quad$ (2) $\quad \bigcirc(\neg a)$
$\quad$ (3) $\quad \bigcirc(c \vee \neg b)$
$\quad$ (4) $\quad \bigcirc(\neg c)$

with $(4) \prec (3) \prec (2) \prec (1)$.

Let $N_1 = \{\bigcirc(a \vee b), \bigcirc(c \vee \neg b), \bigcirc(\neg c)\}$ and $N_2 = \{\bigcirc(\neg a)\}$ be arguments in $\mathcal{N}$. Then N_1 is an argument for $\bigcirc(a)$ and N_2 an argument for $\neg \bigcirc (a)$, since $\bigcirc(\neg a) \rightarrow \neg \bigcirc (a)$ is deduced by axioms (OD) and (OC). Thus, N_1 and N_2 are in conflict.

Example 4.7

$\quad$ (1) $\quad \bigcirc(a)$
$\quad$ (2) $\quad \bigcirc(\neg b)$

$(2) \prec (1)$ and $W(w) = \{a \Rightarrow b\}$.

Let $N_3 = \{\bigcirc(a)\}$ and $N_4 = \{\bigcirc(\neg b)\}$ be arguments in $\mathcal{N}$. Then N_3 is an argument for $\bigcirc(b)$, since $\{a \Rightarrow b\} \cup N_3 \vdash \bigcirc(b)$ and N_4 is an argument for $\neg \bigcirc (b)$. Thus, N_3 and N_4 are in conflict.

4.1. *Defeasibility*

Because the arguments in $\mathcal{N}(w, F)$ can be in conflict, we resolve these deontic conflicts by adopting defeasible reasoning. The defeasibility of norms in $\Delta(w, F)$ determines the validity of these norms. The validity depends on the rules in w. For instance, let $\Delta(w, F) = \{\bigcirc(a), \bigcirc(b)\}$, $\bigcirc(b) \prec \bigcirc(a)$ and $w = \{a \Rightarrow \neg b\}$. Then $\{\bigcirc(a)\}$ is an argument for $\neg \bigcirc (b)$, since $w \cup \{\bigcirc(a)\} \vdash \neg \bigcirc (b)$. Now we say that $\{\bigcirc(a)\}$ defeats $\{\bigcirc(b)\}$, and that $\bigcirc(b)$ is not valid. Suppose that $w = \emptyset$, then $\bigcirc(a)$ and $\bigcirc(b)$ are both valid, because $\{\bigcirc(a)\}$ and $\{\bigcirc(b)\}$ are not in conflict.

Definition 4.8 Let N_1 and N_2 be arguments. Then N_1 is defeated by N_2 ($N_1 \prec^* N_2$) iff N_1 and N_2 are in conflict and

$$\exists_{\psi_1 \in N_1} \forall_{\psi_2 \in N_2} (\psi_1 \preceq \psi_2).$$

The main difference between this definition and definition 3.5 is that here we look at the statements of the two arguments with the lowest priority, and in definition 3.5 we looked at the statements of the two arguments with conflicting conclusions. Note that it is possible that $N_1 \prec^* N_2$ and $N_2 \prec^* N_1$ both hold, but only if the statements with the lowest priority of the two arguments have the same priority. $\prec^*$ is not transitive and not asymmetric.

Example 4.9

$\quad$ Consider example 4.6. N_1 is defeated by N_2, since $\bigcirc(\neg c)$ has a lower priority than all the norms in N_2: $\bigcirc(\neg c) \preceq \bigcirc(\neg a)$.

Now consider example 4.7. N_4 is defeated by N_3, since $\bigcirc(\neg b) \preceq \bigcirc(a)$. If $(1) \sim (2)$, then $N_3 \prec^* N_4$ and $N_4 \prec^* N_3$.

The following three definitions for arguments in $\mathcal{N}$ concerning defeasibility chains, $Ch(N)$ and justified, defensible and overruled arguments are exactly the same as the definitions for arguments in $\mathcal{N}$ (cf. definitions 3.7, 3.8 and 3.9).

Definition 4.10 Let $\mathcal{N} \subseteq \mathcal{N}(w, F)$. A defeasibility chain is a sequence of arguments in $\mathcal{N}$: $N_1 \prec^* N_2 \prec^* \ldots \prec^* N_n$ with the following conditions:

- $\forall_{k,l=1,2,\ldots,n \wedge k<l} N_k \not\subseteq N_l$;
- $\neg\exists_{N_{n+1}\in\mathcal{N}}\{(N_1,\ldots,N_n \not\subseteq N_{n+1}) \to (N_n \prec^* N_{n+1})\}$.

We define $Ch(\mathcal{N})$ as the set of all defeasibility chains in $\mathcal{N}$.

Definition 4.11 Let $\mathcal{N} \subseteq \mathcal{N}(w, F)$. Then $Ch(N)$ is the set of all defeasibility chains in $Ch(\mathcal{N})$ starting with N.

Definition 4.12 Let $N \in \mathcal{N}(w, F)$. Then

- N is a justified argument iff $Ch(N) = \{N\}$ or for all chains $N \prec^* N_1 \prec^* \ldots \prec^* N_n \in Ch(\mathcal{N})$ it holds that

$$n \text{ is even} \quad \wedge \neg\exists_{N'\in\mathcal{N}} N_n \prec^* N' \wedge$$
$$\forall_k \text{ is even} \quad (N_k \text{ is a justified argument}$$
$$\text{assuming } N \text{ is a justified argument}).$$

- N is an overruled argument iff there is a chain $N \prec^* N_1 \prec^* \ldots \prec^* N_n \in Ch(\mathcal{N})$ such that n is odd $\wedge \neg\exists_{N'\in\mathcal{N}} N_n \prec^* N'$.
- N is a defensible argument iff N is neither a justified argument nor an overruled argument.

Note that $\neg\exists_{N'\in\mathcal{N}} N_n \prec^* N'$ is equivalent to $Ch(N_n) = \{N_n\}$.

Example 4.13

Consider example 4.6. Let $\mathcal{N} = \{N_1, N_2, \ldots, N_6\}$, with
$N_1 = \{\bigcirc(a \vee b), \bigcirc(c \vee \neg b), \bigcirc(\neg c)\} \in [\bigcirc(a)]\mathcal{N}$
$N_2 = \{\bigcirc(\neg a)\} \in [\neg \bigcirc (a)]\mathcal{N}$
$N_3 = \{\bigcirc(a \vee b), \bigcirc(\neg a)\} \in [\bigcirc(b)]\mathcal{N}$
$N_4 = \{\bigcirc(c \vee \neg b), \bigcirc(\neg c)\} \in [\neg \bigcirc (b)]\mathcal{N}$
$N_5 = \{\bigcirc(a \vee b), \bigcirc(c \vee \neg b), \bigcirc(\neg a)\} \in [\bigcirc(c)]\mathcal{N}$
$N_6 = \{\bigcirc(\neg c)\} \in [\neg \bigcirc (c)]\mathcal{N}$

Argument N_1 is defeated by justified argument N_2, since $\bigcirc(\neg c) \prec \bigcirc(\neg a)$ and $Ch(N_2) = \{N_2\}$, thus N_1 is an overruled argument. N_3 and N_5 are justified arguments, since $Ch(N_3) = \{N_3\}$ and $Ch(N_5) = \{N_5\}$. N_4 and N_6 are overruled arguments, since $N_4 \prec^* N_3 \in Ch(N_4)$ and $N_6 \prec^* N_5 \in Ch(N_6)$. If $(4) \sim (3) \prec (2) \prec (1)$, then N_5 and N_6 are defensible arguments, since $Ch(N_5) = \{N_5 \prec^* N_6\}$ and $Ch(N_6) = \{N_6 \prec^* N_5\}$.

Example 4.14

Consider example 4.7. N_4 is defeated by justified argument N_3 and $Ch(N_3) = \{N_3\}$, thus N_4 is an overruled argument.

Definition 4.15 Let $\mathcal{N} \subseteq \mathcal{N}(w, F)$ and $\mathcal{N}^*$ be the set of all defensible and justified arguments in $\mathcal{N}$. Then o is a maximal-consistent argument set iff o is the set $\{N_1, N_2, \ldots, N_n\}$ of arguments in $\mathcal{N}^*$, such that

- $N_1 \cup N_2 \cup \ldots \cup N_n \cup \{F_b\} \cup W(w)$ is consistent and
- $\neg\exists_{N \in \mathcal{N}^* \setminus o}(N_1 \cup N_2 \cup \ldots \cup N_n \cup \{F_b\} \cup W(w) \cup N$ is consistent).

$\mathcal{O}(\mathcal{N})$ is defined as the set of all maximal-consistent argument sets o. $Out(o)$ is defined as the set of all outcomes of the arguments $N \in o$.

Corollary 4.16 Let $o \in \mathcal{O}(\mathcal{N})$. Then for all justified arguments N in $\mathcal{N}$ it holds that $N \in o$.

Example 4.17

Consider example 4.13 with the justified arguments N_2, N_3 and N_5. There is one maximal-consistent argument set o: $o = \{N_2, N_3, N_5\}$.

If $(4) \sim (3) \prec (2) \prec (1)$, then N_5 and N_6 are defensible (see example 4.13). Then there are two maximal-consistent argument sets: $o_1 = \{N_2, N_3, N_5\}$ and $o_2 = \{N_2, N_3, N_6\}$, thus $\mathcal{O}(\mathcal{N}) = \{o_1, o_2\}$.

4.2. *Violation*

An obligation is violated iff the obligation is not fulfilled. In SDL, we can represent the violated obligation by $\bigcirc(p) \wedge \neg p$. We define the violated obligation in our theory analogously.

Definition 4.18 Let $\mathcal{N} \subseteq \mathcal{N}(w, F)$, $o \in \mathcal{O}(\mathcal{N})$, $o = \{N_1, \ldots, N_n\}$, $w = \{M_1, \ldots, M_l\}$ and $N_1 \cup N_2 \cup \ldots \cup N_n \cup W(w) \cup \{F_b\} \vdash \bigcirc(\phi)$. The norm $\bigcirc(\phi)$ is violated iff $M_1 \cup M_2 \cup \ldots \cup M_l \cup \{F\} \models \neg\phi$. The set of violated norms will be denoted as $V(o)$.

Example 4.19

Let $o = \{\{\bigcirc(a)\}, \{\bigcirc(b)\}\}$, $W(w) = \{a \Rightarrow c\}$, $\{F_b\} = w = \emptyset$ and F_c: $\neg b \wedge \neg c$. Then $\bigcirc(c) \in V(o)$, since $\{\bigcirc(a)\} \cup \{\bigcirc(b)\} \cup W(w) \vdash \bigcirc(c)$ and $\{F\} \vdash \neg c$ and $\bigcirc(b) \in V(o)$, since $\{\bigcirc(a)\} \cup \{\bigcirc(b)\} \cup W(w) \vdash \bigcirc(b)$ and $\{F\} \vdash \neg b$.

Definition 4.20 Let $\mathcal{N} \subseteq \mathcal{N}(w, F)$, $o \in \mathcal{O}(\mathcal{N})$ and $V(o)$ be the set of violated norms. Then $N \in o$ is a violated argument iff

$$\exists_{\psi \in V(o)} N \cup W(w) \cup \{F_b\} \vdash \psi.$$

$\mathcal{N}(V(o))$ is the set of all the violated arguments with respect to $V(o)$.

Example 4.21

Consider example 4.6:

(1) $\bigcirc(a \vee b)$
(2) $\bigcirc(\neg a)$
(3) $\bigcirc(c \vee \neg b)$
(4) $\bigcirc(\neg c)$

with $(4) \prec (3) \prec (2) \prec (1)$, $W(w) = \{F_b\} = \emptyset$ and $F_c: \neg c$.

Suppose further (see example 4.13) that $\mathcal{N} = \{N_1, N_2, \ldots, N_6\}$, with
$N_1 = \{\bigcirc(a \vee b), \bigcirc(c \vee \neg b), \bigcirc(\neg c)\} \in [\bigcirc(a)]\mathcal{N}$
$N_2 = \{\bigcirc(\neg a)\} \in [\neg \bigcirc (a)]\mathcal{N}$
$N_3 = \{\bigcirc(a \vee b), \bigcirc(\neg a)\} \in [\bigcirc(b)]\mathcal{N}$
$N_4 = \{\bigcirc(c \vee \neg b), \bigcirc(\neg c)\} \in [\neg \bigcirc (b)]\mathcal{N}$
$N_5 = \{\bigcirc(a \vee b), \bigcirc(c \vee \neg b), \bigcirc(\neg a)\} \in [\bigcirc(c)]\mathcal{N}$
$N_6 = \{\bigcirc(\neg c)\} \in [\neg \bigcirc (c)]\mathcal{N}.$

From examples 4.13 and 4.17 it follows that $o = \{N_2, N_3, N_5\}$. $\bigcirc(c) \in V(o)$, since $N_5 \vdash \bigcirc(c)$ and $\{F\} \vdash \neg c$. Therefore, N_5 is a violated argument. N_2 and N_3 are no violated arguments, since $N_2 \nvdash \bigcirc(c)$ and $N_3 \nvdash \bigcirc(c)$.

Definition 4.22 Let $\mathcal{N} \subseteq \mathcal{N}(w, F)$ and $\psi_1, \ldots, \psi_n \in \Delta(w, F)$. Then

$$\mathcal{N} \setminus^* \{\psi_1, \ldots, \psi_n\} = \cup\{N | N \in \mathcal{N} \wedge \forall_{i=1,\ldots,n} \psi_i \notin N\}.$$

Thus $\mathcal{N} \setminus^* \{\psi_1, \ldots, \psi_n\}$ is the set of arguments in $\mathcal{N}$ without the arguments containing a norm of the set $\{\psi_1, \ldots \psi_n\}$.

Example 4.23

A programme committee requires that conference submissions (papers) are sent in by mail. However, if your paper is not sent by mail, then your paper should be sent by fax. And if no fax-machine is available, one should try to send it by e-mail. The facts are that the paper is sent by fax and if you send your paper by fax, then you do not send the paper by e-mail. The formalisation is as follows:

W:
(1) $email \Rightarrow \neg mail$
(2) $fax \Rightarrow \neg mail$

Δ:
(1') $\bigcirc(mail)$
(2') $\neg mail \Rightarrow \bigcirc(fax)$
(3') $\neg fax \Rightarrow \bigcirc(email)$

$F_c: fax$
$F_b: fax \rightarrow \neg email$

with $(2) \prec (1)$ and $(3') \prec (2') \prec (1')$.

Let us consider this example. If the paper is sent by mail, then there is no violation; this is the best situation. However, the norm $\bigcirc(mail)$ is violated, because the paper is not sent by mail. Then the second-best situation is that your paper is sent by fax. We can formalise this process as follows:

$Out(w) = \{\neg mail\}$, $W(w) = \{fax \Rightarrow \neg mail, email \Rightarrow \neg mail\}$
$\Delta(w, F) = \{\bigcirc(mail), \bigcirc(fax)\}$

$\mathcal{N}(w, F) = \{N_1, N_2\}$, with $N_1 = \{\bigcirc(mail)\}$ and $N_2 = \{\bigcirc(fax)\}$.
Note that $\bigcirc(email)$ is not an element of $\Delta(w, F)$, since it is not an applicable
norm: $w \cup \{F\} \not\models \neg fax$.

N_1 is a justified argument, since $Ch(N_1) = \{N_1\}$, and N_2 is an overruled argument, since it is defeated by N_1. N_1 and N_2 are in conflict, since
$\{F_b\} \cup W(w) \cup N_1 \vdash \bigcirc(mail)$ and $\{F_b\} \cup W(w) \cup N_2 \vdash \neg \bigcirc (mail)$ and
$\bigcirc(fax) \prec \bigcirc(mail)$. Thus, $o = \{N_1\}$.

The norm $\bigcirc(mail)$ has a higher priority than the norm $\bigcirc(fax)$. However,
the norm $\bigcirc(mail)$ is violated:

$$V(o) = \{\bigcirc(mail)\} \text{ and } (\mathcal{N}(w, F))(V(o)) = \{N_1\}.$$

Now we consider the norms again without the violated norm, since they can
become valid because of the violation of the norm $\bigcirc(mail)$. Let $\mathcal{N} = \mathcal{N}(w, F) \setminus^* \{\bigcirc(mail)\}$. Then $\mathcal{N} = \{N_2\}$. Argument N_2 is a justified argument. Let $o' \in \mathcal{O}(\mathcal{N})$, then it follows that $o' = \{N_2\}$. N_2 (with $\bigcirc(fax)$
as an outcome) is a justified and non-violated argument with respect to the
violation of the norm $\bigcirc(mail)$. Thus, sending in your paper by fax is the
second-best situation.

5. CONCLUSIONS

In this paper, we presented a theory of defeasible deontic reasoning dealing
with some very common problems of other approaches:

- defeasibility between *groups of conditional norms*;
- the combination of defeasibility of rules and norms;
- the absence of the notion of permission.

However, we do not claim that our theory is completely free from the above-
mentioned problems. Adopting defeasible reasoning for non-deontic constraints (rules) is not trivial, like the study of the validity of deducing $\bigcirc(b)$
from $\bigcirc(a)$ and $a \Rightarrow b$. This corresponds with the choice of rule (ROM2):

$$\frac{\bigcirc(p_1), \bigcirc(p_2), \ldots, \bigcirc(p_n), p_1 \wedge p_2 \wedge \ldots \wedge p_n \Rightarrow q}{\bigcirc(q)}.$$

However, it is also possible to add the default rule schema (RK)

$$(p_1 \wedge p_2 \wedge \ldots \wedge p_n \Rightarrow q) \rightarrow (\bigcirc(p_1) \wedge \bigcirc(p_2) \wedge \ldots \bigcirc(p_n) \Rightarrow \bigcirc(q)),$$

which also allows defaults between norms.

The consequence of the use of rule (ROM2) is that norms are dependent on
rules and that rules are not dependent on norms. This means that rules have
a higher priority than norms. Thus, an argument of rules cannot be defeated
by an argument of norms. If we had not made this distinction between rules
and conditional norms (i.e., if we had opted for (RK) instead of (ROM2)), we
would have got, for example, the following situation:

$W \cup \Delta$: (1) $\bigcirc(a)$ F: $\emptyset$

(2) $\bigcirc(b)$
(3) $a \Rightarrow \neg b$
with $(3) \prec (2) \prec (1)$.

From $\bigcirc(a)$ and $a \Rightarrow \neg b$ we can deduce $\bigcirc(\neg b)$. Thus, $\{\bigcirc(a), a \Rightarrow \neg b\}$ would be an argument for $\bigcirc(\neg b)$. Thus, the set $\{\bigcirc(a), \bigcirc(b), a \Rightarrow \neg b\}$ is incoherent. We cannot deduce $\neg(a \Rightarrow \neg b)$ from $\bigcirc(a)$ and $\bigcirc(b)$ with the (ROM2) rule. However, with (RK) we can derive $\neg(a \Rightarrow \neg b)$ from $\bigcirc(a)$ and $\bigcirc(b)$:

$\bigcirc(a) \wedge \bigcirc(b) \rightarrow \bigcirc(a) \wedge \neg \bigcirc (\neg b)$;
$\bigcirc(a) \wedge \neg \bigcirc (\neg b) \rightarrow \neg(\neg \bigcirc (a) \vee \bigcirc(\neg b))$;
$\neg(\neg \bigcirc (a) \vee \bigcirc(\neg b)) \rightarrow \neg(\bigcirc(a) \rightarrow \bigcirc(b))$;
$\neg(\bigcirc(a) \rightarrow \bigcirc(b)) \rightarrow \neg(a \Rightarrow \neg b)$.

Therefore, $\{\bigcirc(a), \bigcirc(b)\}$ is an argument for $\neg(a \Rightarrow \neg b)$.[8]

The advantage of replacing rule (ROM2) by a stronger rule is that rules and conditional norms do not have to be separated in the arguments, and that, by definition, rules do not have a higher priority than conditional norms, which is a consequence from the theory presented in this paper. At first glance, this seems a good concept for solving the problem of the separation of rules and norms. However, this concept gives rise to some serious problems since the definition of defeating arguments for rules is different from the definition of norms. In the definition of defeating arguments for rules, we only look at single statements with conflicting final conclusions, whereas in the definition of norms we not only look at final conclusions but also at groups of statements deriving conflicting conclusions. Furthermore, the applicability of a conditional norm depends on the facts and the rules. This means that we have to separate rules and conditional norms. We leave this issue of the separation of arguments for rules and conditional norms in deontic reasoning as a future research topic. Another interesting topic for further research is to investigate to what extent the theory developed in (Prakken and Sartor, 1996) corresponds to our theory, and what exactly the differences of both theories are.

Most deontic defeasible reasoning approaches are based on specificity considering the amount of relevant information or supporting evidence. Our approach is based on the more general idea of priority (authority). Other defeasibility criteria can easily be converted to some form of defeasibility on the basis of priority.

Lamber Royakkers
Department of Mathematics and Computer Science
Eindhoven University of Technology

---

[8] As a consequence, we allow negations of default rules. It is not trivial to decide on the meaning of these formulas.

Eindhoven, The Netherlands

Frank Dignum
Department of Mathematics and Computer Science
Eindhoven University of Technology
Eindhoven, The Netherlands

REFERENCES

Alchourrón, C.E. (1986). *Conditionality and the Representation of Legal Norms.* In A.A. Martino and F. Socci Natali (eds.), *Automated Analysis of Legal Texts,* pages 175–186.

Alchourrón, C.E. and D. Makinson (1981). *Hierarchies of Regulations and Their Logic.* In R. Hilpinen (ed), *New Studies in Deontic Logic,* D. Reidel Publishing Company, pages 125–148.

Brewka, G. (1991). *Preferred subtheories: An extended logical framework for default reasoning.* In *Proceedings IJCAI,* pages 1043–1048.

Chellas, B.F. (1980). *Modal Logic: An Introduction.* Cambridge University Press.

Delgrande, J. (1988). An approach to default reasoning based on a first-order conditional logic. *Artificial Intelligence* 36:63–90.

Dung P.(1993). On the acceptability of arguments and its fundamental role in nonmonotonic reasoning and logic programming. In *Proceedings IJCAI,* pages 852–857.

Hart, H.L.A. (1961). *The Concept of Law.* Clarendon Press, Oxford.

Horty, J.F. (1994). Moral Dilemmas and Nonmonotonic Logic. *Journal of Philosophical Logic* 23:35–65.

Loui, R.P. and J. Norman (1995). Rationales and arguments moves. *Artificial Intelligence and Law* 3:159–189.

McDermott, D.V. and J. Doyle (1980). Non-monotonic logic I. *Artificial Intelligence* 13:41–72.

Pollock, J.L. (1987). Defeasible reasoning. *Cognitive Science* 11(4):481–518.

Poole, D. (1988). A logical framework for default reasoning. *Artificial Intelligence* 36:27–47.

Prakken, H. (1993). *Logical Tools for Modeling Legal Argument.* PhD thesis, Amsterdam.

Prakken, H, (1996). Two approaches to defeasible reasoning. *Studia Logica,* forthcoming.

Prakken, H. and G. Sartor (1995). On the relation between legal language and legal argument: Assumptions, applicability and dynamic priorities. In *Proceedings of the Fifth International Conference on Artificial Intelligence and Law,* University of Maryland, pages 1–11.

Prakken, H. and G. Sartor, *Rules About Rules: Assessing Conflicting Arguments in Legal Reasoning,* submitted.

Reiter, R. (1980). A logic for default reasoning. *Artificial Intelligence* 13:81–132.

Reiter, R. (1987). Nonmonotonic reasoning. *Annual Review of Computer Science* 2:147–186.

Rescher, N. (1964). *Hypothetical Reasoning.* North-Holland, Amsterdam.

Royakkers, L.M.M. and F. Dignum (1994). Deontic inconsistencies and authorities In Breuker J. (ed), *Normative Reasoning.*

Ryu, Y.U. (1992). Conditional deontic logic augmented with defeasible reasoning. *Data & Knowledge Engineering* 16:73–91.

Sartor, G. (1993). Defeasibility in legal reasoning. *Rechtstheorie* 24:281–316.

Shoham, Y. (1988). *Reasoning about Change,* MIT Press.

Tan, Y.-H. and L.W.N. van der Torre (1994). Multi preference semantics for a defeasible deontic logic. In Prakken H. (ed.), *Legal Knowledge Based Systems. The Relation with Legal Theory,* Koninklijke Vermande, Lelystad, pages 115–126.

von Wright, G.H. (1951). Deontic logic. *Mind* 60:1–15, .

DONALD NUTE

APPARENT OBLIGATION*

1. INTRODUCTION

I want to contrast three notions of obligation: *prima facie* obligation, *actual* obligation, and what I will call *apparent* obligation. By a *prima facie* obligation, I mean something that is binding *other things being equal*. An example might be the obligation to keep a promise. Of course, we all recognize that the obligation to keep a promise or any other *prima facie* obligation might be overriden by some greater obligation, such as an obligation to prevent harm to a friend. By an *actual* obligation I will mean any obligation that is binding when all relevant circumstances are considered. So our actual obligations are our *overriding* obligations or our obligations *all things considered*. An obligation may be an actual obligation, of course, because it is a *prima facie obligation* and no greater obligation overrides it. A hard fact of our moral existence, though, is that we are often not aware of all morally relevant circumstances of our situation. Indeed, there may be situations in which we *cannot* know all morally relevant circumstances before deciding what we ought to do. In such a situation, we are expected to fulfill those obligations which bind us *given all we know about morally relevant circumstances*. These are what I call our *apparent* obligations.

Let's consider a revision of Plato's example from *The Republic*. A friend has loaned us a weapon and we have promised to return it upon demand. The friend later becomes suicidal and, intent upon taking his life, comes to us to recover his weapon. In Plato's example, we know that our friend is suicidal and our *prima facie* obligation to keep our promise is overriden by our obligation to keep our friend from harm. So our apparent and actual obligation is to deny the weapon to our friend. But suppose there is nothing in our friend's behavior to signal his intent. The way I am using the terms, we nevertheless have both a *prima facie* obligation to return the weapon and

*Many of the ideas that went into this paper were presented at the last two meetings of the Society for Exact Philosophy (Calgary, Ontario, Canada – May 1995, and Johnson City, Tennessee, U.S.A. – October 1996). This material was also discussed frequently in a discussion group devoted to defeasible reasoning that has met at the Artificial Intelligence Center at the University of Georgia over the last year and a half. For their helpful comments and suggestions, I thank Vic Bancroft, David Billington, Daniel Bonevac, Charles Cross, David Goodman, Christopher Henderson, Zachary Hunter, Hong-Gee Kim, Michael Morreau, Henry Prakken, Frank Price, and Xiaochang Yu.

D. Nute (ed.), Defeasible Deontic Logic, 287–315.
© 1997 *Kluwer Academic Publishers. Printed in the Netherlands.*

an actual obligation to deny it. Unfortunately, we cannot discover our actual obligation because all morally relevant circumstances of our situation are not accessible to us. In this situation, our apparent obligation is to return the weapon. Suppose we do so and our friend indeed kills himself. We may feel remorse and say that we should not have given him the weapon because he used it for this purpose. We did not fulfill our actual obligation. Others will tell us that we had no way of knowing what our friend intended and, under the circumstances, *morally* we could have done nothing other than what we did. Of course it would be morally wrong for us to hide our heads in the sand and ignore evidence about morally relevant circumstances of our situation; but the commonsense view seems to be that for the reasonably prudent person, it is apparent obligation rather than actual obligation that guides our lives.

Of course, our apparent obligation will change as we obtain new information. Reasoning about what I call apparent obligation is *defeasible,* that is, an appropriate conclusion about what is apparently the proper course of action may be defeated in light of new information. I propose the notion of apparent obligation because it has been suggested that there can be nothing nonmonotonic or defeasible about actual or all things considered obligation. Either all morally relevant circumstances have been considered or they have not. If they have, then no new evidence can be introduced that could render an actual obligation non-actual. While this is certainly true, it overlooks the realities of moral deliberation. So I surrender this point and insist on another: real moral life requires us to make the best moral choices we can given the information available to us. Moral deliberation has an inescapable epistemological component.

Some normative principles are recognized as taking precedence over others in a principled way. For example, the principle of *lex superior* holds that laws of a higher authority override laws of any lower authority, and the principle of *lex posterior* holds that laws enacted later override earlier laws. Thus, normative principles may be prioritized even when there is no sense that any of the prioritized principles are *prima facie*. Again we see that a normative principle might or might not result in an apparent obligation depending on circumstances. In this case, the circumstances involve complete or partial orderings of norms. These orderings themselves represent a kind of normative metaprinciple. We will want our defeasible deontic system to provide some way to represent the priorities of normative principles, and we want some means for reasoning about these priorities.

The treatment of moral dilemmas is another area where defeasibility may be useful. Standard deontic logic includes the principle $\sim(\bigcirc\phi \wedge \bigcirc\sim\phi)$. This makes moral dilemmas inconsistent. Any set of norms that can lead to a moral dilemma under any possible circumstances is deemed inconsistent. But this runs counter to the intuitions of at least some moral theorists. An important aspect of moral life might be to anticipate and avoid irresolvable moral dilemmas. But if we take this view, we surely do not expect that such moral straits are commonplace. We do not expect every conflicting set of *prima facie* obligations or every conflicting set of prioritized normative principles to produce an irresolvable moral dilemma. And the intuitive way we avoid this is that we expect some normative rules to be overriden by circumstances. If this were not the case, life would be entirely too hard. So our defeasible deontic system will allow for the existence of consistent, rich normative theories that support many normative conclusions, including conflicting ones, but in which moral dilemmas are possible, consistent, and rare.

Some of the most compelling examples motivating investigation of defeasible deontic systems involve contrary-to-duty obligations. There are two classes of paradoxes based on contrary-to-duty obligations. I will call these the Chisholm paradoxes and the Good Samaritan paradoxes. I will quickly review the general forms for these two classes of examples and offer an initial analysis of the Chisholm paradoxes that suggests a way we can use defeasible reasoning to resolve them. I believe the Good Samaritan paradoxes have quite a different analysis and I do not believe defeasible reasoning will play an essential role in their solution.

A Chisholm example consists of four claims which are taken to be logically independent. Furthermore, the four claims taken together do not imply a moral dilemma intuitively. The first claim is that some proposition ϕ ought to be the case. The second is that it ought to be that case that if ϕ is the case, then a second proposition ψ is also the case. The third claim, that if ϕ is not the case, then ψ ought not to be the case, represents the contrary-to-duty obligation. The obligation that ψ not be the case only becomes apparent (or actual) if the obligation that ϕ be the case is violated. The final, purely factual, claim is that ϕ is not the case, that is, that the obligation that ϕ be the case is in fact violated. Intuitively, if the third and fourth premises were absent, the first two premises would imply an obligation that ψ be the case. This pattern of normative inference is often called *deontic detachment*. Also intuitively, the third and fourth premises together, even in the presence of the first two premises, imply an obligation that ψ not be the case. This pattern of inference is often called *factual detachment*. When confronted with a Chisholm example, people generally agree that, clearly, ψ ought not to be the case. The obvious solution is that when a deontic detachment and a factual detachment together would produce a moral dilemma, we should allow the factual detachment to override the deontic detachment. But of course, in a monotonic system we can't both allow a deontic detachment when a competing contrary-to-duty obligation is absent but block it when the competing contrary-to-duty obligation is present. For this we need a nonmonotonic system in which factual detachment has precedence over deontic detachment.

Besides contrary-to-duty obligations, Good Samaritan paradoxes also involve *deontic inheritance*. If ϕ entails ψ, and ϕ ought to be the case, then by deontic inheritance, ψ also ought to be the case. A Good Samaritan example also consists of four claims which intuitively do not imply a moral dilemma. The first claim is that ϕ ought not to be the case. The second claim is the contrary-to-duty claim that if ϕ is the case, then ψ ought also to be the case. The third claim is that ϕ in fact is the case. The fourth claim (often implicit) is that ψ entails ϕ. By factual detachment using the second and third premises, ψ ought to be the case. But using this conclusion together with the fourth premise, deontic inheritance gives us that ϕ ought to be the case. This conflicts with the first premise, producing the apparent moral dilemma. Intuitively, it is the inference that ϕ ought to be the case, the inference based on deontic inheritance, that we want to block. But I think that deontic inheritance should not be defeasible. So I will not attempt to use defeasible reasoning as a basis for a solution to Good Samaritan paradoxes. Instead, I adopt the view that at least some of these examples only appear paradoxical because they have been incompletely and incorrectly formalized.

I will propose a formalism for representing and using the defeasible rules that guide moral reasoning. This formalism is a deontic extension of a defeasible logic developed in an earlier series of papers (Nute, 1992; Nute, 1992; Nute, 1992). I will proceed by first presenting a version of defeasible logic extended only to include deontic operators in its language. This will be enough to introduce a principle of factual detachment. It will also allow us to express *prima facie* obligations, contrary-to-duty obligations, and priorities for normative rules. Then I will extend the proof theory for defeasible logic to include deontic inheritance, deontic detachment, and some additional inference patterns not yet considered. The proof theory will be constructed so that factual detachment overrides deontic detachment when the two conflict. We will see how Chisholm examples are resolved within this formalism. We will also see how deliberation over priorities of normative rules is enabled. Finally, I will take a closer look at Good Samaritan examples, offering a different solution for some of these examples. I am unclear how to resolve others.

2. THE LANGUAGE

We define atomic formulas in the usual way. A literal is any atomic formula or its negation. If ϕ is a literal, then $\bigcirc\phi$ and $\sim\bigcirc\phi$ are deontic formulas. All and only literals and deontic formulas are formulas of our language. Where ϕ is an atomic formula, we say ϕ and $\sim\phi$ are the complements of each other, and where ϕ is a literal we say $\bigcirc\phi$ and $\sim\bigcirc\phi$ are complements of each other. $\neg\phi$ denotes the complement of any formula ϕ, positive or negative. We define $\mathcal{P}\phi$ as $\sim\bigcirc\neg\phi$. So $\neg\mathcal{P}\phi$ is the complement of $\sim\bigcirc\neg\phi$, that is, $\bigcirc\neg\phi$. Where ϕ is an atomic formula, $\mathcal{P}\phi = \sim\bigcirc\sim\phi$ and $\mathcal{P}\sim\phi = \sim\bigcirc\phi$. Technically, $\sim\mathcal{P}\phi$ is not well-formed, but we can allow it as an informal variant of $\neg\mathcal{P}\phi$.

Rules are a class of expressions distinct from formulas. Rules are constructed using three primitive symbols: $\rightarrow$, $\Rightarrow$, and $\rightsquigarrow$. Where $A \cup \{\phi\}$ is a set of formulas, $A \rightarrow \phi$ is a *strict rule*, $A \Rightarrow \phi$ is a *defeasible rule*, and $A \rightsquigarrow \phi$ is an *undercutting defeater*. In each case, we call A the *antecedent* of the rule and we call ϕ the *consequent* of the rule. Where $A = \{\psi\}$, we denote $A \rightarrow \phi$ as $\psi \rightarrow \phi$, and similarly for defeasible rules and defeaters. Antecedents for strict rules and defeaters must be non-empty; antecedents for defeasible rules may be empty. We will call a rule of the form $\emptyset \Rightarrow \phi$ a *presumption* and represent it more simply as $\Rightarrow \phi$.

All rules are read as 'if-then' statements. We read $A \Rightarrow \phi$ as 'If A, then evidently (normally, typically, presumably) ϕ', we read $\Rightarrow \phi$ as 'Presumably, ϕ', and we read $A \rightsquigarrow \phi$ as 'If A, then it might be that ϕ'. The role of a defeater is only to interfere with the process of drawing an inference from a defeasible rule. Defeaters never support inferences directly although they may support inferences indirectly by undercutting potential defeaters. If free variables occur in a rule, we interpret the rule as though all variables were bound by universal quantifiers that have the entire rule within their scope. So, for example, we read $Fx \Rightarrow Gx$ as 'F's are typically G's'.

Rules themselves are conceived as policies for forming and revising beliefs. As such, they can have both justification conditions and compliance conditions, but not truth conditions. A typical example of a defeasible rule in English is 'Birds fly'. We might accept this rule because most birds do fly. We might even call the English sentence true for this reason. But as a *rule*, we reinterpret the sentence to mean something like 'Take a thing's being a bird as evidence that it flies.' This is an imperative and does not have a truth value. We might justify such a policy for forming or revising beliefs in many ways. Compliance conditions, on the other hand, concern the way the rule is to be used once it is accepted. These conditions are procedural or proof theoretic. I expect that any suitable semantics for defeasible logic will be highly procedural and will derive directly from proof theory. I will not explore these issues further here, but a preliminary investigation can be found in (Nute, 1992).

Our formal language lacks the power to describe some situations that we might find interesting, but it is adequate for a wide range of examples. Adding disjunction and existential quantification to the language would increase the expressive power and disjunctive permissions raise interesting logical issues, but these enhancements introduce difficulties that we will not try to resolve here.

3. BASIC DEFEASIBLE LOGIC

Definition 1 *A* **defeasible theory** *is a quadruple* $\langle F, R, C, \prec \rangle$ *such that*

1. F is a set of formulas,

2. R is a set of rules,

3. C is a set of finite sets of formulas such that for every formula ϕ, either $\{\phi\} \in C$ or $\{\neg\phi\} \in C$, or $\{\phi, \neg\phi\} \in C$, and

4. $\prec$ is an acyclic binary relation on the non-strict rules in R.

The set C in a defeasible theory represents minimal sets of conflicting formulas. Conflicting formulas may be inconsistent, as with ϕ and $\neg\phi$. But if we allow the possibility that a moral dilemma might not constitute a contradiction, we still might want to include $\{\bigcirc\phi, \bigcirc\neg\phi\}$ in the conflicts set of a theory. If the strict rule $\{\phi, \psi\}{\rightarrow}\neg\chi$ were in a theory, we might also include $\{\phi, \psi, \chi\}$ in the conflicts set C. If we used this criterion, we would include $\{\phi\}$ in C in peculiar theories where $\{\phi\}{\rightarrow}\neg\phi \in R$. (We will discuss criteria for conflicts sets in more detail below.) We will call the members of C *conflict* (no plural) *sets.* The ultimate purpose of the set of conflict sets is to determine sets of competing rules. This is crucial for our proof theory. We immediately define two further notions involving conflicts sets which will prove useful.

Definition 2 *Let $T = \langle F, R, C, \prec \rangle$ be a defeasible theory and let ϕ be a formula. Then $\phi \asymp_T C_\phi$ iff $\{\phi\} \cup C_\phi \in C$ and $C_\phi \notin C$.*

Definition 3 *Let $T = \langle F, R, C, \prec \rangle$ be a defeasible theory and let S be a set of formulas. Then C_R covers S in T iff C_R is a subset of R such that for each $\phi \in S - F$, there is exactly one rule in C_R that has ϕ as its consequent.*

We want to define a defeasible consequence relation between defeasible theories and formulas. We notice immediately that there should be a distinction between what can be derived from the facts and strict rules in a theory and what can be derived from the entire theory. We also notice that what can be derived from a theory T depends on what cannot be derived from T. Consider a defeasible rule $A{\Rightarrow}\phi$. If $\phi \asymp_T C_\phi$ and C_R covers C_ϕ in T, then before we can detach the consequent of $A{\Rightarrow}\phi$ we will need to show that there is at least one rule $r \in C_R$ such that either the antecedent of r is not derivable from the theory or r cannot be used to defeat $A{\Rightarrow}\phi$ for some other reason such as that it is inferior to $A{\Rightarrow}\phi$ ($r \prec A{\Rightarrow}\phi$). In other words, we will sometimes have to *refute* the antecedent of a rule. As it turns out, we will also need to distinguish between refuting a set of formulas strictly (demonstrating that it cannot be derived strictly) and refuting a set of formulas defeasibly (demonstrating that it cannot be derived even using the defeasible rules in the theory.) So our defeasible consequence relation encompasses four subrelations: strict derivability, strict refutability, defeasible derivability, and defeasible refutability. Rather than a relation between theories and formulas, our defeasible derivability relation will actually be represented as a relation between theories, a set of four symbols ($\vdash$, $\dashv$, $\vdash\!\!\!\sim$, and $\dashv\!\!\!\sim$), and formulas. For convenience, we will define a term that refers to triples with just these components.

Definition 4 *A* **defeasible assertion** *is a triple* $\langle T, \vdash, \phi \rangle$, $\langle T, \dashv, \phi \rangle$, $\langle T, \mathrel{\vdash\!\!\!\sim}, \phi \rangle$, *or* $\langle T, \mathrel{\dashv\!\!\!\sim}, \phi \rangle$ *such that* T *is a defeasible theory and* ϕ *is a formula.*

For notational simplicity, we will write $T \vdash \phi$ for $\langle T, \vdash, \phi \rangle$, etc.

Of course, a defeasible consequence relation can't be just any set of defeasible assertions. Given our intentions, a formula derivable using only the strict rules should certainly be derivable using all the rules, and a demonstration that a formula cannot be derived using all the rules surely should also demonstrate that the same formula cannot be derived using only the strict rules in a theory. Furthermore, a formula should not be both strictly derivable and strictly refutable. Nor should it be both defeasibly derivable and defeasibly refutable. Of course, it may be possible to derive a formula using the defeasible rules in a theory even though it is demonstrably not possible to derive the same formula using only the strict rules in the theory. So a formula might be both defeasibly derivable and strictly refutable. These four conditions constitute coherence conditions on defeasible consequence relations.

Definition 5 *A* **defeasible consequence relation** *is a set* Σ *of defeasible assertions such that for every defeasible theory* T *and every formula* ϕ,

1. *if* $T \vdash \phi \in \Sigma$, *then* $T \mathrel{\vdash\!\!\!\sim} \phi \in \Sigma$,
2. *if* $T \mathrel{\dashv\!\!\!\sim} \phi \in \Sigma$, *then* $T \dashv \phi \in \Sigma$,
3. *if* $T \vdash \phi \in \Sigma$, *then* $T \dashv \phi \notin \Sigma$, *and*
4. *if* $T \mathrel{\vdash\!\!\!\sim} \phi \in \Sigma$, *then* $T \mathrel{\dashv\!\!\!\sim} \phi \notin \Sigma$.

As it is notationally awkward to have to say continually that defeasible assertions are members of consequence relations, we will instead subscript our four symbols $\vdash$, $\dashv$, $\mathrel{\vdash\!\!\!\sim}$, and $\mathrel{\dashv\!\!\!\sim}$ with a term denoting the consequence relation to which the assertion belongs. It will also be convenient to extend this notation to represent a relation between theories and sets of formulas. We include the deontic cases here even though we will not need them in this section.

Definition 6 *Let* Σ *be a defeasible consequence relation,* T *be a defeasible theory,* ϕ *be a formula, and* A *be a set of formulas.*

1. $T \vdash_\Sigma \phi$ *iff* $T \vdash \phi \in \Sigma$.
2. $T \dashv_\Sigma \phi$ *iff* $T \dashv \phi \in \Sigma$.
3. $T \mathrel{\vdash\!\!\!\sim}_\Sigma \phi$ *iff* $T \mathrel{\vdash\!\!\!\sim} \phi \in \Sigma$.
4. $T \mathrel{\dashv\!\!\!\sim}_\Sigma \phi$ *iff* $T \mathrel{\dashv\!\!\!\sim} \phi \in \Sigma$.
5. $T \vdash_\Sigma A$ *iff for every* $\phi \in A$, $T \vdash_\Sigma \phi$.
6. $T \dashv_\Sigma A$ *iff there is* $\phi \in A$ *such that* $T \dashv_\Sigma \phi$.
7. $T \mathrel{\vdash\!\!\!\sim}_\Sigma A$ *iff for every* $\phi \in A$, $T \mathrel{\vdash\!\!\!\sim}_\Sigma \phi$.
8. $T \mathrel{\dashv\!\!\!\sim}_\Sigma A$ *iff there is* $\phi \in A$ *such that* $T \mathrel{\dashv\!\!\!\sim}_\Sigma \phi$.
9. $T \vdash_\Sigma \bigcirc A$ *iff for every literal* $\phi \in A$ *and every deontic formula* $\bigcirc \phi \in A$, $T \vdash_\Sigma \bigcirc \phi$.

10. $T \dashv_\Sigma \bigcirc A$ iff there is literal $\phi \in A$ or deontic formula $\bigcirc\phi \in A$ such that $T \dashv_\Sigma \bigcirc \phi$.

11. $T \vdash_\Sigma \bigcirc A$ iff for every literal $\phi \in A$ and every deontic formula $\bigcirc\phi \in A$, $T \vdash_\Sigma \bigcirc \phi$.

12. $T \nvdash_\Sigma \bigcirc A$ iff there is literal $\phi \in A$ or deontic formula $\bigcirc\phi \in A$ such that $T \nvdash_\Sigma \bigcirc \phi$.

Besides the coherence conditions included in the definition of a defeasible consequence relation, there are other conditions that appear attractive. In stating these, and throughout the rest of this paper, I use F_T to denote the facts, R_T to denote the rules, C_T to denote the conflicts set, and $\prec_T$ to denote the superiority relation for the defeasible theory T.

Strict Derivation: If $\phi \in F_T$ or if there is $A{\rightarrow}\phi \in R_T$ such that $T \vdash_\Sigma A$, then $T \vdash_\Sigma \phi$.

Strict Refutation: If $\phi \notin F_T$ and for all $A{\rightarrow} \in R_T, T \dashv_\Sigma A$, then $T \dashv_\Sigma \phi$.

Immediate Defeasible Derivation: If $T \vdash_\Sigma \phi$, then $T \vdash_\Sigma \phi$.

Semi-strict Derivation: If there is $A{\rightarrow}\phi \in R_T$ such that

1. $T \vdash_\Sigma A$,
2. for all $\phi \asymp_T C_\phi, T \dashv_\Sigma C_\phi$, and
3. for all $\phi \asymp_T C_\phi$ and C_R covering C_ϕ in T such that every member of C_R is strict, there is $B{\rightarrow}\psi \in C_R$ such that $T \nvdash_\Sigma B$,

then $T \vdash_\Sigma \phi$.

Defeasible Derivation: If there is $A{\Rightarrow}\phi \in R_T$ such that

1. $T \vdash_\Sigma A$,
2. for all $\phi \asymp_T C_\phi, T \dashv_\Sigma C_\psi$,
3. for all $\phi \asymp_T C_\phi$ and C_R covering C_ϕ in T, either

   (a) there is $B{\rightarrow}\psi \in C_R$ $[B{\Rightarrow}\psi \in C_R, B{\rightsquigarrow}\psi \in C_R]$ such that $T \nvdash_\Sigma B$, or

   (b) for some $B{\Rightarrow}\psi \in C_R$ $[B{\rightsquigarrow}\psi \in C_R], B{\Rightarrow}\psi \prec_T A{\Rightarrow}\phi$ $[B{\rightsquigarrow}\phi \prec_T A{\Rightarrow}\phi]$.

then $T \vdash_\Sigma \phi$.

Defeasible Refutation: If

1. (NB: Demonstrate that Immediate Defeasible Derivation fails) $T \dashv_\Sigma \phi$ and
2. (NB: Demonstrate that Semi-strict Derivation fails) for each $A{\rightarrow}\phi \in R_T$, either

(a) $T \not\vdash_{\Sigma} A$,

(b) there is $\phi \asymp_T C_\phi$ such that $T \vdash C_\phi$, or

(c) there is $\phi \asymp_T C_\phi$ and C_R covering C_ϕ in T such that every rule in C_R is strict and for each $B \rightarrow \psi \in C_R, T \not\sim_{\Sigma} B$;

and

3. (NB: Demonstrate that Defeasible Derivation fails) for each $A \Rightarrow \phi \in R_T$, either

(a) $T \not\vdash_{\Sigma} A$,

(b) there is $\phi \asymp_T C_\phi$ such that $T \vdash C_\psi$, or

(c) there is $\phi \asymp_T C_\phi$ and C_R covering C_ϕ in T such that

   i. for all $B \rightarrow \psi \in C_R$ $[B \Rightarrow \psi \in C_R, B \leadsto \psi \in C_R], T \vdash B$,

   ii. for all $B \Rightarrow \psi \in C_R$ $[B \leadsto \psi \in R], B \Rightarrow \psi \not\prec A \Rightarrow \phi$ $[B \leadsto \psi \not\prec A \Rightarrow \phi]$.

then $T \not\vdash_{\Sigma} \phi$.

Condition 3.b in the Defeasible Derivation principle might be strengthened. A rule that has been defeated by superior strict and defeasible rules should not be allowed to defeat any other defeasible rule. Its power as a defeater has been *preempted*, and the principle represented by this condition is called *preemption*.

To see how preemption works, consider a "Double Tweety Triangle." We assume that (defeasibly) movie stars are rich, that (defeasibly) movie stars are not Republicans, and that (defeasibly) rich people are Republicans. We also assume that (defeasibly) southerners are conservative, that (defeasibly) southerners are not Republicans, and that (defeasibly) conservatives are Republicans. What are we to make of Kim Bassinger, a southern movie star? The intuitive response seems to be that the evidence is against her being a Republican. But neither of the rules with that conclusion is more specific or in any other way superior to the rules for the contrary conclusion. (We will discuss specificity and the original Tweety Triangle in the next section.) However, since movie stars tend to be rich, the rule for movie stars is more specific than and thus to be preferred over the rule for rich people. Since it has been defeated by a superior rule, the rule for rich people cannot defeat the rule that says southerners tend not to be Republicans. Similarly, since southerners tend to be conservative, the rule for southerners is more specific than and thus to be preferred over the rule for conservatives. Since it has been defeated by a superior rule, the rule for conservatives cannot defeat the rule that says movie stars tend not to be Republicans. So neither of the two rules supporting the conclusion that Kim Bassinger is not a Republican is defeated.

A potential defeater should only be preempted when it is defeated by strict rules or superior *defeasible rules*, not by superior *undercutting defeaters*. For example we know penguins are birds, (defeasibly) birds fly, and (defeasibly) penguins don't fly (the original Tweety Triangle.) But consider a penguin that has been altered genetically so that it has large wings and flight muscles. Would such a penguin fly? Perhaps it would. So we might adopt the undercutting defeater, genetically altered penguins *might* fly. This defeater is more specific than our penguin rule. If we allow it to preempt the penguin rule, then the bird rule is reinstated and we can conclude that our genetically altered penguin (since it is a bird) *does* fly. But intuitively this is too strong: we should reserve judgement. A rule should only be preempted as a potential defeater if it is *rebutted* by superior defeasible rules, but it is not preempted if it is only *undercut* by a superior defeater.

Such a preemption principle would make our proof theory much more complicated. Since preemption doesn't play a role in any familiar examples that involve normative concepts in an essential way, I have not attempted to incorporate preemption in the system presented in this paper.[1]

Next we want to define a defeasible consequence relation that satisfies the conditions listed above. We will do this by defining a proof theory for defeasible logic and then identifying the consequence relation with exactly those defeasible assertions for which proofs exist. A proof will be a finite sequence of defeasible assertions satisfying certain conditions corresponding to the conditions on consequence relations listed above. To make the statement of these conditions simpler, we will first define what it means for certain statements about theories and sets of formulas to succeed at some point in a sequence of defeasible assertions. Again, we include the deontic cases for later use.

Definition 7 *Let σ be a finite sequence of defeasible assertions and let $k \leq \ell(\sigma)$.*

1. *$T \vdash A$ **succeeds at** σ_k iff for every $\phi \in A$, there is $j < k$ such that $\sigma_j = T \vdash \phi$.*
2. *$T \dashv A$ **succeeds at** σ_k iff there is $\phi \in A$ and $j < k$ such that $\sigma_j = T \dashv \phi$.*
3. *$T \mathrel{\vdash\mkern-7mu\sim} A$ **succeeds at** σ_k iff for every $\phi \in A$, there is $j < k$ such that $\sigma_j = T \mathrel{\vdash\mkern-7mu\sim} \phi$.*
4. *$T \mathrel{\dashv\mkern-7mu\sim} A$ **succeeds at** σ_k iff there is $\phi \in A$ and $j < k$ such that $\sigma_j = T \mathrel{\dashv\mkern-7mu\sim} \phi$.*
5. *$T \vdash \bigcirc A$ **succeeds at** σ_k iff for every literal $\phi \in A$ and deontic formula $\bigcirc\phi \in A$, there is $j < k$ such that $\sigma_j = T \vdash \bigcirc \phi$.*
6. *$T \dashv \bigcirc A$ **succeeds at** σ_k iff there is literal $\phi \in A$ or deontic formula $\bigcirc\phi \in A$ such that for some $j < k$, $\sigma_j = T \dashv \bigcirc \phi$.*

---

[1]The versions of Defeasible Derivation and Defeasible Refutation found in (Nute, 1992) got the preemption principle wrong. I thank David Billington for bringing this problem to my attention.

7. $T \mathrel{\not\mapsto} \bigcirc A$ **succeeds at** σ_k *iff for every literal* $\phi \in A$ *and deontic formula* $\bigcirc \phi \in A$, *there is* $j < k$ *such that* $\sigma_j = T \mathrel{\mapsto} \bigcirc \phi$.

8. $T \mathrel{\rightsquigarrow} \bigcirc A$ **succeeds at** σ_k *iff there is literal* $\phi \in A$ *or deontic formula* $\bigcirc \phi \in A$ *such that for some* $j < k$, $\sigma_j = T \mathrel{\rightsquigarrow} \bigcirc \phi$.

Definition 8 *An* **SD-proof** *in a defeasible theory* $T = \langle F, R, C, \prec \rangle$ *is a sequence* σ *of defeasible assertions such that for each* $k \leq \ell(\sigma)$, *one of the following holds.*

$[\mathbf{M^+}]$ $\sigma_k = T \vdash \phi$ and either $\phi \in F$ or there is $A \rightarrow \phi \in R$ such that $T \vdash A$ succeeds at σ_k.

$[\mathbf{M^-}]$ $\sigma_k = T \dashv \phi$, $\phi \notin F$, and for each $A \rightarrow \phi \in R$, $T \dashv A$ succeeds at σ_k.

$[\mathbf{E^+}]$ $\sigma_k = T \mathrel{\not\mapsto} \phi$ and $T \vdash \{\phi\}$ succeeds at σ_k.

$[\mathbf{SS^+}]$ $\sigma_k = T \mathrel{\not\mapsto} \phi$ and there is $A \rightarrow \phi \in R$ such that

1. $T \mathrel{\not\mapsto} A$ succeeds at σ_k,
2. for each $\phi \asymp_T C_\phi$, $T \dashv C_\phi$ succeeds at σ_k, and
3. for each $\phi \asymp_T C_\phi$ and C_R covering C_ϕ in T such that every member of C_R is strict, there is $B \rightarrow \psi \in C_R$ such that $T \mathrel{\rightsquigarrow} B$ succeeds at σ_k.

$[\mathbf{SD^+}]$: $\sigma_k = T \mathrel{\not\mapsto} \phi$ and there is $A \Rightarrow \phi \in R$ such that

1. $T \mathrel{\not\mapsto} A$ succeeds at σ_k,
2. for each $\phi \asymp_T C_\phi$ there is $\psi \in C_\phi$ such that $T \dashv \{\psi\}$ succeeds at σ_k, and
3. for each $\phi \asymp_T C_\phi$ and C_R covering C_ϕ in T, either
   (a) there is $\psi \in C_\phi$ and $B \Rightarrow \psi \in C_R$ $[B \Rightarrow \psi \in C_R, B \rightsquigarrow \psi \in R]$ such that $T \mathrel{\rightsquigarrow} B$ succeeds at σ_k, or
   (b) for some $B \Rightarrow \psi \in C_R$ $[B \rightsquigarrow \psi \in R]$, $B \Rightarrow \psi \prec_T A \Rightarrow \phi$ $[B \rightsquigarrow \psi \prec_T A \Rightarrow \phi]$.

$[\mathbf{SD^-}]$: $\sigma_k = T \mathrel{\rightsquigarrow} \phi$ and

1. (NB: demonstrate that $[\mathbf{E^+}]$ fails.) $T \dashv \{\phi\}$ succeeds at σ_k;
2. (NB: demonstrate that $[\mathbf{SS^+}]$ fails.) for each $A \rightarrow \phi \in R$, either
   (a) $T \mathrel{\rightsquigarrow} A$ succeeds at σ_k,
   (b) there is $\phi \asymp_T C_\phi$ such $T \vdash C_\phi$ succeeds at σ_k, or
   (c) there is $\phi \asymp_T C_\phi$ and C_R covering C_ϕ such that every member of C_R is strict and for each $B \rightarrow \psi \in C_R$, $T \mathrel{\not\mapsto} B$ succeeds at σ_k; and
3. (NB: demonstrate that $[\mathbf{SD^+}]$ fails.) for each $A \Rightarrow \phi \in R$, either
   (a) $T \mathrel{\rightsquigarrow} A$ succeeds at σ_k,
   (b) there is $\phi \asymp_T C_\phi$ such that $T \vdash C_\phi$ succeeds at σ_k, or

(c) there is $\phi \asymp_T C_\phi$ and C_R covering C_ϕ in T such that

    i. for all $B{\rightarrow}\psi \in C_R$ $[B{\Rightarrow}\psi \in C_R,\ B{\rightsquigarrow}\psi \in C_R]$, $T \hspace{0.5pt}\vdash\hspace{-6pt}\shortmid\hspace{2pt} B$ succeeds at σ_k, and

    ii. for all $B{\Rightarrow}\psi \in C_R$ $[B{\rightsquigarrow}\psi \in R]$, $B{\Rightarrow}\psi \not\prec A{\Rightarrow}\phi$ $[B{\rightsquigarrow}\psi \not\prec A{\Rightarrow}\phi]$.

With our proof theory in place, we can define our defeasible consequence relation.

Definition 9 SD $= \{\sigma_{\ell(\sigma)} :$ *for some defeasible theory T, σ is an SD-proof in T*$\}$.

Theorem 1 SD *is a defeasible consequence relation.*

Proof: Condition 1 of Definition 5 follows from E^+, and Condition 2 of Definition 5 follows from Condition 1 of SD^-.

Let σ and τ be **SD**-proofs. We will show by mathematical induction that there is no literal ϕ, $i \le \ell(\sigma)$, and $j \le \ell(\tau)$ such that either $\sigma_i = T \vdash \phi$ and $\tau_j = T \dashv \phi$, or $\sigma_i = T \hspace{0.5pt}\vdash\hspace{-6pt}\shortmid\hspace{2pt} \phi$ and $\tau_j = T \hspace{0.5pt}\dashv\hspace{-8pt}\shortmid\hspace{4pt} \phi$. Since our selection of σ and τ is arbitrary, and by Definition 9, this will show that **SD** satisfies Conditions 4 and 5 of Definition 5.

Basis step: Suppose $\sigma_1 = T \vdash \phi$ and for some $i \le \ell(\tau)$, $\tau_i = T \dashv \phi$. Then by Definition 8, σ_1 satisfies M^+ and τ_i satisfies M^-. But then since σ has no earlier members, $\phi \in F_T$ and $\phi \notin F_T$, which is impossible.

Suppose $\sigma_1 = T \hspace{0.5pt}\vdash\hspace{-6pt}\shortmid\hspace{2pt} \phi$. Then by Definition 8, τ_i satisfies SD^- and $T \dashv \{\phi\}$ succeeds at σ_1. By Definition 7, σ has a member earlier than σ_1. But this is impossible.

Induction step: Let $k > 1$ and suppose that there do not exist literal ϕ, $i < k$, and $j \le \ell(\tau)$ such that either $\sigma_i = T \vdash \phi$ and $\tau_j = T \dashv \phi$, or $\sigma_i = T \hspace{0.5pt}\vdash\hspace{-6pt}\shortmid\hspace{2pt} \phi$ and $\tau_j = T \hspace{0.5pt}\dashv\hspace{-8pt}\shortmid\hspace{4pt} \phi$.

Suppose $\sigma_k = T \vdash \phi$ and for some $i \le \ell(\tau)$, $\tau_i = T \dashv \phi$. Then by Definition 8, σ_k satisfies M^+ and τ_i satisfies M^-. By M^-, $\phi \notin T$. So by M^+, let $A{\rightarrow}\phi \in R_T$ such that $T \dashv A$ succeeds at τ_i. By Definition 7, this contradicts our inductive hypothesis.

Suppose $\sigma_k = T \hspace{0.5pt}\vdash\hspace{-6pt}\shortmid\hspace{2pt} \phi$ and $i \le \ell(\tau)$ such that $\tau_i = T \hspace{0.5pt}\dashv\hspace{-8pt}\shortmid\hspace{4pt} \phi$. Then by Definition 8, σ_k satisfies E^+, SS^+, or SD^+, and τ_i satisfies EE^- or SD^-.

Case 1: σ_k satisfies E^+. Then $T \vdash \{\phi\}$ succeeds at σ_k and $T \dashv \{\phi\}$ succeeds at τ_i. By Definition 7, this contradicts our inductive hypothesis.

Case 2: σ_k satisfies SS^+. Let $A{\rightarrow}\phi \in R_T$ such that $A{\rightarrow}\phi$ satisfies the conditions of SS^+. Without pursuing the details, and since τ_i satisfies SD^-, we see that the three subconditions of Condition 2, SD^- together with the corresponding conditions of SS^+ contradict our inductive hypothesis.

Case 3: σ_k satisfies SD^+. Let $A{\Rightarrow}\phi \in R_T$ satisfy the conditions of SD^+. Then each subcondition of Condition 3, SD^- together with the corresponding condition of SD^+ leads to a contradiction of our inductive hypothesis. ∎

4. CONFLICTS SETS AND PRECEDENCE RELATIONS

By the definition of a conflicts set, every formula conflicts with its complement (unless we have the pathological case where a formula conflicts with itself.) If this is the only kind of conflict we recognize, our conflicts set is minimal. In (Nute, 1992), the implicit conflicts set built into each defeasible theory is minimal in this sense.

Definition 10 $C_{\min} = \{\{\phi, \neg\phi\} : \phi \text{ is a literal }\}$.

We can use the strict rules in a theory to extend the notion of the conflicts set for a theory. This has been suggested in (Schurtz, 1994) and elsewhere.

Definition 11 *Let R be a set of rules. Then C is an R-closed conflicts set iff C is a conflicts set and for every set of literals S, if*

1. *there is a literal ϕ such that $\langle S, R, \emptyset, \emptyset \rangle \vdash_{SD} \phi$ and $\langle S, R, \emptyset, \emptyset \rangle \vdash_{SD} \neg\phi$, and*
2. *there is no literal ϕ and proper subset S^* of S such that $\langle S^*, R, \emptyset, \emptyset \rangle \vdash_{SD} \phi$ and $\langle S^*, R, \emptyset, \emptyset \rangle \vdash_{SD} \neg\phi$,*

then $S \in C$.

Definition 12 *A defeasible theory T is conflict-closed iff C_T is the smallest R_T-closed conflicts set.*

Definition 13 *Let $T = \langle F, R, C, \prec \rangle$ be a defeasible theory. Then T is a deontically-closed theory iff for every set of literals $\{\phi_1, \ldots, \phi_n\} \in C$, $\{\psi_1, \ldots, \psi_n\} \in C$ where for $\psi_1 = \bigcirc\phi_1$ or $\psi_1 = \bigcirc\phi_1$, and for each $1 < i \leq n$, ψ_i is $\bigcirc\phi_i$.*

The point of this definition, of course, is that if some set of literals are in conflict, then there is some constraint against all of them being obligatory, or if all but one of them is obligatory, there is some constraint against permitting the remaining literal which is not obligatory. This will not make it impossible to generate moral dilemmas in deontically closed theories, but it will make it more difficult.

Since the notion of a conflict-closed theory depends only on the strict rules in the theory, one might expect that this notion is monotonic, that is, if T is conflict-closed and we add facts and rules to T, then we need only add sets to C_T to produce a conflict-closed extension T^* of T. But this is incorrect. Suppose $\{\phi, \psi, \chi\} \in C_T$. If we add $\phi \rightarrow \sim \psi$ to R_T, then the appropriate conflicts set for our new conflict-closed extension must contain $\{\phi, \psi\}$. But then $\{\phi, \psi, \chi\}$ is no longer a *smallest* set of the sort required and must be discarded. So, unfortunately, the notion of a conflict-closed theory is nonmonotonic. If we are interested in conflict-closed theories and we add strict rules to a theory, we may well have to recompute the conflicts set for the theory. However, if we extend a conflict-closed theory by adding facts and nonstrict rules to the original theory, the extended theory remains conflict-closed.

It is commonly held that more specific rules are superior to less specific rules. A rule $A \Rightarrow \phi$ is considered more specific than a rule $B \Rightarrow \psi$ [$B \rightsquigarrow \psi$] within a theory T just in case we can derive B from A together with the rules in T (omitting any presumptions in T), but we can't derive all of A from B together with the rules in T (again omitting any presumptions.) To state this condition precisely, we will let $R^\circ = \{r : r \in R$ and the antecedent of r is not empty $\}$.

Definition 14 *Let $\Gamma \subseteq C_T$. Then T is Γ-specific iff for all $r_1, r_2 \in R_T$ such that $(r_1, r_2) \notin \Gamma$, A is the antecedent of r_1, and B is the antecedent of R_2,*

    1. if $\langle A, R_T^\circ, C_T, \prec_T \rangle \vdash_{SD} B$ and $\langle B, R_T^\circ, C_T, \prec_T \rangle \dashv_{SD} A$, then $r_2 \prec_T$ r_1, and

    2. if $\langle A, R_T^\circ, C_T, \prec_T \rangle \dashv_{SD} B$ or $\langle B, R_T^\circ, C_T, \prec_T \rangle \vdash_{SD} A$, then $r_2 \nprec_T r_1$.

An interesting case is the $\emptyset$-specific theory. In such a theory, which we will say **preserves specificity**, one rule takes precedence over another if and only if the first is more specific than the second. But we may want to specify that some rules take precedence over others regardless of specificity, for example, that federal law takes precedence over state law. If we let Γ be the set of pairs (r_s, r_f) where each r_s is the law of some particular state and each r_f is a federal law, then Γ represents this principle of *lex superior*. The corresponding Γ-specific theory will then use specificity alone to adjudicate between two federal laws or two state laws, but any federal law will override any state law regardless of specificity. If a theory T is Γ-specific, we will say that Γ is a *core precedence relation* for T. In our example, we could say informally that *lex superior* was a core precedence relation for our hypothetical legal system. Of course, a theory may have more than one core precedence relation.

Notice that T might be Γ-specific for some Γ and yet the theory $T^* = \langle F_T, R_T \cup R, C_T, \prec_T \rangle$ may not be Γ-specific. Rule r_1 might be more specific than rule r_2 is theory T, but if we add rules to T, we may produce a theory in which this is no longer the case. Consider a theory T such that $R_T = \{\phi \Rightarrow \psi, \psi \Rightarrow \chi, \chi \Rightarrow \theta, \phi \Rightarrow \sim\theta\}$. The two rules $\phi \Rightarrow \sim\theta$ and $\chi \Rightarrow \theta$ will conflict for the minimal conflicts set. In T, $\phi \Rightarrow \sim\theta$ is more specific than $\chi \Rightarrow \theta$. But if we add the rule $\phi \Rightarrow \sim\chi$ to R_T, $\phi \Rightarrow \sim\theta$ is not more specific than $\chi \Rightarrow \theta$ in the resulting theory. So specificity is itself nonmonotonic. However, if we add only facts and presumptions to a Γ-specific theory, the resulting extension will also be Γ-specific.

To see how we can use such definitions for conflicts sets and precedence relations in our derivations, let's consider the simple Tweety Triangle example. Our single initial fact is that Tweety is a penguin. Our rules are that Tweety is a bird if he is a penguin, Tweety defeasibly flies if he is a bird, and Tweety defeasibly does not fly if he is a penguin. Let

$$R = \{p \rightarrow b, b \Rightarrow f, p \Rightarrow \sim f\}$$

and let

$$T = \langle \{p\}, R, C_{\min}, \prec \rangle$$

such that T preserves specificity. We want to show that $T \mathrel{\vdash\mkern-10mu\vee} \sim f$. First, we need two subderivations. The first shows that $p \Rightarrow \sim f$ is at least as specific as $b \Rightarrow f$.

1. $\langle \{p\}, R^\circ, C_{\min}, \prec \rangle \vdash p$ by M^+.
2. $\langle \{p\}, R^\circ, C_{\min}, \prec \rangle \vdash b$ by M^+.
3. $\langle \{p\}, R^\circ, C_{\min}, \prec \rangle \mathrel{\vdash\mkern-10mu\vee} b$ by E^+.

The second subderivation shows that $b \Rightarrow f$ is not at least as specific as $p \Rightarrow \sim f$.

1. $\langle \{b\}, R^\circ, C_{\min}, \prec \rangle \dashv p$ by M^-.
2. $\langle \{b\}, R^\circ, C_{\min}, \prec \rangle \mathrel{\dashv\mkern-10mu\wedge} p$ by SD^- (since there are no rules with p as consequent.)

Since T preserves specificity, this shows that

$$b \Rightarrow f \prec p \Rightarrow \sim f$$

Now we have our main derivation:

1. $T \vdash p$ by M^+.
2. $T \mathrel{\vdash\mkern-10mu\vee} p$ by E^+.
3. $T \dashv \sim f$ by M^-.
4. $T \mathrel{\vdash\mkern-10mu\vee} \sim f$ by SD^+.

The last line in this derivation requires some comment. Since $\{f, \sim f\}$ is the only member of $C_{\min}$ containing f, $\{\sim f\}$ is the only set S such that $\phi \asymp_T S$. By examination of T, we see that $\{b \Rightarrow \sim f\}$ is the only subset of R covering $\{\sim f\}$. Thus, since $b \Rightarrow f \prec p \Rightarrow \sim f$, all the conditions of SD^+ hold.

When we turn to normative reasoning, we will be interested primarily in deontically-closed theories that have an explicit core precedence relation.

5. DEFEASIBLE DEONTIC INFERENCES

Recall that we want a deontic extension of defeasible logic that supports deontic inheritance, factual detachment, and deontic detachment. Furthermore, factual detachment should override deontic detachment whenever the two conflict. We haven't yet incorporated deontic inheritance and deontic detachment into our system, but both strict and defeasible factual detachment are integral components of **SD**, since Strict Derivation amounts to strict factual detachment and Defeasible Derivation amounts to defeasible factual detachment. We also have the ability in **SD** to prioritize normative rules. We will quickly consider some of the features of **SD** important for normative reasoning and then take on the task of extending **SD** to include our peculiarly deontic inference patterns.

We can represent *prima facie* and contrary-to-duty obligations using defeasible rules. The *prima facie* obligation that promises ought to be kept becomes $PromisedToDo(x, A) \Rightarrow \bigcirc Does(x, A)$. A conflicting rule might be $Disastrous(A) \rightarrow \bigcirc \sim Does(x, A)$ or $Disastrous(A) \Rightarrow \bigcirc \sim Does(x, A)$. Being strict, the first conflicting rule would always override the *prima facie* obligation to keep promises. For a defeasible competing rule, both the *prima facie* obligation and its competitor would be defeated unless the competitor was superior. Contrary-to-duty obligations such as the obligation to make reparations might look like $Harms(x, y) \Rightarrow \bigcirc MakesReparationsTo(x, y)$. What makes this a contrary-to-duty obligation is just that $\bigcirc \sim Harms(x, y)$ (or perhaps $\Rightarrow \bigcirc \sim Harms(x, y)$) is also in our theory.

Entailments are represented within our defeasible system by strict rules. Deontic inheritance, then, tells us that the consequent of a strict rule ought to be the case if its antecedent ought to be the case. For these purposes, it appears to make no difference whether the strict rule has the form $A \rightarrow \phi$ where ϕ is a literal, or the form $A \rightarrow \bigcirc \phi$ (which we might also classify as strict defeasible detachment.) We will include both versions when we formulate a new strict inference principle.

We want no corresponding principle of deontic inheritance for defeasible rules since deontic inheritance should hold only for entailments, that is, for strict rules. But we are left with the possibility of a semi-strict deontic inheritance and a semi-strict deontic detachment where the antecedent of the strict rule is only defeasibly obligatory. That is, suppose we have $T \vdash\!\!\!\sim \bigcirc A$ and either $A \rightarrow \phi \in R_T$ or $A \rightarrow \bigcirc \phi \in R_T$. Then we certainly have evidence that $\bigcirc \phi$. How does the strength of this evidence compare with various other cases? I propose that the strength of the various classes of possible principles should be in the order in which they appear in the following table.

Strict Principles:

$A \rightarrow \phi \in R_T$	and	$T \vdash A$	supports	$T \vdash \phi$
$A \rightarrow \phi \in R_T$	and	$T \vdash \bigcirc A$	supports	$T \vdash \bigcirc \phi$
$A \rightarrow \bigcirc \phi \in R_T$	and	$T \vdash \bigcirc A$	supports	$T \vdash \bigcirc \phi$

Semi-strict Principles:

$A \rightarrow \phi \in R_T$	and	$T \vdash\!\!\!\sim A$	supports	$T \vdash\!\!\!\sim \phi$
$A \rightarrow \phi \in R_T$	and	$T \vdash\!\!\!\sim \bigcirc A$	supports	$T \vdash\!\!\!\sim \bigcirc \phi$
$A \rightarrow \bigcirc \phi \in R_T$	and	$T \vdash\!\!\!\sim \bigcirc A$	supports	$T \vdash\!\!\!\sim \bigcirc \phi$

Defeasible Factual Detachment:

$A \Rightarrow \phi \in R_T$	and	$T \vdash\!\!\!\sim A$	supports	$T \vdash\!\!\!\sim \phi$

Defeasible Deontic Detachment:

$$A \Rightarrow \bigcirc \phi \in R_T \quad \text{and} \quad T \hspace{0.5mm}\vdash\hspace{-2mm}\sim\hspace{0.5mm} \bigcirc A \quad \text{supports} \quad T \hspace{0.5mm}\vdash\hspace{-2mm}\sim\hspace{0.5mm} \bigcirc \phi$$

Each group in this taxonomy is weaker than the group before it. Strict inferences cannot be defeated under any circumstances. Semi-strict inferences can be defeated by strict inferences or other semi-strict inferences. Defeasible factual detachments can be defeated by strict or semi-strict inferences or by other factual defeasible detachments. And defeasible deontic detachments can be defeated by any of the kinds of inference included in the taxonomy including other defeasible deontic detachments. Since we reject defeasible deontic inheritance, this taxonomy includes all relevant combinations of rules and ways to satisfy the antecedents of rules.

We begin developing our proof theory for defeasible deontic logic, then, by supplementing $[\mathbf{M}^+]$ with a new condition that incorporates all of our strict deontic inference principles.

$[\mathbf{DM}^+]$ $\sigma_k = T \vdash \bigcirc \phi$ and there is $A \rightarrow \phi \in R_T$ or $A \rightarrow \bigcirc \phi \in R_T$ such that $T \vdash \bigcirc A$ succeeds at σ_k.

Since we are adding $[\mathbf{DM}^+]$ to our proof theory, we need to replace $[\mathbf{M}^-]$ with a stronger refutation principle. This is necessary because a strict refutation must now demonstrate that both $[\mathbf{M}^+]$ and $[\mathbf{DM}^+]$ fail.

$[\mathbf{DM}^-]$ $\sigma_k = T \dashv \phi$,

1. $\phi \notin F$,
2. for each $A \rightarrow \phi \in R_T$, $T \dashv A$ succeeds at σ_k, and
3. if $\phi = \bigcirc \psi$, then for each $A \rightarrow \psi \in R$ or $A \rightarrow \bigcirc \psi \in R_T$, $T \dashv \bigcirc A$ succeeds at σ_k.

We cannot simply add a semi-strict deontic inference principle to our proof theory because the new deontic principles have the potential for defeating our previous semi-strict factual inferences. We will also have to replace $[\mathbf{SS}^+]$ with a new condition. But before we do this, we must modify the notion of a set of rules covering a set of literals. We must do this to take into account the possibility that we might detach $\bigcirc \phi$ from a rule that has ϕ as consequent.

Definition 15 *Let $T = \langle F, R, C, \prec \rangle$ be a defeasible theory and let S be a set of formulas. Then C_R **d-covers** S in T iff C_R is a subset of R such that for each $\phi \in S - F$, there is exactly one rule r in C_R such that either*

1. *ϕ is the consequent of r, or*
2. *r is strict, ψ is the consequent of r, and $\phi = \bigcirc \psi$.*

With this notion of a set of rules that deontically covers a set of literals, we are ready to formulate our replacement for $[\mathbf{SS}^+]$ and our new condition for semi-strict defeasible inheritance.

[SS$_\mathbf{D}^+$] $\sigma_k = T \mathrel{\vdash\!\!\!\!\!\!\vdash} \phi$ and there is $A\to\phi \in R_T$ such that

1. $T \mathrel{\vdash\!\!\!\!\!\!\vdash} A$ succeeds at σ_k,
2. for each $\phi \asymp_T C_\phi$ there is $\psi \in C_\phi$ such that $T \dashv \psi$ succeeds at σ_k, and
3. for each $\phi \asymp_T C_\phi$ and C_R d-covering C_ϕ in T such that every rule in C_R is strict, either

    (a) there is a literal $\psi \in C_\phi$ and $B\to\psi \in C_R$ such that $T \mathrel{\righttail} B$ succeeds at σ_k,

    (b) there is $\bigcirc\psi \in C_\phi$ and $B\to\psi \in C_R$ such that $T \mathrel{\righttail} \bigcirc B$ succeeds at σ_k, or

    (c) there is $\bigcirc\psi \in C_\phi$ and $B\to \bigcirc\psi \in C_R$ such that both $T \mathrel{\righttail} B$ and $T \mathrel{\righttail} \bigcirc B$ succeed at σ_k.

[DSS$^+$] $\sigma_k = T \mathrel{\vdash\!\!\!\!\!\!\vdash} \bigcirc\phi$ and there is $A\to\phi \in R_T$ or $A\to \bigcirc\phi \in R_T$ such that

1. $T \mathrel{\vdash\!\!\!\!\!\!\vdash} \bigcirc A$ succeeds at σ_k,
2. for each $\bigcirc\phi \asymp_T C_{\bigcirc\phi}$ there is $\psi \in C_{\bigcirc\phi}$ such that $T \dashv \psi$ succeeds at σ_k, and
3. for each $\bigcirc\phi \asymp_T C_{\bigcirc\phi}$ and C_R d-covering $C_{\bigcirc\phi}$ in T such that every rule in C_R is strict, either

    (a) there is a literal $\psi \in C_{\bigcirc\phi}$ and $B\to\psi \in C_R$ such that $T \mathrel{\righttail} B$ succeeds at σ_k,

    (b) there is $\bigcirc\psi \in C_{\bigcirc\phi}$ and $B\to\psi \in C_R$ such that $T \mathrel{\righttail} \bigcirc B$ succeeds at σ_k, or

    (c) there is $\bigcirc\psi \in C_{\bigcirc\phi}$ and $B\to \bigcirc\psi \in C_R$ such that both $T \mathrel{\righttail} B$ and $T \mathrel{\righttail} \bigcirc B$ succeed at σ_k.

We have to reformulate **[SD$^+$]** since it can now be defeated by semi-strict deontic inferences.

[DSD$^+$] $\sigma_k = T \mathrel{\vdash\!\!\!\!\!\!\vdash} \phi$ and there is $A\Rightarrow\phi \in R_T$ such that

1. $T \mathrel{\vdash\!\!\!\!\!\!\vdash} A$ succeeds at σ_k,
2. for each $\phi \asymp_T C_\phi$, there is $\psi \in C_\phi$ such that $T \dashv \psi$ succeeds at σ_k,
3. for each $\phi \asymp_T C_\phi$ and C_R d-covering C_ϕ in T, either

    (a) there is a literal $\psi \in C_\phi$ and $B\to\psi \in C_R$ such that $T \mathrel{\righttail} B$ succeeds at σ_k,

    (b) there is $\bigcirc\psi \in C_\phi$ and $B\to\psi \in C_R$ such that $T \mathrel{\righttail} \bigcirc B$ succeeds at σ_k,

    (c) there is $\bigcirc\psi \in C_\phi$ and $B\to \bigcirc\psi \in C_R$ such that both $T \mathrel{\righttail} B$ and $T \mathrel{\righttail} \bigcirc B$ succeed at σ_k, or

    (d) there is $B\Rightarrow\psi \in C_R$ $[B\rightsquigarrow\psi \in C_R]$ such that either

i. $T \dashv B$ succeeds at σ_k, or

ii. $B \Rightarrow \psi \prec_T A \Rightarrow \phi \ [B \leadsto \psi \prec_T A \Rightarrow \phi]$.

Next we formulate the condition for defeasible deontic detachment which is the weakest of our detachment principles. The basic requirements for defeasible deontic detachment, of course, will be that $A \Rightarrow \bigcirc \phi \in R_T$ and that $T \mathrel{\vdash\!\!\!\sim} \bigcirc A$. The conclusion of the corresponding defeasible deontic detachment will be that $T \mathrel{\vdash\!\!\!\sim} \bigcirc \phi$.

[**DDD$^+$**] $\sigma_k = T \mathrel{\vdash\!\!\!\sim} \bigcirc \phi$ and there is $A \Rightarrow \bigcirc \phi \in R_T$ such that

1. $T \mathrel{\vdash\!\!\!\sim} \bigcirc A$ succeeds at σ_k,
2. for each $\bigcirc \phi \asymp_T C_{\bigcirc \phi}$, there is $\psi \in C_{\bigcirc \phi}$ such that $T \dashv \psi$ succeeds at σ_k, and
3. for each $\bigcirc \phi \asymp_T C_{\bigcirc \phi}$ and C_R d-covering $C_{\bigcirc \phi}$ in T, either

   (a) there is a literal $\psi \in C_{\bigcirc \phi}$ and $B \rightarrow \psi \in C_R$ such that $T \dashv B$ succeeds at σ_k,

   (b) there is $\bigcirc \psi \in C_{\bigcirc \phi}$ and $B \rightarrow \psi \in C_R$ such that $T \dashv \bigcirc B$ succeeds at σ_k,

   (c) there is $\bigcirc \psi \in C_{\bigcirc \phi}$ and $B \rightarrow \bigcirc \psi \in C_R$ such that both $T \dashv B$ and $T \dashv \bigcirc B$ succeed at σ_k,

   (d) there is $B \Rightarrow \psi \in C_R \ [B \leadsto \psi \in C_R]$ such that either

      i. $T \dashv B$ succeeds at σ_k, or

      ii. $B \Rightarrow \psi \prec_T A \Rightarrow \bigcirc \phi \ [B \leadsto \psi \prec_T A \Rightarrow \bigcirc \phi]$, or

   (e) there is $B \Rightarrow \bigcirc \psi \in C_R \ [B \leadsto \bigcirc \psi \in C_R]$ such that either

      i. both $T \dashv B$ and $T \dashv \bigcirc B$ succeed at σ_k, or

      ii. $B \Rightarrow \bigcirc \psi \prec_T A \Rightarrow \bigcirc \phi \ [B \leadsto \bigcirc \psi \prec_T A \Rightarrow \bigcirc \phi]$.

This rule is so complex because there are so many ways that a defeasible deontic detachment can be defeated. Before we can perform a defeasible deontic detachment, we must demonstrate that the rule whose consequent we want to detach is not defeated in any of these ways. [**DSD$^+$**] and [**DDD$^+$**] are alike except for the extra Condition 3.e in [**DDD$^+$**]. In both cases, Condition 2 guarantees that the inference is not defeated by a competing strict factual inference, Condition 3.a guarantees that it is not defeated by a competing semi-strict factual inference, Conditions 3.b-c guarantee that it is not defeated by a competing strict or semi-strict deontic inheritance (or deontic detachment,) Condition 3.d, guarantees that the inference is not defeated by a competing defeasible factual inference, and Condition 3.e (occurring only in [**DDD$^+$**]), guarantees that the inference is not defeated by a competing defeasble deontic inference.

Finally, we will need a new rule for defeasible refutation. This rule will necessarily be quite complex since a defeasible refutation must include demonstrations that none of our positive rules succeeds.

[DSD⁻] $\sigma_k = T \not\vdash \phi$ and

1. (NB: demonstrate that **[M⁺]**, **[DM⁺]**, and **[E⁺]** fail.) $T \not\vdash \{\phi\}$ succeeds at σ_k;

2. (NB: demonstrate that **[SS⁺$_D$]** fails.) for each $A{\to}\phi \in R_T$, either

    (a) $T \not\vdash A$ succeeds at σ_k,

    (b) there is $\phi \asymp_T C_\phi$ such that $T \mathbin{\vdash\!\!\!\sim} C_\phi$ succeeds at σ_k, or

    (c) there is $\phi \asymp_T C_\phi$ and C_R d-covering C_ϕ in T such that every rule in C_R is strict,

        i. for each literal $\psi \in C_\phi$ and $B{\to}\psi \in C_R$, $T \mathbin{\vdash\!\!\!\sim} B$ succeeds in σ_k,

        ii. for each $\bigcirc\psi \in C_\phi$ and $B{\to}\psi \in C_R$, $T \mathbin{\vdash\!\!\!\sim} \bigcirc B$ succeeds at σ_k,

        iii. for each $\bigcirc\psi \in C_\phi$ and $B{\to} \bigcirc \psi \in C_R$, either $T \mathbin{\vdash\!\!\!\sim} B$ or $T \mathbin{\vdash\!\!\!\sim} \bigcirc B$ succeeds at σ_k,

3. (NB: demonstrate that **[DSS⁺]** fails.) for each $A{\to}\psi \in R_T$ or $A{\to} \bigcirc \psi \in R_T$ such that $\phi = \bigcirc\psi$, either

    (a) $T \not\vdash A$ and $T \not\vdash \bigcirc A$ both succeed at σ_k,

    (b) there is $\phi \asymp_T C_\phi$ such that for each $\psi \in C_\phi$, $T \vdash \psi$ succeeds at σ_k, or

    (c) there is $\phi \asymp_T C_\phi$ and C_R d-covering C_ϕ in T such that every rule in C_R is strict,

        i. for each literal $\chi \in C_\phi$ and $B{\to}\chi \in C_R$, $T \mathbin{\vdash\!\!\!\sim} B$ succeeds in σ_k,

        ii. for each $\bigcirc\chi \in C_\phi$ and $B{\to}\chi \in C_R$, $T \mathbin{\vdash\!\!\!\sim} \bigcirc B$ succeeds at σ_k,

        iii. for each $\bigcirc\chi \in C_\phi$ and $B{\to} \bigcirc \chi \in C_R$, either $T \mathbin{\vdash\!\!\!\sim} B$ or $T \mathbin{\vdash\!\!\!\sim} \bigcirc B$ succeeds at σ_k,

4. (NB: demonstrate that **[DSD⁺]** fails.) for each $A{\Rightarrow}\phi \in R_T$, either

    (a) $T \not\vdash A$ succeeds at σ_k,

    (b) there is $\phi \asymp_T C_\phi$ such that $T \vdash C_\phi$ succeeds at σ_k, or

    (c) there is $\phi \asymp_T C_\phi$ and C_R d-covering C_ϕ in T such that

        i. for each literal $\psi \in C_\phi$ and $B{\to}\psi \in C_R$, $T \mathbin{\vdash\!\!\!\sim} B$ succeeds at σ_k,

ii. for each $\bigcirc\psi \in C_\phi$ and $B{\rightarrow}\psi \in C_R$, $T \mathrel{\v:} \bigcirc B$ succeeds at σ_k, and

iii. for each $\bigcirc\psi \in C_\phi$ and $B{\rightarrow}\bigcirc\psi \in C_R$, either $T \mathrel{\v:} B$ or $T \mathrel{\v:} \bigcirc B$ succeeds at σ_k, and

iv. for every $B{\Rightarrow}\psi \in C_R$ [$B{\rightsquigarrow}\psi \in C_R$],

   A. $T \mathrel{\v:} B$ succeeds at σ_k, and

   B. $B{\Rightarrow}\psi \not\prec_T A{\Rightarrow}\phi$ [$B{\rightsquigarrow}\psi \not\prec_T A{\Rightarrow}\phi$],

5. (NB: demonstrate that [**DDD$^+$**] fails.) if $\phi = \bigcirc\psi$, then for each $A{\Rightarrow}\bigcirc\psi \in R_T$, either

(a) $T \mathrel{\rightthreetimes} \bigcirc A$ succeeds at σ_k,

(b) there is $\bigcirc\psi \asymp_T C_{\bigcirc\psi}$ such that $T \vdash C_{\bigcirc\psi}$ succeeds at σ_k, or

(c) there is $\bigcirc\psi \asymp_T C_{\bigcirc\psi}$ and C_R d-covering $C_{\bigcirc\psi}$ in T such that

  i. for each literal $\chi \in C_{\bigcirc\psi}$ and $B{\rightarrow}\chi \in C_R$, $T \mathrel{\v:} B$ succeeds at σ_k,

  ii. for each $\bigcirc\chi \in C_{\bigcirc\psi}$ and $B{\rightarrow}\bigcirc\chi \in C_R$, $T \mathrel{\rightthreetimes} B$ succeeds in σ_k,

  iii. for each $\bigcirc\chi \in C_{\bigcirc\psi}$ and $B{\rightarrow}\bigcirc\chi \in C_R$, either $T \mathrel{\v:} B$ or $T \mathrel{\v:} \bigcirc B$ succeeds at σ_k,

  iv. for each $B{\Rightarrow}\chi \in C_R$ [$B{\rightsquigarrow}\chi \in C_R$],

    A. $T \mathrel{\v:} B$ succeeds at σ_k,

    B. $B{\Rightarrow}\chi \not\prec_T A{\Rightarrow}\bigcirc\psi$ [$B{\rightsquigarrow}\chi \not\prec_T A{\Rightarrow}\bigcirc\psi$],

  v. for each $B{\Rightarrow}\bigcirc\chi \in C_R$ [$B{\rightsquigarrow}\bigcirc\chi \in C_R$],

    A. either $T \mathrel{\v:} B$ or $T \mathrel{\v:} \bigcirc B$ succeeds at σ_k,

    B. $B{\Rightarrow}\bigcirc\chi \not\prec_T A{\Rightarrow}\bigcirc\psi$ [$B{\rightsquigarrow}\bigcirc\chi \not\prec_T A{\Rightarrow}\bigcirc\psi$].

Definition 16 *A* **DSD-proof** *in a defeasible theory* $T = \langle F, R, C, \prec \rangle$ *is a sequence σ of defeasible assertions such that for each $k \leq \ell(\sigma)$, one of* [**M$^+$**], [**DM$^+$**], [**DM$^-$**], [**E$^+$**], [**E$^-$**], [**SS$_\mathbf{D}^+$**], [**DSS$^+$**], [**DSD$^+$**], [**DDD$^+$**], *or* [**DSD$^-$**] *hold.*

A precise statement of our proof theory is quite complicated. But the intuitions are fairly clear. All we need to remember is the taxonomy of inference principles at the beginning of this section.

1. Strict inferences are never defeated and defeat all non-strict competing principles. Familiar deontic inheritance is a strict inference.
2. Semi-strict principles can only be defeated by strict inferences and by other semi-strict inferences. We discovered a semi-strict version of deontic inheritance.
3. Defeasible factual detachment is weaker than any strict or semi-strict inferences. Defeasible factual detachments can also be defeated by other potential defeasible factual detachments.

4. Defeasible deontic detachment is the weakest kind of inference in our
   defeasible deontic logic.

Definition 17 DSD = $\{\sigma_{\ell(\sigma)} : for\ some\ defeasible\ theory\ T,\ \sigma\ is\ a\ DSD\text{-}proof$
in $T\}$.

Theorem 2 DSD *is a defeasible consequence relation.*

Proof: The proof is similar to that for Theorem 1.   ∎

6. PUZZLES AND PARADOXES

6.1. *Chisholm Examples*

Chisholm examples are easily resolved in **DSD**. Consider a typical example.
Jones ought to visit his mother. If Jones visits his mother, he ought to call her
and tell her he is coming. It ought to be that if Jones doesn't visit his mother,
he doesn't call her and tell her he is coming. In fact, Jones does not visit his
mother. The corresponding theory includes two facts and two rules.

1. $\bigcirc v$
2. $v \Rightarrow \bigcirc c$
3. $\sim v \Rightarrow \bigcirc \sim c$
4. $\sim v$

We will use $C_{\min}$ as our conflicts set and an empty precedence relation
to complete our theory T. We get the intuitive conclusion, $T \vdash_{DSD} \bigcirc \sim c$
from 3 and 4 by [**DSD**$^+$]. Furthermore, we get $T \nvdash_{DSD} \bigcirc c$ by [**DSD**$^-$]
because the application of [**DDD**$^+$] to 1 and 2 is barred since 2 and 3 compete
and [**DSD**$^+$] (factual detachment) takes precedence over [**DDD**$^+$] (deontic
detachment.)

6.2. *Reykjavik Examples*

Chisholm Examples involve a violated obligation where the obligation is
usually represented as an incontrovertible fact. Another kind of example
can be resolved if we represent certain initial obligations as *prima facie*
obligations using presumptions. Suppose there is a disarmament conference
at Reykjavik involving representatives of the United States, Russia, and Great
Britain. The U.S. President instructs his spokesperson not to reveal a certain
piece of information to either the Russian or the British negotiator. But he
also tells his spokesperson that if she should reveal the information to the
Russian negotiator, then she should reveal it to the British negotiator; and if
she reveals it to the British negotiator, then she should reveal it to the Russian
negotiator. Our theory then has four rules.

1. $\Rightarrow \bigcirc \sim r$
2. $\Rightarrow \bigcirc \sim b$

3. $r \Rightarrow \bigcirc b$
4. $b \Rightarrow \bigcirc r$

We complete our defeasible deontic theory T by adopting $C_{\mathbf{min}}$ as our conflicts set and making our theory specificity preserving. With no facts, we can derive $T \vdash_{DSD} \bigcirc \sim r$, $T \vdash_{DSD} \bigcirc \sim b$, $T \not\vdash_{DSD} \bigcirc r$, and $T \not\vdash_{DSD} \bigcirc b$. But if we add either r or b to our theory, we can derive $T \vdash_{DSD} \bigcirc r$, $T \vdash_{DSD} \bigcirc b$, $T \not\vdash_{DSD} \bigcirc \sim r$, and $T \not\vdash_{DSD} \bigcirc \sim b$. Once their antecedent conditions become apparent, the more specific rules override the competing presumptions as we would expect.

6.3. *Good Samaritan Examples*

I suggested earlier that defeasible reasoning did not hold the answer to the paradoxes of the Good Samaritan or the Gentle Murderer. I think the proper response to many of these examples is a more sophisticated representation of the cases described in these examples.

Let's take a closer look at the example of the Gentle Murderer. Stated in simple English, the example goes like this. Smith ought not to kill his mother, but if he does kill her, he ought to kill her gently. In fact he does kill his mother. Of course, killing his mother gently entails that he kills her. Since Jones kills his mother, we conclude by factual detachment that he ought to kill her gently. But since this entails killing her, we conclude by deontic inheritance that he ought to kill her. This violates our intuitions.

Below we have a representation of the example in our defeasible deontic language.

1. $\bigcirc \sim kill$
2. $kill \Rightarrow \bigcirc gently$
3. $gently \rightarrow kill$
4. $kill$

At best, using 2, we would derive $T \vdash_{DSD} \bigcirc gently$. Then we could only hope to obtain the objectionable conclusion $T \vdash_{DSD} \bigcirc kill$ by applying semi-strict inheritance to 3. But since 1 is a fact, we have $T \vdash_{DSD} \bigcirc \sim kill$ which blocks the competing semi-strict inference. So we don't get the objectionable result after all. As we would hope, $T \not\vdash_{DSD} \bigcirc kill$.

But we haven't really escaped the paradox. Another intuition is that Jones does have an apparent obligation to commit his murder gently. Suppose our theory T containing these facts and rules is deontically-closed. Then $(gently, \sim kill) \in C_T$ by 3, and $(\bigcirc gently, \bigcirc \sim kill) \in C_T$. Then

$$\bigcirc gently \asymp_T \{\bigcirc \sim kill\}$$

and there is $\bigcirc gently \asymp_T C$ such that $T \vdash_{DSD} C$. Thus, we can't derive $T \vdash_{DSD} \bigcirc gently$ as we want. We have escaped the objectionable result at the price of losing the force of the contrary-to-duty obligation.

Another way we might try to resolve the paradox is by insisting that the obligation not to kill is only a *prima facie* obligation. Then we would replace 1 with $\Rightarrow \bigcirc \sim kill$. But if our theory is deontically closed, this new presumption still competes with 2. We will only ever be able to detach the consequent of one of these defeasible rules no matter how we play with the precedence relation. And now that we have replaced 1 with a presumption, we will be forced to accept $T \vdash_{DSD} \bigcirc murder$ by semi-strict deontic inheritance if we ever derive $T \vdash_{DSD} \bigcirc gently$.

I think we must reject the rule 2 in the example and insist that this is an inadequate representation of the contrary-to-duty obligation in the example. What we must do is adopt a formalism in which we quantify over events and represent obligations that events have certain qualities. Then 2 becomes

$$Killing(e) \Rightarrow Gentle(e)$$

Where k is the event of Jones' kiling his mother, an instance of this general prescription would be

$$Killing(k) \Rightarrow Gentle(k)$$

What we require is not that the unfortunate event be a gentle *murder*, but that if his act is a murder, then it should be a *gentle* act. Then we do not have

$$Gentle(e) \rightarrow Killing(e)$$

since certainly not every gentle event is a killing. We are no longer blocked from concluding (with appropriate modifications to T) that we can derive all of the following.

1. $T \vdash_{DSD} \bigcirc \sim Killing(k)$
2. $T \vdash_{DSD} \bigcirc Gentle(k)$
3. $T \nvdash_{DSD} \bigcirc Killing(k)$

The Good Samaritan Paradox has a similar formulation, but the solution I would support is a bit different. I think this putative paradox rests on a confusion about the relative scopes of deontic operators and quantifiers, but I will not pursue the details here.

An interesting example that belongs to the general class of Good Samaritan examples is the Knower's Paradox.[2] The Knower's Paradox will not submit to the kind of event analysis I have put forward for the Gentle Murderer. Suppose an office manager has a responsibility to know when something happens in the office that shouldn't. suppose further that something happens in the office, say, an embezzlement, that shouldn't happen. Then the office manager ought to know that it happened. But if the office manager knows that it happened, this entails that it did happen. So once again by deontic inheritance, the embezzlement ought to have happened.

---

[2] I have not been able to locate this example in the literature, but I first heard it from Hector Casteñeda almost exactly twenty-five years ago.

I find it puzzling that so much effort has been spent on the Good Samaritan and the Gentle Murderer and so little on the Knower's Paradox. Somehow, this example has avoided much attention even though I think it is much more difficult. Solutions to the Good Samaritan and the Gentle Murder that seem adequate to me cannot be converted into solutions for the Knower's Paradox.

In any event, defeasible reasoning offers no solution to any of these puzzles. However, I do not see this as a deficiency of defeasible deontic logic. These puzzles simply require a different kind of solution.

6.4. *Moral Dilemmas*

We can show that if $T \hspace{0.1em}\not\vdash_{DSD} \phi$ and $T \hspace{0.1em}\not\vdash_{DSD} \neg\phi$, then $T \vdash_{DSD} \phi$ and $T \vdash_{DSD} \neg\phi$. Furthermore, if T is deontically closed, $T \hspace{0.1em}\not\vdash_{DSD} \bigcirc \phi$, and $T \hspace{0.1em}\not\vdash_{DSD} \bigcirc \neg\phi$, then $T \vdash_{DSD} \bigcirc \phi$ and $T \vdash_{DSD} \bigcirc \neg\phi$. So the only way a moral dilemma can arise in our theory is if it is implied by the strict rules alone. Thus there will be no moral dilemmas if our moral theory includes only *prima facie* obligations.

Once an agent is in an irresolvable moral dilemma, every outcome must be tragic. The real importance of moral dilemmas as a guide to conduct seems to be this: we should anticipate and avoid moral dilemmas. That is, we should act in such a way that we do not find ourselves in a situation where we have obligations to perform incompatible actions. A principle like this cannot be stated directly in our defeasible deontic formalism, but this is not too surprising. It is, after all, quite an abstract principle. But we can represent it as a condition on defeasible consequence relations.

Definition 18 *Let Σ be a defeasible consequence relation and let T be a defeasible theory. Then T is* **tragic in** Σ *iff there is a literal ϕ such that $T \vdash_\Sigma \bigcirc \phi$ and $T \vdash_\Sigma \bigcirc \neg\phi$.*

Definition 19 *A defeasible consequence relation is* **prudential** *iff for each defeasible theory $T = \langle F, R, C, \prec \rangle$ and each literal ϕ, if T is not tragic in Σ but $\langle F \cup \{\phi\}, R, C, \prec \rangle$ is tragic in Σ, then $T \vdash_\Sigma \bigcirc \neg\phi$.*

So a prudential defeasible consequence relation is one that prohibits actions which would lead to an irresolvable moral dilemma.

There is another kind of situation has some of the character of a moral dilemma. Suppose we have *prima facie* obligations to keep promises and to avoid harming others. The interesting case, of course, is when these two *prima facie* obligations come into conflict. Here are formulations of facts and rules for a propositional version of such a theory.

1. *promised*
2. *promised* $\Rightarrow \bigcirc act$
3. $\Rightarrow \bigcirc \sim harm$
4. *act* $\Rightarrow harm$

If our theory is conflict-closed, then 2 and 3 compete. Assuming our theory preserves specificity, we would derive $T \vdash_{DSD} \bigcirc act$ since 2 is more specific than 3. Here specificity supports a suspicious result. If anything, the prohibition against harming others intuitively is stronger than the prohibition against breaking promises. Of course, we can enforce such an intuition by making

$$promised \Rightarrow \bigcirc act \prec_T \Rightarrow \bigcirc \sim harm$$

But suppose our precedence relation is completely empty. Then we have both $T \not\vdash_{DSD} \bigcirc act$ and $T \not\vdash_{DSD} \bigcirc \sim harm$. Here we have a dilemma in which we don't conclude that two incompatible moral obligations are both apparently (or even actually) binding. Instead, we have two *prima facie* obligations which seem to cancel each other out in an unintuitive way! Even if we can't accomplish both, it would seem that we should *either* keep our promise *or* refrain from causing another harm. But according to our logic, neither is an apparent obligation. Of course, we can't represent disjunctive obligations in our language. Both language and logic seem too weak to represent the case properly. Perhaps we could add enough to our theory to get the desired result in this case, but we shouldn't have to add extra rules or beef up our precedence relation for each conflict that comes along. We prefer a general principle that says when we have to competing defeasible obligations, we have an *apparent* disjunctive obligation to fulfill at least one of the defeasible obligations. Finding a formalism in which we capture such a general principle is a task for another occasion.

Moral dilemmas directly concern obligations, but the rejection of moral dilemmas by classical deontic logic also has consequences for our understanding of permissions. The classical theorem $\sim(\bigcirc \phi \wedge \bigcirc \sim \phi)$ is logically equivalent to $\mathcal{P}\phi \vee \mathcal{P} \sim \phi$. If we allow moral dilemmas, what more can or should we say about the relationship between obligation and permission?

First, we recall that for any literal ϕ, $\mathcal{P}\phi$ is defined as $\sim\bigcirc\neg\phi$. So we have the immediate result that if $T \vdash_{DSD} \bigcirc\neg\phi$, then $T \vdash_{DSD} \neg\mathcal{P}\phi$. We preserve the principle that whatever is forbidden is not permitted.

When we encounter a moral dilemma, then even though both ϕ and $\sim\phi$ are obligatory, neither is permitted. We retain some of the force of the classical rejection of moral dilemmas if we adopt the view that we should expect at least *defeasibly* that all obligatory propositions are permitted. Rather than further complicate our proof theory, I propose we do this by defining a class of theories in which we have rules supporting this expectation.

Definition 20 *A defeasible theory T is* **optimistic** *if and only if for every literal ϕ, $O\phi \Rightarrow P\phi \in T$.*

Of course, the expectations engendered by these optimistic axioms are defeated in the case of moral dilemmas since these are always strict.

7. THEORIES ABOUT PRECEDENCE

In law and other normative contexts, much deliberation is often directed toward resolving issues of precedence, that is, toward deciding which of several relevant but jointly incompatible principles should apply in a particular case. In the context of the formalism presented here, the material for such deliberations could also be represented as by a set of strict and defeasible rules where the consequents of the rules made claims about the precedence relation for a defeasible deontic theory. One might, as Prakken and Sartor do ((Prakken and Sartor, 1996)) try to incorporate such rules into the very theory to whose precedence relation the rules refer. I prefer to take a different approach and will discuss some of the issues that arise when we try to build a defeasible theory $T_\prec$ for the precedence relation of another defeasible theory $T = \langle F, R, C, \prec \rangle$.

To begin, the language for $T_\prec$ must include names for each of the rules in T. It will also include a binary predicate $\sqsubseteq$ which will be the syntactic counterpart for the precedence relation $\prec$ in T. Let's suppose we want to capture the principles of *lex superior* and *lex posterior* in our precedence theory. We will assume that all rules in our object theory T arise from either the higher authority or the lower authority. We introduce predicates H and L where $H(r)$ says r arises from the higher authority and $L(r)$ says r arises from the lower authority. We will also need an earlier-than predicate E. So $E(r_1, r_2)$ will say that r_1 was enacted earlier than r_2. We will assume that $T_\prec$ includes facts telling us from which authority each rule arises and sufficient facts and rules to tell us, at least for any two rules arising from the same authority, which rule was enacted first.

I think the following set of rules captures our two principles of *lex superior* and *lex posterior*.

$$\Rightarrow r_1 \not\sqsubseteq r_2$$
$$\{L(r_1), H(r_2)\} \Rightarrow r_1 \sqsubseteq r_2$$
$$\{H(r_1), H(r_2), E(r_1, r_2)\} \Rightarrow r_1 \sqsubseteq r_2$$
$$\{L(r_1), L(r_2), E(r_1, r_2)\} \Rightarrow r_1 \sqsubseteq r_2$$

The initial presumption allows us to conclude that one rule does not take precedence over another where no evidence of precedence is available. The second rule captures the principle of *lex superior*. The third and forth rules capture the priciple of *lex posterior* for the higher and lower authorities respectively.

We will assume that $T_\prec$ preserves specificity. So no rule in $T_\prec$ takes precedence over any other except for reasons of specificity. Figuring out the conflicts set for $T_\prec$ is where some serious questions arise about this approach. We want to say that either that $T_\prec$ completely determines the precedence relation for T or that $T_\prec$ determines a relation Γ such that T is Γ-specific.

Let's begin with the easier case: $r_1 \prec r_2$ if and only if $T_\prec \vdash_{SD} r_1 \sqsubset r_2$. We are supposing that specificity has no role in resolving conflicts between rules in T. Still, $\prec$ must be acyclic or T is not a defeasible theory. So for every set of rules $\{r_1, r_2, \ldots, r_n\} \in R$, the set of literals $\{r_1 \sqsubset r_2, r_2 \sqsubset r_3, \ldots, r_n \sqsubset r_1\}$ should be in $C_\prec$, the conflicts set for $T_\prec$. Let $C_\prec$ be the smallest conflicts set for the language of $T_\prec$ containing all these "loops." Then as long as $T_\prec$ contains no strict rules, as in our example for *lex superior* and *lex posterior*, $T_\prec$ will determine an acyclic precedence relation for T. Whether or not we have strict rules in $T_\prec$, and whether or not we take $T_\prec$ to determine the whole of the precedence relation for T or only the core of the precedence relation for T, $T_\prec$ can *only* serve as a precedence theory for T if $\{(r_1, r_2) : T_\prec \vdash_{SD} r_1 \sqsubset r_2\}$ is acyclic.

If we want to add specificity as a criterion for resolving conflicts in T, the situation becomes more complicated. Suppose r_1 is $\Rightarrow \phi$, r_2 is $\psi \Rightarrow \sim \phi$, $H(r_1)$, and $L(r_2)$. In this case, if we make T Γ-specific where $T_\prec$ determines Γ, then we have $r_2 \prec r_1$ and specificity is overriden. But suppose a bit more complicated case: r_1 is $\Rightarrow \phi_1$, r_2 is $\psi \Rightarrow \phi_2$, r_3 is $\{\psi, \chi\} \Rightarrow \phi_3$, $\{\phi_1, \phi_2, \phi_3\} \in C_T$, $H(r_1)$, and $L(r_3)$. Then we will have $T_\prec \vdash r_3 \sqsubset r_1$ and $r_3 \prec r_1$, and we must reject either $r_1 \prec r_2$ or $r_2 \prec r_3$ to avoid a loop in our precedence relation. Which do we reject? If we have $H(r_2)$, we can resolve the problem since we must reject $r_2 \prec r_3$, and if we have $L(r_2)$, we resolve the problem by rejecting $r_1 \prec r_2$. so *lex superior* saves us. But suppose we had two lower authorities, L_1 and L_2 neither of which was higher than the other. If we had $L_1(r_2)$ and $L_2(r_3)$, we could not use *lex superior* to decide which pair to exclude from our precedence relation for T. Nor could we use *lex posterior* since it only applies to rules arising from the same authority.

I have no general solution to the problem raised here. Indeed, I think it is unlikely that we can come up with a formal solution to the problem. In a case like this, we must decide how to resolve the details of the precedence relation based on the content of the rules involved. We cannot decide on the basis of superior authority or time of enactment. Of course, once we resolve the matter we can put $r_1 \sqsubset r_2$ or $r_2 \sqsubset r_3$ in $T_\prec$. Then the problem will not arise when we implement specificity in T. And perhaps this is the best we can hope for. Formal considerations can never resolve all normative disputes or even all disputes about the priorities of normative principles, but at least our formalism gives us some indication of what is required of an adequate theory about the precedence relation for a defeasible deontic theory.

Donald Nute
Department of Philosophy and Artificial Intelligence Center
The University of Georgia

REFERENCES

Nute, Donald (1992). Basic defeasible logic. In Fariñas del Cerro, L., and Penttonen, M. (eds.), *Intensional Logics for Programming,* Oxford University Press.

Nute, Donald (1993). Inference, rules, and instrumentalism. *International Journal of Expert Systems Research and Applications,* 5:267–274.

Nute, Donald (1994). A decidable quantified defeasible logic. In Prawitz, D., Skyrms, B., and Westerstahl, D. (eds.), *Logic, Methodology and Philosophy of Science IX,* Elsevier Science B. V., New York, pages 263–284.

Nute, Donald (1996). d-Prolog: an implementation of defeasible logic in Prolog. In *Non-monotonic Extensions of Logic Programming: Theory, Implementation and Applications,* (Proceedings of the JICSLP 96 Postconference Workshop W1), Bad Honnef, Germany, pages 161-182.

Prakken, Henry and Sartor, Giovanni (1996). Rules about rules: assessing conflicting arguments in legal reasoning. *Artificial Intelligence and Law,* to appear.

Schurtz, G (1994). Defeasible reasoning based on constructive and cumulative rules. In Casati, R., Smith, B., and White, G. (eds.), *Philosophy and Cognitive Sciences,* Hölder-Pichler-Tempsky, pages 297–310.

JOSÉ CARMO AND ANDREW J. I. JONES

A NEW APPROACH TO CONTRARY-TO-DUTY OBLIGATIONS

1. CONTRARY-TO-DUTY OBLIGATIONS AND THE CHISHOLM SET

Since the publication of (Chisholm, 1963), deontic logicians have struggled with the problem of supplying an adequate formal characterisation of the distinction between primary obligations and those obligations - called "contrary–to–duty" by Chisholm - which come into force when some other obligation is violated.

Consider Example 1, the four sentences of the "Chisholm set" :

Example 1

 (a) It ought to be that a certain man go to help his neighbours.
 (b) It ought to be that if he goes he tell them he is coming.
 (c) If he does not go, he ought not to tell them he is coming.
 (d) He does not go.

There is widespread *agreement* in the literature that, from the intuitive point of view, this set is consistent, and its members logically independent of each other. However, attempts to formalize it in SDL (Standard Deontic Logic), which is a normal modal system of type KD according to the classification of (Chellas, 1980), result either in inconsistency or in failure of logical independence.[1]

There is a good deal of *disagreement* in the literature as regards which *further* requirements, in addition to consistency and logical independence, an adequate formal representation of the Chisholm set should meet. For instance, there is the question whether the two conditional sentences, (b) and (c), should be given fundamentally distinct logical forms; the surface structure of (b) suggests that the deontic modality has the entire conditional within its scope, whereas the surface structure of (c) suggests that the deontic modality governs only the consequent of the conditional.

In what follows, however, we shall develop a theory which offers a uniform treatment of deontic conditionals. Our view is that, in the absence of strong arguments to the contrary, the surface form of (b) and (c) should be deemed to be merely stylistic variants of essentially the same type of underlying logical structure. In particular, we reject the position taken in (Prakken and Sergot, 1994; Prakken and Sergot, 1996), where it is argued that (b) and (c)

---

[1]We take this result to be well established. For details, see, e.g., (Jones and Pörn, 1985).

D. Nute (ed.), Defeasible Deontic Logic, 317–344.
© 1997 *Kluwer Academic Publishers. Printed in the Netherlands.*

should be given distinct logical representations just because (c), unlike (b), is a contrary–to–duty (C-T-D) conditional, expressing as it does the obligation which comes into force when the obligation expressed by line (a) is violated. It is clear that Prakken and Sergot's approach makes the assignment of logical form to deontic conditionals a highly context–dependent matter. We here present an alternative theory in which that kind of "context dependence of the representation" is avoided.

Initially then, as we see it, an adequate formalization of the Chisholm set must meet three requirements:

(i) consistency of the set;
(ii) logical independence of the members;
(iii) analogous logical structures for the two conditional sentences, (b) and (c).

2. DYADIC DEONTIC LOGICS AND THE CHISHOLM SET

One important group of logics which satisfy these three requirements employ a primitive dyadic conditional obligation operator $\bigcirc$ (-/-), where expressions of the form $\bigcirc$ (B/A) are read "it is obligatory (or ought to be the case) that B, given that A". Ordinarily, these logics take the unconditional obligation $\bigcirc$ B to be equivalent to $\bigcirc$ (B/$\top$), where $\top$ is any tautology. They would represent the Chisholm set in the following fashion, where "tell" and "help" are used in an obvious way as abbreviations for the sentences concerned:

(a) $\bigcirc$ (help / $\top$)
(b) $\bigcirc$ (tell / help)
(c) $\bigcirc$ ($\neg$ tell / $\neg$ help)
(d) $\neg$ help

In (Loewer and Belzer, 1983), Loewer and Belzer distinguish between two main "families" of dyadic deontic logics. One of these accepts the "factual detachment" principle

$$\text{(FD)} \quad \vdash A \wedge \bigcirc (B/A) \rightarrow \bigcirc B$$

and we may accordingly call it the "FD–family".[2] This principle permits the derivation of the *actual obligations* of the agent, i.e., the obligations which arise given the actual facts of the situation.

The other family accepts the "deontic detachment" principle

$$\text{(DD)} \quad \vdash \bigcirc A \wedge \bigcirc (B/A) \rightarrow \bigcirc B$$

---

[2](Loewer and Belzer, 1983) mention (Mott, 1973), (al–Hibri, 1978) and (Chellas, 1974) as representatives of the FD–family. As regards the last of these, however, it should be noted that it is not entirely clear whether Chellas commits himself to acceptance of the principle (FD).

and may be called the "DD–family".[3] This principle permits the derivation of the *ideal obligations* of the agent, i.e., the further obligations which arise if he behaves in a way which conforms with some existing set of obligations.

Returning again to the Chisholm set, it is clear that acceptance of *both* (FD) *and* (DD) would permit the derivation of $\bigcirc \neg$ tell (by (FD) on lines (c) and (d)) and $\bigcirc$ tell (by (DD) on lines (a) and (b)). If the (D)–schema

$$(D) \quad \vdash \bigcirc A \rightarrow \neg \bigcirc \neg A$$

is accepted, then the situation arising from adoption of both (FD) and (DD) would of course be one of *logical* inconsistency. But even if the (D)–schema is not accepted, so that the conjunction $\bigcirc$ tell $\wedge \bigcirc \neg$ tell is not deemed to be *logically* inconsistent, the derivation from the Chisholm set of a *conflict of obligations* of the type expressed by this conjunction is surely unacceptable from the intuitive point of view. The situation described by the Chisholm set does not present the agent concerned with a *moral dilemma*, on our view. Requirement (i), above, should be understood as one to the effect that a conjunction of the form $\bigcirc A \wedge \bigcirc \neg A$ should not be derivable from the formal representation of the set, regardless of whether that conjunction is deemed *logically* inconsistent.

Of course, neither the FD–family nor the DD–family accepts *both* (FD) and (DD). Nevertheless, it might be suggested that a fully adequate representation of the Chisholm set should be able to capture, in a way which generates neither inconsistency nor a moral dilemma, both the fact that - given the circumstances, and particularly the occurrence of the violation of the obligation expressed by line (a) - the agent's actual obligation is not to tell his neighbours he is coming, *and* the fact that - under ideal circumstances, in the absence of violation of the obligation expressed by line (a) - the agent's obligation would be to tell his neighbours he is coming. Accepting this suggestion, we offer three further requirements which we believe an adequate representation of the Chisholm set should meet:

(iv) capacity to derive *actual obligations*;
(v) capacity to derive *ideal obligations* (perhaps these might be called *prima facie obligations*);
(vi) capacity to represent the fact that a *violation* of obligation has occurred.

Neither the FD–family nor the DD–family meet both (iv) and (v). We return below to the issues raised by (vi).[4]

---

[3] (Lewis, 1974) presents an overview of several members of the DD–family.

[4] In (Jones, 1993), where issues regarding default reasoning in deontic logic are discussed, it is argued that a further problem for the FD–family resides in the fact that they reject the "strengthening–of–the–antecedent" principle

$$(SA) \quad \bigcirc (B/A) \rightarrow \bigcirc (B/A \wedge C)$$

3. SOME OTHER APPROACHES, AND THE "PRAGMATIC ODDITY"

On the basis of analysis comparable to the above, (Loewer and Belzer, 1983) and (Jones and Pörn, 1985; Jones, 1993) reach mutually distinct conclusions and proposals. (Loewer and Belzer, 1983) maintain that the problems raised by the Chisholm set essentially involve a temporal dimension, and that previously proposed solutions fail in as much as they do not capture this dimension. Temporal approaches to the semantics of deontic notions are generally based on tree–structures, and reflect the linguistic dimension syntactically in one of two ways: either by means of obligation operators indexed by temporal terms (as in (VanEck, 1981) and (Loewer and Belzer, 1983)), or by means of combining deontic operators and temporal operators in sequence ((Chellas, 1980, sections 6.3 and 6.4), (Åqvist and Hopepelman, 1981), (Thomason, 1981; Thomason, 1984) and (Brown, 1996)).

By contrast, (Jones and Pörn, 1985) and (Jones, 1993)[5] claim that, although the temporal dimension is present in some versions of the Chisholm set, this is not an inherent, essential feature of the problems which that set exhibits. They offer an alternative, rather simple logical analysis, which takes as its point of departure the observation that SDL fails in its attempt to capture C–T–Ds because - from the semantical point of view - SDL considers only the *ideal* versions of any world. They propose, in addition, an accessibility relation which picks out the *sub–ideal* versions of a given world, and they introduce into the logical language two modal necessity operators, here denoted by $\boxed{i}$ and $\boxed{s}$. The first of these is just the obligation operator of SDL, so that an expression of the form $\boxed{i}$ A is true at a given world w iff A is true at all of the ideal versions of w. By contrast, an expression of the form $\boxed{s}$ A is true at a given world w iff A is true at all of the sub–ideal versions of w. (A sub–ideal version w1, of w, is a version of w in which at least one of the obligations in force at w is violated.) The duals of $\boxed{i}$ and $\boxed{s}$ are, respectively, $\diamondsuit\!\!\!\!{\scriptstyle i}$ and $\diamondsuit\!\!\!\!{\scriptstyle s}$. A deontic necessity operator $\boxed{}$ is defined as follows: $\boxed{}$ A $=_{df}$ $\boxed{i}$ A $\wedge$ $\boxed{s}$ A and an actual–obligation operator $\bigcirc$ught is defined by

$$\bigcirc\text{ught } A =_{df} \boxed{i}\, A \wedge \diamondsuit\!\!\!\!{\scriptstyle s}\, \neg A^{6}$$

---

whilst at the same time accepting unrestricted factual detachment. The problem is that one main reason for rejecting (SA) is that one wants to be able to permit consistent expression of such conjunctions as $\bigcirc$ (B/A) $\wedge$ $\bigcirc$ ($\neg$ B/A $\wedge$ C), even in circumstances in which both A and C are true. "Consistent" is again here meant to be interpreted as "without logical inconsistency or moral dilemma of the form $\bigcirc$ B $\wedge$ $\bigcirc$ $\neg$ B".

[5]In (Jones, 1993) the logic described in (Jones and Pörn, 1985) is modified in such a way as to invalidate the principle of strengthening of the antecedent and the principle of unrestricted factual detachment. Some suggestions are made about the drawing of default conclusions in reasoning with deontic–conditionals–which–allow–exceptions.

[6]The second conjunct here guarantees that $\vdash$ $\neg\bigcirc$ught $\top$. Note that the notation employed here for the operators differs in most cases from that used in (Jones and Pörn, 1985).

In (Jones and Pörn, 1985) the Chisholm set was represented as follows:

(a) $\bigcirc$ught help
(b) $\boxminus$ (help $\rightarrow$ $\bigcirc$ught tell)
(c) $\boxminus$ ($\neg$help $\rightarrow$ $\bigcirc$ught $\neg$tell)
(d) $\neg$help

The set, on this representation, is consistent and its members are logically independent of each other. Lines (c) and (d) imply $\bigcirc$ught $\neg$tell,[7] but lines (a) and (b) imply $\boxminus\bigcirc$ught tell. Furthermore, the conjunction of lines (a) and (d) may be taken as expressing the fact that the unconditional obligation to help the neighbours has been violated; and, had it been the case that

(d') help

rather than (d) were true, then from (b) one could deduce the actual obligation to tell, $\bigcirc$ught tell. Apparently, all is well...!

However, (Prakken and Sergot, 1996) point out that the Jones and Pörn treatment of Chisholm, in common with a number of others, generates what they call the "pragmatic oddity": line (a), together with the derived actual obligation $\bigcirc$ught $\neg$ tell, require that, in all ideal versions of the given world, the agent concerned goes to help his neighbours but does not tell them he is coming - a result which (for reasons we shall explore below) appears highly counterintuitive.

Prakken and Sergot correctly point out that, for a number of cases, a reasonable temporal interpretation is available which would enable the pragmatic oddity to be avoided. For instance, perhaps the obligation expressed in line (a) would ordinarily be understood as an obligation to go to help the neighbours *no later than a particular time, t*. Then, if line (d) were to be true after time t, the accessible deontically ideal worlds would be characterized in such a way that, after time t, these worlds would require that the agent does not tell his neighbours he is coming (but they would not, of course, also require that he goes to help, since it would then be too late).

However, Prakken and Sergot also point out that there are instances of the Chisholm set which may be interpreted in such a way that the temporal dimension is completely absent.[8] Consider the following:

Example 2

(a) There ought to be no dog
(b) If there is no dog, there ought to be no warning sign
(c) If there is a dog, there ought to be a warning sign
(d) There is a dog

One very ordinary way of understanding this set, surely, takes each sentence to be true at one and the same moment of time, and - without any insertion of

---

[7]Note that it is a feature of the logic of (Jones and Pörn, 1985) that $\vdash$ $\boxminus$ A $\rightarrow$ A.
[8]*cf.* (Jones, 1993, pp.153–4), which makes a similar point.

temporal qualifications concerning *when* there ought to be no dog, or *when* there ought to be a warning sign - allows the conclusion to be drawn that there ought, in the circumstances, to be a warning sign, *without* thereby generating the pragmatic oddity, i.e., *without* forcing the further conclusion that, in all ideal versions of the given situation, there is no dog but there is a sign warning of one.

Unfortunately, Prakken and Sergot offer little by way of explanation of the pragmatic oddity. They say little about what it is that creates the sense of oddity. However, we want here to suggest an explanation which exploits a parallel between examples of type 2 (above), which exhibit the pragmatic oddity *simpliciter*, and examples of the following kind (also due to Prakken and Sergot) which, in virtue of some implicitly assumed logical truth, are inconsistent when formalized in the style of (Jones and Pörn, 1985):

Example 3

(a) There must be no fence
(c) If there is a fence then it must be a white fence
(d) There is a fence

Lines (c) and (d) together imply that there must be a white fence, which in turn implies (because of line (a)) that in all ideal versions of the given world there is a white fence and no fence at all, which is inconsistent.[9] The parallel with Example 2 is this, we suggest: as represented in the language of (Jones and Pörn, 1985), Example 2 exhibits the pragmatic oddity because an inconsistency *would be* generated were one to add to the example the further requirement that it ought not to be the case that there is both no dog and a sign warning of one. The sense of oddity arises because there is an interpretation of the set of sentences according to which it remains consistent even if supplemented with the further constraint that it ought not to be the case that there is both no dog and a sign warning of one. What is unsatisfactory about the attempt to formalize Example 2 in the logic of (Jones and Pörn, 1985) is that it fails to capture *that* interpretation.

With this diagnosis of the nature of the pragmatic oddity in mind, we add a seventh requirement which an adequate treatment of the Chisholm set and C–T–Ds should satisfy:

(vii) capacity to avoid the pragmatic oddity.

---

[9] Assuming validity of the (D)–schema, i.e., assuming that there is at least one ideal version of the given world. See, above, section 2, for comments on the (D)–schema, inconsistency and conflict of obligations.

4. TWO ATTEMPTS TO RESOLVE THE PRAGMATIC ODDITY

Prakken and Sergot argue that the proper response to the problems raised by Example 2 - and in particular the problem of pragmatic oddity - is to assign distinct logical forms to primary obligations, on the one hand, and C–T–D obligations, on the other. For C–T–D obligations, they relativize an obligation operator to a specific "context of violation" ; more precisely, an expression of the form $\bigcirc_B A$ "is intended to be read as 'there is a secondary obligation that A given that, or presupposing, the sub–ideal context B', or 'given that B, which is a violation of some primary obligation, there is a secondary, compromise obligation that A'" (Prakken and Sergot, 1996, section 5). They emphasise that expressions of type $\bigcirc_B A$ are not to be read as conditional primary obligations. "The expression $\bigcirc_B A$... represents a particular kind of obligation. There is no meaningful sense ... in which the obligation $\bigcirc A$ can be detached from the expression $\bigcirc_B A$" [*loc.cit.*]. Their representation of Example 2 would take the following form:

(a) $\bigcirc \neg \text{dog}$
(b) $\neg \text{dog} \rightarrow \bigcirc \neg \text{sign}$
(c) $\text{dog} \rightarrow \bigcirc_{\text{dog}} \text{sign}$
(d) dog

We shall not pursue the Prakken and Sergot treatment of C–T–Ds further here. Suffice it to say that their approach rejects the third of our requirements, listed above, for a satisfactory theory in this area. For them, the choice of logical form for an apparently conditional deontic sentence will itself be dependent on which other norms are contained in, or derivable from, the set of norms being formalized. One consequence of this can be that the form initially assigned to a given sentence will have to be *revised* in virtue of what turns out to be derivable from other sentences; for instance, one might initially assign the form $A \rightarrow \bigcirc B$ to the sentence "if A then it ought to be the case that B" - but if it later transpires that the obligation sentence $\bigcirc \neg A$ is derivable from some other members of the given set of norms, then $A \rightarrow \bigcirc B$ will have to be replaced by $A \rightarrow \bigcirc_A B$. This is a highly unsatisfactory situation to be in, particularly if the task is to represent formally a relatively large corpus of norms.[10]

---

[10]Indeed *any* insertion or deletion of a norm may require that some revision be made to the formalization of some other norm in the set. There are some further difficulties in understanding how expressions of the form $\bigcirc_B A$ should be interpreted, particularly since Prakken and Sergot insist that B (in $\bigcirc_B A$) necessarily represents a context of violation. For instance, the formula

$$(\mathcal{P}B \wedge \bigcirc_B A) \rightarrow \bigcirc A$$

is *valid*, on their account (where $\mathcal{P}$ is the permission operator), but not trivially so. As we see it, the conjunction in the antecedent of this conditional (given their reading of $\bigcirc_B A$) could only be false, so the validity of the conditional would be entirely trivial. Furthermore, what can

In (Carmo and Jones, 1995)[11] we attempted a different kind of approach to the problem of the pragmatic oddity, distinguishing between "ideal obligations" (line (a) in Examples 1 and 2, for instance) and "actual obligations", which indicate what ought to be done given the (perhaps less–than–ideal) circumstances. The operator $\bigcirc_a$, for representing actual obligations, was defined in the same way as the $\bigcirc$ught –operator of (Jones and Pörn, 1985), described above. As regards ideal obligations, the basic model–theoretic idea was to distinguish between ideal *versions* of a given world (the fundamental feature of the semantics of SDL), and *ideal worlds themselves*. Accordingly, we divided the set of possible worlds into two mutually exclusive sub–sets, the set of ideal worlds and the set of sub–ideal worlds; importantly for our purposes, we allowed that a world w1 could be an ideal *version* of a given (*sub–ideal*) world w *without* also itself being an ideal *world*. And we fixed truth conditions for expressions of the form $\bigcirc_i$ A ("it ought ideally to be the case that A") in terms of truth of A *in all ideal worlds* and falsity of A *in some sub–ideal world*.[12]

We represented Example 2 in the following way:

(a) $\bigcirc_i \neg$ dog
(b) $\boxminus$ ($\neg$ dog $\rightarrow \bigcirc_a \neg$ sign)
(c) $\boxminus$ (dog $\rightarrow \bigcirc_a$ sign)
(d) dog

All of the requirements (i) - (vii) are met by this analysis. In particular, the pragmatic oddity disappears because the conjunction $\bigcirc_i \neg$ dog $\wedge \bigcirc_a$ sign, which is clearly derivable from (a) - (d), does *not* imply that, in all ideal versions of the given world, there is no dog but a sign warning of one. What that conjunction *does* say, essentially, is that in all ideal *worlds* there is no dog, but in all ideal *versions* of the given (clearly sub–ideal) world there is a warning sign.

The proposal worked well for this and a number of other examples. But serious difficulties arose as soon as a second level of C–T–Ds was considered. Suppose that lines (e) and (f), below, are added to Example 2:

(e) If there is a dog and no warning sign, there ought to be a high fence.
(f) There is no warning sign.

The (Carmo and Jones, 1995) representation of this extended set is:

---

they possibly mean by the claim that $\bigcirc$ A is an abbreviation of $\bigcirc_\top$ A? Are we to suppose that it is obligatory that A only if the tautology represents a context of violation?

[11]We there adapt the logic proposed in (Carmo and Jones, 1994; Carmo and Jones, 1996) for the analysis of deontic integrity constraints.

[12]The second conjunct simply guarantees the violability of ideal obligations, i.e. it grants validity to $\neg \bigcirc_i \top$. (Carmo and Jones, 1995) contains discussion of possible connections between the notions of ideal/sub–ideal *world* and ideal/sub–ideal *versions of a world*. But we omit those details here.

(a) $O_i \neg$ dog
(b) $\boxminus (\neg$ dog $\rightarrow O_a \neg$ sign$)$
(c) $\boxminus ($dog $\rightarrow O_a$ sign$)$
(d) dog
(e) $\boxminus ($dog $\wedge \neg$ sign $\rightarrow O_a$ fence$)$
(f) $\neg$ sign

The pragmatic oddity now re–appears, since the conjunction O_a sign $\wedge$ O_a fence is derivable. So, in all ideal versions of the given world, there is a sign and a fence. (If this does not seem "odd", imagine that the sign says "Beware of the unfenced dog" : it may well be forbidden to have both a sign of that kind and a fence. Thus the pragmatic oddity, in the sense of our earlier diagnosis, here re–emerges.)

The problem of further levels of C–T–Ds forces the (Carmo and Jones, 1995) approach to allow the possibility of an infinity of obligation operators: the need to associate (in some way or other) a context to each obligation seems to re–appear.

Note that, on one very common interpretation of the set (a) - (f), the actual obligation which *applies* in the circumstances is the obligation to put up a fence, and it applies because the other two obligations (not to have a dog, and to put up a sign if there is a dog) have been violated. It is not that the obligations to have no dog, and to put up a sign if there is a dog, have been *defeated*, or *overturned*; they have been *violated*, and any proper representation of the situation must register that fact. And it must also register the fact that, because of these violations, the obligation which becomes actual is the obligation to erect a fence. But how are these points to be articulated in a formal theory? To that question we now turn.

5. TOWARDS A SOLUTION

Consider again Example 2, particularly lines (a), (c) and (d). The norms governing, or in force in, the situation are that there ought to be no dog, and that if there is a dog there ought to be a warning sign; and the relevant fact is that there is a dog. So what is the actual obligation, of the agent concerned, in these circumstances? To erect a warning sign? But why not insist on getting rid of the dog, rather than on erecting a warning sign?[13] We wish to suggest that the answer to such questions turns on the *status* assigned to the fact that there is a dog - in the following sense: so long as there is a dog, but this, for one reason or another, is not deemed to be a *fixed*, *unalterable* feature of the situation, then the actual obligation which applies is that there ought to be no dog. However, as soon as, for one reason or another, the fact that there is a

---

[13]Remember that, in keeping with our analysis of the pragmatic oddity, we seek an answer to these questions which is compatible with a further assumption to the effect that there ought not to be *both* no dog *and* a warning sign.

dog is deemed *fixed*, i.e., it is seen as a *necessary*, unavoidable feature of the situation, so that - in consequence - the practical possibility of satisfying the obligation that there be no dog has to all intents and purposes been eliminated, then the actual obligation which applies is that there ought to be a warning sign.[14]

What do we mean when we say that *for some reason or another* a fact of the situation - in this case that there is a dog - may be deemed a fixed, necessary, unalterable feature of that situation? Well, there are various ways in which this arises; those who focussed on temporal solutions to the problems associated with C–T–Ds latched on to *one* of these ways. If books shall be returned by date due, then if you still have the books after the date due there is no way *that* obligation can be met. It is too late! It is unalterably the case that the books are not returned by the date due, and consequently the possibility of satisfying the obligation to return the books by date due has been eliminated. As far as further deliberation about obligations (e.g., that you shall pay a fine) is concerned, there is no question of your being able to satisfy the norm requiring books to be returned by date due.

But temporal reasons, although very common, are not the only reasons why things become fixed, in the sense of necessity or unalterability we here seek to explicate; for instance, it is not for temporal reasons that the deed of killing, once done, cannot be undone. What explains fixity in this case is not temporal necessity, but rather causal necessity. Nor need temporal considerations have any role to play in explaining why the presence of a dog may be, to all intents and purposes, an unavoidable feature of the situation; its owner, let us suppose, stubbornly refuses to remove it, and nobody else dares attempt the feat. The presence of the dog is a fixed fact: the dog remains unless the intervention of some agent leads to its removal, and no agent is prepared to perform the required action.

From the practical point of view - from the point of view of deciding which obligation actually applies to the situation - the key feature is that the possibility of satisfaction of the requirement that there be no dog is effectively eliminated.

6. THE NEW THEORY AND ITS FUNDAMENTAL SEMANTIC FEATURES

We now present the basic features of a modal–logical language designed to capture the approach to C–T–Ds described above in a way which conforms to the constraints, or requirements, (i) - (vii). We shall then show how the new language may be applied to the Chisholm set, and to the analysis of

---

[14]Some remarks in a similar spirit are to be found in (Hansson, 1971, section XIII: "on the interpretation of 'circumstances'").

some other problematic C–T–D "scenarios" which have been discussed in the literature.[15]

We adopt the following approach to the formal representation of these scenarios: their *deontic component* (the obligation norms which they explicitly contain) will be represented throughout in terms of a dyadic, conditional obligation operator $\bigcirc$ (-/-); their *factual component* will be represented by means of either unmodalized sentences, or modalized sentences in two categories. These two categories correspond to two notions of necessity (and their associated dual notions of possibility) which we shall employ to articulate the ideas regarding fixity, or unalterability, of facts alluded to in the previous section.

From the deontic and factual components taken together, some further obligation–sentences may be derivable. The *derived obligation–sentences* are of two types, pertaining to *actual* obligations and *ideal* obligations, respectively. As will be explained below, there is an intimate conceptual connection between these two notions of derived obligation, on the one hand, and the two notions of necessity/possibility used in characterising the factual component, on the other.

Consider first the dyadic conditional obligation operator. How do we wish to interpret a sentence of the kind "if there is a dog then there shall be a warning sign" ? On our view, this sentence is to be understood as saying that in any context in which the presence of a dog is a fixed, unalterable fact, it is obligatory to have a warning sign if it is possible to have a warning sign. We think of a context as a set of worlds - the set of relevant worlds for the situation at hand. So the above sentence is to be understood as saying that, for any context in which there is a dog (i.e., for any context in which there is a dog in each world of that context), if it is possible to have a warning sign then it is obligatory to have a warning sign. In order to capture this idea we introduce in our models a function $\mathrm{pi} : \wp(w) \rightarrow \wp(\wp(w))$ which picks out, for each context, the propositions which represent that which is obligatory in that context. That is, $\|B\| \in \mathrm{pi}(X)$ if and only if the proposition expressed by B represents something obligatory in the context X. Accordingly, we say that a sentence of the form $\bigcirc$ (B/A) is true in a model if and only if, in any context X where A is true and B is possible (i.e., in any context having A true in each of its worlds and B true in at least one of its worlds), it is obligatory that B.[16]

On the basis of this operator we could now derive the obligations that were applicable in each context, assuming that our language contains a means of representing contexts. The question is: what are the types of contexts that we

---

[15] (Prakken and Sergot, 1996) provides an excellent survey of the principal examples in this domain.

[16] We also add the further requirement that the conjunction of A and B is not contradictory, in order to avoid absurd vacuous conditional obligations.

need to be able to talk about in our formal language, given that we want to be able to derive obligation sentences of two kinds, describing *actual* obligations and *ideal* obligations, respectively? We answer this question in terms of the two notions of necessity to be introduced next.

The first of these will be denoted by ⊟, and its dual possibility notion denoted by ◇. Intuitively, ⊟ is intended to capture that which - in a particular situation - is *actually* fixed, or unalterable, given (*among other factors*) what the agents concerned have done, and what they have decided to do and not to do. For instance, in the "dog scenario" (Example 2) it may be the case both that the owner of the (prohibited) dog has firmly resolved not to remove the dog, and that nobody else is prepared to secure its removal. Then it would be appropriate to say that, to all intents and purposes, the presence of the dog is a fixed feature of the situation; in all of the *actually* possible alternatives to the situation it is the case that there is a dog. The presence of the dog is actually an unalterable fact, and the sentence ⊟ dog is true of the situation. On the other hand, if some actual possibility existed for getting rid of the dog, then the situation would be appropriately described by ◇ ¬ dog (i.e., ¬⊟ dog). Which *actual obligations* arise in the dog scenario will depend in part, as we see it, on whether or not ◇ ¬ dog is true. We should point out immediately one important difference between this notion of necessity/possibility and the second one to be introduced below: a sentence of the form ⊟ A might be true even though the agents concerned have the ability and the opportunity to see to it that ¬ A. For, despite their abilities and opportunities for action, the agents may have firmly resolved not to see to it that ¬ A, and the situation may be such that - given that this is what the agents have decided - there is no actual way A could be false; there is no actual possibility of any other form of intervention in the situation which could make it the case that ¬ A, and so - to all intents and purposes - the truth of A is an actual necessity.[17]

Our semantical models will contain a function, va, which picks out (for any given world w) a set of worlds va(w) - the set of worlds which are the *actual alternative versions* of w, those which constitute the context that it is actually relevant to take into account in determining which obligations are actually in force, or actually apply, at w. Accordingly, a sentence of the form ⊟ A will be said to be true at a given world w if and only if A is true at *all* of the worlds contained in va(w).

---

[17]It is not our intention to discuss in detail the grounds upon which a decision might be made regarding whether or not some state of affairs was actually possible in a given situation. We want merely to claim that judgments of this kind are in fact made - for instance in courts of law - and that they play a crucial part in determining which obligations actually arise. The task of our *logic*, as we see it, is just to show which actual obligations can be derived, *given that* a particular judgment has been made regarding the status of the facts with respect to questions of fixity. Our thanks to Layman Allen for raising a question at the Sesimbra ΔEON Workshop related to this point.

Given the way the function pi is understood, the set of propositions pi(va(w)) will be the set of propositions which represent that which is obligatory in the context va(w); that is to say, these propositions represent the obligations which are in force in the actual alternative versions of the world w. In line with this, we shall say that a sentence of the form $\bigcirc_a$ A (read as "it is actually obligatory that A", or "it actually ought to be the case that A") is true at a world w only if the proposition expressed by A is one of those propositions picked out by pi for the argument va(w). In addition, the truth of $\bigcirc_a$ A at w will require that there is at least one world in va(w) where the sentence A is false; the reason for this second requirement is that that which is actually obligatory might actually fail to obtain.

The second of the two notions of necessity will be denoted by $\square$, and its dual possibility notion denoted by $\diamondsuit$. Intuitively, $\square$ is intended to capture that which - in a particular situation - is not only actually fixed, but would still be fixed even if different decisions were to be made, by the agents concerned, regarding how they were going to behave. For instance, certain features of the situation will be such that it is beyond the power of the agents to change them - they may lack the ability, or the opportunity, or both. Of such features it is appropriate to say that they are fixed in the sense that they *could not have been* avoided by the agents concerned, no matter what they had done. It is not even potentially possible for the agents to alter them. In the original Chisholm scenario, for example, if there is no telephone system available to the agent, then clearly it is a necessary feature of the situation, in this second sense of necessity, that he does not telephone the neighbour. This is to be understood in contrast to the situation in which there is a functioning telephone system available, but the agent has made a definite decision, from which he will not budge, not to use it. His will is firm, and thus it is not *actually* possible that he will telephone the neighbour. But given that he has the ability and opportunity to telephone, it is *potentially* possible - in the sense expressed by the $\diamondsuit$ operator - that he does so.[18]

To articulate the semantics of the second pair of notions of necessity and possibility, we introduce into the models a function vp, which picks out (for any given world w) a set of worlds vp(w) - the set of worlds which are the *potential alternative versions* of w. (These worlds will constitute the context that it is relevant to take into account in determining which *ideal* obligations hold at w.) A sentence of the form $\square$ A will be said to be true at a given world

---

[18]So the best short readings for these two pairs of operators we can offer are the following:
$\diamondsuit_a$ A : it is actually possible that A
$\diamondsuit$ A : it is potentially possible that A
$\boxminus_a$ A : it is not actually possible that ¬ A
$\square$ A : it is not potentially possible that ¬ A
(In a number of cases, the natural reading of statements about potential possibility will be in the past tense.)

w if and only if A is true at all of the worlds contained in vp(w). Furthermore, given the way the function pi is understood, the set of propositions pi(vp(w)) will be the set of propositions which represent that which is obligatory in the context vp(w); that is to say, these propositions represent the obligations which are in force in the potential alternative versions of the world w. Then we shall say that a sentence of the form $\bigcirc_i$ A (read as "it is ideally obligatory that A", or "it ideally ought to be the case that A") is true at a world w only if the proposition expressed by A is one of the propositions picked out by pi for the argument vp(w). In addition, the truth of $\bigcirc_i$ A at w will require that there is at least one world in vp(w) where the sentence A is false - since that which is ideally obligatory might potentially fail to obtain.

We shall define the notion of *violation* in terms of the notion of ideal obligation, as follows:

$$\text{viol (A)} =_{df} \bigcirc_i A \wedge \neg A$$

The reason for this choice of definition of violation is essentially connected with our treatment of the pragmatic oddity and other features of C–T–D scenarios, and will become clearer below, where a number of examples are analysed in some detail. But, briefly, the main points may be explained as follows: in, for instance, the dog scenario, if it is a fixed fact that there is a dog (i.e., if $\boxminus$ dog is true), but it is *actually* possible that a sign may be erected and *potentially* possible that there is no dog, then we shall be able to derive that it is actually obligatory that a sign is erected and ideally obligatory that there is no dog. The pragmatic oddity will be avoided because it will not, in *these* circumstances, be possible to derive an actual obligation that there be no dog. Nevertheless, we still of course want to say that an obligation (that there be no dog) has been violated, and this result is secured if violation is characterised as above.[19] As the formal analysis of this example will show, we shall also be able to derive a second violation in this situation, if no sign has been erected.

The semantical models described in the next section will be subject to various constraints, designed to achieve a particular pattern of relationships between the dyadic obligation operator, the two types of necessity/possibility operators, and the operators for actual and ideal obligation. The principal consequences of the adoption of these constraints are given in the form of a list of "results" - valid sentence schemas which (as will be seen) play a key role in determining what may or may not be derived from any chosen representation of a C–T–D scenario.

Although, as would be expected, the set va(w) will be required to be a subset of the set vp(w), for any given w (so that actual possibility entails potential possibility), there will be no direct logical connection between the notions of actual and ideal obligation. However, in the concluding remarks

---

[19]We shall return to the issue of the characterisation of violation in our concluding remarks.

we shall suggest a possible modification which, if accepted, would supply a bridge between the two monadic obligation operators.

7. SYNTAX AND SEMANTICS OF THE FORMAL LANGUAGE

Syntax

Alphabet

*	a set of letters$\{$ p, q, r,...$\}$	(for atomic sentences)
*	$\neg$, $\wedge$, $\vee$, $\rightarrow$, $\leftrightarrow$	(sentential connectives)
*	$($, $)$	(parentheses)
*	⊟	(dual: $\diamondsuit$ $=_{df}$ $\neg$⊟$\neg$)
*	□	(dual: $\diamondsuit$ $=_{df}$ $\neg$□$\neg$)
*	$\bigcirc$ $(/)$	(dyadic deontic operator)
*	$\bigcirc_a$	(monadic deontic operator - for actual obligations)
*	$\bigcirc_i$	(monadic deontic operator - for ideal or *prima facie* obligations)

* *Rules for construction of well–formed sentences*: as usual. We employ capital letters (A, B, C, ...) to stand for arbitrary well–formed sentences.

As indicated in the previous section, we also employ the definition:

* viol $(A) =_{df} \bigcirc_i A \wedge \neg A$

Semantics

Models:

$\mathcal{M} = \langle W, va, vp, pi, V \rangle$, where:

1) $W \neq \emptyset$
2) V – a function assigning a truth set to each atomic sentence
3) $va : W \rightarrow \wp(W)$ (alternatively: Ra $\subseteq$ W$\times$W and
   such that: va(w)=$\{$w1: w Ra w1$\}$)
   3-a) $w \in va(w)$
4) $vp : W \rightarrow \wp(W)$ (alternatively: Ri $\subseteq$ W$\times$W and
   such that: vi(w)=$\{$w1: w Ri w1$\}$)
   4-a) $va(w) \subseteq vp(w)$
5) $pi : \wp(W) \rightarrow \wp(\wp(W))$ such that
   (where X, Y, Z designate arbitrary sets of members of W) : [20]
   5-a) $\emptyset \notin pi(X)$
   5-b) if $Y \cap X = Z \cap X$, then ($Y \in pi(X)$ iff $Z \in pi(X)$)
   5-c) if $Y, Z \in pi(X)$, then $Y \cap Z \in pi(X)$
   5-d) if $Y \subseteq X$ and $Y \in pi(X)$ and $X \subseteq Z$,
          then $((Z-X) \cup Y) \in pi(Z)$

---

[20]Note, in particular, that it is a consequence of the conditions which follow that "if $Z \in$ pi(X) and $Z \in$ pi(Y), then $Z \in$ pi(X $\cup$ Y)".

Truth in a world w *in a model* $\mathcal{M} = \langle W, va, vp, pi, V \rangle$ is characterised as follows:
(Note that $\|A\| = \|A\|^{\mathcal{M}} = \{w \in W : \mathcal{M}\models_w A\}$)

$$\mathcal{M}\models_w p \qquad \text{iff} \quad w \in V(p)$$

... (the usual truth conditions for the connectives $\neg, \wedge, \vee, \rightarrow$ and $\leftrightarrow$)

$\mathcal{M}\models_w \boxminus A$	iff	$va(w) \subseteq \|A\|$
$\mathcal{M}\models_w \Box A$	iff	$vp(w) \subseteq \|A\|$
$\mathcal{M}\models_w \bigcirc (B/A)$	iff	$\|A\| \cap \|B\| \neq \emptyset$ and
		$(\forall X)(\text{if } X \subseteq \|A\| \text{ and } X \cap \|B\| \neq \emptyset,$
		$\text{then } \|B\| \in pi(X))^{21}$
$\mathcal{M}\models_w \bigcirc_a A$	iff	$\|A\| \in pi(va(w)) \text{ and } va(w) \cap (W - \|A\|) \neq \emptyset$
$\mathcal{M}\models_w \bigcirc_i A$	iff	$\|A\| \in pi(vp(w)) \text{ and } vp(w) \cap (W - \|A\|) \neq \emptyset$

$\mathcal{M}\models A$ iff $\|A\|^{\mathcal{M}} = W$ ($\mathcal{M} = \langle W, va, vp, pi, V \rangle$)
and $\models A$ iff $\mathcal{M}\models A$ in all models $\mathcal{M}$.

<u>Some fundamental results</u>

It is easy to verify that $\Box$ and $\boxminus$ are normal modal operators of type T; that $\bigcirc$ (-/-) is a classical operator with respect to each of its arguments; and that $\bigcirc_a$ (respectively: $\bigcirc_i$) are classical modal operators for which the following schemas are valid:

($\neg$N)	$\neg \bigcirc_a \top$	(resp.: $\neg \bigcirc_i \top$)
(OD)	$\neg \bigcirc_a \bot$	(resp.: $\neg \bigcirc_i \bot$)
(C)	$\bigcirc_a A \wedge \bigcirc_a B \rightarrow \bigcirc_a (A \wedge B)$	(resp.: $\bigcirc_i A \wedge \bigcirc_i B \rightarrow \bigcirc_i (A \wedge B)$)

(Note: a classical operator which validates (OD) and (C) also validates the schema (D); on the other hand, it is important that neither $\bigcirc_a$ nor $\bigcirc_i$ validates the schema (M) - the converse of (C).)

As regards the relationships between the different operators, the following results are the most important. (Some further results concerning the dyadic operator are in the Appendix.)

Result 1 $\models \diamondsuit\!\!\!\!\diamond A \rightarrow \diamondsuit A$

Result 2 ("Restricted factual detachment")
(a) $\models \bigcirc (B/A) \wedge \boxminus A \wedge \diamondsuit\!\!\!\!\diamond B \wedge \diamondsuit\!\!\!\!\diamond \neg B \rightarrow \bigcirc_a B$
(b) $\models \bigcirc (B/A) \wedge \Box A \wedge \diamondsuit B \wedge \diamondsuit \neg B \rightarrow \bigcirc_i B$

---

[21]Note that this definition entails that "if $\mathcal{M}\models_w \bigcirc (B/A)$, then $\|B\| \in pi(\|A\|)$".

Result 3

(a) $\models \bigcirc (B/A) \wedge \diamondsuit (A \wedge B) \wedge \diamondsuit (A \wedge \neg B) \rightarrow \bigcirc_a (A \rightarrow B)$

(b) $\models \bigcirc (B/A) \wedge \diamondsuit (A \wedge B) \wedge \diamondsuit (A \wedge \neg B) \rightarrow \bigcirc_i (A \rightarrow B)$

Result 4   ("Restricted deontic detachment")

(a) $\models \bigcirc_a A \wedge \bigcirc (B/A) \wedge \diamondsuit (A \wedge B) \rightarrow \bigcirc_a (A \wedge B)$
(but not $\cdots \rightarrow \bigcirc_a B$)

(b) $\models \bigcirc_i A \wedge \bigcirc (B/A) \wedge \diamondsuit (A \wedge B) \rightarrow \bigcirc_i (A \wedge B)$
(but not $\cdots \rightarrow \bigcirc_i B)^{22}$

Result 5

(a) $\models \boxminus A \rightarrow (\neg \bigcirc_a A \wedge \neg \bigcirc_a \neg A)^{23}$

(b) $\models \square A \rightarrow (\neg \bigcirc_i A \wedge \neg \bigcirc_i \neg A)$

Result 6

(a) $\models \boxminus (A \leftrightarrow B) \rightarrow (\bigcirc_a A \leftrightarrow \bigcirc_a B)^{24}$

(b) $\models \square (A \leftrightarrow B) \rightarrow (\bigcirc_i A \leftrightarrow \bigcirc_i B)$

---

[22] Although it may seem, at first sight, that the failure of this implication represents a weakness of the logic, the analysis of some examples, to follow, indicates that it is - on the contrary - an advantage.

[23] The counterpart of this result also held in the system DL of (Jones and Pörn, 1985), where their modality Ought represented actual obligation. The point captured by this result is as follows: if it is not actually possible that A is false, then A is not actually obligatory (for it is guaranteed that A is true, so any such obligation has been discharged); and, in addition, ¬ A is not actually obligatory (for that which it is not actually possible to realize cannot be actually obligatory). However, as the earlier discussion of our approach has attempted to indicate, and as will be made clearer through the discussion of further examples below, the fact that it is not actually possible that ¬ A does not rule out the possibility that, ideally, it ought not to be the case that A.

[24] It has been suggested to us that the following example may be a counter-instance to 5(a)(and to the semantical condition 5-b) on which, essentially, the validity of 5(a) turns). Suppose j has decided that he will help his friend move on Saturday if and only if the weather is good, and suppose that j has also decided that he will borrow his brother's convertible on Saturday if and only if the weather is good. Suppose that j is firmly committed to both of these propositions, so that both H↔G and B↔G must be deemed to be actual necessities. In that case it follows that $\boxminus$(H↔B) is true. Even so, the suggestion goes, j might have an actual obligation to help his friend, but not an actual obligation to borrow the convertible; that is, it may consistently be supposed that $\bigcirc_a$ H and $\neg \bigcirc_a$ B.

One problem about interpreting this example, from our point of view, is that it is presumably not within j's effective power to influence the weather, whereas he does determine (we may suppose) whether or not he will help his friend and whether or not he will borrow the convertible. But let us put that point to one side, and replace G by C: j cleans his apartment on Friday night - a state of affairs which may be assumed to be under j's control. Suppose then the the result of j's decision may properly be characterised by the conjunction $\boxminus$(H↔C) $\wedge$ $\boxminus$(B↔C) which entails $\boxminus$(H↔B). Can it now be consistently supposed that it is actually obligatory that j helps his friend but not actually obligatory that j borrows the convertible? The answer is definitely negative. The central point, on our view, is that the truth of $\boxminus$(H↔B) means that it is not actually possible that either j helps his friend and does not borrow the convertible or j borrows the convertible and does not help his friend. Given that actual impossibility, there can

Corollary:

(a) $\models \boxminus A \rightarrow (\bigcirc_a B \rightarrow \bigcirc_a (A \wedge B))$
(b) $\models \Box A \rightarrow (\bigcirc_i B \rightarrow \bigcirc_i (A \wedge B))$

Regarding the semantic conditions necessary for the previous results, we may briefly say that:

> Result 1 comes directly from the relevant truth conditions;
> and in addition to the role of the relevant truth conditions, we should point out that:
> Result 2 turns essentially on condition 5-d);
> Result 3 turns essentially on conditions 5-c) and 5-d);
> Result 4 uses conditions 5-a) and 5-b);
> Result 5 is a consequence of 5-b).

8. APPLYING THE THEORY TO THE ANALYSIS OF SOME SCENARIOS WHICH EXHIBIT C--T--D STRUCTURES

We shall focus on three scenarios: the Chisholm set - Example 1; the extended version of Example 2 - the "dog scenario" - involving "contrary–to–contrary–to–duties"; and the so–called "Reykjavik scenario" [25]. We offer patterns of representation which - we would claim - are more abstract and simpler than, but at least as expressively rich as, those which might be supplied by approaches which explicitly represent actions and/or the temporal dimension.

Scenario 1:   *The Chisholm Set*

The deontic component
(d1) It ought to be that a certain man go to help his neighbours
(d2) It ought to be that if he goes he tell them he is coming
(d3) If he does not go, he ought not to tell them he is coming
Logical representation
(d1) $\bigcirc$ (help / $\top$)
(d2) $\bigcirc$ (tell / help)
(d3) $\bigcirc$ ($\neg$ tell / $\neg$ help)

---

be an actual obligation to help the friend if and only if there is an actual obligation to borrow the convertible. The fact that the decision to help a friend involves a commitment to another person, whereas the decision to borrow the car perhaps does not, is irrelevant to the conception of actual obligation we wish to explicate. (Our thanks to Donald Nute for suggesting the example; it points in the direction of an alternative conception of actual obligation, which we hope to investigate in future work.)

[25] This scenario, discussed in (Belzer, 1987) and (McCarty, 1994), is one of the many examples considered in (Prakken and Sergot, 1994; Prakken and Sergot, 1996).

Case 1.1
  Factual component

  (f1) X (the agent concerned) decides not to go to help his neighbour
  (f2) But it is potentially possible that X both helps and tells that he is coming
  (f3) X has not in fact told that he is coming, although it is still actually possible that he does tell

Logical representation

  (f1) $\boxminus \neg$ help
  (f2) $\diamondsuit$(help $\wedge$ tell)
  (f3) $\neg$ tell $\wedge \diamondsuit$ tell   (note that $\neg$ tell $\rightarrow \diamondsuit \neg$ tell)

Conclusions

  In virtue of Result 1, we may derive the following:
  *   viol(help) $\wedge \bigcirc_a \neg$ tell
  that is to say, X violates his obligation to help his neighbours, and is actually (given the circumstances) under an obligation not to tell them he is coming. On the other hand, it is also possible to derive the conclusion that X violates his obligation to "help and tell", since it is also possible to deduce, in virtue of Result 3, that $\bigcirc_i$ (help $\wedge$ tell). Note here (and *cf.* footnote 22 above) that it is not also possible to conclude that X has violated an obligation to tell *simpliciter*, since that particular obligation would not come into effect until X's helping was a fixed fact. This result seems to accord well with intuition.
  Note, also, that the pragmatic oddity, as we have diagnosed it, is avoided, for we could consistently add to the deontic component above an obligation to the effect that X ought not both go to help and not say that he is coming, i.e., an obligation of the form $\bigcirc$ ($\neg$ help $\vee$ tell / $\top$).

Case 1.2
  Factual component

  (f1) It is not actually possible that it is not the case that X both helps his neighbours and tells them he is coming (i.e., it is actually a fixed fact that X both helps his neighbours and tells them that he is coming)
  (f2) But it was potentially possible that X did not help his neighbours

Logical representation

  (f1) $\boxminus$ (help $\wedge$ tell)
  (f2) $\diamondsuit \neg$ help

Conclusions

We may derive the following:

* $\bigcirc_i$ help $\wedge \bigcirc_i$ (help $\wedge$ tell) $\wedge$ help $\wedge$ tell

i.e., X meets his ideal obligations, and no actual obligations are derivable.

Case 1.3

Factual component

(f1) It is actually a fixed fact that X both helps his neighbours and does not tell them he is coming, but it was potentially possible that he both helped and told.

Logical representation

(f1) $\boxminus$ (help $\wedge \neg$ tell) $\wedge \diamondsuit$ (help $\wedge$ tell)

Conclusions

We may derive the following:

* $\bigcirc_i$ help $\wedge$ help $\wedge$ viol(help $\wedge$ tell)

i.e., X meets his ideal obligation to help, but violates his obligation to help and tell; no actual obligation arises.

Case 1.4

Factual component

(f1) It is actually a fixed fact that X helps his neighbours, although it was potentially possible that he did not help them; and it is potentially impossible for X to tell his neighbours he is coming (imagine that there is no available means of communication).

Logical representation

(f1) $\boxminus$ help $\wedge \diamondsuit \neg$ help $\wedge \square \neg$ tell

Conclusions

We may derive the following:

* $\bigcirc_i$ help $\wedge$ help

i.e., X has not violated any ideal obligation (the obligation sentence $\bigcirc_i$ (help $\wedge$ tell) cannot be derived because it would be impossible to satisfy that obligation); furthermore, X has met his ideal obligation to help. No actual obligations are derivable.

Case 1.5

Factual component

(f1) It is not potentially possible for X to help his neighbours (for some reason or other - perhaps, for instance, there are no available means for X to travel to his neighbours' house); however, X tells his neighbours he is coming, but he might not have told them so.

Logical representation

(f1) $\square \neg$ help $\wedge \boxminus$ tell $\wedge \diamondsuit \neg$ tell

Conclusions

We may derive the following:

* viol($\neg$ tell)

Scenario 2:   *The dog example - extended with a second–level C–T–D*

The deontic component
(d1) There ought to be no dog
(d2) If there is no dog, there ought not to be a warning sign
(d3) If there is a dog, there ought to be a warning sign
(d4) If there is a dog and no warning sign, there ought to be a high fence
Logical representation
(d1) $\bigcirc$ ($\neg$ dog / $\top$)
(d2) $\bigcirc$ ($\neg$ sign / $\neg$ dog)
(d3) $\bigcirc$ (sign / dog)
(d4) $\bigcirc$ (fence / dog $\wedge \neg$ sign)

Case 2.1

Factual component

(f1) There is a dog, but it is actually possible not to have a dog (and there is no information regarding the possibility of having, or not, a sign or a fence)

Logical representation

(f1) dog $\wedge \diamondsuit \neg$ dog

Conclusions

We may derive the following regarding violation and actual obligation:

* viol($\neg$ dog) $\wedge \bigcirc_a \neg$ dog

There is a violation of the obligation not to have a dog, and there is an actual obligation to get rid of it.

Case 2.2

Factual component

(f1) It is not actually possible that there is not a dog (i.e., the presence of a dog is actually a fixed fact), but it was potentially possible that there was no dog.

Logical representation

(f1) $\boxminus$ dog $\wedge \diamondsuit \neg$ dog

Conclusions

We may derive the following regarding violation and actual obligation:
*   viol($\neg$ dog)

There is a violation of the prohibition against having a dog, and no actual obligations may be derived - although it is possible to deduce that

$$\diamondsuit \text{ sign} \wedge \diamondsuit \neg \text{ sign} \rightarrow \bigcirc_a \text{ sign}$$

Case 2.3

Factual component

(f1) It is actually necessary that there is a dog (i.e., it is not practically possible that there is not a dog), but there might potentially have been no dog

(f2) It is not actually possible that there is a sign, but there might potentially have been both a dog and a sign

(f3) There is not a fence, but it is actually possible that there could be a fence

Logical representation

(f1) $\boxminus$ dog $\wedge \diamondsuit \neg$ dog
(f2) $\boxminus \neg$ sign $\wedge \diamondsuit$ (dog $\wedge$ sign)
(f3) $\neg$ fence $\wedge \diamondsuit$ fence

Conclusions

We may derive, in particular, the following violations and actual obligation:
*   viol($\neg$ dog) $\wedge$ viol(dog$\rightarrow$ sign) $\wedge$ viol(dog $\wedge \neg$ sign$\rightarrow$fence) $\wedge$
     $\bigcirc_a$ fence

The ideal obligation that there be no dog is obtained by applying Result 1. By application of Result 2, we also derive (i) that there is an ideal obligation that if there is a dog then there is a sign, and (ii) that there is an ideal obligation that if there is a dog and no sign, then there is a fence. If we further assume that it is potentially possible that there is both no dog and no sign, then we may derive (using Result 3) that it is ideally obligatory that there is neither a dog nor a sign. Result 1 enables us to derive that, given the circumstances, the actual obligation is to put up a fence.

Scenario 3:   *The Reykjavik scenario*

The deontic component

Consider the following instructions given to officials accompanying Reagan and Gorbachov at the Reykjavik meeting:

(d1) The secret shall be told neither to Reagan nor to Gorbachov

(d2) But if the secret is told to Reagan it shall also be told to Gorbachov

(d3) And if the secret is told to Gorbachov it shall also be told to Reagan

Logical representation

Suppose that 'r' represents 'Reagan knows the secret', and that 'g' represents 'Gorbachov knows the secret':

(d1) $\bigcirc (\neg r \wedge \neg g / \top)$

(d2) $\bigcirc (g / r)$

(d3) $\bigcirc (r / g)$

Comments on the logical representation of the deontic component

(a) Sentence (d1) ought to be represented in the form indicated and not as $\bigcirc (\neg r / \top) \wedge \bigcirc (\neg g / \top)$. The reason for this is that there is no "absolute" obligation according to which, e.g., Reagan is not to know the secret (in just any context in which that would be possible); what is "absolutely" obligatory is that neither of them knows the secret. In fact, if the above alternative formulation of (d1) were to be employed, then in the situation where, for instance, the secret has been told to Gorbachov but not to Reagan it will be possible to derive contradictory actual obligations; this situation would indeed be intuitively incoherent, and it is a merit of the logic proposed that it would detect that incoherence. (A similar point is made in (Prakken and Sergot, 1996), in their discussion of this scenario.)

(b) A possible alternative representation of (d2)+(d3) would be (d2+3): $\bigcirc (g \wedge r / g \vee r)$ (although it would obviously then be necessary to employ different derivations to generate the same results).

Assumptions regarding the representation of the facts

(a) $r \rightarrow \boxminus r$

(b) $g \rightarrow \boxminus g$

(c) $\diamondsuit (r \wedge g)$ (which gives: $\diamondsuit r$ and $\diamondsuit g$, as well as $\diamondsuit (r \wedge g)$)

Case 3.1

Factual component

(f1) The secret has not yet been told to either of them

Logical representation

(f1) $\neg r \wedge \neg g$

Conclusions

* $O_i (\neg r \wedge \neg g) \wedge \neg r \wedge \neg g \wedge O_a (\neg r \wedge \neg g)$

The obligation to tell the secret to neither of them has not been violated, and persists as an actual obligation. Application of Result 1 (both parts) is instrumental in the derivation of these conclusions.

Case 3.2

Factual component

(f1) Reagan knows the secret but Gorbachov does not

(f2) But it was potentially possible that neither of them knew

Logical representation

(f1) $r \wedge \neg g$

(f2) $\Diamond (\neg r \wedge \neg g)$

Conclusions

* $\text{viol}(\neg r \wedge \neg g) \wedge O_a g$ (it suffices to use Result 1)

We may also derive $O_a (r \wedge g)$, by direct application of the corollary to Result 5, on the basis of the prior derivation of $O_a g$. On the other hand, if we employ (d2+3) instead of (d2) and (d3), we get $O_a (r \wedge g)$ by direct application of Result 1, and then on the basis of that result we can use Result 5 to obtain $O_a g$.

Case 3.3

Factual component

(f1) The secret has been told at the same time to both Reagan and Gorbachov

Logical representation

(f1) $r \wedge g \wedge \Diamond (\neg r \wedge \neg g)$

Conclusions

* $\text{viol}(\neg r \wedge \neg g)$

There is violation of the obligation to tell neither of them, and no actual obligations are now derivable.

Case 3.4

Factual component

(f1) One, and only one, of Reagan and Gorbachov has been told the secret

(f2) It might potentially have been the case that neither of them was told

Logical representation

(f1) $(r \vee g) \wedge \neg (r \wedge g)$

(f2) $\Diamond (\neg r \wedge \neg g)$

Conclusions

* $\text{viol}(\neg\, r \wedge \neg\, g) \wedge \bigcirc_a (r \wedge g)$

Note that the derivation of $\bigcirc_a (r \wedge g)$ requires the use of Result 1, and then the application of the corollary to Result 5; the derivation could be made directly by application of Result 1 if (d2+3) were used to represent the second and third lines of the deontic component.

9. CONCLUDING REMARKS

The above discussion of various C–T–D scenarios illustrates the expressive capacity of our formal language, and indicates how these scenarios can be analyzed in ways which conform to requirements (i)–(vii), described in sections (1)–(3). A number of issues remain unresolved, of course, and we here briefly mention three of them, since they will be the focus of our attempts to develop this theory further.

One specific issue concerns the characterisation of violation. In certain contexts it may be natural to distinguish between the violation of an obligation, on the one hand, and the situation in which an obligation has yet to be fulfilled, on the other. It might be suggested that the way we have defined violation above really corresponds to the latter, weaker notion, since that definition does not rule out the actual possibility of fulfilling the (ideal) obligation concerned; whereas violation in the full sense of the obligation $\bigcirc_i A$ implies that the falsity of A is an actual necessity. In summary, we might consider the alternative definitions:

$$\text{not–yet–fulfilled}(A) =_{df} \bigcirc_i A \wedge \neg\, A$$

$$\text{violated}(A) =_{df} \bigcirc_i A \wedge \boxminus \neg\, A$$

This distinction suggests, in turn, a possible way of linking the notions of ideal and actual obligation, since it would appear reasonable to require that an ideal obligation which is not yet fulfilled entails an actual obligation, if that which is ideally obligatory is still actually possible. That is:

$$\bigcirc_i A \wedge \diamondsuit A \wedge \neg\, A \rightarrow \bigcirc_a A$$

Validity of this schema would be secured were the following model condition to be adopted:

5-e)   if $Y \subseteq X$ and $Z \in \text{pi}(X)$ and $Y \cap Z \neq \emptyset$, then $Z \in \text{pi}(Y)$

It remains to be seen what the consequences of adopting changes of these kinds might be, in regard to our analysis of C–T–D scenarios.

The two pairs of notions of necessity and possibility are at the core of our understanding of C–T–D problems; the way we have attempted to characterise these notions intuitively, indicates a close connection between them and concepts in the theory and logic of action. Actual possibility was understood, essentially, in terms of the alternatives available in a particular situation, given what the agents therein have done or have firmly decided to do, or not to do. Whereas potential possibility was understood, essentially, in terms of the alternatives available in a particular situation given both the capabilities of the agents therein, and their opportunities for action. In contrast to a number of other approaches to C–T–D problems, our treatment of C–T–D scenarios has not involved an explicit representation of actions; nor have we felt a need for such representations. Nevertheless, it would be interesting to explore ways of defining our two pairs of necessity/possibility notions in terms of concepts drawn from the logic of action, pertaining to decision, volition, ability and opportunity.

Another point of difference between our approach and that favoured by other attempts to deal with C–T–D problems, is that we do not at any stage employ techniques drawn from the study of default reasoning. In this respect our approach follows the same line as that adopted in the earlier sections of (Prakken and Sergot, 1996), where the need to distinguish between the defeasibility and violation of obligations is emphasised. Consider, for instance, a conditional obligation to the effect that, if your aged mother is sick, then you ought to help her. Such a conditional obligation might well leave room for exceptions, just as penguins might be the exception to the generalisation that birds fly; supposing for example that your young child has been injured in a car accident, and urgently needs you at the hospital, the obligation to help your sick, aged mother may well be deemed to have been defeated, or overturned. Your going to the hospital to be with your child would not then ordinarily be seen as an act violating an obligation to help your aged mother. And there, precisely, is an essential contrast between this "defeasibility scenario", and the kind of C–T–D scenario we have discussed above, where you have a dog and have not put up a warning sign - and where, in consequence, your actual obligation is to erect a fence. Here, as we have stressed, the obligations not to have a dog, and to put up a sign if you do have a dog, have not been overturned, or defeated - they have been violated.

Nevertheless it is clear that a general theory of deontic conditionals should encompass both phenomena of the C–T–D type and the fact deontic conditionals usually permit exceptions. So one further task we are setting ourselves is the integration of our analysis of C–T–Ds within a theory of default deontic conditionals.

APPENDIX: SOME OTHER RESULTS FOR THE DYADIC
OPERATOR $\bigcirc$ (-/-)

Although the logic of the dyadic conditional obligation operator has not been completely characterised from the axiomatic point of view, we list here some schemas which might be employed in an axiomatisation (in addition to the property, mentioned above, that this operator is classical with respect to both of its arguments)

* $\models\bigcirc (B/A) \rightarrow \bigcirc (A \wedge B/A)$
* $\models\diamondsuit(A \wedge B) \wedge \bigcirc (A \rightarrow B/\top) \rightarrow \bigcirc (B/A)$
* $\models\diamondsuit (A \wedge B \wedge C) \wedge \bigcirc (C/B) \rightarrow \bigcirc (C/A \wedge B)$
  (*restricted version of the principle of strengthening of the antecedent*)
* $\models \bigcirc (B/A) \rightarrow \bigcirc (B/A \wedge B)$
* $\models \bigcirc (B/A) \wedge \bigcirc (C/A) \rightarrow \bigcirc (B \wedge C/A)$
* $\models \neg\bigcirc (A/\bot)$
* $\models \neg\bigcirc (\neg A/A)$

ACKNOWLEDGMENTS

Part of the background to this paper is an invited talk given by Andrew Jones t the Third International Workshop on Deontic Logic in Computer Science, held in Sesimbra, Portugal, January 1996. Andrew Jones wishes to thank the organizers of that workshop for their kind invitation, and the PRAXIS XXI Programme of the Portuguese Research Council for its support in the Spring of 1996. Some of the research here reported has been carried out within the Portuguese research project no. PCSH/C/OGE/1038/95–MAGO, financially supported by JNICT, and the ESPRIT Basic Research Working Group 8319 MODELAGE ("A Common Formal Model of Cooperating Intelligent Agents").

José Carmo
Department of Mathematics
Instuto Superior Técnico
Lisboa, Portugal

Andrew J. I. Jones
Department of Philosophy
University of Oslo

REFERENCES

al–Hibri, A. (1978). *Deontic Logic: A Comprehensive Appraisal and a New Proposal.* University Press of America, Washington, D.C..

Åqvist, L. and Hoepelman, J. (1981). Some theorems about a 'tree' system of deontic tense logic. In Hilpinen, R. (ed.), *New Studies in Deontic Logic,* D. Reidel, Dordrecht, pages 187–221.

Belzer, M. (1987). Legal reasoning in 3–D. In *Proc. of the First International Conference in Artificial Intelligence and Law,* ACM Press, Boston, pages 155–163.

Brown, M. (1996). Doing as we ought: Towards a logic of simply dischargeable obligations. In Brown, M. and Carmo, J. (eds.), *Deontic Logic, Agency and Normative Systems (Proc. of the Third International Workshop on Deontic Logic in Computer Science)*, Springer, Workshops in Computing Series, pages 47–65.

Carmo, J. and Jones, A. J. I. (1994). Deontic database constraints and the characterisation of recovery. In Jones, A.J.I. and Sergot, M.J.(eds.), *Proc. of the Second International Workshop on Deontic Logic in Computer Science,* pages 56–85.

Carmo, J. and Jones, A. J. I. (1995). Deontic logic and different levels of ideality. *RRDMIST.*

Carmo, J. and Jones, A. J. I. (1996). Deontic database constraints, violation and recovery. to appear in *Studia Logica,* 1/2 (57).

Chellas, B. J. (1974). Conditional obligation. In Stenlund (ed.), *Logical Theory and Semantic Analysis,* D. Reidel, Dordrecht, pages 23–33.

Chellas, B. J. (1980). *Modal Logic - An Introduction.* Cambridge University Press.

Chisholm, R. M. (1963). Contrary–to–duty imperatives and deontic logic. *Analysis* 24:33–36.

Hansson, B. (1971). An analysis of some deontic logics. In Hilpinen, R. (ed.), *Deontic Logic: Introductory and Systematic Readings,* D. Reidel, Dordrecht, pages 121–147, (2$\underline{nd}$ ed. 1981).

Jones, A. J. I. (1993). Towards a formal theory of defeasible deontic conditionals. *Annals of Mathematics and Artificial Intelligence* 9:151–166.

Jones, A. J. I. and Pörn, I. (1985). Ideality, sub–ideality and deontic logic. *Synthese* 65:275–290.

Lewis, D. (1974). Semantic analysis for dyadic deontic logic. In Stenlund (ed.), *Logical Theory and Semantic Analysis,* D. Reidel, Dordrecht, pages 1–14.

Loewer, B. and Belzer, M. (1983). Dyadic deontic detachment. *Synthese* 54:295–318.

McCarty, L. T. (1994). Defeasible deontic reasoning. *Fundamenta Informaticae* 21:125–148.

Mott, P. L. (1973). On Chisholm's paradox. *Journal of Philosophical Logic* 2:197–211.

Prakken, H. and Sergot, M. J. (1994). Contrary–to–duty imperatives, defeasibility and violability. In Jones, A.J.I. and Sergot, M.J. (eds.), *Proc. of the Second International Workshop on Deontic Logic in Computer Science,* pages 296–318.

Prakken, H. and Sergot, M. J. (1996). Contrary–to–duty obligations and defeasible deontic reasoning. to appear in *Studia Logica* 1/2 (57).

Thomason, R. H. (1981). Deontic logic as founded on tense logic. In Hilpinen, R. (ed.), *New Studies in Deontic Logic,* D. Reidel, Dordrecht, pages 165–176.

Thomason, R. H. (1984). Combinations of tense and modality. In Gabbay, D. and Guenthner, F. (eds.), *Handbook of Philosophical Logic,* D. Reidel, Dordrecht, Volume II: pages 135–165.

van Eck, J. (1981). *A System of Temporally Relative Modal and Deontic Predicate Logic and its Philosophical Applications.* Ph. D. thesis, Rijksuniversiteit te Gronigen.

R. P. LOUI

ALCHOURRÓN AND VON WRIGHT ON CONFLICT AMONG NORMS

1. INTRODUCTION

In an impassioned defense of deontic logic (1993), Carlos Alchourrón provided us with a clear statement of many of his final positions on the subtle relations between defeasibility, deontic modality, and belief revision. Alchourrón, the Argentine gentleman lawyer and polymath, stood at the apex where met three of this half-century's most important developments in reasoning and the mathematical modeling of reasoning. His passing must be marked with the particular sadness of the loss of the rare opposing thinker worth forthrightly engaging (although it must be confessed that this author never succeeded in doing so).

Alchourrón understood defeasibility and its implications better than all others who failed to embrace it.[1] Defeasibility was for him a competitor. It was an insurgent idea backed by the sheer volume and number of formalists in artificial intelligence, knowledge representation and non-monotonic reasoning, their incessance, their unchecked onslaught. It was floodwater. It was to be opposed because it was so plausible a substitute for Alchourrón's own favorite logical developments. Of course, as a co-founder with Peter Gärdenfors and David Makinson of AGM belief revision (Alchourrón et al., 1985), and as co-author with Eugenio Bulygin on the understanding of legal reasoning through deontic logic (Alchourrón et al., 1971), Alchourrón's loyalties were determined.

Unlike other opponents of defeasibility, Alchourrón was a legal scholar who had every reason to know the origins of defeasibility in contract and property law; he could appreciate the concepts of burden-shifting and process, upon which a proper understanding of defeasibility depends. In his paper, we find the depth of his appreciation of defeasibility, and through his concern with

---

[1]For example, Alchourrón understands that defeasibility is ampliative (Alchourrón, 1993, p. 83), that it creates "contributory" conditions rather than conditions necessary or sufficient [p. 82], that it is not always reducible to probabilistic relations [p. 69], that it is fundamental to the philosophy of law [p. 67], that it demotes its conclusions to a secondary status relative to its premises [p. 83], that it militates against the modularity of rules [p. 67], that it creates conditionals that lack truth values [p. 44] and that are not falsifiable [p. 83], and that it is closely related to belief revision [p. 83]. Inexplicably, Alchourrón fails to note its burden-shifting, its relativizing warrant to partial computation.

D. Nute (ed.), Defeasible Deontic Logic, 345–351.
© 1997 Kluwer Academic Publishers. Printed in the Netherlands.

von Wright's conditional norms, we find the source of his recalcitrance.

2. ALCHOURRON'S ATTACK

Alchourrón's text shows his concern over the popularity of the newcomer and an obvious effort at restraint. His defense of deontic logic takes the form of an attack on defeasibility. Defeasibility invokes a "possible confusion of logic and revision," (Alchourrón, 1993, p. 69) providing new mechanisms for which "there is no need" [p. 44], and which anyway hides its "conceptually weaker conclusions" in a "quiet darkness" [p. 83].

The principal conclusion is that

> If x is a bird then (defeasibly) x flies

is not the proper way to "give formal expression of the cognitive situations of ... incomplete knowledge". When a bird is subsumed under this rule, the defeasible conclusion thereby (defeasibly) warranted, that it flies, has a questionable epistemic status. To Alchourrón, the better approach is to use the Russell/Frege/Peirce conditional,

> If x is a bird then (materially) x flies

and to revise that conditional as necessary if and when conflict arises. The revision of the conditional depends on the actual conflicts that the epistemic agent has suffered; for Alchourrón,

> If x is a bird and x is not a penguin and x is not dead,
> then (materially) x flies

is a reasonable stage to reach *post revision*.

This move is of course well known (though not always well understood). H. L. A. Hart, in the paper that brought defeasibility forward from medieval English law to modern logico-linguistics (Hart, 1952), entertained such a move in a footnote, regarding it as trivial at best and misleading at worst.[2] AI writers have built their industry on the correct perception that the antecedent

---

[2]Alchourrón cites other work by Hart and the prior work of Sir W. D. Ross (1930), but does not show an awareness of this principal work of Hart. This is quite clear in Alchourrón's analogy that Dworkin is to Hart as Ross is to Kant: the implication is that Dworkin's principles, like Ross's *prima facie* duties, make room for defeasibility while Hart's positive rules, like Kant's absolute duties, do not. This cannot be right. No scholar in possession of Hart's early paper would take Hart to be in contrast to Ross, since Hart's paper on defeasible concepts is the historical extension of Ross's *prima facie* duties. Perhaps Alchourrón knew the paper, but simply did not fully care, or was following too closely Dworkin's twisted prose. Although Hart trades the defeasibility of the conditional for the defeasibility of the predication, the sentiment

cannot thus be gerrymandered. Something that has become important about the intertwining of computation and specification, about *prima facie* warrant's localization in a rule, about the incompleteness of computation, accounts for the transformation's failure. In plain language,

> If x is a bird then (defeasibly) x flies and
> If x is a penguin then (defeasibly) x does not fly

is not equivalent to

> If x is a bird and x is not a penguin then (materially) x flies and
> If x is a penguin then (materially) x does not fly.

Neither do the pairs of rules behave the same at various levels of computation, nor do they behave the same at various levels of epistemic improvement.

This much is a standard lesson in knowledge representation and reasoning. The usual response among classically trained thinkers is that logic should be about commitment, not computation, and that one who uses the rule that birds fly without explicit commitment to whether the bird is a penguin, implicitly asserts that it is not a penguin. It is a response that retraces its steps rather than steps forward.

Alchourrón takes us farther. He too embraces epistemic commitment as the goal of logic and denies the importance of computation. But he understands that defeasibility is part of a constructive model of belief. Construction is different from constraint. Defeasible rules prescribe the construction of warrant based on what can be computed or asserted so far. Alchourrón's model of belief revision can describe the dynamics of belief, so he too can give an account of construction. He can do more than indulge the insistence of deductivists. He can supplement conditionals with revision.

Alchourrón notes that what is at stake is ampliative reasoning. Ampliative reasoning is the great logical territory unconquered by earlier mathematical models. Probabilists and inductivists thought they had accounts of it, as did philosophers of scientific explanation. Alchourrón believed that his theory of revision (with Gärdenfors and Makinson) provided the best qualitative understanding of ampliative reasoning. Of course, AGM revision theory occurs shortly after Gärdenfors's feud with Isaac Levi on indeterminate decision; historically and technically, I find belief revision's paternity in Levi's work on confirmational conditionalization and non-Bayesian shifts. So perhaps AGM revision theory's ampliativity is not so different from inductive ampliativity.

For Alchourrón, the state of belief depends on the epistemic agent's experience. The posterior nature of the revised conditional is important. Adding

---

is the same, and is largely present in the work of Hart that Alchourrón cites (Ross, 1961) under the new term, "open-texture".

the explicit conditions of the bird not being dead and not being a penguin are for Alchourrón dependent on the particular conflicts and revisions that were endured at earlier times. "It seems to me unquestionable that the main [conditions] are the formal representation of the revisions effectively performed by an agent and of his dispositions to revise. ... We will probably need different choice functions [i.e., conditions] for the same sentences in different moments of his life." (p. 81) In AGM, revisions are constrained but not uniquely constrained. There is some indeterminacy of the resulting state of belief. This indeterminacy together with the contingency of the agent's revisions accounts for Alchourrón's view of the result as ampliative. The result is certainly not contained wholly within the language of the original, unrevised state of belief, and it is not predictable even if one has been given the sentences that force revisions.

Defeasible reasoning likewise permits indeterminacy of the result, a freeing (or indexing) of the connection between input and output. The antecedent of a defeasible rule is a contributory condition, not a sufficient condition. Its sufficiency depends on what other conditions might be found in conflicting rules. This in turn depends on which rules have been considered by the search and inference procedures which are indeterminate, unspecified computations.[3] There is no question that the result of defeasible reasoning is an ampliative procedure. Computational indeterminacy permits entailments to be independent of their premises in a sense that can be found in none of the competing accounts of ampliative reasoning. Defeasible entailments are computationally ampliative.

Alchourrón's claim in the paper, that there is no need for a logic of defeasible norms, is more the consequence of his fancy for revision than his fixation upon deontic modalities. Nevertheless, we may find in von Wright what is at stake for deontic logic, and what is surely a precursor of Alchourrón's view.

3. VON WRIGHT'S STAND

von Wright(1982) responds to Roderick Chisholm's (1963) puzzle of Contrary-to-Duty imperatives. According to the puzzle, it is possible that

$$\bigcirc (p \to q), \bigcirc p \to r), \text{ and } \bigcirc (\sim p)$$

can co-exist in a corpus. Worse,

---

[3] Isaac Levi (1996) writes that this view might merely reinforce our human irrationality, our bad habits of reasoning. Levi, too, views logic as the specification of ideal belief commitments, finding no place in the model for computation or construction. He does not say whether he thinks there can be analysis of the canons for regulating the constructions that might be used in case humans fall short of the ideals, in case societies insist on procedural justice, in case rule-makers decide to write regulations for constructions, or in case we discover that the classical ideals merely affect our language but do not help fix our beliefs.

$$\bigcirc(\sim p) \text{ technically entails } \bigcirc (p \to x)$$

for any x! von Wright goes to some length to distinguish deontic obligation from technical, or derived obligation, to avoid this representational embarrassment. But the main point is that the norms are not in conflict unless p, which is prohibited, occurs. The addition of p would require the subtraction of $\bigcirc(\sim p)$. This would be a revision, and the revision might as well include the resolution of whether q or r (or x) is the appropriate sanction. von Wright says as much:

> [The coexistence] in itself, need not lead to trouble. It only means that, if the prohibition is violated, the coordinated Contrary-to-Duty imperatives require, for their satisfaction, that both q and that r come true. ... If ... the conjunction of the two states that q and r is a logical impossibility ..., if a case like this occurred "in real life", the legislator would presumably take steps to remove the conflict – say by derogating one of the conditional norms or by making them, somehow, consonant. (vonWright, 1982, p. 157)

von Wright presses further into the question of deontic modeling:

> Such contradictions cannot be "solved" in logic, only in the practice of norm-giving. ... The legislator is well advised to amend legislation. The *logician* cannot help him. (vonWright, 1982, p. 158)

In no less a pair of legal authorities than John Austin and Hans Kelsen does von Wright find a distinction between laws that norm action, and laws that specify sanctions for delicts. Some laws delimit right and wrong. Some laws specify consequences. von Wright wishes here to keep them separate, as primary and secondary norms, as two different deontic environments between which one passes when one retracts an *a priori* $\bigcirc(\sim p)$ in favor of an *a posteriori* p.

Alchourrón likewise discusses a problem of conflicting norms (Alchourrón, 1993, pp. 60–61). From

$$\bigcirc(A/B);$$
$$\bigcirc(\sim A/C),$$

he derives

$$\sim(B\&C).$$

That is, if B and C can co-occur, then the authority has inconsistently normed. Hence, conditional norms with inconsistent consequents B and C cannot jointly apply because B and C cannot co-occur.

A set of conditional general norms entails (in the logic of norms) a non-tautological sentence (has a factual or contradictory consequence) iff it follows in the logic for normative propositions that the authority has inconsistently normed some action for some circumstance. (Chisholm, 1963, p. 61)

The problem is that in real normative systems, conflicting norms seem to occur. In a legal code, conflicting norms might be the natural, most literal interpretation of the "duties imposed." The law might prohibit people from making p true, and might additionally specify the sanctions q and r in the case of p. In case of a crime of one foreign national upon another, perhaps one rule prescribes extradition while another recommends imprisonment. Sometimes the conflict is resolved by ordering the rules, by considerations of jurisdiction, rank, or recency. Sometimes the rules are unorderable and an adjudicator sets a precedent with deliberation and opinion.

This situation is the normal problem for juridical decision. The problem is not that two rules are in direct conflict. The problem is usually that the current fact situation can be subsumed under two (or more) rules with equal probity. The problem is not, as Richard Wasserstrom muses (1961) as he attempts to escape the dominant deductivism of the time, that there is no precedent that governs a case. The problem is that with no disingenuity, two or more precedents can be brought to bear on the case at hand.

In a slightly different example, p might be the killing of a person by accident, for which there is one remedy for killing in general, and one remedy for manslaughter in particular. p is thus separable as $p_1\&p_2$, stating the killing and the accidental nature of the killing, respectively. So the literal "duties" might be

$$\bigcirc(p_1 \to q);$$

$$\bigcirc(p_1\&p_2 \to r).$$

Nevertheless, from $\bigcirc(p_1 \to q)$, many can derive $\bigcirc(p_1\&p_2 \to q)$. This is exactly the kind of situation in which the law's *lex specialis* recommends the more specific rule. The deference of one rule to the other, or "derogation", can also be governed by (meta-)rule, principle, or precedent. In logics of defeasible reasoning the more specific antecedent dominates (for example, (Nute, 1985)) or else there are rules that have as their consequents that one rule is preferred to the other (for example, (Prakken and Sartor, 1996)).

Instead of specifying in a mathematically precise way how this deference, derogation, or defeat occurs, von Wright regards the question as extra-logical. Somehow, consistency is restored. Alchourrón hides the defeat within the "choice functions" that arise during "contingent" revisions. Somehow, the legislator or adjudicator makes the right revisions.

"The particular details of the revisions (and the choice functions) are never analyzed by a logician (as a logician), since at the logical level any empirical analysis is out of question." (Alchourrón, 1993, p. 83). The alternative paradigm, says Alchourrón, hides its conclusions in an epistemic status that is tentative and subordinate. Defeasibility is sneaky science. It is disrespectful of the *status quo*; it flaunts the weaker status of its defeasible conclusions.

But the defeasible logics describe exactly how conflicting norms are processed. The defeasible logics do not need to pretend that there are no conflicts, or that someone else will solve the problem somehow. The defeasible logics provide a place for computation.

Alchourrón left us at this same point: a choice between two paths, neither of which he could ascertain to have *a priori* superiority. Like the revisions of the agents he proposes with Gärdenfors and Makinson, the only constraint is for the final snapshot to have the dignity of consistency. Alchourrón could only hope that we would choose well. I however, am able to believe consistently that inquiry will dignify other conclusions.[4]

R. P. Loui
Department of Computer Science
Washington University
St. Louis

REFERENCES

Alchourrón, Carlos, and Bulygin, Eugenio (1971). *Normative Systems*. Springer.
Alchourrón, Carlos, Gärdenfors, Peter, and Makinson, David (1985). On the logic of theory change: partial meet contraction and revision functions. *Journal of Symbolic Logic* 50.
Alchourrón, Carlos (1993). Philosophical foundations of deontic logic and the logic of defeasible conditionals. In Meyer, J. J., and Wieringa, R. (eds.), *Deontic Logic in Computer Science: Normative System Specification*, Wiley.
Chisholm, Roderick (1963). Contrary-to-duty imperatives and deontic logic. *Analysis* 24.
Hart, H. L. A. (1952). The ascription of responsibility and rights, In Flew, A. (ed.), *Logic and Language*, Oxford.
Levi, Isaac (1996). *For The Sake of Argument*. Cambridge.
Nute, Donald (1986). LDR: a logic for defeasible reasoning. *Technical Report ACMC 01-0013*, Artificial Intelligence Center, The University of Georgia.
Prakken, Henry and Sartor, Giovanni (1996). Rules about rules. *in this volume*.
Ross, W. D. (1930). *The Right and the Good*. Oxford.
Ross, W. D. (1961). *Concept of Law*. Oxford.
von Wright, G. H. (1982). Norms, truth and logic, In Martino, A.A. (ed.), *Deontic Logic, Computational Linguistics, and Legal Information Systems,* North-Holland.
von Wright, G. H. (1983). *Practical Reason: Philosophical Papers.* v. I, Cornell.
Wasserstrom, Richard (1961). *The Judicial Decision*. Stanford.

---

[4]Dr. Fernando Tohmé gave important encouragement in the preparation of this paper and graciously recalled his meetings with Professor Alchourrón.

INDEX

Åqvist, L., 223, 246, 320

al–Hibri, A., 11, 318
Alchourrón, C., 80, 81, 115, 123, 125, 263, 265, 345, 346, 349, 350
Anderson, A. R., 59
Aristotle, 159, 166
Arlo-Costas, H., 54

Becher, V., 107
Belnap, N., 20, 33, 42
Belzer, M., 93, 104, 123, 227, 234–236, 239, 318, 320, 334
Bonevac, D., 123
Boutilier, C., 41, 42, 81, 85, 93, 100, 107
Brewka, G., 83, 92, 116, 263
Brown, A. L., 89, 257, 320
Bulygin, E., 345

Carmo, J., 240, 245
Castañeda, H.-N., 4, 9, 45, 161, 223
Causey, R., 131
Chellas, B., 20, 21, 39, 48, 81, 83, 85, 89, 99, 149, 223, 231, 257, 279, 317, 318, 320
Chisholm, R., 6, 48, 79, 80, 83–89, 91–94, 97, 98, 100, 108, 118, 123, 132, 162, 186, 200, 201, 240, 245, 246, 248, 317–322, 326, 329, 334, 348, 350
Clark, K. L., 129

Decew, J., 12
Delgrande, J., 41, 264
Dennett, D., 20
Donagan, A., 19, 32
Doyle, J., 263
Dung, P., 264
Dworkin, R., 54, 218

Feldman, F., 8, 48
Fodor, J., 140
Foot, P., 19
Forrester, J., 4, 79, 80, 83–85, 87, 100, 118, 161, 223

Frankena, W., 160
Føllesdal, D., 8, 124, 129

Gabbay, D., 90
Gardner, A. v. d., 123
Geffner, H., 41, 82, 117, 124
Goble, L., 5, 184, 188
Greenspan, P., 6, 123, 186
Gärdenfors, P., 107

Hansson, B., 14, 34, 59–61, 82, 93, 95, 98, 99, 115, 123, 227–229, 231–236, 238–242, 245, 247–251, 254, 259, 260, 326
Hansson, S., 5, 89
Hart, H. L. A., 123, 264, 346
Hempel, C., 140
Hilpinen, R., 8, 124, 129–130, 224
Hintikka, J., 4, 34, 35, 129, 238
Hoepelman, J., 223, 246, 320
Horty, J., 83, 100, 124, 131, 133, 134, 162, 163, 188, 189, 211, 212, 224, 238, 263, 265
Humberstone, I., 48

Jackson, F., 5
Jennings, R. E., 94
Jones, A., 162, 186, 220, 224, 239, 240, 245

Kant, I., 167
Koons, R., 54
Kraus, S., 82

Lehman, D., 82
Lemmon, J., 19
Levesque, H., 81, 91
Levi, I., 347, 348
Lewis, D., 11, 14, 34, 48, 53, 60–62, 80, 84, 123, 143, 188, 189, 199, 224, 227–232, 235, 239–243, 245, 254–256, 258, 260, 319
Loewer, B., 93, 159, 184, 188, 195, 198–200, 227, 234–236, 239, 318, 320

Loui, R., 131, 264

MacCormick, D. N., 123
Magidor, M., 82
Makinson, D., 110, 112, 123, 125, 237,
    239, 263
Mantha, S., 89
Marcus, R. B., 19, 32, 174
McCarthy, J., 157
McCarty, T., 80, 85, 87, 106, 227, 334
McDermott, J., 26, 263
McArthur, R., 11, 12
Mill, J. S., 160, 167, 168, 196
Montague, R., 123
Morreau, M., 83, 113, 162, 164–165, 170,
    180–181, 237
Mott, P., 11, 89, 318

Nickle, J., 168
Norman, J., 264
Nozick, R., 45
Nute, D., 124, 125, 129, 130, 132, 350

Pearl, J., 27, 42, 82, 83, 91, 107, 109, 117,
    205, 211–213
Pietroski, P., 140, 167, 169, 194–196
Pollock, J, 41, 49, 130, 147, 263
Poole, D., 124, 263
Pope, A., 163, 188, 189, 191, 193
Pörn, I., 224, 239, 240, 317, 320–322, 324,
    333
Powers, L., 85
Prakken, H., 80, 93, 100, 124–125, 133,
    135, 263–264, 267–268, 285,
    313, 317, 321, 323, 327, 334,
    339, 342, 350
Prior, A., 4, 34, 36
Przymusinska, H., 35

Raz, J., 49, 153, 155
Reiter, R.,13, 17, 18, 24–26, 28, 39, 79, 93,
    124, 129, 133, 134, 263–265
Rescher, N., 60, 264
Rey, G., 140
Ross, W. D., 4, 83, 113, 115, 123, 159,
    163, 195, 223, 236, 346
Ryan, M., 252, 253, 261
Ryle, G., 169
Ryu, Y., 263

Sartor, G., 264, 265, 267–268, 285, 313,
    350

Sartre, J., 19
Schiffer, S., 140
Schurtz, G., 299
Schobbens, P.-T., 253
Sergot, M., 80, 93, 100, 124–125, 133,
    135, 317, 321, 323, 327, 334,
    339, 342
Seung, T. K., 54, 163, 195
Shapiro, S., 54
Shoham, Y., 263
Sinnott-Armstrong, W., 5
Smith, T., 80
Sophocles, 208, 212
Stalnaker, R., 35, 143

Tan, Y.-H., 224, 256, 263, 265
Taylor, P., 168
Thomason, R., 35, 48, 85, 143, 184, 188,
    189, 320
Tomberlin, J., 9, 12, 85, 89

Ullman-Margalit, E., 27

Van der Torre, L., 224, 256, 263, 265
van Eck, J. A., 242, 243, 246, 259, 320
van Fraassen, B., 17, 22, 34, 123, 133, 163,
    195
von Wright, H., 2, 7, 8, 17, 34, 60, 81, 83,
    94, 123, 160, 279, 348, 349
Vorobej, M., 10
Vreeswijk, G., 83

Wasserstrom, R., 350
Williams, B., 19, 22, 169, 174, 209

163. D. Mayr and G. Süssmann (eds.), *Space, Time, and Mechanics*. Basic Structures of a Physical Theory. 1983　　　　　　　　　　　　　　ISBN 90-277-1525-4
164. D. Gabbay and F. Guenthner (eds.), *Handbook of Philosophical Logic*. Vol. I: Elements of Classical Logic. 1983　　　　　　　　　　　ISBN 90-277-1542-4
165. D. Gabbay and F. Guenthner (eds.), *Handbook of Philosophical Logic*. Vol. II: Extensions of Classical Logic. 1984　　　　　　　　　ISBN 90-277-1604-8
166. D. Gabbay and F. Guenthner (eds.), *Handbook of Philosophical Logic*. Vol. III: Alternative to Classical Logic. 1986　　　　　　　　ISBN 90-277-1605-6
167. D. Gabbay and F. Guenthner (eds.), *Handbook of Philosophical Logic*. Vol. IV: Topics in the Philosophy of Language. 1989　　　　ISBN 90-277-1606-4
168. A. J. I. Jones, *Communication and Meaning*. An Essay in Applied Modal Logic. 1983
　　　　　　　　　　　　　　　　　　　　　　　ISBN 90-277-1543-2
169. M. Fitting, *Proof Methods for Modal and Intuitionistic Logics*. 1983
　　　　　　　　　　　　　　　　　　　　　　　ISBN 90-277-1573-4
170. J. Margolis, *Culture and Cultural Entities*. Toward a New Unity of Science. 1984
　　　　　　　　　　　　　　　　　　　　　　　ISBN 90-277-1574-2
171. R. Tuomela, *A Theory of Social Action*. 1984　　　ISBN 90-277-1703-6
172. J. J. E. Gracia, E. Rabossi, E. Villanueva and M. Dascal (eds.), *Philosophical Analysis in Latin America*. 1984　　　　　　　　　　　ISBN 90-277-1749-4
173. P. Ziff, *Epistemic Analysis*. A Coherence Theory of Knowledge. 1984
　　　　　　　　　　　　　　　　　　　　　　　ISBN 90-277-1751-7
174. P. Ziff, *Antiaesthetics*. An Appreciation of the Cow with the Subtle Nose. 1984
　　　　　　　　　　　　　　　　　　　　　　　ISBN 90-277-1773-7
175. W. Balzer, D. A. Pearce, and H.-J. Schmidt (eds.), *Reduction in Science*. Structure, Examples, Philosophical Problems. 1984　　　ISBN 90-277-1811-3
176. A. Peczenik, L. Lindahl and B. van Roermund (eds.), *Theory of Legal Science*. Proceedings of the Conference on Legal Theory and Philosophy of Science (Lund, Sweden, December 1983). 1984　　　　　　　　　　　ISBN 90-277-1834-2
177. I. Niiniluoto, *Is Science Progressive?* 1984　　　ISBN 90-277-1835-0
178. B. K. Matilal and J. L. Shaw (eds.), *Analytical Philosophy in Comparative Perspective*. Exploratory Essays in Current Theories and Classical Indian Theories of Meaning and Reference. 1985　　　　　　　　　　　　ISBN 90-277-1870-9
179. P. Kroes, *Time: Its Structure and Role in Physical Theories*. 1985
　　　　　　　　　　　　　　　　　　　　　　　ISBN 90-277-1894-6
180. J. H. Fetzer, *Sociobiology and Epistemology*. 1985
　　　　　　　　　　　　　ISBN 90-277-2005-3; Pb 90-277-2006-1
181. L. Haaparanta and J. Hintikka (eds.), *Frege Synthesized*. Essays on the Philosophical and Foundational Work of Gottlob Frege. 1986　ISBN 90-277-2126-2
182. M. Detlefsen, *Hilbert's Program*. An Essay on Mathematical Instrumentalism. 1986
　　　　　　　　　　　　　　　　　　　　　　　ISBN 90-277-2151-3
183. J. L. Golden and J. J. Pilotta (eds.), *Practical Reasoning in Human Affairs*. Studies in Honor of Chaim Perelman. 1986　　　　　　ISBN 90-277-2255-2
184. H. Zandvoort, *Models of Scientific Development and the Case of Nuclear Magnetic Resonance*. 1986　　　　　　　　　　　　　　ISBN 90-277-2351-6
185. I. Niiniluoto, *Truthlikeness*. 1987　　　　　　　ISBN 90-277-2354-0
186. W. Balzer, C. U. Moulines and J. D. Sneed, *An Architectonic for Science*. The Structuralist Program. 1987　　　　　　　　　　ISBN 90-277-2403-2
187. D. Pearce, *Roads to Commensurability*. 1987　　　ISBN 90-277-2414-8
188. L. M. Vaina (ed.), *Matters of Intelligence*. Conceptual Structures in Cognitive Neuroscience. 1987　　　　　　　　　　　　　　ISBN 90-277-2460-1
189. H. Siegel, *Relativism Refuted*. A Critique of Contemporary Epistemological Relativism. 1987　　　　　　　　　　　　　　　ISBN 90-277-2469-5

190. W. Callebaut and R. Pinxten, *Evolutionary Epistemology*. A Multiparadigm Program, with a Complete Evolutionary Epistemology Bibliograph. 1987   ISBN 90-277-2582-9
191. J. Kmita, *Problems in Historical Epistemology*. 1988   ISBN 90-277-2199-8
192. J. H. Fetzer (ed.), *Probability and Causality*. Essays in Honor of Wesley C. Salmon, with an Annotated Bibliography. 1988   ISBN 90-277-2607-8; Pb 1-5560-8052-2
193. A. Donovan, L. Laudan and R. Laudan (eds.), *Scrutinizing Science*. Empirical Studies of Scientific Change. 1988   ISBN 90-277-2608-6
194. H.R. Otto and J.A. Tuedio (eds.), *Perspectives on Mind*. 1988   ISBN 90-277-2640-X
195. D. Batens and J.P. van Bendegem (eds.), *Theory and Experiment*. Recent Insights and New Perspectives on Their Relation. 1988   ISBN 90-277-2645-0
196. J. Österberg, *Self and Others*. A Study of Ethical Egoism. 1988   ISBN 90-277-2648-5
197. D.H. Helman (ed.), *Analogical Reasoning*. Perspectives of Artificial Intelligence, Cognitive Science, and Philosophy. 1988   ISBN 90-277-2711-2
198. J. Wolenski, *Logic and Philosophy in the Lvov-Warsaw School*. 1989
ISBN 90-277-2749-X
199. R. Wójcicki, *Theory of Logical Calculi*. Basic Theory of Consequence Operations. 1988
ISBN 90-277-2785-6
200. J. Hintikka and M.B. Hintikka, *The Logic of Epistemology and the Epistemology of Logic*. Selected Essays. 1989   ISBN 0-7923-0040-8; Pb 0-7923-0041-6
201. E. Agazzi (ed.), *Probability in the Sciences*. 1988   ISBN 90-277-2808-9
202. M. Meyer (ed.), *From Metaphysics to Rhetoric*. 1989   ISBN 90-277-2814-3
203. R.L. Tieszen, *Mathematical Intuition*. Phenomenology and Mathematical Knowledge. 1989   ISBN 0-7923-0131-5
204. A. Melnick, *Space, Time, and Thought in Kant*. 1989   ISBN 0-7923-0135-8
205. D.W. Smith, *The Circle of Acquaintance*. Perception, Consciousness, and Empathy. 1989
ISBN 0-7923-0252-4
206. M.H. Salmon (ed.), *The Philosophy of Logical Mechanism*. Essays in Honor of Arthur W. Burks. With his Responses, and with a Bibliography of Burk's Work. 1990
ISBN 0-7923-0325-3
207. M. Kusch, *Language as Calculus vs. Language as Universal Medium*. A Study in Husserl, Heidegger, and Gadamer. 1989   ISBN 0-7923-0333-4
208. T.C. Meyering, *Historical Roots of Cognitive Science*. The Rise of a Cognitive Theory of Perception from Antiquity to the Nineteenth Century. 1989   ISBN 0-7923-0349-0
209. P. Kosso, *Observability and Observation in Physical Science*. 1989
ISBN 0-7923-0389-X
210. J. Kmita, *Essays on the Theory of Scientific Cognition*. 1990   ISBN 0-7923-0441-1
211. W. Sieg (ed.), *Acting and Reflecting*. The Interdisciplinary Turn in Philosophy. 1990
ISBN 0-7923-0512-4
212. J. Karpiński, *Causality in Sociological Research*. 1990   ISBN 0-7923-0546-9
213. H.A. Lewis (ed.), *Peter Geach: Philosophical Encounters*. 1991   ISBN 0-7923-0823-9
214. M. Ter Hark, *Beyond the Inner and the Outer*. Wittgenstein's Philosophy of Psychology. 1990   ISBN 0-7923-0850-6
215. M. Gosselin, *Nominalism and Contemporary Nominalism*. Ontological and Epistemological Implications of the Work of W.V.O. Quine and of N. Goodman. 1990
ISBN 0-7923-0904-9
216. J.H. Fetzer, D. Shatz and G. Schlesinger (eds.), *Definitions and Definability*. Philosophical Perspectives. 1991   ISBN 0-7923-1046-2
217. E. Agazzi and A. Cordero (eds.), *Philosophy and the Origin and Evolution of the Universe*. 1991   ISBN 0-7923-1322-4
218. M. Kusch, *Foucault's Strata and Fields*. An Investigation into Archaeological and Genealogical Science Studies. 1991   ISBN 0-7923-1462-X

219. C.J. Posy, *Kant's Philosophy of Mathematics*. Modern Essays. 1992
ISBN 0-7923-1495-6

220. G. Van de Vijver, *New Perspectives on Cybernetics*. Self-Organization, Autonomy and Connectionism. 1992　　　　ISBN 0-7923-1519-7

221. J.C. Nyíri, *Tradition and Individuality*. Essays. 1992　　ISBN 0-7923-1566-9

222. R. Howell, *Kant's Transcendental Deduction*. An Analysis of Main Themes in His Critical Philosophy. 1992　　　　ISBN 0-7923-1571-5

223. A. García de la Sienra, *The Logical Foundations of the Marxian Theory of Value*. 1992
ISBN 0-7923-1778-5

224. D.S. Shwayder, *Statement and Referent*. An Inquiry into the Foundations of Our Conceptual Order. 1992　　　　ISBN 0-7923-1803-X

225. M. Rosen, *Problems of the Hegelian Dialectic*. Dialectic Reconstructed as a Logic of Human Reality. 1993　　　　ISBN 0-7923-2047-6

226. P. Suppes, *Models and Methods in the Philosophy of Science: Selected Essays*. 1993
ISBN 0-7923-2211-8

227. R. M. Dancy (ed.), *Kant and Critique: New Essays in Honor of W. H. Werkmeister*. 1993
ISBN 0-7923-2244-4

228. J. Woleński (ed.), *Philosophical Logic in Poland*. 1993　　ISBN 0-7923-2293-2

229. M. De Rijke (ed.), *Diamonds and Defaults*. Studies in Pure and Applied Intensional Logic. 1993　　　　ISBN 0-7923-2342-4

230. B.K. Matilal and A. Chakrabarti (eds.), *Knowing from Words*. Western and Indian Philosophical Analysis of Understanding and Testimony. 1994　　ISBN 0-7923-2345-9

231. S.A. Kleiner, *The Logic of Discovery*. A Theory of the Rationality of Scientific Research. 1993　　　　ISBN 0-7923-2371-8

232. R. Festa, *Optimum Inductive Methods*. A Study in Inductive Probability, Bayesian Statistics, and Verisimilitude. 1993　　　　ISBN 0-7923-2460-9

233. P. Humphreys (ed.), *Patrick Suppes: Scientific Philosopher*. Vol. 1: Probability and Probabilistic Causality. 1994　　　　ISBN 0-7923-2552-4

234. P. Humphreys (ed.), *Patrick Suppes: Scientific Philosopher*. Vol. 2: Philosophy of Physics, Theory Structure, and Measurement Theory. 1994　　ISBN 0-7923-2553-2

235. P. Humphreys (ed.), *Patrick Suppes: Scientific Philosopher*. Vol. 3: Language, Logic, and Psychology. 1994　　　　ISBN 0-7923-2862-0
Set ISBN (Vols 233–235) 0-7923-2554-0

236. D. Prawitz and D. Westerståhl (eds.), *Logic and Philosophy of Science in Uppsala*. Papers from the 9th International Congress of Logic, Methodology, and Philosophy of Science. 1994　　　　ISBN 0-7923-2702-0

237. L. Haaparanta (ed.), *Mind, Meaning and Mathematics*. Essays on the Philosophical Views of Husserl and Frege. 1994　　　　ISBN 0-7923-2703-9

238. J. Hintikka (ed.), *Aspects of Metaphor*. 1994　　　　ISBN 0-7923-2786-1

239. B. McGuinness and G. Oliveri (eds.), *The Philosophy of Michael Dummett*. With Replies from Michael Dummett. 1994　　　　ISBN 0-7923-2804-3

240. D. Jamieson (ed.), *Language, Mind, and Art*. Essays in Appreciation and Analysis, In Honor of Paul Ziff. 1994　　　　ISBN 0-7923-2810-8

241. G. Preyer, F. Siebelt and A. Ulfig (eds.), *Language, Mind and Epistemology*. On Donald Davidson's Philosophy. 1994　　　　ISBN 0-7923-2811-6

242. P. Ehrlich (ed.), *Real Numbers, Generalizations of the Reals, and Theories of Continua*. 1994　　　　ISBN 0-7923-2689-X

243. G. Debrock and M. Hulswit (eds.), *Living Doubt*. Essays concerning the epistemology of Charles Sanders Peirce. 1994　　　　ISBN 0-7923-2898-1

244. J. Srzednicki, *To Know or Not to Know*. Beyond Realism and Anti-Realism. 1994
ISBN 0-7923-2909-0

245. R. Egidi (ed.), *Wittgenstein: Mind and Language*. 1995　　ISBN 0-7923-3171-0

246. A. Hyslop, *Other Minds*. 1995   ISBN 0-7923-3245-8

247. L. Pólos and M. Masuch (eds.), *Applied Logic: How, What and Why*. Logical Approaches to Natural Language. 1995   ISBN 0-7923-3432-9

248. M. Krynicki, M. Mostowski and L.M. Szczerba (eds.), *Quantifiers: Logics, Models and Computation*. Volume One: Surveys. 1995   ISBN 0-7923-3448-5

249. M. Krynicki, M. Mostowski and L.M. Szczerba (eds.), *Quantifiers: Logics, Models and Computation*. Volume Two: Contributions. 1995   ISBN 0-7923-3449-3
Set ISBN (Vols 248 + 249) 0-7923-3450-7

250. R.A. Watson, *Representational Ideas from Plato to Patricia Churchland*. 1995
ISBN 0-7923-3453-1

251. J. Hintikka (ed.), *From Dedekind to Gödel*. Essays on the Development of the Foundations of Mathematics. 1995   ISBN 0-7923-3484-1

252. A. Wiśniewski, *The Posing of Questions*. Logical Foundations of Erotetic Inferences. 1995   ISBN 0-7923-3637-2

253. J. Peregrin, *Doing Worlds with Words*. Formal Semantics without Formal Metaphysics. 1995   ISBN 0-7923-3742-5

254. I.A. Kieseppä, *Truthlikeness for Multidimensional, Quantitative Cognitive Problems*. 1996   ISBN 0-7923-4005-1

255. P. Hugly and C. Sayward: *Intensionality and Truth*. An Essay on the Philosophy of A.N. Prior. 1996   ISBN 0-7923-4119-8

256. L. Hankinson Nelson and J. Nelson (eds.): *Feminism, Science, and the Philosophy of Science*. 1997   ISBN 0-7923-4162-7

257. P.I. Bystrov and V.N. Sadovsky (eds.): *Philosophical Logic and Logical Philosophy*. Essays in Honour of Vladimir A. Smirnov. 1996   ISBN 0-7923-4270-4

258. Å.E. Andersson and N-E. Sahlin (eds.): *The Complexity of Creativity*. 1996
ISBN 0-7923-4346-8

259. M.L. Dalla Chiara, K. Doets, D. Mundici and J. van Benthem (eds.): *Logic and Scientific Methods*. Volume One of the Tenth International Congress of Logic, Methodology and Philosophy of Science, Florence, August 1995. 1997   ISBN 0-7923-4383-2

260. M.L. Dalla Chiara, K. Doets, D. Mundici and J. van Benthem (eds.): *Structures and Norms in Science*. Volume Two of the Tenth International Congress of Logic, Methodology and Philosophy of Science, Florence, August 1995. 1997   ISBN 0-7923-4384-0
Set ISBN (Vols 259 + 260) 0-7923-4385-9

261. A. Chakrabarti: *Denying Existence*. The Logic, Epistemology and Pragmatics of Negative Existentials and Fictional Discourse. 1997   ISBN 0-7923-4388-3

262. A. Biletzki: *Talking Wolves*. Thomas Hobbes on the Language of Politics and the Politics of Language. 1997   ISBN 0-7923-4425-1

263. D. Nute (ed.): *Defeasible Deontic Logic*. 1997   ISBN 0-7923-4630-0